C++ CRASH COURSE

C++ CRASH COURSE

A Fast-Paced Introduction

by Josh Lospinoso

San Francisco

Printed in USA

First printing

23 22 21 20 19   1 2 3 4 5 6 7 8 9

ISBN-10: 1-59327-888-8
ISBN-13: 978-1-59327-888-5

Publisher: William Pollock
Production Editors: Meg Sneeringer and Riley Hoffman
Cover Illustration: Josh Ellingson
Interior Design: Octopod Studios
Developmental Editors: Chris Cleveland and Patrick DiJusto
Technical Reviewer: Kyle Willmon
Copyeditor: Anne Marie Walker
Compositors: Happenstance Type-O-Rama, Riley Hoffman, and Meg Sneeringer
Proofreader: Paula L. Fleming

For information on distribution, translations, or bulk sales, please contact No Starch Press, Inc. directly:

No Starch Press, Inc.
245 8th Street, San Francisco, CA 94103
phone: 1.415.863.9900; info@nostarch.com
www.nostarch.com

Library of Congress Cataloging-in-Publication Data

Names: Lospinoso, Josh, author.
Title: C++ crash course : a fast-paced introduction / Josh Lospinoso.
Description: First edition. | San Francisco, CA : No Starch Press, Inc., [2019]
Identifiers: LCCN 2019020529 (print) | LCCN 2019022057 (ebook) | ISBN 9781593278892 (epub) | ISBN 1593278896 (epub) | ISBN 9781593278885 (print) | ISBN 1593278888 (print)
Subjects: LCSH: C++ (Computer program language) | Computer programming.
Classification: LCC QA76.73.C153 (ebook) | LCC QA76.73.C153 L67 2019 (print) | DDC 005.13/3--dc23
LC record available at https://lccn.loc.gov/2019020529

```
#include <algorithm>
#include <iostream>
#include <string>

int main() {
  auto i{ 0x01B99644 };
  std::string x{ " DFaeeillnor" };
  while (i--) std::next_permutation(x.begin(), x.end());
  std::cout << x;
}
```

About the Author

Josh Lospinoso, PhD, is an entrepreneur who served 15 years in the US Army. As a cyber officer, Josh wrote dozens of infosec tools and taught C++ to junior developers. He has spoken at a wide range of conferences, published over 20 peer-reviewed articles, is a Rhodes Scholar, and holds a patent. In 2012, he co-founded a successfully acquired security company. He keeps a blog and is an active contributor to open source software.

About the Technical Reviewer

Kyle Willmon is a systems developer with 12 years of C++ experience. He has worked in the information security community for 7 years utilizing C++, Python, and Go across a variety of projects. Kyle currently works as a developer for Sony's Global Threat Emulation Team.

BRIEF CONTENTS

CONTENTS IN DETAIL

13 CONTAINERS 407

14 ITERATORS 463

15 STRINGS 481

18 ALGORITHMS 573

FOREWORD

"C++ is a complicated language." This is a reputation C++ has earned across a number of decades of use, and not always for the right reasons. Often, this is used as a reason to disallow people from learning C++, or as a reason why a different programming language would be better. These arguments are hard to substantiate because the basic premise they rely on is wrong: C++ is not a complicated language. The biggest problem C++ has is its reputation, and the second biggest problem is the lack of high-quality educational materials for learning it.

The language itself has evolved over the past four decades from C. It started off as being a fork of C (with minor additions) and a pre-compiler called Cfront, which compiles early C++ code to C that is then to be processed with the C compiler. Hence the name Cfront—in front of C. After a few years of progress and development, this proved to limit the language too much and work was undertaken to create an actual compiler. This compiler, written by Bjarne Stroustrup (the original inventor of the language), could compile a C++ program stand-alone. Other companies were also interested in continuing from basic C support and made their own C++ compilers, mostly compatible with either Cfront or the newer compiler.

This proved to be untenable because the language was unportable and wildly incompatible between compilers. Not to mention the fact that keeping all decisions and direction within the hands of a single person is not the way to make a cross-company international standard—there are standard procedures for that, and organizations that manage them. C++ was thus moved to become an ISO standard belonging to the International Standards Organization. After a number of years of development, the first official C++ standard came out in 1998, and people rejoiced.

They rejoiced for only a short while though, because while C++98 was a good definition, it had included a few new developments that people didn't see coming, and had some features that interacted in weird ways. In some cases the features themselves were well-written, but the interaction between common features was just not present—for example, being able to have a filename as a `std::string` and then opening a file with that.

Another late addition was support of templates, which was the main underlying technology supporting the Standard Template Library, one of the most important pieces in C++ today. Only after its release did people discover that it itself is Turing complete, and that many advanced constructs could be done by doing computations at compile time. This greatly enhanced the ability for library writers to write generic code that would be able to handle arbitrarily complex deductions, which was unlike anything other languages in existence at the time could do.

A final complication was that while C++98 was good, many compilers were not suited for implementing templates. The two major compilers of the time, GNU GCC 2.7 and Microsoft Visual C++ 6.0, were both unable to do a two-step name lookup required by templates. The only way to fully get this right was to do a full compiler rewrite. . .

GNU tried to keep adding onto its existing code base, but finally went for a rewrite around the 2.95 time frame. This meant that there were no new features or releases for a multi-year period, and many were unhappy with this. Some companies took the code base and tried to continue its development, creating 2.95.2, 2.95.3 and 2.96—all three of which are remembered for their lack of stability. Finally, the completed rewrite GCC 3.0 came out. It was not very successful initially, because while it would compile templates and C++ code much better than 2.95 ever did, it would not compile the Linux kernel to a working binary. The Linux community plainly objected to modifying their code to adapt to the new compiler, insisting that the compiler was broken. Eventually, around the 3.2 timeframe, the Linux community came around and the Linux world recentered around GCC 3.2 and up.

Microsoft tried to avoid rewriting their compiler for as long as they could. They added cornercase upon cornercase and heuristic methods to guess whether something should have been resolved in the first or second template name lookup pass. This worked nearly completely, but libraries written in the early 2010s showed that there was no possible way to make all of them work—not even with source modifications. Microsoft finally rewrote their parser and released the updated version in 2018—but many people did not enable the new parser. In 2019 the new parser was finally included by default on new projects.

But before 2019, there was a major event in 2011: the release of C++11. After C++98 was released, major new features were proposed and worked on. But due to one feature in particular not working out quite as was expected, the new C++ release was postponed from around 2006 until around 2009. During that time attempts were made to make it work with the new feature. In 2009 it was finally removed and the rest was fixed up for release, and the 1998 version of C++ was finally updated. There were a ton of new features and library enhancements. Compilers were again slow to catch up, and most of the compilers could compile most of C++11 only by the end of 2013.

The C++ committee had learned from their earlier failure, and now had a battle plan of creating a new release every three years. The plan was to conjure and test new features in one year, integrate them well in the next, and stabilize and officially release in the third, and repeat this process every three years. C++11 was the first instance, and 2014 was the year for the second. Much to their credit, the committee did exactly as they had promised, making a major update over C++11 and enabling the C++11 features to be much more usable than they had been. In most of the places where careful limits had been implemented, the limits were moved to what was then considered acceptable—in particular around `constexpr`.

Compiler writers who were still trying to get all the C++11 features running well now realized that they needed to adjust their pace or be left behind. By 2015 all compilers supported just about all of C++14—a remarkable feat, given what happened to C++98 and C++11 before. This also renewed participation in the C++ committee from all major compiler writers—if you know about a feature before it's released, you can be the leading compiler supporting it. And if you find that a certain feature does not match your compiler's design, you can influence the C++ committee to adjust it in a way that makes it much easier for you to support, allowing people to use it sooner.

C++ is now experiencing a rebirth. This period started around 2011 when C++11 was introduced and the "Modern C++" programming style that it enabled was adopted. It has improved only so far though, because all the ideas from C++11 were fine-tuned in C++14 and C++17, and all compilers now fully support all of the features that you would expect. Even better, the new standard for C++20 will soon be released, and all compilers in their most up-to-date versions already support major parts of it.

Modern C++ allows developers to skip most of the original trouble of trying to first learn C, then C++98, then C++11 and then unlearning all the parts of C and C++98 that had been fixed. Most courses used to start with an introduction about the history of C++ because it was necessary to understand why some things were as weird as they were. For this book though, I'm including this information in the foreword because Josh rightfully left it out.

You don't need to know this history anymore to learn C++. Modern C++ style allows you to skip it entirely and write well-designed programs knowing just the basic tenets of C++. There is no better time to start learning C++ than now.

But now to return to an earlier point—the lack of high-quality educational opportunities and materials for learning C++. High-quality C++ education is now being provided within the C++ committee itself—there's a study group dedicated just to teaching C++!—and the latter issue is in my opinion completely resolved by the very book you're holding.

Unlike all other C++ books I've read, this book teaches you the basics and the principles. It teaches you how to reason, and then lets you reason through the things that the Standard Template Library offers you. The payoff may take a bit longer, but you will be so much more satisfied to see your first results compile and run when you fully understand how C++ works. This book even includes topics that most C++ books shy away from: setting up your environment and testing your code before running the full program.

Enjoy reading this book and trying out all its exercises, and good luck on your C++ journey!

Peter Bindels
Principal Software Engineer, TomTom

ACKNOWLEDGMENTS

Above all, I thank my family for giving me creative space. It took twice as long to write half of what I proposed, and for your patience I owe you immeasurably.

I'm indebted to Kyle Willmon and Aaron Bray, who taught me C++; to Tyler Ortman, who shepherded this book from a proposal; to Bill Pollock, who rehabilitated my expositive style; to Chris Cleveland, Patrick De Justo, Anne Marie Walker, Annie Choi, Meg Sneeringer, and Riley Hoffman, whose top-notch editing benefited this book enormously; and to the many early readers who transmuted raw chapters into inestimable feedback.

And finally I thank Jeff Lospinoso, who bequeathed to his wide-eyed, ten-year-old nephew the well-thumbed, coffee-stained Camel Book that ignited the spark.

INTRODUCTION

Grab the ol' brush and paint along with us.
—Bob Ross

The demand for system programming is enormous. With the ubiquity of web browsers, mobile devices, and the Internet of Things, there has perhaps never been a better time to be a system programmer. Efficient, maintainable, and correct code is desired in all cases, and it's my firm belief that C++ is the right language for the job *in general.*

In the hands of a knowledgeable programmer, C++ can produce smaller, more efficient, and more readable code than any other system programming language on the planet. It's a language committed to the ideal of zero-overhead abstraction mechanisms—so your programs are fast and quick to program—as well as simple, direct mapping to hardware—so you have low-level control when you need it. When you program in C++, you stand on the shoulders of giants who have spent decades crafting an incredibly powerful and flexible language.

A huge benefit of learning C++ is that you gain access to the C++ Standard Library, the *stdlib*, free of charge. The stdlib is composed of three interlocking parts: containers, iterators, and algorithms. If you've ever written your own quicksort algorithm by hand or if you've programmed system code and been bitten by buffer overflows, dangling pointers, use-after frees, and double frees, you'll enjoy getting acquainted with the stdlib. It provides you with an unrivaled combination of type safety, correctness, and efficiency. In addition, you'll like how compact and expressive your code can be.

At the core of the C++ programming model is the *object life cycle*, which gives you strong guarantees that resources your program uses, such as files, memory, and network sockets, release correctly, even when error conditions occur. When used effectively, exceptions can clean out large amounts of error-condition-checking clutter from your code. Also, move/copy semantics provide safety, efficiency, and flexibility to manage resource ownership in a way that earlier system programming languages, like C, simply don't provide.

C++ is a living, breathing language; after more than 30 years, the International Organization for Standardization (ISO) committee for C++ regularly makes improvements in the language. Several updates to the standard have been released in the past decade: C++11, C++14, and C++17, which were released in 2011, 2014, and 2017, respectively. You can expect a new C++20 in 2020.

When I use the term *modern C++*, I mean the latest C++ version that embraces the features and paradigms presented in these additions. These updates have made serious refinements to the language that improve its expressiveness, efficiency, safety, and overall usability. By some measures, the language has never been more popular, and it's not going away any time soon. If you decide to invest in learning C++, it will pay dividends for years to come.

About This Book

Although a number of very high-quality books are available to modern C++ programmers, such as Scott Meyer's *Effective Modern C++* and Bjarne Stroustrup's *The C++ Programming Language*, 4th Edition, they're generally quite advanced. Some introductory C++ texts are available, but they often skip over crucial details because they're geared to those totally new to programming. For the experienced programmer, it's not clear where to dive into the C++ language.

I prefer to learn about complicated topics deliberately, building concepts from their fundamental elements. C++ has a daunting reputation because its fundamental elements nest so tightly together, making it difficult to construct a complete picture of the language. When I learned C++, I struggled to get my mind around the language, bouncing among books, videos, and exhausted colleagues. So I wrote the book I wish I'd had five years ago.

Who Should Read This Book?

This book is intended for intermediate to advanced programmers already familiar with basic programming concepts. If you don't specifically have *system* programming experience, that's okay. Experienced application programmers are welcome.

NOTE *If you're a seasoned C programmer or an aspiring system programmer wondering whether you should invest in learning C++, be sure to read An Overture to C Programmers on page xxxvii for a detailed examination.*

What's in This Book?

The book is divided into two parts. Part I covers the core C++ language. Rather than presenting the C++ language chronologically (from old-style C++ 98 to modern C++11/14/17), you'll learn idiomatic, modern C++ directly. Part II introduces you to the world of the C++ Standard Library (stdlib) where you'll learn the most important and essential concepts.

Part I: The C++ Core Language

Chapter 1: Up and Running This introductory chapter will help you set up a C++ development environment. You'll compile and run your first program, and you'll learn how to debug it.

Chapter 2: Types Here you'll explore the C++ type system. You'll learn about the fundamental types, the foundation upon which all other types are built. Next, you'll learn about plain-old-data types and fully featured classes. You'll delve into the role of constructors, initialization, and destructors.

Chapter 3: Reference Types This chapter introduces you to objects that store the memory addresses of other objects. These types are the cornerstone of many important programming patterns, and they allow you to produce flexible, efficient code.

Chapter 4: The Object Life Cycle The discussion of class invariants and the constructor is continued within the context of storage durations. The destructor is introduced alongside the resource acquisition is initialization (RAII) paradigm. You'll learn about exceptions and how they enforce class invariants and complement RAII. After a discussion of move and copy semantics, you'll explore how to operationalize them with constructors and assignment operators.

Chapter 5: Runtime Polymorphism Here you'll be introduced to interfaces, a programming concept that allows you to write code that's polymorphic at runtime. You'll learn the basics of inheritance and object composition, which underpin how you can operationalize interfaces in C++.

Chapter 6: Compile-Time Polymorphism This chapter introduces templates, a language feature that allows you to write polymorphic code. You'll also explore concepts, a language feature that will be added to a future C++ release, and named conversion functions, which allow you to convert objects from one type to another.

Chapter 7: Expressions Now you'll dive deeply into operands and operators. With a firm grasp of types, the object life cycle, and templates, you'll be ready to plunge into the core components of the C++ language, and expressions are the first waypoint.

Chapter 8: Statements This chapter explores the elements that comprise functions. You'll learn about expression statements, compound statements, declaration statements, iteration statements, and jump statements.

Chapter 9: Functions The final chapter of Part I expands on the discussion of how to arrange statements into units of work. You'll learn the details of function definitions, return types, overload resolution, variadic functions, variadic templates, and function pointers. You'll also learn how to create invokable user-defined types using the function call operator and lambda expressions. You'll explore `std::function`, a class that provides a uniform container for storing invokable objects.

Part II: C++ Libraries and Frameworks

Chapter 10: Testing This chapter introduces you to the wonderful world of unit testing and mocking frameworks. You'll practice test-driven development to develop software for an autonomous driving system while learning about frameworks, such as Boost Test, Google Test, Google Mock, and others.

Chapter 11: Smart Pointers The special utility classes that the stdlib provides for handling ownership of dynamic objects are explained.

Chapter 12: Utilities Here you'll get an overview of the types, classes, and functions at your disposal in the stdlib and Boost libraries for tackling common programming problems. You'll learn about data structures, numeric functions, and random number generators.

Chapter 13: Containers This chapter surveys the many special data structures in the Boost libraries and stdlib that help you organize data. You'll learn about sequence containers, associative containers, and unordered associative containers.

Chapter 14: Iterators This is the interface between the containers you learned about in the previous chapter and the strings of the next chapter. You'll learn about the different kinds of iterators and how their design provides you with incredible flexibility.

Chapter 15: Strings This chapter teaches you how to handle human language data in a single family of containers. You'll also learn about the special facilities built into strings that allow you to perform common tasks.

Chapter 16: Streams You'll be introduced here to the major concept underpinning input and output operations. You'll learn how to handle input and output streams with formatted and unformatted operations, as well as how to employ manipulators. You'll also learn how to read and write data from and to files.

Chapter 17: Filesystems Here you'll get an overview of the facilities in the stdlib for manipulating filesystems. You'll learn how to construct and manipulate paths, inspect files and directories, and enumerate directory structures.

Chapter 18: Algorithms This is a quick reference to the dozens of problems you can solve easily from within the stdlib. You'll learn about the impressive scope of the high-quality algorithms available to you.

Chapter 19: Concurrency and Parallelism This chapter teaches you some simple methods for multithreaded programming that are part of the stdlib. You'll learn about futures, mutexes, condition variables, and atomics.

Chapter 20: Network Programming with Boost Asio Here you'll learn how to build high-performance programs that communicate over networks. You'll see how to use Boost Asio with blocking and non-blocking input and output.

Chapter 21: Writing Applications This final chapter rounds out the book with a discussion of several important topics. You'll learn about program support facilities that allow you to hook into the application life cycle. You'll also learn about Boost ProgramOptions, a library that makes writing console applications that accept user input straightforward.

NOTE *Visit the companion site* https://ccc.codes/ *to access the code listings contained in this book.*

AN OVERTURE TO C PROGRAMMERS

ARTHUR DENT: What's the matter with him?
HIG HURTENFLURST: His feet are the wrong size for his shoes.
—Douglas Adams, The Hitchhiker's Guide to the Galaxy, *"Fit the Eleventh"*

This preface is meant for experienced C programmers who are considering whether or not to read this book. Non–C programmers are welcome to skip this prelude.

Bjarne Stroustrup developed C++ from the C programming language. Although C++ isn't completely compatible with C, well-written C programs are often also valid C++ programs. Case in point, every example in *The C Programming Language* by Brian Kernighan and Dennis Ritchie is a legal C++ program.

One primary reason for C's ubiquity in the system-programming community is that C allows programmers to write at a higher level of abstraction than assembly programming does. This tends to produce clearer, less error-prone, and more maintainable code.

Generally, system programmers aren't willing to pay overhead for programming convenience, so C adheres to the zero-overhead principle: *what you don't use, you don't pay for*. The strong type system is a prime example of a zero-overhead abstraction. It's used only at compile time to check for program correctness. After compile time, the types will have disappeared, and the emitted assembly code will show no trace of the type system.

As a descendant of C, C++ also takes zero-overhead abstraction and direct mapping to hardware very seriously. This commitment goes beyond just the C language features that C++ supports. Everything that C++ builds on top of C, including new language features, upholds these principles, and departures from either are made very deliberately. In fact, some C++ features incur even less overhead than corresponding C code. The `constexpr` keyword is one such example. It instructs the compiler to evaluate the expression at compile time (if possible), as shown in the program in Listing 1.

```
#include <cstdio>

constexpr int isqrt(int n) {
  int i=1;
  while (i*i<n) ++i;
  return i-(i*i!=n);
}

int main() {
  constexpr int x = isqrt(1764); ❶
  printf("%d", x);
}
```

Listing 1: A program illustrating `constexpr`

The `isqrt` function computes the square root of the argument `n`. Starting at `1`, the function increments the local variable `i` until `i*i` is greater than or equal to `n`. If `i*i == n`, it returns `i`; otherwise, it returns `i-1`. Notice that the invocation of `isqrt` has a literal value, so the compiler could theoretically compute the result for you. The result will only ever take on one value ❶.

Compiling Listing 1 on GCC 8.3 targeting x86-64 with `-O2` yields the assembly in Listing 2.

```
.LC0:
        .string "%d"
main:
        sub     rsp, 8
        mov     esi, 42 ❶
        mov     edi, OFFSET FLAT:.LC0
        xor     eax, eax
        call    printf
        xor     eax, eax
        add     rsp, 8
        ret
```

Listing 2: The assembly produced after compiling Listing 1

The salient result here is the second instruction in `main` ❶; rather than evaluating the square root of `1764` at runtime, the compiler evaluates it and outputs instructions to treat `x` as `42`. Of course, you could calculate the square root using a calculator and insert the result manually, but using `constexpr` provides lots of benefits. This approach can mitigate many errors associated with manually copying and pasting, and it makes your code more expressive.

NOTE *If you're not familiar with x86 assembly, refer to* The Art of Assembly Language, *2nd Edition, by Randall Hyde and* Professional Assembly Language *by Richard Blum.*

Upgrading to Super C

Modern C++ compilers will accommodate most of your C programming habits. This makes it easy to embrace a few of the tactical niceties that the C++ language affords you while deliberately avoiding the language's deeper themes. This style of C++—let's call it *Super C*—is important to discuss for several reasons. First, seasoned C programmers can immediately benefit from applying simple, tactical-level C++ concepts to their programs. Second, Super C is *not* idiomatic C++. Simply sprinkling references and instances of `auto` around a C program might make your code more robust and readable, but you'll need to learn other concepts to take full advantage of it. Third, in some austere environments (for example, embedded software, some operating system kernels, and heterogeneous computing), the available tool chains have incomplete C++ support. In such situations, it's possible to benefit from at least some C++ idioms, and Super C is likely to be supported. This section covers some Super C concepts you can apply to your code immediately.

NOTE *Some C-supported constructs won't work in C++. See the links section of this book's companion site,* https://ccc.codes.

Function Overloading

Consider the following conversion functions from the standard C library:

```
char* itoa(int value, char* str, int base);
char* ltoa(long value, char* buffer, int base);
char* ultoa(unsigned long value, char* buffer, int base);
```

These functions achieve the same goal: they convert an integral type to a C-style string. In C, each function must have a unique name. But in C++ functions can share names as long as their arguments differ; this is called *function overloading.* You can use function overloading to create your own conversion functions, as Listing 3 illustrates.

```
char* toa(int value, char* buffer, int base) {
  --snip--
}

char* toa(long value, char* buffer, int base)
  --snip--
}

char* toa(unsigned long value, char* buffer, int base) {
  --snip--
}
```

```
int main() {
  char buff[10];
  int a = 1; ❶
  long b = 2; ❷
  unsigned long c = 3; ❸
  toa(a, buff, 10);
  toa(b, buff, 10);
  toa(c, buff, 10);
}
```

Listing 3: Calling overloaded functions

The data type of the first argument in each of the functions differs, so the C++ compiler has enough information from the arguments passed into `toa` to call the correct function. Each `toa` call is to a unique function. Here, you create the variables `a` ❶, `b` ❷, and `c` ❸, which are different types of `int` objects that correspond with one of the three `toa` functions. This is more convenient than defining separately named functions, because you just need to remember one name and the compiler figures out which function to call.

References

Pointers are a crucial feature of C (and by extension most system programming). They enable you to handle large amounts of data efficiently by passing around data addresses instead of the actual data. Pointers are equally crucial to C++, but you have additional safety features available that defend against null dereferences and unintentional pointer reassignments.

References are a major improvement to handling pointers. They're similar to pointers, but with some key differences. Syntactically, references differ from pointers in two important ways. First, you declare them with `&` rather than `*`, as Listing 4 illustrates.

```
struct HolmesIV {
  bool is_sentient;
  int sense_of_humor_rating;
};
void mannie_service(HolmesIV*); // Takes a pointer to a HolmesIV
void mannie_service(HolmesIV&); // Takes a reference to a HolmesIV
```

Listing 4: Code illustrating how to declare functions taking pointers and references

Second, you interact with members using the dot operator `.` rather than the arrow operator `->`, as Listing 5 illustrates.

```
void make_sentient(HolmesIV* mike) {
  mike->is_sentient = true;
}

void make_sentient(HolmesIV& mike) {
  mike.is_sentient = true;
}
```

Listing 5: A program illustrating the use of the dot and arrow operators

Under the hood, references are equivalent to pointers because they're also a zero-overhead abstraction. The compiler produces similar code. To illustrate this, consider the results of compiling the `make_sentient` functions on GCC 8.3 targeting x86-64 with `-O2`. Listing 6 contains the assembly generated by compiling Listing 5.

```
make_sentient(HolmesIV*):
        mov     BYTE PTR [rdi], 1
        ret
make_sentient(HolmesIV&):
        mov     BYTE PTR [rdi], 1
        ret
```

Listing 6: The assembly generated from compiling Listing 5

However, at compile time, references provide some safety over raw pointers because, generally speaking, they cannot be null.

With pointers, you might add a `nullptr` check to be safe. For example, you might add a check to `make_sentient`, as in Listing 7.

```
void make_sentient(HolmesIV* mike) {
  if(mike == nullptr) return;
  mike->is_sentient = true;
}
```

Listing 7: A refactor of `make_sentient` from Listing 5 so it performs a `nullptr` check

Such a check is unnecessary when taking a reference; however, this doesn't mean that references are always valid. Consider the following function:

```
HolmesIV& not_dinkum() {
  HolmesIV mike;
  return mike;
}
```

The `not_dinkum` function returns a reference, which is guaranteed to be non-null. But it's pointing to garbage memory (probably in the returned-from stack frame of `not_dinkum`). You must never do this. The result will be utter misery, also known as *undefined runtime behavior:* it might crash, it might give you an error, or it might do something completely unexpected.

One other safety feature of references is that they can't be *reseated.* In other words, once a reference is initialized, it can't be changed to point to another memory address, as Listing 8 shows.

```
int main() {
  int a = 42;
  int& a_ref = a; ❶
  int b = 100;
  a_ref = b; ❷
}
```

Listing 8: A program illustrating that references cannot be reseated

You declare a_ref as a reference to int a ❶. There is no way to reseat a_ref to point to another int. You might try to reseat a with *operator=* ❷, but this actually sets the value of a to the value of b instead of setting a_ref to reference b. After the snippet is run both a and b are equal to 100, and a_ref still points to a. Listing 9 contains equivalent code using pointers instead.

```
int main() {
  int a = 42;
  int* a_ptr = &a; ❶
  int b = 100;
  *a_ptr = b; ❷
}
```

Listing 9: An equivalent program to Listing 8 using pointers

Here, you declare the pointer with a * instead of a & ❶. You assign the value of b to the memory pointed to by a_ptr ❷. With references, you don't need any decoration on the left side of the equal sign. But if you omit the * in *a_ptr, the compiler would complain that you're trying to assign an int to a pointer type.

References are just pointers with extra safety precautions and a sprinkle of syntactic sugar. When you put a reference on the left side of an equal sign, you're setting the pointed-to value equal to the right side of the equal sign.

auto Initialization

C often requires you to repeat type information more than once. In C++, you can express a variable's type information just once by utilizing the auto keyword. The compiler will know the variable's type because it knows the type of the value being used to initialize the variable. Consider the following C++ variable initializations:

```
int x = 42;
auto y = 42;
```

Here, x and y are both of int type. You might be surprised to know that the compiler can deduce the type of y, but consider that 42 is an integer literal. With auto, the compiler deduces the type on the right side of the equal sign = and sets the variable's type to the same. Because an integer literal is of int type, in this example the compiler deduces that the type of y is also an int. This doesn't seem like much of a benefit in such a simple example, but consider initializing a variable with a function's return value, as Listing 10 illustrates.

```
#include <cstdlib>

struct HolmesIV {
  --snip--
};
```

```
HolmesIV* make_mike(int sense_of_humor) {
  --snip--
}

int main() {
  auto mike = make_mike(1000);
  free(mike);
}
```

Listing 10: A toy program initializing a variable with the return value of a function

The auto keyword is easier to read and is more amenable to code refactoring than explicitly declaring a variable's type. If you use auto freely while declaring a function, there will be less work to do later if you need to change the return type of make_mike. The case for auto strengthens with more complex types, such as those involved with the template-laden code of the stdlib. The auto keyword makes the compiler do all the work of type deduction for you.

NOTE *You can also add* const, volatile, &, *and* * *qualifiers to* auto.

Namespaces and Implicit typedef of struct, union, and enum

C++ treats type tags as implicit typedef names. In C, when you want to use a struct, union, or enum, you have to assign a name to the type you've created using the typedef keyword. For example:

```
typedef struct Jabberwocks {
  void* tulgey_wood;
  int is_galumphing;
} Jabberwock;
```

In C++ land, you chortle at such code. Because the typedef keyword can be implicit, C++ allows you instead to declare the Jabberwock type like this:

```
struct Jabberwock {
  void* tulgey_wood;
  int is_galumphing;
};
```

This is more convenient and saves some typing. What happens if you also want to define a Jabberwock function? Well, you shouldn't, because reusing the same name for a data type and a function is likely to cause confusion. But if you're really committed to it, C++ allows you to declare a namespace to create different scopes for identifiers. This helps to keep user types and functions tidy, as shown in Listing 11.

```
#include <cstdio>

namespace Creature { ❶
  struct Jabberwock {
    void* tulgey_wood;
    int is_galumphing;
```

```
  };
}
namespace Func { ❷
  void Jabberwock() {
    printf("Burble!");
  }
}
```

Listing 11: Using namespaces to disambiguate functions and types with identical names

In this example, `Jabberwock` the `struct` and `Jabberwock` the function now live together in frabjous harmony. By placing each element in its own `namespace`—the `struct` in the `Creature` namespace ❶ and the function in the `Jabberwock` namespace ❷–you can disambiguate which Jabberwock you mean. You can do such disambiguation in several ways. The simplest is to qualify the name with its `namespace`, for example:

```
Creature::Jabberwock x;
Func::Jabberwock();
```

You can also employ a `using` directive to import all the names in a `namespace`, so you'd no longer need to use the fully qualified element name. Listing 12 uses the `Creature namespace`.

```
#include <cstdio>

namespace Creature {
  struct Jabberwock {
    void* tulgey_wood;
    int is_galumphing;
  };
}

namespace Func {
  void Jabberwock() {
    printf("Burble!");
  }
}

using namespace Creature; ❶

int main() {
  Jabberwock x; ❷
  Func::Jabberwock();
}
```

Listing 12: Employing `using` namespace to refer to a type within the `Creature` namespace

The `using namespace` ❶ enables you to omit the `namespace` qualification ❷. But you still need a qualifier on `Func::Jabberwock`, because it isn't part of the `Creature namespace`.

Use of a namespace is idiomatic C++ and is a zero-overhead abstraction. Just like the rest of a type's identifiers, the namespace is erased by the compiler when emitting assembly code. In large projects, it's incredibly helpful for separating code in different libraries.

Intermingling C and C++ Object Files

C and C++ code can coexist peacefully if you're careful. Sometimes, it's necessary for a C compiler to link object files emitted by a C++ compiler (and vice versa). Although this is possible, it requires a bit of work.

Two issues are related to linking the files. First, the calling conventions in the C and C++ code could potentially be mismatched. For example, the protocols for how the stack and registers are set when you call a function could be different. These calling conventions are language-level mismatches and aren't generally related to how you've written your functions. Second, C++ compilers emit different symbols than C compilers do. Sometimes the linker must identify an object by name. C++ compilers assist by decorating the object, associating a string called a *decorated name* with the object. Because of function overloads, calling conventions, and namespace usage, the compiler must encode additional information about a function beyond just its name through decoration. This is done to ensure that the linker can uniquely identify the function. Unfortunately, there is no standard for how this decoration occurs in C++ (which is why you should use the same tool chain and settings when linking between translation units). C linkers know nothing about C++ name decoration, which can cause problems if decoration isn't suppressed whenever you link against C code within C++ (and vice versa).

The fix is simple. You wrap the code you want to compile with C-style linkages using the statement extern "C", as in Listing 13.

```
// header.h
#ifdef __cplusplus
extern "C" {
#endif
void extract_arkenstone();

struct MistyMountains {
  int goblin_count;
};
#ifdef __cplusplus
}
#endif
```

Listing 13: Employing C-style linkage

This header can be shared between C and C++ code. It works because __cplusplus is a special identifier that the C++ compiler defines (but the C compiler doesn't). Accordingly, the C compiler sees the code in Listing 14 after preprocessing completes. Listing 14 illustrates the code that remains.

```
void extract_arkenstone();

struct MistyMountains {
  int goblin_count;
};
```

Listing 14: The code remaining after the preprocessor processes Listing 13 in a C environment

This is just a simple C header. The code between the `#ifdef __cplusplus` statements is removed during preprocessing, so the `extern "C"` wrapper isn't visible. For the C++ compiler, `__cplusplus` *is* defined in `header.h`, so it sees the contents of Listing 15.

```
extern "C" {
  void extract_arkenstone();

  struct MistyMountains {
    int goblin_count;
  };
}
```

Listing 15: The code remaining after the preprocessor processes Listing 13 in a C++ environment

Both `extract_arkenstone` and `MistyMountains` are now wrapped with `extern "C"`, so the compiler knows to use C linkage. Now your C source can call into compiled C++ code, and your C++ source can call into compiled C code.

C++ Themes

This section takes you on a brief tour of some core themes that make C++ the premier system-programming language. Don't worry too much about the details. The point of the following subsections is to whet your appetite.

Expressing Ideas Concisely and Reusing Code

Well-crafted C++ code has an elegant, compact quality. Consider the evolution from ANSI-C to modern C++ in the following simple operation: looping over some array `v` with `n` elements, as Listing 16 illustrates.

```
#include <cstddef>

int main() {
  const size_t n{ 100 };
  int v[n];

  // ANSI-C
  size_t i;
  for (i=0; i<n; i++) v[i] = 0; ❶
```

```
  // C99
  for (size_t i=0; i<n; i++)  v[i] = 0; ❷

  // C++17
  for (auto& x : v) x = 0; ❸
}
```

Listing 16: A program illustrating several ways to iterate over an array

This code snippet shows the different ways to declare loops in ANSI-C, C99, and C++. The index variable `i` in the ANSI-C ❶ and C99 ❷ examples are ancillary to what you're trying to accomplish, which is to access each element of `v`. The C++ version ❸ utilizes a *range-based* `for` loop, which loops over in the range of values in `v` while hiding the details of how iteration is achieved. Like a lot of the zero-overhead abstractions in C++, this construct enables you to focus on meaning rather than syntax. Range-based `for` loops work with many types, and you can even make them work with user-defined types.

Speaking of user-defined types, they allow you to express ideas directly in code. Suppose you want to design a function, `navigate_to`, that tells a hypothetical robot to navigate to some position given x and y coordinates. Consider the following prototype function:

```
void navigate_to(double x, double y);
```

What are `x` and `y`? What are their units? Your user must read the documentation (or possibly the source) to find out. Compare the following improved prototype:

```
struct Position{
--snip--
};
void navigate_to(const Position& p);
```

This function is far clearer. There is no ambiguity about what `navigate_to` accepts. As long as you have a validly constructed `Position`, you know exactly how to call `navigate_to`. Worrying about units, conversions, and so on is now the responsibility of whoever constructs the `Position` class.

You can also come close to this clarity in C99/C11 using a `const` pointer, but C++ also makes return types compact and expressive. Suppose you want to write a corollary function for the robot called `get_position` that—you guessed it—gets the position. In C, you have two options, as shown in Listing 17.

```
Position* get_position(); ❶
void get_position(Position* p); ❷
```

Listing 17: A C-style API for returning a user-defined type

In the first option, the caller is responsible for cleaning up the return value ❶, which has probably incurred a dynamic allocation (although this is unclear from the code). The caller is responsible for allocating a `Position` somewhere and passing it into get_position ❷. This latter approach is more idiomatic C-style, but the language is getting in the way: you're just trying to get a position object, but you have to worry about whether the caller or the called function is responsible for allocating and deallocating memory. C++ lets you do all of this succinctly by returning user-defined types directly from functions, as shown in Listing 18.

```
Position❶ get_position() {
  --snip--
}
void navigate() {
  auto p = get_position(); ❷
  // p is now available for use
  --snip--
}
```

Listing 18: Returning a user-defined type by value in C++

Because get_position returns a value ❶, the compiler can *elide the copy*, so it's as if you've constructed an automatic Position variable directly ❷; there's no runtime overhead. Functionally, you're in very similar territory to the C-style pass by reference of Listing 17.

The C++ Standard Library

The C++ Standard Library (stdlib) is a major reason for migrating from C. It contains high-performance, generic code that is guaranteed to be available right out of the standards-conforming box. The three broad components of the stdlib are containers, iterators, and algorithms.

Containers are the data structures. They're responsible for holding sequences of objects. They're correct, safe, and (usually) at least as efficient as what you could accomplish manually, meaning that writing your own versions of these containers would take great effort and wouldn't turn out better than the stdlib containers. Containers are neatly partitioned into two categories: *sequence containers* and *associative containers*. The sequence containers are conceptually similar to arrays; they provide accesses to sequences of elements. Associative containers contain key/value pairs, so elements in the containers can be looked up by key.

The stdlib *algorithms* are general-purpose functions for common programming tasks, such as counting, searching, sorting, and transforming. Much like containers, the stdlib algorithms are extremely high quality and broadly applicable. Users should very rarely have to implement their own version, and using the stdlib algorithms greatly increases programmer productivity, code safety, and readability.

Iterators connect containers with algorithms. For many stdlib algorithm applications, the data you want to operate on resides in a container. Containers expose iterators to provide an even, common interface, and the algorithms consume the iterators, keeping programmers (including the implementers of the stdlib) from having to implement a custom algorithm for each container type.

Listing 19 shows how to sort a container of values using a few lines of code.

```
#include <vector>
#include <algorithm>
#include <iostream>

int main() {
  std::vector<int> x{ 0, 1, 8, 13, 5, 2, 3 }; ❶
  x[0] = 21; ❷
  x.push_back(1); ❸
  std::sort(x.begin(), x.end()); ❹
  std::cout << "Printing " << x.size() << " Fibonacci numbers.\n"; ❺
  for (auto number : x) {
    std::cout << number << std::endl; ❻
  }
}
```

Listing 19: Sorting a container of values using the stdlib

A good amount of computation is going on in the background, yet the code is compact and expressive. First, you initialize a `std::vector` container ❶. *Vectors* are the stdlib's dynamically sized arrays. The *initializer braces* (the `{0, 1, ...}`) set the initial values contained in `x`. You can access the elements of a `vector` just like the elements of an array using brackets (`[]`) and the index number. You use this technique to set the first element equal to `21` ❷. Because `vector` arrays are dynamically sized, you can append values to them using the `push_back` method ❸. The seemingly magical invocation of `std::sort` showcases the power of the algorithms in stdlib ❹. The methods `x.begin()` and `x.end()` return iterators that `std::sort` uses to sort `x` in place. The `sort` algorithm is decoupled from `vector` through the use of iterators.

Thanks to iterators, you can use other containers in stdlib similarly. For example, you could use a `list` (the stdlib's doubly linked list) rather than using a `vector`. Because `list` also exposes iterators through `.begin()` and `.end()` methods, you could call `sort` on the `list` iterators in the same way.

Additionally, Listing 19 uses iostreams. *Iostreams* are the stdlib's mechanism for performing buffered input and output. You use the put-to operator (`<<`) to stream the value of `x.size()` (the number of elements in `x`), some string literals, and the Fibonacci element `number` to `std::cout`, which encapsulates stdout ❺ ❻. The `std::endl` object is an I/O manipulator that writes `\n` and flushes the buffer, ensuring that the entire stream is written to stdout before executing the next instruction.

Now, just imagine all the hoops you'd have to jump through to write an equivalent program in C, and you'll see why the stdlib is such a valuable tool.

Lambdas

Lambdas, also called *unnamed* or *anonymous functions* in some circles, are another powerful language feature that improve the locality of code. In some cases, you should pass pointers to functions to use a pointer as the target of a newly created thread or to perform some transformation on each element of a sequence. It's generally inconvenient to define a one-time-use free function. That's where lambdas come in. A lambda is a new, custom function *defined inline with the other parameters of an invocation.* Consider the following one-liner, which computes the count of even numbers in x:

```
auto n_evens = std::count_if(x.begin(), x.end(),
                             [] (auto number) { return number % 2 == 0; });
```

This snippet uses the stdlib's count_if algorithm to count the even numbers in x. The first two arguments to std::count_if match std::sort; they're the iterators that define the range over which the algorithm will operate. The third argument is the lambda. The notation probably looks a bit foreign, but the basics are quite simple:

```
[capture] (arguments) { body }
```

Capture contains any objects you need from the scope where the lambda is defined to perform computation in the body. *Arguments* define the names and types of arguments the lambda expects to be invoked with. The *body* contains any computation that you want completed upon invocation. It might or might not return a value. The compiler will deduce the function prototype based on the types you've implied.

In the std::count_if invocation above, the lambda didn't need to capture any variables. All the information it needs is taken as a single argument number. Because the compiler knows the type of the elements contained in x, you declare the type of number with auto so the compiler can deduce it for you. The lambda is invoked with each element of x passed in as the number parameter. In the body, the lambda returns true only when number is divisible by 2, so only the even numbers are included in the count.

Lambdas don't exist in C, and it's not really possible to reconstruct them. You'd need to declare a separate function each time you need a function object, and it's not possible to capture objects into a function in the same way.

Generic Programming with Templates

Generic programming is writing code once that works with different types rather than having to repeat the same code multiple times by copying and pasting each type you want to support. In C++, you use *templates* to produce generic code. Templates are a special kind of parameter that tells the compiler to represent a wide range of possible types.

You've already used templates: all of the stdlib's containers use templates. For the most part, the type of the objects in these containers doesn't matter. For example, the logic for determining the number of elements in a container or returning its first element doesn't depend on the element's type.

Suppose you want to write a function that adds three numbers of the same type. You want to accept any addable type. In C++, this is a straightforward generic programming problem that you can solve directly with templates, as Listing 20 illustrates.

```
template <typename T>
T add(T x, T y, T z) { ❶
  return x + y + z;
}

int main() {
  auto a = add(1, 2, 3);       // a is an int
  auto b = add(1L, 2L, 3L);    // b is a long
  auto c = add(1.F, 2.F, 3.F); // c is a float
}
```

Listing 20: Using templates to create a generic add function

When you declare `add` ❶, you don't need to know `T`. You only need to know that all the arguments and the return value are of type `T` and that `T` is addable. When the compiler encounters `add` being called, it deduces `T` and generates a bespoke function on your behalf. That's some serious code reuse!

Class Invariants and Resource Management

Perhaps the single greatest innovation C++ brings to system programming is the *object life cycle*. This concept has its roots in C, where objects have different storage durations depending on how you declare them in your code.

C++ builds on top of this memory management model with constructors and destructors. These special functions are methods that belong to *user-defined types*. User-defined types are the basic building blocks of C++ applications. Think of them as `struct` objects that can also have functions.

An object's constructor is called just after its storage duration begins, and the destructor is called just before its storage duration ends. Both the constructor and destructor are functions with no return type and the same name as the enclosing class. To declare a destructor, add a ~ to the beginning of the class name, as Listing 21 illustrates.

```
#include <cstdio>

struct Hal {
  Hal() : version{ 9000 } { // Constructor ❶
    printf("I'm completely operational.\n");
  }
  ~Hal() { // Destructor ❷
    printf("Stop, Dave.\n");
  }
  const int version;
};
```

Listing 21: A `Hal` class containing a constructor and a destructor

The first method in `Hal` is the *constructor* ❶. It sets up the `Hal` object and establishes its *class invariants*. Invariants are features of a class that don't change once they've been constructed. With some help from the compiler and the runtime, the programmer decides what the invariants of a class are and ensures that their code enforces them. In this case, the constructor sets the version, which is an invariant, to 9000. The *destructor* is the second method ❷. Whenever Hal is about to be deallocated, it prints "Stop, Dave." to the console. (Getting Hal to sing "Daisy Bell" is left as an exercise to the reader.)

The compiler makes sure the constructor and destructor are invoked automatically for objects with static, local, and thread local storage duration. For objects with dynamic storage duration, you use the keywords new and delete to replace malloc and free, Listing 22 illustrates.

```
#include <cstdio>

struct Hal {
--snip--
};

int main() {
  auto hal = new Hal{};  // Memory is allocated, then constructor is called
  delete hal;            // Destructor is called, then memory is deallocated
}
```

```
I'm completely operational.
Stop, Dave.
```

Listing 22: A program that creates and destroys a Hal *object*

If (for whatever reason) the constructor is unable to achieve a good state, it typically throws an *exception*. As a C programmer, you might have dealt with exceptions when programming with some operating system APIs (for example, Windows Structured Exception Handling). When an exception is thrown, the stack unwinds until an exception handler is found, at which point the program recovers. Judicious use of exceptions can clean up code because you only have to check for error conditions where it makes sense to do so. C++ has language-level support for exceptions, as Listing 23 illustrates.

```
#include <exception>

try {
  // Some code that might throw a std::exception ❶
} catch (const std::exception &e) {
  // Recover the program here. ❷
}
```

Listing 23: A try-catch block

You can put your code that might throw an exception in the block immediately following try ❶. If at any point an exception is thrown, the stack will unwind (graciously destructing any objects that go out of scope) and run any code that you've put after the catch expression ❷. If no exception is thrown, this catch code never executes.

Constructors, destructors, and exceptions are closely related to another core C++ theme, which is tying an object's life cycle to the resources it owns.

This is the resource allocation is initialization (RAII) concept (sometimes also called *constructor acquires, destructor releases*). Consider the C++ class in Listing 24.

```
#include <system_error>
#include <cstdio>

struct File {
  File(const char* path, bool write) { ❶
    auto file_mode = write ? "w" : "r"; ❷
    file_pointer = fopen(path, file_mode); ❸
    if (!file_pointer) throw std::system_error(errno, std::system_category()); ❹
  }
  ~File() {
    fclose(file_pointer);
  }
  FILE* file_pointer;
};
```

Listing 24: A `File` class

The constructor of `File` ❶ takes two arguments. The first argument corresponds with the `path` of the file, and the second is a `bool` corresponding to whether the file mode should be open for write (`true`) or read (`false`). This argument's value sets `file_mode` ❷ via the *ternary operator* `? :`. The ternary operator evaluates a Boolean expression and returns one of two values depending on the Boolean value. For example:

```
x ? val_if_true : val_if_false
```

If the Boolean expression `x` is `true`, the expression's value is `val_if_true`. If `x` is `false`, the value is `val_if_false` instead.

In the `File` constructor code snippet in Listing 24, the constructor attempts to open the file at `path` with read/write access ❸. If anything goes wrong, the call will set `file_pointer` to `nullptr`, a special C++ value that's similar to 0. When this happens, you throw a `system_error` ❹. A `system_error` is just an object that encapsulates the details of a system error. If `file_pointer` isn't `nullptr`, it's valid to use. That's this class's invariant.

Now consider the program in Listing 25, which employs `File`.

```
#include <cstdio>
#include <system_error>
#include <cstring>

struct File {
--snip--
};

int main() {
  { ❶
    File file("last_message.txt", true); ❷
    const auto message = "We apologize for the inconvenience.";
```

```
    fwrite(message, strlen(message), 1, file.file_pointer);
  } ❸
  // last_message.txt is closed here!
  {
    File file("last_message.txt", false); ❹
    char read_message[37]{};
    fread(read_message, sizeof(read_message), 1, file.file_pointer);
    printf("Read last message: %s\n", read_message);
  }
}
```

```
We apologize for the inconvenience.
```

Listing 25: A program employing the `File` class

The braces ❶ ❸ define a scope. Because the first `file` resides within this scope, the scope defines the lifetime of `file`. Once the constructor returns ❷, you know that `file.file_pointer` is valid thanks to the class invariant; based on the design of the constructor of `File`, you know `file.file_pointer` must be valid for the lifetime of the `File` object. You write a message using `fwrite`. There's no need to call `fclose` explicitly, because `file` expires and the destructor cleans up `file.file_pointer` for you ❷. You open `File` again but this time for read access ❹. As long as the constructor returns, you know that *last_message .txt* was opened successfully and continue on reading into `read_message`. After printing the message, the destructor of `file` is called, and the `file.file_pointer` is again cleaned up.

Sometimes you need the flexibility of dynamic memory allocation, but you still want to lean on the object life cycle of C++ to ensure that you don't leak memory or accidentally "use after free." This is exactly the role of *smart pointers*, which manage the life cycle of dynamic objects through an ownership model. Once no smart pointer owns a dynamic object, the object destructs.

One such smart pointer is `unique_ptr`, which models exclusive ownership. Listing 26 illustrates its basic usage.

```
#include <memory>

struct Foundation{
  const char* founder;
};

int main() {
  std::unique_ptr<Foundation> second_foundation{ new Foundation{} }; ❶
  // Access founder member variable just like a pointer:
  second_foundation->founder = "Wanda";
} ❷
```

Listing 26: A program employing a `unique_ptr`

You dynamically allocate a `Foundation`, and the resulting `Foundation*` pointer is passed into the constructor of `second_foundation` using the braced-initialization syntax ❶. The `second_foundation` has type `unique_ptr`, which is just an RAII object wrapping the dynamic `Foundation`. When `second_foundation` is destructed ❷, the dynamic `Foundation` destructs appropriately.

Smart pointers differ from regular, *raw* pointers because a raw pointer is simply a memory address. You must orchestrate all the memory management that's involved with the address manually. On the other hand, smart pointers handle all these messy details. By wrapping a dynamic object with a smart pointer, you can rest assured that memory will be cleaned up appropriately as soon as the object is no longer needed. The compiler knows that the object is no longer needed because the smart pointer's destructor is called when it falls out of scope.

Move Semantics

Sometimes, you want to transfer ownership of an object; this comes up often, for example, with `unique_ptr`. You can't copy a `unique_ptr`, because once one of the copies of the `unique_ptr` is destructed, the remaining `unique_ptr` would hold a reference to the deleted object. Rather than copying the object, you use the `move` semantics of C++ to transfer ownership from one unique pointer to another, as Listing 27 illustrates.

```
#include <memory>

struct Foundation{
  const char* founder;
};

struct Mutant {
  // Constructor sets foundation appropriately:
  Mutant(std::unique_ptr<Foundation> foundation)
    : foundation(std::move(foundation)) {}
  std::unique_ptr<Foundation> foundation;
};

int main() {
  std::unique_ptr<Foundation> second_foundation{ new Foundation{} }; ❶
  // ... use second_foundation
  Mutant the_mule{ std::move(second_foundation) }; ❷
  // second_foundation is in a 'moved-from' state
  // the_mule owns the Foundation
}
```

Listing 27: A program moving a unique_ptr

As before, you create `unique_ptr<Foundation>` ❶. You use it for some time and then decide to transfer ownership to a `Mutant` object. The `move` function tells the compiler that you want to make the transfer. After constructing `the_mule` ❷, the lifetime of `Foundation` is tied to the lifetime of `the_mule` through its member variable.

Relax and Enjoy Your Shoes

C++ is *the* premier system programming language. Much of your C knowledge will map directly into C++, but you'll also learn many new concepts. You can start gradually incorporating C++ into your C programs using Super C. As you become competent in some of the deeper themes of C++, you'll find that writing modern C++ brings with it many substantial advantages over C. You'll be able to express ideas concisely in code, capitalize on the impressive stdlib to work at a higher level of abstraction, employ templates to improve runtime performance and code reuse, and lean on the C++ object life cycle to manage resources.

I expect that the investment you'll make learning C++ will yield vast dividends. After reading this book, I think you'll agree.

PART I

THE C++ CORE LANGUAGE

First we crawl. Later we crawl on broken glass.
—*Scott Meyers,* Effective STL

Part I teaches you the crucial concepts in the C++ Core Language. Chapter 1 sets up a working environment and bootstraps some language constructs, including the basics of objects, the primary abstraction you use to program C++.

The next five chapters examine objects and types—the heart and soul of C++. Unlike some other programming books, you won't be building web servers or launching rocket ships from the get-go. All the programs in Part I simply print to the command line. The focus is on building your mental model of the language instead of instant gratification.

Chapter 2 takes an extensive look at types, the language construct that defines your objects.

Chapter 3 extends the discussion of Chapter 2 to discuss reference types, which describe objects that refer to other objects.

Chapter 4 describes the object life cycle, one of the most powerful aspects of C++.

Chapters 5 and 6 explore compile-time polymorphism with templates and runtime polymorphism with interfaces, which allow you to write loosely coupled and highly reusable code.

Armed with a foundation in C++'s object model, you'll be ready to dive into Chapters 7 through 9. These chapters present expressions, statements, and functions, which you use to get work done in the language. It might seem odd that these language constructs appear at the end of Part I, but without a strong knowledge of objects and their life cycles, all but the most basic features of these language constructs would be impossible to understand.

As a comprehensive, ambitious, powerful language, C++ can overwhelm the newcomer. To make it approachable, Part I is sequential, cohesive, and meant to be read like a story.

Part I is an entry fee. All your hard work learning the C++ Core Language buys you admission into the all-you-can-eat buffet of libraries and frameworks in Part II.

1

UP AND RUNNING

. . . with such violence I fell to the ground that I found myself stunned, and in a hole nine fathoms under the grass. . . . Looking down, I observed that I had on a pair of boots with exceptionally sturdy straps. Grasping them firmly, I pulled (repeatedly) with all my might.
—*Rudolph Raspe,* The Singular Adventures of Baron Munchausen

In this chapter, you'll begin by setting up a C++ *development environment,* which is the collection of tools that enables you to develop C++ software. You'll use the development environment to compile your first C++ *console application,* a program that you can run from the command line. Then you'll learn the main components of the development environment along with the role they play in generating the application you'll write. The chapters that follow will cover enough C++ essentials to construct useful example programs.

C++ has a reputation for being hard to learn. It's true that C++ is a big, complex, and ambitious language and that even veteran C++ programmers regularly learn new patterns, features, and usages.

A major source of nuance is that C++ features mesh together so tightly. Unfortunately, this often causes some distress to newcomers. Because C++ concepts are so tightly coupled, it's just not clear where to jump in. Part I of this book charts a deliberate, methodical course through the tumult, but it has to begin somewhere. This chapter covers just enough to get you started. Don't sweat the details too much!

The Structure of a Basic C++ Program

In this section, you'll write a simple C++ program and then compile and run it. You write C++ source code into human-readable text files called *source files*. Then you use a compiler to convert your C++ into executable machine code, which is a program that computers can run.

Let's dive in and create your first C++ source file.

Creating Your First C++ Source File

Open your favorite text editor. If you don't have a favorite just yet, try Vim, Emacs, or gedit on Linux; TextEdit on Mac; or Notepad on Windows. Enter the code in Listing 1-1 and save the resulting file to your desktop as *main.cpp*.

```
#include <cstdio> ❶

int main❷(){
  printf("Hello, world!"); ❸
  return 0; ❹
}
--------------------------------------------------------------------------
Hello, world! ❸
```

Listing 1-1: Your first C++ program prints `Hello, world!` to the screen.

The Listing 1-1 source file compiles to a program that prints the characters `Hello, world!` to the screen. By convention, C++ source files have a *.cpp* extension.

NOTE *In this book, listings will include any program output immediately after the program's source; the output will appear in gray. Numerical annotations will correspond with the line that produced the output. The `printf` statement in Listing 1-1, for example, is responsible for the output `Hello, world!`, so these share the same annotation ❸.*

Main: A C++ Program's Starting Point

As shown in Listing 1-1, C++ programs have a single entry point called the `main` function ❷. An *entry point* is a function that executes when a user runs a program. *Functions* are blocks of code that can take inputs, execute some instructions, and return results.

Within `main`, you call the function `printf`, which prints the characters `Hello, world!` to the console ❸. Then the program exits by returning the exit code `0` to the operating system ❹. *Exit codes* are integer values that the operating system uses to determine how well a program ran. Generally, a zero (`0`) exit code means the program ran successfully. Other exit codes might indicate a problem. Having a return statement in `main` is optional; the exit code defaults to `0`.

The `printf` function is not defined in the program; it's in the `cstdio` library ❶.

Libraries: Pulling in External Code

Libraries are helpful code collections you can import into your programs to prevent having to reinvent the wheel. Virtually every programming language has some way of incorporating library functionality into a program:

- Python, Go, and Java have `import`.
- Rust, PHP, and C# have `use`/`using`.
- JavaScript, Lua, R, and Perl have `require`/`requires`.
- C and C++ have `#include`.

Listing 1-1 included `cstdio` ❶, a library that performs input/output operations, such as printing to the console.

The Compiler Tool Chain

After writing the source code for a C++ program, the next step is to turn your source code into an executable program. The *compiler tool chain* (or *tool chain*) is a collection of three elements that run one after the other to convert source code into a program:

1. The **preprocessor** performs basic source code manipulation. For example, `#include <cstdio>` ❶ is a directive that instructs the preprocessor to include information about the `cstdio` library directly into your program's source code. When the preprocessor finishes processing a source file, it produces a single translation unit. Each translation unit is then passed to the compiler for further processing.
2. The **compiler** reads a translation unit and generates an *object file*. Object files contain an intermediate format called object code. These files contain data and instructions in an intermediate format that most humans wouldn't understand. Compilers work on one translation unit at a time, so each translation unit corresponds to a single object file.
3. The **linker** generates programs from object files. Linkers are also responsible for finding the libraries you've included within your source code. When you compile Listing 1-1, for example, the linker will find the `cstdio` library and include everything your program needs to use the `printf` function. Note that the `cstdio` header is distinct from the `cstdio` library. The header contains information about how to use the library. You'll learn more about libraries and source code organization in Chapter 21.

Setting Up Your Development Environment

All C++ development environments contain a way to edit source code and a compiler tool chain to turn that source code into a program. Often, development environments also contain a *debugger*—an invaluable program that lets you step through a program line by line to find errors.

When all of these tools—the text editor, the compiler tool chain, and the debugger—are bundled into a single program, that program is called an *interactive development environment (IDE)*. For beginners and veterans alike, IDEs can be a huge productivity booster.

NOTE *Unfortunately, C++ doesn't have an interpreter with which to interactively execute C++ code snippets. This is different from other languages like Python, Ruby, and JavaScript, which do have interpreters. Some web applications exist that allow you to test and share small C++ code snippets. See Wandbox (*https://wandbox.org/*), which allows you to compile and run code, and Matt Godbolt's Compiler Explorer (*https://www.godbolt.org/*), which allows you to inspect the assembly code that your code generates. Both work on a variety of compilers and systems.*

Each operating system has its own source code editors and compiler tool chain, so this section is broken out by operating system. Skip to the one that is relevant to you.

Windows 10 and Later: Visual Studio

At press time, the most popular C++ compiler for Microsoft Windows is the Microsoft Visual C++ Compiler (MSVC). The easiest way to obtain MSVC is to install the Visual Studio 2017 IDE as follows:

1. Download the Community version of Visual Studio 2017. A link is available at *https://ccc.codes/*.
2. Run the installer, allowing it to update if required.
3. At the Installing Visual Studio screen, ensure that **Desktop Development with C++ Workload** is selected.
4. Click **Install** to install Visual Studio 2017 along with MSVC.
5. Click **Launch** to launch Visual Studio 2017. The entire process might take several hours depending on the speed of your machine and your selections. Typical installations require 20GB to 50GB.

Set up a new project:

1. Select **File ▸ New ▸ Project**.
2. In **Installed**, click **Visual C++** and select **General**. Select **Empty Project** in the center panel.

3. Enter **hello** as the name of your project. Your window should look like Figure 1-1, but the Location will vary depending on your username. Click **OK**.

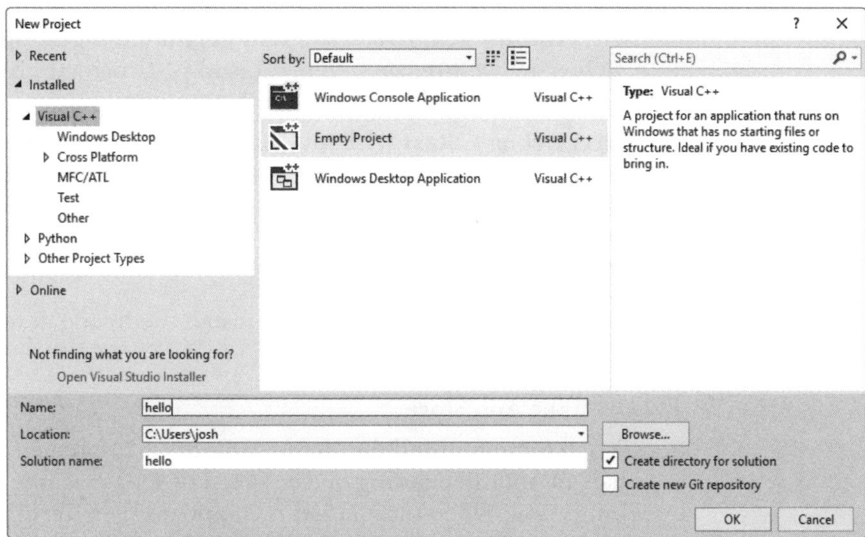

Figure 1-1: The Visual Studio 2017 New Project wizard

4. In the **Solution Explorer** pane on the left side of the workspace, right-click the **Source Files** folder and select **Add ▸ Existing Item**. See Figure 1-2.

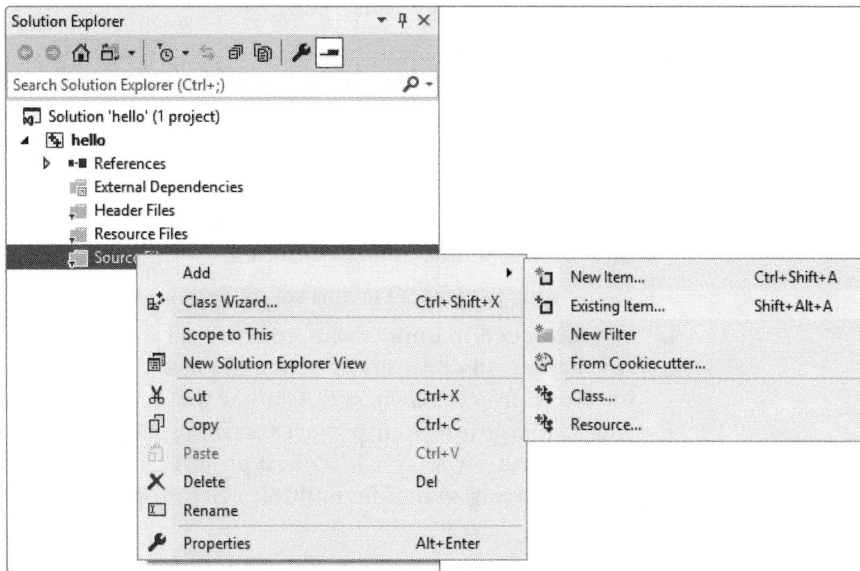

Figure 1-2: Adding an existing source file to a Visual Studio 2017 project

5. Select the *main.cpp* file that you created earlier in Listing 1-1. (Alternatively, if you haven't yet created this file, select **New Item** instead of **Existing Item**. Name the file *main.cpp* and type the contents of Listing 1-1 into the resulting editor window.)
6. Select **Build ▸ Build Solution**. If any error messages appear in the output box, make sure you've typed Listing 1-1 correctly. If you still get error messages, read them carefully for hints.
7. Select **Debug ▸ Start Without Debugging** or press CTRL-F5 to run your program. The letters `Hello, world!` should print to the console (followed by `Press Any Key to Continue`).

macOS: Xcode

If you're running macOS, you should install the Xcode development environment.

1. Open the **App Store**.
2. Search for and install the **Xcode** IDE. Installation might take more than an hour depending on the speed of your machine and internet connection. When installation is complete, open **Terminal** and navigate to the directory where you've saved *main.cpp*.
3. Enter **`clang++ main.cpp -o hello`** in the Terminal to compile your program. The `-o` option tells the tool chain where to write the output. (If any compiler errors appear, check that you've entered the program correctly.)
4. Enter **`./hello`** in the Terminal to run your program. The text `Hello, world!` should appear onscreen.

To compile and run your program, open the Xcode IDE and follow these steps:

1. Select **File ▸ New ▸ Project**.
2. Select **macOS ▸ Command Line Tool** and click **Next**. In the next dialog, you can modify where to create the project's file directory. For now, accept the defaults and click **Create**.
3. Name your project **`hello`** and set its **Type** to **C++**. See Figure 1-3.
4. You now need to import your code from Listing 1-1 into your project. An easy way to do this is to copy and paste the contents of *main.cpp* into your project's *main.cpp*. Another way is to use Finder to replace your *main.cpp* into your project's *main.cpp*. (Normally you won't have to handle this when creating new projects. It's just an artifact of this tutorial having to handle multiple operating environments.)
5. Click **Run**.

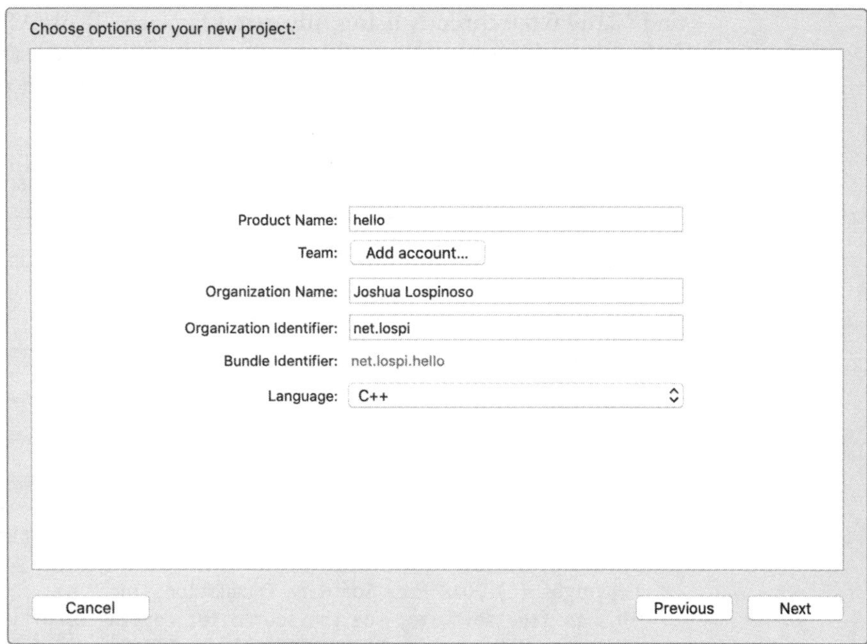

Figure 1-3: The New Project dialog in Xcode

Linux and GCC

On Linux, you can choose between two main C++ compilers: GCC and Clang. At press time, the latest stable release is 9.1 and the latest major Clang release is 8.0.0. In this section, you'll install both. Some users find the error messages from one to be more helpful than the other.

NOTE GCC *is an initialism for* GNU Compiler Collection. *GNU, pronounced "guh-NEW," is a recursive acronym for "GNU's Not Unix!" GNU is a Unix-like operating system and a collection of computer software.*

Try to install GCC and Clang from your operating system's package manager, but beware. Your default repositories might have old versions that may or may not have C++ 17 support. If your version doesn't have C++ 17 support, you won't be able to compile some examples in the book, so you'll need to install updated versions of GCC or Clang. For brevity, this chapter covers how to do this on Debian and from source. You can either investigate how to perform corollary actions on your chosen Linux flavor or set up a development environment with one of the operating systems listed in this chapter.

Installing GCC and Clang on Debian

Depending on what software the Personal Package Archives contain when you're reading this chapter, you might be able to install GCC 8.1

and Clang 6.0.0 directly using Advanced Package Tool (APT), which is Debian's package manager. This section shows how to install GCC and Clang on Ubuntu 18.04, the latest LTS Ubuntu version at press time.

1. Open a terminal.
2. Update and upgrade your currently installed packages:

```
$ sudo apt update && sudo apt upgrade
```

3. Install GCC 8 and Clang 6.0:

```
$ sudo apt install g++-8 clang-6.0
```

4. Test GCC and Clang:

```
$ g++-8 -version
g++-8 (Ubuntu 8-20180414-1ubuntu2) 8.0.1 20180414 (experimental) [trunk
revision 259383]
Copyright (C) 2018 Free Software Foundation, Inc.
This is free software; see the source for copying conditions.  There is NO
warranty; not even for MERCHANTABILITY or FITNESS FOR A PARTICULAR
PURPOSE.
$ clang++-6.0 --version
clang version 6.0.0-1ubuntu2 (tags/RELEASE_600/final)
Target: x86_64-pc-linux-gnu
Thread model: posix
InstalledDir: /usr/bin
```

If either command returns an error stating that the command wasn't found, the corresponding compiler did not install correctly. Try searching for information on the error you receive, especially in the documentation and forums for your respective package manager.

Installing GCC from Source

If you can't find the latest GCC or Clang versions with your package manager (or your Unix variant doesn't have one), you can always install GCC from source. Note that this takes a lot of time (as much as several hours), and you might need to get your hands dirty: installation often runs into errors that you'll need to research to resolve. To install GCC, follow the instructions available at *https://gcc.gnu.org/*. This section summarizes the far more extensive documentation available on that site.

NOTE *For brevity, this tutorial doesn't detail Clang installation. Refer to* https://clang.llvm.org/ *for more information.*

To install GCC 8.1 from source, do the following:

1. Open a terminal.

2. Update and upgrade your currently installed packages. For example, with APT you would issue the following command:

```
$ sudo apt update && sudo apt upgrade
```

3. From one of the available mirrors at *https://gcc.gnu.org/mirrors.html*, download the files *gcc-8.1.0.tar.gz* and *gcc-8.1.0.tar.gz.sig*. These files can be found in *releases/gcc-8.1.0*.
4. (Optional) Verify the integrity of the package. First, import the relevant GnuPG keys. You can find these listed on the mirrors site. For example:

```
$ gpg --keyserver keyserver.ubuntu.com --recv C3C45C06
gpg: requesting key C3C45C06 from hkp server keyserver.ubuntu.com
gpg: key C3C45C06: public key "Jakub Jelinek <jakub@redhat.com>" imported
gpg: key C3C45C06: public key "Jakub Jelinek <jakub@redhat.com>" imported
gpg: no ultimately trusted keys found
gpg: Total number processed: 2
gpg:               imported: 2  (RSA: 1)
```

Verify what you downloaded:

```
$ gpg --verify gcc-8.1.0.tar.gz.sig gcc-8.1.0.tar.gz
gpg: Signature made Wed 02 May 2018 06:41:51 AM DST using DSA key ID
C3C45C06
gpg: Good signature from "Jakub Jelinek <jakub@redhat.com>"
gpg: WARNING: This key is not certified with a trusted signature!
gpg:          There is no indication that the signature belongs to the
owner.
Primary key fingerprint: 33C2 35A3 4C46 AA3F FB29  3709 A328 C3A2 C3C4
5C06
```

The warnings you see mean that I haven't marked the signer's certificate as trusted on my machine. To verify that the signature belongs to the owner, you'll need to verify the signing key using some other means (for example, by meeting the owner in person or by verifying the primary key fingerprint out of band). For more information about GNU Privacy Guard (GPG), refer to *PGP & GPG: Email for the Practical Paranoid* by Michael W. Lucas or browse to *https://gnupg.org/download/integrity_check.html* for specific information about GPG's integrity-checking facilities.

5. Decompress the package (this command might take a few minutes):

```
$ tar xzf gcc-8.1.0.tar.gz
```

6. Navigate to the newly created *gcc-8.1.0* directory:

```
$ cd gcc-8.1.0
```

7. Download GCC's prerequisites:

```
$ ./contrib/download_prerequisites
--snip--
gmp-6.1.0.tar.bz2: OK
mpfr-3.1.4.tar.bz2: OK
mpc-1.0.3.tar.gz: OK
isl-0.18.tar.bz2: OK
All prerequisites downloaded successfully.
```

8. Configure GCC using the following commands:

```
$ mkdir objdir
$ cd objdir
$ ../configure --disable-multilib
checking build system type... x86_64-pc-linux-gnu
checking host system type... x86_64-pc-linux-gnu
--snip--
configure: creating ./config.status
config.status: creating Makefile
```

   Instructions are available at *https://gcc.gnu.org/install/configure.html.*

9. Build the GCC binaries (perhaps do this overnight, because it can take hours):

```
$ make
```

   Full instructions are available at *https://gcc.gnu.org/install/build.html.*

10. Test whether your GCC binaries built correctly:

```
$ make -k check
```

   Full instructions are available at *https://gcc.gnu.org/install/test.html.*

11. Install GCC:

```
$ make install
```

   This command places a handful of binaries into your operating system's default executable directory, which is usually */usr/local/bin*. Full instructions are available at *https://gcc.gnu.org/install/.*

12. Verify that GCC installed correctly by issuing the following command:

```
$ x86_64-pc-linux-gnu-gcc-8.1.0 --version
```

   If you get an error indicating that the command was not found, your installation did not succeed. Refer to the gcc-help mailing list at *https://gcc.gnu.org/ml/gcc-help/.*

NOTE *You might want to alias the cumbersome* x86_64-pc-linux-gnu-gcc-8.1.0 *to something like* g++8*, for example, using a command like this:*

```
$ sudo ln -s /usr/local/bin/x86_64-pc-linux-gnu-gcc-8.1.0 /usr/local/bin/g++8
```

13. Navigate to the directory where you've saved *main.cpp* and compile your program with GCC:

```
$ x86_64-pc-linux-gnu-gcc-8.1.0 main.cpp -o hello
```

14. The `-o` flag is optional; it tells the compiler what to name the resulting program. Because you specified the program name as `hello`, you should be able to run your program by entering **`./hello`**. If any compiler errors appear, ensure that you input the program's text correctly. (The compiler errors should help you determine what went wrong.)

Text Editors

If you'd rather not work with one of the aforementioned IDEs, you can write C++ code using a simple text editor like Notepad (Windows), TextEdit (Mac), or Vim (Linux); however, a number of excellent editors are designed specifically for C++ development. Choose the environment that makes you most productive.

If you're running Windows or macOS, you already have a high-quality, fully featured IDE at your disposal, namely Visual Studio or Xcode. Linux options include Qt Creator (*https://www.qt.io/ide/*), Eclipse CDT (*https://eclipse.org/cdt/*), and JetBrains's CLion (*https://www.jetbrains.com/clion/*). If you're a Vim or Emacs user, you'll find plenty of C++ plug-ins.

NOTE *If cross-platform C++ is important to you, I highly recommend taking a look at Jetbrains's CLion. Although CLion is a paid product, unlike many of its competitors, at press time Jetbrains does offer reduced-price and free licenses for students and open source project maintainers.*

Bootstrapping C++

This section gives you just enough context to support the example code in the chapters to come. You'll have questions about the details, and the coming chapters will answer them. Until then, don't panic!

The C++ Type System

C++ is an object-oriented language. Objects are abstractions with state and behavior. Think of a real-world object, such as a light switch. You can describe its *state* as the condition that the switch is in. Is it on or off? What is the maximum voltage it can handle? What room in the house is it in? You could also describe the switch's *behavior*. Does it toggle from one state (on) to another state (off)? Or is it a dimmer switch, which can be set to many different states between on and off?

The collection of behaviors and states describing an object is called its *type*. C++ is a *strongly typed language*, meaning each object has a predefined data type.

C++ has a built-in integer type called `int`. An `int` object can store whole numbers (its state), and it supports many math operations (its behavior).

To perform any meaningful tasks with `int` types, you'll create some `int` objects and name them. Named objects are called *variables*.

Declaring Variables

You declare variables by providing their type, followed by their name, followed by a semicolon. The following example declares a variable called `the_answer` with type `int`:

```
int❶ the_answer❷;
```

The type, `int` ❶, is followed by the variable name, `the_answer` ❷.

Initializing a Variable's State

When you declare variables, you initialize them. *Object initialization* establishes an object's initial state, such as setting its value. We'll delve into the details of initialization in Chapter 2. For now, you can use the equal sign (`=`) following a variable declaration to set the variable's initial value. For example, you could declare and assign `the_answer` in one line:

```
int the_answer = 42;
```

After running this line of code, you have a variable called `the_answer` with type `int` and value 42. You can assign variables equal to the result of math expressions, such as:

```
int lucky_number = the_answer / 6;
```

This line evaluates the expression `the_answer / 6` and assigns the result to `lucky_number`. The `int` type supports many other operations, such as addition `+`, subtraction `-`, multiplication `*`, and modulo division `%`.

NOTE *If you aren't familiar with modulo division or are wondering what happens when you divide two integers and there's a remainder, you're asking great questions. And those great questions will be answered in detail in Chapter 7.*

Conditional Statements

Conditional statements allow you to make decisions in your programs. These decisions rest on Boolean expressions, which evaluate to true or false. For example, you can use *comparison operators*, such as "greater than" or "not equal to," to build Boolean expressions.

Some basic comparison operators that work with `int` types appear in the program in Listing 1-2.

```
int main() {
  int x = 0;
  42  == x;  // Equality
  42  != x;  // Inequality
  100 >  x;  // Greater than
  123 >= x;  // Greater than or equal to
  -10 <  x;  // Less than
  -99 <= x;  // Less than or equal to
}
```

Listing 1-2: A program using comparison operators

This program produces no output (compile and run Listing 1-2 to verify this). While the program doesn't produce any output, compiling it helps to verify that you've written valid C++. To generate more interesting programs, you'd use a conditional statement like `if`.

An `if` statement contains a Boolean expression and one or more nested statements. Depending on whether the Boolean evaluates to true or false, the program decides which nested statement to execute. There are several forms of `if` statements, but the basic usage follows:

```
if (❶boolean-expression) ❷statement
```

If the Boolean expression ❶ is true, the nested statement ❷ executes; otherwise, it doesn't.

Sometimes, you'll want a group of statements to run rather than a single statement. Such a group is called a *compound statement*. To declare a compound statement, simply wrap the group of statements in braces { }. You can use compound statements within `if` statements as follows:

```
if (❶boolean-expression) { ❷
  statement1;
  statement2;
  --snip--
}
```

If the Boolean expression ❶ is true, all the statements in the compound statement ❷ execute; otherwise, none of them do.

You can elaborate the if statement using else if and else statements. These optional additions allow you to describe more complicated branching behavior, as shown in Listing 1-3.

```
❶ if (boolean-expression-1) statement-1
❷ else if (boolean-expression-2) statement-2
❸ else statement-3
```

Listing 1-3: An `if` *statement with* `else if` *and* `else` *branches*

First, *`boolean-expression-1`* ❶ is evaluated. If *`boolean-expression-1`* is true, *`statement-1`* is evaluated, and the if statement stops executing. If *`boolean-expression-1`* is false, *`boolean-expression-2`* ❷ is evaluated. If true, *`statement-2`* is evaluated. Otherwise, *`statement-3`* ❸ is evaluated. Note that *`statement-1`*, *`statement-2`*, and *`statement-3`* are mutually exclusive and together they cover all possible outcomes of the if statement. Only one of the three will be evaluated.

You can include any number of else if clauses or omit them entirely. As with the initial if statement, the Boolean expression for each else if clause is evaluated in order. When one of these Boolean expressions evaluates to true, evaluation stops and the corresponding statement executes. If no else if evaluates to true, the else clause's *`statement-3`* *always* executes. (As with the else if clauses, the else is optional.)

Consider Listing 1-4, which uses an if statement to determine which statement to print.

```
#include <cstdio>

int main() {
  int x = 0; ❶
  if (x > 0) printf("Positive.");
  else if (x < 0) printf("Negative.");
  else printf("Zero.");
}
--------------------------------------------------------------------------
Zero.
```

Listing 1-4: A program with conditional behavior

Compile the program and run it. Your result should also be `Zero`. Now change the `x` value ❶. What does the program print now?

NOTE *Notice that* `main` *in Listing 1-4 omits a return statement. Because* `main` *is a special function, return statements are optional.*

Functions

Functions are blocks of code that accept any number of input objects called *parameters* or *arguments* and can return output objects to their callers.

You declare functions according to the general syntax shown in Listing 1-5.

```
return-type❶ function_name❷(par-type1 par_name1❸, par-type2 par_name2❹) {
  --snip--
  return❺ return-value;
}
```

Listing 1-5: The general syntax for a C++ function

The first part of this function declaration is the type of the return variable ❶, such as `int`. When the function returns a value ❺, the type of `return-value` must match `return-type`.

Then you declare the function's name ❷ after declaring the return type. A set of parentheses following the function name contains any number of comma-separated input parameters that the function requires. Each parameter also has a type and a name.

Listing 1-5 has two parameters. The first parameter ❸ has type `par-type1` and is named `par_name1`, and the second parameter ❹ has type `par-type2` and is named `par_name2`. Parameters represent the objects passed into a function.

A set of braces following that list contains the function's body. This is a compound statement that contains the function's logic. Within this logic, the function might decide to return a value to the function's caller. Functions that return values will have one or more `return` statements. Once a function returns, it stops executing, and the flow of the program returns to whatever called the function. Let's look at an example.

Example: A Step Function

For demonstration purposes, this section shows how to build a mathematical function called `step_function` that returns `-1` for all negative arguments, `0` for a zero-valued argument, and `1` for all positive arguments. Listing 1-6 shows how you might write the `step_function`.

```
int step_function(int ❶x) {
  int result = 0; ❷
  if (x < 0) {
    result = -1; ❸
  } else if (x > 0) {
    result = 1; ❹
  }
  return result; ❺
}
```

Listing 1-6: A step function that returns `-1` for negative values, `0` for zero, and `1` for positive values

The `step_function` takes a single argument `x` ❶. The `result` variable is declared and initialized to `0` ❷. Next, the `if` statement sets `result` to `-1` ❸ if `x` is less than `0`. If `x` is greater than `0`, the `if` statement sets `result` to `1` ❹. Finally, `result` is returned to the caller ❺.

Calling Functions

To call (or *invoke*) a function, you use the name of the desired function, parentheses, and a comma-separated list of the required parameters. The compiler reads files from top to bottom, so the function's declaration must appear before its point of first use.

Consider the program in Listing 1-7, which uses the step_function.

```
int step_function(int x) {
  --snip--
}

int main() {
  int value1 = step_function(100); // value1 is  1
  int value2 = step_function(0);   // value2 is  0
  int value3 = step_function(-10); // value3 is -1
}
```

Listing 1-7: A program using the step_function. (This program produces no output.)

Listing 1-7 calls step_function three times with different arguments and assigns the results to the variables value1, value2, and value3.

Wouldn't it be nice if you could print these values? Fortunately, you can use the printf function to build output from different variables. The trick is to use printf format specifiers.

printf Format Specifiers

In addition to printing constant strings (like Hello, world! in Listing 1-1), printf can combine multiple values into a nicely formatted string; it is a special kind of function that can take one or more arguments.

The first argument to printf is always a *format string*. The format string provides a template for the string to be printed, and it contains any number of special *format specifiers*. Format specifiers tell printf how to interpret and format the arguments following the format string. All format specifiers begin with %.

For example, the format specifier for an int is %d. Whenever printf sees a %d in the format string, it knows to expect an int argument following the format specifier. Then printf replaces the format specifier with the argument's actual value.

NOTE *The printf function is a derivative of the writef function offered in BCPL, a defunct programming language designed by Martin Richards in 1967. Providing the specifiers %H, %I, and %O to writef resulted in hexadecimal and octal output via the functions WRITEHEX, WRITED, and WRITEOCT. It's unclear where the %d specifier comes from (perhaps the D in WRITED?), but we're stuck with it.*

Consider the following `printf` call, which prints the string `Ten 10, Twenty 20, Thirty 30`:

```
printf("Ten %d❶, Twenty %d❷, Thirty %d❸", 10❹, 20❺, 30❻);
```

The first argument, `"Ten %d, Twenty %d, Thirty %d"`, is the format string. Notice that there are three format specifiers `%d` ❶ ❷ ❸. There are also three arguments after the format string ❹ ❺ ❻. When `printf` builds the output, it replaces the argument at ❶ with the one at ❹, the argument at ❷ with the one at ❺, and the argument at ❸ with the one at ❻.

IOSTREAMS, PRINTF, AND INPUT OUTPUT PEDAGOGY

People have really strong opinions about which standard output method to teach C++ newcomers. One option is `printf`, which has a lineage that traces back to C. Another option is `cout`, which is part of the C++ standard library's `iostream` library. This book teaches both: `printf` in Part I and `cout` in Part II. Here's why.

This book builds your C++ knowledge brick by brick. Each chapter is designed sequentially so you don't need a leap of faith to understand code examples. More or less, you'll know exactly what every line does. Because `printf` is fairly primitive, you'll have enough knowledge by Chapter 3 to know exactly how it works.

In contrast, `cout` involves a whole lot of C++ concepts, and you won't have sufficient background to understand how it works until the end of Part I. (What's a stream buffer? What's `operator<<`? What's a method? How does `flush()` work? Wait, `cout` flushes automatically in the destructor? What's a destructor? What's `setf`? Actually, what's a format flag? A `BitmaskType`? Oh my, what's a manipulator? And so on.)

Of course, `printf` has issues, and once you've learned `cout`, you should prefer it. With `printf` you can easily introduce mismatches between format specifiers and arguments, and this can cause strange behavior, program crashes, and even security vulnerabilities. Using `cout` means you don't need format strings, so you don't need to remember format specifiers. You'll never get mismatches between format strings and arguments. Iostreams are also *extensible*, meaning you can integrate input and output functionality into your own types.

This book teaches modern C++ directly, but on this particular topic it compromises a bit of modernist dogma in exchange for a deliberate, linear approach. As an ancillary benefit, you'll be prepared to encounter `printf` specifiers, which is likely to happen at some point in your programming career. Most languages, such as C, Python, Java, and Ruby, have facilities for `printf` specifiers, and there are analogs in C#, JavaScript, and other languages.

Revisiting step_function

Let's look at another example that uses step_function. Listing 1-8 incorporates variable declarations, function calls, and printf format specifiers.

```
#include <cstdio> ❶

int step_function(int x) { ❷
  --snip--
}

int main() { ❸
    int num1 = 42; ❹
    int result1 = step_function(num1); ❺

    int num2 = 0;
    int result2 = step_function(num2);

    int num3 = -32767;
    int result3 = step_function(num3);

    printf("Num1: %d, Step: %d\n", num1, result1); ❻
    printf("Num2: %d, Step: %d\n", num2, result2);
    printf("Num3: %d, Step: %d\n", num3, result3);

    return 0;
}
```

```
Num1: 42, Step: 1 ❻
Num2: 0, Step: 0
Num3: -32767, Step: -1
```

Listing 1-8: A program that prints the results of applying step_function to several integers

Because the program uses printf, cstdio ❶ is included. The step_function ❷ is defined so you can use it later in the program, and main ❸ establishes the defined entry point.

NOTE *Some listings in this book will build on one another. To save trees, you'll see the use of the --snip-- notation to denote no changes to the reused portion.*

Inside main, you initialize a few int types, like num1 ❹. Next, you pass these variables to step_function and initialize result variables to store the returned values, like result1 ❺.

Finally, you print the returned values by invoking printf. Each invocation starts with a format string, like "Num1: %d, Step: %d\n" ❻. There are two %d format specifiers embedded in each format string. Per the requirements of printf, there are two parameters following the format string, num1 and result1, that correspond to these two format specifiers.

Comments

Comments are human-readable annotations that you can place into your source code. You can add comments to your code using the notation // or /**/. These symbols, // or /**/, tell the compiler to ignore everything from the first forward slash to the next newline, which means you can put comments in-line with your code as well as on their own lines:

```
// This comment is on its own line
int the_answer = 42; // This is an in-line comment
```

You can use the /**/ notation to include multiline comments in your code:

```
/*
 *  This is a comment
 *  That lives on multiple lines
 *  Don't forget to close
 */
```

The comment starts with /* and ends with */. (The asterisks on the lines between the starting and ending forward slash are optional but are commonly used.)

When to use comments is a matter of eternal debate. Some programming luminaries suggest that code should be so expressive and self-explanatory as to render comments largely unnecessary. They might say that descriptive variable names, short functions, and good tests are usually all the documentation you need. Other programmers like to place comments all over the place.

You can cultivate your own philosophy. The compiler will totally ignore whatever you do because it never interprets comments.

Debugging

One of the most important skills for a software engineer is efficient, effective debugging. Most development environments have debugging tools. On Windows, macOS, and Linux, the debugging tools are excellent. Learning to use them well is an investment that pays off very quickly. This section provides a quick tour of how to use a debugger to step through the program in Listing 1-8. You can skip to whichever environment is most relevant to you.

Visual Studio

Visual Studio has an excellent, built-in debugger. I suggest that you debug programs in its *Debug* configuration. This causes the tool chain to build a target that enhances the debugging experience. The only reason to debug in *Release* mode is to diagnose some rare conditions that occur in Release mode but not in Debug mode.

1. Open *main.cpp* and locate the first line of `main`.
2. Click the margin just to the left of the line number corresponding to the first line of `main` to insert a breakpoint. A red circle appears where you clicked, as shown in Figure 1-4.

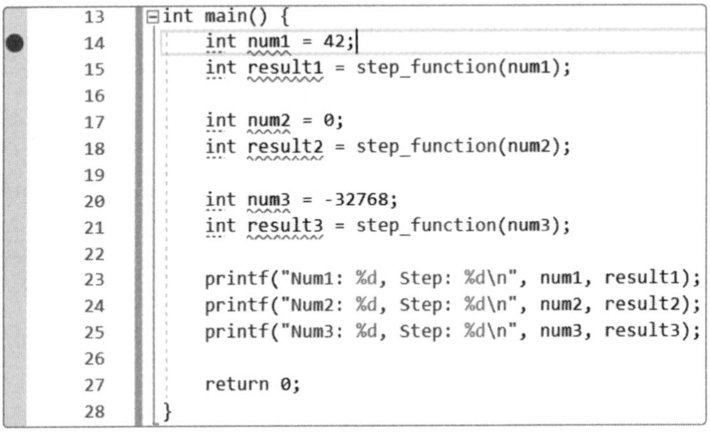

```
int main() {
    int num1 = 42;
    int result1 = step_function(num1);

    int num2 = 0;
    int result2 = step_function(num2);

    int num3 = -32768;
    int result3 = step_function(num3);

    printf("Num1: %d, Step: %d\n", num1, result1);
    printf("Num2: %d, Step: %d\n", num2, result2);
    printf("Num3: %d, Step: %d\n", num3, result3);

    return 0;
}
```

Figure 1-4: Inserting a breakpoint

3. Select **Debug ▸ Start Debugging**. The program will run up to the line where you've inserted a breakpoint. The debugger will halt program execution, and a yellow arrow will appear to indicate the next instruction to be run, as shown in Figure 1-5.

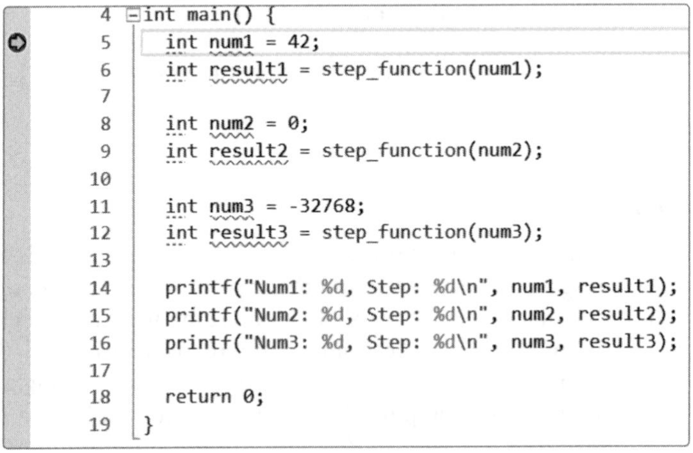

```
int main() {
    int num1 = 42;
    int result1 = step_function(num1);

    int num2 = 0;
    int result2 = step_function(num2);

    int num3 = -32768;
    int result3 = step_function(num3);

    printf("Num1: %d, Step: %d\n", num1, result1);
    printf("Num2: %d, Step: %d\n", num2, result2);
    printf("Num3: %d, Step: %d\n", num3, result3);

    return 0;
}
```

Figure 1-5: The debugger halts execution at the breakpoint.

4. Select **Debug ▸ Step Over**. The step over operation executes the instruction without "stepping into" any function calls. By default, the keyboard shortcut for step over is F10.

5. Because the next line calls `step_function`, select **Debug ▸ Step Into** to call `step_function` and break on the first line. You can continue debugging this function by stepping into/over its instructions. By default, the keyboard shortcut for step into is F11.
6. To allow execution to return to `main`, select **Debug ▸ Step Out**. By default, the keyboard shortcut for this operation is SHIFT-F11.
7. Inspect the Autos window by selecting **Debug ▸ Windows ▸ Auto**. You can see the current value of some of the important variables, as shown in Figure 1-6.

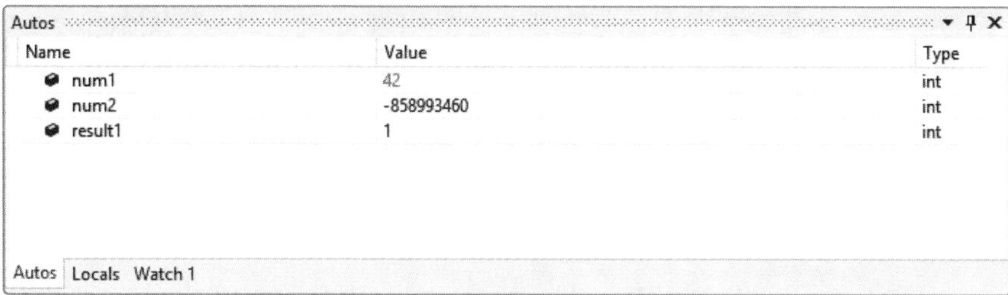

Figure 1-6: The Autos window shows the values of variables at the current breakpoint.

You can see `num1` is set to 42 and `result1` is set to 1. Why does `num2` have a gibberish value? Because the initialization to 0 hasn't happened yet: it's the next instruction to execute.

NOTE *The debugger has just emphasized a very important low-level detail: allocating an object's storage and initializing an object's value are two distinct steps. You'll learn more about storage allocation and object initialization in Chapter 4.*

The Visual Studio debugger supports many more features. For more information, check out the Visual Studio documentation link available at *https://ccc.codes/*.

Xcode

Xcode also has an excellent, built-in debugger that's completely integrated into the IDE.

1. Open *main.cpp* and locate the first line of `main`.
2. Click the first line and then select **Debug ▸ Breakpoints ▸ Add Breakpoint at Current Line**. A breakpoint appears, as shown in Figure 1-7.

```
#include "step_function.h"
#include <cstdio>

int main() {
  int num1 = 42;
  int result1 = step_function(num1);

  int num2 = 0;
  int result2 = step_function(num2);

  int num3 = -32768;
  int result3 = step_function(num3);

  printf("Num1: %d, Step: %d\n", num1, result1);
  printf("Num2: %d, Step: %d\n", num2, result2);
  printf("Num3: %d, Step: %d\n", num3, result3);

  return 0;
}
```

Figure 1-7: Inserting a breakpoint

3. Select **Run**. The program will run up to the line with the inserted breakpoint. The debugger will halt program execution, and a green arrow will appear to indicate the next instruction to be run, as shown in Figure 1-8.

```
#include "step_function.h"
#include <cstdio>

int main() {
  int num1 = 42;                              Thread 1: breakpoint 1.1
  int result1 = step_function(num1);

  int num2 = 0;
  int result2 = step_function(num2);

  int num3 = -32768;
  int result3 = step_function(num3);

  printf("Num1: %d, Step: %d\n", num1, result1);
  printf("Num2: %d, Step: %d\n", num2, result2);
  printf("Num3: %d, Step: %d\n", num3, result3);

  return 0;
}
```

Figure 1-8: The debugger halts execution at the breakpoint.

4. Select **Debug ▸ Step Over** to execute the instruction without "stepping into" any function calls. By default, the keyboard shortcut for step over is F6.
5. Because the next line calls `step_function`, select **Debug ▸ Step Into** to call `step_function` and break on the first line. You can continue debugging this function by stepping into/over its instructions. By default, the keyboard shortcut for step into is F7.

6. To allow execution to return to main, select **Debug ▸ Step Out**. By default, the keyboard shortcut for step out is F8.
7. Inspect the Autos window at the bottom of the *main.cpp* screen. You can see the current value of some of the important variables, as shown in Figure 1-9.

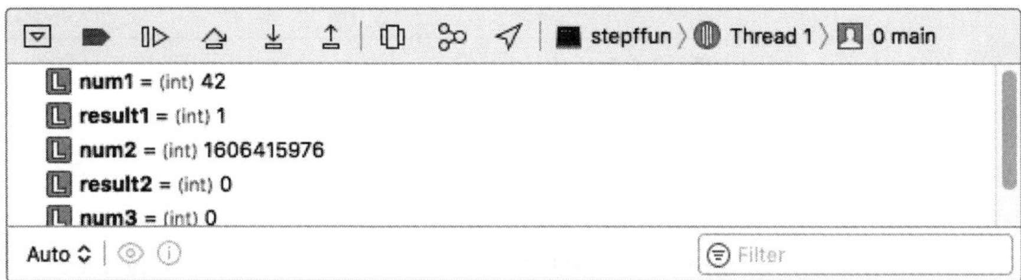

Figure 1-9: The Autos window shows the values of variables at the current breakpoint.

You can see num1 is set to 42 and result1 is set to 1. Why does num2 have a gibberish value? Because the initialization to 0 hasn't happened yet: it's the next instruction to execute.

The Xcode debugger supports many more features. For more information, check out the Xcode documentation link at *https://ccc.codes/*.

GCC and Clang Debugging with GDB and LLDB

The GNU Project Debugger (GDB) is a powerful debugger (*https://www.gnu.org/software/gdb/*). You can interact with GDB using the command line. To enable debugging support during compilation with g++ or clang++, you must add the -g flag.

Your package manager will most likely have GDB. For example, to install GDB with Advanced Package Tool (APT), enter the following command:

```
$ sudo apt install gdb
```

Clang also has an excellent debugger called the Low Level Debugger (LLDB), which you can download at *https://lldb.llvm.org/*. It was designed to work with the GDB commands in this section, so for brevity I won't cover LLDB explicitly. You can debug programs compiled with GCC debug support using LLDB, and you can debug programs compiled with Clang debug support using GDB.

NOTE *Xcode uses LLDB in the background.*

To debug the program in Listing 1-8 (on page 20) using GDB, follow these steps:

1. In a command line, navigate to the folder where you've stored your header and source files.

2. Compile your program with debug support:

```
$ g++-8 main.cpp -o stepfun -g
```

3. Debug your program using gdb; you should see the following interactive console session:

```
$ gdb stepfun
GNU gdb (Ubuntu 7.7.1-0ubuntu5~14.04.2) 7.7.1
Copyright (C) 2014 Free Software Foundation, Inc.
License GPLv3+: GNU GPL version 3 or later <http://gnu.org/licenses/gpl.
html>
This is free software: you are free to change and redistribute it.
There is NO WARRANTY, to the extent permitted by law.  Type "show copying"
and "show warranty" for details.
This GDB was configured as "x86_64-linux-gnu".
Type "show configuration" for configuration details.
For bug reporting instructions, please see:
<http://www.gnu.org/software/gdb/bugs/>.
Find the GDB manual and other documentation resources online at:
<http://www.gnu.org/software/gdb/documentation/>.
For help, type "help".
Type "apropos word" to search for commands related to "word"...
Reading symbols from stepfun...done.
(gdb)
```

4. To insert a breakpoint, use the command `break`, which takes a single argument corresponding to the name of the source file and the line where you want to break, separated by a colon (`:`). For example, suppose you want to break on the first line of *main.cpp*. In Listing 1-8, that is on line 5 (although you might need to adjust placement depending on how you've written the source). You can create a breakpoint using the following command at the `(gdb)` prompt:

```
(gdb) break main.cpp:5
```

5. You can also tell `gdb` to break at a particular function by name:

```
(gdb) break main
```

6. Either way, you can now execute your program:

```
(gdb) run
Starting program: /home/josh/stepfun
Breakpoint 1, main () at main.cpp:5
5         int num1 = 42;
(gdb)
```

7. To single step into an instruction, you use the step command to follow each line of the program, including steps into functions:

```
(gdb) step
6         int result1 = step_function(num1);
```

8. To continue stepping, press ENTER to repeat the last command:

```
(gdb)
step_function (x=42) at step_function.cpp:4
```

9. To step back out of a function invocation, you use the finish command:

```
(gdb) finish
Run till exit from #0  step_function (x=42) at step_function.cpp:7
0x0000000000400546 in main () at main.cpp:6
6         int result1 = step_function(num1);
Value returned is $1 = 1
```

10. To execute an instruction without stepping into a function call, you use the next command:

```
(gdb) next
8         int num2 = 0;
```

11. To inspect the current value of variables, you use the info locals command:

```
(gdb) info locals
num2 = -648029488
result2 = 32767
num1 = 42
result1 = 1
num3 = 0
result3 = 0
```

Notice that any variables that have not yet been initialized will not have sensible values.

12. To continue execution until the next breakpoint (or until the program completes), use the continue command:

```
(gdb) continue
Continuing.
Num1: 42, Step: 1
Num2: 0, Step: 0
Num3: -32768, Step: -1
[Inferior 1 (process 1322) exited normally]
```

13. Use the quit command to exit gdb at any time.

GDB supports many more features. For more information, check out the documentation at *https://sourceware.org/gdb/current/onlinedocs/gdb/*.

Summary

This chapter got you up and running with a working C++ development environment, and you compiled your first C++ program. You learned about the components of a build tool chain and the roles they play in the compilation process. Then you explored a few essential C++ topics, such as types, declaring variables, statements, conditionals, functions, and `printf`. The chapter wrapped up with a tutorial on setting up a debugger and stepping through your project.

NOTE *If you have problems setting up your environment, search on your error messages online. If that fails, post your question to Stack Overflow at* https://stackoverflow.com/, *the C++ subreddit at* https://www.reddit.com/r/cpp_questions/, *or the C++ Slack channel at* https://cpplang.now.sh/.

EXERCISES

Try these exercises to practice what you've learned in this chapter. (The book's companion code is available at *https://ccc.codes.*)

1-1. Create a function called `absolute_value` that returns the absolute value of its single argument. The absolute value of an integer x is the following: x (itself) if x is greater than or equal to 0; otherwise, it is x times −1. You can use the program in Listing 1-9 as a template:

```
#include <cstdio>

int absolute_value(int x) {
  // Your code here
}

int main() {
  int my_num = -10;
  printf("The absolute value of %d is %d.\n", my_num,
         absolute_value(my_num));
}
```

Listing 1-9: A template for a program that uses an `absolute_value` *function*

1-2. Try running your program with different values. Did you see the values you expect?

1-3. Run your program with a debugger, stepping through each instruction.

1-4. Write another function called `sum` that takes two `int` arguments and returns their sum. How can you modify the template in Listing 1-9 to test your new function?

1-5. C++ has a vibrant online community, and the internet is awash with excellent C++ related material. Investigate the CppCast podcast at *http://cppcast.com/*. Search for CppCon and C++Now videos available on YouTube. Add *https://cppreference.com/* and *http://www.cplusplus.com/* to your browser's bookmarks.

1-6. Finally, download a copy of the International Organization for Standardization (ISO) C++ 17 Standard from *https://isocpp.org/std/the-standard/*. Unfortunately, the official ISO standard is copyrighted and must be purchased. Fortunately, you can download a "draft," free of charge, that differs only cosmetically from the official version.

Note *Because the ISO standard's page numbers differ from version to version, this book will refer to specific sections using the same naming schema as the standard itself. This schema cites sections by enclosing the section name with square brackets. Subsections are appended with period separation. For example, to cite the section on the C++ Object Model, which is contained in the Introduction section, you would write [intro.object].*

FURTHER READING

- *The Pragmatic Programmer: From Journeyman to Master* by Andrew Hunt and David Thomas (Addison-Wesley Professional, 2000)
- *The Art of Debugging with GDB, DDD, and Eclipse* by Norman Matloff and Peter Jay Salzman (No Starch Press, 2008)
- *PGP & GPG: Email for the Practical Paranoid* by Michael W. Lucas (No Starch Press, 2006)
- *The GNU Make Book* by John Graham-Cumming (No Starch Press, 2015)

2

TYPES

Hardin once said, "To succeed, planning alone is insufficient. One must improvise as well." I'll improvise.
—Isaac Asimov, Foundation

As discussed in Chapter 1, a type declares how an object will be interpreted and used by the compiler. Every object in a C++ program has a type. This chapter begins with a thorough discussion of fundamental types and then introduces user-defined types. Along the way, you'll learn about several control flow structures.

Fundamental Types

Fundamental types are the most basic types of object and include integer, floating-point, character, Boolean, `byte`, `size_t`, and `void`. Some refer to fundamental types as *primitive* or *built-in* types because they're part of the core language and almost always available to you. These types will work on any platform, but their features, such as size and memory layout, depend on implementation.

Fundamental types strike a balance. On one hand, they try to map a direct relationship from C++ construct to computer hardware; on the other hand, they simplify writing cross-platform code by allowing a programmer to write code once that works on many platforms. The sections that follow provide additional detail about these fundamental types.

Integer Types

Integer types store whole numbers: those that you can write without a fractional component. The four sizes of integer types are *short int*, *int*, *long int*, and *long long int*. Each can be either signed or unsigned. A *signed* variable can be positive, negative, or zero, and an *unsigned* variable must be non-negative.

Integer types are signed and `int` by default, which means you can use the following shorthand notations in your programs: `short`, `long`, and `long long` rather than `short int`, `long int`, and `long long int`. Table 2-1 lists all available C++ integer types, whether each is signed or unsigned, the size of each (in bytes) across platforms, as well as the format specifier for each.

Table 2-1: Integer Types, Sizes, and Format Specifiers

		Size in bytes				
		32-bit OS		64-bit OS		`printf` format
Type	**Signed**	**Windows**	**Linux/Mac**	**Windows**	**Linux/Mac**	**specifier**
`short`	Yes	2	2	2	2	`%hd`
`unsigned short`	No	2	2	2	2	`%hu`
`int`	Yes	4	4	4	4	`%d`
`unsigned int`	No	4	4	4	4	`%u`
`long`	Yes	4	4	4	8	`%ld`
`unsigned long`	No	4	4	4	8	`%lu`
`long long`	Yes	8	8	8	8	`%lld`
`unsigned long long`	No	8	8	8	8	`%llu`

Notice that the integer type sizes vary across platforms: 64-bit Windows and Linux/Mac have different sizes for a `long` integer (4 and 8, respectively).

Usually, a compiler will warn you of a mismatch between format specifier and integer type. But you must ensure that the format specifiers are correct when you're using them in `printf` statements. Format specifiers appear here so you can print integers to console in examples to follow.

NOTE *If you want to enforce guaranteed integer sizes, you can use integer types in the* `<cstdint>` *library. For example, if you need a signed integer with exactly 8, 16, 32, or 64 bits, you could use* `int8_t`, `int16_t`, `int32_t`, *or* `int64_t`. *You'll find options for the fastest, smallest, maximum, signed, and unsigned integer types to meet your requirements. But because this header is not always available in every platform, you should only use* `cstdint` *types when there is no other alternative.*

A *literal* is a hardcoded value in a program. You can use one of four hardcoded, *integer literal* representations:

binary Uses the prefix 0b

octal Uses the prefix 0

decimal This is the default

hexadecimal Uses the prefix 0x

These are four different ways of writing the same set of whole numbers. For example, Listing 2-1 shows how you might assign several integer variables with integer literals using each of the non-decimal representations.

```
#include <cstdio>

int main() {
  unsigned short a = 0b10101010; ❶
  printf("%hu\n", a);
  int b = 0123; ❷
  printf("%d\n", b);
  unsigned long long d = 0xFFFFFFFFFFFFFFFF; ❸
  printf("%llu\n", d);
}
--------------------------------------------------------------------------------
170 ❶
83 ❷
18446744073709551615 ❸
```

Listing 2-1: A program that assigns several integer variables and prints them with the appropriate format specifier

This program uses each of the non-decimal integer representations (binary ❶, octal ❷, and hexadecimal ❸) and prints each with `printf` using the appropriate format specifier listed in Table 2-1. The output from each `printf` appears as a following comment.

NOTE *Integer literals can contain any number of single quotes (') for readability. These are completely ignored by the compiler. For example,* `1000000` *and* `1'000'000` *are both integer literals equal to one million.*

Sometimes, it's useful to print an unsigned integer in its hexadecimal representation or (rarely) its octal representation. You can use the `printf` specifiers `%x` and `%o` for these purposes, respectively, as shown in Listing 2-2.

```
#include <cstdio>

int main() {
  unsigned int a = 3669732608;
  printf("Yabba %x❶!\n", a);
  unsigned int b = 69;
  printf("There are %u❷,%o❸ leaves here.\n", b❹, b❺);
}
```

```
Yabba dabbad00❶!
There are 69❷,105❸ leaves here.
```

Listing 2-2: A program that uses octal and hexadecimal representations of unsigned integers

The hexadecimal representation of the decimal 3669732608 is dabbad00, which appears in the first line of output as a result of the hexadecimal format specifier %x ❶. The decimal 69 is 105 in octal. The format specifiers for unsigned integer %u ❷ and octal integer %o ❸ correspond with the arguments at ❹ and ❺, respectively. The printf statement substitutes these quantities ❷❸ into the format string, yielding the message There are 69,105 leaves in here.

WARNING *The octal prefix is a holdover from the B language, back in the days of the PDP-8 computer and ubiquitous octal literals. C, and by extension C++, continues the dubious tradition. You must be careful, for example, when you're hardcoding ZIP codes:*

```
int mit_zip_code = 02139; // Won't compile
```

Eliminate leading zeros on decimal literals; otherwise, they'll cease to be decimal. This line doesn't compile because 9 is not an octal digit.

By default, an integer literal's type is one of the following: int, long, or long long. An integer literal's type is the smallest of these three types that fits. (This is defined by the language and will be enforced by the compiler.)

If you want more control, you can supply *suffixes* to an integer literal to specify its type (suffixes are case insensitive, so you can choose the style you like best):

- The unsigned suffix u or U
- The long suffix l or L
- The long long suffix ll or LL

You can combine the unsigned suffix with either the long or the long long suffix to specify signed-ness and size. Table 2-2 shows the possible types that a suffix combination can take. Allowed types are shown with a check mark (✓). For binary, octal, and hexadecimal literals, you can omit the u or U suffix. These are depicted with an asterisk (*).

Table 2-2: Integer Suffixes

Type	(none)	l/L	ll/LL	u/U	ul/UL	ull/ULL
int	✓					
long	✓	✓				
long long	✓	✓	✓			
unsigned int	*			✓		
unsigned long	*	*		✓	✓	
unsigned long long	*	*	*	✓	✓	✓

The smallest allowed type that still fits the integer literal is the resulting type. This means that among all types allowed for a particular integer, the smallest type will apply. For example, the integer literal `112114` could be an `int`, a `long`, or a `long long`. Since an `int` can store 112114, the resulting integer literal is an `int`. If you really want, say, a `long`, you can instead specify `112114L` (or `112114l`).

Floating-Point Types

Floating-point types store approximations of real numbers (which in our case can be defined as any number that has a decimal point and a fractional part, such as 0.33333 or 98.6). Although it's not possible to represent an arbitrary real number exactly in computer memory, it's possible to store an approximation. If this seems hard to believe, just think of a number like π, which has infinitely many digits. With finite computer memory, how could you possibly represent infinitely many digits?

As with all types, floating-point types take up a finite amount of memory, which is called the type's *precision*. The more precision a floating-point type has, the more accurate it will be at approximating a real number. C++ offers three levels of precision for approximations:

`float` single precision

`double` double precision

`long double` extended precision

As with integer types, each floating-point representation depends on implementation. This section won't go into detail about floating-point types, but note that there is substantial nuance involved in these implementations.

On major desktop operating systems, the `float` level usually has 4 bytes of precision. The `double` and `long double` levels usually have 8 bytes of precision (*double precision*).

Most users not involved in scientific computing applications can safely ignore the details of floating-point representation. In such cases, a good general rule is to use a `double`.

NOTE *For those who cannot safely ignore the details, look at the floating-point specification relevant to your hardware platform. The predominant implementation of floating-point storage and arithmetic is outlined in* The IEEE Standard for Floating-Point Arithmetic, IEEE 754.

Floating-Point Literals

Floating-point literals are double precision by default. If you need single precision, use an `f` or `F` suffix; for extended precision, use `l` or `L`, as shown here:

```
float a = 0.1F;
double b = 0.2;
long double c = 0.3L;
```

You can also use scientific notation in literals:

```
double plancks_constant = 6.62607004❶e-34❷;
```

No spaces are permitted between the *significand* (the base ❶) and the *suffix* (the exponential portion ❷).

Floating-Point Format Specifiers

The format specifier `%f` displays a `float` with decimal digits, whereas `%e` displays the same number in scientific notation. You can let `printf` decide which of these two to use with the `%g` format specifier, which selects the more compact of `%e` or `%f`.

For `double`, you simply prepend an `l` (lowercase *L*) to the desired specifier; for `long double`, prepend an `L`. For example, if you wanted a `double` with decimal digits, you would specify `%lf`, `%le`, or `%lg`; for a long double, you would specify `%Lf`, `%Le`, or `%Lg`.

Consider Listing 2-3, which explores the different options for printing floating points.

```
#include <cstdio>

int main() {
  double an = 6.0221409e23; ❶
  printf("Avogadro's Number:  %le❷ %lf❸ %lg❹\n", an, an, an);
  float hp = 9.75; ❺
  printf("Hogwarts' Platform: %e %f %g\n", hp, hp, hp);
}
--------------------------------------------------------------------------------
Avogadro's Number:  6.022141e+23❷ 602214090000000006225920.000000❸
6.02214e+23❹
Hogwarts' Platform: 9.750000e+00 9.750000 9.75
```

Listing 2-3: A program printing several floating points

This program declares a `double` called `an` ❶. The format specifier `%le` ❷ gives you scientific notation `6.022141e-23`, and `%lf` ❸ gives the decimal representation `602214090000000006225920.000000`. The `%lg` ❹ specifier chose the scientific notation `6.02214e-23`. The `float` called `hp` ❺ produces similar `printf` output using the `%e` and `%f` specifiers. But the format specifier `%g` decided to provide the decimal representation 9.75 rather than scientific notation.

As a general rule, use `%g` to print floating-point types.

NOTE *In practice, you can omit the* `l` *prefix on the format specifiers for* `double`*, because* `printf` *promotes* `float` *arguments to* `double` *precision.*

Character Types

Character types store human language data. The six character types are:

`char` The default type, always 1 byte. May or may not be signed. (Example: ASCII.)

`char16_t` Used for 2-byte character sets. (Example: UTF-16.)

`char32_t` Used for 4-byte character sets. (Example: UTF-32.)

`signed char` Same as `char` but guaranteed to be signed.

`unsigned char` Same as `char` but guaranteed to be unsigned.

`wchar_t` Large enough to contain the largest character of the implementation's locale. (Example: Unicode.)

The character types `char`, `signed char`, and `unsigned char` are called *narrow characters*, whereas `char16_t`, `char32_t`, and `wchar_t` are called *wide characters* due to their relative storage requirements.

Character Literals

A *character literal* is a single, constant character. Single quotation marks (`' '`) surround all characters. If the character is any type but `char`, you must also provide a prefix: `L` for `wchar_t`, `u` for `char16_t`, and `U` for `char32_t`. For example, `'J'` declares a `char` literal and `L'J'` declares a `wchar_t`.

Escape Sequences

Some characters don't display on the screen. Instead, they force the display to do things like move the cursor to the left side of the screen (carriage return) or move the cursor down one line (newline). Other characters can display onscreen, but they're part of the C++ language syntax, such as single or double quotes, so you must use them very carefully. To put these characters into a `char`, you use the *escape sequences*, as listed in Table 2-3.

Table 2-3: Reserved Characters and Their Escape Sequences

Value	Escape sequence
Newline	`\n`
Tab (horizontal)	`\t`
Tab (vertical)	`\v`
Backspace	`\b`
Carriage return	`\r`
Form feed	`\f`
Alert	`\a`
Backslash	`\\`
Question mark	`?` or `\?`
Single quote	`\'`
Double quote	`\"`
The null character	`\0`

Unicode Escape Characters

You can specify Unicode character literals using the *universal character names*, and you can form a universal character name in one of two ways: the prefix `\u` followed by a 4-digit Unicode code point or the prefix `\U` followed by an 8-digit Unicode code point. For example, you can represent the `A` character as `'\u0041'` and represent the beer mug character 🍺 as `U'\U0001F37A'`.

Format Specifiers

The `printf` format specifier for `char` is `%c`. The `wchar_t` format specifier is `%lc`.

Listing 2-4 initializes two character literals, `x` and `y`. You use these variables to build a `printf` call.

```
#include <cstdio>

int main() {
  char x = 'M';
  wchar_t y = L'Z';
  printf("Windows binaries start with %c%lc.\n", x, y);
}
--------------------------------------------------------------------------------
Windows binaries start with MZ.
```

Listing 2-4: A program that assigns several character-typed variables and prints them

This program outputs *Windows binaries start with MZ.* Even though the *M* is a narrow character `char` and the *Z* is a wide character, `printf` works because the program uses the correct format specifiers.

NOTE *The first two bytes of all Windows binaries are the characters* M *and* Z, *an homage to Mark Zbikowski, the designer of the MS-DOS executable binary file format.*

Boolean Types

Boolean types have two states: true and false. The sole Boolean type is `bool`. Integer types and the `bool` types convert readily: the `true` state converts to 1, and `false` converts to 0. Any non-zero integer converts to true, and 0 converts to `false`.

Boolean Literals

To initialize Boolean types, you use two Boolean literals, `true` and `false`.

Format Specifiers

There is no format specifier for `bool`, but you can use the `int` format specifier `%d` within `printf` to yield a `1` for true and a `0` for false. The reason is that `printf` promotes any integral value smaller than an `int` to an `int`. Listing 2-5 illustrates how to declare a Boolean variable and inspect its value.

```
#include <cstdio>

int main() {
  bool b1 = true;  ❶ // b1 is true
  bool b2 = false; ❷ // b2 is false
  printf("%d %d\n", b1, b2); ❸
}
--------------------------------------------------------------------------
1 0 ❸
```

Listing 2-5: Printing `bool` variables with a `printf` statement

You initialize `b1` to `true` ❶ and `b2` to `false` ❷. By printing `b1` and `b2` as integers (using `%d` format specifiers), you get 1 for `b1` and 0 for `b2` ❸.

Comparison Operators

Operators are functions that perform computations on *operands*. Operands are simply objects. ("Logical Operators" on page 182 covers a full menu of operators.) In order to have meaningful examples using `bool` types, you'll take a quick look at comparison operators in this section and logical operators in the next.

You can use several operators to build Boolean expressions. Recall that comparison operators take two arguments and return a `bool`. The available operators are equality (`==`), inequality (`!=`), greater than (`>`), less than (`<`), greater than or equal to (`>=`), and less than or equal to (`<=`).

Listing 2-6 shows how you can use these operators to produce Booleans.

```
#include <cstdio>

int main() {
  printf(" 7 ==  7: %d❶\n", 7  ==  7❷);
  printf(" 7 !=  7: %d\n", 7  !=  7);
  printf("10 >  20: %d\n", 10 >  20);
  printf("10 >= 20: %d\n", 10 >= 20);
  printf("10 <  20: %d\n", 10 <  20);
  printf("20 <= 20: %d\n", 20 <= 20);
}
--------------------------------------------------------------------------
 7 ==  7: 1 ❶
 7 !=  7: 0
10 >  20: 0
10 >= 20: 0
10 <  20: 1
20 <= 20: 1
```

Listing 2-6: Using comparison operators

Each comparison produces a Boolean result ❷, and the `printf` statement prints the Boolean as an `int` ❶.

Logical Operators

Logical operators evaluate Boolean logic on `bool` types. You characterize operators by how many operands they take. A *unary operator* takes a single operand, a *binary operator* takes two, a *ternary operator* takes three, and so on. You categorize operators further by describing the types of their operands.

The unary *negation* operator (`!`) takes a single operand and returns its opposite. In other words, `!true` yields `false`, and `!false` yields `true`.

The logical operators AND (`&&`) and OR (`||`) are binary. Logical AND returns `true` only if both of its operands are `true`. Logical OR returns `true` if either or both of its operands are `true`.

NOTE *When you're reading a Boolean expression, the* `!` *is pronounced "not," as in "a and not b" for the expression* `a && !b`.

Logical operators might seem confusing at first, but they quickly become intuitive. Listing 2-7 showcases the logical operators.

```
#include <cstdio>

int main() {
  bool t = true;
  bool f = false;
  printf("!true: %d\n", !t); ❶
  printf("true  &&  false: %d\n", t &&  f); ❷
  printf("true  && !false: %d\n", t && !f); ❸
  printf("true  ||  false: %d\n", t ||  f); ❹
  printf("false ||  false: %d\n", f ||  f); ❺
}
```

```
!true: 0 ❶
true  &&  false: 0 ❷
true  && !false: 1 ❸
true  ||  false: 1 ❹
false ||  false: 0 ❺
```

Listing 2-7: A program that illustrates the use of logical operators

Here, you see the negation operator ❶, the logical AND operator ❷❸, and the logical OR operator ❹❺.

The std::byte Type

System programmers sometimes work directly with *raw memory*, which is a collection of bits without a type. Employ the `std::byte` type, available in the `<cstddef>` header, in such situations. The `std::byte` type permits bitwise logical operations (which you'll meet in Chapter 7) and little else. Using this type for raw data rather than an integral type can help to avoid common sources of difficult-to-debug programming errors.

Note that unlike most other fundamental types in `<cstddef>`, `std::byte` doesn't have an exact corollary type in the C language (a "C type"). Like C++, C has `char` and `unsigned char`. These types are less safe to use because they support many operations that std::byte doesn't. For example, you can perform arithmetic, like addition (+), on a char but not a std::byte. The odd-looking std:: prefix is called a *namespace*, which you'll meet in "Namespaces" on page 216 (for now, just think of the namespace std:: as part of the type name).

NOTE *There are two schools of thought on how to pronounce* std. *One is to treat it as an initialism, as in "ess-tee-dee," and another is to treat it as an acronym, as in "stood." When referring to a class in the* std *namespace, speakers typically imply the namespace operator* ::. *So you could pronounce* std::byte *as "stood byte" or, if you're not into the whole brevity thing, as "ess-tee-dee colon colon byte."*

The size_t Type

You use the size_t type, also available in the <cstddef> header, to encode size of objects. The size_t objects guarantee that their maximum values are sufficient to represent the maximum size in bytes of all objects. Technically, this means a size_t could take 2 bytes or 200 bytes depending on the implementation. In practice, it's usually identical to an unsigned long long on 64-bit architectures.

NOTE *The type* size_t *is a C type in the* <stddef> *header, but it's identical to the C++ version, which resides in the* std *namespace. Occasionally, you'll see the (technically correct) construction* std::size_t *instead.*

sizeof

The unary operator sizeof takes a type operand and returns the size (in bytes) of that type. The sizeof operator always returns a size_t. For example, sizeof(float) returns the number of bytes of storage a float takes.

Format Specifiers

The usual format specifiers for a size_t are %zd for a decimal representation or %zx for a hexadecimal representation. Listing 2-8 shows how you might check a system for several integer types' sizes.

```
#include <cstddef>
#include <cstdio>

int main() {
  size_t size_c = sizeof(char); ❶
  printf("char: %zd\n", size_c);
  size_t size_s = sizeof(short); ❷
  printf("short: %zd\n", size_s);
  size_t size_i = sizeof(int); ❸
  printf("int: %zd\n", size_i);
  size_t size_l = sizeof(long); ❹
  printf("long: %zd\n", size_l);
```

```
  size_t size_ll = sizeof(long long); ❺
  printf("long long: %zd\n", size_ll);
}
--------------------------------------------------------------------------------
char: 1 ❶
short: 2 ❷
int: 4 ❸
long: 4 ❹
long long: 8 ❺
```

Listing 2-8: A program that prints the sizes in bytes of several integer types. (The output comes from a Windows 10 x64 machine.)

Listing 2-8 evaluates the sizeof a char ❶, a short ❷, an int ❸, a long ❹, and a long long ❺ and prints their sizes using the %zd format specifier. Results will vary depending on the operating system. Recall from Table 2-1 that each environment defines its own sizes for the integer types. Pay special attention to the return value of long in Listing 2-8; Linux and macOS define 8-byte long types.

void

The void type has an empty set of values. Because a void object cannot hold a value, C++ disallows void objects. You use void in special situations, such as the return type for functions that don't return any value. For example, the function taunt doesn't return a value, so you declare its return type void:

```
#include <cstdio>

void taunt() {
  printf("Hey, laser lips, your mama was a snow blower.");
}
```

In Chapter 3, you'll learn about other special void uses.

Arrays

Arrays are sequences of identically typed variables. *Array types* include the contained type and the number of contained elements. You weave this information together in the declaration syntax: the element type precedes square brackets enclosing the array's size.

For example, the following line declares an array of 100 int objects:

```
int my_array[100];
```

Array Initialization

There's a shortcut for initializing arrays with values using braces:

```
int array[] = { 1, 2, 3, 4 };
```

You can omit the length of the array because it can be inferred from the number of elements in the braces at compile time.

Accessing Array Elements

You access array elements by using square brackets to enclose the desired index. Array indexing is zero based in C++, so the first element is at index 0, the tenth element is at index 9, and so on. Listing 2-9 illustrates reading and writing array elements.

```
#include <cstdio>

int main() {
  int arr[] = { 1, 2, 3, 4 }; ❶
  printf("The third element is %d.\n", arr[2]❷);
  arr[2] = 100; ❸
  printf("The third element is %d.\n", arr[2]❹);
}
--------------------------------------------------------------------------
The third element is 3. ❷
The third element is 100. ❹
```

Listing 2-9: A program that indexes into an array

This code declares a four-element array named arr containing the elements 1, 2, 3, and 4 ❶. On the next line ❷, it prints the third element. It then assigns the third element to 100 ❸, so when it reprints the third element ❹, the value is 100.

A Nickel Tour of for Loops

A for loop lets you repeat (or iterate) the execution of a statement a specified number of times. You can stipulate a starting point and other conditions. The *init statement* executes before the first iteration executes, so you can initialize variables used in the for loop. The *conditional* is an expression that is evaluated before each iteration. If it evaluates to true, iteration proceeds. If false, the for loop terminates. The *iteration statement* executes after each iteration, which is useful in situations where you must increment a variable to cover a range of values. The for loop syntax is as follows:

```
for(init-statement; conditional; iteration-statement) {
  --snip--
}
```

For example, Listing 2-10 shows you how to use a for loop to find the maximum of an array.

```
#include <cstddef>
#include <cstdio>

int main() {
  unsigned long maximum = 0; ❶
```

```
  unsigned long values[] = { 10, 50, 20, 40, 0 }; ❷
  for(size_t i=0; i < 5; i++) { ❸
    if (values[i] > maximum❹) maximum = values[i]; ❺
  }
  printf("The maximum value is %lu", maximum); ❻
}
--------------------------------------------------------------------------
The maximum value is 50 ❻
```

Listing 2-10: Finding the maximum value contained in an array

You initialize `maximum` ❶ to the smallest value possible; here that's 0 because it's unsigned. Next, you initialize the array `values` ❷, which you iterate over using the `for` loop ❸. The iterator variable `i` ranges from 0 to 4 inclusive. Within the `for` loop, you access each element of `values` and check whether the element is greater than the current `maximum` ❹. If it is, you set `maximum` to that new value ❺. When the loop is complete, `maximum` will equal the greatest value in the array, which prints the value of `maximum` ❻.

NOTE *If you've programmed C or C++ before, you might be wondering why Listing 2-10 employs `size_t` instead of an `int` for the type of `i`. Consider that `values` could theoretically take up the maximum storage allowed. Although `size_t` is guaranteed to be able to index any value within it, `int` is not. In practice, it makes little difference, but technically `size_t` is correct.*

The Range-Based for Loop

In Listing 2-10, you saw how to use the `for` loop at ❸ to iterate over the elements of the array. You can eliminate the iterator variable `i` by using a *range-based for loop*. For certain objects like arrays, `for` understands how to iterate over the range of values within an object. Here's the syntax for a range-based for loop:

```
for(element-type❶ element-name❷ : array-name❸) {
  --snip--
}
```

You declare an iterator variable `element-name` ❷ with type `element-type` ❶. The `element-type` must match the types within the array you're iterating over. This array is called `array-name` ❸.

Listing 2-11 refactors Listing 2-10 with a range-based `for` loop.

```
#include <cstdio>

int main() {
  unsigned long maximum = 0;
  unsigned long values[] = { 10, 50, 20, 40, 0 };
  for(unsigned long value : values❶) {
    if (value❷ > maximum) maximum = value❸;
  }
```

```
  printf("The maximum value is %lu.", maximum);
}
-------------------------------------------------------------------------
The maximum value is 50.
```

Listing 2-11: Refactoring Listing 2-10 with a range-based `for` *loop*

NOTE *You'll learn about expressions in Chapter 7. For now, think of an expression as some bit of code that produces an effect on your program.*

Listing 2-11 greatly improves Listing 2-10. At a glance, you know that the `for` loop iterates over `values` ❶. Because you've discarded the iterator variable `i`, the body of the `for` loop simplifies nicely; for that reason, you can use each element of values directly ❷❸.

Use range-based `for` loops generously.

Number of Elements in an Array

Use the `sizeof` operator to obtain the total size in bytes of an array. You can use a simple trick to determine the number of elements in an array: divide the size of the array by the size of a single constituent element:

```
short array[] = { 104, 105, 32, 98, 105, 108, 108, 0 };
size_t n_elements = sizeof(array)❶ / sizeof(short)❷;
```

On most systems, `sizeof(array)` ❶ will evaluate to 16 bytes and `sizeof(short)` ❷ will evaluate to 2 bytes. Regardless of the size of a `short`, `n_elements` will always initialize to 8 because the factor will cancel. This evaluation happens at compile time, so there is no runtime cost in evaluating the length of an array in this way.

The `sizeof(x)/sizeof(y)` construction is a bit of a hack, but it's widely used in older code. In Part II, you'll learn other options for storing data that don't require external computation of their lengths. If you really must use an array, you can safely obtain the number of elements using the `std::size` function available in the `<iterator>` header.

NOTE *As an additional benefit,* `std::size` *can be used with any container that exposes a* `size` *method. This includes all the containers in Chapter 13. This is especially useful when writing generic code, a topic you'll explore in Chapter 6. Further, it will refuse to compile if you accidentally pass an unsupported type, like a pointer.*

C-Style Strings

Strings are contiguous blocks of characters. A *C-style string* or *null-terminated string* has a zero-byte appended to its end (a null) to indicate the end of the string. Because array elements are contiguous, you can store strings in arrays of character types.

String Literals

Declare string literals by enclosing text in quotation marks (""). Like character literals, string literals support Unicode: just prepend the literal with the appropriate prefix, such as `L`. The following example assigns string literals to the arrays `english` and `chinese`:

```
char english[] = "A book holds a house of gold.";
char16_t chinese[] = u"\u4e66\u4e2d\u81ea\u6709\u9ec4\u91d1\u5c4b";
```

NOTE *Surprise! You've been using string literals all along: the format strings of your* `printf` *statements are string literals.*

This code generates two variables: `english`, which contains `A book holds a house of gold.`, and `chinese`, which contains the Unicode characters for 书中自有黄金屋.

Format Specifier

The format specifier for narrow strings (`char*`) is `%s`. For example, you can incorporate strings into format strings as follows:

```
#include <cstdio>

int main() {
  char house[] = "a house of gold.";
  printf("A book holds %s\n ", house);
}
--------------------------------------------------------------------------
A book holds a house of gold.
```

NOTE *Printing Unicode to the console is surprisingly complicated. Typically, you need to ensure that the correct* code page *is selected, and this topic is well beyond the scope of this book. If you need to embed Unicode characters into a string literal, look at* `wprintf` *in the* `<cwchar>` *header.*

Consecutive string literals get concatenated together, and any intervening whitespaces or newlines get ignored. So, you can place string literals on multiple lines in your source, and the compiler will treat them as one. For example, you could refactor this example as follows:

```
#include <cstdio>

int main() {
  char house[] = "a "
      "house "
      "of " "gold.";
  printf("A book holds %s\n ", house);
}
--------------------------------------------------------------------------
A book holds a house of gold.
```

Usually, such constructions are useful for readability only when you have a long string literal that would span multiple lines in your source code. The generated programs are identical.

ASCII

The *American Standard Code for Information Interchange (ASCII)* table assigns integers to characters. Table 2-4 shows the ASCII table. For each integer value in decimal (0d) and hex (0x), the given control code or printable character is shown.

Table 2-4: The ASCII Table

Control codes			Printable characters								
0d	**0x**	**Code**	**0d**	**0x**	**Char**	**0d**	**0x**	**Char**	**0d**	**0x**	**Char**
0	0	NULL	32	20	SPACE	64	40	@	96	60	`
1	1	SOH	33	21	!	65	41	A	97	61	a
2	2	STX	34	22	"	66	42	B	98	62	b
3	3	ETX	35	23	#	67	43	C	99	63	c
4	4	EOT	36	24	$	68	44	D	100	64	d
5	5	ENQ	37	25	%	69	45	E	101	65	e
6	6	ACK	38	26	&	70	46	F	102	66	f
7	7	BELL	39	27	'	71	47	G	103	67	g
8	8	BS	40	28	(	72	48	H	104	68	h
9	9	HT	41	29	)	73	49	I	105	69	i
10	0a	LF	42	2a	*	74	4a	J	106	6a	j
11	0b	VT	43	2b	+	75	4b	K	107	6b	k
12	0c	FF	44	2c	,	76	4c	L	108	6c	l
13	0d	CR	45	2d	-	77	4d	M	109	6d	m
14	0e	SO	46	2e	.	78	4e	N	110	6e	n
15	0f	SI	47	2f	/	79	4f	O	111	6f	o
16	10	DLE	48	30	0	80	50	P	112	70	p
17	11	DC1	49	31	1	81	51	Q	113	71	q
18	12	DC2	50	32	2	82	52	R	114	72	r
19	13	DC3	51	33	3	83	53	S	115	73	s
20	14	DC4	52	34	4	84	54	T	116	74	t
21	15	NAK	53	35	5	85	55	U	117	75	u
22	16	SYN	54	36	6	86	56	V	118	76	v
23	17	ETB	55	37	7	87	57	W	119	77	w
24	18	CAN	56	38	8	88	58	X	120	78	x

(continued)

Table 2-4: The ASCII Table (continued)

<table>
<tr><th colspan="3">Control codes</th><th colspan="9">Printable characters</th></tr>
<tr><th>Od</th><th>Ox</th><th>Code</th><th>Od</th><th>Ox</th><th>Char</th><th>Od</th><th>Ox</th><th>Char</th><th>Od</th><th>Ox</th><th>Char</th></tr>
<tr><td>25</td><td>19</td><td>EM</td><td>57</td><td>39</td><td>9</td><td>89</td><td>59</td><td>Y</td><td>121</td><td>79</td><td>y</td></tr>
<tr><td>26</td><td>1a</td><td>SUB</td><td>58</td><td>3a</td><td>:</td><td>90</td><td>5a</td><td>Z</td><td>122</td><td>7a</td><td>z</td></tr>
<tr><td>27</td><td>1b</td><td>ESC</td><td>59</td><td>3b</td><td>;</td><td>91</td><td>5b</td><td>[</td><td>123</td><td>7b</td><td>{</td></tr>
<tr><td>28</td><td>1c</td><td>FS</td><td>60</td><td>3c</td><td><</td><td>92</td><td>5c</td><td>\</td><td>124</td><td>7c</td><td>|</td></tr>
<tr><td>29</td><td>1d</td><td>GS</td><td>61</td><td>3d</td><td>=</td><td>93</td><td>5d</td><td>]</td><td>125</td><td>7d</td><td>}</td></tr>
<tr><td>30</td><td>1e</td><td>RS</td><td>62</td><td>3e</td><td>></td><td>94</td><td>5e</td><td>^</td><td>126</td><td>7e</td><td>~</td></tr>
<tr><td>31</td><td>1f</td><td>US</td><td>63</td><td>3f</td><td>?</td><td>95</td><td>5f</td><td>_</td><td>127</td><td>7f</td><td>DEL</td></tr>
</table>

ASCII codes 0 to 31 are the *control code characters* that control devices. These are mostly anachronisms. When the American Standards Association formalized ASCII in the 1960s, modern devices included teletype machines, magnetic tape readers, and dot-matrix printers. Some control codes still in common use are the following:

- 0 (NULL) is used as a string terminator by programming languages.
- 4 (EOT), the end of transmission, terminates shell sessions and PostScript printer communications.
- 7 (BELL) causes a device to make a noise.
- 8 (BS), the backspace, causes the device to erase the last character.
- 9 (HT), the horizontal tab, moves a cursor several spaces to the right.
- 10 (LF), the line feed, is used as the end-of-line marker on most operating systems.
- 13 (CR), the carriage return, is used in combination with LF as the end-of-line marker on Windows systems.
- 26 (SUB), the substitute character/end of file/CTRL-Z, suspends the currently executing interactive process on most operating systems.

The remainder of the ASCII table, codes from 32 to 127, is the printable characters. These represent the English characters, digits, and punctuation.

On most systems, the `char` type's representation is ASCII. Although this relationship is not strictly guaranteed, it is a de facto standard.

Now it's time to combine your knowledge of `char` types, arrays, `for` loops, and the ASCII table. Listing 2-12 shows how to build an array with the letters of the alphabet, print the result, and then convert this array to uppercase and print again.

```
#include <cstdio>

int main() {
  char alphabet[27]; ❶
  for (int i = 0; i<26; i++) {
```

```
    alphabet[i] = i + 97; ❷
  }
  alphabet[26] = 0; ❸
  printf("%s\n", alphabet); ❹
  for (int i = 0; i<26; i++) {
    alphabet[i] = i + 65; ❺
  }
  printf("%s", alphabet); ❻
}
--------------------------------------------------------------------------
abcdefghijklmnopqrstuvwxyz❹
ABCDEFGHIJKLMNOPQRSTUVWXYZ❻
```

Listing 2-12: Printing the letters of the alphabet in lowercase and uppercase using ASCII

First, you declare a `char` array of length 27 to hold the 26 English letters plus a null terminator ❶. Next, employ a `for` loop to iterate from 0 to 25 using the iterator `i`. The letter *a* has the value 97 in ASCII. By adding 97 to the iterator `i`, you can generate all the lowercase letters in the `alphabet` ❷. To make `alphabet` a null-terminated string, you set `alphabet[26]` to 0 ❸. You then print the result ❹.

Next, you print the uppercase alphabet. The letter *A* has the value 65 in ASCII, so you reset each element of the alphabet accordingly ❺ and invoke `printf` again ❻.

User-Defined Types

User-defined types are types that the user can define. The three broad categories of user-defined types are these:

Enumerations The simplest of the user-defined types. The values that an enumeration can take are restricted to a set of possible values. Enumerations are excellent for modeling categorical concepts.

Classes More fully featured types that give you flexibility to pair data and functions. Classes that only contain data are called plain-old-data classes; you'll learn about them in this section.

Unions A boutique user-defined type. All members share the same memory location. Unions are dangerous and easy to misuse.

Enumeration Types

Declare enumerations using the keywords `enum class` followed by the type name and a listing of the values it can take. These values are arbitrary alphanumeric strings that will represent whatever categories you want to represent. Under the hood, these values are simply integers, but they allow you to write safer, more expressive code by using programmer-defined types rather than integers that could mean anything. For example, Listing 2-13 declares an `enum class` called `Race` that can take one of seven values.

```
enum class Race {
  Dinan,
```

```
  Teklan,
  Ivyn,
  Moiran,
  Camite,
  Julian,
  Aidan
};
```

Listing 2-13: An enumeration class containing all the races from Neal Stephenson's Seveneves

To initialize an enumeration variable to a value, use the name of the type followed by two colons `::` and the desired value. For example, here's how to declare the variable `langobard_race` and initialize its value to `Aidan`:

```
Race langobard_race = Race::Aidan;
```

NOTE *Technically, an* `enum class` *is one of two kinds of enumerations: it's called a* scoped enum. *For compatibility with C, C++ also supports an* unscoped enum, *which is declared with* `enum` *rather than* `enum class`. *The major difference is that scoped enums require the enum's type followed by* `::` *to precede the values, whereas unscoped enums don't. Unscoped* `enum` *classes are less safe to use than scoped enums, so shy away from them unless absolutely necessary. They're supported in C++ for mainly historical reasons, especially interoperation with C code. See* Effective Modern C++ *by Scott Meyers, Item 10, for details.*

Switch Statements

The *switch statement* transfers control to one of several statements depending on the value of a *condition*, which evaluates to either an integer or enumeration type. The `switch` keyword denotes a switch statement.

Switch statements provide conditional branching. When a switch statement executes, control transfers to the *case* fitting the condition or to a *default condition* if no case matches the condition expression. The `case` keyword denotes a case, whereas the `default` keyword denotes the default condition.

Somewhat confusingly, execution will continue until the end of the switch statement or the `break` keyword. You'll almost always find a `break` at the end of each condition.

Switch statements have a lot of components. Listing 2-14 shows how they fit together.

```
switch❶(condition❷) {
  case❸ (case-a❹): {
    // Handle case a here
    --snip--
  }❺ break❻;
  case (case-b): {
    // Handle case b here
    --snip--
  } break;
```

```
    // Handle other conditions as desired
    --snip--
  default❼: {
    // Handle the default case here
    --snip--
  }
}
```

Listing 2-14: A sketch of how switch statements fit together

All switch statements begin with the `switch` keyword ❶ followed by the `condition` in parentheses ❷. Each case begins with the `case` keyword ❸ followed by the case's enumeration or integral value ❹. If `condition` ❷ equals `case-a` ❹, for example, the code in the block containing `Handle case a here` will execute. After each statement following a case ❺, you place a `break` keyword ❻. If `condition` matches none of the cases, the `default` case ❼ executes.

NOTE *The braces enclosing each case are optional but highly recommended. Without them, you'll sometimes get surprising behavior.*

Using a Switch Statement with an Enumeration Class

Listing 2-15 uses a switch statement on a `Race` enumeration class to generate a bespoke greeting.

```
#include <cstdio>

enum class Race { ❶
  Dinan,
  Teklan,
  Ivyn,
  Moiran,
  Camite,
  Julian,
  Aidan
};

int main() {
  Race race = Race::Dinan; ❷

  switch(race) { ❸
  case Race::Dinan: { ❹
      printf("You work hard.");
    } break;  ❺
  case Race::Teklan: {
      printf("You are very strong.");
    } break;
  case Race::Ivyn: {
      printf("You are a great leader.");
    } break;
  case Race::Moiran: {
      printf("My, how versatile you are!");
    } break;
```

```
  case Race::Camite: {
    printf("You're incredibly helpful.");
  } break;
  case Race::Julian: {
    printf("Anything you want!");
  } break;
  case Race::Aidan: {
    printf("What an enigma.");
  } break;
  default: {
    printf("Error: unknown race!"); ❻
  }
 }
}
--------------------------------------------------------------------------
You work hard.
```

Listing 2-15: A program that prints a greeting that depends on the `Race` selected

The `enum class` ❶ declares the enumeration type `Race`, which you use to initialize `race` to `Dinan` ❷. The switch statement ❸ evaluates the condition `race` to determine which condition to hand control to. Because you hardcoded this to `Dinan` earlier in the code, execution transfers to ❹, which prints `You work hard`. The `break` at ❺ terminates the switch statement.

The `default` condition at ❻ is a safety feature. If someone adds a new `Race` value to the enumeration class, you'll detect that unknown race at runtime and print an error message.

Try setting `race` ❷ to different values. How does the output change?

Plain-Old-Data Classes

Classes are user-defined types that contain data and functions, and they're the heart and soul of C++. The simplest kind of classes are *plain-old-data classes (PODs)*. PODs are simple containers. Think of them as a sort of heterogeneous array of elements of potentially *different* types. Each element of a class is called a *member*.

Every POD begins with the keyword `struct` followed by the POD's desired name. Next, you list the members' types and names. Consider the following `Book` class declaration with four members:

```
struct Book {
  char name[256]; ❶
  int year; ❷
  int pages; ❸
  bool hardcover; ❹
};
```

A single `Book` contains a `char` array called `name` ❶, an `int year` ❷, an `int pages` ❸, and a `bool hardcover` ❹.

You declare POD variables just like any other variables: by type and name. You can then access members of the variable using the dot operator (`.`).

Listing 2-16 uses the Book type.

```
#include <cstdio>

struct Book {
  char name[256];
  int year;
  int pages;
  bool hardcover;
};

int main() {
  Book neuromancer; ❶
  neuromancer.pages = 271; ❷
  printf("Neuromancer has %d pages.", neuromancer.pages); ❸
}
--------------------------------------------------------------------------
Neuromancer has 271 pages. ❸
```

Listing 2-16: Example using the POD type Book *to read and write members*

First, you declare a Book variable neuromancer ❶. Next, you set the number of pages of neuromancer to 271 using the dot operator (.) ❷. Finally, you print a message and extract the number of pages from neuromancer, again using the dot operator ❸.

NOTE *PODs have some useful low-level features: they're C compatible, you can employ machine instructions that are highly efficient to copy or move them, and they can be efficiently represented in memory.*

C++ guarantees that members will be sequential in memory, although some implementations require members to be aligned along word boundaries, which depend on CPU register length. As a general rule, you should order members from largest to smallest within POD definitions.

Unions

The union is a cousin of the POD that puts all of its members in the same place. You can think of unions as different views or interpretations of a block of memory. They can be useful in some low-level situations, such as when marshalling structures that must be consistent across architectures, dealing with type-checking issues related to C/C++ interoperation, and even when packing bitfields.

Listing 2-17 illustrates how you declare a union: simply use the union keyword instead of struct.

```
union Variant {
  char string[10];
  int integer;
  double floating_point;
};
```

Listing 2-17: An example union

The union Variant can be interpreted as a char[10], an int, or a double. It takes up only as much memory as its largest member (probably string in this case).

You use the dot operator (.) to specify a union's interpretation. Syntactically, this looks like accessing a member of a POD, but it's completely different under the hood.

Because all members of a union are in the same place, you can cause data corruption very easily. Listing 2-18 illustrates the danger.

```
#include <cstdio>

union Variant {
  char string[10];
  int integer;
  double floating_point;
};

int main() {
  Variant v; ❶
  v.integer = 42; ❷
  printf("The ultimate answer: %d\n", v.integer); ❸
  v.floating_point = 2.7182818284; ❹
  printf("Euler's number e:    %f\n", v.floating_point); ❺
  printf("A dumpster fire:     %d\n", v.integer); ❻
}
--------------------------------------------------------------------------------
The ultimate answer: 42 ❸
Euler's number e:    2.718282 ❺
A dumpster fire:     -1961734133 ❻
```

Listing 2-18: A program using the union Variant from Listing 2-17

You declare a Variant v at ❶. Next, you interpret v as an integer, set its value to 42 ❷, and print it ❸. You then reinterpret v as a float and reassign its value ❹. You print it to the console, and all appears well ❺. So far so good.

Disaster strikes only when you try to interpret v as an integer again ❻. You clobbered over the original value of v (42) ❷ when assigning Euler's number ❹.

That's the main problem with unions: it's up to you to keep track of which interpretation is appropriate. The compiler won't help you.

You should avoid using unions in all but the rarest of cases, and you won't see them in this book. "variant" on page 379 discusses some safer options when you require poly-type functionality.

Fully Featured C++ Classes

POD classes contain only data members, and sometimes that's all you want from a class. However, designing a program using only PODs can create a lot of complexity. You can fight such complexity with *encapsulation*, a design pattern that binds data with the functions that manipulate it. Placing related functions and data together helps to simplify code in at least two ways. First, you can put related code in one place, which helps you to reason about your program. You can understand how a code segment works because it describes in one place both program state and how your code modifies that state. Second, you can hide some of a class's code and data from the rest of your program using a practice called *information hiding*.

In C++, you achieve encapsulation by adding methods and access controls to class definitions.

Methods

Methods are member functions. They create an explicit connection among a class, its data members, and some code. Defining a method is as simple as adding a function to a class definition. Methods have access to all of a class's members.

Consider an example class `ClockOfTheLongNow` that keeps track of the year. You define an `int year` member and an `add_year` method that increments it:

```
struct ClockOfTheLongNow {
  void add_year() { ❶
    year++; ❷
  }
  int year; ❸
};
```

The `add_year` method's declaration ❶ looks like any other function that takes no parameters and returns no value. Within the method, you increment ❷ the member `year` ❸. Listing 2-19 shows how you can use the class to keep track of a year.

```
#include <cstdio>

struct ClockOfTheLongNow {
  --snip--
};

int main() {
  ClockOfTheLongNow clock; ❶
  clock.year = 2017; ❷
  clock.add_year(); ❸
  printf("year: %d\n", clock.year); ❹
  clock.add_year(); ❺
  printf("year: %d\n", clock.year); ❻
}
--------------------------------------------------------------------------
year: 2018 ❹
year: 2019 ❻
```

Listing 2-19: A program using the `ClockOfTheLongNow` struct

You declare the ClockOfTheLongNow instance clock ❶ and then set the year of clock to 2017 ❷. Next, you call the add_year method on clock ❸ and then print the value of clock.year ❹. You complete the program by incrementing ❺ and printing ❻ once more.

Access Controls

Access controls restrict class-member access. *Public* and *private* are the two major access controls. Anyone can access a public member, but only a class can access its private members. All struct members are public by default.

Private members play an important role in encapsulation. Consider again the ClockOfTheLongNow class. As it stands, the year member can be accessed from anywhere—for both reading and writing. Suppose you want to protect against the value of the year being less than 2019. You can accomplish this in two steps: you make year private, and you require anyone using the class (consumers) to interact with year only through the struct's methods. Listing 2-20 illustrates this approach.

```
struct ClockOfTheLongNow {
  void add_year() {
    year++;
  }
  bool set_year(int new_year) { ❶
    if (new_year < 2019) return false; ❷
    year = new_year;
    return true;
  }
  int get_year() { ❸
    return year;
  }
private: ❹
  int year;
};
```

Listing 2-20: An updated ClockOfTheLongNow from Listing 2-19 that encapsulates year

You've added two methods to ClockOfTheLongNow: a *setter* ❶ and a *getter* ❸ for year. Rather than allowing a user of ClockOfTheLongNow to modify year directly, you set the year with set_year. This addition of input validation ensures that new_year will never be less than 2019 ❷. If it is, the code returns false and leaves year unmodified. Otherwise, year is updated and returns true. To obtain the value of year, the user calls get_year.

You've used the access control label private ❹ to prohibit consumers from accessing year. Now, users can access year only from within ClockOfTheLongNow.

The class Keyword

You can replace the struct keyword with the class keyword, which declares members private by default. Aside from default access control, classes declared with the struct and class keywords are the same. For example, you could declare ClockOfTheLongNow in the following way:

```
class ClockOfTheLongNow {
  int year;
public:
  void add_year() {
    --snip--
  }
  bool set_year(int new_year) {
    --snip--
  }
  int get_year() {
    --snip--
  }
};
```

Which way you declare classes is a matter of style. There is absolutely no difference between struct and class aside from the default access control. I prefer using struct keywords because I like having the public members listed first. But you'll see all kinds of conventions out in the wild. Cultivate a style and stick to it.

Initializing Members

Having encapsulated year, you must now use methods to interact with ClockOfTheLongNow. Listing 2-21 shows how you can stitch these methods together into a program that attempts to set the year to 2018. This fails, and the program then sets the year to 2019, increments the year, and prints its final value.

```
#include <cstdio>

struct ClockOfTheLongNow {
  --snip--
}

int main() {
  ClockOfTheLongNow clock; ❶
  if(!clock.set_year(2018)) { ❷ // will fail; 2018 < 2019
    clock.set_year(2019); ❸
  }
  clock.add_year(); ❹
  printf("year: %d", clock.get_year());
}
--------------------------------------------------------------------------
year: 2020 ❺
```

Listing 2-21: A program using the ClockOfTheLongNow to illustrate the use of methods

You declare a clock ❶ and attempt to set its year to 2018 ❷. This fails because 2018 is less than 2019, and the program then sets the year to 2019 ❸. You increment the year once ❹ and then print its value.

In Chapter 1, you saw how uninitialized variables can contain random data as you stepped through the debugger. The ClockOfTheLongNow struct has the same problem: when clock is declared ❶, year is uninitialized. You want to guarantee that year is never less than 2019 *under any circumstances*. Such a requirement is called a *class invariant*: a feature of a class that is always true (that is, it never varies).

In this program, clock eventually gets into a good state ❸, but you can do better by employing a *constructor*. Constructors initialize objects and enforce class invariants from the very beginning of an object's life.

Constructors

Constructors are special methods with special declarations. Constructor declarations don't state a return type, and their name matches the class's name. For example, the constructor in Listing 2-22 takes no arguments and sets year to 2019, which causes year to default to 2019.

```
#include <cstdio>

struct ClockOfTheLongNow {
  ClockOfTheLongNow() { ❶
    year = 2019; ❷
  }
  --snip--
};

int main() {
  ClockOfTheLongNow clock; ❸
  printf("Default year: %d", clock.get_year()); ❹
}
```

```
Default year: 2019 ❹
```

Listing 2-22: Improving Listing 2-21 with a parameterless constructor

The constructor takes no arguments ❶ and sets year to 2019 ❷. When you declare a new ClockOfTheLongNow ❸, year defaults to 2019. You access year using get_year and print it to the console ❹.

What if you want to initialize a ClockOfTheLongNow with a custom year? Constructors can take any number of arguments. You can implement as many constructors as you'd like, as long as their argument types differ.

Consider the example in Listing 2-23 where you add a constructor taking an int. The constructor initializes year to the argument's value.

```
#include <cstdio>

struct ClockOfTheLongNow {
  ClockOfTheLongNow(int year_in) { ❶
    if(!set_year(year_in)) { ❷
      year = 2019; ❸
    }
  }
```

```
  --snip--
};

int main() {
  ClockOfTheLongNow clock{ 2020 }; ❹
  printf("Year: %d", clock.get_year()); ❺
}
```
```
Year: 2020 ❺
```

Listing 2-23: Elaborating Listing 2-22 with another constructor

The new constructor ❶ takes a single year_in argument of type int. You call set_year with year_in ❷. If set_year returns false, the caller provided bad input, and you override year_in with the default value of 2019 ❸. In main, you make a clock with the new constructor ❹ and then print the result ❺.

The conjuration ClockOfTheLongNow clock{ 2020 }; is called an initialization.

NOTE *You might not like the idea that invalid year_in instances were silently corrected to 2019 ❸. I don't like it either. Exceptions solve this problem; you'll learn about them in "Exceptions" on page 98.*

Initialization

Object initialization, or simply *initialization,* is how you bring objects to life. Unfortunately, object initialization syntax is complicated. Fortunately, the initialization process is straightforward. This section distills the bubbling cauldron of C++ object initialization into a palatable narrative.

Initializing a Fundamental Type to Zero

Let's start by initializing an object of fundamental type to zero. There are four ways to do so:

```
int a = 0;     ❶// Initialized to 0
int b{};       ❷// Initialized to 0
int c = {};    ❸// Initialized to 0
int d;         ❹// Initialized to 0 (maybe)
```

Three of these are reliable: explicitly set the value using a literal ❶, use braces {} ❷, or use the equals-plus-braces approach = {} ❸. Declaring the object with no extra notation ❹ is unreliable; it works only in certain situations. Even if you know what these situations are, you should avoid relying on this behavior because it sows confusion.

Using braces {} to initialize a variable is, unsurprisingly, called *braced initialization.* Part of the reason C++ initialization syntax is such a mess is that the language grew out of C, where object life cycles are primitive, into a language with a robust and featureful object life cycle. Language designers incorporated braced initialization into modern C++ to help smooth over the sharp corners this has caused in the initialization syntax. In short, no matter the object's scope or type, *braced initialization is always applicable*, whereas the other notations are not. Later in the chapter, you'll learn a general rule that encourages widespread use of braced initialization.

Initializing a Fundamental Type to an Arbitrary Value

Initializing to an arbitrary value is similar to initializing a fundamental type to zero:

```
int e = 42;       ❶ // Initialized to 42
int f{ 42 };      ❷ // Initialized to 42
int g = { 42 };❸ // Initialized to 42
int h(42);        ❹ // Initialized to 42
```

There are four ways: equals ❶, braced initialization ❷, equals-plus-braces initialization ❸, and parentheses ❹. All of these produce identical code.

Initializing PODs

The notation for initializing a POD mostly follows fundamental types. Listing 2-24 illustrates the similarity by declaring a POD type containing three members and initializing instances of it with various values.

```
#include <cstdint>

struct PodStruct {
  uint64_t a;
  char b[256];
  bool c;
};

int main() {
  PodStruct initialized_pod1{};      ❶   // All fields zeroed
  PodStruct initialized_pod2 = {}; ❷   // All fields zeroed

  PodStruct initialized_pod3{ 42, "Hello" }; ❸        // Fields a & b set; c = 0
  PodStruct initialized_pod4{ 42, "Hello", true }; ❹ // All fields set
}
```

Listing 2-24: A program illustrating various ways to initialize a POD

Initializing a POD object to zero is similar to initializing objects of fundamental types to zero. The braces ❶ and equals-plus-braces ❷ approaches produce the same code: fields initialize to zero.

WARNING *You cannot use the equals-zero approach with PODs. The following will not compile because it's expressly forbidden in the language rules:*

```
PodStruct initialized_pod = 0;
```

Initializing PODs to Arbitrary Values

You can initialize fields to arbitrary values using braced initializers. The arguments within braced initializers must match types with POD members. The order of arguments from left to right matches the order of members from top to bottom. Any omitted members are zeroed. Members a and b initialize to 42 and Hello after the initialization of initialized_pod3 ❸, and c is zeroed (set to false) because you omitted it from the braced initialization. The initialization of initialized_pod4 ❹ includes an argument for c (true), so its value is set to true after initialization.

The equals-plus-braces initialization works identically. For example, you could replace ❹ with this:

```
PodStruct initialized_pod4 = { 42, "Hello", true };
```

You can only omit fields from right to left, so the following won't compile:

```
PodStruct initialized_pod4 = { 42, true };
```

WARNING *You cannot use parentheses to initialize PODs. The following will not compile:*

```
PodStruct initialized_pod(42, "Hello", true);
```

Initializing Arrays

You initialize arrays like PODs. The main difference between array and POD declarations is that arrays specify length. Recall that this argument goes in square brackets [].

When you use braced initializers to initialize arrays, the length argument becomes optional; the compiler can infer the size argument from the number of braced initializer arguments.

Listing 2-25 illustrates some ways to initialize an array.

```
int main() {
  int array_1[]{ 1, 2, 3 };  ❶ // Array of length 3; 1, 2, 3
  int array_2[5]{};          ❷ // Array of length 5; 0, 0, 0, 0, 0
  int array_3[5]{ 1, 2, 3 }; ❸ // Array of length 5; 1, 2, 3, 0, 0
  int array_4[5];            ❹ // Array of length 5; uninitialized values
}
```

Listing 2-25: A program listing various ways to initialize an array

The array array_1 has length three, and its elements equal 1, 2, and 3 ❶. The array array_2 has length five because you specified a length argument ❷. The braced initializer is empty, so all five elements initialize to zero. The array array_3 also has length five, but the braced initializer is not empty. It contains three elements, so the remaining two elements initialize to zero ❸. The array array_4 has no braced initializer, so it contains uninitialized objects ❹.

WARNING *Whether* `array_5` *is initialized or not actually depends on the same rules as does initializing a fundamental type. The object's storage duration, which you'll learn about in "An Object's Storage Duration" on page 89, determines the rules. You don't have to memorize these rules if you're explicit about initialization.*

Fully Featured Classes

Unlike fundamental types and PODs, fully featured classes are *always initialized*. In other words, one of a fully featured class's constructors always gets called during initialization. Which constructor is called depends on the arguments given during initialization.

The class in Listing 2-26 helps clarify how to use fully featured classes.

```
#include <cstdio>

struct Taxonomist {
  Taxonomist() { ❶
    printf("(no argument)\n");
  }
  Taxonomist(char x) { ❷
    printf("char: %c\n", x);
  }
  Taxonomist(int x) { ❸
    printf("int: %d\n", x);
  }
  Taxonomist(float x) { ❹
    printf("float: %f\n", x);
  }
};
```

Listing 2-26: A class announcing which of its several constructors gets called during initialization

The `Taxonomist` class has four constructors. If you supply no argument, the constructor with no arguments gets called ❶. If you supply a `char`, `int`, or `float` during initialization, the corresponding constructor gets called: ❷, ❸, or ❹, respectively. In each case, the constructor alerts you with a `printf` statement.

Listing 2-27 initializes several `Taxonomists` using different syntaxes and arguments.

```
#include <cstdio>

struct Taxonomist {
  --snip--
};

int main() {
  Taxonomist t1; ❶
  Taxonomist t2{ 'c' }; ❷
  Taxonomist t3{ 65537 }; ❸
  Taxonomist t4{ 6.02e23f }; ❹
  Taxonomist t5('g'); ❺
```

```
  Taxonomist t6 = { 'l' }; ❻
  Taxonomist t7{}; ❼
  Taxonomist t8(); ❽
}
```

```
(no argument) ❶
char: c ❷
int: 65537 ❸
float: 6020000172718952229464576.000000 ❹
char: g ❺
char: l ❻
(no argument) ❼
```

Listing 2-27: A program using the `Taxonomist` class with various initialization syntaxes

Without any braces or parentheses, the no argument constructor gets called ❶. Unlike with POD and fundamental types, you can rely on this initialization no matter where you've declared the object. With braced initializers, the `char` ❷, `int` ❸, and `float` ❹ constructors get called as expected. You can also use parentheses ❺ and the equals-plus-braces syntaxes ❻; these invoke the expected constructors.

Although fully featured classes always get initialized, some programmers like the uniformity of using the same initialization syntax for all objects. This is no problem with braced initializers; the default constructor gets invoked as expected ❼.

Unfortunately, using parentheses ❽ causes some surprising behavior. You get no output.

If you squint a little bit, this initialization ❽ looks like a function declaration, and that's because it is. Because of some arcane language-parsing rules, what you've declared to the compiler is that a yet-to-be-defined function `t8` takes no arguments and returns an object of type `Taxonomist`. Ouch.

NOTE *"Function Declarations" on page 244 covers function declarations in more detail. But for now, just know that you can provide a function declaration that defines a function's modifiers, name, arguments, and return type and then later provide the body in its definition.*

This widely known problem is called the *most vexing parse*, and it's a major reason why the C++ community added braced initialization syntax to the language. *Narrowing conversions* are another problem.

Narrowing Conversions

Braced initialization will generate warnings whenever implicit narrowing conversions are encountered. This is a nice feature that can save you from nasty bugs. Consider the following example:

```
float a{ 1 };
float b{ 2 };
int narrowed_result(a/b); ❶ // Potentially nasty narrowing conversion
int result{ a/b };        ❷ // Compiler generates warning
```

Dividing two float literals yields a float. When initializing narrowed_result ❶, the compiler silently narrows the result of a/b (0.5) to 0 because you've used parentheses ( ) to initialize. When you use braced initializers, the compiler generates a warning ❷.

Initializing Class Members

You can use braced initializers to initialize the members of classes, as demonstrated here:

```
struct JohanVanDerSmut {
  bool gold = true; ❶
  int year_of_smelting_accident{ 1970 }; ❷
  char key_location[8] = { "x-rated" }; ❸
};
```

The gold member is initialized using the equals initialization ❶, year_of_smelting_accident using braced initialization ❷, and key_location using braces-plus-equals initialization ❸. It's not possible to use parentheses to initialize member variables.

Brace Yourself

The options for initializing objects bewilder even experienced C++ programmers. Here's a general rule to make initialization simple: *use braced initializers everywhere.* Braced initializers work as intended almost everywhere, and they cause the fewest surprises. For this reason, braced initialization is also called *uniform initialization.* The remainder of the book follows this guidance.

WARNING *You'll break the* use braced initializers everywhere *rule for certain classes in C++ stdlib. Part II will make these exceptions to the rule very clear.*

The Destructor

An object's *destructor* is its cleanup function. The destructor is invoked before an object is destroyed. Destructors are almost never called explicitly: the compiler will ensure that each object's destructor is called as appropriate. You declare a class's destructor with the tilde ~ followed by the name of the class.

The following Earth class has a destructor that prints Making way for hyperspace bypass:

```
#include <cstdio>

struct Earth {
  ~Earth() { // Earth's destructor
       printf("Making way for hyperspace bypass");
  }
}
```

Defining a destructor is optional. If you do decide to implement a destructor, it must not take any arguments. Examples of actions you might want to take in a destructor include releasing file handles, flushing network sockets, and freeing dynamic objects.

If you don't define a destructor, a default destructor is automatically generated. The default destructor's behavior is to perform no action.

You'll learn a whole lot more about destructors in "Tracing the Object Life Cycle" on page 96.

Summary

This chapter presented the foundation of C++, which is its type system. You first learned about fundamental types, the building blocks of all other types. Then you continued with user-defined types, including the `enum class`, POD classes, and fully featured C++ classes. You capped off your tour of classes with a discussion of constructors, initialization syntax, and destructors.

EXERCISES

2-1. Create an `enum class Operation` that has values `Add`, `Subtract`, `Multiply`, and `Divide`.

2-2. Create a `struct Calculator`. It should have a single constructor that takes an `Operation`.

2-3. Create a method on `Calculator` called `int calculate(int a, int b)`. Upon invocation, this method should perform addition, subtraction, multiplication, or division based on its constructor argument and return the result.

2-4. Experiment with different means of initializing `Calculator` instances.

FURTHER READING

- *ISO International Standard ISO/IEC (2017) – Programming Language C++* (International Organization for Standardization; Geneva, Switzerland; *https://isocpp.org/std/the-standard/*)
- *The C++ Programming Language*, 4th Edition, by Bjarne Stroustrup (Pearson Education, 2013)
- *Effective Modern C++* by Scott Meyers (O'Reilly Media, 2014)
- "C++ Made Easier: Plain Old Data" by Andrew Koenig and Barbara E. Moo (Dr. Dobb's, 2002; *http://www.drdobbs.com/c-made-easier-plain-old-data/184401508/*)

3

REFERENCE TYPES

Everyone knows that debugging is twice as hard as writing a program in the first place. So if you're as clever as you can be when you write it, how will you ever debug it?
—Brian Kernighan

Reference types store the memory addresses of objects. These types enable efficient programming, and many elegant design patterns feature them. In this chapter, I'll discuss the two kinds of reference types: pointers and references. I'll also discuss `this`, `const`, and `auto` along the way.

Pointers

Pointers are the fundamental mechanism used to refer to memory addresses. Pointers encode both pieces of information required to interact with another object—that is, the object's address and the object's type.

You can declare a pointer's type by appending an asterisk (*) to the pointed-to type. For example, you declare a pointer to `int` called `my_ptr` as follows:

```
int* my_ptr;
```

The format specifier for a pointer is `%p`. For example, to print the value in `my_ptr`, you could use the following:

```
printf("The value of my_ptr is %p.", my_ptr);
```

Pointers are very low-level objects. Although they play a central role in most C programs, C++ offers higher-level, sometimes more efficient, constructs that obviate the need to deal with memory addresses directly. Nonetheless, pointers are a foundational concept that you'll no doubt come across in your system-programming travels.

In this section, you'll learn how to find the address of an object and how to assign the result to a pointer variable. You'll also learn how to perform the opposite operation, which is called *dereferencing*: given a pointer, you can obtain the object residing at the corresponding address.

You'll learn more about *arrays*, the simplest construct for managing an object collection, as well as how arrays relate to pointers. As low-level constructs, arrays and pointers are relatively dangerous. You'll learn about what can go wrong when pointer- and array-based programs go awry.

This chapter introduces two special kinds of pointers: `void` pointers and `std::byte` pointers. These very useful types have some special behaviors that you'll need to keep in mind. Additionally, you'll learn how to encode empty pointers with `nullptr` and how to use pointers in Boolean expressions to determine whether they're empty.

Addressing Variables

You can obtain the address of a variable by prepending the *address-of operator* (`&`). You might want to use this operator to initialize a pointer so it "points to" the corresponding variable. Such programming requirements arise very often in operating systems programming. For example, major operating systems, such as Windows, Linux, and FreeBSD, have interfaces that use pointers heavily.

Listing 3-1 demonstrates how to obtain the address of an `int`.

```
#include <cstdio>

int main() {
  int gettysburg{}; ❶
  printf("gettysburg: %d\n", gettysburg); ❷
  int *gettysburg_address = &gettysburg; ❸
  printf("&gettysburg: %p\n", gettysburg_address); ❹
}
```

Listing 3-1: A program featuring the address-of operator & and a terrible pun

First, you declare the integer gettysburg ❶ and print its value ❷. Then you declare a pointer, called gettysburg_address, to that integer's address ❸; notice that the asterisk prepends the pointer and the ampersand prepends gettysburg. Finally, you print the pointer to the screen ❹ to reveal the gettysburg integer's address.

If you run Listing 3-1 on Windows 10 (x86), you should see the following output:

```
gettysburg: 0
&gettysburg: 0053FBA8
```

Running the same code on Windows 10 x64 yields the following output:

```
gettysburg: 0
&gettysburg: 0000007DAB53F594
```

Your output should have an identical value for gettysburg, but gettysburg_address should be different each time. This variation is due to *address space layout randomization*, which is a security feature that scrambles the base address of important memory regions to hamper exploitation.

ADDRESS SPACE LAYOUT RANDOMIZATION

Why does address space layout randomization hamper exploitation? When a hacker finds an exploitable condition in a program, they can sometimes cram a malicious payload into user-provided input. One of the first security features designed to prevent a hacker from getting this malicious payload to execute is to make all data sections non-executable. If the computer attempts to execute data as code, then the theory is that it knows something's amiss and should terminate the program with an exception.

Some exceedingly clever hackers figured out how to repurpose executable code instructions in totally unforeseen ways by carefully crafting exploits containing so-called *return-oriented programs*. These exploits could arrange to invoke the relevant system APIs to mark their payload executable, hence defeating the non-executable-memory mitigation.

Address space layout randomization combats return-oriented programming by randomizing memory addresses, making it difficult to repurpose existing code because the attacker doesn't know where it resides in memory.

Also note that in the outputs for Listing 3-1, gettysburg_address contains 8 hexadecimal digits (4 bytes) for an x86 architecture and 16 hexadecimal digits (8 bytes) for an x64 architecture. This should make some sense because on modern desktop systems, the pointer size is the same as the CPU's general-purpose register. An x86 architecture has 32-bit (4-byte) general-purpose registers, whereas an x64 architecture has 64-bit (8-byte) general-purpose registers.

Dereferencing Pointers

The *dereference operator* (*) is a unary operator that accesses the object to which a pointer refers. This is the inverse operation of the address-of operator. Given an address, you can obtain the object residing there. Like the address-of operator, system programmers use the dereference operator very often. Many operating system APIs will return pointers, and if you want to access the referred-to object, you'll use the dereference operator.

Unfortunately, the dereference operator can cause a lot of notation-based confusion for beginners because the dereference operator, the pointer declaration, and multiplication all use asterisks. Remember that you append an asterisk to the end of the pointed-to object's type to declare a pointer; however, you prepend the dereference operator—an asterisk—to the pointer, like this:

```
*gettysburg_address
```

After accessing an object by prepending the dereference operator to a pointer, you can treat the result like any other object of the pointed-to type. For example, because gettysburg is an integer, you can write the value 17325 into gettysburg using gettysburg_address. The correct syntax is as follows:

```
*gettysburg_address = 17325;
```

Because the dereferenced pointer—that is, *gettysburg_address—appears on the left side of the equal sign, you're writing to the address where gettysburg is stored.

If a dereferenced pointer appears anywhere except the left side of an equal sign, you're reading from the address. To retrieve the int pointed to by gettysburg_address, you just tack on the dereference operator. For instance, the following statement will print the value stored in gettysburg:

```
printf("%d", *gettysburg_address);
```

Listing 3-2 uses the dereference operator to read and write.

```
#include <cstdio>

int main() {
  int gettysburg{};
  int* gettysburg_address = &gettysburg; ❶
  printf("Value at gettysburg_address: %d\n", *gettysburg_address); ❷
  printf("Gettysburg Address: %p\n", gettysburg_address); ❸
  *gettysburg_address = 17325; ❹
  printf("Value at gettysburg_address: %d\n", *gettysburg_address); ❺
  printf("Gettysburg Address: %p\n", gettysburg_address); ❻
}
```

```
Value at gettysburg_address: 0 ❷
Gettysburg Address: 000000B9EEEFFB04 ❸
```

```
Value at gettysburg_address: 17325 ❺
Gettysburg Address: 000000B9EEEFFB04 ❻
```

Listing 3-2: An example program illustrating reads and writes using a pointer (output is from a Windows 10 x64 machine)

First, you initialize gettysburg to zero. Then, you initialize the pointer gettysburg_address to the address of gettysburg ❶. Next, you print the int pointed to by gettysburg_address ❷ and the value of gettysburg_address itself ❸.

You write the value 17325 into the memory pointed to by gettysburg_address ❹ and then print the pointed-to value ❺ and address ❻ again.

Listing 3-2 would be functionally identical if you assigned the value 17325 directly to gettysburg instead of to the gettysburg_address pointer, like this:

```
gettysburg = 17325;
```

This example illustrates the close relationship between a pointed-to object (gettysburg) and a dereferenced pointer to that object (*gettysburg_address).

The Member-of-Pointer Operator

The *member-of-pointer operator*, or *arrow operator* (->), performs two simultaneous operations:

- It dereferences a pointer.
- It accesses a member of the pointed-to object.

You can use this operator to reduce *notational friction*, the resistance a programmer feels in expressing their intent in code, when you're handling pointers to classes. You'll need to handle pointers to classes in a variety of design patterns. For example, you might want to pass a pointer to a class as a function parameter. If the receiving function needs to interact with a member of that class, the member-of-pointer operator is the tool for the job.

Listing 3-3 employs the arrow operator to read the year from a ClockOfTheLongNow object (which you implemented in Listing 2-22 on page 58).

```
#include <cstdio>

struct ClockOfTheLongNow {
  --snip--
};

int main() {
  ClockOfTheLongNow clock;
  ClockOfTheLongNow* clock_ptr = &clock; ❶
  clock_ptr->set_year(2020); ❷
```

```
  printf("Address of clock: %p\n", clock_ptr); ❸
  printf("Value of clock's year: %d", clock_ptr->get_year()); ❹
}
--------------------------------------------------------------------------
Address of clock: 000000C6D3D5FBE4 ❸
Value of clock's year: 2020 ❹
```

Listing 3-3: Using a pointer and the arrow operator to manipulate the `ClockOfTheLongNow` object (output is from a Windows 10 x64 machine)

You declare a `clock` and then store its address in `clock_ptr` ❶. Next, you use the arrow operator to set the year member of `clock` to 2020 ❷. Finally, you print the address of `clock` ❸ and the value of year ❹.

You could achieve an identical result using the dereference (`*`) and member of (`.`) operators. For example, you could have written the last line of Listing 3-3 as follows:

```
  printf("Value of clock's year: %d", (*clock_ptr).get_year());
```

First, you dereference `clock_ptr`, and then you access the year. Although this is equivalent to invoking the pointer-to-member operator, it's a more verbose syntax and provides no benefit over its simpler alternative.

NOTE *For now, use parentheses to emphasize the order of operations. Chapter 7 walks through the precedents rules for operators.*

Pointers and Arrays

Pointers share several characteristics with arrays. Pointers encode object location. Arrays encode the location and length of contiguous objects.

At the slightest provocation, an array will *decay* into a pointer. A decayed array loses length information and converts to a pointer to the array's first element. For example:

```
int key_to_the_universe[]{ 3, 6, 9 };
int* key_ptr = key_to_the_universe; // Points to 3
```

First, you initialize an `int` array `key_to_the_universe` with three elements. Next, you initialize the `int` pointer `key_ptr` to `key_to_the_universe`, which decays into a pointer. After initialization, `key_ptr` points to the first element of `key_to_the_universe`.

Listing 3-4 initializes an array containing `College` objects and passes the array to a function as a pointer.

```
#include <cstdio>

struct College {
  char name[256];
};
```

```
void print_name(College* college_ptr❶) {
  printf("%s College\n", college_ptr->name❷);
}

int main() {
  College best_colleges[] = { "Magdalen", "Nuffield", "Kellogg" };
  print_name(best_colleges);
}
--------------------------------------------------------------------------
Magdalen College ❷
```

Listing 3-4: A program illustrating array decay into a pointer

The `print_name` function takes a pointer-to-`College` argument ❶, so the `best_colleges` array decays into a pointer when you call `print_name`. Because arrays decay into pointers to their first element, `college_ptr` at ❶ points to the first `College` in `best_colleges`.

There's another array decay in Listing 3-4 ❷ as well. You use the arrow operator (`->`) to access the `name` member of the `College` pointed to by `college_ptr`, which is itself a `char` array. The `printf` format specifier `%s` expects a C-style string, which is a `char` pointer, and `name` decays into a pointer to satisfy `printf`.

Handling Decay

Often, you pass arrays as two arguments:

- A pointer to the first array element
- The array's length

The mechanism that enables this pattern is square brackets (`[]`), which work with pointers just as with arrays. Listing 3-5 employs this technique.

```
#include <cstdio>

struct College {
  char name[256];
};

void print_names(College* colleges❶, size_t n_colleges❷) {
  for (size_t i = 0; i < n_colleges; i++) { ❸
    printf("%s College\n", colleges[i]❹.name❺);
  }
}

int main() {
  College oxford[] = { "Magdalen", "Nuffield", "Kellogg" };
  print_names(oxford, sizeof(oxford) / sizeof(College));
}
```

```
Magdalen College
Nuffield College
Kellogg College
```

Listing 3-5: A program illustrating a common idiom for passing arrays to functions

The print_names function accepts an array in two arguments: a pointer to the first College element ❶ and the number of elements n_colleges ❷. Within print_names, you iterate with a for loop and an index i. The value of i iterates from 0 to n_colleges-1 ❸.

You extract the corresponding college name by accessing the ith element ❹ and then get the name member ❺.

This pointer-plus-size approach to passing arrays is ubiquitous in C-style APIs, for example, in Windows or Linux system programming.

Pointer Arithmetic

To obtain the address of the nth element of an array, you have two options. First, you can take the direct approach of obtaining the nth element with square brackets ([]) and then use the address-of (&) operator:

```
College* third_college_ptr = &oxford[2];
```

Pointer arithmetic, the set of rules for addition and subtraction on pointers, provides an alternate approach. When you add or subtract integers to pointers, the compiler figures out the correct byte offset using the size of the pointed-to type. For example, adding 4 to a uint64_t pointer adds 32 bytes: a uint64_t takes up 8 bytes, so 4 of them take up 32 bytes. The following is therefore equivalent to the previous option of obtaining the address of the nth element of an array:

```
College* third_college_ptr = oxford + 2;
```

Pointers Are Dangerous

It's not possible to convert a pointer to an array, which is a good thing. You shouldn't need to, and besides it wouldn't be possible in general for a compiler to recover the size of the array from a pointer. But the compiler can't save you from all the dangerous things you might try to do.

Buffer Overflows

For arrays and pointers, you can access arbitrary array elements with the bracket operator ([]) or with pointer arithmetic. These are very powerful tools for low-level programming because you can interact with memory more or less without abstraction. This gives you exquisite control over the system, which you need in some environments (for example, in system programming contexts like implementing network protocols or with embedded controllers). With great power comes great responsibility, however, and you must be very careful. Simple mistakes with pointers can have catastrophic and mysterious consequences.

Listing 3-6 performs low-level manipulation on two strings.

```
#include <cstdio>
int main() {
  char lower[] = "abc?e";
  char upper[] = "ABC?E";
  char* upper_ptr = upper;      ❶ // Equivalent: &upper[0]

  lower[3] = 'd';               ❷ // lower now contains a b c d e \0
  upper_ptr[3] = 'D';             // upper now contains A B C D E \0

  char letter_d = lower[3];     ❸ // letter_d equals 'd'
  char letter_D = upper_ptr[3];   // letter_D equals 'D'

  printf("lower: %s\nupper: %s", lower, upper); ❹

  lower[7] = 'g';               ❺ // Super bad. You must never do this.
}
--------------------------------------------------------------------------
lower: abcde ❹
upper: ABCDE
The time is 2:14 a.m. Eastern time, August 29th. Skynet is now online. ❺
```

Listing 3-6: A program containing a buffer overflow

After initializing the strings `lower` and `upper`, you initialize `upper_ptr` pointing to the first element ❶ in `upper`. You then reassign the fourth elements of both `lower` and `upper` (the question marks) to `d` and `D` ❷❸. Notice that `lower` is an array and `upper_ptr` is a pointer, but the mechanism is the same. So far, so good.

Finally, you make a major boo-boo by writing out-of-bounds memory ❺. By accessing the element at index `7` ❹, you've gone past the storage allotted to `lower`. No bounds checking occurs; this code compiles without warning.

At runtime, you get *undefined behavior*. Undefined behavior means the C++ language specification doesn't prescribe what happens, so your program might crash, open a security vulnerability, or spawn an artificial general intelligence ❺.

The Connection Between Brackets and Pointer Arithmetic

To understand the ramifications of out-of-bounds access, you must understand the connection between bracket operators and pointer arithmetic. Consider that you could have written Listing 3-6 with pointer arithmetic and dereference operators rather than bracket operators, as demonstrated in Listing 3-7.

```
#include <cstdio>
int main() {
```

```
    char lower[] = "abc?e";
    char upper[] = "ABC?E";
    char* upper_ptr = &upper[0];

    *(lower + 3) = 'd';
    *(upper_ptr + 3) = 'D';

    char letter_d = *(lower + 4); // lower decays into a pointer when we add
    char letter_D = *(upper_ptr + 4);

    printf("lower: %s\nupper: %s", lower, upper);

    *(lower + 7) = 'g'; ❶
}
```

Listing 3-7: An equivalent program to Listing 3-6 that uses pointer arithmetic

The `lower` array has length 6 (the letters *a*–*e* plus a null terminator). It should now be clear why assigning `lower[7]` ❶ is perilous. In this case, you're writing to some memory that doesn't belong to `lower`. This can result in access violations, program crashes, security vulnerabilities, and corrupted data. These kinds of errors can be very insidious, because the point at which the bad write occurs might be far removed from the point at which the bug manifests.

void Pointers and std::byte Pointers

Sometimes the pointed-to type is irrelevant. In such situations, you use the *void pointer* `void*`. The `void` pointers have important restrictions, the principal of which is that you cannot dereference a `void*`. Because the pointed-to type has been erased, dereferencing makes no sense (recall that the set of values for `void` objects is empty). For similar reasons, C++ forbids `void` pointer arithmetic.

Other times, you want to interact with raw memory at the byte level. Examples include low-level operations like copying raw data between files and memory, encryption, and compression. You cannot use a `void` pointer for such purposes because bit-wise and arithmetic operations are disabled. In such situations, you can use a `std::byte` pointer.

nullptr and Boolean Expressions

Pointers can have a special literal value, `nullptr`. Generally, a pointer that equals `nullptr` doesn't point to anything. You could use `nullptr` to indicate, for example, that there's no more memory left to allocate or that some error occurred.

Pointers have an implicit conversion to `bool`. Any value that is not `nullptr` converts implicitly to `true`, whereas `nullptr` converts implicitly to `false`. This is useful when a function returning a pointer ran successfully. A common idiom is that such a function returns `nullptr` in the case of failure. The canonical example is memory allocation.

References

References are safer, more convenient versions of pointers. You declare references with the & declarator appended to the type name. References cannot be assigned to null (easily), and they cannot be *reseated* (or reassigned). These characteristics eliminate some bugs endemic to pointers.

The syntax for dealing in references is much cleaner than for pointers. Rather than using the member-of-pointer and dereference operators, you use references exactly as if they're of the pointed-to type.

Listing 3-8 features a reference argument.

```
#include <cstdio>

struct ClockOfTheLongNow {
  --snip--
};

void add_year(ClockOfTheLongNow&❶ clock) {
  clock.set_year(clock.get_year() + 1); ❷ // No deref operator needed
}

int main() {
  ClockOfTheLongNow clock;
  printf("The year is %d.\n", clock.get_year()); ❸
  add_year(clock); ❹ // Clock is implicitly passed by reference!
  printf("The year is %d.\n", clock.get_year()); ❺
}
--------------------------------------------------------------------------
The year is 2019. ❸
The year is 2020. ❺
```

Listing 3-8: A program using references

You declare the clock argument as a ClockOfTheLongNow reference using the ampersand rather than the asterisk ❶. Within add_year, you use clock as if it were of type ClockOfTheLongNow ❷: there's no need to use clumsy dereference and pointer-to-reference operators. First, you print the value of year ❸. Next, at the call site, you pass a ClockOfTheLongNow object directly into add_year ❹: there's no need to take its address. Finally, you print the value of year again to illustrate that it has incremented ❺.

Usage of Pointers and References

Pointers and references are largely interchangeable, but both have trade-offs. If you must sometimes change your reference type's value—that is, if you must change what your reference type refers to—you must use a pointer. Many data structures (including forward-linked lists, which are covered in the next section) require that you be able to change a pointer's value. Because references cannot be reseated and they shouldn't generally be assigned to nullptr, they're sometimes not suitable.

Forward-Linked Lists: The Canonical Pointer-Based Data Structure

A *forward-linked list* is a simple data structure made up of a series of elements. Each element holds a pointer to the next element. The last element in the linked list holds a `nullptr`. Inserting elements into a linked list is very efficient, and elements can be discontinuous in memory. Figure 3-1 illustrates their layout.

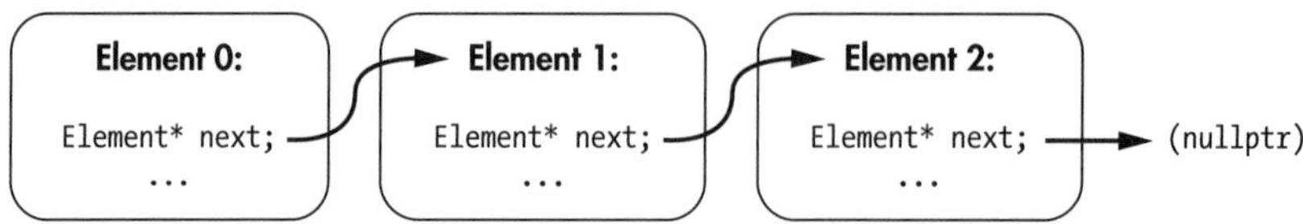

Figure 3-1: A linked list

Listing 3-9 demonstrates a possible implementation of a singly linked list element.

```
struct Element {
  Element* next{}; ❶
  void insert_after(Element* new_element) { ❷
    new_element->next = next; ❸
    next = new_element; ❹
  }
  char prefix[2]; ❺
  short operating_number; ❻
};
```

Listing 3-9: An implementation of a linked list `Element` with an operating number

Each `element` has a pointer to the `next` element in the linked list ❶, which initializes to `nullptr`. You insert a new element using the `insert_after` method ❷. It sets the `next` member of `new_element` to the `next` of `this` ❸ and then sets `next` of `this` to `new_element` ❹. Figure 3-2 illustrates this insertion. You haven't changed the memory location of any `Element` objects in this listing; you're only modifying pointer values.

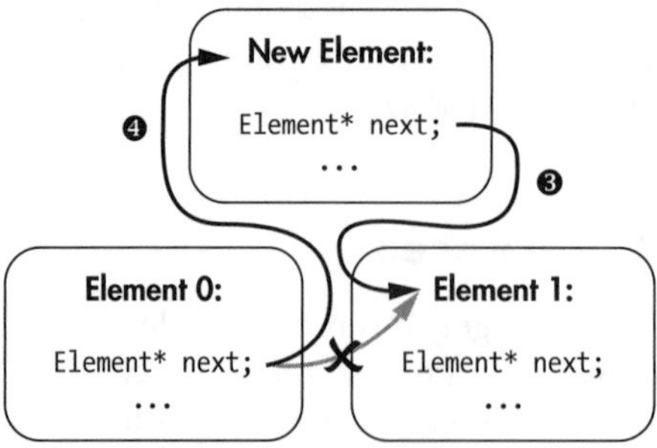

Figure 3-2: Inserting an element into a linked list

Each `Element` also contains a `prefix` array ❺ and an `operating_number` pointer ❻.

Listing 3-10 traverses a linked list of stormtroopers of type Element, printing their operating numbers along the way.

```
#include <cstdio>

struct Element {
  --snip--
};

int main() {
  Element trooper1, trooper2, trooper3; ❶
  trooper1.prefix[0] = 'T';
  trooper1.prefix[1] = 'K';
  trooper1.operating_number = 421;
  trooper1.insert_after(&trooper2); ❷
  trooper2.prefix[0] = 'F';
  trooper2.prefix[1] = 'N';
  trooper2.operating_number = 2187;
  trooper2.insert_after(&trooper3); ❸
  trooper3.prefix[0] = 'L';
  trooper3.prefix[1] = 'S';
  trooper3.operating_number = 005; ❹

  for (Element *cursor = &trooper1❺; cursor❻; cursor = cursor->next❼) {
    printf("stormtrooper %c%c-%d\n",
           cursor->prefix[0],
           cursor->prefix[1],
           cursor->operating_number); ❽
  }
}
--------------------------------------------------------------------------
stormtrooper TK-421 ❽
stormtrooper FN-2187 ❽
stormtrooper LS-5 ❽
```

Listing 3-10: A program illustrating a forward-linked list

Listing 3-10 initializes three stormtroopers ❶. The element trooper1 is assigned the operating number TK-421, and then you insert it as the next element in the list ❷. The elements trooper2 and trooper3 have operating numbers FN-2187 and LS-005 and are also inserted into the list ❸❹.

The for loop iterates through the linked list. First, you assign the cursor pointer to the address of trooper1 ❺. This is the beginning of the list. Before each iteration, you make sure that cursor is not nullptr ❻. After each iteration, you set cursor to the next element ❼. Within the loop, you print each stormtrooper's operating number ❽.

Employing References

Pointers provide a lot of flexibility, but this flexibility comes at a safety cost. If you don't need the flexibility of reseatability and nullptr, references are the go-to reference type.

Let's drive home the point that references cannot be reseated. Listing 3-11 initializes an int reference and then attempts to reseat it with a new_value.

```
#include <cstdio>

int main() {
  int original = 100;
  int& original_ref = original;
  printf("Original:  %d\n", original); ❶
  printf("Reference: %d\n", original_ref); ❷

  int new_value = 200;
  original_ref = new_value; ❸
  printf("Original:  %d\n", original); ❹
  printf("New Value: %d\n", new_value); ❺
  printf("Reference: %d\n", original_ref); ❻
}
```

```
Original:  100 ❶
Reference: 100 ❷
Original:  200 ❹
New Value: 200 ❺
Reference: 200 ❻
```

Listing 3-11: A program illustrating that you cannot reseat references

This program initializes an int called original to 100. Then it declares a reference to original called original_ref. From this point on, original_ref will *always* refer to original. This is illustrated by printing the value of original ❶ and the value referred to by original_ref ❷. They're the same.

Next, you initialize another int called new_value to 200 and assign original to it ❸. Read that carefully: this assignment ❸ doesn't reseat original_ref so that it points to new_value. Rather, it assigns the value of new_value to the object it points to (original).

The upshot is that all of these variables—original, original_ref, and new_value—evaluate to 200 ❹❺❻.

this Pointers

Remember that methods are associated with classes and that instances of classes are objects. When you program a method, sometimes you need to access the *current object*, which is the object that is executing the method.

Within method definitions, you can access the current object using the this pointer. Usually, this isn't needed, because this is implicit when accessing members. But sometimes you might need to disambiguate—for example, if you declare a method parameter whose name collides with a member variable. For example, you can rewrite Listing 3-9 to make explicit which Element you're referring to, as demonstrated in Listing 3-12.

```
struct Element {
  Element* next{};
  void insert_after(Element* new_element) {
```

```
    new_element->next = this->next; ❶
    this->next ❷ = new_element;
  }
  char prefix[2];
  short operating_number;
};
```

Listing 3-12: A rewriting of Listing 3-9 using the this pointer

Here, next is replaced with this->next ❶❷. The listings are functionally identical.

Sometimes, you need this to resolve ambiguity between members and arguments, as demonstrated in Listing 3-13.

```
struct ClockOfTheLongNow {
  bool set_year(int year❶) {
    if (year < 2019) return false;
    this->year = year; ❷
    return true;
  }
--snip--
private:
  int year; ❸
};
```

Listing 3-13: A verbose ClockOfTheLongNow definition using this

The year argument ❶ has the same name as the year member ❸. Method arguments will always mask members, meaning when you type year within this method, it refers to the year argument ❶, not the year member ❸. That's no problem: you disambiguate with this ❷.

const Correctness

The keyword const (short for "constant") roughly means "I promise not to modify." It's a safety mechanism that prevents unintended (and potentially catastrophic) modifications of member variables. You'll use const in function and class definitions to specify that a variable (usually a reference or a pointer) won't be modified by that function or class. If code attempts to modify a const variable, the compiler will emit an error. When used correctly, const is one of the most powerful language features in all modern programming languages because it helps you to eliminate many kinds of common programming mistakes at compile time.

Let's look at a few common usages of const.

const Arguments

Marking an argument const precludes its modification within a function's scope. A const pointer or reference provides you with an efficient mechanism to pass an object into a function for read-only use. The function in Listing 3-14 takes a const pointer.

```
void petruchio(const char* shrew❶) {
  printf("Fear not, sweet wench, they shall not touch thee, %s.", shrew❷);
  shrew[0] = "K"; ❸ // Compiler error! The shrew cannot be tamed.
}
```

Listing 3-14: A function taking a const pointer (This code doesn't compile.)

The petruchio function takes a shrew string by const reference ❶. You can read from shrew ❷, but attempting to write to it results in a compiler error ❸.

const Methods

Marking a method const communicates that you promise not to modify the current object's state within the const method. Put another way, these are read-only methods.

To mark a method const, place the const keyword after the argument list but before the method body. For example, you could update the ClockOfTheLongNow object's get_year with const, as demonstrated in Listing 3-15.

```
struct ClockOfTheLongNow {
  --snip--
  int get_year() const ❶{
      return year;
  }
private:
  int year;
};
```

Listing 3-15: Updating ClockOfTheLongNow with const

All you need to do is place const between the argument list and the method body ❶. Had you attempted to modify year within get_year, the compiler would have generated an error.

Holders of const references and pointers cannot invoke methods that are not const, because methods that are not const might modify an object's state.

The is_leap_year function in Listing 3-16 takes a const ClockOfTheLongNow reference and determines whether it's a leap year.

```
bool is_leap_year(const ClockOfTheLongNow& clock) {
  if (clock.get_year() % 4 > 0) return false;
  if (clock.get_year() % 100 > 0) return true;
  if (clock.get_year() % 400 > 0) return false;
  return true;
}
```

Listing 3-16: A function for determining leap years

Had get_year not been marked a const method, Listing 3-16 would not compile because clock is a const reference and cannot be modified within is_leap_year.

const Member Variables

You can mark member variables const by adding the keyword to the member's type. The const member variables cannot be modified after their initialization.

In Listing 3-17, the Avout class contains two member variables, one const and one not const.

```
struct Avout {
  const❶ char* name = "Erasmas";
  ClockOfTheLongNow apert; ❷
};
```

Listing 3-17: An Avout *class with a* const *member*

The name member is const, meaning the pointed-to value cannot be modified ❶. On the other hand, apert is not const ❷.

Of course, a const Avout reference cannot be modified, so the usual rules would still apply to apert:

```
void does_not_compile(const Avout& avout) {
  avout.apert.add_year(); // Compiler error: avout is const
}
```

Sometimes you want the safety of marking a member variable const but would also like to initialize the member with arguments passed into a constructor. For this, you employ member initializer lists.

Member Initializer Lists

Member initializer lists are the primary mechanism for initializing class members. To declare a member initializer list, place a colon after the argument list in a constructor. Then insert one or more comma-separated *member initializers*. A member initializer is the name of the member followed by a braced initialization { }. Member initializers allow you to set the value of const fields at runtime.

The example in Listing 3-18 improves Listing 3-17 by introducing a member initialization list.

```
#include <cstdio>

struct ClockOfTheLongNow {
  --snip--
};

struct Avout {
  Avout(const char* name, long year_of_apert) ❶
    :❷ name❸{ name }❹, apert❺{ year_of_apert }❻ {
  }
  void announce() const { ❼
    printf("My name is %s and my next apert is %d.\n", name, apert.get_year());
  }
```

```
  const char* name;
  ClockOfTheLongNow apert;
};

int main() {
  Avout raz{ "Erasmas", 3010 };
  Avout jad{ "Jad", 4000 };
  raz.announce();
  jad.announce();
}
```

```
My name is Erasmas and my next apert is 3010.
My name is Jad and my next apert is 4000.
```

Listing 3-18: A program declaring and announcing two `Avout` objects

The `Avout` constructor takes two arguments, a `name` and the `year_of_apert` ❶. A member initializer list is added by inserting a colon ❷ followed by the names of each member you're initializing ❸❺ and braced initializations ❹❻. A `const` method `announce` is also added to print the `Avout` constructor's status ❼.

All member initializations execute before the constructor's body. This has two advantages:

- It ensures validity of all members before the constructor executes, so you can focus on initialization logic rather than member error checking.
- The members initialize once. If you reassign members in the constructor, you potentially do extra work.

NOTE *You should order the member initializers in the same order they appear in the class definition, because their constructors will be called in this order.*

Speaking of eliminating extra work, it's time to meet `auto`.

auto Type Deduction

As a strongly typed language, C++ affords its compiler a lot of information. When you initialize elements or return from functions, the compiler can divine type information from context. The `auto` keyword tells the compiler to perform such a divination for you, relieving you from inputting redundant type information.

Initialization with auto

In almost all situations, the compiler can determine the correct type of an object using the initialization value. This assignment contains redundant information:

```
int answer = 42;
```

The compiler knows answer is an int because 42 is an int.

You can use auto instead:

```
auto the_answer { 42 };            // int
auto foot { 12L };                 // long
auto rootbeer { 5.0F };            // float
auto cheeseburger { 10.0 };        // double
auto politifact_claims { false };  // bool
auto cheese { "string" };          // char[7]
```

This also works when you're initializing with parentheses () and the lone =:

```
auto the_answer = 42;
auto foot(12L);
--snip--
```

Because you've committed to universal initialization with {} as much as possible, this section will say no more of these alternatives.

Alone, all of this simple initialization help doesn't buy you much; however, when types become more complicated—for example, dealing with iterators from stdlib containers—it really saves quite a bit of typing. It also makes your code more resilient to refactoring.

auto and Reference Types

It's common to add modifiers like &, *, and const to auto. Such modifications add the intended meanings (reference, pointer, and const, respectively):

```
auto year { 2019 };              // int
auto& year_ref = year;           // int&
const auto& year_cref = year;    // const int&
auto* year_ptr = &year;          // int*
const auto* year_cptr = &year;   // const int*
```

Adding modifiers to the auto declaration behaves just as you'd expect: if you add a modifier, the resulting type is guaranteed to have that modifier.

auto and Code Refactorings

The auto keyword assists in making code simpler and more resilient to refactoring. Consider the example in Listing 3-19 with a range-based for loop.

```
struct Dwarf {
  --snip--
};

Dwarf dwarves[13];

struct Contract {
  void add(const Dwarf&);
};
```

```
void form_company(Contract &contract) {
  for (const auto& dwarf : dwarves) { ❶
    contract.add(dwarf);
  }
}
```

Listing 3-19: An example using auto in a range-based for loop

If ever the type of dwarves changes, the assignment in the range-based for loop ❶ doesn't need to change. The dwarf type will adapt to its surroundings, in much the same way that the dwarves of Middle Earth don't.

As a general rule, use auto always.

NOTE *There are some corner cases to using braced initialization where you might get surprising results, but these are few, especially after C++17 fixed some pedantic nonsense behavior. Prior to C++17, using auto with braces {} specified a special object called a std::initializer_list, which you'll meet in Chapter 13.*

Summary

This chapter covered the two reference types: references and pointers. Along the way, you learned about the member-of-pointer operator, how pointers and arrays interplay, and void/byte pointers. You also learned about the meaning of const and its basic usage, the this pointer, and member initializer lists. Additionally, the chapter introduced auto type deduction.

EXERCISES

3-1. Read about CVE-2001-0500, a buffer overflow in Microsoft's Internet Information Services. (This vulnerability is commonly referred to as the Code Red worm vulnerability.)

3-2. Add a read_from and a write_to function to Listing 3-6. These functions should read or write to upper or lower as appropriate. Perform bounds checking to prevent buffer overflows.

3-3. Add an Element* previous to Listing 3-9 to make a *doubly linked list*. Add an insert_before method to Element. Traverse the list from front to back, then from back to front, using two separate for loops. Print the operating_number inside each loop.

3-4. Reimplement Listing 3-11 using no explicit types. (Hint: use auto.)

3-5. Scan the listings in Chapter 2. Which methods could be marked const? Where could you use auto?

FURTHER READING

- *The C++ Programming Language*, 4th Edition, by Bjarne Stroustrup (Pearson Education, 2013)
- "C++ Core Guidelines" by Bjarne Stroustrup and Herb Sutter (*https://github.com/isocpp/CppCoreGuidelines/*)
- "East End Functions" by Phil Nash (2018; *https://levelofindirection.com/blog/east-end-functions.html*)
- "References FAQ" by the Standard C++ Foundation (*https://isocpp.org/wiki/faq/references/*)

4

THE OBJECT LIFE CYCLE

Things you used to own, now they own you.
—Chuck Palahniuk, Fight Club

The object life cycle is the series of stages a C++ object goes through during its lifetime. This chapter begins with a discussion of an object's storage duration, the time during which storage is allocated for an object. You'll learn about how the object life cycle dovetails with exceptions to handle error conditions and cleanup in a robust, safe, and elegant way. The chapter closes with a discussion of move and copy semantics that provides you with granular control over an object's life cycle.

An Object's Storage Duration

An *object* is a region of storage that has a type and a value. When you declare a variable, you create an object. A variable is simply an object that has a name.

Allocation, Deallocation, and Lifetime

Every object requires storage. You reserve storage for objects in a process called *allocation*. When you're done with an object, you release the object's storage in a process called *deallocation*.

An object's *storage duration* begins when the object is allocated and ends when the object is deallocated. The *lifetime* of an object is a runtime property that is bound by the object's storage duration. An object's lifetime begins once its constructor completes, and it ends just before a destructor is invoked. In summary, each object passes through the following stages:

1. The object's storage duration begins, and storage is allocated.
2. The object's constructor is called.
3. The object's lifetime begins.
4. You can use the object in your program.
5. The object's lifetime ends.
6. The object's destructor is called.
7. The object's storage duration ends, and storage is deallocated.

Memory Management

If you've been programming in an application language, chances are you've used an *automatic memory manager*, or a *garbage collector*. At runtime, programs create objects. Periodically, the garbage collector determines which objects are no longer required by the program and safely deallocates them. This approach frees the programmer from worrying about managing an object's life cycle, but it incurs several costs, including runtime performance, and requires some powerful programming techniques like deterministic resource management.

C++ takes a more efficient approach. The trade-off is that C++ programmers must have intimate knowledge of storage durations. It's *our* job, not the garbage collector's, to craft object lifetimes.

Automatic Storage Duration

An *automatic object* is allocated at the beginning of an enclosing code block, and it's deallocated at the end. The enclosing block is the automatic object's *scope*. Automatic objects are said to have *automatic storage duration*. Note that function parameters are automatic, even though notationally they appear outside the function body.

In Listing 4-1, the function `power_up_rat_thing` is the scope for the automatic variables `nuclear_isotopes` and `waste_heat`.

```
void power_up_rat_thing(int nuclear_isotopes) {
  int waste_heat = 0;
  --snip--
}
```

Listing 4-1: A function with two automatic variables, nuclear_isotopes and waste_heat

Both nuclear_isotopes and waste_heat are allocated each time power_up_rat_thing is invoked. Just before power_up_rat_thing returns, these variables are deallocated.

Because you cannot access these variables outside of power_up_rat_thing, automatic variables are also called *local variables*.

Static Storage Duration

A *static object* is declared using the static or extern keyword. You declare static variables at the same level you declare functions—at global scope (or *namespace scope*). Static objects with global scope have *static storage duration* and are allocated when the program starts and deallocated when the program stops.

The program in Listing 4-2 powers up a Rat Thing with nuclear isotopes by calling the power_up_rat_thing function. When it does, the Rat Thing's power increases, and the variable rat_things_power keeps track of the power level between power-ups.

```
#include <cstdio>

static int rat_things_power = 200; ❶

void power_up_rat_thing(int nuclear_isotopes) {
  rat_things_power = rat_things_power + nuclear_isotopes; ❷
  const auto waste_heat = rat_things_power * 20; ❸
  if (waste_heat > 10000) { ❹
    printf("Warning! Hot doggie!\n"); ❺
  }
}

int main() {
  printf("Rat-thing power: %d\n", rat_things_power); ❻
  power_up_rat_thing(100); ❼
  printf("Rat-thing power: %d\n", rat_things_power);
  power_up_rat_thing(500);
  printf("Rat-thing power: %d\n", rat_things_power);
}
--------------------------------------------------------------------------
Rat-thing power: 200
Rat-thing power: 300
Warning! Hot doggie! ❽
Rat-thing power: 800
```

Listing 4-2: A program with a static variable and several automatic variables

The variable rat_things_power ❶ is a static variable because it's declared at global scope with the static keyword. Another feature of being declared at global scope is that power_up_rat_thing can be accessed from any function in the translation unit. (Recall from Chapter 1 that a translation unit is what a preprocessor produces after acting on a single source file.) At ❷, you see power_up_rat_thing increasing rat_things_power by the number of nuclear_isotopes. Because rat_things_power is a static variable—and hence its lifetime is the program's lifetime—each time you call power_up_rat_thing, the value of rat_things_power carries over into the next call.

Next, you calculate how much waste heat is produced given the new value of rat_things_power, and you store the result in the automatic variable waste_heat ❸. Its storage duration begins when power_up_rat_thing is called and ends when power_up_rat_thing returns, so its values aren't saved between function calls. Finally, you check whether waste_heat is over a threshold value of 10000 ❹. If it is, you print a warning message ❺.

Within main, you alternate between printing the value of rat_things_power ❻ and calling power_up_rat_thing ❼.

Once you've increased the Rat Thing's power from 300 to 800, you get the warning message in the output ❽. The effects of modifying rat_things_power last for the lifetime of the program due to its static storage duration.

When you use the static keyword, you specify *internal linkage*. Internal linkage means that a variable is inaccessible to other translation units. You can alternately specify *external linkage*, which makes a variable accessible to other translation units. For external linkage, you use the extern keyword instead of static.

You could modify Listing 4-2 in the following way to achieve external linkage:

```
#include <cstdio>

extern int rat_things_power = 200; // External linkage
--snip--
```

With extern rather than static, you can access rat_things_power from other translation units.

Local Static Variables

A *local static variable* is a special kind of static variable that is a local—rather than global—variable. Local static variables are declared at function scope, just like automatic variables. But their lifetimes begin upon the first invocation of the enclosing function and end when the program exits.

For example, you could refactor Listing 4-2 to make rat_things_power a local static variable, as demonstrated in Listing 4-3.

```
#include <cstdio>

void power_up_rat_thing(int nuclear_isotopes) {
  static int rat_things_power = 200;
  rat_things_power = rat_things_power + nuclear_isotopes;
  const auto waste_heat = rat_things_power * 20;
  if (waste_heat > 10000) {
    printf("Warning! Hot doggie!\n");
  }
  printf("Rat-thing power: %d\n", rat_things_power);
}
```

```
int main() {
  power_up_rat_thing(100);
  power_up_rat_thing(500);
}
```

Listing 4-3: A refactor of Listing 4-2 using a local static variable.

Unlike in Listing 4-2, you cannot refer to `rat_things_power` from outside of the `power_up_rat_thing` function due to its local scope. This is an example of a programming pattern called *encapsulation*, which is the bundling of data with a function that operates on that data. It helps to protect against unintended modification.

Static Members

Static members are members of a class that aren't associated with a particular instance of the class. Normal class members have lifetimes nested within the class's lifetime, but static members have static storage duration.

These members are essentially similar to static variables and functions declared at global scope; however, you must refer to them by the containing class's name, using the scope resolution operator `::`. In fact, you must initialize static members at global scope. You cannot initialize a static member within a containing class definition.

NOTE *There is an exception to the static member initialization rule: you can declare and define integral types within a class definition as long as they're also* `const`.

Like other static variables, static members have only a single instance. All instances of a class with static members share the same member, so if you modify a static member, *all* class instances will observe the modification. To illustrate, you could convert `power_up_rat_thing` and `rat_things_power` in Listing 4-2 to static members of a `RatThing` class, as shown in Listing 4-4.

```
#include <cstdio>

struct RatThing {
  static int rat_things_power; ❶
  static❷ void power_up_rat_thing(int nuclear_isotopes) {
    rat_things_power❸ = rat_things_power + nuclear_isotopes;
    const auto waste_heat = rat_things_power * 20;
    if (waste_heat > 10000) {
      printf("Warning! Hot doggie!\n");
    }
    printf("Rat-thing power: %d\n", rat_things_power);
  }
};

int RatThing::rat_things_power = 200; ❹

int main() {
```

```
  RatThing::power_up_rat_thing(100); ❺
  RatThing::power_up_rat_thing(500);
}
```

Listing 4-4: A refactor of Listing 4-2 using static members

The `RatThing` class contains `rat_things_power` as a static member variable ❶ and `power_up_rat_thing` as a static method ❷. Because `rat_things_power` is a member of `RatThing`, you don't need the scope resolution operator ❸; you access it like any other member.

You see the scope resolution operator in action where `rat_things_power` is initialized ❹ and where you invoke the static method `power_up_rat_thing` ❺.

Thread-Local Storage Duration

One of the fundamental concepts in concurrent programs is the *thread*. Each program has one or more threads that can perform independent operations. The sequence of instructions that a thread executes is called its *thread of execution*.

Programmers must take extra precautions when using more than one thread of execution. Code that multiple threads can execute safely is called *thread-safe code*. Mutable global variables are the source of many thread safety issues. Sometimes, you can avoid these issues by giving each thread its own copy of a variable. You can do this by specifying that an object has *thread storage duration*.

You can modify any variable with static storage duration to have thread-local storage duration by adding the `thread_local` keyword to the `static` or `extern` keyword. If only `thread_local` is specified, `static` is assumed. The variable's linkage is unchanged.

Listing 4-3 is not thread safe. Depending on the order of reads and writes, `rat_things_power` could become corrupted. You could make Listing 4-3 thread safe by specifying `rat_things_power` as `thread_local`, as demonstrated here:

```
#include <cstdio>

void power_up_rat_thing(int nuclear_isotopes) {
  static thread_local int rat_things_power = 200; ❶
  --snip--
}
```

Now each thread would represent its own Rat Thing; if one thread modifies its `rat_things_power`, the modification will not affect the other threads. Each copy of `rat_things_power` is initialized to 200 ❶.

NOTE *Concurrent programming is discussed in more detail in Chapter 19. Thread storage duration is presented here for completeness.*

Dynamic Storage Duration

Objects with *dynamic storage duration* are allocated and deallocated on request. You have manual control over when a *dynamic object*'s life begins and when it ends. Dynamic objects are also called *allocated objects* for this reason.

The primary way to allocate a dynamic object is with a *new expression*. A new expression begins with the `new` keyword followed by the desired type of the dynamic object. New expressions create objects of a given type and then return a pointer to the newly minted object.

Consider the following example where you create an `int` with dynamic storage duration and save it into a pointer called `my_int_ptr`:

```
int*❶ my_int_ptr = new❷ int❸;
```

You declare a pointer to `int` and initialize it with the result of the new expression on the right side of the equal sign ❶. The new expression is composed of the `new` keyword ❷ followed by the desired type `int` ❸. When the new expression executes, the C++ runtime allocates memory to store an `int` and then returns its pointer.

You can also initialize a dynamic object within a new expression, as shown here:

```
int* my_int_ptr = new int{ 42 }; // Initializes dynamic object to 42
```

After allocating storage for the `int`, the dynamic object will be initialized as usual. After initialization completes, the dynamic object's lifetime begins.

You deallocate dynamic objects using the *delete expression*, which is composed of the `delete` keyword followed by a pointer to the dynamic object. Delete expressions always return `void`.

To deallocate the object pointed to by `my_int_ptr`, you would use the following delete expression:

```
delete my_int_ptr;
```

The value contained in memory where the deleted object resided is undefined, meaning the compiler can produce code that leaves anything there. In practice, major compilers will try to be as efficient as possible, so typically the object's memory will remain untouched until the program reuses it for some other purposes. You would have to implement a custom destructor to, for example, zero out some sensitive contents.

NOTE *Because the compiler doesn't typically clean up memory after an object is deleted, a subtle and potentially serious type of bug called a* use after free *can occur. If you delete an object and accidentally reuse it, your program might appear to function correctly because the deallocated memory might still contain reasonable values. In some situations, the problems don't manifest until the program has been in production for a long time—or until a security researcher finds a way to exploit the bug and discloses it!*

Dynamic Arrays

Dynamic arrays are arrays with dynamic storage duration. You create dynamic arrays with *array new expressions*. Array new expressions have the following form:

```
new MyType[n_elements] { init-list }
```

MyType is the desired type of the array elements, n_elements is the length of the desired array, and the optional init-list is an initialization list to initialize the array. Array new expressions return a pointer to the first element of the newly allocated array.

In the following example, you allocate an int array of length 100 and save the result into a pointer called my_int_array_ptr:

```
int* my_int_array_ptr = new int[100❶];
```

The number of elements ❶ doesn't need to be constant: the size of the array can be determined at runtime, meaning the value between brackets ❶ could be a variable rather than a literal.

To deallocate a dynamic array, use the *array delete expression*. Unlike the array new expression, the array delete expression doesn't require a length:

```
delete[] my_int_ptr;
```

Like the delete expression, the array delete expression returns void.

Memory Leaks

With privilege comes responsibility, so you must make sure that dynamic objects you allocate are also deallocated. Failure to do so causes *memory leaks* in which memory that is no longer needed by your program isn't released. When you leak memory, you use up a resource in your environment that you'll never reclaim. This can cause performance problems or worse.

NOTE *In practice, your program's operating environment might clean up leaked resources for you. For example, if you've written user-mode code, modern operating systems will clean up the resources when the program exits. However, if you've written kernel code, those operating systems won't clean up the resources. You'll only reclaim them when the computer reboots.*

Tracing the Object Life Cycle

The object life cycle is as daunting to newcomers as it is powerful. Let's clarify with an example that explores each of the storage durations.

Consider the Tracer class in Listing 4-5, which prints a message whenever a Tracer object is constructed or destructed. You can use this class to investigate object life cycles, because each Tracer clearly indicates when its life is beginning and ending.

```
#include <cstdio>

struct Tracer {
  Tracer(const char* name❶) : name{ name }❷ {
    printf("%s constructed.\n", name); ❸
  }
  ~Tracer() {
    printf("%s destructed.\n", name); ❹
  }
private:
  const char* const name;
};
```

Listing 4-5: A `Tracer` *class that announces construction and destruction*

The constructor takes a single parameter ❶ and saves it into the member `name` ❷. It then prints a message containing `name` ❸. The destructor ❹ also prints a message with `name`.

Consider the program in Listing 4-6. Four different `Tracer` objects have different storage durations. By looking at the order of the program's `Tracer` output, you can verify what you've learned about storage durations.

```
#include <cstdio>

struct Tracer {
  --snip--
};

static Tracer t1{ "Static variable" }; ❶
thread_local Tracer t2{ "Thread-local variable" }; ❷

int main() {
  printf("A\n"); ❸
  Tracer t3{ "Automatic variable" }; ❹
  printf("B\n");
  const auto* t4 = new Tracer{ "Dynamic variable" }; ❺
  printf("C\n");
}
```

Listing 4-6: A program using the `Tracer` *class in Listing 4-5 to illustrate storage duration*

Listing 4-6 contains a `Tracer` with static duration ❶, thread local duration ❷, automatic duration ❹, and dynamic duration ❺. Between each line in `main`, you print the character `A`, `B`, or `C` for reference ❸.

Running the program yields Listing 4-7.

```
Static variable constructed.
Thread-local variable constructed.
A ❸
```

```
Automatic variable constructed.
B
Dynamic variable constructed.
C
Automatic variable destructed.
Thread-local variable destructed.
Static variable destructed.
```

Listing 4-7: Sample output from running Listing 4-6

Before the first line of `main` ❸, the static and thread local variables `t1` and `t2` have been initialized ❶ ❷. You can see this in Listing 4-7: both variables have printed their initialization messages before `A`. As an automatic variable, the scope of `t3` is bounded by the enclosing function `main`. Accordingly, `t3` is constructed where it is initialized just after `A`.

After `B`, you see the message corresponding to the initialization of `t4` ❺. Notice that there's no corresponding message generated by the dynamic destructor of `Tracer`. The reason is that you've (intentionally) leaked the object pointed to by `t4`. Because there's no command to `delete t4`, the destructor is never called.

Just before `main` returns, `C` prints. Because `t3` is an automatic variable whose scope is `main`, it's destroyed at this point because `main` is returning.

Finally, the static and thread-local variables `t1` and `t2` are destroyed just before program exit, yielding the final two messages in Listing 4-7.

Exceptions

Exceptions are types that communicate an error condition. When an error condition occurs, you *throw* an exception. After you throw an exception, it's *in flight.* When an exception is in flight, the program stops normal execution and searches for an *exception handler* that can manage the in-flight exception. Objects that fall out of scope during this process are destroyed.

In situations where there's no good way to handle an error locally, such as in a constructor, you generally use exceptions. Exceptions play a crucial role in managing object life cycles in such circumstances.

The other option for communicating error conditions is to return an error code as part of a function's prototype. These two approaches are complementary. In situations where an error occurs that can be dealt with locally or that is expected to occur during the normal course of a program's execution, you generally return an error code.

The throw Keyword

To throw an exception, use the `throw` keyword followed by a throwable object.

Most objects are throwable. But it's good practice to use one of the exceptions available in stdlib, such as `std::runtime_error` in the `<stdexcept>` header. The `runtime_error` constructor accepts a null-terminated `const char*` describing the nature of the error condition. You can retrieve this message via the `what` method, which takes no parameters.

The Groucho class in Listing 4-8 throws an exception whenever you invoke the forget method with an argument equal to 0xFACE.

```
#include <stdexcept>
#include <cstdio>

struct Groucho {
  void forget(int x) {
    if (x == 0xFACE) {
      throw❶ std::runtime_error❷{ "I'd be glad to make an exception." };
    }
    printf("Forgot 0x%x\n", x);
  }
};
```

Listing 4-8: The Groucho class

To throw an exception, Listing 4-8 uses the throw keyword ❶ followed by a std::runtime_error object ❷.

Using try-catch Blocks

You use try-catch blocks to establish exception handlers for a block of code. Within the try block, you place code that might throw an exception. Within the catch block, you specify a handler for each exception type you can handle.

Listing 4-9 illustrates the use of a try-catch block to handle exceptions thrown by a Groucho object.

```
#include <stdexcept>
#include <cstdio>

struct Groucho {
  --snip--
};

int main() {
  Groucho groucho;
  try { ❶
    groucho.forget(0xC0DE); ❷
    groucho.forget(0xFACE); ❸
    groucho.forget(0xC0FFEE); ❹
  } catch (const std::runtime_error& e❺) {
    printf("exception caught with message: %s\n", e.what()); ❻
  }
}
```

Listing 4-9: The use of try-catch to handle the exceptions of the Groucho class

In main, you construct a Groucho object and then establish a try-catch block ❶. Within the try portion, you invoke the groucho class's forget method with several different parameters: 0xC0DE ❷, 0xFACE ❸, and 0xC0FFEE ❹. Within the catch portion, you handle any std::runtime_error exceptions ❺ by printing the message to the console ❻.

When you run the program in Listing 4-9, you get the following output:

```
Forgot 0xc0de
exception caught with message: I'd be glad to make an exception.
```

When you invoked `forget` with the argument `0xC0DE` ❷, `groucho` printed `Forgot 0xc0de` and returned. When you invoked `forget` with the argument `0xFACE` ❸, `groucho` threw an exception. This exception stopped normal program execution, so `forget` is never invoked again ❹. Instead, the in-flight exception is caught ❺, and its message is printed ❻.

A CRASH COURSE IN INHERITANCE

Before introducing the stdlib exceptions, you need to understand simple C++ class inheritance at a very high level. Classes can have *subclasses* that inherit the functionality of their *superclasses*. The syntax in Listing 4-10 defines this relationship.

```
struct Superclass {
  int x;
};

struct Subclass : Superclass { ❶
  int y;
  int foo() {
    return x + y; ❷
  }
};
```

Listing 4-10: Defining superclasses and subclasses

There's nothing special about `Superclass`. But the declaration of `Subclass` ❶ is special. It defines the inheritance relationship using the `: Superclass` syntax. `Subclass` inherits members from `Superclass` that are not marked `private`. You can see this in action where `Subclass` uses the field `x` ❷. This is a field belonging to `Superclass`, but because `Subclass` inherits from `Superclass`, `x` is accessible.

Exceptions use these inheritance relationships to determine whether a handler catches an exception. Handlers will catch a given type *and* any of its parents' types.

stdlib Exception Classes

You can arrange classes into parent-child relationships using *inheritance*. Inheritance has a big impact on how the code handles exceptions. There is a nice, simple hierarchy of existing exception types available for use in the stdlib. You should try to use these types for simple programs. Why reinvent the wheel?

Standard Exception Classes

The stdlib provides you with the *standard exception classes* in the <stdexcept> header. These should be your first port of call when you're programming exceptions. The superclass for all the standard exception classes is the class `std::exception`. All the subclasses in `std::exception` can be partitioned into three groups: logic errors, runtime errors, and language support errors. While language support errors are not generally relevant to you as a programmer, you'll definitely encounter logic errors and runtime errors. Figure 4-1 summarizes their relationship.

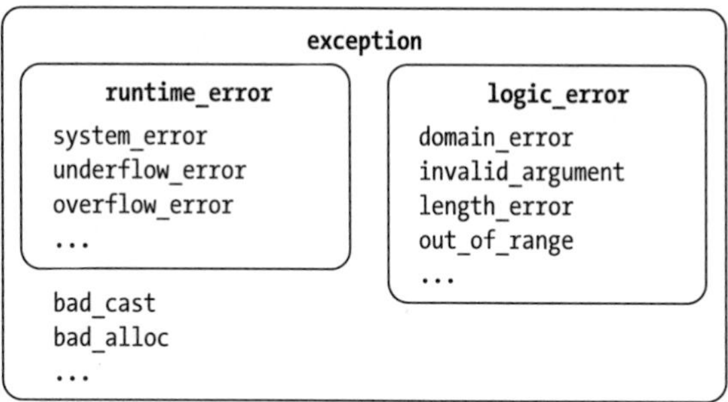

Figure 4-1: How stdlib exceptions are nested under `std::exception`

Logic Errors

Logic errors derive from the `logic_error` class. Generally, you could avoid these exceptions through more careful programming. A primary example is when a logical precondition of a class isn't satisfied, such as when a class invariant cannot be established. (Remember from Chapter 2 that a class invariant is a feature of a class that is always true.)

Since a class invariant is something that the programmer defines, neither the compiler nor the runtime environment can enforce it without help. You can use a class constructor to check for various conditions, and if you cannot establish a class invariant, you can throw an exception. If the failure is the result of, say, passing an incorrect parameter to the constructor, a `logic_error` is an appropriate exception to throw.

The `logic_error` has several subclasses that you should be aware of:

- The `domain_error` reports errors related to valid input range, especially for math functions. The square root, for example, only supports nonnegative numbers (in the real case). If a negative argument is passed, a square root function could throw a `domain_error`.
- The `invalid_argument` exception reports generally unexpected arguments.
- The `length_error` exception reports that some action would violate a maximum size constraint.
- The `out_of_range` exception reports that some value isn't in an expected range. The canonical example is bounds-checked indexing into a data structure.

Runtime Errors

Runtime errors derive from the runtime_error class. These exceptions help you report error conditions that are outside the program's scope. Like logic_error, runtime_error has some subclasses that you might find useful:

- The system_error reports that the operating system encountered some error. You can get a lot of mileage out of this kind of exception. Inside of the <system_error> header, there's a large number of *error codes* and *error conditions*. When a system_error is constructed, information about the error is packed in so you can determine the nature of the error. The .code() method returns an enum class of type std::errc that has a large number of values, such as bad_file_descriptor, timed_out, and permission_denied.
- The overflow_error and underflow_error report arithmetic overflow and underflow, respectively.

Other errors inherit directly from exception. A common one is the bad_alloc exception, which reports that new failed to allocate the required memory for dynamic storage.

Language Support Errors

You won't use language support errors directly. They exist to indicate that some core language feature failed at runtime.

Handling Exceptions

The rules for exception handling are based on class inheritance. When an exception is thrown, a catch block handles the exception if the thrown exception's type matches the catch handler's exception type or if the thrown exception's type *inherits from* the catch handler's exception type.

For example, the following handler catches any exception that inherits from std::exception, including a std::logic_error:

```
try {
  throw std::logic_error{ "It's not about who wrong "
                          "it's not about who right" };
} catch (std::exception& ex) {
  // Handles std::logic_error as it inherits from std::exception
}
```

The following special handler catches *any* exception regardless of its type:

```
try {
  throw 'z'; // Don't do this.
} catch (...) {
  // Handles any exception, even a 'z'
}
```

Special handlers are typically used as a safety mechanism to log the program's catastrophic failure to catch an exception of a specific type.

You can handle different types of exceptions originating from the same try block by chaining together catch statements, as demonstrated here:

```
try {
  // Code that might throw an exception
  --snip--
} catch (const std::logic_error& ex) {
  // Log exception and terminate the program; there is a programming error!
  --snip--
} catch (const std::runtime_error& ex) {
  // Do our best to recover gracefully
  --snip--
} catch (const std::exception& ex) {
  // This will handle any exception that derives from std:exception
  // that is not a logic_error or a runtime_error.
  --snip--
} catch (...) {
  // Panic; an unforeseen exception type was thrown
  --snip--
}
```

It's common to see such code in a program's entry point.

RETHROWING AN EXCEPTION

In a catch block, you can use the throw keyword to resume searching for an appropriate exception handler. This is called *rethrowing an exception*. There are some unusual but important cases where you might want to further inspect an exception before deciding to handle it, as shown in Listing 4-11.

```
try {
  // Some code that might throw a system_error
  --snip--
} catch(const std::system_error& ex) {
  if(ex.code()!= std::errc::permission_denied){
    // Not a permission denied error
    throw; ❶
  }
  // Recover from a permission denied
  --snip--
}
```

Listing 4-11: Rethrowing an error

(continued)

In this example, some code that might throw a system_error is wrapped in a try-catch block. All system_errors are handled, but unless it's an EACCES (permission denied) error, you *rethrow* the exception ❶. There are some performance penalties to this approach, and the resulting code is often needlessly convoluted.

Rather than rethrowing, you can define a new exception type and create a separate catch handler for the EACCES error, as demonstrated in Listing 4-12.

```
try {
  // Throw a PermissionDenied instead
  --snip--
} catch(const PermissionDenied& ex) {
  // Recover from an EACCES error (Permission Denied) ❶
  --snip--
}
```

Listing 4-12: Catching a specific exception rather than rethrowing

If a std::system_error is thrown, the PermissionDenied handler ❶ won't catch it. (Of course, you could still keep the std::system_error handler to catch such exceptions if you wish.)

User-Defined Exceptions

You can define your own exceptions whenever you'd like; usually, these *user-defined exceptions* inherit from std::exception. All the classes from stdlib use exceptions that derive from std::exception. This makes it easy to catch all exceptions, whether from your code or from the stdlib, with a single catch block.

The noexcept Keyword

The keyword noexcept is another exception-related term you should know. You can, and should, mark any function that cannot possibly throw an exception noexcept, as in the following:

```
bool is_odd(int x) noexcept {
  return 1 == (x % 2);
}
```

Functions marked noexcept make a rigid contract. When you're using a function marked noexcept, you can rest assured that the function cannot throw an exception. In exchange, you must be extremely careful when you mark your own function noexcept, since the compiler won't check for you. If your code throws an exception inside a function marked noexcept, it's bad juju. The C++ runtime will call the function `std::terminate`, a function that by default will exit the program via `abort`. Your program cannot recover:

```
void hari_kari() noexcept {
  throw std::runtime_error{ "Goodbye, cruel world." };
}
```

Marking a function `noexcept` enables some code optimizations that rely on the function's not being able to throw an exception. Essentially, the compiler is liberated to use move semantics, which may be faster (more about this in "Move Semantics" on page 122).

NOTE *Check out Item 16 of* Effective Modern C++ *by Scott Meyers for a thorough discussion of* `noexcept`. *The gist is that some move constructors and move assignment operators might throw an exception, for example, if they need to allocate memory and the system is out. Unless a move constructor or move assignment operator specifies otherwise, the compiler must assume that a move could cause an exception. This disables certain optimizations.*

Call Stacks and Exceptions

The *call stack* is a runtime structure that stores information about active functions. When a piece of code (the *caller*) invokes a function (the *callee*), the machine keeps track of who called whom by pushing information onto the call stack. This allows programs to have many function calls nested within each other. The callee could then, in turn, become the caller by invoking another function.

Stacks

A stack is a flexible data container that can hold a dynamic number of elements. There are two essential operations that all stacks support: *pushing* elements onto the top of the stack and *popping* those elements off. It is a last-in, first-out data structure, as illustrated in Figure 4-2.

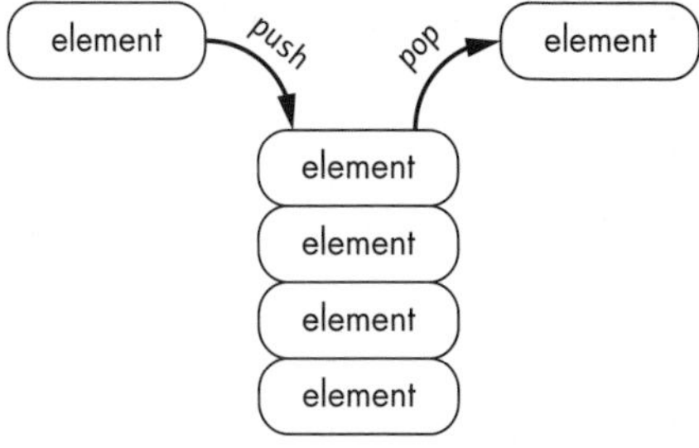

Figure 4-2: Elements being pushed onto and popped off of a stack

As its name suggests, the call stack is functionally similar to its namesake data container. Each time a function is invoked, information about the function invocation is arranged into a *stack frame* and pushed onto the call stack. Because a new stack frame is pushed onto the stack for every function call, a callee is free to call other functions, forming arbitrarily deep call chains. Whenever a function returns, its stack frame is popped off the top of the call stack, and execution control resumes as indicated by the previous stack frame.

Call Stacks and Exception Handling

The runtime seeks the closest exception handler to a thrown exception. If there is a matching exception handler in the current stack frame, it will handle the exception. If no matching handler is found, the runtime will unwind the call stack until it finds a suitable handler. Any objects whose lifetimes end are destroyed in the usual way.

Throwing in Destructors

If you throw an exception in a destructor, you are juggling with chainsaws. Such an exception absolutely must be caught within the destructor.

Suppose an exception is thrown, and during stack unwinding, another exception is thrown by a destructor during normal cleanup. Now you have *two* exceptions in flight. How should the C++ runtime handle such a situation?

You can have an opinion on the matter, but the runtime will call `terminate`. Consider Listing 4-13, which illustrates what can happen when you throw an exception from a destructor:

```
#include <cstdio>
#include <stdexcept>

struct CyberdyneSeries800 {
  CyberdyneSeries800() {
    printf("I'm a friend of Sarah Connor."); ❶
  }
  ~CyberdyneSeries800() {
    throw std::runtime_error{ "I'll be back." }; ❷
  }
};

int main() {
  try {
    CyberdyneSeries800 t800; ❸
    throw std::runtime_error{ "Come with me if you want to live." }; ❹
  } catch(const std::exception& e) { ❺
    printf("Caught exception: %s\n", e.what()); ❻
  }
}
```

```
I'm a friend of Sarah Connor. ❶
```

Listing 4-13: A program illustrating the perils of throwing an exception within a destructor

NOTE *Listing 4-13 calls `std::terminate`, so depending on your environment, you might get a nasty pop-up indicating this.*

First, you declare the `CyberdyneSeries800` class, which has a simple constructor that prints a message ❶ and a thoroughly belligerent destructor that throws an uncaught exception ❷. Within `main`, you set up a `try` block where you initialize a `CyberdyneSeries800` called `t800` ❸ and throw a `runtime_error` ❹. Under better circumstances, the `catch` block ❺ would handle this exception, print its message ❻, and exit gracefully. Because `t800` is an automatic variable within the `try` block, it destructs during the normal process of finding a handler for the exception you've thrown ❹. And because `t800` throws an exception in its destructor ❷, your program invokes `std::terminate` and ends abruptly.

As a general rule, treat destructors as if they were `noexcept`.

A SimpleString Class

Using an extended example, let's explore how constructors, destructors, members, and exceptions gel together. The `SimpleString` class in Listing 4-14 allows you to add C-style strings together and print the result.

```
#include <stdexcept>

struct SimpleString {
  SimpleString(size_t max_size) ❶
    : max_size{ max_size }, ❷
      length{} { ❸
    if (max_size == 0) {
      throw std::runtime_error{ "Max size must be at least 1." }; ❹
    }
    buffer = new char[max_size]; ❺
    buffer[0] = 0; ❻
  }

  ~SimpleString() {
    delete[] buffer; ❼
  }
--snip--
private:
  size_t max_size;
  char* buffer;
  size_t length;
};
```

Listing 4-14: The constructor and destructor of a `SimpleString` class

The constructor ❶ takes a single `max_size` argument. This is the maximum length of your string, which includes a null terminator. The member initializer ❷ saves this length into the `max_size` member variable. This value is also used in the array new expression to allocate a buffer to store your string ❺. The resulting pointer is stored into `buffer`. You initialize length to zero ❸ and ensure that there is at least enough size for a null byte ❹. Because the string is initially empty, you assign the first byte of the buffer to zero ❻.

NOTE *Because* `max_size` *is a* `size_t`*, it is unsigned and cannot be negative, so you don't need to check for this bogus condition.*

The `SimpleString` class owns a resource—the memory pointed to by `buffer`—which must be released when it's no longer needed. The destructor contains a single line ❼ that deallocates `buffer`. Because you've paired the allocation and deallocation of `buffer` with the constructor and destructor of `SimpleString`, you'll never leak the storage.

This pattern is called *resource acquisition is initialization (RAII)* or *constructor acquires, destructor releases (CADRe)*.

NOTE *The* `SimpleString` *class still has an implicitly defined* copy constructor. *Although it might never leak the storage, it will potentially double free if copied. You'll learn about copy constructors in "Copy Semantics" on page 115. Just be aware that Listing 4-14 is a teaching tool, not production-worthy code.*

Appending and Printing

The `SimpleString` class isn't of much use yet. Listing 4-15 adds the ability to print the string and append a line to the end of the string.

```
#include <cstdio>
#include <cstring>
#include <stdexcept>

struct SimpleString {
  --snip--
  void print(const char* tag) const { ❶
    printf("%s: %s", tag, buffer);
  }

  bool append_line(const char* x) { ❷
    const auto x_len = strlen❸(x);
    if (x_len + length + 2 > max_size) return false; ❹
    std::strncpy❺(buffer + length, x, max_size - length);
    length += x_len;
    buffer[length++] = '\n';
    buffer[length] = 0;
    return true;
  }
--snip--
};
```

Listing 4-15: The `print` *and* `append_line` *methods of* `SimpleString`

The first method `print` ❶ prints your string. For convenience, you can provide a `tag` string so you can match an invocation of `print` with the result. This method is `const` because it doesn't need to modify the state of a `SimpleString`.

The `append_line` method ❷ takes a null-terminated string `x` and adds its contents—plus a newline character—to `buffer`. It returns `true` if `x` was successfully appended and `false` if there wasn't enough space. First, `append_line` must determine the length of `x`. For this, you employ the `strlen` function ❸ from the <cstring> header, which accepts a null-terminated string and returns its length:

```
size_t strlen(const char* str);
```

You use `strlen` to compute the length of `x` and initialize `x_len` with the result. This result is used to compute whether appending `x` (a newline character) and a null byte to the current string would result in a string with length greater than `max_size` ❹. If it would, `append_line` returns `false`.

If there is enough room to append `x`, you need to copy its bytes into the correct location in `buffer`. The `std::strncpy` function ❺ from the <cstring> header is one possible tool for this job. It accepts three arguments: the `destination` address, the `source` address, and the `num` of characters to copy:

```
char* std::strncpy(char* destination, const char* source, std::size_t num);
```

The `strncpy` function will copy up to `num` bytes from `source` into `destination`. Once complete, it will return `destination` (which you discard).

After adding the number of bytes `x_len` copied into `buffer` to `length`, you finish by adding a newline character `\n` and a null byte to the end of `buffer`. You return `true` to indicate that you've successfully appended the input `x` as a line to the end of `buffer`.

WARNING *Use* `strncpy` *very carefully. It's too easy to forget the null-terminator in the* `source` *string or not allocate enough space in the* `destination` *string. Both errors will cause undefined behavior. We'll cover a safer alternative in Part II of the book.*

Using SimpleString

Listing 4-16 illustrates an example use of `SimpleString` where you append several strings and print intermediate results to the console.

```
#include <cstdio>
#include <cstring>
#include <exception>

struct SimpleString {
  --snip--
}
```

```
int main() {
  SimpleString string{ 115 }; ❶
  string.append_line("Starbuck, whaddya hear?");
  string.append_line("Nothin' but the rain."); ❷
  string.print("A: "); ❸
  string.append_line("Grab your gun and bring the cat in.");
  string.append_line("Aye-aye sir, coming home."); ❹
  string.print("B: "); ❺
  if (!string.append_line("Galactica!")) { ❻
    printf("String was not big enough to append another message."); ❼
  }
}
```

Listing 4-16: The methods of `SimpleString`

First, you create a `SimpleString` with `max_length=115` ❶. You use the `append_line` method twice ❷ to add some data to `string` and then print the contents along with the tag `A` ❸. You then append more text ❹ and print the contents again, this time with the tag `B` ❺. When `append_line` determines that `SimpleString` has run out of space ❻, it returns `false` ❼. (It's your responsibility as a user of `string` to check for this condition.)

Listing 4-17 contains output from running this program.

```
A: Starbuck, whaddya hear? ❶
Nothin' but the rain.
B: Starbuck, whaddya hear? ❷
Nothin' but the rain.
Grab your gun and bring the cat in.
Aye-aye sir, coming home.
String was not big enough to append another message. ❸
```

Listing 4-17: Output from running the program in Listing 4-16

As expected, the string contains `Starbuck, whaddya hear?\nNothin' but the rain.\n` at `A` ❶. (Recall from Chapter 2 that `\n` is the newline special character.) After appending `Grab your gun and bring the cat in.` and `Aye-aye sir, coming home.`, you get the expected output at `B` ❷.

When Listing 4-17 tries to append `Galactica!` to `string`, `append_line` returns `false` because there is not enough space in `buffer`. This causes the message `String was not big enough to append another message` to print ❸.

Composing a SimpleString

Consider what happens when you define a class with a `SimpleString` member, as demonstrated in Listing 4-18.

```
#include <stdexcept>

struct SimpleStringOwner {
  SimpleStringOwner(const char* x)
    : string{ 10 } { ❶
    if (!string.append_line(x)) {
      throw std::runtime_error{ "Not enough memory!" };
```

```
    }
    string.print("Constructed: ");
  }
  ~SimpleStringOwner() {
    string.print("About to destroy: "); ❷
  }
private:
  SimpleString string;
};
```

Listing 4-18: The implementation of `SimpleStringOwner`

As suggested by the member initializer ❶, `string` is fully constructed, and its class invariants are established once the constructor of `SimpleStringOwner` executes. This illustrates the order of an object's members during construction: *members are constructed before the enclosing object's constructor.* This makes sense: how can you establish a class's invariants if you don't know about its members' invariants?

Destructors work the opposite way. Inside `~SimpleStringOwner()` ❷, you need the class invariants of `string` to hold so you can print its contents. *All members are destructed after the object's destructor is invoked.*

Listing 4-19 exercises a `SimpleStringOwner`.

```
--snip--
int main() {
  SimpleStringOwner x{ "x" };
  printf("x is alive\n");
}
```

```
Constructed: x ❶
x is alive
About to destroy: x ❷
```

Listing 4-19: A program containing a `SimpleStringOwner`

As expected, the member `string` of `x` is created appropriately because *an object's member constructors are called before the object's constructor,* resulting in the message `Constructed: x` ❶. As an automatic variable, `x` is destroyed just before `main` returns, and you get `About to destroy: x` ❷. The member `string` is still valid at this point because member destructors are called after the enclosing object's destructor.

Call Stack Unwinding

Listing 4-20 demonstrates how exception handling and stack unwinding work together. You establish a `try`-`catch` block in `main` and then make a series of function calls. One of these calls causes an exception.

```
--snip--
void fn_c() {
  SimpleStringOwner c{ "cccccccccc" }; ❶
}
```

```
void fn_b() {
  SimpleStringOwner b{ "b" };
  fn_c(); ❷
}

int main() {
  try { ❸
    SimpleStringOwner a{ "a" };
    fn_b(); ❹
    SimpleStringOwner d{ "d" }; ❺
  } catch(const std::exception& e) { ❻
    printf("Exception: %s\n", e.what());
  }
}
```

Listing 4-20: A program illustrating the use of `SimpleStringOwner` and call stack unwinding

Listing 4-21 shows the results of running the program in Listing 4-20.

```
Constructed: a
Constructed: b
About to destroy: b
About to destroy: a
Exception: Not enough memory!
```

Listing 4-21: Output from running the program in Listing 4-20

You've set up a `try-catch` block ❸. The first `SimpleStringOwner`, `a`, gets constructed without incident, and you see `Constructed: a` printed to the console. Next, `fn_b` is called ❹. Notice that you're still in the `try-catch` block, so any `exception` that gets thrown *will* be handled. Inside `fn_b`, another `SimpleStringOwner`, `b`, gets constructed successfully, and `Constructed: b` is printed to the console. Next, there's a call into yet another function, `fn_c` ❷.

Let's pause for a moment to take an account of what the call stack looks like, what objects are alive, and what the exception-handling situation looks like. You have two `SimpleStringOwner` objects alive and valid: `a` and `b`. The call stack looks like `fn()` → `fn_b()` → `fn_c()`, and you have an exception handler set up inside `main` to handle any exceptions. Figure 4-3 summarizes this situation.

At ❶, you run into a little problem. Recall that `SimpleStringOwner` has a member `SimpleString` that is always initialized with a `max_size` of 10. When you try to construct `c`, the constructor of `SimpleStringOwner` throws an `exception` because you've tried to append `"cccccccccc"`, which has length 10 and is too big to fit alongside a newline and a null terminator.

Now you have an exception in flight. The stack will unwind until an appropriate handler is found, and all objects that fall out of scope as a result of this unwinding will be destructed. The handler is all the way up the stack ❻, so `fn_c` and `fn_b` unwind. Because `SimpleStringOwner b` is an automatic variable in `fn_b`, it gets destructed and you see `About to destroy: b` printed to the console. After `fn_b`, the automatic variables inside try{} are destroyed. This includes `SimpleStringOwner a`, so you see `About to destroy: a` printed to the console.

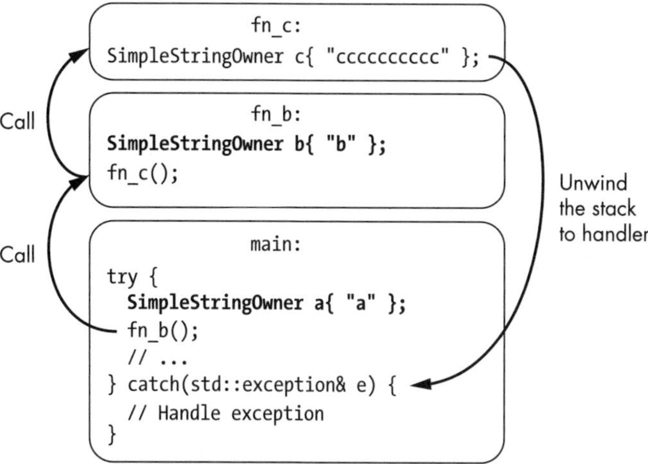
fn_c:
SimpleStringOwner c{ "cccccccccc" };
Call
fn_b:
SimpleStringOwner b{ "b" };
fn_c();
Unwind
the stack
to handler
Call
main:
try {
SimpleStringOwner a{ "a" };
fn_b();
// ...
} catch(std::exception& e) {
// Handle exception
}

Figure 4-3: The call stack when fn_c calls the constructor of `SimpleStringOwner c`

Once an exception occurs in a `try{}` block, no further statements execute. As a result, `d` never initializes ❺, and you never see the constructor of `d` print to console. After the call stack is unwound, execution proceeds immediately to the `catch` block. In the end, you print the message `Exception: Not enough memory!` to the console ❻.

Exceptions and Performance

In your programs, you must handle errors; errors are unavoidable. When you use exceptions correctly and no errors occur, your code is faster than manually error-checked code. If an error does occur, exception handling can sometimes be slower, but you make huge gains in robustness and maintainability over the alternative. Kurt Guntheroth, the author of *Optimized C++*, puts it well: "use of exception handling leads to programs that are faster when they execute normally, and better behaved when they fail." When a C++ program executes normally (without exceptions being thrown), there is no runtime overhead associated with checking exceptions. It's only when an exception is thrown that you pay overhead.

Hopefully, you're convinced of the central role exceptions play in idiomatic C++ programs. Sometimes, unfortunately, you won't be able to use exceptions. One example is embedded development where real-time guarantees are required. Tools simply don't (yet) exist in this setting. With luck, this will change soon, but for now, you're stuck without exceptions in most embedded contexts. Another example is with some legacy code. Exceptions are elegant because of how they fit in with RAII objects. When destructors are responsible for cleaning up resources, stack unwinding is a direct and effective way to guarantee against resource leakages. In legacy code, you might find manual resource management and error handling instead of RAII objects. This makes using exceptions very dangerous, because stack unwinding is safe only with RAII objects. Without them, you could easily leak resources.

Alternatives to Exceptions

In situations where exceptions are not available, all is not lost. Although you'll need to keep track of errors manually, there are some helpful C++ features that you can employ to take the sting out a bit. First, you can manually enforce class invariants by exposing some method that communicates whether the class invariants could be established, as shown here:

```
struct HumptyDumpty {
   HumptyDumpty();
   bool is_together_again();
  --snip--
};
```

In idiomatic C++, you would just throw an exception in the constructor, but here you must remember to check and treat the situation as an error condition in your calling code:

```
bool send_kings_horses_and_men() {
  HumptyDumpty hd{};
  if (hd.is_together_again()) return false;
  // Class invariants of hd are now guaranteed.
  // Humpty Dumpty had a great fall.
  --snip--
  return true;
}
```

The second, complementary coping strategy is to return multiple values using *structured binding declaration*, a language feature that allows you to return multiple values from a function call. You can use this feature to return success flags alongside the usual return value, as demonstrated in Listing 4-22.

```
struct Result { ❶
  HumptyDumpty hd;
  bool success;
};

Result make_humpty() { ❷
  HumptyDumpty hd{};
  bool is_valid;
  // Check that hd is valid and set is_valid appropriately
  return { hd, is_valid };
}

bool send_kings_horses_and_men() {
  auto [hd, success] = make_humpty(); ❸
  if(!success) return false;
  // Class invariants established
  --snip--
  return true;
}
```

Listing 4-22: A code segment illustrating structured binding declaration

First, you declare a POD that contains a HumptyDumpty and a success flag ❶. Next, you define the function make_humpty ❷, which builds and validates a HumptyDumpty. Such methods are called *factory methods*, because their purpose is to initialize objects. The make_humpty function packs this and the success flag into a Result when it returns. The syntax at the call site ❸ illustrates how you can unpack the Result into multiple, auto-type-deduced variables.

NOTE *You'll explore structured bindings in more detail in "Structured Bindings" on page 222.*

Copy Semantics

Copy semantics is "the meaning of copy." In practice, programmers use the term to mean the rules for making copies of objects: after x is *copied into* y, they're *equivalent* and *independent*. That is, x == y is true after a copy (equivalence), and a modification to x doesn't cause a modification of y (independence).

Copying is extremely common, especially when passing objects to functions by value, as demonstrated in Listing 4-23.

```
#include <cstdio>

int add_one_to(int x) {
  x++; ❶
  return x;
}

int main() {
  auto original = 1;
  auto result = add_one_to(original); ❷
  printf("Original: %d; Result: %d", original, result);
}
--------------------------------------------------------------------------
Original: 1; Result: 2
```

Listing 4-23: A program illustrating that passing by value generates a copy

Here, add_one_to takes its argument x by value. It then modifies the value of x ❶. This modification is isolated from the caller ❷; original is unaffected because add_one_to gets a copy.

For user-defined POD types, the story is similar. Passing by value causes each member value to be copied into the parameter (a *member-wise copy*), as demonstrated in Listing 4-24.

```
struct Point {
  int x, y;
};

Point make_transpose(Point p) {
  int tmp = p.x;
  p.x = p.y;
```

```
  p.y = tmp;
  return p;
}
```

Listing 4-24: The function `make_transpose` generates a copy of the POD type `Point`.

When `make_transpose` is invoked, it receives a copy `Point` in `p`, and the original is unaffected.

For fundamental and POD types, the story is straightforward. Copying these types is memberwise, which means each member gets copied into its corresponding destination. This is effectively a bitwise copy from one memory address to another.

Fully featured classes require some more thought. The default copy semantics for fully featured classes is also the memberwise copy, and this can be extremely dangerous. Consider again the `SimpleString` class. You would invite disaster if you allowed a user to make a memberwise copy of a live `SimpleString` class. Two `SimpleString` classes would point to the same `buffer`. With both of the copies appending to the same `buffer`, they'll clobber each other. Figure 4-4 summarizes the situation.

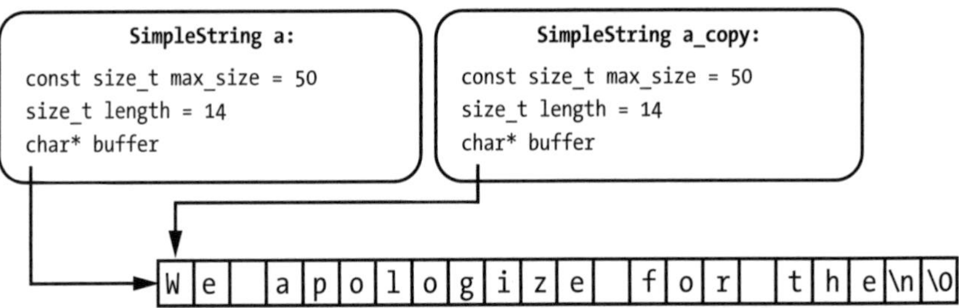

Figure 4-4: A depiction of default copy semantics on the `SimpleString` class

This result is bad, but even worse things happen when the `SimpleString` classes start destructing. When one of the `SimpleString` classes is destructed, `buffer` will be freed. When the remaining `SimpleString` class tries to write its `buffer`—bang!—you have undefined behavior. At some point, this remaining `SimpleString` class will be destructed and free `buffer` again, resulting in what is commonly called a *double free*.

NOTE *Like its nefarious cousin the use after free, the double free can result in subtle and hard-to-diagnose bugs that manifest only very infrequently. A double free occurs when you deallocate an object twice. Recall that once you've deallocated an object, its storage lifetime ends. This memory is now in an undefined state, and if you destruct an object that's already been destructed, you've got undefined behavior. In certain situations, this can cause serious security vulnerabilities.*

You can avoid this dumpster fire by taking control of copy semantics. You can specify copy constructors and copy assignment operators, as described in the following sections.

Copy Constructors

There are two ways to copy an object. One is to use *copy construction*, which creates a copy and assigns it to a brand-new object. The copy constructor looks like other constructors:

```
struct SimpleString {
  --snip--
  SimpleString(const SimpleString& other);
};
```

Notice that other is const. You're copying from some original SimpleString, and you have no reason to modify it. You use the copy constructor just like other constructors, using the uniform initialization syntax of braced initializers:

```
SimpleString a;
SimpleString a_copy{ a };
```

The second line invokes the copy constructor of SimpleString with a to yield a_copy.

Let's implement the copy constructor of SimpleString. You want what is known as a *deep copy* where you copy the data pointed to by the original buffer into a new buffer, as depicted in Figure 4-5.

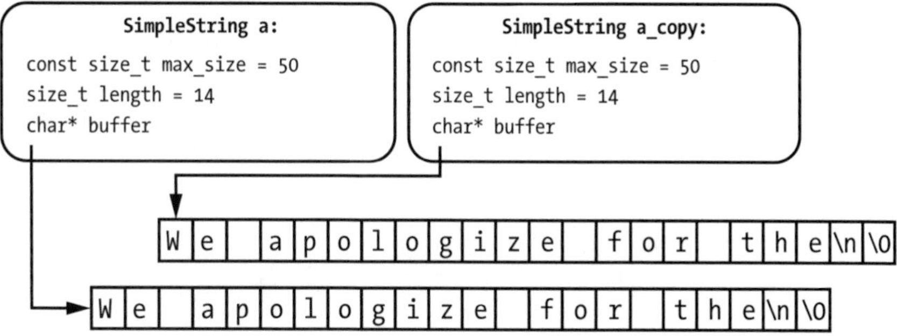

Figure 4-5: A depiction of a deep copy on the SimpleString *class*

Rather than copying the pointer buffer, you'll make a new allocation on the free store and then copy all the data pointed to by the original buffer. This gives you two independent SimpleString classes. Listing 4-25 implements the copy constructor of SimpleString:

```
SimpleString(const SimpleString& other)
  : max_size{ other.max_size }, ❶
    buffer{ new char[other.max_size] }, ❷
    length{ other.length } { ❸
    std::strncpy(buffer, other.buffer, max_size); ❹
}
```

Listing 4-25: SimpleString *class's copy constructor*

You use member initializers for max_size ❶, buffer ❷, and length ❸ and pass in the corresponding fields on other. You can use array new ❶ to initialize buffer because you know other.max_size is greater than 0. The copy constructor's body contains a single statement ❹ that copies the contents pointed to by other.buffer into the array pointed to by buffer.

Listing 4-26 uses this copy constructor by initializing a SimpleString with an existing SimpleString:

```
--snip--
int main() {
  SimpleString a{ 50 };
  a.append_line("We apologize for the");
  SimpleString a_copy{ a }; ❶
  a.append_line("inconvenience."); ❷
  a_copy.append_line("incontinence."); ❸
  a.print("a");
  a_copy.print("a_copy");
}
```

```
a: We apologize for the
inconvenience.
a_copy: We apologize for the
incontinence.
```

Listing 4-26: A program using SimpleString class's copy constructor

In the program, SimpleString a_copy ❶ is copy constructed from a. It's equivalent to—and independent from—the original. You can append different messages to the end of a ❷ and a_copy ❸, and the changes are isolated.

The copy constructor is invoked when passing SimpleString into a function by value, as demonstrated in Listing 4-27.

```
--snip--
void foo(SimpleString x) {
  x.append_line("This change is lost.");
}

int main() {
  SimpleString a { 20 };
  foo(a); // Invokes copy constructor
  a.print("Still empty");
}
```

```
Still empty:
```

Listing 4-27: A program illustrating that copy constructors get invoked when passing an object by value

NOTE *You shouldn't pass by value to avoid modification. Use a const reference.*

The performance impact of copying can be substantial, especially in a situation where free store allocations and buffer copies are involved. For example, suppose you have a class that manages the life cycle of a gigabyte of data. Each time you copy the object, you'll need to allocate and copy a gigabyte of data. This can take a lot of time, so you should be absolutely sure you need the copy. If you can get away with passing a `const` reference, strongly prefer it.

Copy Assignment

The other way to make a copy in C++ is with the *copy assignment operator*. You can create a copy of an object and assign it to another existing object, as demonstrated in Listing 4-28.

```
--snip--
void dont_do_this() {
  SimpleString a{ 50 };
  a.append_line("We apologize for the");
  SimpleString b{ 50 };
  b.append_line("Last message");
  b = a; ❶
}
```

Listing 4-28: Using the default copy assignment operator to create a copy of an object and assign it to another existing object

NOTE *The code in Listing 4-28 causes undefined behavior because it doesn't have a user-defined copy assignment operator.*

The line at ❶ *copy assigns* `a` to `b`. The major difference between copy assignment and copy construction is that in copy assignment, `b` might already have a value. You must clean up `b`'s resources before copying `a`.

WARNING *The default copy assignment operator for simple types just copies the members from the source object to the destination object. In the case of* `SimpleString`*, this is very dangerous for two reasons. First, the original* `SimpleString` *class's buffer gets rewritten without freeing the dynamically allocated* `char` *array. Second, now two* `SimpleString` *classes own the same buffer, which can cause dangling pointers and double frees. You must implement a copy assignment operator that performs a clean hand-off.*

The copy assignment operator uses the `operator=` syntax, as demonstrated in Listing 4-29.

```
struct SimpleString {
  --snip--
  SimpleString& operator=(const SimpleString& other) {
    if (this == &other) return *this; ❶
    --snip--
    return *this; ❷
  }
}
```

Listing 4-29: A user-defined copy assignment operator for `SimpleString`

The copy assignment operator returns a reference to the result, which is always `*this` ❷. It's also generally good practice to check whether `other` refers to `this` ❶.

You can implement copy assignment for `SimpleString` by following these guidelines: free the current `buffer` of `this` and then copy `other` as you did in copy construction, as shown in Listing 4-30.

```
SimpleString& operator=(const SimpleString& other) {
  if (this == &other) return *this;
  const auto new_buffer = new char[other.max_size]; ❶
  delete[] buffer; ❷
  buffer = new_buffer; ❸
  length = other.length; ❹
  max_size = other.max_size; ❺
  strcpy_s(buffer, max_size, other.buffer); ❻
  return *this;
}
```

Listing 4-30: A copy assignment operator for `SimpleString`

The copy assignment operator starts by allocating a `new_buffer` with the appropriate size ❶. Next, you clean up `buffer` ❷. The rest is essentially identical to the copy constructor in Listing 4-25. You copy `buffer` ❸, `length` ❹, and `max_size` ❺ and then copy the contents from `other.buffer` into your own `buffer` ❻.

Listing 4-31 illustrates how `SimpleString` copy assignment works (as implemented in Listing 4-30).

```
--snip--
int main() {
  SimpleString a{ 50 };
  a.append_line("We apologize for the"); ❶
  SimpleString b{ 50 };
  b.append_line("Last message"); ❷
  a.print("a"); ❸
  b.print("b"); ❹
  b = a; ❺
  a.print("a"); ❻
  b.print("b"); ❼
}
--------------------------------------------------------------------------
a: We apologize for the ❸
b: Last message ❹
a: We apologize for the ❻
b: We apologize for the ❼
```

Listing 4-31: A program illustrating copy assignment with the `SimpleString` class

You begin by declaring two `SimpleString` classes with different messages: the string `a` contains `We apologize for the` ❶, and `b` contains `Last` message ❷. You print these strings to verify that they contain the text you've specified ❸❹. Next, you copy assign b equal to a ❺. Now, a and b contain copies of the same message, We apologize for the ❻❼. But—and this is important—that message resides in two separate memory locations.

Default Copy

Often, the compiler will generate default implementations for copy construction and copy assignment. The default implementation is to invoke copy construction or copy assignment on each of a class's members.

Any time a class manages a resource, you must be extremely careful with default copy semantics; they're likely to be wrong (as you saw with SimpleString). Best practice dictates that you explicitly declare that default copy assignment and copy construction are acceptable for such classes using the default keyword. The Replicant class, for example, has default copy semantics, as demonstrated here:

```
struct Replicant {
  Replicant(const Replicant&) = default;
  Replicant& operator=(const Replicant&) = default;
  --snip--
};
```

Some classes simply cannot or should not be copied—for example, if your class manages a file or if it represents a mutual exclusion lock for concurrent programming. You can suppress the compiler from generating a copy constructor and a copy assignment operator using the delete keyword. The Highlander class, for example, cannot be copied:

```
struct Highlander {
  Highlander(const Highlander&) = delete;
  Highlander& operator=(const Highlander&) = delete;
  --snip--
};
```

Any attempt to copy a Highlander will result in a compiler error:

```
--snip--
int main() {
  Highlander a;
  Highlander b{ a }; // Bang! There can be only one.
}
```

I highly recommend that you explicitly define the copy assignment operator and copy constructor for *any* class that owns a resource (like a printer, a network connection, or a file). If custom behavior is not needed, use either default or delete. This will save you from a lot of nasty and difficult-to-debug errors.

Copy Guidelines

When you implement copy behavior, think about the following criteria:

Correctness You must ensure that class invariants are maintained. The `SimpleString` class demonstrated that the default copy constructor can violate invariants.

Independence After copy assignment or copy construction, the original object and the copy shouldn't change each other's state during modification. Had you simply copied `buffer` from one `SimpleString` to another, writing to one `buffer` could overwrite the data from the other.

Equivalence The original and the copy should be the *same*. The semantics of sameness depend on context. But generally, an operation applied to the original should yield the same result when applied to the copy.

Move Semantics

Copying can be quite time-consuming at runtime when a large amount of data is involved. Often, you just want to *transfer ownership* of resources from one object to another. You could make a copy and destroy the original, but this is often inefficient. Instead, you can *move*.

Move semantics is move's corollary to copy semantics, and it requires that after an object `y` is *moved into* an object `x`, `x` is equivalent to the former value of `y`. After the move, `y` is in a special state called the *moved-from* state. You can perform only two operations on moved-from objects: (re)assign them or destruct them. Note that moving an object `y` into an object `x` isn't just a renaming: these are separate objects with separate storage and potentially separate lifetimes.

Similar to how you specify copying behavior, you specify how objects move with *move constructors* and *move assignment operators*.

Copying Can Be Wasteful

Suppose you want to move a `SimpleString` into a `SimpleStringOwner` in the following way:

```
--snip--
void own_a_string() {
  SimpleString a{ 50 };
  a.append_line("We apologize for the");
  a.append_line("inconvenience.");
  SimpleStringOwner b{ a };
  --snip--
}
```

You could add a constructor for `SimpleStringOwner` and then copy-construct its `SimpleString` member, as demonstrated in Listing 4-32.

```
struct SimpleStringOwner {
  SimpleStringOwner(const SimpleString& my_string) : string{ my_string }❶ { }
  --snip--
private:
  SimpleString string; ❷
};
```

Listing 4-32: A naive approach to member initialization containing a wasteful copy

There is hidden waste in this approach. You have a copy construction ❶, but the caller never uses the pointed-to object again after constructing `string` ❷. Figure 4-6 illustrates the issue.

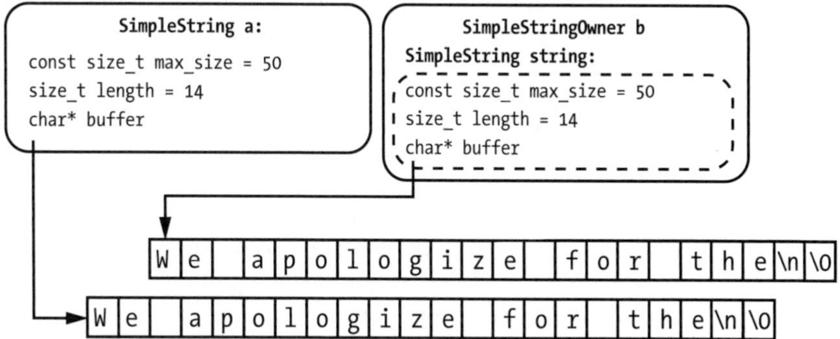

Figure 4-6: Using the copy constructor for `string` is wasteful.

You should move the guts of `SimpleString a` into the `string` field of `SimpleStringOwner`. Figure 4-7 shows what you want to achieve: `SimpleString Owner b` steals `buffer` and sets `SimpleString a` into a destructible state.

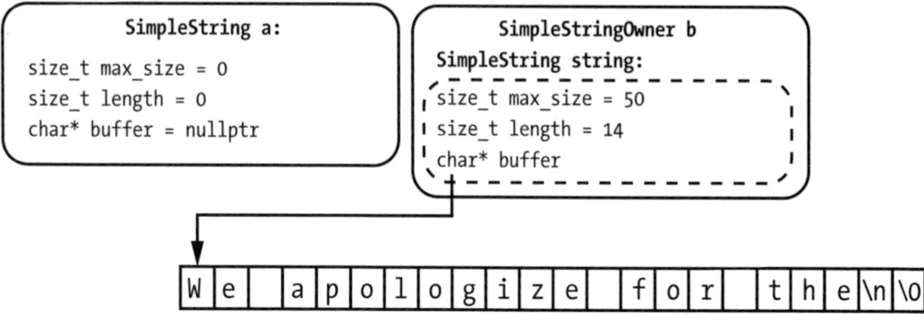

Figure 4-7: Swapping the buffer of `a` into `b`

After moving `a`, the `SimpleString` of `b` is equivalent to the former state of `a`, and `a` is destructible.

Moving can be dangerous. If you accidentally use moved-from `a`, you'd invite disaster. The class invariants of `SimpleString` aren't satisfied when `a` is moved from.

Fortunately, the compiler has built-in safeguards: lvalues and rvalues.

Value Categories

Every expression has two important characteristics: its *type* and its *value category*. A value category describes what kinds of operations are valid for the expression. Thanks to the evolutionary nature of C++, value categories are complicated: an expression can be a "generalized lvalue" (*glvalue*), a "pure rvalue" (*prvalue*), an "expiring value" (*xvalue*), an *lvalue* (a glvalue that isn't an xvalue), or an *rvalue* (a prvalue or an xvalue). Fortunately for the newcomer, you don't need to know much about most of these value categories.

We'll consider a very simplified view of value categories. For now, you'll just need a general understanding of lvalues and rvalues. An lvalue is any value that has a name, and an rvalue is anything that isn't an lvalue.

Consider the following initializations:

```
SimpleString a{ 50 };
SimpleStringOwner b{ a };                   // a is an lvalue
SimpleStringOwner c{ SimpleString{ 50 } };  // SimpleString{ 50 } is an rvalue
```

The etymology of these terms is *right value* and *left value*, referring to where each appears with respect to the equal sign in construction. In the statement `int x = 50;`, `x` is left of the equal sign (lvalue) and `50` is right of the equal sign (rvalue). These terms aren't totally accurate because you can have an lvalue on the right side of an equal sign (as in copy assignment, for example).

NOTE *The ISO C++ Standard details Value Categories in [basic] and [expr].*

lvalue and rvalue References

You can communicate to the compiler that a function accepts lvalues or rvalues using *lvalue references* and *rvalue references*. Up to this point in this book, every reference parameter has been an lvalue reference, and these are denoted with a single `&`. You can also take a parameter by rvalue reference using `&&`.

Fortunately, the compiler does an excellent job of determining whether an object is an lvalue or an rvalue. In fact, you can define multiple functions with the same name but with different parameters, and the compiler will automatically call the correct version depending on what arguments you provide when you invoke the function.

Listing 4-33 contains two functions with the name `ref_type` function to discern whether the invoker passed an lvalue or an rvalue reference.

```
#include <cstdio>

void ref_type(int &x) { ❶
  printf("lvalue reference %d\n", x);
}
```

```
void ref_type(int &&x) { ❷
  printf("rvalue reference %d\n", x);
}

int main() {
  auto x = 1;
  ref_type(x); ❸
  ref_type(2); ❹
  ref_type(x + 2); ❺
}
--------------------------------------------------------------------------
lvalue reference 1 ❸
rvalue reference 2 ❹
rvalue reference 3 ❺
```

Listing 4-33: A program containing an overloaded function with lvalue and rvalue references

The `int &x` version ❶ takes an lvalue reference, and the `int &&x` version ❷ takes an rvalue reference. You invoke `ref_type` three times. First, you invoke the lvalue reference version, because `x` is an lvalue (it has a name) ❸. Second, you invoke the rvalue reference version because `2` is an integer literal without a name ❹. Third, the result of adding 2 to `x` is not bound to a name, so it's an rvalue ❺.

NOTE *Defining multiple functions with the same name but different parameters is called* function overloading, *a topic you'll explore in detail in Chapter 9.*

The std::move Function

You can cast an lvalue reference to an rvalue reference using the `std::move` function from the `<utility>` header. Listing 4-34 updates Listing 4-33 to illustrate the use of the `std::move` function.

```
#include <utility>
--snip--
int main() {
  auto x = 1;
  ref_type(std::move(x)); ❶
  ref_type(2);
  ref_type(x + 2);
}
--------------------------------------------------------------------------
rvalue reference 1 ❶
rvalue reference 2
rvalue reference 3
```

Listing 4-34: An update to Listing 4-33 using `std::move` to cast `x` to an rvalue

As expected, `std::move` changes the lvalue `x` into an rvalue ❶. You never call the lvalue `ref_type` overload.

NOTE *The C++ committee probably should have named `std::move` as `std::rvalue`, but it's the name we're stuck with. The `std:move` function doesn't actually move anything—it casts.*

Be very careful when you're using `std::move`, because you remove the safeguards keeping you from interacting with a moved-from object. You can perform two actions on a moved-from object: destroy it or reassign it.

How lvalue and rvalue semantics enable move semantics should now be clear. If an lvalue is at hand, moving is suppressed. If an rvalue is at hand, moving is enabled.

Move Construction

Move constructors look like copy constructors except they take rvalue references instead of lvalue references.

Consider the `SimpleString` move constructor in Listing 4-35.

```
SimpleString(SimpleString&& other) noexcept
  : max_size{ other.max_size }, ❶
  buffer(other.buffer),
  length(other.length) {
  other.length = 0; ❷
  other.buffer = nullptr;
  other.max_size = 0;
}
```

Listing 4-35: A move constructor for `SimpleString`

Because `other` is an rvalue reference, you're allowed to cannibalize it. In the case of `SimpleString`, this is easy: just copy all fields of `other` into `this` ❶ and then zero out the fields of `other` ❷. The latter step is important: it puts `other` in a moved-from state. (Consider what would happen upon the destruction of `other` had you not cleared its members.)

Executing this move constructor is a *lot* less expensive than executing the copy constructor.

The move constructor is designed to *not* throw an exception, so you mark it `noexcept`. Your preference should be to use `noexcept` move constructors; often, the compiler cannot use exception-throwing move constructors and will use copy constructors instead. Compilers prefer slow, correct code instead of fast, incorrect code.

Move Assignment

You can also create a move analogue to copy assignment via `operator=`. The move assignment operator takes an rvalue reference rather than a `const` lvalue reference, and you usually mark it `noexcept`. Listing 4-36 implements such a move assignment operator for `SimpleString`.

```
SimpleString& operator=(SimpleString&& other) noexcept { ❶
  if (this == &other) return *this; ❷
  delete[] buffer; ❸
```

```
  buffer = other.buffer; ❹
  length = other.length;
  max_size = other.max_size;
  other.buffer = nullptr; ❺
  other.length = 0;
  other.max_size = 0;
  return *this;
}
```

Listing 4-36: A move assignment operator for `SimpleString`

You declare the move assignment operator using the rvalue reference syntax and the `noexcept` qualifier, as with the move constructor ❶. The self-reference check ❷ handles the move assignment of a `SimpleString` to itself. You clean up `buffer` ❸ before assigning the fields of `this` to the fields of `other` ❹ and zero out the fields of `other` ❺. Aside from the self-reference check ❷ and the cleanup ❸, the move assignment operator and the move constructor are functionally identical.

Now that `SimpleString` is movable, you can complete the `SimpleString` constructor of `SimpleStringOwner`:

```
SimpleStringOwner(SimpleString&& x) : string{ std::move(x)❶ } { }
```

The `x` is an lvalue, so you must `std::move x` into the move constructor of `string` ❶. You might find `std::move` odd, because `x` is an rvalue reference. Recall that lvalue/rvalue and lvalue reference/rvalue reference are distinct descriptors.

Consider if `std::move` weren't required here: what if you moved from `x` and then used it inside the constructor? This could lead to bugs that are hard to diagnose. Remember that you cannot use moved-from objects except to reassign or destruct them. Doing anything else is undefined behavior.

Listing 4-37 illustrates the `SimpleString` move assignment.

```
--snip--
int main() {
  SimpleString a{ 50 };
  a.append_line("We apologize for the"); ❶
  SimpleString b{ 50 };
  b.append_line("Last message"); ❷
  a.print("a"); ❸
  b.print("b"); ❹
  b = std::move(a); ❺
  // a is "moved-from"
  b.print("b"); ❻
}
--------------------------------------------------------------------------
a: We apologize for the ❸
b: Last message ❹
b: We apologize for the ❻
```

Listing 4-37: A program illustrating move assignment with the `SimpleString` *class*

As in Listing 4-31, you begin by declaring two SimpleString classes with different messages: the string a contains We apologize for the ❶, and b contains Last message ❷. You print these strings to verify that they contain the strings you've specified ❸❹. Next, you move assign b equal to a ❺. Note that you had to cast a to an rvalue using std::move. After the move assignment, a is in a moved-from state, and you can't use it unless you reassign it to a new value. Now, b owns the message that a used to own, We apologize for the ❻.

The Final Product

You now have a fully implemented SimpleString that supports move and copy semantics. Listing 4-38 brings these all together for your reference.

```
#include <cstdio>
#include <cstring>
#include <stdexcept>
#include <utility>

struct SimpleString {
  SimpleString(size_t max_size)
    : max_size{ max_size },
    length{} {
    if (max_size == 0) {
      throw std::runtime_error{ "Max size must be at least 1." };
    }
    buffer = new char[max_size];
    buffer[0] = 0;
  }
  ~SimpleString() {
    delete[] buffer;
  }
  SimpleString(const SimpleString& other)
    : max_size{ other.max_size },
    buffer{ new char[other.max_size] },
    length{ other.length } {
    std::strncpy(buffer, other.buffer, max_size);
  }
  SimpleString(SimpleString&& other) noexcept
    : max_size(other.max_size),
    buffer(other.buffer),
    length(other.length) {
    other.length = 0;
    other.buffer = nullptr;
    other.max_size = 0;
  }
  SimpleString& operator=(const SimpleString& other) {
    if (this == &other) return *this;
    const auto new_buffer = new char[other.max_size];
    delete[] buffer;
    buffer = new_buffer;
    length = other.length;
    max_size = other.max_size;
    std::strncpy(buffer, other.buffer, max_size);
```

```
    return *this;
  }
  SimpleString& operator=(SimpleString&& other) noexcept {
    if (this == &other) return *this;
    delete[] buffer;
    buffer = other.buffer;
    length = other.length;
    max_size = other.max_size;
    other.buffer = nullptr;
    other.length = 0;
    other.max_size = 0;
    return *this;
  }
  void print(const char* tag) const {
    printf("%s: %s", tag, buffer);
  }
  bool append_line(const char* x) {
    const auto x_len = strlen(x);
    if (x_len + length + 2 > max_size) return false;
    std::strncpy(buffer + length, x, max_size - length);
    length += x_len;
    buffer[length++] = '\n';
    buffer[length] = 0;
    return true;
  }
private:
  size_t max_size;
  char* buffer;
  size_t length;
};
```

Listing 4-38: A fully specified `SimpleString` class supporting copy and move semantics

Compiler-Generated Methods

Five methods govern move and copy behavior:

- The destructor
- The copy constructor
- The move constructor
- The copy assignment operator
- The move assignment operator

The compiler can generate default implementations for each under certain circumstances. Unfortunately, the rules for which methods get generated are complicated and potentially uneven across compilers.

You can eliminate this complexity by setting these methods to `default`/`delete` or by implementing them as appropriate. This general rule is the *rule of five*, because there are five methods to specify. Being explicit costs a little time, but it saves a lot of future headaches.

The alternative is memorizing Figure 4-8, which summarizes the interactions between each of the five functions you implement and each that the compiler generates on your behalf.

If you explicitly define:

You'll end up with:	Nothing	Destructor	Copy Constructor	Copy Assignment	Move Constructor	Move Assignment
Destructor `~Foo()`	✓	✓	✓	✓	✓	✓
Copy Constructor `Foo(const Foo&)`	✓	✓	✓	✓		
Copy Assignment `Foo& operator=(const Foo&)`	✓	✓	✓	✓		
Move Constructor `Foo(Foo&&)`	✓		Copies are used in place of moves	Copies are used in place of moves	✓	✓
Move Assignment `Foo& operator=(Foo&&)`	✓		Copies are used in place of moves	Copies are used in place of moves		

Figure 4-8: A chart illustrating which methods the compiler generates when given various inputs

If you provide nothing, the compiler will generate all five destruct/copy/move functions. This is the *rule of zero*.

If you explicitly define any of destructor/copy constructor/copy assignment operator, you get all three. This is dangerous, as demonstrated earlier with `SimpleString`: it's too easy to get into an unintended situation in which the compiler will essentially convert all your moves into copies.

Finally, if you provide only move semantics for your class, the compiler will not automatically generate anything except a destructor.

Summary

You've completed the exploration of the object life cycle. Your journey began in storage durations, where you saw an object lifetime from construction to destruction. Subsequent study of exception handling illustrated deft, lifetime-aware error handling and enriched your understanding of RAII. Finally, you saw how copy and move semantics grant you granular control over object lifetimes.

EXERCISES

4-1. Create a `struct TimerClass`. In its constructor, record the current time in a field called `timestamp` (compare with the POSIX function `gettimeofday`).

4-2. In the destructor of `TimerClass`, record the current time and subtract the time at construction. This time is roughly the *age* of the timer. Print this value.

4-3. Implement a copy constructor and a copy assignment operator for `TimerClass`. The copies should share `timestamp` values.

4-4. Implement a move constructor and a move assignment operator for `TimerClass`. A moved-from `TimerClass` shouldn't print any output to the console when it gets destructed.

4-5. Elaborate the `TimerClass` constructor to accept an additional `const char*` name parameter. When `TimerClass` is destructed and prints to stdout, include the name of the timer in the output.

4-6. Experiment with your `TimerClass`. Create a timer and move it into a function that performs some computationally intensive operation (for example, lots of math in a loop). Verify that your timer behaves as you expect.

4-7. Identify each method in the `SimpleString` class (Listing 4-38). Try reimplementing it from scratch without referring to the book.

FURTHER READING

- *Optimized C++: Proven Techniques for Heightened Performance* by Kurt Guntheroth (O'Reilly Media, 2016)
- *Effective Modern C++: 42 Specific Ways to Improve Your Use of C++11 and C++14* by Scott Meyers (O'Reilly Media, 2015)

5

RUNTIME POLYMORPHISM

One day Trurl the constructor put together a machine that could create anything starting with n.
—*Stanislaw Lem,* The Cyberiad

In this chapter, you'll learn what polymorphism is and the problems it solves. You'll then learn how to achieve runtime polymorphism, which allows you to change the behavior of your programs by swapping out components during program execution. The chapter starts with a discussion of several crucial concepts in runtime polymorphic code, including interfaces, object composition, and inheritance. Next, you'll develop an ongoing example of logging bank transactions with multiple kinds of loggers. You'll finish the chapter by refactoring this initial, naive solution with a more elegant, interface-based solution.

Polymorphism

Polymorphic code is code you write once and can reuse with different types. Ultimately, this flexibility yields loosely coupled and highly reusable code. It eliminates tedious copying and pasting, making your code more maintainable and readable.

C++ offers two polymorphic approaches. *Compile-time polymorphic code* incorporates polymorphic types you can determine at compile time. The other approach is *runtime polymorphism*, which instead incorporates types determined at runtime. Which approach you choose depends on whether you know the types you want to use with your polymorphic code at compile time or at runtime. Because these closely related topics are fairly involved, they're separated into two chapters. Chapter 6 will focus on compile-time polymorphism.

A Motivating Example

Suppose you're in charge of implementing a `Bank` class that transfers money between accounts. Auditing is very important for the `Bank` class's transactions, so you provide support for logging with a `ConsoleLogger` class, as shown in Listing 5-1.

```
#include <cstdio>

struct ConsoleLogger {
  void log_transfer(long from, long to, double amount) { ❶
    printf("%ld -> %ld: %f\n", from, to, amount); ❷
  }
};

struct Bank {
  void make_transfer(long from, long to, double amount) { ❸
    --snip-- ❹
    logger.log_transfer(from, to, amount); ❺
  }
  ConsoleLogger logger;
};

int main() {
  Bank bank;
  bank.make_transfer(1000, 2000, 49.95);
  bank.make_transfer(2000, 4000, 20.00);
}
```

```
1000 -> 2000: 49.950000
2000 -> 4000: 20.000000
```

Listing 5-1: A `ConsoleLogger` and a `Bank` class that uses it

First, you implement `ConsoleLogger` with a `log_transfer` method ❶, which accepts the details of a transaction (sender, recipient, amount) and prints them ❷. The Bank class has the make_transfer method ❸, which (notionally) processes the transaction ❹ and then uses the logger member ❺ to log the transaction. The Bank and the ConsoleLogger have separate concerns—the Bank deals with bank logic, and the ConsoleLogger deals with logging.

Suppose you have a requirement to implement different kinds of loggers. For example, you might require a remote server logger, a local file logger, or even a logger that sends jobs to a printer. In addition, you must be able to change how the program logs at runtime (for example, an administrator might need to switch from logging over the network to logging to the local filesystem because of some server maintenance).

How can you accomplish such a task?

A simple approach is to use an enum class to switch between the various loggers. Listing 5-2 adds a FileLogger to Listing 5-1.

```
#include <cstdio>
#include <stdexcept>

struct FileLogger {
  void log_transfer(long from, long to, double amount) { ❶
    --snip--
    printf("[file] %ld,%ld,%f\n", from, to, amount);
  }
};

struct ConsoleLogger {
  void log_transfer(long from, long to, double amount) {
    printf("[cons] %ld -> %ld: %f\n", from, to, amount);
  }
};

enum class LoggerType { ❷
  Console,
  File
};

struct Bank {
  Bank() : type { LoggerType::Console } { } ❸

  void set_logger(LoggerType new_type) { ❹
    type = new_type;
  }

  void make_transfer(long from, long to, double amount) {
    --snip--
    switch(type) { ❺
    case LoggerType::Console: {
      consoleLogger.log_transfer(from, to, amount);
      break;
    } case LoggerType::File: {
      fileLogger.log_transfer(from, to, amount);
      break;
    } default: {
```

```
      throw std::logic_error("Unknown Logger type encountered.");
    } }
  }
private:
  LoggerType type;
  ConsoleLogger consoleLogger;
  FileLogger fileLogger;
};

int main() {
  Bank bank;
  bank.make_transfer(1000, 2000, 49.95);
  bank.make_transfer(2000, 4000, 20.00);
  bank.set_logger(LoggerType::File); ❻
  bank.make_transfer(3000, 2000, 75.00);
}
```

```
[cons] 1000 -> 2000: 49.950000
[cons] 2000 -> 4000: 20.000000
[file] 3000,2000,75.000000
```

Listing 5-2: An updated Listing 5-1 with a runtime polymorphic logger

You (notionally) add the ability to log to a file ❶ by implementing a `FileLogger`. You also create an `enum class LoggerType` ❷ so you can switch logging behavior at runtime. You initialize the type field to `Console` within the `Bank` constructor ❸. Within the updated `Bank` class, you add a `set_logger` function ❹ to perform the desired logging behavior. You use the `type` within `make_transfer` to `switch` on the correct logger ❺. To alter a `Bank` class's logging behavior, you use the `set_logger` method ❻, and the object handles dispatching internally.

Adding New Loggers

Listing 5-2 works, but this approach suffers from several design problems. Adding a new kind of logging requires you to make several updates throughout the code:

1. You need to write a new logger type.
2. You need to add a new `enum` value to the `enum class LoggerType`.
3. You must add a new case in the `switch` statement ❺.
4. You must add the new logging class as a member to `Bank`.

That's a lot of work for a simple change!

Consider an alternative approach where `Bank` holds a pointer to a logger. This way, you can set the pointer directly and get rid of `LoggerType` entirely. You exploit the fact that your loggers have the same function prototype. This is the idea behind an interface: the `Bank` class doesn't need to know the implementation details of the `Logger` reference it holds, just how to invoke its methods.

Wouldn't it be nice if we could swap out the `ConsoleLogger` for another type that supports the same operations? Say, a `FileLogger`?

Allow me to introduce you to the interface.

Interfaces

In software engineering, an *interface* is a shared boundary that contains no data or code. It defines function signatures that all implementations of the interface agree to support. An *implementation* is code or data that declares support for an interface. You can think of an interface as a contract between classes that implement the interface and users (also called *consumers*) of that class.

Consumers know how to use implementations because they know the contract. In fact, the consumer never needs to know the underlying implementation type. For example, in Listing 5-1 `Bank` is a consumer of `ConsoleLogger`.

Interfaces impose stringent requirements. A consumer of an interface can use only the methods explicitly defined in the interface. The `Bank` class doesn't need to know anything about how `ConsoleLogger` performs its function. All it needs to know is how to call the `log_transfer` method.

Interfaces promote highly reusable and loosely coupled code. You can understand the notation for specifying an interface, but you'll need to know a bit about object composition and implementation inheritance.

Object Composition and Implementation Inheritance

Object composition is a design pattern where a class contains members of other class types. An alternate, antiquated design pattern called *implementation inheritance* achieves runtime polymorphism. Implementation inheritance allows you to build hierarchies of classes; each child inherits functionality from its parents. Over the years, accumulated experience with implementation inheritance has convinced many that it's an anti-pattern. For example, Go and Rust—two new and increasingly popular system-programming languages—have zero support for implementation inheritance. A brief discussion of implementation inheritance is warranted for two reasons:

- You might encounter it infecting legacy code.
- The quirky way you define C++ interfaces has a shared lineage with implementation inheritance, so you'll be familiar with the mechanics anyway.

NOTE *If you're dealing with implementation inheritance–laden C++ code, see Chapters 20 and 21 of* The C++ Programming Language, *4th Edition, by Bjarne Stroustrup.*

Defining Interfaces

Unfortunately, there's no `interface` keyword in C++. You have to define interfaces using antiquated inheritance mechanisms. This is just one of those archaisms you have to deal with when programming in a 40+ year-old language.

Listing 5-3 illustrates a fully specified `Logger` interface and a corresponding `ConsoleLogger` that implements the interface. At least four constructions in Listing 5-3 will be unfamiliar to you, and this section covers each of them.

```
#include <cstdio>

struct Logger {
  virtual❶ ~Logger()❷ = default;
  virtual void log_transfer(long from, long to, double amount) = 0❸;
};

struct ConsoleLogger : Logger ❹ {
  void log_transfer(long from, long to, double amount) override ❺ {
    printf("%ld -> %ld: %f\n", from, to, amount);
  }
};
```

Listing 5-3: A `Logger` interface and a refactored `ConsoleLogger`

To parse Listing 5-3, you'll need to understand the `virtual` keyword ❶, the virtual destructor ❷, the `=0` suffix and pure-virtual methods ❸, base class inheritance ❹, and the `override` keyword ❺. Once you understand these, you'll know how to define an interface. The sections that follow discuss these concepts in detail.

Base Class Inheritance

Chapter 4 delved into how the `exception` class is the base class for all other stdlib exceptions and how the `logic_error` and `runtime_error` classes derived from `exception`. These two classes, in turn, form the base classes for other derived classes that describe error conditions in even greater detail, such as `invalid_argument` and `system_error`. Nested exception classes form an example of a class hierarchy and represent an implementation inheritance design.

You declare derived classes using the following syntax:

```
struct DerivedClass : BaseClass {
  --snip--
};
```

To define an inheritance relationship for `DerivedClass`, you use a colon (`:`) followed by the name of the base class, `BaseClass`.

Derived classes are declared just like any other class. The benefit is that you can treat derived class references as if they were of base class reference type. Listing 5-4 uses a `DerivedClass` reference in place of a `BaseClass` reference.

```
struct BaseClass {}; ❶
struct DerivedClass : BaseClass {}; ❷
void are_belong_to_us(BaseClass& base) {} ❸

int main() {
  DerivedClass derived;
  are_belong_to_us(derived); ❹
}
```

Listing 5-4: A program using a derived class in place of a base class

The DerivedClass ❷ derives from BaseClass ❶. The are_belong_to_us function takes a reference-to-BaseClass argument base ❸. You can invoke it with an instance of a DerivedClass because DerivedClass derives from BaseClass ❹.

The opposite is not true. Listing 5-5 attempts to use a base class in place of a derived class.

```
struct BaseClass {}; ❶
struct DerivedClass : BaseClass {}; ❷
void all_about_that(DerivedClass& derived) {} ❸

int main() {
  BaseClass base;
  all_about_that(base); // No! Trouble! ❹
}
```

Listing 5-5: This program attempts to use a base class in place of a derived class. (This listing won't compile.)

Here, BaseClass ❶ doesn't derive from DerivedClass ❷. (The inheritance relationship is the other way around.) The all_about_that function takes a DerivedClass argument ❸. When you attempt to invoke all_about_that with a BaseClass ❹, the compiler yields an error.

The main reason you'd want to derive from a class is to inherit its members.

Member Inheritance

Derived classes inherit non-private members from their base classes. Classes can use inherited members just like normal members. The supposed benefit of member inheritance is that you can define functionality once in a base class and not have to repeat it in the derived classes. Unfortunately, experience has convinced many in the programming community to avoid member inheritance because it can easily yield brittle, hard-to-reason-about code compared to composition-based polymorphism. (This is why so many modern programming languages exclude it.)

The class in Listing 5-6 illustrates member inheritance.

```
#include <cstdio>

struct BaseClass {
  int the_answer() const { return 42; } ❶
```

```
  const char* member = "gold"; ❷
private:
  const char* holistic_detective = "Dirk Gently"; ❸
};

struct DerivedClass : BaseClass ❹ {};

int main() {
  DerivedClass x;
  printf("The answer is %d\n", x.the_answer()); ❺
  printf("%s member\n", x.member); ❻
  // This line doesn't compile:
  // printf("%s's Holistic Detective Agency\n", x.holistic_detective); ❼
}
--------------------------------------------------------------------------
The answer is 42 ❺
gold member ❻
```

Listing 5-6: A program using inherited members

Here, `BaseClass` has a public method ❶, a public field ❷, and a private field ❸. You declare a `DerivedClass` deriving from `BaseClass` ❹ and then use it in `main`. Because they're inherited as public members, `the_answer` ❺ and `member` ❻ are available on the `DerivedClass x`. However, uncommenting ❼ yields a compiler error because `holistic_detective` is private and thus not inherited by derived classes.

virtual Methods

If you want to permit a derived class to override a base class's methods, you use the `virtual` keyword. By adding `virtual` to a method's definition, you declare that a derived class's implementation should be used if one is supplied. Within the implementation, you add the `override` keyword to the method's declaration, as demonstrated in Listing 5-7.

```
#include <cstdio>

struct BaseClass {
  virtual❶ const char* final_message() const {
    return "We apologize for the incontinence.";
  }
};

struct DerivedClass : BaseClass ❷ {
  const char* final_message() const override ❸ {
    return "We apologize for the inconvenience.";
  }
};

int main() {
  BaseClass base;
  DerivedClass derived;
  BaseClass& ref = derived;
```

```
  printf("BaseClass:    %s\n", base.final_message()); ❹
  printf("DerivedClass: %s\n", derived.final_message()); ❺
  printf("BaseClass&:   %s\n", ref.final_message()); ❻
}
--------------------------------------------------------------------------
BaseClass:    We apologize for the incontinence. ❹
DerivedClass: We apologize for the inconvenience. ❺
BaseClass&:   We apologize for the inconvenience. ❻
```

Listing 5-7: A program using virtual members

The BaseClass contains a virtual member ❶. In the DerivedClass ❷, you override the inherited member and use the override keyword ❸. The implementation of BaseClass is used only when a BaseClass instance is at hand ❹. The implementation of DerivedClass is used when a DerivedClass instance is at hand ❺, even if you're interacting with it through a BaseClass reference ❻.

If you want to *require* a derived class to implement the method, you can append the =0 suffix to a method definition. You call methods with both the virtual keyword and =0 suffix pure virtual methods. You can't instantiate a class containing any pure virtual methods. In Listing 5-8, consider the refactor of Listing 5-7 that uses a pure virtual method in the base class.

```
#include <cstdio>

struct BaseClass {
  virtual const char* final_message() const = 0; ❶
};

struct DerivedClass : BaseClass ❷ {
  const char* final_message() const override ❸ {
    return "We apologize for the inconvenience.";
  }
};

int main() {
  // BaseClass base; // Bang! ❹
  DerivedClass derived;
  BaseClass& ref = derived;
  printf("DerivedClass: %s\n", derived.final_message()); ❺
  printf("BaseClass&:   %s\n", ref.final_message()); ❻
}
--------------------------------------------------------------------------
DerivedClass: We apologize for the inconvenience. ❺
BaseClass&:   We apologize for the inconvenience. ❻
```

Listing 5-8: A refactor of Listing 5-7 using a pure virtual method

The =0 suffix specifies a pure virtual method ❶, meaning you can't instantiate a BaseClass—only derive from it. DerivedClass still derives from BaseClass ❷, and you provide the requisite final_message ❸. Attempting to instantiate a BaseClass would result in a compiler error ❹. Both DerivedClass and the BaseClass reference behave as before ❺❻.

NOTE *Virtual functions can incur runtime overhead, although the cost is typically low (within 25 percent of a regular function call). The compiler generates* virtual function tables (vtables) *that contain function pointers. At runtime, a consumer of an interface doesn't generally know its underlying type, but it knows how to invoke the interface's methods (thanks to the vtable). In some circumstances, the linker can detect all uses of an interface and* devirtualize *a function call. This removes the function call from the vtable and thus eliminates associated runtime cost.*

Pure-Virtual Classes and Virtual Destructors

You achieve interface inheritance through deriving from base classes that contain only pure-virtual methods. Such classes are referred to as *pure-virtual classes*. In C++, interfaces are always pure-virtual classes. Usually, you add virtual destructors to interfaces. In some rare circumstances, it's possible to leak resources if you fail to mark destructors as virtual. Consider Listing 5-9, which illustrates the danger of not adding a virtual destructor.

```
#include <cstdio>

struct BaseClass {};

struct DerivedClass : BaseClass❶ {
  DerivedClass() { ❷
    printf("DerivedClass() invoked.\n");
  }
  ~DerivedClass() { ❸
    printf("~DerivedClass() invoked.\n");
  }
};

int main() {
  printf("Constructing DerivedClass x.\n");
  BaseClass* x{ new DerivedClass{} }; ❹
  printf("Deleting x as a BaseClass*.\n");
  delete x; ❺
}
```

```
Constructing DerivedClass x.
DerivedClass() invoked.
Deleting x as a BaseClass*.
```

Listing 5-9: An example illustrating the dangers of non-virtual destructors in base classes

Here you see a `DerivedClass` deriving from `BaseClass` ❶. This class has a constructor ❷ and destructor ❸ that print when they're invoked. Within `main`, you allocate and initialize a `DerivedClass` with `new` and set the result to a `BaseClass` pointer ❹. When you `delete` the pointer ❺, the `BaseClass` destructor gets invoked, but the `DerivedClass` destructor doesn't!

Adding virtual to the `BaseClass` destructor solves the problem, as demonstrated in Listing 5-10.

```
#include <cstdio>

struct BaseClass {
  virtual ~BaseClass() = default; ❶
};

struct DerivedClass : BaseClass {
  DerivedClass() {
    printf("DerivedClass() invoked.\n");
  }
  ~DerivedClass() {
    printf("~DerivedClass() invoked.\n"); ❷
  }
};

int main() {
  printf("Constructing DerivedClass x.\n");
  BaseClass* x{ new DerivedClass{} };
  printf("Deleting x as a BaseClass*.\n");
  delete x; ❸
}
--------------------------------------------------------------------------------
Constructing DerivedClass x.
DerivedClass() invoked.
Deleting x as a BaseClass*.
~DerivedClass() invoked. ❷
```

Listing 5-10: A refactor of Listing 5-9 with a virtual destructor

Adding the virtual destructor ❶ causes the `DerivedClass` destructor to get invoked when you delete the `BaseClass` pointer ❸, which results in the `DerivedClass` destructor printing the message ❷.

Declaring a virtual destructor is optional when declaring an interface, but beware. If you forget that you haven't implemented a virtual destructor in the interface and accidentally do something like Listing 5-9, you can leak resources, and the compiler won't warn you.

NOTE *Declaring a protected non-virtual destructor is a good alternative to declaring a public virtual destructor because it will cause a compilation error when writing code that deletes a base class pointer. Some don't like this approach because you eventually have to make a class with a public destructor, and if you derive from that class, you run into the same issues.*

Implementing Interfaces

To declare an interface, declare a pure virtual class. To implement an interface, derive from it. Because the interface is pure virtual, an implementation must implement all of the interface's methods.

It's good practice to mark these methods with the override keyword. This communicates that you intend to override a virtual function, allowing the compiler to save you from simple mistakes.

Using Interfaces

As a consumer, you can only deal in references or pointers to interfaces. The compiler cannot know ahead of time how much memory to allocate for the underlying type: if the compiler could know the underlying type, you would be better off using templates.

There are two options for how to set the member:

Constructor injection With constructor injection, you typically use an interface reference. Because references cannot be reseated, they won't change for the lifetime of the object.

Property injection With property injection, you use a method to set a pointer member. This allows you to change the object to which the member points.

You can combine these approaches by accepting an interface pointer in a constructor while also providing a method to set the pointer to something else.

Typically, you'll use constructor injection when the injected field won't change throughout the lifetime of the object. If you need the flexibility of modifying the field, you'll provide methods to perform property injection.

Updating the Bank Logger

The Logger interface allows you to provide multiple logger implementations. This allows a Logger consumer to log transfers with the log_transfer method without having to know the logger's implementation details. You've already implemented a ConsoleLogger in Listing 5-2, so let's consider how you can add another implementation called FileLogger. For simplicity, in this code you'll only modify the log output's prefix, but you can imagine how you might implement some more complicated behavior.

Listing 5-11 defines a FileLogger.

```
#include <cstdio>

struct Logger {
  virtual ~Logger() = default; ❶
  virtual void log_transfer(long from, long to, double amount) = 0; ❷
};

struct ConsoleLogger : Logger ❸ {
  void log_transfer(long from, long to, double amount) override ❹ {
    printf("[cons] %ld -> %ld: %f\n", from, to, amount);
  }
};
```

```
struct FileLogger : Logger ❺ {
  void log_transfer(long from, long to, double amount) override ❻ {
    printf("[file] %ld,%ld,%f\n", from, to, amount);
  }
};
```

Listing 5-11: `Logger`, `ConsoleLogger`, and `FileLogger`

`Logger` is a pure virtual class (interface) with a default virtual destructor ❶ and a single method `log_transfer` ❷. `ConsoleLogger` and `FileLogger` are `Logger` implementations, because they derive from the interface ❸❺. You've implemented `log_transfer` and placed the `override` keyword on both ❹❻.

Now we'll look at how you could use either constructor injection or property injection to update `Bank`.

Constructor Injection

Using constructor injection, you have a `Logger` reference that you pass into the `Bank` class's constructor. Listing 5-12 adds to Listing 5-11 by incorporating the appropriate `Bank` constructor. This way, you establish the kind of logging that a particular `Bank` instantiation will perform.

```
--snip--
// Include Listing 5-11
struct Bank {
  Bank(Logger& logger) : logger{ logger }❶ { }
  void make_transfer(long from, long to, double amount) {
    --snip--
    logger.log_transfer(from, to, amount);
  }
private:
  Logger& logger;
};

int main() {
  ConsoleLogger logger;
  Bank bank{ logger }; ❷
  bank.make_transfer(1000, 2000, 49.95);
  bank.make_transfer(2000, 4000, 20.00);
}
```

```
[cons] 1000 -> 2000: 49.950000
[cons] 2000 -> 4000: 20.000000
```

Listing 5-12: Refactoring Listing 5-2 using constructor injection, interfaces, and object composition to replace the clunky `enum class` approach

The `Bank` class's constructor sets the value of `logger` using a member initializer ❶. References can't be reseated, so the object that `logger` points to doesn't change for the lifetime of `Bank`. You fix your logger choice upon `Bank` construction ❷.

Property Injection

Instead of using constructor injection to insert a Logger into a Bank, you could use property injection. This approach uses a pointer instead of a reference. Because pointers can be reseated (unlike references), you can change the behavior of Bank whenever you like. Listing 5-13 is a property-injected variant of Listing 5-12.

```
--snip--
// Include Listing 5-10

struct Bank {
  void set_logger(Logger* new_logger) {
    logger = new_logger;
  }
  void make_transfer(long from, long to, double amount) {
    if (logger) logger->log_transfer(from, to, amount);
  }
private:
  Logger* logger{};
};

int main() {
  ConsoleLogger console_logger;
  FileLogger file_logger;
  Bank bank;
  bank.set_logger(&console_logger); ❶
  bank.make_transfer(1000, 2000, 49.95); ❷
  bank.set_logger(&file_logger); ❸
  bank.make_transfer(2000, 4000, 20.00); ❹
}
```

```
[cons] 1000 -> 2000: 49.950000 ❷
[file] 2000,4000,20.000000 ❹
```

Listing 5-13: Refactoring Listing 5-12 using property injection

The set_logger method enables you to inject a new logger into a Bank object at any point during the life cycle. When you set the logger to a ConsoleLogger instance ❶, you get a [cons] prefix on the logging output ❷. When you set the logger to a FileLogger instance ❸, you get a [file] prefix ❹.

Choosing Constructor or Property Injection

Whether you choose constructor or property injection depends on design requirements. If you need to be able to modify underlying types of an object's members throughout the object's life cycle, you should choose pointers and the property injector method. But the flexibility of using pointers and property injection comes at a cost. In the Bank example in this chapter, you must make sure that you either don't set logger to nullptr or that you check for this condition before using logger. There's also the question of what the default behavior is: what is the initial value of logger?

One possibility is to provide constructor and property injection. This encourages anyone who uses your class to think about initializing it. Listing 5-14 illustrates one way to implement this strategy.

```
#include <cstdio>

struct Logger {
  --snip--
};

struct Bank {
  Bank(Logger* logger) : logger{ logger } () ❶
  void set_logger(Logger* new_logger) { ❷
    logger = new_logger;
  }
  void make_transfer(long from, long to, double amount) {
    if (logger) logger->log_transfer(from, to, amount);
  }
private:
    Logger* logger;
};
```

Listing 5-14: A refactor of the `Bank` to include constructor and property injection

As you can see, you can include a constructor ❶ and a setter ❷. This requires the user of a `Bank` to initialize logger with a value, even if it's just `nullptr`. Later on, the user can easily swap out this value using property injection.

Summary

In this chapter, you learned how to define interfaces, the central role that virtual functions play in making inheritance work, and some general rules for using constructor and property injectors. Whichever approach you choose, the combination of interface inheritance and composition provides sufficient flexibility for most runtime polymorphic applications. You can achieve type-safe runtime polymorphism with little or no overhead. Interfaces encourage encapsulation and loosely coupled design. With simple, focused interfaces, you can encourage code reuse by making your code portable across projects.

EXERCISES

5-1. You didn't implement an accounting system in your `Bank`. Design an interface called `AccountDatabase` that can retrieve and set amounts in bank accounts (identified by a `long id`).

5-2. Generate an `InMemoryAccountDatabase` that implements `AccountDatabase`.

5-3. Add an `AccountDatabase` reference member to `Bank`. Use constructor injection to add an `InMemoryAccountDatabase` to the `Bank`.

5-4. Modify `ConsoleLogger` to accept a `const char*` at construction. When `ConsoleLogger` logs, prepend this string to the logging output. Notice that you can modify logging behavior without having to modify `Bank`.

FURTHER READING

- *API Design for C++* by Martin Reddy (Elsevier, 2011)

6

COMPILE-TIME POLYMORPHISM

The more you adapt, the more interesting you are.
—Martha Stewart

In this chapter, you'll learn how to achieve compile-time polymorphism with templates. You'll learn how to declare and use templates, enforce type safety, and survey some of the templates' more advanced usages. This chapter concludes with a comparison of runtime and compile-time polymorphism in C++.

Templates

C++ achieves compile-time polymorphism through *templates*. A template is a class or function with template parameters. These parameters can stand in for any type, including fundamental and user-defined types. When the compiler sees a template used with a type, it stamps out a bespoke template instantiation.

Template instantiation is the process of creating a class or a function from a template. Somewhat confusingly, you can also refer to "a template instantiation" as the result of the template instantiation process. Template instantiations are sometimes called concrete classes and concrete types.

The big idea is that, rather than copying and pasting common code all over the place, you write a single template; the compiler generates new template instances when it encounters a new combination of types in the template parameters.

Declaring Templates

You declare templates with a *template prefix*, which consists of the keyword `template` followed by angle brackets `< >`. Within the angle brackets, you place the declarations of one or more template parameters. You can declare template parameters using either the `typename` or `class` keywords followed by an identifier. For example, the template prefix `template<typename T>` declares that the template takes a template parameter `T`.

NOTE *The coexistence of the* `typename` *and* `class` *keywords is unfortunate and confusing. They mean the same thing. (They're both supported for historical reasons.) This chapter always uses* `typename`.

Template Class Definitions

Consider `MyTemplateClass` in Listing 6-1, which takes three template parameters: `X`, `Y`, and `Z`.

```
template❶<typename X, typename Y, typename Z> ❷
struct MyTemplateClass❸ {
  X foo(Y&); ❹
private:
  Z* member; ❺
};
```

Listing 6-1: A template class with three template parameters

The `template` keyword ❶ begins the template prefix, which contains the template parameters ❷. This `template` preamble leads to something special about the remaining declaration of `MyTemplateClass` ❸. Within `MyTemplateClass`, you use `X`, `Y`, and `Z` as if they were any fully specified type, like an `int` or a user-defined class.

The `foo` method takes a `Y` reference and returns an `X` ❹. You can declare members with types that include template parameters, like a pointer to `Z` ❺. Besides the special prefix beginning ❶, this template class is essentially identical to a non-template class.

Template Function Definitions

You can also specify template functions, like the `my_template_function` in Listing 6-2 that also takes three template parameters: `X`, `Y`, and `Z`.

```
template<typename X, typename Y, typename Z>
X my_template_function(Y& arg1, const Z* arg2) {
  --snip--
}
```

Listing 6-2: A template function with three template parameters

Within the body of `my_template_function`, you can use `arg1` and `arg2` however you'd like, as long as you return an object of type `X`.

Instantiating Templates

To instantiate a template class, use the following syntax:

```
tc_name❶<t_param1❷, t_param2, ...> my_concrete_class{ ... }❸;
```

The *tc_name* ❶ is where you place the template class's name. Next, you fill in your template parameters ❷. Finally, you treat this combination of template name and parameters as if it were a normal type: you use whatever initialization syntax you like ❸.

Instantiating a template function is similar:

```
auto result = tf_name❶<t_param1❷, t_param2, ...>(f_param1❸, f_param2, ...);
```

The *tf_name* ❶ is where you put the template function's name. You fill in the parameters just as you do for template classes ❷. You use the combination of template name and parameters as if it were a normal type. You invoke this template function instantiation with parentheses and function parameters ❸.

All this new notation might be daunting to a newcomer, but it's not so bad once you get used to it. In fact, it's used in a set of language features called named conversion functions.

Named Conversion Functions

Named conversions are language features that explicitly convert one type into another type. You use named conversions sparingly in situations where you cannot use implicit conversions or constructors to get the types you need.

All named conversions accept a single object parameter, which is the object you want to cast *object-to-cast*, and a single type parameter, which is the type you want to cast to *desired-type*:

```
named-conversion<desired-type>(object-to-cast)
```

For example, if you need to modify a const object, you would first need to cast away the const qualifier. The named conversion function const_cast allows you to perform this operation. Other named conversions help you to reverse implicit casts (static_cast) or reinterpret memory with a different type (reinterpret_cast).

NOTE *Although named conversion functions aren't technically template functions, they are conceptually very close to templates—a relationship reflected in their syntactic similarity.*

const_cast

The const_cast function shucks away the const modifier, allowing the modification of const values. The *object-to-cast* is of some const type, and the *desired-type* is that type minus the const qualifier.

Consider the carbon_thaw function in Listing 6-3, which takes a const reference to an encased_solo argument.

```
void carbon_thaw(const❶ int& encased_solo) {
  //encased_solo++; ❷ // Compiler error; modifying const
  auto& hibernation_sick_solo = const_cast❸<int&❹>(encased_solo❺);
  hibernation_sick_solo++; ❻
}
```

Listing 6-3: A function using const_cast. Uncommenting yields a compiler error.

The encased_solo parameter is const ❶, so any attempt to modify it ❷ would result in a compiler error. You use const_cast ❸ to obtain the non-const reference hibernation_sick_solo. The const_cast takes a single template parameter, the type you want to cast into ❹. It also takes a function parameter, the object you want to remove const from ❺. You're then free to modify the int pointed to by encased_solo via the new, non-const reference ❻.

Only use const_cast to obtain write access to const objects. Any other type conversion will result in a compiler error.

NOTE *Trivially, you can use const_cast to add const to an object's type, but you shouldn't because it's verbose and unnecessary. Use an implicit cast instead. In Chapter 7, you'll learn what the volatile modifier is. You can also use const_cast to remove the volatile modifier from an object.*

static_cast

The static_cast reverses a well-defined implicit conversion, such as an integer type to another integer type. The *object-to-cast* is of some type that the *desired-type* implicitly converts to. The reason you might need static_cast is that, generally, implicit casts aren't reversible.

The program in Listing 6-4 defines an increment_as_short function that takes a void pointer argument. It employs a static_cast to create a short pointer from this argument, increment the pointed-to short, and return the result. In some low-level applications, such as network programming or handling binary file formats, you might need to interpret raw bytes as an integer type.

```
#include <cstdio>

short increment_as_short(void*❶ target) {
  auto as_short = static_cast❷<short*❸>(target❹);
  *as_short = *as_short + 1;
  return *as_short;
}

int main() {
  short beast{ 665 };
  auto mark_of_the_beast = increment_as_short(&beast);
  printf("%d is the mark_of_the_beast.", mark_of_the_beast);
}
--------------------------------------------------------------------------
666 is the mark_of_the_beast.
```

Listing 6-4: A program using `static_cast`

The target parameter is a void pointer ❶. You employ static_cast to cast target into a short* ❷. The template parameter is the desired type ❸, and the function parameter is the object you want to cast into ❹.

Notice that the implicit conversion of short* to void* is well defined. Attempting ill-defined conversions with static_cast, such as converting a char* to a float*, will result in a compiler error:

```
float on = 3.5166666666;
auto not_alright = static_cast<char*>(&on); // Bang!
```

To perform such chainsaw juggling, you need to use reinterpret_cast.

reinterpret_cast

Sometimes in low-level programming, you must perform type conversions that are not well defined. In system programming and especially in embedded environments, you often need complete control over how to interpret memory. The reinterpret_cast gives you such control, but ensuring the correctness of these conversions is entirely your responsibility.

Suppose your embedded device keeps an unsigned long timer at memory address 0x1000. You could use reinterpret_cast to read from the timer, as demonstrated in Listing 6-5.

```
#include <cstdio>

int main() {
  auto timer = reinterpret_cast❶<const unsigned long*❷>(0x1000❸);
  printf("Timer is %lu.", *timer);
}
```

Listing 6-5: A program using `reinterpret_cast`. This program will compile, but you should expect a runtime crash unless 0x1000 is readable.

The reinterpret_cast ❶ takes a type parameter corresponding to the desired pointer type ❷ and the memory address the result should point to ❸.

Of course, the compiler has no idea whether the memory at address 0x1000 contains an unsigned long. It's entirely up to you to ensure correctness. Because you're taking full responsibility for this very dangerous construction, the compiler forces you to employ reinterpret_cast. You couldn't, for example, replace the initialization of timer with the following line:

```
const unsigned long* timer{ 0x1000 };
```

The compiler will grumble about converting an int to a pointer.

narrow_cast

Listing 6-6 illustrates a custom static_cast that performs a runtime check for *narrowing*. Narrowing is a loss in information. Think about converting from an int to a short. As long as the value of int fits into a short, the conversion is reversible and no narrowing occurs. If the value of int is too big for the short, the conversion isn't reversible and results in narrowing.

Let's implement a named conversion called narrow_cast that checks for narrowing and throws a runtime_error if it's detected.

```
#include <stdexcept>

template <typename To❶, typename From❷>
To❸ narrow_cast(From❹ value) {
  const auto converted = static_cast<To>(value); ❺
  const auto backwards = static_cast<From>(converted); ❻
  if (value != backwards) throw std::runtime_error{ "Narrowed!" }; ❼
  return converted; ❽
}
```

Listing 6-6: A narrow_cast definition

The narrow_cast function template takes two template parameters: the type you're casting To ❶ and the type you're casting From ❷. You can see these template parameters in action as the return type of the function ❸ and the type of the parameter value ❹. First, you perform the requested conversion using static_cast to yield converted ❺. Next, you perform the conversion in the opposite direction (from converted to type From) to yield backwards ❻. If value doesn't equal backwards, you've narrowed, so you throw an exception ❼. Otherwise, you return converted ❽.

You can see narrow_cast in action in Listing 6-7.

```
#include <cstdio>
#include <stdexcept>

template <typename To, typename From>
To narrow_cast(From value) {
  --snip--
}
```

```
int main() {
  int perfect{ 496 }; ❶
  const auto perfect_short = narrow_cast<short>(perfect); ❷
  printf("perfect_short: %d\n", perfect_short); ❸
  try {
    int cyclic{ 142857 }; ❹
    const auto cyclic_short = narrow_cast<short>(cyclic); ❺
    printf("cyclic_short: %d\n", cyclic_short);
  } catch (const std::runtime_error& e) {
    printf("Exception: %s\n", e.what()); ❻
  }
}
--------------------------------------------------------------------------
perfect_short: 496 ❸
Exception: Narrowed! ❻
```

Listing 6-7: A program using `narrow_cast`. (The output comes from an execution on Windows 10 x64.)

You first initialize `perfect` to 496 ❶ and then `narrow_cast` it to the short `perfect_short` ❷. This proceeds without exception because the value 496 fits easily into a 2-byte short on Windows 10 x64 (maximum value 32767). You see the output as expected ❸. Next, you initialize cyclic to 142857 ❹ and attempt to `narrow_cast` to the short cyclic_short ❺. This throws a `runtime_error` because 142857 is greater than the short's maximum value of 32767. The check within `narrow_cast` will fail. You see the exception printed in the `output` ❻.

Notice that you need to provide only a single template parameter, the return type, upon instantiation ❶❹. The compiler can deduce the `From` parameter based on usage.

mean: A Template Function Example

Consider the function in Listing 6-8 that computes the mean of a `double` array using the sum-and-divide approach.

```
#include <cstddef>

double mean(const double* values, size_t length) {
  double result{}; ❶
  for(size_t i{}; i<length; i++) {
    result += values[i]; ❷
  }
  return result / length; ❸
}
```

Listing 6-8: A function for computing the mean of an array

You initialize a `result` variable to zero ❶. Next, you sum over `values` by iterating over each index `i`, adding the corresponding element to `result` ❷. Then you divide `result` by `length` and `return` ❸.

Genericizing mean

Suppose you want to support mean calculations for other numeric types, such as float or long. You might be thinking, "That's what function overloads are for!" Essentially, you would be correct.

Listing 6-9 overloads mean to accept a long array. The straightforward approach is to copy and paste the original, then replace instances of double with long.

```
#include <cstddef>

long❶ mean(const long*❷ values, size_t length) {
  long result{}; ❸
  for(size_t i{}; i<length; i++) {
    result += values[i];
  }
  return result / length;
}
```

Listing 6-9: An overload of Listing 6-8 accepting a long array

That sure is a lot of copying and pasting, and you've changed very little: the return type ❶, the function argument ❷, and result ❸.

This approach doesn't scale as you add more types. What if you want to support other integral types, such as short types or uint_64 types? What about float types? What if, later on, you want to refactor some logic in mean? You're in for a lot of tedious and error-prone maintenance.

There are three changes to mean in Listing 6-9, and all of them involve finding and replacing double types with long types. Ideally, you could have the compiler automatically generate versions of the function for you whenever it encounters usage with a different type. The key is that none of the logic changes—only the types.

What you need to solve this copy-and-paste problem is *generic programming*, a programming style where you program with yet-to-be-specified types. You achieve generic programming using the support C++ has for templates. Templates allow the compiler to instantiate a custom class or function based on the types in use.

Now that you know how to declare templates, consider the mean function again. You still want mean to accept a wide range of types—not just double types—but you don't want to have to copy and paste the same code over and over again.

Consider how you can refactor Listing 6-8 into a template function, as demonstrated in Listing 6-10.

```
#include <cstddef>

template<typename T> ❶
T❷ mean(T*❸ values, size_t length) {
  T❹ result{};
  for(size_t i{}; i<length; i++) {
    result += values[i];
```

```
  }
  return result / length;
}
```

Listing 6-10: Refactoring Listing 6-8 into a template function

Listing 6-10 kicks off with a template prefix ❶. This prefix communicates a single template parameter `T`. Next, you update `mean` to use `T` instead of `double` ❷❸❹.

Now you can use `mean` with many different types. Each time the compiler encounters a usage of `mean` with a new type, it performs template instantiation. It's *as if* you had done the copy-paste-and-replace-types procedure, but the compiler is much better at doing detail-oriented, monotonous tasks than you are. Consider the example in Listing 6-11, which computes means for `double`, `float`, and `size_t` types.

```
#include <cstddef>
#include <cstdio>

template<typename T>
T mean(const T* values, size_t length) {
  --snip--
}

int main() {
  const double nums_d[] { 1.0, 2.0, 3.0, 4.0 };
  const auto result1 = mean<double>(nums_d, 4); ❶
  printf("double: %f\n", result1);

  const float nums_f[] { 1.0f, 2.0f, 3.0f, 4.0f };
  const auto result2 = mean<float>(nums_f, 4); ❷
  printf("float: %f\n", result2);

  const size_t nums_c[] { 1, 2, 3, 4 };
  const auto result3 = mean<size_t>(nums_c, 4); ❸
  printf("size_t: %zd\n", result3);
}
--------------------------------------------------------------------------
double: 2.500000
float: 2.500000
size_t: 2
```

Listing 6-11: A program using the template function `mean`

Three templates are instantiated ❶❷❸; it's as if you generated the overloads isolated in Listing 6-12 by hand. (Each template instantiation contains types, shown in bold, where the compiler substituted a type for a template parameter.)

```
double mean(const double* values, size_t length) {
  double result{};
  for(size_t i{}; i<length; i++) {
    result += values[i];
  }
```

```
  return result / length;
}

float mean(const float* values, size_t length) {
  float result{};
  for(size_t i{}; i<length; i++) {
    result += values[i];
  }
  return result / length;
}

char mean(const char* values, size_t length) {
  char result{};
  for(size_t i{}; i<length; i++) {
    result += values[i];
  }
  return result / length;
}
```

Listing 6-12: The template instantiations for Listing 6-11

The compiler has done a lot of work for you, but you might have noticed that you had to type the pointed-to array type twice: once to declare an array and again to specify a template parameter. This gets tedious and can cause errors. If the template parameter doesn't match, you'll likely get a compiler error or cause unintended casting.

Fortunately, you can generally omit the template parameters when invoking a template function. The process that the compiler uses to determine the correct template parameters is called *template type deduction.*

Template Type Deduction

Generally, you don't have to provide template function parameters. The compiler can deduce them from usage, so a rewrite of Listing 6-11 without them is shown in Listing 6-13.

```
#include <cstddef>
#include <cstdio>

template<typename T>
T mean(const T* values, size_t length) {
  --snip--
}

int main() {
  const double nums_d[] { 1.0, 2.0, 3.0, 4.0 };
  const auto result1 = mean(nums_d, 4); ❶
  printf("double: %f\n", result1);

  const float nums_f[] { 1.0f, 2.0f, 3.0f, 4.0f };
  const auto result2 = mean(nums_f, 4); ❷
  printf("float: %f\n", result2);

  const size_t nums_c[] { 1, 2, 3, 4 };
```

```
  const auto result3 = mean(nums_c, 4); ❸
  printf("size_t: %zd\n", result3);
}
```

```
double: 2.500000
float: 2.500000
size_t: 2
```

Listing 6-13: A refactor of Listing 6-11 without explicit template parameters

It's clear from usage that the template parameters are `double` ❶, `float` ❷, and `size_t` ❸.

NOTE *Template type deduction mostly works the way you might expect, but there is some nuance you'll want to become familiar with if you're writing a lot of generic code. For more information, see the ISO standard [temp]. Also, refer to Item 1 of* Effective Modern C++ *by Scott Meyers and Section 23.5.1 of* The C++ Programming Language, *4th Edition, by Bjarne Stroustrup.*

Sometimes, template arguments cannot be deduced. For example, if a template function's return type is a template argument, you must specify template arguments explicitly.

SimpleUniquePointer: A Template Class Example

A *unique pointer* is an RAII wrapper around a free-store-allocated object. As its name suggests, the unique pointer has a single owner at a time, so when a unique pointer's lifetime ends, the pointed-to object gets destructed.

The underlying object's type in unique pointers doesn't matter, making them a prime candidate for a template class. Consider the implementation in Listing 6-14.

```
template <typename T> ❶
struct SimpleUniquePointer {
  SimpleUniquePointer() = default; ❷
  SimpleUniquePointer(T* pointer)
    : pointer{ pointer } { ❸
  }
  ~SimpleUniquePointer() { ❹
    if(pointer) delete pointer;
  }
  SimpleUniquePointer(const SimpleUniquePointer&) = delete;
  SimpleUniquePointer& operator=(const SimpleUniquePointer&) = delete; ❺
  SimpleUniquePointer(SimpleUniquePointer&& other) noexcept ❻
    : pointer{ other.pointer } {
    other.pointer = nullptr;
  }
  SimpleUniquePointer& operator=(SimpleUniquePointer&& other) noexcept { ❼
    if(pointer) delete pointer;
    pointer = other.pointer;
    other.pointer = nullptr;
    return *this;
```

```
  }
  T* get() { ❽
    return pointer;
  }
private:
  T* pointer;
};
```

Listing 6-14: A simple unique pointer implementation

You announce the template class with a template prefix ❶, which establishes T as the wrapped object's type. Next, you specify a default constructor using the default keyword ❷. (Recall from Chapter 4 that you need default when you want both a default constructor *and* a non-default constructor.) The generated default constructor will set the private member T* pointer to nullptr thanks to default initialization rules. You have a non-default constructor that takes a T* and sets the private member pointer ❸. Because the pointer is possibly nullptr, the destructor checks before deleting ❹.

Because you want to allow only a single owner of the pointed-to object, you delete the copy constructor and the copy-assignment operator ❺. This prevents double-free issues, which were discussed in Chapter 4. However, you can make your unique pointer moveable by adding a move constructor ❻. This steals the value of pointer from other and then sets the pointer of other to nullptr, handing responsibility of the pointed-to object to this. Once the move constructor returns, the moved-from object is destroyed. Because the moved-from object's pointer is set to nullptr, the destructor will not delete the pointed-to object.

The possibility that this already owns an object complicates the move assignment ❼. You must check explicitly for prior ownership, because failure to delete a pointer leaks a resource. After this check, you perform the same operations as in the copy constructor: you set pointer to the value of other.pointer and then set other.pointer to nullptr. This ensures that the moved-from object doesn't delete the pointed-to object.

You can obtain direct access to the underlying pointer by calling the get method ❽.

Let's enlist our old friend Tracer from Listing 4-5 to investigate SimpleUniquePointer. Consider the program in Listing 6-15.

```
#include <cstdio>
#include <utility>

template <typename T>
struct SimpleUniquePointer {
  --snip--
};

struct Tracer {
  Tracer(const char* name) : name{ name } {
    printf("%s constructed.\n", name); ❶
  }
  ~Tracer() {
```

```
    printf("%s destructed.\n", name); ❷
  }
private:
  const char* const name;
};

void consumer(SimpleUniquePointer<Tracer> consumer_ptr) {
  printf("(cons) consumer_ptr: 0x%p\n", consumer_ptr.get()); ❸
}

int main() {
  auto ptr_a = SimpleUniquePointer(new Tracer{ "ptr_a" });
  printf("(main) ptr_a: 0x%p\n", ptr_a.get()); ❹
  consumer(std::move(ptr_a));
  printf("(main) ptr_a: 0x%p\n", ptr_a.get()); ❺
}
--------------------------------------------------------------------------
ptr_a constructed. ❶
(main) ptr_a: 0x000001936B5A2970 ❹
(cons) consumer_ptr: 0x000001936B5A2970 ❸
ptr_a destructed. ❷
(main) ptr_a: 0x0000000000000000 ❺
```

Listing 6-15: A program investigating `SimpleUniquePointers` with the `Tracer` class

First, you dynamically allocate a `Tracer` with the message `ptr_a`. This prints the first message ❶. You use the resulting `Tracer` pointer to construct a `SimpleUniquePointer` called `ptr_a`. Next, you use the `get()` method of `ptr_a` to retrieve the address of its `Tracer`, which you print ❹. Then you use `std::move` to relinquish the `Tracer` of `ptr_a` to the `consumer` function, which moves `ptr_a` into the `consumer_ptr` argument.

Now, `consumer_ptr` owns the `Tracer`. You use the `get()` method of `consumer_ptr` to retrieve the address of `Tracer`, then print ❸. Notice this address matches the one printed at ❹. When `consumer` returns, `consumer_ptr` dies because its storage duration is the scope of `consumer`. As a result, `ptr_a` gets destructed ❷.

Recall that `ptr_a` is in a moved-from state—you moved its `Tracer` into `consumer`. You use the `get()` method of `ptr_a` to illustrate that it now holds a `nullptr` ❺.

Thanks to `SimpleUniquePointer`, you won't leak a dynamically allocated object; also, because the `SimpleUniquePointer` is just carrying around a pointer under the hood, move semantics are efficient.

NOTE *The `SimpleUniquePointer` is a pedagogical implementation of the stdlib's `std::unique_ptr`, which is a member of the family of RAII templates called smart pointers. You'll learn about these in Part II.*

Type Checking in Templates

Templates are type safe. During template instantiation, the compiler pastes in the template parameters. If the resulting code is incorrect, the compiler will not generate the instantiation.

Consider the template function in Listing 6-16, which squares an element and returns the result.

```
template<typename T>
T square(T value) {
  return value * value; ❶
}
```

Listing 6-16: A template function that squares a value

The T has a silent requirement: it must support multiplication ❶.

If you try to use square with, say, a char*, the compilation will fail, as shown in Listing 6-17.

```
template<typename T>
T square(T value) {
  return value * value;
}

int main() {
  char my_char{ 'Q' };
  auto result = square(&my_char); ❶ // Bang!
}
```

Listing 6-17: A program with a failed template instantiation. (This program fails to compile.)

Pointers don't support multiplication, so template initialization fails ❶.

The square function is trivially small, but the failed template initialization's error message isn't. On MSVC v141, you get this:

```
main.cpp(3): error C2296: '*': illegal, left operand has type 'char *'
main.cpp(8): note: see reference to function template instantiation 'T
*square<char*>(T)' being compiled
        with
        [
            T=char *
        ]
main.cpp(3): error C2297: '*': illegal, right operand has type 'char *'
```

And on GCC 7.3, you get this:

```
main.cpp: In instantiation of 'T square(T) [with T = char*]':
main.cpp:8:32:   required from here
main.cpp:3:16: error: invalid operands of types 'char*' and 'char*' to binary
'operator*'
   return value * value;
          ~~~~~~^~~~~~~
```

These error messages exemplify the notoriously cryptic error messages emitted by template initialization failures.

Although template instantiation ensures type safety, the checking happens very late in the compilation process. When the compiler instantiates a template, it pastes the template parameter types into the template. After type insertion, the compiler attempts to compile the result. If instantiation fails, the compiler emits the dying words inside the template instantiation.

C++ template programming shares similarities with *duck-typed languages*. Duck-typed languages (like Python) defer type checking until runtime. The underlying philosophy is that if an object looks like a duck and quacks like a duck, then it must be type duck. Unfortunately, this means you can't generally know whether an object supports a particular operation until you execute the program.

With templates, you cannot know whether an instantiation will succeed until you try to compile it. Although duck-typed languages might blow up at runtime, templates might blow up at compile time.

This situation is widely regarded as unacceptable by right-thinking people in the C++ community, so there is a splendid solution called concepts.

Concepts

Concepts constrain template parameters, allowing for parameter checking at the point of instantiation rather than the point of first use. By catching usage issues at the point of instantiation, the compiler can give you a friendly, informative error code—for example, "You tried to instantiate this template with a `char*`, but this template requires a type that supports multiplication."

Concepts allow you to express requirements on template parameters directly in the language.

Unfortunately, concepts aren't yet officially part of the C++ standard, although they've been voted into C++ 20. At press time, GCC 6.0 and later support the Concepts Technical Specification, and Microsoft is actively working toward implementing concepts in its C++ compiler, MSVC. Regardless of its unofficial status, it's worth exploring concepts in some detail for a few reasons:

- They'll fundamentally change the way you achieve compile-time polymorphism. Familiarity with concepts will pay major dividends.
- They provide a conceptual framework for understanding some of the makeshift solutions that you can put in place to get better compiler errors when templates are misused.
- They provide an excellent conceptual bridge from compile-time templates to interfaces, the primary mechanism for runtime polymorphism (covered in Chapter 5).
- If you can use GCC 6.0 or later, concepts *are* available by turning on the `-fconcepts` compiler flag.

WARNING *C++ 20's final concept specification will almost certainly deviate from the Concepts Technical Specification. This section presents concepts as specified in the Concepts Technical Specification so you can follow along.*

Defining a Concept

A concept is a template. It's a constant expression involving template arguments, evaluated at compile time. Think of a concept as one big *predicate*: a function that evaluates to true or false.

If a set of template parameters meets the criteria for a given concept, that concept evaluates to true when instantiated with those parameters; otherwise, it will evaluate to false. When a concept evaluates to false, template instantiation fails.

You declare concepts using the keyword concept on an otherwise familiar template function definition:

```
template<typename T1, typename T2, ...>
concept bool ConceptName() {
  --snip--
}
```

Type Traits

Concepts validate type parameters. Within concepts, you manipulate types to inspect their properties. You can hand roll these manipulations, or you can use the type support library built into the stdlib. The library contains utilities for inspecting type properties. These utilities are collectively called *type traits*. They're available in the <type_traits> header and are part of the std namespace. Table 6-1 lists some commonly used type traits.

NOTE *See Chapter 5.4 of* The C++ Standard Library, *2nd Edition, by Nicolai M. Josuttis for an exhaustive listing of type traits available in the stdlib.*

Table 6-1: Selected Type Traits from the <type_traits> Header

Type trait	Checks if template argument is . . .
is_void	void
is_null_pointer	nullptr
is_integral	bool, a char type, an int type, a short type, a long type, or a long long type
is_floating_point	float, double, or long double
is_fundamental	Any of is_void, is_null_pointer, is_integral, or is_floating_point
is_array	An array; that is, a type containing square brackets []
is_enum	An enumeration type (enum)
is_class	A class type (but not a union type)
is_function	A function
is_pointer	A pointer; function pointers count, but pointers to class members and nullptr do not
is_reference	A reference (either lvalue or rvalue)
is_arithmetic	is_floating_point or is_integral

Type trait	Checks if template argument is . . .
is_pod	A plain-old-data type; that is, a type that can be represented as a data type in plain C
is_default_constructible	Default constructible; that is, it can be constructed without arguments or initialization values
is_constructible	Constructible with the given template parameters: this type trait allows the user to provide additional template parameters beyond the type under consideration
is_copy_constructible	Copy constructible
is_move_constructible	Move constructible
is_destructible	Destructible
is_same	The same type as the additional template parameter type (including const and volatile modifiers)
is_invocable	Invocable with the given template parameters: this type trait allows the user to provide additional template parameters beyond the type under consideration

Each type trait is a template class that takes a single template parameter, the type you want to inspect. You extract the results using the template's static member `value`. This member equals `true` if the type parameter meets the criteria; otherwise, it's `false`.

Consider the type trait classes `is_integral` and `is_floating_point`. These are useful for checking if a type is (you guessed it) integral or floating point. Both of these templates take a single template parameter. The example in Listing 6-18 investigates type traits with several types.

```
#include <type_traits>
#include <cstdio>
#include <cstdint>

constexpr const char* as_str(bool x) { return x ? "True" : "False"; } ❶

int main() {
  printf("%s\n", as_str(std::is_integral<int>::value)); ❷
  printf("%s\n", as_str(std::is_integral<const int>::value)); ❸
  printf("%s\n", as_str(std::is_integral<char>::value)); ❹
  printf("%s\n", as_str(std::is_integral<uint64_t>::value)); ❺
  printf("%s\n", as_str(std::is_integral<int&>::value)); ❻
  printf("%s\n", as_str(std::is_integral<int*>::value)); ❼
  printf("%s\n", as_str(std::is_integral<float>::value)); ❽
}
--------------------------------------------------------------------------
True ❷
True ❸
True ❹
True ❺
False ❻
False ❼
False ❽
```

Listing 6-18: A program using type traits

Listing 6-18 defines the convenience function `as_str` ❶ to print Boolean values with the string `True` or `False`. Within `main`, you print the result of various type trait instantiations. The template parameters `int` ❷, `const int` ❸, `char` ❹, and `uint64_t` ❺ all return `true` when passed to `is_integral`. Reference types ❻❼ and floating-point types ❽ return `false`.

NOTE *Recall that `printf` doesn't have a format specifier for `bool`. Rather than using the integer format specifier `%d` as a stand-in, Listing 6-18 employs the `as_str` function, which returns the string literal `True` or `False` depending on the value of the `bool`. Because these values are string literals, you can capitalize them however you like.*

Type traits are often the building blocks for a concept, but sometimes you need more flexibility. Type traits tell you *what* types are, but sometimes you must also specify *how* the template will use them. For this, you use requirements.

Requirements

Requirements are ad hoc constraints on template parameters. Each concept can specify any number of requirements on its template parameters. Requirements are encoded into requires expressions denoted by the `requires` keyword followed by function arguments and a body.

A sequence of syntactic requirements comprises the requirements expression's body. Each syntactic requirement puts a constraint on the template parameters. Together, requires expressions have the following form:

```
requires (arg-1, arg-2, ...❶) {
  { expression1❷ } -> return-type1❸;
  { expression2 } -> return-type2;
  --snip--
}
```

Requires expressions take arguments that you place after the `requires` keyword ❶. These arguments have types derived from template parameters. The syntactic requirements follow, each denoted with `{ } ->`. You put an arbitrary expression within each of the braces ❷. This expression can involve any number of the arguments to the argument expression.

If an instantiation causes a syntactic expression not to compile, that syntactic requirement fails. Supposing the expression evaluates without error, the next check is whether the return type of that expression matches the type given after the arrow `->` ❸. If the expression result's evaluated type can't implicitly convert to the return type ❸, the syntactic requirement fails.

If any of the syntactic requirements fail, the requires expression evaluates to `false`. If all of the syntactic requirements pass, the requires expression evaluates to `true`.

Suppose you have two types, `T` and `U`, and you want to know whether you can compare objects of these types using the equality `==` and inequality `!=` operators. One way to encode this requirement is to use the following expression.

```
// T, U are types
requires (T t, U u) {
  { t == u } -> bool; // syntactic requirement 1
  { u == t } -> bool; // syntactic requirement 2
  { t != u } -> bool; // syntactic requirement 3
  { u != t } -> bool; // syntactic requirement 4
}
```

The requires expression takes two arguments, one each of types `T` and `U`. Each of the syntactic requirements contained in the requires expression is an expression using `t` and `u` with either `==` or `!=`. All four syntactic requirements enforce a `bool` result. Any two types that satisfy this requires expression are guaranteed to support comparison with `==` and `!=`.

Building Concepts from Requires Expressions

Because requires expressions are evaluated at compile time, concepts can contain any number of them. Try to construct a concept that guards against the misuse of `mean`. Listing 6-19 annotates some of the implicit requirements used earlier in Listing 6-10.

```
template<typename T>
T mean(T* values, size_t length) {
  T result{}; ❶
  for(size_t i{}; i<length; i++) {
    result ❷+= values[i];
  }
  ❸return result / length;
}
```

Listing 6-19: A relisting of 6-10 with annotations for some implicit requirements on `T`

You can see three requirements implied by this code:

- `T` must be default constructible ❶.
- `T` supports `operator+=` ❷.
- Dividing a `T` by a `size_t` yields a `T` ❸.

From these requirements, you could create a concept called `Averageable`, as demonstrated in Listing 6-20.

```
template<typename T>
concept bool Averageable() {
  return std::is_default_constructible<T>::value ❶
    && requires (T a, T b) {
      { a += b } -> T; ❷
      { a / size_t{ 1 } } -> T; ❸
    };
}
```

Listing 6-20: An `Averageable` concept. Annotations are consistent with the requirements and the body of `mean`.

You use the type trait is_default_constructible to ensure that T is default constructible ❶, that you can add two T types ❷, and that you can divide a T by a size_t ❸ and get a result of type T.

Recall that concepts are just predicates; you're building a Boolean expression that evaluates to true when the template parameters are supported and false when they're not. The concept is composed of three Boolean expressions AND-ed (&&) together: two type traits ❶❸ and a requires expression. If any of the three returns false, the concept's constraints are not met.

Using Concepts

Declaring concepts is a lot more work than using them. To use a concept, just use the concept's name in place of the typename keyword.

For example, you can refactor Listing 6-13 with the Averageable concept, as shown in Listing 6-21.

```
#include <cstddef>
#include <type_traits>

template<typename T>
concept bool Averageable() { ❶
  --snip--
}

template<Averageable❷ T>
T mean(const T* values, size_t length) {
  --snip--
}

int main() {
  const double nums_d[] { 1.0f, 2.0f, 3.0f, 4.0f };
  const auto result1 = mean(nums_d, 4);
  printf("double: %f\n", result1);

  const float nums_f[] { 1.0, 2.0, 3.0, 4.0 };
  const auto result2 = mean(nums_f, 4);
  printf("float: %f\n", result2);

  const size_t nums_c[] { 1, 2, 3, 4 };
  const auto result3 = mean(nums_c, 4);
  printf("size_t: %d\n", result3);
}
```

```
double: 2.500000
float: 2.500000
size_t: 2
```

Listing 6-21: A refactor of Listing 6-13 using Averageable

After defining Averageable ❶, you just use it in place of typename ❷. No further modification is necessary. The code generated from compiling Listing 6-13 is identical to the code generated from compiling Listing 6-21.

The payoff is when you get to try to use mean with a type that is not Averageable: you get a compiler error at the point of instantiation. This produces much better compiler error messages than you would obtain from a raw template.

Look at the instantiation of mean in Listing 6-22 where you "accidentally" try to average an array of double pointers.

```
--snip-
int main() {
  auto value1 = 0.0;
  auto value2 = 1.0;
  const double* values[] { &value1, &value2 };
  mean(values❶, 2);
}
```

Listing 6-22: A bad template instantiation using a non-Averageable argument

There are several problems with using values ❶. What can the compiler tell you about those problems?

Without concepts, GCC 6.3 produces the error message shown in Listing 6-23.

```
<source>: In instantiation of 'T mean(const T*, size_t) [with T = const
double*; size_t = long unsigned int]':
<source>:17:17:   required from here
<source>:8:12: error: invalid operands of types 'const double*' and 'const
double*' to binary 'operator+'
     result += values[i]; ❶
     ~~~~~~~^~~~~~~~~~
<source>:8:12: error:   in evaluation of 'operator+=(const double*, const
double*)'
<source>:10:17: error: invalid operands of types 'const double*' and 'size_t'
{aka 'long unsigned int'} to binary 'operator/'
   return result / length; ❷
          ~~~~~~~^~~~~~~~
```

Listing 6-23: Error message from GCC 6.3 when compiling Listing 6-22

You might expect a casual user of mean to be extremely confused by this error message. What is i ❶? Why is a const double* involved in division ❷?

Concepts provide a far more illuminating error message, as Listing 6-24 demonstrates.

```
<source>: In function 'int main()':
<source>:28:17: error: cannot call function 'T mean(const T*, size_t) [with T
= const double*; size_t = long unsigned int]'
   mean(values, 2); ❶
                 ^
<source>:16:3: note:   constraints not satisfied
 T mean(const T* values, size_t length) {
   ^~~~
<source>:6:14: note: within 'template<class T> concept bool Averageable()
[with T = const double*]'
```

```
concept bool Averageable() {
             ^~~~~~~~~~~
<source>:6:14: note:     with 'const double* a'
<source>:6:14: note:     with 'const double* b'
<source>:6:14: note: the required expression '(a + b)' would be ill-formed ❷
<source>:6:14: note: the required expression '(a / b)' would be ill-formed ❸
```

Listing 6-24: Error message from GCC 7.2 when compiling Listing 6-22 with concepts enabled

This error message is fantastic. The compiler tells you which argument (`values`) didn't meet a constraint ❶. Then it tells you that `values` is not `Averageable` because it doesn't satisfy two required expressions ❷❸. You know immediately how to modify your arguments to make this template instantiation successful.

When concepts incorporate into the C++ standard, it's likely that the stdlib will include many concepts. The design goal of concepts is that a programmer shouldn't have to define very many concepts on their own; rather, they should be able to combine concepts and ad hoc requirements within a template prefix. Table 6-2 provides a partial listing of some concepts you might expect to be included; these are borrowed from Andrew Sutton's implementation of concepts in the Origins Library.

NOTE *See* https://github.com/asutton/origin/ *for more information on the Origins Library. To compile the examples that follow, you can install Origins and use GCC version 6.0 or later with the* `-fconcepts` *flag.*

Table 6-2: The Concepts Contained in the Origins Library

Concept	A type that . . .
`Conditional`	Can be explicitly converted to `bool`
`Boolean`	Is `Conditional` and supports `!`, `&&`, and `||` Boolean operations
`Equality_comparable`	Supports `==` and `!=` operations returning a `Boolean`
`Destructible`	Can be destroyed (compare `is_destructible`)
`Default_constructible`	Is default constructible (compare `is_default_constructible`)
`Movable`	Supports move semantics: it must be move assignable and move constructible (compare `is_move_assignable`, `is_move_constructible`)
`Copyable`	Supports copy semantics: it must be copy assignable and copy constructible (compare `is_copy_assignable`, `is_copy_constructible`)
`Regular`	Is default constructible, copyable, and `Equality_comparable`
`Ordered`	Is `Regular` and is totally ordered (essentially, it can be sorted)
`Number`	Is `Ordered` and supports math operations like `+`, `-`, `/`, and `*`
`Function`	Supports invocation; that is, you can call it (compare `is_invocable`)
`Predicate`	Is a `Function` and returns `bool`
`Range`	Can be iterated over in a range-based `for` loop

There are several ways to build constraints into a template prefix. If a template parameter is only used to declare the type of a function parameter, you can omit the template prefix entirely:

```
return-type function-name(Concept1❶ arg-1, ...) {
  --snip--
}
```

Because you use a concept rather than a typename to define an argument's type ❶, the compiler knows that the associated function is a template. You are even free to mix concepts and concrete types in the argument list. In other words, whenever you use a concept as part of a function definition, that function becomes a template.

The template function in Listing 6-25 takes an array of Ordered elements and finds the minimum.

```
#include <origin/core/concepts.hpp>
size_t index_of_minimum(Ordered❶* x, size_t length) {
  size_t min_index{};
  for(size_t i{ 1 }; i<length; i++) {
    if(x[i] < x[min_index]) min_index = i;
  }
  return min_index;
}
```

Listing 6-25: A template function using the Ordered *concept*

Even though there's no template prefix, index_of_minimum is a template because Ordered ❶ is a concept. This template can be instantiated in the same way as any other template function, as demonstrated in Listing 6-26.

```
#include <cstdio>
#include <cstdint>
#include <origin/core/concepts.hpp>

struct Goblin{};

size_t index_of_minimum(Ordered* x, size_t length) {
  --snip--
}

int main() {
  int x1[] { -20, 0, 100, 400, -21, 5123 };
  printf("%zd\n", index_of_minimum(x1, 6)); ❶

  unsigned short x2[] { 42, 51, 900, 400 };
  printf("%zd\n", index_of_minimum(x2, 4)); ❷

  Goblin x3[] { Goblin{}, Goblin{} };
  //index_of_minimum(x3, 2); ❸ // Bang! Goblin is not Ordered.
}
```

```
4 ❶
0 ❷
```

Listing 6-26: A listing employing `index_of_minimum` from Listing 6-25. Uncommenting ❸ causes compilation to fail.

The instantiations for `int` ❶ and `unsigned short` ❷ arrays succeed because types are `Ordered` (see Table 6-2).

However, the `Goblin` class is not `Ordered`, and template instantiation would fail if you tried to compile ❸. Crucially, the error message would be informative:

```
error: cannot call function 'size_t index_
of_minimum(auto:1*, size_t) [with auto:1 = Goblin; size_t = long unsigned int]'
   index_of_minimum(x3, 2); // Bang! Goblin is not Ordered.
                         ^
note:   constraints not satisfied
 size_t index_of_minimum(Ordered* x, size_t length) {
        ^~~~~~~~~~~~~~~~
note: within 'template<class T> concept bool origin::Ordered() [with T =
Goblin]'
 Ordered()
```

You know that the `index_of_minimum` instantiation failed and that the issue is with the `Ordered` concept.

Ad Hoc Requires Expressions

Concepts are fairly heavyweight mechanisms for enforcing type safety. Sometimes, you just want to enforce some requirement directly in the template prefix. You can embed requires expressions directly into the template definition to accomplish this. Consider the `get_copy` function in Listing 6-27 that takes a pointer and safely returns a copy of the pointed-to object.

```
#include <stdexcept>

template<typename T>
  requires❶ is_copy_constructible<T>::value ❷
T get_copy(T* pointer) {
  if (!pointer) throw std::runtime_error{ "Null-pointer dereference" };
  return *pointer;
}
```

Listing 6-27: A template function with an ad hoc requires expression

The template prefix contains the `requires` keyword ❶, which begins the requires expression. In this case, the type trait `is_copy_constructible` ensures that `T` is copyable ❷. This way, if a user accidentally tries to `get_copy` with a pointer that points to an uncopyable object, they'll be presented with a clear explanation of why template instantiation failed. Consider the example in Listing 6-28.

```
#include <stdexcept>
#include <type_traits>

template<typename T>
  requires std::is_copy_constructible<T>::value
T get_copy(T* pointer) { ❶
  --snip--
}

struct Highlander {
  Highlander() = default; ❷
  Highlander(const Highlander&) = delete; ❸
};

int main() {
  Highlander connor; ❹
  auto connor_ptr = &connor; ❺
  auto connor_copy = get_copy(connor_ptr); ❻
}
--------------------------------------------------------------------------------
In function 'int main()':
error: cannot call function 'T get_copy(T*) [with T = Highlander]'
   auto connor_copy = get_copy(connor_ptr);
                                         ^
note:   constraints not satisfied
 T get_copy(T* pointer) {
   ^~~~~~~~
note: 'std::is_copy_constructible::value' evaluated to false
```

Listing 6-28: Program using the get_copy template in Listing 6-27. This code doesn't compile.

The definition of get_copy ❶ is followed by a Highlander class definition, which contains a default constructor ❷ and a deleted copy constructor ❸. Within main, you've initialized a Highlander ❹, taken its reference ❺, and attempted to instantiate get_copy with the result ❻. Because there can be only one Highlander (it's not copyable), Listing 6-28 produces an exquisitely clear error message.

static_assert: The Preconcepts Stopgap

As of C++17, concepts aren't part of the standard, so they're not guaranteed to be available across compilers. There is a stopgap you can apply in the interim: the static_assert expression. These assertions evaluate at compile time. If an assertion fails, the compiler will issue an error and optionally provide a diagnostic message. A static_assert has the following form:

```
static_assert(boolean-expression, optional-message);
```

In the absence of concepts, you can include one or more static_assert expressions in the bodies of templates to assist users in diagnosing usage errors.

Suppose you want to improve the error messages of mean without leaning on concepts. You can use type traits in combination with static_assert to achieve a similar result, as demonstrated in Listing 6-29.

```
#include <type_traits>

template <typename T>
T mean(T* values, size_t length) {
  static_assert(std::is_default_constructible<T>(),
    "Type must be default constructible."); ❶
  static_assert(std::is_copy_constructible<T>(),
    "Type must be copy constructible."); ❷
  static_assert(std::is_arithmetic<T>(),
    "Type must support addition and division."); ❸
  static_assert(std::is_constructible<T, size_t>(),
    "Type must be constructible from size_t."); ❹
  --snip--
}
```

Listing 6-29: Using static_assert expressions to improve compile time errors in mean in Listing 6-10.

You see the familiar type traits for checking that T is default ❶ and copy constructible ❷, and you provide error methods to help users diagnose issues with template instantiation. You use is_arithmetic ❸, which evaluates to true if the type parameter supports arithmetic operations (+, -, /, and *), and is_constructible ❹, which determines whether you can construct a T from a size_t.

Using static_assert as a proxy for concepts is a hack, but it's widely used. Using type traits, you can limp along until concepts are included in the standard. You'll often see static_assert if you use modern third-party libraries; if you're writing code for others (including future you), consider using static_assert and type traits.

Compilers, and often programmers, don't read documentation. By baking requirements directly into the code, you can avoid stale documentation. In the absence of concepts, static_assert is a fine stopgap.

Non-Type Template Parameters

A template parameter declared with the typename (or class) keyword is called a *type template parameter*, which is a stand-in for some yet-to-be-specified type. Alternatively, you can use *non-type template parameters*, which are stand-ins for some yet-to-be-specified value. Non-type template parameters can be any of the following:

- An integral type
- An lvalue reference type
- A pointer (or pointer-to-member) type

- A std::nullptr_t (the type of nullptr)
- An enum class

Using a non-type template parameter allows you to inject a value into the generic code at compile time. For example, you can construct a template function called get that checks for out-of-bounds array access at compile time by taking the index you want to access as a non-type template parameter.

Recall from Chapter 3 that if you pass an array to a function, it decays into a pointer. You can instead pass an array reference with a particularly off-putting syntax:

```
element-type(param-name&)[array-length]
```

For example, Listing 6-30 contains a get function that makes a first attempt at performing bounds-checked array access.

```
#include <stdexcept>

int& get(int (&arr)[10]❶, size_t index❷) {
  if (index >= 10) throw std::out_of_range{ "Out of bounds" }; ❸
  return arr[index]; ❹
}
```

Listing 6-30: A function for accessing array elements with bounds checking

The get function accepts a reference to an int array of length 10 ❶ and an index to extract ❷. If index is out of bounds, it throws an out_of_bounds exception ❸; otherwise, it returns a reference to the corresponding element ❹.

You can improve Listing 6-30 in three ways, which are all enabled by non-type template parameters genericizing the values out of get.

First, you can relax the requirement that arr refer to an int array by making get a template function, as in Listing 6-31.

```
#include <stdexcept>

template <typename T❶>
T&❷ get(T❸ (&arr)[10], size_t index) {
  if (index >= 10) throw std::out_of_range{ "Out of bounds" };
  return arr[index];
}
```

Listing 6-31: A refactor of Listing 6-30 to accept an array of a generic type

As you've done throughout this chapter, you've genericized the function by replacing a concrete type (here, int) with a template parameter ❶❷❸.

Second, you can relax the requirement that arr refer to an array of length 10 by introducing a non-type template parameter Length. Listing 6-32 shows how: simply declare a size_t Length template parameter and use it in place of 10.

```
#include <stdexcept>

template <typename T, size_t Length❶>
T& get (T(&arr)[Length❷], size_t index) {
  if (index >= Length❸) throw std::out_of_range{ "Out of bounds" };
  return arr[index];
}
```

Listing 6-32: A refactor of Listing 6-31 to accept an array of a generic length

The idea is the same: rather than replacing a specific type (`int`), you've replaced a specific integral value (`10`) ❶❷❸. Now you can use the function with arrays of any size.

Third, you can perform compile time bounds checking by taking `size_t index` as another non-type template parameter. This allows you to replace the `std::out_of_range` with a `static_assert`, as in Listing 6-33.

```
#include <cstdio>

template <size_t Index❶, typename T, size_t Length>
T& get(T (&arr)[Length]) {
  static_assert(Index < Length, "Out-of-bounds access"); ❷
  return arr[Index❸];
}

int main() {
  int fib[]{ 1, 1, 2, 0 }; ❹
  printf("%d %d %d ", get<0>(fib), get<1>(fib), get<2>(fib)); ❺
  get<3>(fib) = get<1>(fib) + get<2>(fib); ❻
  printf("%d", get<3>(fib)); ❼
  //printf("%d", get<4>(fib)); ❽
}
--------------------------------------------------------------------------
1 1 2 ❺3 ❼
```

Listing 6-33: A program using compile time bounds-checked array accesses

You've moved the `size_t` index parameter into a non-type template parameter ❶ and updated the array access with the correct name `Index` ❸. Because `Index` is now a compile time constant, you also replace the `logic_error` with a `static_assert`, which prints the friendly message `Out-of-bounds access` whenever you accidentally try to access an out-of-bounds element ❷.

Listing 6-33 also contains example usage of get in `main`. You've first declared an `int` array `fib` of length 4 ❹. You then print the first three elements of the array using get ❺, set the fourth element ❻, and print it ❼. If you uncomment the out-of-bounds access ❽, the compiler will generate an error thanks to the `static_assert`.

Variadic Templates

Sometimes, templates must take in an unknown number of arguments. The compiler knows these arguments at template instantiation, but you want to avoid having to write many different templates each for different numbers of arguments. This is the raison d'être of variadic templates. *Variadic templates* take a variable number of arguments.

You denote variadic templates using a final template parameter that has a special syntax, namely `typename... arguments`. The ellipsis indicates that `arguments` is a *parameter pack type*, meaning you can declare parameter packs within your template. A parameter pack is a template argument that accepts zero or more function arguments. These definitions can seem a bit abstruse, so consider the following sample variadic template that builds upon `SimpleUniquePointer`.

Recall from Listing 6-14 that you pass a raw pointer into the constructor of `SimpleUniquePointer`. Listing 6-34 implements a `make_simple_unique` function that handles construction of the underlying type.

```
template <typename T, typename... Arguments❶>
SimpleUniquePointer<T> make_simple_unique(Arguments... arguments❷) {
  return SimpleUniquePointer<T>{ new T{ arguments...❸ } };
}
```

Listing 6-34: Implementing a `make_simple_unique` function to ease `SimpleUniquePointer` usage

You define the parameter pack type `Arguments` ❶, which declares `make_simple_unique` as a variadic template. This function passes arguments ❷ to the constructor of template parameter `T` ❸.

The upshot is you can now create `SimpleUniquePointers` very easily, even when the pointed-to object has a non-default constructor.

NOTE *There is a slightly more efficient implementation of Listing 6-34. If* `arguments` *is an rvalue, you can move it directly into the constructor of* `T`*. The stdlib contains a function called* `std::forward` *in the* `<utility>` *header that will detect whether* `arguments` *is an lvalue or rvalue and perform a copy or move, respectively. See Item 23 in* Effective Modern C++ *by Scott Meyers.*

Advanced Template Topics

For everyday polymorphic programming, templates are your go-to tool. It turns out that templates are also used in a wide range of advanced settings, especially in implementing libraries, high-performance programs, and embedded system firmware. This section outlines some of the major terrain features of this vast space.

Template Specialization

To understand advanced template usage, you must first understand template specialization. Templates can actually take more than just `concept` and `typename` parameters (type parameters). They can also accept fundamental types, like `char` (value parameters), as well as other templates. Given the tremendous flexibility of template parameters, you can make a lot of compile-time decisions about their features. You could have different versions of templates depending on the characteristics of these parameters. For example, if a type parameter is `Ordered` instead of `Regular`, you might be able to make a generic program more efficient. Programming this way is called *template specialization*. Refer to the ISO standard [temp.spec] for more information about template specialization.

Name Binding

Another critical component of how templates get instantiated is name binding. Name binding helps determine the rules for when the compiler matches a named element within a template to a concrete implementation. The named element could, for example, be part of the template definition, a local name, a global name, or from some named namespace. If you want to write heavily templated code, you need to understand how this binding occurs. If you're in such a situation, refer to Chapter 9, "Names in Templates," in *C++ Templates: The Complete Guide* by David Vandevoorde et al. and to [temp.res].

Type Function

A *type function* takes types as arguments and returns a type. The type traits with which you build up concepts are closely related to type functions. You can combine type functions with compile time control structures to do general computation, such as programming control flow, at compile time. Generally, programming using these techniques is called *template metaprogramming*.

Template Metaprogramming

Template metaprogramming has a deserved reputation for resulting in code that is exceedingly clever and absolutely inscrutable to all but the mightiest of wizards. Fortunately, once concepts are part of the C++ standard, template metaprogramming should become more approachable to us mere mortals. Until then, tread carefully. For those interested in further detail on this topic, refer to *Modern C++ Design: Generic Programming and Design Patterns Applied* by Andrei Alexandrescu and *C++ Templates: The Complete Guide* by David Vandevoorde et al.

Template Source Code Organization

Each time a template is instantiated, the compiler must be able to generate all the code necessary to use the template. This means all the information about how to instantiate a custom class or function must be available within the same translation unit as the template instantiation. By far, the most popular way to achieve this is to implement templates entirely within header files.

There are some modest inconveniences associated with this approach. Compile times can increase, because templates with the same parameters might get instantiated multiple times. It also decreases your ability to hide implementation details. Fortunately, the benefits of generic programming far outweigh these inconveniences. (Major compilers will probably minimize the problems of compile times and code duplication anyway.)

There are even a few advantages to having header-only templates:

- It's very easy for others to use your code: it's a matter of applying `#include` to some headers (rather than compiling the library, ensuring the resulting object files are visible to the linker, and so on).
- It's trivially easy for compilers to inline header-only templates, which can lead to faster code at runtime.
- Compilers can generally do a better job of optimizing code when all of the source is available.

Polymorphism at Runtime vs. Compile Time

When you want polymorphism, you should use templates. But sometimes you can't use templates because you won't know the types used with your code until runtime. Remember that template instantiation only occurs when you pair a template's parameters with types. At this point, the compiler can instantiate a custom class for you. In some situations, you might not be able to perform such pairings until your program is executing (or, at least, performing such pairing at compile time would be tedious).

In such cases, you can use runtime polymorphism. Whereas the template is the mechanism for achieving compile-time polymorphism, the runtime mechanism is the interface.

Summary

In this chapter, you explored polymorphism in C++. The chapter started with a discussion of what polymorphism is and why it's so tremendously useful. You explored how to achieve polymorphism at compile time with templates. You learned about type checking with concepts and then explored some advanced topics, such as variadic templates and template metaprogramming.

EXERCISES

6-1. The mode of a series of values is the value that appears most commonly. Implement a mode function using the following signature: `int mode(const int* values, size_t length)`. If you encounter an error condition, such as input having multiple modes and no values, return zero.

6-2. Implement `mode` as a template function.

6-3. Modify mode to accept an `Integer` concept. Verify that mode fails to instantiate with floating types like `double`.

6-4. Refactor `mean` in Listing 6-13 to accept an array rather than pointer and length arguments. Use Listing 6-33 as a guide.

6-5. Using the example from Chapter 5, make `Bank` a template class that accepts a template parameter. Use this type parameter as the type of an account rather than `long`. Verify that your code still works using a `Bank<long>` class.

6-6. Implement an `Account` class and instantiate a `Bank<Account>`. Implement functions in `Account` to keep track of balances.

6-7. Make `Account` an interface. Implement a `CheckingAccount` and `SavingsAccount`. Create a program with several checking and savings accounts. Use a `Bank<Account>` to make several transactions between the accounts.

FURTHER READING

- *C++ Templates: The Complete Guide*, 2nd Edition, by David Vandevoorde, Nicolai M. Josuttis, and Douglas Gregor (Addison-Wesley, 2017)
- *Effective Modern C++: 42 Specific Ways to Improve Your Use of C++11 and C++14* by Scott Meyers (O'Reilly Media, 2015)
- *The C++ Programming Language*, 4th Edition, by Bjarne Stroustrup (Pearson Education, 2013)
- *Modern C++ Design: Generic Programming and Design Patterns Applied* by Andrei Alexandrescu (Addison-Wesley, 2001)

EXPRESSIONS

Here is the essence of mankind's creative genius: not the edifices of civilization nor the bang-flash weapons which can end it, but the words which fertilize new concepts like spermatozoa attacking an ovum.
—*Dan Simmons,* Hyperion

Expressions are computations that produce results and side effects. Generally, expressions contain operands and operators that do work on them. A number of operators are baked into the core language, and you'll see a majority of them in this chapter. The chapter begins with a discussion of built-in operators before moving on to discuss the overloading operator `new` and user-defined literals and then diving into an exploration of type conversions. When you create your own user-defined types, you'll often need to describe how these types convert into other types. You'll explore these user-defined conversions before learning about `constexpr` constant expressions and the widely misunderstood `volatile` keyword.

Operators

Operators, such as the addition (+) and address-of (&) operators, do work on arguments called operands, such as numerical values or objects. In this section, we'll look at logical, arithmetic, assignment, increment/decrement, comparison, member access, ternary conditional, and comma operators.

Logical Operators

The C++ expression suite includes a full complement of logical operators. Within this category are the (regular) operators AND (`&&`), OR (`||`), and NOT (`!`), which take `bool`-convertible operands and return an object of type `bool`. Also, *bitwise logical operators* work on integral types like `bool`, `int`, and `unsigned long`. These operators include AND (`&`), OR (`|`), XOR (`^`), complement (`~`), left shift (`<<`), and right shift (`>>`). Each performs a Boolean operation at the bit level and returns an integral type matching its operands.

Table 7-1 lists all of these logical operators alongside some examples.

Table 7-1: Logical Operators

Operator	Name	Example expression	Result
`x & y`	Bitwise AND	`0b1100 & 0b1010`	`0b1000`
`x | y`	Bitwise OR	`0b1100 | 0b1010`	`0b1110`
`x ^ y`	Bitwise XOR	`0b1100 ^ 0b1010`	`0b0110`
`~x`	Bitwise complement	`~0b1010`	`0b0101`
`x << y`	Bitwise left shift	`0b1010 << 2` `0b0011 << 4`	`0b101000` `0b110000`
`x >> y`	Bitwise right shift	`0b1010 >> 2` `0b10110011 >> 4`	`0b10` `0b1011`
`x && y`	AND	`true && false` `true && true`	`false` `true`
`x || y`	OR	`true || false` `false || false`	`true` `false`
`!x`	NOT	`!true` `!false`	`false` `true`

Arithmetic Operators

Additional unary and binary *arithmetic operators* work with both integral and floating-point types (also called the *arithmetic types*). You'll use built-in arithmetic operators wherever you need to perform mathematical computations. They perform some of the most basic elements of work, whether you're incrementing an index variable or performing computationally intensive statistical simulations.

Unary Arithmetic Operators

The *unary plus* `+` and *unary minus* `-` operators take a single arithmetic operand. Both operators *promote* their operands to `int`. So, if the operand is of type `bool`, `char`, or `short int`, the result of the expression is an `int`.

Unary plus doesn't do much besides promotion; unary minus, on the other hand, will flip the sign of the operand. For example, given `char x = 10`, `+x` results in an `int` with a value of 10 and `-x` results in an `int` with a value of –10.

Binary Arithmetic Operators

Aside from the two unary arithmetic operators, there are five *binary* arithmetic operators: *addition* `+`, *subtraction* `-`, *multiplication* `*`, *division* `/`, and *modulo* `%`. These operators take two operands and perform the indicated mathematical operation. Like their unary counterparts, these binary operators cause integer promotion on their operands. For example, adding two `char` operands will result in an `int`. There are floating-point promotion rules, too:

- If an operand is `long double`, the other operand is promoted to `long double`.
- If an operand is `double`, the other operand is promoted to `double`.
- If an operand is `float`, the other operand is promoted to `float`.

If none of the floating-point promotion rules apply, you then check whether either argument is signed. If so, both operands become signed. Finally, as with the promotion rules for floating-point types, the size of the largest operand is used to promote the other operand:

- If an operand is `long long`, the other operand is promoted to `long long`.
- If an operand is `long`, the other operand is promoted to `long`.
- If an operand is `int`, the other operand is promoted to `int`.

Although these rules are not too complicated to memorize, I recommend checking your work by leaning on `auto` type deduction. Just assign the result of an expression to an `auto`-declared variable and check the deduced type.

Don't confuse casting and promotion. Casting is when you have an object of one type and need to convert it to another type. Promotion is the set of rules for interpreting literals. For example, if you have a platform with a 2-byte `short` and you performed signed conversion on an `unsigned short` with a value of 40000, the result is an integer overflow and undefined behavior. This is entirely different from processing promotion rules on the literal 40000. If it needs to be signed, the literal's type is signed `int`, because a signed `short` is not large enough to hold such a value.

NOTE *You can use your IDE or even RTTI's* `typeid` *to print the type to console.*

Table 7-2 summarizes the arithmetic operators.

Table 7-2: Arithmetic Operators

Operator	Name	Examples	Result
+x	Unary plus	+10	10
-x	Unary minus	-10	-10
x + y	Binary addition	1 + 2	3
x - y	Binary subtraction	1 - 2	-1
x * y	Binary multiplication	10 * 20	200
x / y	Binary division	300 / 15	20
x % y	Binary modulo	42 % 5	2

Many of the binary operators in Tables 7-1 and 7-2 have corollary as *assignment operators* as well.

Assignment Operators

An assignment operator performs a given operation and then assigns the result to the first operand. For example, the *addition assignment* `x += y` computes the value `x + y` and assigns `x` equal to the result. You can achieve similar results with the expression `x = x + y`, but the *assignment operator* is more syntactically compact and at least as runtime efficient. Table 7-3 summarizes all of the available assignment operators.

Table 7-3: Assignment Operators

Operator	Name	Examples	Result (value of x)
x = y	Simple assignment	x = 10	10
x += y	Addition assignment	x += 10	15
x -= y	Subtraction assignment	x -= 10	-5
x *= y	Multiplication assignment	x *= 10	50
x /= y	Division assignment	x /= 2	2
x %= y	Modulo assignment	x %= 2	1
x &= y	Bitwise AND assignment	x &= 0b1100	0b0100
x |= y	Bitwise OR assignment	x |= 0b1100	0b1101
x ^= y	Bitwise XOR assignment	x ^= 0b1100	0b1001
x <<= y	Bitwise left-shift assignment	x <<= 2	0b10100
x >>= y	Bitwise right-shift assignment	x >>= 2	0b0001

NOTE *Promotion rules don't really apply when using assignment operators; the type of the assigned to operand won't change. For example, given* `int x = 5`*, the type of* `x` *after* `x /= 2.0f` *is still* `int`.

Increment and Decrement Operators

There are four (unary) *increment/decrement* operators, as outlined in Table 7-4.

Table 7-4: The Increment and Decrement Operators (values given for x=5)

Operator	Name	Value of x after evaluation	Value of expression
++x	Prefix increment	6	6
x++	Postfix increment	6	5
--x	Prefix decrement	4	4
x--	Postfix decrement	4	5

As Table 7-4 shows, increment operators increase the value of their operand by 1, whereas decrement operators decrease by 1. The value returned by the operator depends on whether it is prefix or postfix. A prefix operator will return the value of the operand after modification, whereas a postfix operator will return the value before modification.

Comparison Operators

Six comparison operators compare the given operands and evaluate to a `bool`, as outlined in Table 7-5. For arithmetic operands, the same type conversions (promotions) occur as with the arithmetic operators. The comparison operators also work with pointers, and they work approximately how you would expect them to.

NOTE *There are some nuances to pointer comparison. Interested readers should refer to* [expr.rel].

Table 7-5: The Comparison Operators

Operator	Name	Examples (all evaluate to `true`)
x == y	Equal-to operator	`100 == 100`
x != y	Not-equal-to operator	`100 != 101`
x < y	Less-than operator	`10 < 20`
x > y	Greater-than operator	`-10 > -20`
x <= y	Less-than-or-equal-to operator	`10 <= 10`
x >= y	Greater-than-or-equal-to operator	`20 >= 10`

Member Access Operators

You use *member access operators* to interact with pointers, arrays, and many of the classes you'll meet in Part II. The six such operators include *subscript* `[]`, *indirection* `*`, *address-of* `&`, *member-of-object* `.`, and *member-of-pointer* `->`. You met these operators in Chapter 3, but this section provides a brief summary.

NOTE *There are also* pointer-to-member-of-object `.*` *and* pointer-to-member-of-pointer `->*` *operators, but these are uncommon. Refer to [expr.mptr.oper].*

The subscript operator `x[y]` provides access to the yth element of the array pointed to by `x`, whereas the indirection operator `*x` provides access to the element pointed to by `x`. You can create a pointer to an element `x` using the address-of operator `&x`. This is essentially the inverse operation to the indirection operator. For elements `x` with a member `y`, you use the member-of-object operator `x.y`. You can also access members of a pointed-to object; given a pointer `x`, you use the member-of-pointer operator `x->y` to access an object pointed to by `x`.

Ternary Conditional Operator

The *ternary conditional operator* `x ? y : z` is a lump of syntactic sugar that takes three operands (hence "ternary"). It evaluates the first operand `x` as a Boolean expression and returns the second operand `y` or the third operand `z` depending on whether the Boolean is `true` or `false` (respectively). Consider the following step function that returns 1 if the parameter `input` is positive; otherwise, it returns zero:

```
int step(int input) {
  return input > 0 ? 1 : 0;
}
```

Using an equivalent if-then statement, you could also implement `step` the following way:

```
int step(int input) {
  if (input > 0) {
    return 1;
  } else {
    return 0;
  }
}
```

These two approaches are runtime equivalent, but the ternary conditional operator requires less typing and usually results in cleaner code. Use it generously.

NOTE *The conditional ternary operator has a more fashionable moniker: the* Elvis operator. *If you rotate the book 90 degrees clockwise and squint, you'll see why:* `?:`

The Comma Operator

The *comma operator*, on the other hand, doesn't usually promote cleaner code. It allows several expressions separated by commas to be evaluated within a larger expression. The expressions evaluate from left to right, and the rightmost expression is the return value, as Listing 7-1 illustrates.

```
#include <cstdio>

int confusing(int &x) {
  return x = 9, x++, x / 2;
}

int main() {
  int x{}; ❶
  auto y = confusing(x); ❷
  printf("x: %d\ny: %d", x, y);
}
--------------------------------------------------------------------------
x: 10
y: 5
```

Listing 7-1: A confusing function employing the comma operator

After invoking `confusing`, `x` equals `10` ❶ and `y` equals `5` ❷.

NOTE *A vestigial structure from C's wilder and altogether less-inhibited college days, the comma operator permits a particular kind of expression-oriented programming. Eschew the comma operator; its use is exceedingly uncommon and likely to sow confusion.*

Operator Overloading

For each fundamental type, some portion of the operators covered in this section will be available. For user-defined types, you can specify custom behavior for these operators by employing *operator overloading*. To specify behavior for an operator in a user-defined class, simply name the method with the word `operator` immediately followed by the operator; ensure that the return types and parameters match the types of the operands you want to deal with.

Listing 7-2 defines a `CheckedInteger`.

```
#include <stdexcept>

struct CheckedInteger {
  CheckedInteger(unsigned int value) : value{ value } ❶ { }

  CheckedInteger operator+(unsigned int other) const { ❷
    CheckedInteger result{ value + other }; ❸
    if (result.value < value) throw std::runtime_error{ "Overflow!" }; ❹
    return result;
  }

  const unsigned int value; ❺
};
```

Listing 7-2: A `CheckedInteger` class that detects overflow at runtime

In this class, you've defined a constructor that takes a single `unsigned int`. This argument is used ❶ to member initialize the private field `value` ❺. Because `value` is `const`, `CheckedInteger` is *immutable*—after construction, it's not possible to modify the state of a `CheckedInteger`. The method of interest here is `operator+` ❷, which allows you to add an ordinary `unsigned int` to a `CheckedInteger` to produce a new `CheckedInteger` with the correct `value`. The return value of `operator+` is constructed at ❸. Whenever addition results in the overflow of an `unsigned int`, the result will be less than the original values. You check for this condition at ❹. If an overflow is detected, you throw an exception.

Chapter 6 described `type_traits`, which allow you to determine features of your types at compile time. A related family of type support is available in the `<limits>` header, which allows you to query various properties of arithmetic types.

Within `<limits>`, the template class `numeric_limits` exposes a number of member constants that provide information about the template parameter. One such example is the `max()` method, which returns the highest finite value of a given type. You can use this method to kick the tires of the `CheckedInteger` class. Listing 7-3 illustrates the behavior of the `CheckedInteger`.

```
#include <limits>
#include <cstdio>
#include <stdexcept>

struct CheckedInteger {
  --snip--
};

int main() {
  CheckedInteger a{ 100 }; ❶
  auto b = a + 200; ❷
  printf("a + 200 = %u\n", b.value);
  try {
    auto c = a + std::numeric_limits<unsigned int>::max(); ❸
  } catch(const std::overflow_error& e) {
    printf("(a + max) Exception: %s\n", e.what());
  }
}
```

```
a + 200 = 300
(a + max) Exception: Overflow!
```

Listing 7-3: A program illustrating the use of `CheckedInteger`

After constructing a `CheckedInteger` ❶, you can add it to an `unsigned int` ❷. Because the resulting value, 300, is guaranteed to fit inside an `unsigned int`, this statement executes without throwing an exception. Next, you add the same `CheckedInteger a` to the maximum value of an `unsigned int` via `numeric_limits` ❸. This causes an overflow, which is detected by the `operator+` overload and results in a thrown `overflow_error`.

Overloading Operator new

Recall from Chapter 4 that you allocate objects with dynamic storage duration using operator `new`. By default, operator `new` will allocate memory on the free store to make space for your dynamic objects. The *free store*, also known as the *heap*, is an implementation-defined storage location. On desktop operating systems, the kernel usually manages the free store (see the `HeapAlloc` on Windows and `malloc` on Linux and macOS) and is generally vast.

Free Store Availability

In some environments, like the Windows kernel or embedded systems, there is no free store available to you by default. In other settings, such as game development or high-frequency trading, free store allocations simply involve too much latency, because you've delegated its management to the operating system.

You could try to avoid using the free store entirely, but this is severely limiting. One major limitation this would introduce is to preclude the use of stdlib containers, which after reading Part II you'll agree is a major loss. Rather than settling for these severe restrictions, you can overload the free store operations and take control over allocations. You do this by overloading operator `new`.

The <new> Header

In environments that support free store operations, the `<new>` header contains the following four operators:

- `void* operator new(size_t);`
- `void operator delete(void*);`
- `void* operator new[](size_t);`
- `void operator delete[](void*);`

Notice that the return type of operator `new` is `void*`. The free store operators deal in raw, uninitialized memory.

It's possible to provide your own versions of these four operators. All you do is define them once in your program. The compiler will use your versions rather than the defaults.

Free store management is a surprisingly complicated task. One of the major issues is *memory fragmentation*. Over time, large numbers of memory allocations and releases can leave free blocks of memory scattered throughout the region dedicated for the free store. It's possible to get into situations where there is plenty of free memory, but it's scattered across allocated memory. When this happens, large requests for memory will fail, even though there is technically enough free memory to provide to the requester. Figure 7-1 illustrates such a situation. There is plenty of memory for the desired allocation, but the available memory is noncontiguous.

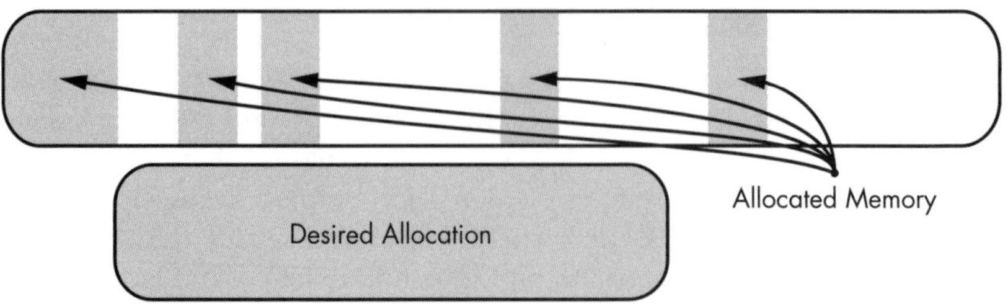

Figure 7-1: The memory fragmentation problem

Buckets

One approach is to chop allocated memory into so-called *buckets* of a fixed size. When you request memory, the environment allocates a whole bucket, even if you didn't request all the memory. For example, Windows provides two functions for allocating dynamic memory: `VirtualAllocEx` and `HeapAlloc`.

The `VirtualAllocEx` function is low level, which allows you to provide many options, such as which process to allocate memory into, the preferred memory address, the requested size, and permissions, like whether the memory should be readable, writable, and executable. This function will never allocate fewer than 4096 bytes (a so-called *page*).

On the other hand, `HeapAlloc` is a higher-level function that hands out less than a page of memory when it can; otherwise, it will invoke `VirtualAllocEx` on your behalf. At least with the Visual Studio compiler, `new` will call `HeapAlloc` by default.

This arrangement prevents memory fragmentation in exchange for some overhead associated with rounding up allocations to bucket size. Modern operating systems like Windows will have fairly complex schemes for allocating memory of different sizes. You don't see any of this complexity unless you want to take control.

Taking Control of the Free Store

Listing 7-4 demonstrates implementing very simple `Bucket` and `Heap` classes. These will facilitate taking control over dynamic memory allocation:

```
#include <cstddef>
#include <new>

struct Bucket { ❶
  const static size_t data_size{ 4096 };
  std::byte data[data_size];
};

struct Heap {
  void* allocate(size_t bytes) { ❷
    if (bytes > Bucket::data_size) throw std::bad_alloc{};
    for (size_t i{}; i < n_heap_buckets; i++) {
      if (!bucket_used[i]) {
        bucket_used[i] = true;
        return buckets[i].data;
```

```
      }
    }
    throw std::bad_alloc{};
  }

  void free(void* p) { ❸
    for (size_t i{}; i < n_heap_buckets; i++) {
      if (buckets[i].data == p) {
        bucket_used[i] = false;
        return;
      }
    }
  }
  static const size_t n_heap_buckets{ 10 };
  Bucket buckets[n_heap_buckets]{}; ❹
  bool bucket_used[n_heap_buckets]{}; ❺
};
```

Listing 7-4: Heap and Bucket classes

The Bucket class ❶ is responsible for taking up space in memory. As an homage to the Windows heap manager, the bucket size is hardcoded to 4096. All of the management logic goes into the Heap class.

Two important accounting members are in Heap: buckets ❹ and bucket_used ❺. The buckets member houses all the Buckets, neatly packed into a contiguous string. The bucket_used member is a relatively tiny array containing objects of type bool that keeps track of whether a Bucket in buckets with the same index has been loaned out yet. Both members are initialized to zero.

The Heap class has two methods: allocate ❷ and free ❸. The allocate method first checks whether the number of bytes requested is greater than the bucket size. If it is, it throws a std::bad_alloc exception. Once the size check passes, Heap iterates through the buckets looking for one that isn't marked true in bucket_used. If it finds one, it returns the data member pointer for the associated Bucket. If it can't find an unused Bucket, it throws a std::bad_alloc exception. The free method accepts a void* and iterates through all the buckets looking for a matching data member pointer. If it finds one, it sets bucket_used for the corresponding bucket to false and returns.

Using Our Heap

One way to allocate a Heap is to declare it at namespace scope so it has static storage duration. Because its lifetime begins when the program starts, you can use it inside the operator new and operator delete overrides, as shown in Listing 7-5.

```
Heap heap; ❶

void* operator new(size_t n_bytes) {
  return heap.allocate(n_bytes); ❷
}
```

```
void operator delete(void* p) {
  return heap.free(p); ❸
}
```

Listing 7-5: Overriding the new *and* delete *operators to use the* Heap *class from Listing 7-4*

Listing 7-5 declares a Heap ❶ and uses it inside the operator new overload ❷ and the operator delete overload ❸. Now if you use new and delete, dynamic memory management will use heap instead of the default free store offered by the environment. Listing 7-6 kicks the tires of the overloaded dynamic memory management.

```
#include <cstdio>
--snip--
int main() {
  printf("Buckets:   %p\n", heap.buckets); ❶
  auto breakfast = new unsigned int{ 0xC0FFEE };
  auto dinner = new unsigned int { 0xDEADBEEF };
  printf("Breakfast: %p 0x%x\n", breakfast, *breakfast); ❷
  printf("Dinner:    %p 0x%x\n", dinner, *dinner); ❸
  delete breakfast;
  delete dinner;
  try {
    while (true) {
      new char;
      printf("Allocated a char.\n"); ❹
    }
  } catch (const std::bad_alloc&) {
    printf("std::bad_alloc caught.\n"); ❺
  }
}
--------------------------------------------------------------------------
Buckets:   00007FF792EE3320 ❶
Breakfast: 00007FF792EE3320 0xc0ffee ❷
Dinner:    00007FF792EE4320 0xdeadbeef ❸
Allocated a char. ❹
Allocated a char.
Allocated a char.
Allocated a char.
Allocated a char.
Allocated a char.
Allocated a char.
Allocated a char.
Allocated a char.
Allocated a char.
std::bad_alloc caught. ❺
```

Listing 7-6: A program illustrating the use of Heap *to manage dynamic allocations*

You've printed the memory address of the first buckets element of the heap ❶. This is the memory location loaned out to the first new invocation. You verify that this is the case by printing the memory address and value pointed to by breakfast ❷. Notice that the memory address matches the memory address of the first Bucket in heap. You've done the same for the memory pointed to by `dinner` ❸. Notice that the memory address is exactly `0x1000` greater than that of `breakfast`. This coincides exactly with the 4096-byte length of a `Bucket`, as defined in the `const static` member `Bucket::data_size`.

After printing ❷❸, you delete `breakfast` and `dinner`. Then, you allocate `char` objects with reckless abandon until a `std::bad_alloc` is thrown when `heap` runs out of memory. Each time you make an allocation, you print `Allocated a char.` starting at ❹. There are 10 lines before you see a `std::bad_alloc` exception ❺. Notice that this is exactly the number of buckets you've set in `Heap::n_heap_buckets`. This means that, for each `char` you've allocated, you've taken up 4096 bytes of memory!

Placement Operators

Sometimes, you don't want to override *all* free store allocations. In such situations, you can use the placement operators, which perform the appropriate initialization on preallocated memory:

- `void* operator new(size_t, void*);`
- `void operator delete(size_t, void*);`
- `void* operator new[](void*, void*);`
- `void operator delete[](void*, void*);`

Using placement operators, you can manually construct objects in arbitrary memory. This has the advantage of enabling you to manually manipulate an object's lifetime. However, you cannot use `delete` to release the resulting dynamic objects. You must call the object's destructor directly (and exactly once!), as demonstrated in Listing 7-7.

```
#include <cstdio>
#include <cstddef>
#include <new>

struct Point {
  Point() : x{}, y{}, z{} {
    printf("Point at %p constructed.\n", this); ❶
  }
  ~Point() {
    printf("Point at %p destructed.\n", this); ❷
  }
  double x, y, z;
};

int main() {
  const auto point_size = sizeof(Point);
  std::byte data[3 * point_size];
  printf("Data starts at %p.\n", data); ❸
  auto point1 = new(&data[0 * point_size]) Point{}; ❹
  auto point2 = new(&data[1 * point_size]) Point{}; ❺
  auto point3 = new(&data[2 * point_size]) Point{}; ❻
  point1->~Point(); ❼
```

```
  point2->~Point(); ❽
  point3->~Point(); ❾
}
--------------------------------------------------------------------------
Data starts at 0000004D290FF8E8. ❸
Point at 0000004D290FF8E8 constructed. ❹
Point at 0000004D290FF900 constructed. ❺
Point at 0000004D290FF918 constructed. ❻
Point at 0000004D290FF8E8 destructed. ❼
Point at 0000004D290FF900 destructed. ❽
Point at 0000004D290FF918 destructed. ❾
```

Listing 7-7: Using placement new to initialize dynamic objects

The constructor ❶ prints a message indicating that a `Point` at a particular address was constructed, and the destructor ❷ prints a corresponding message indicating that the `Point` is getting destructed. You've printed the address of `data`, which is the first address where placement `new` initializes a `Point` ❸.

Observe that each placement `new` has allocated the `Point` within the memory occupied by your `data` array ❹❺❻. You must invoke each destructor individually ❼❽❾.

Operator Precedence and Associativity

When more than one operator appears in an expression, *operator precedence* and *operator associativity* decide how the expression parses. Operators with higher precedence are bound tighter to their arguments than operators with lower precedence. If two operators have the same precedence, their associativity breaks the tie to decide how arguments bind. Associativity is either *left to right* or *right to left*.

Table 7-6 contains every C++ operator sorted by its precedence and annotated with its associativity. Each row contains one or more operators with the same precedence along with a description and its associativity. Higher rows have higher precedence.

Table 7-6: Operator Precedence and Associativity

Operator	Description	Associativity
`a::b`	Scope resolution	Left to right

`a++`
`a--`
`fn()`
`a[b]`
`a->b`
`a.b`
`Type(a)`
`Type{ a }`
	Postfix increment
	Postfix decrement
	Function call
	Subscript
	Member of pointer
	Member of object
	Functional cast
	Functional cast
		Left to right

<table>
<tr><th>Operator</th><th>Description</th><th>Associativity</th></tr>
<tr><td>++a</td><td>Prefix increment</td><td>Right to left</td></tr>
<tr><td>--a</td><td>Prefix decrement</td><td></td></tr>
<tr><td>+a</td><td>Unary plus</td><td></td></tr>
<tr><td>-a</td><td>Unary minus</td><td></td></tr>
<tr><td>!a</td><td>Logical NOT</td><td></td></tr>
<tr><td>~a</td><td>Bitwise complement</td><td></td></tr>
<tr><td>(Type)a</td><td>C-style cast</td><td></td></tr>
<tr><td>*a</td><td>Dereference</td><td></td></tr>
<tr><td>&a</td><td>Address of</td><td></td></tr>
<tr><td>sizeof(Type)</td><td>Size of</td><td></td></tr>
<tr><td>new Type</td><td>Dynamic allocation</td><td></td></tr>
<tr><td>new Type[]</td><td>Dynamic allocation (array)</td><td></td></tr>
<tr><td>delete a</td><td>Dynamic deallocation</td><td></td></tr>
<tr><td>delete[] a</td><td>Dynamic deallocation (array)</td><td></td></tr>
<tr><td>.*</td><td>Pointer-to-member-of-pointer</td><td>Left to right</td></tr>
<tr><td>->*</td><td>Pointer-to-member-of-object</td><td></td></tr>
<tr><td>a * b</td><td>Multiplication</td><td>Left to right</td></tr>
<tr><td>a / b</td><td>Division</td><td></td></tr>
<tr><td>a % b</td><td>Modulo division</td><td></td></tr>
<tr><td>a + b</td><td>Addition</td><td>Left to right</td></tr>
<tr><td>a - b</td><td>Subtraction</td><td></td></tr>
<tr><td>a << b</td><td>Bitwise left shift</td><td>Left to right</td></tr>
<tr><td>a >> b</td><td>Bitwise right shift</td><td></td></tr>
<tr><td>a < b</td><td>Less than</td><td>Left to right</td></tr>
<tr><td>a > b</td><td>Greater than</td><td></td></tr>
<tr><td>a <= b</td><td>Less than or equal to</td><td></td></tr>
<tr><td>a >= b</td><td>Greater than or equal to</td><td></td></tr>
<tr><td>a == b</td><td>Equals</td><td>Left to right</td></tr>
<tr><td>a != b</td><td>Not equals</td><td></td></tr>
<tr><td>a & b</td><td>Bitwise AND</td><td>Left to right</td></tr>
<tr><td>a ^ b</td><td>Bitwise AND</td><td>Left to right</td></tr>
<tr><td>a | b</td><td>Bitwise OR</td><td>Left to right</td></tr>
<tr><td>a && b</td><td>Logical AND</td><td>Left to right</td></tr>
<tr><td>a || b</td><td>Logical OR</td><td>Left to right</td></tr>
<tr><td>a ? b : c</td><td>Ternary</td><td>Right to left</td></tr>
<tr><td>throw a</td><td>Throw</td><td></td></tr>
<tr><td>a = b</td><td>Assignment</td><td></td></tr>
<tr><td>a += b</td><td>Sum assignment</td><td></td></tr>
<tr><td>a -= b</td><td>Difference assignment</td><td></td></tr>
<tr><td>a *= b</td><td>Product assignment</td><td></td></tr>
<tr><td>a /= b</td><td>Quotient assignment</td><td></td></tr>
<tr><td>a %= b</td><td>Remainder assignment</td><td></td></tr>
<tr><td>a <<= b</td><td>Bitwise-left-shift assignment</td><td></td></tr>
<tr><td>a >>= b</td><td>Bitwise-right-shift assignment</td><td></td></tr>
<tr><td>a &= b</td><td>Bitwise AND assignment</td><td></td></tr>
<tr><td>a ^= b</td><td>Bitwise XOR assignment</td><td></td></tr>
<tr><td>a |= b</td><td>Bitwise OR assignment</td><td></td></tr>
<tr><td>a, b</td><td>Comma</td><td>Left to right</td></tr>
</table>

NOTE *You haven't yet met the scope resolution operator (it first appears in Chapter 8), but Table 7-6 includes it for completeness.*

Because C++ has many operators, the operator precedence and associativity rules can be hard to keep track of. For the mental health of those reading your code, try to make expressions as clear as possible.

Consider the following expression:

```
*a++ + b * c
```

Because postfix addition has higher precedence than the dereference operator `*`, it binds first to the argument `a`, meaning the result of `a++` is the argument to the dereference operator. Multiplication `*` has higher precedence than addition `+`, so the multiplication operator `*` binds to `b` and `c`, and the addition operator `+` binds to the results of `*a++` and `b * c`.

You can impose precedence within an expression by adding parentheses, which have higher precedence than any operator. For example, you can rewrite the preceding expression using parentheses:

```
(*(a++)) + (b * c)
```

As a general rule, add parentheses wherever a reader could become confused about operator precedence. If the result is a bit ugly (as in this example), your expression is probably too complicated; you might consider breaking it up into multiple statements.

Evaluation Order

Evaluation order determines the execution sequence of operators in an expression. A common misconception is that precedence and evaluation order are equivalent: they are not. *Precedence* is a compile time concept that drives how operators bind to operands. *Evaluation order* is a runtime concept that drives the scheduling of operator execution.

In general, C++ has no clearly specified execution order for operands. Although operators bind to operands in the well-defined way explained in the preceding sections, those operands evaluate in an undefined order. The compiler can order operand evaluation however it likes.

You might be tempted to think that the parentheses in the following expression drive evaluation order for the functions `stop`, `drop`, and `roll`, or that some left-to-right associativity has some runtime effect:

```
(stop() + drop()) + roll()
```

They do not. The `roll` function might execute before, after, or between evaluations of `stop` and `drop`. If you require operations to execute in a specific order, simply place them into separate statements in the desired sequence, as shown here:

```
auto result = stop();
result = result + drop();
result = result + roll();
```

If you aren't careful, you can even get undefined behavior. Consider the following expression:

```
b = ++a + a;
```

Because the ordering of the expressions `++a` and `a` is not specified, and because the value of `++a + a` depends on which expression evaluates first, the value of `b` cannot be well defined.

In some special situations, execution order is specified by the language. The most commonly encountered scenarios are as follows:

- The built-in logical AND operator `a && b` and built-in logical OR operator `a || b` guarantee that `a` executes before `b`.
- The ternary operator `a ? b : c` guarantees that `a` executes before `b` and `c`.
- The comma operator `a, b` guarantees that `a` executes before `b`.
- The constructor arguments in a `new` expression evaluate before the call to the allocator function.

You might be wondering why C++ doesn't enforce execution order, say from left to right, to avoid confusion. The answer is simply that by not arbitrarily constraining execution order, the language is allowing compiler writers to find clever optimization opportunities.

NOTE *For more information on execution order, see [expr].*

User-Defined Literals

Chapter 2 covered how to declare literals, constant values that you use directly in your programs. These help the compiler to turn embedded values into the desired types. Each fundamental type has its own syntax for literals. For example, a `char` literal is declared in single quotes like `'J'`, whereas a `wchar_t` is declared with an `L` prefix like `L'J'`. You can specify the precision of floating-point numbers using either the `F` or `L` suffix.

For convenience, you can also make your own *user-defined literals*. As with the baked-in literals, these provide you with some syntactical support for giving type information to the compiler. Although you'd rarely ever need to declare a user-defined literal, it's worth mentioning because you might find them in libraries. The stdlib `<chrono>` header uses literals extensively to give programmers a clean syntax for using time types—for example, `700ms` denotes 700 milliseconds. Because user-defined literals are fairly rare, I won't cover them in any more detail here.

NOTE *For further reference, see Section 19.2.6 of* The C++ Programming Language, *4th Edition, by Bjarne Stroustrup.*

Type Conversions

You perform type conversions when you have one type but want to convert it to another type. Depending on the situation, type conversions can be explicit or implicit. This section treats both sorts of conversions while covering promotions, floating-point-to-integer conversions, integer-to-integer conversions, and floating-point-to-floating-point conversions.

Type conversions are fairly common. For example, you might need to compute the mean of some integers given a count and a sum. Because the count and sum are stored in variables of integral type (and you don't want to truncate fractional values), you'll want to compute the mean as a floating-point number. To do this, you'll need to use type conversion.

Implicit Type Conversions

Implicit type conversions can occur anywhere a particular type is called for but you provide a different type. These conversions occur in several different contexts.

"Binary Arithmetic Operators" on page 183 outlined so-called *promotion rules*. In fact, these are a form of implicit conversion. Whenever an arithmetic operation occurs, shorter integral types are promoted to `int` types. Integral types can also be promoted to floating-point types during arithmetic operation. All of this happens in the background. The result is that, in most situations, the type system simply gets out of your way so you can focus on programming logic.

Unfortunately, in some situations, C++ is a bit overzealous in silently converting types. Consider the following implicit conversion from a `double` to a `uint_8`:

```
#include <cstdint>

int main() {
  auto x = 2.7182818284590452353602874713527L;
  uint8_t y = x; // Silent truncation
}
```

You should hope that the compiler will generate a warning here, but technically this is valid C++. Because this conversion loses information, it's a narrowing conversion that would be prevented by braced initialization {}:

```
#include <cstdint>

int main() {
```

```
  auto x = 2.7182818284590452353602874713527L;
  uint8_t y{ x }; // Bang!
}
```

Recall that braced initialization doesn't permit narrowing conversions. Technically, the braced initializer is an explicit conversion, so I'll discuss that in "Explicit Type Conversion" on page 201.

Floating-Point-to-Integer Conversion

Floating-point and integral types can coexist peacefully within arithmetic expressions. The reason is implicit type conversion: when the compiler encounters mixed types, it performs the necessary promotions so arithmetic proceeds as expected.

Integer-to-Integer Conversion

Integers can be converted into other integer types. If the destination type is `signed`, all is well, as long as the value can be represented. If it cannot, the behavior is implementation defined. If the destination type is `unsigned`, the result is as many bits as can fit into the type. In other words, the high-order bits are lost.

Consider the example in Listing 7-8, which demonstrates how you can get undefined behavior resulting from signed conversion.

```
#include <cstdint>
#include <cstdio>

int main() {
  // 0b111111111 = 511
  uint8_t x = 0b111111111; ❶// 255
  int8_t y =  0b111111111; ❷// Implementation defined.
  printf("x: %u\ny: %d", x, y);
}
--------------------------------------------------------------------------
x: 255 ❶
y: -1 ❷
```

Listing 7-8: Undefined behavior resulting from signed conversion

Listing 7-8 implicitly casts an integer that is too big to fit in an 8-bit integer (511, or 9 bits of ones) into `x` and `y`, which are `unsigned` and `signed`. The value of `x` is guaranteed to be 255 ❶, whereas the value of `y` is implementation dependent. On a Windows 10 x64 machine, `y` equals `-1` ❷. The assignment of both `x` and `y` involve narrowing conversions that could be avoided using the braced initialization syntax.

Floating-Point-to-Floating-Point Conversions

Floating-point numbers can be implicitly cast to and from other floating-point numbers. As long as the destination value can fit the source value, all is well. When it cannot, you have undefined behavior. Again, braced initialization can prevent potentially dangerous conversions. Consider the example in Listing 7-9, which demonstrates undefined behavior resulting from a narrowing conversion.

```
#include <limits>
#include <cstdio>

int main() {
  double x = std::numeric_limits<float>::max(); ❶
  long double y = std::numeric_limits<double>::max(); ❷
  float z = std::numeric_limits<long double>::max(); ❸  // Undefined Behavior
  printf("x: %g\ny: %Lg\nz: %g", x, y, z);
}
```

```
x: 3.40282e+38
y: 1.79769e+308
z: inf
```

Listing 7-9: Undefined behavior resulting from narrowing conversion

You have completely safe implicit conversions from `float` to `double` ❶ and `double` to `long double` ❷ respectively. Unfortunately, assigning the maximum value of a `long double` to a `float` results in undefined behavior ❸.

Conversion to bool

Pointers, integers, and floating-point numbers can all be implicitly converted to `bool` objects. If the value is nonzero, the result of implicit conversion is `true`. Otherwise, the result is `false`. For example, the value `int{ 1 }` converts to `true`, and the value `int{}` converts to `false`.

Pointer to void*

Pointers can always be implicitly converted to `void*`, as demonstrated in Listing 7-10.

```
#include <cstdio>

void print_addr(void* x) {
  printf("0x%p\n", x);
}

int main() {
  int x{};
  print_addr(&x); ❶
  print_addr(nullptr); ❷
}
```

```
0x000000F79DCFFB74 ❶
0x0000000000000000 ❷
```

Listing 7-10: Implicit pointer conversion to void. Output is from a Windows 10 x64 machine.*

Listing 7-10 compiles thanks to the pointers' implicit conversion to void*. The address refers to the address of x ❶ and prints 0 ❷.

Explicit Type Conversion

Explicit type conversions are also called *casts*. The first port of call for conducting an explicit type conversion is braced initialization {}. This approach has the major benefit of being fully type safe and non-narrowing. The use of braced initialization ensures at compile time that only safe, well-behaved, non-narrowing conversions are allowed. Listing 7-11 shows an example.

```
#include <cstdio>
#include <cstdint>

int main() {
  int32_t a = 100;
  int64_t b{ a }; ❶
  if (a == b) printf("Non-narrowing conversion!\n"); ❷
  //int32_t c{ b }; // Bang! ❸
}
--------------------------------------------------------------------------
Non-narrowing conversion! ❷
```

Listing 7-11: Explicit type conversion for 4- and 8-byte integers

This simple example uses braced initialization ❶ to build an int64_t from an int32_t. This is a well-behaved conversion because you're guaranteed not to have lost any information. You can always store 32 bits inside 64 bits. After a well-behaved conversion of a fundamental type, the original will always equal the result (according to operator==).

The example attempts a badly behaved (narrowing) conversion ❸. The compiler will generate an error. If you hadn't used the braced initializer {}, the compiler wouldn't have complained, as demonstrated in Listing 7-12.

```
#include <limits>
#include <cstdio>
#include <cstdint>

int main() {
  int64_t b = std::numeric_limits<int64_t>::max();
  int32_t c(b); ❶ // The compiler abides.
  if (c != b) printf("Narrowing conversion!\n"); ❷
}
--------------------------------------------------------------------------
Narrowing conversion! ❷
```

Listing 7-12: A refactor of Listing 7-11 without the braced initializer.

You make a narrowing conversion from a 64-bit integer to a 32-bit integer ❶. Because this narrows, the expression c != b evaluates to true ❷. This behavior is very dangerous, which is why Chapter 2 recommends using the braced initializer as much as possible.

C-Style Casts

Recall from Chapter 6 that the named conversion functions allow you to perform dangerous casts that braced initialization won't permit. You can also perform C-style casts, but this is done mainly to maintain some compatibility between the languages. Their usage is as follows:

```
(desired-type)object-to-cast
```

For each C-style cast, there exists some incantation of `static_casts`, `const_casts`, and `reinterpret_casts` that would achieve the desired type conversion. C-style casts are far more dangerous than the named casts (and this is saying quite a bit).

The syntax of the C++ explicit casts is intentionally ugly and verbose. This calls attention to a point in the code where the rigid rules of the type system are being bent or broken. The C-style cast doesn't do this. In addition, it's not clear from the cast what kind of conversion the programmer is intending. When you use finer instruments like the named casts, the compiler can at least enforce *some* constraints. For example, it's all too easy to forget `const` correctness when using a C-style cast when you only intended a `reinterpret_cast`.

Suppose you wanted to treat a `const char*` array as unsigned within the body of a function. It would be too easy to write code like that demonstrated in Listing 7-13.

```
#include <cstdio>

void trainwreck(const char* read_only) {
  auto as_unsigned = (unsigned char*)read_only;
  *as_unsigned = 'b'; ❶ // Crashes on Windows 10 x64
}

int main() {
  auto ezra = "Ezra";
  printf("Before trainwreck: %s\n", ezra);
  trainwreck(ezra);
  printf("After trainwreck: %s\n", ezra);
}
--------------------------------------------------------------------------
Before trainwreck: Ezra
```

Listing 7-13: A train wreck of a C-style cast that accidentally gets rid of the const qualifier on `read_only`. (This program has undefined behavior; output is from a Windows 10 x64 machine.)

Modern operating systems enforce memory access patterns. Listing 7-13 attempts to write into the memory storing the string literal `Ezra` ❶. On Windows 10 x64, this crashes the program with a memory access violation (it's read-only memory).

If you tried this with a `reinterpret_cast`, the compiler would generate an error, as Listing 7-14 demonstrates.

```
#include <cstdio>

void trainwreck(const char* read_only) {
  auto as_unsigned = reinterpret_cast<unsigned char*>(read_only); ❶
  *as_unsigned = 'b'; // Crashes on Windows 10 x64
}

int main() {
  auto ezra = "Ezra";
  printf("Before trainwreck: %s\n", ezra);
  trainwreck(ezra);
  printf("After trainwreck: %s\n", ezra);
}
```

Listing 7-14: A refactor of Listing 7-13 using a `static_cast`. (This code does not compile.)

If you really intended to throw away `const` correctness, you'd need to tack on a `const_cast` here ❶. The code would self-document these intentions and make such intentional rule breakages easy to find.

User-Defined Type Conversions

In user-defined types, you can provide user-defined conversion functions. These functions tell the compiler how your user-defined types behave during implicit and explicit type conversion. You can declare these conversion functions using the following usage pattern:

```
struct MyType {
  operator destination-type() const {
    // return a destination-type from here.
  --snip--
  }
}
```

For example, the struct in Listing 7-15 can be used like a read-only `int`.

```
struct ReadOnlyInt {
  ReadOnlyInt(int val) : val{ val } { }
  operator int() const { ❶
    return val;
  }
private:
  const int val;
};
```

Listing 7-15: A `ReadOnlyInt` class containing a user-defined type conversion to an `int`

The `operator int` method at ❶ defines the user-defined type conversion *from* a `ReadOnlyInt` *to* an `int`. You can now use `ReadOnlyInt` types just like regular `int` types thanks to implicit conversion:

```
struct ReadOnlyInt {
  --snip--
```

```
};
int main() {
  ReadOnlyInt the_answer{ 42 };
  auto ten_answers = the_answer * 10; // int with value 420
}
```

Sometimes, implicit conversions can cause surprising behavior. You should always try to use explicit conversions, especially with user-defined types. You can achieve explicit conversions with the `explicit` keyword. Explicit constructors instruct the compiler not to consider the constructor as a means for implicit conversion. You can provide the same guidelines for your user-defined conversion functions:

```
struct ReadOnlyInt {
  ReadOnlyInt(int val) : val{ val } { }
  explicit operator int() const {
    return val;
  }
private:
  const int val;
};
```

Now, you must explicitly cast a `ReadOnlyInt` to an `int` using `static_cast`:

```
struct ReadOnlyInt {
  --snip--
};
int main() {
  ReadOnlyInt the_answer{ 42 };
  auto ten_answers = static_cast<int>(the_answer) * 10;
}
```

Generally, this approach tends to promote less ambiguous code.

Constant Expressions

Constant expressions are expressions that can be evaluated at compile time. For performance and safety reasons, whenever a computation can be done at compile time rather than runtime, you should do it. Simple mathematical operations involving literals are an obvious example of expressions that can be evaluated at compile time.

You can extend the reach of the compiler by using the expression `constexpr`. Whenever all the information required to compute an expression is present at compile time, the compiler is *compelled to do so* if that expression is marked `constexpr`. This simple commitment can enable a surprisingly large impact on code readability and runtime performance.

Both `const` and `constexpr` are closely related. Whereas `constexpr` enforces that an expression is compile time evaluable, `const` enforces that a variable cannot change within some scope (at runtime). All `constexpr` expressions are `const` because they're always fixed at runtime.

All constexpr expressions begin with one or more fundamental types (int, float, whchar_t, and so on). You can build on top of these types by using operators and constexpr functions. Constant expressions are used mainly to replace manually computed values in your code. This generally produces code that is more robust and easier to understand, because you can eliminate so-called *magic values*—manually calculated constants copy and pasted directly into source code.

A Colorful Example

Consider the following example where some library you're using for your project uses Color objects that are encoded using the hue-saturation-value (HSV) representation:

```
struct Color {
  float H, S, V;
};
```

Very roughly, hue corresponds with a family of colors like red, green, or orange. Saturation corresponds with colorfulness or intensity. Value corresponds with the color's brightness.

Suppose you want to instantiate Color objects using red-green-blue (RGB) representations. You could use a converter to calculate the RGB to HSV manually, but this is a prime example where you can use constexpr to eliminate magic values. Before you can write the conversion function, you need a few utility functions, namely min, max, and modulo. Listing 7-16 implements these functions.

```
#include <cstdint>
constexpr uint8_t max(uint8_t a, uint8_t b) { ❶
  return a > b ? a : b;
}
constexpr uint8_t max(uint8_t a, uint8_t b, uint8_t c) { ❷
  return max(max(a, b), max(a, c));
}
constexpr uint8_t min(uint8_t a, uint8_t b) { ❸
  return a < b ? a : b;
}
constexpr uint8_t min(uint8_t a, uint8_t b, uint8_t c) { ❹
  return min(min(a, b), min(a, c));
}
constexpr float modulo(float dividend, float divisor) { ❺
  const auto quotient = dividend / divisor; ❻
  return divisor * (quotient - static_cast<uint8_t>(quotient));
}
```

Listing 7-16: Several constexpr functions for manipulating uint8_t objects

Each function is marked constexpr, which tells the compiler that the function must be evaluable at compile time. The max function ❶ uses the ternary operator to return the value of the argument that is greatest. The three-argument version of max ❷ uses the transitive property of comparison; by evaluating the two-argument max for the pairs a, b and a, c, you can find the max of this intermediate result to find the overall max. Because the two-argument version of max is constexpr, this is totally legal.

NOTE *You can't use fmax from the* <math.h> *header for the same reason: it's not* constexpr.

The min versions ❸ ❹ follow exactly with the obvious modification that the comparison is flipped. The modulo function ❺ is a quick-and-dirty, constexpr version of the C function fmod, which computes the floating-point remainder of dividing the first argument (dividend) by the second argument (divisor). Because fmod is *not* constexpr, you've hand-rolled your own. First, you obtain the quotient ❻. Next, you subtract the integral part of quotient using a static_cast and a subtraction. Multiplying the decimal portion of the quotient by divisor yields the result.

With a collection of constexpr utility functions in your arsenal, you can now implement your conversion function rgb_to_hsv, as demonstrated in Listing 7-17.

```
--snip--
constexpr Color rgb_to_hsv(uint8_t r, uint8_t g, uint8_t b) {
  Color c{}; ❶
  const auto c_max = max(r, g, b);
  c.V = c_max / 255.0f; ❷

  const auto c_min = min(r, g, b);
  const auto delta = c.V - c_min / 255.0f;
  c.S = c_max == 0 ? 0 : delta / c.V; ❸

  if (c_max == c_min) { ❹
    c.H = 0;
    return c;
  }
  if (c_max == r) {
    c.H = (g / 255.0f - b / 255.0f) / delta;
  } else if (c_max == g) {
    c.H = (b / 255.0f - r / 255.0f) / delta + 2.0f;
  } else if (c_max == b) {
    c.H = (r / 255.0f - g / 255.0f) / delta + 4.0f;
  }
  c.H *= 60.0f;
  c.H = c.H >= 0.0f ? c.H : c.H + 360.0f;
  c.H = modulo(c.H, 360.0f); ❺
  return c;
}
```

Listing 7-17: A constexpr conversion function from RGB to HSV

You've declared and initialized Color c ❶, which will eventually get returned by rgb_to_hsv. The value of the Color, V, is computed at ❷ by scaling the maximum value of r, g, and b. Next, the saturation S is calculated by computing the distance between the minimum and maximum RGB values and scaling by V ❸. If you imagine the HSV values as existing inside a cylinder, *saturation* is the distance along the horizontal axis and *value* is the distance along the vertical axis. *Hue* is the angle. For brevity, I won't go into detail about how this angle is computed, but the calculation is implemented between ❹ and ❺. Essentially, it entails computing the angle as an offset from the dominant color component's angle. This is scaled and modulo-ed to fit on the 0- to 360-degree interval and stored into H. Finally, c is returned.

NOTE *For an explanation of the formula used to convert HSV to RGB, refer to* https://en.wikipedia.org/wiki/HSL_and_HSV#Color_conversion_formulae.

There's quite a bit going on here, but it's all computed at compile time. This means when you initialize colors, the compiler initializes a Color with all of the HSV field floats filled in:

```
--snip--
int main() {
  auto black   = rgb_to_hsv(0,      0,   0);
  auto white   = rgb_to_hsv(255, 255, 255);
  auto red     = rgb_to_hsv(255,    0,   0);
  auto green   = rgb_to_hsv(  0, 255,   0);
  auto blue    = rgb_to_hsv(  0,    0, 255);
  // TODO: Print these, output.
}
```

You've told the compiler that each of these color values is compile-time evaluable. Depending on how you use these values within the rest of the program, the compiler can decide whether or not to evaluate them at compile time or runtime. The upshot is that the compiler can usually emit instructions with hardcoded *magic numbers* corresponding to the correct HSV values for each Color.

The Case for constexpr

There are some restrictions on what sorts of functions can be constexpr, but these restrictions have been relaxed with each new C++ version.

In certain contexts, like embedded development, constexpr is indispensable. In general, if an expression can be declared constexpr, you should strongly consider doing so. Using constexpr rather than manually calculated literals can make your code more expressive. Often, it can also seriously boost performance and safety at runtime.

Volatile Expressions

The volatile keyword tells the compiler that every access made through this expression must be treated as a visible side effect. This means access cannot be optimized out or reordered with another visible side effect. This keyword is crucial in some settings, like embedded programming, where reads and writes to some special portions of memory have effects on the underlying system. The volatile keyword keeps the compiler from optimizing such accesses away. Listing 7-18 illustrates why you might need the volatile keyword by containing instructions that the compiler would normally optimize away.

```
int foo(int& x) {
  x = 10; ❶
  x = 20; ❷
  auto y = x; ❸
  y = x; ❹
  return y;
}
```

Listing 7-18: A function containing a dead store and a redundant load

Because x is assigned ❶ but never used before getting reassigned ❷, it's called a *dead store* and is a straightforward candidate for getting optimized away. There's a similar story where x is used to set the value of y twice without any intervening instructions ❸❹. This is called a *redundant load* and is also a candidate for optimization.

You might expect any decent compiler to optimize the preceding function into something resembling Listing 7-19.

```
int foo(int& x) {
  x = 20;
  return x;
}
```

Listing 7-19: A plausible optimization of Listing 7-18

In some settings, the redundant reads and dead stores might have visible side effects on the system. By adding the volatile keyword to the argument of foo, you can avoid the optimizer getting rid of these important accesses, as demonstrated in Listing 7-20.

```
int foo(volatile int& x) {
  x = 10;
  x = 20;
  auto y = x;
  y = x;
  return y;
}
```

Listing 7-20: A volatile modification of Listing 7-18

Now the compiler will emit instructions to perform each of the reads and writes you've programmed.

A common misconception is that volatile has to do with concurrent programming. It does not. Variables marked volatile are not generally thread safe. Part II discusses std::atomic, which guarantees certain thread safe primitives on types. Too often, volatile is confused with atomic!

Summary

This chapter covered the major features of operators, which are the fundamental units of work in a program. You explored several aspects of type conversions and took control of dynamic memory management from the environment. You were also introduced to `constexpr`/`volatile` expressions. With these tools in hand, you can perform almost any system-programming task.

EXERCISES

7-1. Create an `UnsignedBigInteger` class that can handle numbers bigger than a `long`. You can use a byte array as the internal representation (for example, `uint8_t[]` or `char[]`). Implement operator overloads for `operator+` and `operator-`. Perform runtime checks for overflow. For the intrepid, also implement `operator*`, `operator/`, and `operator%`. Make sure that your operator overloads work for both `int` types and `UnsignedBigInteger` types. Implement an `operator int` type conversion. Perform a runtime check if narrowing would occur.

7-2. Create a `LargeBucket` class that can store up to 1MB of data. Extend the `Heap` class so it gives out a `LargeBucket` for allocations greater than 4096 bytes. Make sure that you still throw `std::bad_alloc` whenever the `Heap` is unable to allocate an appropriately sized bucket.

FURTHER READING

- *ISO International Standard ISO/IEC (2017) — Programming Language C++* (International Organization for Standardization; Geneva, Switzerland; *https://isocpp.org/std/the-standard/*)

STATEMENTS

Progress doesn't come from early risers—progress is made by lazy men looking for easier ways to do things.
—Robert A. Heinlein, Time Enough for Love

Each C++ function comprises a sequence of *statements*, which are programming constructs that specify the order of execution. This chapter uses an understanding of the object life cycle, templates, and expressions to explore the nuances of statements.

Expression Statements

An *expression statement* is an expression followed by a semicolon (`;`). Expression statements comprise most of the statements in a program. You can turn any expression into a statement, which you should do whenever you need to evaluate an expression but want to discard the result. Of course, this is only useful if evaluating that expression causes a side effect, like printing to the console or modifying the program's state.

Listing 8-1 contains several expression statements.

```
#include <cstdio>

int main() {
  int x{};
  ++x; ❶
  42; ❷
  printf("The %d True Morty\n", x); ❸
}
```

```
The 1 True Morty ❸
```

Listing 8-1: A simple program containing several expression statements

The expression statement at ❶ has a side effect (incrementing x), but the one at ❷ doesn't. Both are valid (although the one at ❷ isn't useful). The function call to printf ❸ is also an expression statement.

Compound Statements

Compound statements, also called *blocks*, are a sequence of statements enclosed by braces { }. Blocks are useful in control structures like if statements, because you might want multiple statements to execute rather than one.

Each block declares a new scope, which is called a *block scope*. As you learned in Chapter 4, objects with automatic storage duration declared within a block scope have lifetimes bound by the block. Variables declared within a block get destroyed in a well-defined order: the reverse of the order in which they were declared.

Listing 8-2 uses the trusty Tracer class from Listing 4-5 (on page 97) to explore block scope.

```
#include <cstdio>

struct Tracer {
  Tracer(const char* name) : name{ name } {
    printf("%s constructed.\n", name);
  }
  ~Tracer() {
    printf("%s destructed.\n", name);
  }
private:
  const char* const name;
};

int main() {
  Tracer main{ "main" }; ❶
  {
    printf("Block a\n"); ❷
    Tracer a1{ "a1" }; ❸
    Tracer a2{ "a2" }; ❹
```

```
  }
  {
    printf("Block b\n"); ❺
    Tracer b1{ "b1" }; ❻
    Tracer b2{ "b2" }; ❼
  }
}
```

```
main constructed. ❶
Block a ❷
a1 constructed. ❸
a2 constructed.  ❹
a2 destructed.
a1 destructed.
Block b ❺
b1 constructed. ❻
b2 constructed. ❼
b2 destructed.
b1 destructed.
main destructed.
```

Listing 8-2: A program exploring compound statements with the `Tracer` class

Listing 8-2 begins by initializing a `Tracer` called `main` ❶. Next, you generate two compound statements. The first compound statement begins with a left brace { followed by the block's first statement, which prints `Block a` ❷. You create two `Tracers`, `a1` ❸ and `a2` ❹, and then close the block with a right brace }. These two tracers get destructed once execution passes through `Block a`. Notice that these two tracers destruct in reverse order from their initialization: `a2` then `a1`.

Also notice another compound statement following `Block a`, where you print `Block b` ❺ and then construct two tracers, `b1` ❻ and `b2` ❼. Its behavior is identical: `b2` destructs followed by `b1`. Once execution passes through `Block b`, the scope of `main` ends and `Tracer main` finally destructs.

Declaration Statements

Declaration statements (or just *declarations*) introduce identifiers, such as functions, templates, and namespaces, into your programs. This section explores some new features of these familiar declarations, as well as type aliases, attributes, and structured bindings.

NOTE *The expression `static_assert`, which you learned about in Chapter 6, is also a declaration statement.*

Functions

A *function declaration*, also called the function's *signature* or *prototype*, specifies a function's inputs and outputs. The declaration doesn't need to include parameter names, only their types. For example, the following line declares a function called `randomize` that takes a `uint32_t` reference and returns `void`:

```
void randomize(uint32_t&);
```

Functions that aren't member functions are called *non-member functions*, or sometimes *free functions*, and they're always declared outside of `main()` at namespace scope. A *function definition* includes the function declaration as well as the function's body. A function's declaration defines a function's interface, whereas a function's definition defines its implementation. For example, the following definition is one possible implementation of the `randomize` function:

```
void randomize(uint32_t& x) {
  x = 0x3FFFFFFF & (0x41C64E6D * x + 12345) % 0x80000000;
}
```

NOTE *This* `randomize` *implementation is a linear congruential generator, a primitive kind of random number generator. See "Further Reading" on page 241 for sources of more information on generating random numbers.*

As you've probably noticed, function declarations are optional. So why do they exist?

The answer is that you can use declared functions throughout your code as long as they're eventually defined somewhere. Your compiler tool chain can figure it out. (You'll learn how this works in Chapter 21.)

The program in Listing 8-3 determines how many iterations the random number generator takes to get from the number 0x4c4347 to the number 0x474343.

```
#include <cstdio>
#include <cstdint>

void randomize(uint32_t&); ❶

int main() {
  size_t iterations{}; ❷
  uint32_t number{ 0x4c4347 }; ❸
  while (number != 0x474343) { ❹
    randomize(number); ❺
    ++iterations; ❻
  }
  printf("%zd", iterations); ❼
}

void randomize(uint32_t& x) {
  x = 0x3FFFFFFF & (0x41C64E6D * x + 12345) % 0x80000000; ❽
}
```

```
927393188 ❼
```

Listing 8-3: A program that uses a function in `main` that isn't defined until later

First, you declare `randomize` ❶. Within `main`, you initialize an `iterations` counter variable to zero ❷ and a `number` variable to 0x4c4347 ❸. A `while` loop checks whether `number` equals the target 0x4c4347 ❹. If it doesn't, you invoke `randomize` ❺ and increment `iterations` ❻. Notice that you haven't yet defined `randomize`. Once `number` equals the target, you print the number of `iterations` ❼ before returning from `main`. Finally, you define `randomize` ❽. The program's output shows that it takes almost a billion iterations to randomly draw the target value.

Try to delete the definition of `randomize` and recompile. You should get an error stating that the definition of `randomize` couldn't be found.

You can similarly separate method declarations from their definitions. As with non-member functions, you can declare a method by omitting its body. For example, the following `RandomNumberGenerator` class replaces the `randomize` function with `next`:

```
struct RandomNumberGenerator {
  explicit RandomNumberGenerator(uint32_t seed) ❶
    : number{ seed } {} ❷
  uint32_t next(); ❸
private:
  uint32_t number;
};
```

You can construct a `RandomNumberGenerator` with a `seed` value ❶, which it uses to initialize the `number` member variable ❷. You've declared the `next` function using the same rules as non-member functions ❸. To provide the definition of `next`, you must use the scope resolution operator and the class name to identify which method you want to define. Otherwise, defining a method is the same as defining a non-member function:

```
uint32_t❶ RandomNumberGenerator::❷next() {
  number = 0x3FFFFFFF & (0x41C64E6D * number + 12345) % 0x80000000; ❸
  return number; ❹
}
```

This definition shares the same return type as the declaration ❶. The `RandomNumberGenerator::` construct specifies that you're defining a method ❷. The function details are essentially the same ❸, except you're returning a copy of the random number generator's state rather than writing into a parameter reference ❹.

Listing 8-4 illustrates how you can refactor Listing 8-3 to incorporate `RandomNumberGenerator`.

```
#include <cstdio>
#include <cstdint>
```

```
struct RandomNumberGenerator {
  explicit RandomNumberGenerator(uint32_t seed)
    : iterations{}❶, number { seed }❷ {}
  uint32_t next(); ❸
  size_t get_iterations() const; ❹
private:
  size_t iterations;
  uint32_t number;
};

int main() {
  RandomNumberGenerator rng{ 0x4c4347 }; ❺
  while (rng.next() != 0x474343) { ❻
    // Do nothing...
  }
  printf("%zd", rng.get_iterations()); ❼
}

uint32_t RandomNumberGenerator::next() { ❽
  ++iterations;
  number = 0x3FFFFFFF & (0x41C64E6D * number + 12345) % 0x80000000;
  return number;
}

size_t RandomNumberGenerator::get_iterations() const { ❾
  return iterations;
}
--------------------------------------------------------------------------------
927393188 ❼
```

Listing 8-4: A refactor of Listing 8-3 using a `RandomNumberGenerator` class

As in Listing 8-3, you've separated declaration from definition. After declaring a constructor that initializes an `iterations` member to zero ❶ and sets its `number` member to a seed ❷, the `next` ❸ and `get_iterations` ❹ method declarations don't contain implementations. Within `main`, you initialize the `RandomNumberGenerator` class with your seed value of 0x4c4347 ❺ and invoke the `next` method to extract new random numbers ❻. The results are the same ❼. As before, the definitions of `next` and `get_iterations` follow their use in `main` ❽❾.

NOTE *The utility of separating definition and declaration might not be apparent because you've been dealing with single-source-file programs so far. Chapter 21 explores multiple-source-file programs where separating declaration and definition provides major benefits.*

Namespaces

Namespaces prevent naming conflicts. In large projects or when importing libraries, namespaces are essential for disambiguating exactly the symbols you're looking for.

Placing Symbols Within Namespaces

By default, all symbols you declare go into the *global namespace*. The global namespace contains all the symbols that you can access without adding any namespace qualifiers. Aside from several classes in the `std` namespace, you've been using objects living exclusively in the global namespace.

To place a symbol within a namespace other than the global namespace, you declare the symbol within a *namespace block*. A namespace block has the following form:

```
namespace BroopKidron13 {
  // All symbols declared within this block
  // belong to the BroopKidron13 namespace
}
```

Namespaces can be nested in one of two ways. First, you can simply nest namespace blocks:

```
namespace BroopKidron13 {
  namespace Shaltanac {
    // All symbols declared within this block
    // belong to the BroopKidron13::Shaltanac namespace
  }
}
```

Second, you can use the scope-resolution operator:

```
namespace BroopKidron13::Shaltanac {
  // All symbols declared within this block
  // belong to the BroopKidron13::Shaltanac namespace
}
```

The latter approach is more succinct.

Using Symbols in Namespaces

To use a symbol within a namespace, you can always use the scope-resolution operator to specify the fully qualified name of a symbol. This allows you to prevent naming conflicts in large projects or when you're using a third-party library. If you and another programmer use the same symbol, you can avoid ambiguity by placing the symbol within a namespace.

Listing 8-5 illustrates how you can use fully qualified symbol names to access a symbol within a namespace.

```
#include <cstdio>

namespace BroopKidron13::Shaltanac { ❶
  enum class Color { ❷
    Mauve,
    Pink,
    Russet
```

```
  };
}

int main() {
  const auto shaltanac_grass{ BroopKidron13::Shaltanac::Color::Russet❸ };
  if(shaltanac_grass == BroopKidron13::Shaltanac::Color::Russet) {
    printf("The other Shaltanac's joopleberry shrub is always "
           "a more mauvey shade of pinky russet.");
  }
}
```

```
The other Shaltanac's joopleberry shrub is always a more mauvey shade of pinky
russet.
```

Listing 8-5: Nested namespace blocks using the scope-resolution operator

Listing 8-5 uses nested namespaces ❶ and declares a `Color` type ❷. To use `Color`, you apply the scope-resolution operator to specify the full name of the symbol, `BroopKidron13::Shaltanac::Color`. Because `Color` is an `enum class`, you use the scope-resolution operator to access its values, as when you assign `shaltanac_grass` to `Russet` ❸.

Using Directives

You can employ a `using` *directive* to avoid a lot of typing. A `using` directive imports a symbol into a block or, if you declare a `using` directive at namespace scope, into the current namespace. Either way, you have to type the full namespace path only once. The usage has the following pattern:

```
using my-type;
```

The corresponding *my-type* gets imported into the current namespace or block, meaning you no longer have to use its full name. Listing 8-6 refactors Listing 8-5 with a using directive.

```
#include <cstdio>

namespace BroopKidron13::Shaltanac {
  enum class Color {
    Mauve,
    Pink,
    Russet
  };
}

int main() {
  using BroopKidron13::Shaltanac::Color; ❶
  const auto shaltanac_grass = Color::Russet❷;
  if(shaltanac_grass == Color::Russet❸) {
    printf("The other Shaltanac's joopleberry shrub is always "
           "a more mauvey shade of pinky russet.");
  }
}
```

```
The other Shaltanac's joopleberry shrub is always a more mauvey shade of pinky
russet.
```

Listing 8-6: A refactor of Listing 8-5 employing a using directive

With a `using` directive ❶ within `main`, you no longer have to type the namespace `BroopKidron13::Shaltanac` to use `Color` ❷❸.

If you're careful, you can introduce all the symbols from a given namespace into the global namespace with the `using namespace` directive.

Listing 8-7 elaborates Listing 8-6: the namespace `BroopKidron13::Shaltanac` contains multiple symbols, which you want to import into the global namespace to avoid a lot of typing.

```
#include <cstdio>

namespace BroopKidron13::Shaltanac {
  enum class Color {
    Mauve,
    Pink,
    Russet
  };

  struct JoopleberryShrub {
    const char* name;
    Color shade;
  };

  bool is_more_mauvey(const JoopleberryShrub& shrub) {
    return shrub.shade == Color::Mauve;
  }
}

using namespace BroopKidron13::Shaltanac; ❶

int main() {
  const JoopleberryShrub❷ yours{
    "The other Shaltanac",
    Color::Mauve❸
  };

  if (is_more_mauvey(yours)❹) {
    printf("%s's joopleberry shrub is always a more mauvey shade of pinky"
           "russet.", yours.name);
  }
}
```

```
The other Shaltanac's joopleberry shrub is always a more mauvey shade of pinky
russet.
```

Listing 8-7: A refactor of Listing 8-6 with multiple symbols imported into the global namespace

With a `using namespace` directive ❶, you can use classes ❷, enum classes ❸, functions ❹, and so on within your program without having to type fully qualified names. Of course, you need to be very careful about clobbering existing types in the global namespace. Usually, it's a bad idea to have too many `using namespace` directives appear in a single translation unit.

NOTE *You should never put a* `using namespace` *directive within a header file. Every source file that includes your header will dump all the symbols from that using directive into the global namespace. This can cause issues that are very difficult to debug.*

Type Aliasing

A *type alias* defines a name that refers to a previously defined name. You can use a type alias as a synonym for the existing type name.

There is no difference between a type and any type aliases referring to it. Also, type aliases cannot change the meaning of an existing type name.

To declare a type alias, you use the following format, where *type-alias* is the type alias name and *type-id* is the target type:

```
using type-alias = type-id;
```

Listing 8-8 employs two type aliases, `String` and `ShaltanacColor`.

```
#include <cstdio>

namespace BroopKidron13::Shaltanac {
  enum class Color {
    Mauve,
    Pink,
    Russet
  };
}

using String = const char[260]; ❶
using ShaltanacColor = BroopKidron13::Shaltanac::Color; ❷

int main() {
  const auto my_color{ ShaltanacColor::Russet }; ❸
  String saying { ❹
    "The other Shaltanac's joopleberry shrub is "
    "always a more mauvey shade of pinky russet."
  };
  if (my_color == ShaltanacColor::Russet) {
    printf("%s", saying);
  }
}
```

Listing 8-8: A refactor of Listing 8-7 with a type alias

Listing 8-8 declares a type alias `String` that refers to a `const char[260]` ❶. This listing also declares a `ShaltanacColor` type alias, which refers to

BroopKidron13::Shaltanac::Color ❷. You can use these type aliases as drop-in replacements to clean up code. Within main, you use ShaltanacColor to remove all the nested namespaces ❸ and String to make the declaration of saying cleaner ❹.

NOTE *Type aliases can appear in any scope—block, class, or namespace.*

You can introduce template parameters into type aliases. This enables two important usages:

- You can perform partial application on template parameters. *Partial application* is the process of fixing some number of arguments to a template, producing another template with fewer template parameters.
- You can define a type alias for a template with a fully specified set of template parameters.

Template instantiations can be quite verbose, and type aliases help you avoid carpal tunnel syndrome.

Listing 8-9 declares a NarrowCaster class with two template parameters. You then use a type alias to partially apply one of its parameters and produce a new type.

```
#include <cstdio>
#include <stdexcept>

template <typename To, typename From>
struct NarrowCaster const { ❶
  To cast(From value) {
    const auto converted = static_cast<To>(value);
    const auto backwards = static_cast<From>(converted);
    if (value != backwards) throw std::runtime_error{ "Narrowed!" };
    return converted;
  }
};

template <typename From>
using short_caster = NarrowCaster<short, From>; ❷

int main() {
  try {
    const short_caster<int> caster; ❸
    const auto cyclic_short = caster.cast(142857);
    printf("cyclic_short: %d\n", cyclic_short);
  } catch (const std::runtime_error& e) {
    printf("Exception: %s\n", e.what()); ❹
  }
}
```

```
Exception: Narrowed! ❹
```

Listing 8-9: A partial application of the NarrowCaster class using a type alias

First, you implement a NarrowCaster template class that has the same functionality as the narrow_cast function template in Listing 6-6 (on page 154): it will perform a static_cast and then check for narrowing ❶. Next, you declare a type alias short_caster that partially applies short as the To type to NarrowCast. Within main, you declare a caster object of type short_caster<int> ❸. The single template parameter in the short_caster type alias gets applied to the remaining type parameter from the type alias—From ❷. In other words, the type short_cast<int> is synonymous with NarrowCaster<short, int>. In the end, the result is the same: with a 2-byte short, you get a narrowing exception when trying to cast an int with the value 142857 into a short ❹.

Structured Bindings

Structured bindings enable you to unpack objects into their constituent elements. Any type whose non-static data members are public can be unpacked this way—for example, the POD (plain-old-data class) types introduced in Chapter 2. The *structured binding syntax* is as follows:

```
auto [object-1, object-2, ...] = plain-old-data;
```

This line will initialize an arbitrary number of objects (*object-1*, *object-2*, and so on) by peeling them off a POD object one by one. The objects peel off the POD from top to bottom, and they fill in the structured binding from left to right. Consider a read_text_file function that takes a string argument corresponding to the file path. Such a function might fail, for example, if a file is locked or doesn't exist. You have two options for handling errors:

- You can throw an exception within read_text_file.
- You can return a success status code from the function.

Let's explore the second option.

The POD type in Listing 8-10 will serve as a fine return type from the read_text_file function.

```
struct TextFile {
  bool success; ❶
  const char* contents; ❷
  size_t n_bytes; ❸
};
```

Listing 8-10: A TextFile type that will be returned by the read_text_file function

First, a flag communicates to the caller whether the function call was a success ❶. Next is the contents of the file ❷ and its size n_bytes ❸.

The prototype of read_text_file looks like this:

```
TextFile read_text_file(const char* path);
```

You can use a structured binding declaration to unpack a TextFile into its parts within your program, as in Listing 8-11.

```
#include <cstdio>

struct TextFile { ❶
  bool success;
  const char* data;
  size_t n_bytes;
};

TextFile read_text_file(const char* path) { ❷
  const static char contents[]{ "Sometimes the goat is you." };
  return TextFile{
    true,
    contents,
    sizeof(contents)
  };
}

int main() {
  const auto [success, contents, length]❸ = read_text_file("REAMDE.txt"); ❹
  if (success❺) {
    printf("Read %zd bytes: %s\n", length❻, contents❼);
  } else {
    printf("Failed to open REAMDE.txt.");
  }
}
--------------------------------------------------------------------------------
Read 27 bytes: Sometimes the goat is you.
```

Listing 8-11: A program simulating the reading of a text file that returns a POD that you use in a structured binding

You've declared the TextFile ❶ and then provided a dummy definition for read_text_file ❷. (It doesn't actually read a file; more on that in Part II.)

Within main, you invoke read_text_file ❹ and use a structured binding declaration to unpack the results into three distinct variables: success, contents, and length ❸. After structured binding, you can use all these variables as though you had declared them individually ❺❻❼.

NOTE *The types within a structured binding declaration don't have to match.*

Attributes

Attributes apply implementation-defined features to an expression statement. You introduce attributes using double brackets [[ ]] containing a list of one or more comma-separated attribute elements.

Table 8-1 lists the standard attributes.

Table 8-1: The Standard Attributes

Attribute	Meaning
`[[noreturn]]`	Indicates that a function doesn't return.
`[[deprecated("reason")]]`	Indicates that this expression is deprecated; that is, its use is discouraged. The `"reason"` is optional and indicates the reason for deprecation.
`[[fallthrough]]`	Indicates that a switch case intends to fall through to the next switch case. This avoids compiler errors that will check for switch case fallthrough, because it's uncommon.
`[[nodiscard]]`	Indicates that the following function or type declaration should be used. If code using this element discards the value, the compiler should emit a warning.
`[[maybe_unused]]`	Indicates that the following element might be unused and that the compiler shouldn't warn about it.
`[[carries_dependency]]`	Used within the `<atomic>` header to help the compiler optimize certain memory operations. You're unlikely to encounter this directly.

Listing 8-12 demonstrates using the `[[noreturn]]` attribute by defining a function that never returns.

```
#include <cstdio>
#include <stdexcept>

[[noreturn]] void pitcher() { ❶
  throw std::runtime_error{ "Knuckleball." }; ❷
}

int main() {
  try {
    pitcher(); ❸
  } catch(const std::exception& e) {
    printf("exception: %s\n", e.what()); ❹
  }
}
--------------------------------------------------------------------------
Exception: Knuckleball. ❹
```

Listing 8-12: A program illustrating the use of the `[[noreturn]]` attribute

First, you declare the `pitcher` function with the `[[noreturn]]` attribute ❶. Within this function, you throw an exception ❷. Because you always throw an exception, `pitcher` never returns (hence the `[[noreturn]]` attribute). Within `main`, you invoke `pitcher` ❸ and handle the caught exception ❹. Of course, this listing works without the `[[noreturn]]` attribute. But giving this information to the compiler allows it to reason more completely on your code (and potentially to optimize your program).

The situations in which you'll need to use an attribute are rare, but they convey useful information to the compiler nonetheless.

Selection Statements

Selection statements express conditional control flow. The two varieties of selection statements are the `if` statement and the `switch` statement.

if Statements

The `if` statement has the familiar form shown in Listing 8-13.

```
if (condition-1) {
  // Execute only if condition-1 is true ❶
} else if (condition-2) { // optional
  // Execute only if condition-2 is true ❷
}
// ... as many else ifs as desired
--snip--
} else { // optional
  // Execute only if none of the conditionals is true ❸
}
```

Listing 8-13: The syntax of the `if` *statement*

Upon encountering an `if` statement, you evaluate the *condition-1* expression first. If it's `true`, the block at ❶ is executed and the `if` statement stops executing (none of the `else if` or `else` statements are considered). If it's `false`, the `else if` statements' conditions evaluate in order. These are optional, and you can supply as many as you like.

If *condition-2* evaluates to `true`, for example, the block at ❷ will execute and none of the remaining `else if` or `else` statements are considered. Finally, the `else` block at ❸ executes if all of the preceding conditions evaluate to `false`. Like the `else if` blocks, the `else` block is optional.

The function template in Listing 8-14 converts an `else` argument into `Positive`, `Negative`, or `Zero`.

```
#include <cstdio>

template<typename T>
constexpr const char* sign(const T& x) {
  const char* result{};
  if (x == 0) { ❶
    result = "zero";
  } else if (x > 0) { ❷
    result = "positive";
  } else { ❸
    result = "negative";
  }
  return result;
}

int main() {
  printf("float 100 is %s\n", sign(100.0f));
  printf("int  -200 is %s\n", sign(-200));
```

```
  printf("char    0 is %s\n", sign(char{}));
}
--------------------------------------------------------------------------------
float 100 is positive
int  -200 is negative
char    0 is zero
```

Listing 8-14: An example usage of the `if` *statement*

The `sign` function takes a single argument and determines if it's equal to 0 ❶, greater than 0 ❷, or less than 0 ❸. Depending on which condition matches, it sets the automatic variable `result` equal to one of three strings—`zero`, `positive`, or `negative`—and returns this value to the caller.

Initialization Statements and if

You can bind an object's scope to an `if` statement by adding an `init-statement` to `if` and `else if` declarations, as demonstrated in Listing 8-15.

```
if (init-statement; condition-1) {
  // Execute only if condition-1 is true
} else if (init-statement; condition-2) { // optional
  // Execute only if condition-2 is true
}
--snip--
```

Listing 8-15: An `if` *statement with initializations*

You can use this pattern with structured bindings to produce elegant error handling. Listing 8-16 refactors Listing 8-11 using the initialization statement to scope a `TextFile` to the `if` statement.

```
#include <cstdio>

struct TextFile {
  bool success;
  const char* data;
  size_t n_bytes;
};

TextFile read_text_file(const char* path) {
  --snip--
}

int main() {
  if(const auto [success, txt, len]❶ = read_text_file("REAMDE.txt"); success❷)
  {
    printf("Read %d bytes: %s\n", len, txt); ❸
  } else {
    printf("Failed to open REAMDE.txt."); ❹
  }
}
```

```
--------------------------------------------------------------------------
Read 27 bytes: Sometimes the goat is you. ❸
```

Listing 8-16: An extension of Listing 8-11 using structured binding and an `if` statement to handle errors

You've moved the structured binding declaration into the initialization statement portion of the `if` statement ❶. This scopes each of the unpacked objects—`success`, `txt`, and `len`—to the `if` block. You use `success` directly within the conditional expression of `if` to determine whether `read_text_file` was successful ❷. If it was, you print the contents of `REAMDE.txt` ❸. If it wasn't, you print an error message ❹.

constexpr if Statements

You can make an `if` statement `constexpr`; such statements are known as `constexpr if` statements. A `constexpr if` statement is evaluated at compile time. Code blocks that correspond to `true` conditions get emitted, and the rest is ignored.

Usage of the `constexpr if` follows usage for a regular `if` statement, as demonstrated in Listing 8-17.

```
if constexpr (condition-1) {
  // Compile only if condition-1 is true
} else if constexpr (condition-2) { // optional; can be multiple else ifs
  // Compile only if condition-2 is true
}
--snip--
} else { // optional
  // Compile only if none of the conditionals is true
}
```

Listing 8-17: Usage of the `constexpr if` statement

In combination with templates and the `<type_traits>` header, `constexpr if` statements are extremely powerful. A major use for `constexpr if` is to provide custom behavior in a function template depending on some attributes of type parameters.

The function template `value_of` in Listing 8-18 accepts pointers, references, and values. Depending on which kind of object the argument is, `value_of` returns either the pointed-to value or the value itself.

```
#include <cstdio>
#include <stdexcept>
#include <type_traits>

template <typename T>
auto value_of(T x❶) {
  if constexpr (std::is_pointer<T>::value) { ❷
    if (!x) throw std::runtime_error{ "Null pointer dereference." }; ❸
    return *x; ❹
```

```
  } else {
    return x; ❺
  }
}

int main() {
  unsigned long level{ 8998 };
  auto level_ptr = &level;
  auto &level_ref = level;
  printf("Power level = %lu\n", value_of(level_ptr)); ❻
  ++*level_ptr;
  printf("Power level = %lu\n", value_of(level_ref)); ❼
  ++level_ref;
  printf("It's over %lu!\n", value_of(level++)); ❽
  try {
    level_ptr = nullptr;
    value_of(level_ptr);
  } catch(const std::exception& e) {
    printf("Exception: %s\n", e.what()); ❾
  }
}
```

```
Power level = 8998 ❻
Power level = 8999 ❼
It's over 9000! ❽
Exception: Null pointer dereference. ❾
```

Listing 8-18: An example function template, `value_of`, employing a `constexpr if` statement

The `value_of` function template accepts a single argument `x` ❶. You determine whether the argument is a pointer type using the `std::is_pointer<T>` type trait as the conditional expression in a `constexpr if` statement ❷. In case `x` is a pointer type, you check for `nullptr` and throw an exception if one is encountered ❸. If `x` isn't a `nullptr`, you dereference it and return the result ❹. Otherwise, `x` is not a pointer type, so you return it (because it is therefore a value) ❺.

Within `main`, you instantiate `value_of` multiple times with an `unsigned long` pointer ❻, an `unsigned long` reference ❼, an `unsigned long` ❽, and a `nullptr` ❾ respectively.

At runtime, the `constexpr if` statement disappears; each instantiation of `value_of` contains one branch of the selection statement or the other. You might be wondering why such a facility is useful. After all, programs are meant to do something useful at runtime, not at compile time. Just flip back to Listing 7-17 (on page 206), and you'll see that compile time evaluation can substantially simplify your programs by eliminating magic values.

There are other examples where compile time evaluation is popular, especially when creating libraries for others to use. Because library writers usually cannot know all the ways their users will utilize their library, they need to write generic code. Often, they'll use techniques like those you learned in Chapter 6 so they can achieve compile-time polymorphism. Constructs like `constexpr` can help when writing this kind of code.

NOTE *If you have a C background, you'll immediately recognize the utility of compile time evaluation when considering that it almost entirely replaces the need for preprocessor macros.*

switch Statements

Chapter 2 first introduced the venerable `switch` statement. This section delves into the addition of the initialization statement into the `switch` declaration. The usage is as follows:

```
switch (init-expression❶; condition) {
  case (case-a): {
    // Handle case-a here
  } break;
  case (case-b): {
    // Handle case-b here
  } break;
    // Handle other conditions as desired
  default: {
    // Handle the default case here
  }
}
```

As with `if` statements, you can instantiate within `switch` statements ❶. Listing 8-19 employs an initialization statement within a `switch` statement.

```
#include <cstdio>

enum class Color { ❶
  Mauve,
  Pink,
  Russet
};

struct Result { ❷
  const char* name;
  Color color;
};

Result observe_shrub(const char* name) { ❸
  return Result{ name, Color::Russet };
}

int main() {
  const char* description;
  switch (const auto result❹ = observe_shrub("Zaphod"); result.color❺) {
  case Color::Mauve: {
    description = "mauvey shade of pinky russet";
    break;
  } case Color::Pink: {
    description = "pinky shade of mauvey russet";
    break;
  } case Color::Russet: {
```

```
      description = "russety shade of pinky mauve";
      break;
    } default: {
      description = "enigmatic shade of whitish black";
    }}
    printf("The other Shaltanac's joopleberry shrub is "
           "always a more %s.", description); ❻
}
--------------------------------------------------------------------------
The other Shaltanac's joopleberry shrub is always a more russety shade of
pinky mauve. ❻
```

Listing 8-19: Using an initialization expression in a `switch` *statement*

You declare the familiar `Color enum class` ❶ and join it with a `char*` member to form the POD type `Result` ❷. The function `observe_shrub` returns a `Result` ❸. Within `main`, you call `observe_shrub` within the initialization expression and store the result in the `result` variable ❹. Within the conditional expression of `switch`, you extract the `color` element of this `result` ❺. This element determines the case that executes (and sets the `description` pointer) ❻.

As with the `if`-statement-plus-initializer syntax, any object initialized in the initialization expression is bound to the scope of the `switch` statement.

Iteration Statements

Iteration statements execute a statement repeatedly. The four kinds of iteration statements are the `while` loop, the `do`-`while` loop, the `for` loop, and the range-based `for` loop.

while Loops

The `while` loop is the basic iteration mechanism. The usage is as follows:

```
while (condition) {
  // The statement in the body of the loop
  // executes upon each iteration
}
```

Before executing an iteration of the loop, the `while` loop evaluates the `condition` expression. If true, the loop continues. If `false`, the loop terminates, as demonstrated in Listing 8-20.

```
#include <cstdio>
#include <cstdint>

bool double_return_overflow(uint8_t& x) { ❶
  const auto original = x;
  x *= 2;
  return original > x;
}
```

```
int main() {
  uint8_t x{ 1 }; ❷
  printf("uint8_t:\n===\n");
  while (!double_return_overflow(x)❸) {
    printf("%u ", x); ❹
  }
}
-----------------------------------------------------------------------
uint8_t:
===
2 4 8 16 32 64 128 ❹
```

Listing 8-20: A program that doubles a `uint8_t` and prints the new value on each iteration

You declare a `double_return_overflow` function taking an 8-bit, unsigned integer by reference ❶. This function doubles the argument and checks whether this causes an overflow. If it does, it returns `true`. If no overflow occurs, it returns `false`.

You initialize the variable `x` to 1 before entering the `while` loop ❷. The conditional expression in the `while` loop evaluates `double_return_overflow(x)` ❸. This has the side effect of doubling `x`, because you've passed it by reference. It also returns a value telling you whether the doubling caused `x` to overflow. The loop will execute when the conditional expression evaluates to `true`, but `double_return_overflow` is written so it returns `true` when the loop should stop. You fix this problem by prepending the logical negation operator (`!`). (Recall from Chapter 7 that this turns `true` to `false` and `false` to `true`.) So the `while` loop is actually asking, "If it's NOT true that `double_return_overflow` is true . . ."

The end result is that you print the values 2, then 4, then 8, and so on to 128 ❹.

Notice that the value 1 never prints, because evaluating the conditional expression doubles `x`. You can modify this behavior by putting the conditional statement at the end of a loop, which yields a `do`-`while` loop.

do-while Loops

A `do`-`while` loop is identical to a `while` loop, except the conditional statement evaluates after a loop completes rather than before. Its usage is as follows:

```
do {
  // The statement in the body of the loop
  // executes upon each iteration
} while (condition);
```

Because the condition evaluates at the end of a loop, you guarantee that the loop will execute at least once.

Listing 8-21 refactors Listing 8-20 into a `do`-`while` loop.

```
#include <cstdio>
#include <cstdint>

bool double_return_overflow(uint8_t& x) {
  --snip--
```

```
}

int main() {
  uint8_t x{ 1 };
  printf("uint8_t:\n===\n");
  do {
    printf("%u ", x); ❶
  } while (!double_return_overflow(x)❷);
}
--------------------------------------------------------------------------
uint8_t:
===
1 2 4 8 16 32 64 128 ❶
```

Listing 8-21: A program that doubles a `uint8_t` and prints the new value on each iteration

Notice that the output from Listing 8-21 now begins with 1 ❶. All you needed to do was reformat the `while` loop to put the condition at the end of the loop ❷.

In most situations involving iterations, you have three tasks:

1. Initialize some object.
2. Update the object before each iteration.
3. Inspect the object's value for some condition.

You can use a `while` or `do-while` loop to accomplish part of these tasks, but the `for` loop provides built-in facilities that make life easier.

for Loops

The `for` loop is an iteration statement containing three special expressions: *initialization*, *conditional*, and *iteration*, as described in the sections that follow.

The Initialization Expression

The initialization expression is like the initialization of `if`: it executes only once before the first iteration executes. Any objects declared within the initialization expression have lifetimes bound by the scope of the `for` loop.

The Conditional Expression

The `for` loop conditional expression evaluates just before each iteration of the loop. If the conditional evaluates to `true`, the loop continues to execute. If the conditional evaluates to `false`, the loop terminates (this behavior is exactly like the conditional of the `while` and `do-while` loops).

Like `if` and `switch` statements, `for` permits you to initialize objects with scope equal to the statement's.

The Iteration Expression

After each iteration of the `for` loop, the iteration expression evaluates. This happens before the conditional expression evaluates. Note that the iteration expression evaluates after a successful iteration, so the iteration expression won't execute before the first iteration.

To clarify, the following list outlines the typical execution order in a `for` loop:

1. Initialization expression
2. Conditional expression
3. (Loop body)
4. Iteration expression
5. Conditional expression
6. (Loop body)

Steps 4 through 6 repeat until a conditional expression returns `false`.

Usage

Listing 8-22 demonstrates the use of a `for` loop.

```
for(initialization❶; conditional❷; iteration❸) {
  // The statement in the body of the loop
  // executes upon each iteration
}
```

Listing 8-22: Using a `for` *loop*

The initialization ❶, conditional ❷, and iteration ❸ expressions reside in parentheses preceding the body of the `for` loop.

Iterating with an Index

The `for` loops are excellent at iterating over an array-like object's constituent elements. You use an auxiliary *index* variable to iterate over the range of valid indices for the array-like object. You can use this index to interact with each array element in sequence. Listing 8-23 employs an index variable to print each element of an array along with its index.

```
#include <cstdio>

int main() {
  const int x[]{ 1, 1, 2, 3, 5, 8 }; ❶
  printf("i: x[i]\n"); ❷
  for (int i{}❸; i < 6❹; i++❺) {
    printf("%d: %d\n", i, x[i]);
  }
}
--------------------------------------------------------------------------
i: x[i] ❷
0: 1
1: 1
2: 2
3: 3
```

```
4: 5
5: 8
```

Listing 8-23: A program iterating over an array of Fibonacci numbers

You initialize an int array called x with the first six Fibonacci numbers ❶. After printing a header for the output ❷, you build a for loop containing your initialization ❸, conditional ❹, and iteration ❺ expressions. The initialization expression executes first, and it initializes the index variable i to zero.

Listing 8-23 shows a coding pattern that hasn't changed since the 1950s. You can eliminate a lot of boilerplate code by using the more modern range-based for loop.

Ranged-Based for Loops

The range-based for loop iterates over a *range* of values without needing an index variable. A range (or *range expression*) is an object that the range-based for loop knows how to iterate over. Many C++ objects are valid range expressions, including arrays. (All of the stdlib containers you'll learn about in Part II are also valid range expressions.)

Usage

Ranged-based for loop usage looks like this:

```
for(range-declaration : range-expression) {
  // The statement in the body of the loop
  // executes upon each iteration
}
```

A *range declaration* declares a named variable. This variable must have the same type as implied by the range expression (you can use auto).

Listing 8-24 refactors Listing 8-23 to use a range-based for loop.

```
#include <cstdio>

int main() {
  const int x[]{ 1, 1, 2, 3, 5, 8 }; ❶
  for (const auto element❷ : x❸) {
    printf("%d ", element❹);
  }
}
--------------------------------------------------------------------------------
1 1 2 3 5 8
```

Listing 8-24: A range-based for loop iterating over the first six Fibonacci numbers

You still declare an array x containing six Fibonacci numbers ❶. The range-based for loop contains a range-declaration expression ❷ where you declare the element variable to hold each element of the range. It also contains the range expression x ❸, which contains the elements you want to iterate over to print ❹.

This code is a whole lot cleaner!

Range Expressions

You can define your own types that are also valid range expressions. But you'll need to specify several functions on your type.

Every range exposes a `begin` and an `end` method. These functions represent the common interface that a range-based `for` loop uses to interact with a range. Both methods return *iterators*. An iterator is an object that supports `operator!=`, `operator++`, and `operator*`.

Let's look at how all these pieces fit together. Under the hood, a range-based `for` loop looks just like the loop in Listing 8-25.

```
const auto e = range.end();❶
for(auto b = range.begin()❷; b != e❸; ++b❹) {
  const auto& element❺ = *b;
}
```

Listing 8-25: A `for` *loop simulating a range-based* `for` *loop*

The initialization expression stores two variables, `b` ❷ and `e` ❶, which you initialize to `range.begin()` and `range.end()` respectively. The conditional expression checks whether `b` equals `e`, in which case the loop has completed ❸ (this is by convention). The iteration expression increments `b` with the prefix operator ❹. Finally, the iterator supports the dereference operator `*`, so you can extract the pointed-to element ❺.

NOTE *The types returned by* `begin` *and* `end` *don't need to be the same. The requirement is that* `operator!=` *on* `begin` *accepts an* `end` *argument to support the comparison* `begin != end`*.*

A Fibonacci Range

You can implement a `FibonacciRange`, which will generate an arbitrarily long sequence of Fibonacci numbers. From the previous section, you know that this range must offer a `begin` and an `end` method that returns an iterator. This iterator, which is called `FibonacciIterator` in this example, must in turn offer `operator!=`, `operator++`, and `operator*`.

Listing 8-26 implements a `FibonacciIterator` and a `FibonacciRange`.

```
struct FibonacciIterator {
  bool operator!=(int x) const {
    return x >= current; ❶
  }

  FibonacciIterator& operator++() {
    const auto tmp = current; ❷
    current += last; ❸
    last = tmp; ❹
    return *this; ❺
  }

  int operator*() const {
    return current; ❻
```

```
  }
private:
  int current{ 1 }, last{ 1 };
};

struct FibonacciRange {
  explicit FibonacciRange(int max❼) : max{ max } { }
  FibonacciIterator begin() const { ❽
    return FibonacciIterator{};
  }
  int end() const { ❾
    return max;
  }
private:
  const int max;
};
```

Listing 8-26: An implementation of `FibonacciIterator` and `FibonacciRange`

The `FibonacciIterator` has two fields, `current` and `last`, which are initialized to 1. These keep track of two values in the Fibonacci sequence. Its `operator!=` checks whether the argument is greater than or equal to `current` ❶. Recall that this argument is used within the range-based `for` loop in the conditional expression. It should return `true` if elements remain in the range; otherwise, it returns `false`. The `operator++` appears in the iteration expression and is responsible for setting up the iterator for the next iteration. You first save `current` value into the temporary variable `tmp` ❷. Next, you increment `current` by `last`, yielding the next Fibonacci number ❸. (This follows from the definition of a Fibonacci sequence.) Then you set `last` equal to `tmp` ❹ and return a reference to `this` ❺. Finally, you implement `operator*`, which returns `current` ❻ directly.

`FibonacciRange` is much simpler. Its constructor takes a `max` argument that defines an upper limit for the range ❼. The `begin` method returns a fresh `FibonacciIterator` ❽, and the `end` method returns `max` ❾.

It should now be apparent why you need to implement `bool operator!=(int x)` on `FibonacciIterator` rather than, for example, `bool operator!=(const FibonacciIterator& x)`: a `FibonacciRange` returns an `int` from `end()`.

You can use the `FibonacciRange` in a ranged-based `for` loop, as demonstrated in Listing 8-27.

```
#include <cstdio>

struct FibonacciIterator {
  --snip--
};

struct FibonacciRange {
  --snip--;
};

int main() {
```

```
  for (const auto i : FibonacciRange{ 5000 }❶) {
    printf("%d ", i); ❷
  }
}
--------------------------------------------------------------------------------
1 2 3 5 8 13 21 34 55 89 144 233 377 610 987 1597 2584 4181 ❷
```

Listing 8-27: Using `FibonacciRange` *in a program*

It took a little work to implement `FibonacciIterator` and `FibonacciRange` in Listing 8-26, but the payoff is substantial. Within `main`, you simply construct a `FibonacciRange` with the desired upper limit ❶, and the range-based `for` loop takes care of everything else for you. You simply use the resulting elements within the `for` loop ❷.

Listing 8-27 is functionally equivalent to Listing 8-28, which converts the range-based `for` loop to a traditional `for` loop.

```
#include <cstdio>

struct FibonacciIterator {
  --snip--
};

struct FibonacciRange {
  --snip--;
};

int main() {
  FibonacciRange range{ 5000 };
  const auto end = range.end();❶
  for (const auto x = range.begin()❷; x != end ❸; ++x ❹) {
    const auto i = *x;
    printf("%d ", i);
  }
}
--------------------------------------------------------------------------------
1 2 3 5 8 13 21 34 55 89 144 233 377 610 987 1597 2584 4181
```

Listing 8-28: A refactor of Listing 8-27 using a traditional for *loop*

Listing 8-28 demonstrates how all of the pieces fit together. Calling `range.begin()` ❷ yields a `FibonacciIterator`. When you call `range.end()` ❶, it yields an `int`. These types come straight from the method definitions of `begin()` and `end()` on `FibonacciRange`. The conditional statement ❸ uses `operator!=(int)` on `FibonacciIterator` to get the following behavior: if the iterator `x` has gone past the `int` argument to `operator!=`, the conditional evaluates to `false` and the loop ends. You've also implemented `operator++` on `FibonacciIterator` so `++x` ❹ increments the Fibonacci number within `FibonacciIterator`.

When you compare Listings 8-27 and 8-28, you can see just how much tedium range-based `for` loops hide.

NOTE *You might be thinking, "Sure, the range-based* `for` *loop looks a lot cleaner, but implementing* `FibonacciIterator` *and* `FibonacciRange` *is a lot of work." That's a great point, and for one-time-use code, you probably wouldn't refactor code in this way. Ranges are mainly useful if you're writing library code, writing code that you'll reuse often, or simply consuming ranges that someone else has written.*

Jump Statements

Jump statements, including the `break`, `continue`, and `goto` statements, transfer control flow. Unlike selection statements, jump statements are not conditional. You should avoid using them because they can almost always be replaced with higher-level control structures. They're discussed here because you might see them in older C++ code and they still play a central role in a lot of C code.

break Statements

The `break` statement terminates execution of the enclosing iteration or `switch` statement. Once `break` completes, execution transfers to the statement immediately following the `for`, range-based `for`, `while`, `do-while`, or `switch` statement.

You've already used `break` within `switch` statements; once a case completes, the `break` statement terminates the `switch`. Recall that, without a `break` statement, the `switch` statement would continue executing all of the following cases.

Listing 8-29 refactors Listing 8-27 to break out of a range-based `for` loop if the iterator `i` equals 21.

```
#include <cstdio>

struct FibonacciIterator {
  --snip--
};

struct FibonacciRange {
  --snip--;
};

int main() {
  for (auto i : FibonacciRange{ 5000 }) {
    if (i == 21) { ❶
      printf("*** "); ❷
      break; ❸
    }
    printf("%d ", i);
  }
}
```

```
1 2 3 5 8 13 *** ❷
```

Listing 8-29: A refactor of Listing 8-27 that breaks if the iterator equals 21

An if statement is added that checks whether i is 21 ❶. If it is, you print three asterisks *** ❷ and break ❸. Notice the output: rather than printing 21, the program prints three asterisks and the for loop terminates. Compare this to the output of Listing 8-27.

continue Statements

The continue statement skips the remainder of an enclosing iteration statement and continues with the next iteration. Listing 8-30 replaces the break in Listing 8-29 with a continue.

```
#include <cstdio>

struct FibonacciIterator {
  --snip--
};

struct FibonacciRange {
  --snip--;
};

int main() {
  for (auto i : FibonacciRange{ 5000 }) {
    if (i == 21) {
      printf("*** "); ❶
      continue; ❷
    }
    printf("%d ", i);
  }
}
```

```
1 2 3 5 8 13 *** ❶34 55 89 144 233 377 610 987 1597 2584 4181
```

Listing 8-30: A refactor of Listing 8-29 to use continue instead of break

You still print three asterisks ❶ when i is 21, but you use continue instead of break ❷. This causes 21 not to print, like Listing 8-29; however, unlike Listing 8-29, Listing 8-30 continues iterating. (Compare the output.)

goto Statements

The goto statement is an unconditional jump. The target of a goto statement is a label.

Labels

Labels are identifiers you can add to any statement. Labels give statements a name, and they have no direct impact on the program. To assign a label, prepend a statement with the desired name of the label followed by a semicolon.

Listing 8-31 adds the labels luke and yoda to a simple program.

```
#include <cstdio>

int main() {
luke: ❶
  printf("I'm not afraid.\n");
yoda: ❷
  printf("You will be.");
}
--------------------------------------------------------------------------------
I'm not afraid.
You will be.
```

Listing 8-31: A simple program with labels

The labels ❶❷ do nothing on their own.

goto Usage

The goto statement's usage is as follows:

```
goto label;
```

For example, you can employ goto statements to needlessly obfuscate the simple program in Listing 8-32.

```
#include <cstdio>

int main() {
  goto silent_bob; ❶
luke:
  printf("I'm not afraid.\n");
  goto yoda; ❸
silent_bob:
  goto luke; ❷
yoda:
  printf("You will be.");
}
--------------------------------------------------------------------------------
I'm not afraid.
You will be.
```

Listing 8-32: Spaghetti code showcasing the goto statement

Control flow in Listing 8-32 passes to silent_bob ❶, then to luke ❷, and then to yoda ❸.

The Role of goto in Modern C++ Programs

In modern C++, there is no good role for goto statements. Don't use them.

NOTE *In poorly written C++ (and in most C code), you might see* `goto` *used as a primitive error-handling mechanism. A lot of system programming entails acquiring resources, checking for error conditions, and cleaning up resources. The RAII paradigm neatly abstracts all of these details, but C doesn't have RAII available. See the Overture to C Programmers on page xxxvii for more information.*

Summary

In this chapter, you worked through different kinds of statements you can employ in your programs. They included declarations and initializations, selection statements, and iteration statements.

NOTE *Keep in mind that* `try-catch` *blocks are also statements, but they were already discussed in great detail in Chapter 4.*

EXERCISES

8-1. Refactor Listing 8-27 into separate translation units: one for `main` and another for `FibonacciRange` and `FibonacciIterator`. Use a header file to share definitions between the two translation units.

8-2. Implement a `PrimeNumberRange` class that can be used in a range exception to iterate over all prime numbers less than a given value. Again, use a separate header and source file.

8-3. Integrate `PrimeNumberRange` into Listing 8-27, adding another loop that generates all prime numbers less than 5,000.

FURTHER READING

- *ISO International Standard ISO/IEC (2017) — Programming Language C++* (International Organization for Standardization; Geneva, Switzerland; *https://isocpp.org/std/the-standard/*)
- *Random Number Generation and Monte Carlo Methods*, 2nd Edition, by James E. Gentle (Springer-Verlag, 2003)
- *Random Number Generation and Quasi-Monte Carlo Methods* by Harald Niederreiter (SIAM Vol. 63, 1992)

9

FUNCTIONS

Functions should do one thing. They should do it well. They should do it only.
—Robert C. Martin, Clean Code

This chapter rounds out the ongoing discussion of functions, which encapsulate code into reusable components. Now that you're armed with a strong background in C++ fundamentals, this chapter first revisits functions with a far more in-depth treatment of modifiers, specifiers, and return types, which appear in function declarations and specialize the behavior of your functions.

Then you'll learn about overload resolution and accepting variable numbers of arguments before exploring function pointers, type aliases, function objects, and the venerable lambda expression. The chapter closes with an introduction to the `std::function` before revisiting the `main` function and accepting command line arguments.

Function Declarations

Function declarations have the following familiar form:

```
prefix-modifiers return-type func-name(arguments) suffix-modifiers;
```

You can provide a number of optional *modifiers* (or *specifiers*) to functions. Modifiers alter a function's behavior in some way. Some modifiers appear at the beginning in the function's declaration or definition (*prefix modifiers*), whereas others appear at the end (*suffix modifiers*). The prefix modifiers appear before the return type. The suffix modifiers appear after the argument list.

There isn't a clear language reason why certain modifiers appear as prefixes or suffixes: because C++ has a long history, these features evolved incrementally.

Prefix Modifiers

At this point, you already know several prefix modifiers:

- The prefix `static` indicates that a function that isn't a member of a class has internal linkage, meaning the function won't be used outside of this translation unit. Unfortunately, this keyword does double duty: if it modifies a method (that is, a function inside a class), it indicates that the function isn't associated with an instantiation of the class but rather with the class itself (see Chapter 4).
- The modifier `virtual` indicates that a method can be overridden by a child class. The `override` modifier indicates to the compiler that a child class intends to override a parent's virtual function (see Chapter 5).
- The modifier `constexpr` indicates that the function should be evaluated at compile time if possible (see Chapter 7).
- The modifier `[[noreturn]]` indicates that this function won't return (see Chapter 8). Recall that this attribute helps the compiler to optimize your code.

Another prefix modifier is `inline`, which plays a role in guiding the compiler when optimizing code.

On most platforms, a function call compiles into a series of instructions, such as the following:

1. Place arguments into registers and on the call stack.
2. Push a return address onto the call stack.
3. Jump to the called function.
4. After the function completes, jump to the return address.
5. Clean up the call stack.

These steps typically execute very quickly, and the payoff in reduced binary size can be substantial if you use a function in many places.

Inlining a function means copying and pasting the contents of the function directly into the execution path, eliminating the need for the five steps outlined. This means that as the processor executes your code, it will immediately execute your function's code rather than executing the (modest) ceremony required for function invocation. If you prefer this marginal increase in speed over the commensurate cost in increased binary size, you can use the `inline` keyword to indicate this to the compiler. The `inline` keyword hints to the compiler's optimizer to put a function directly inline rather than perform a function call.

Adding `inline` to a function doesn't change its behavior; it's purely an expression of preference to the compiler. You must ensure that if you define a function `inline`, you do so in all translation units. Also note that modern compilers will typically inline functions where it makes sense—especially if a function isn't used outside of a single translation unit.

Suffix Modifiers

At this point in the book, you already know two suffix modifiers:

- The modifier `noexcept` indicates that the function will *never* throw an exception. It enables certain optimizations (see Chapter 4).
- The modifier `const` indicates that the method won't modify an instance of its class, allowing `const` references types to invoke the method (see Chapter 4).

This section explores three more suffix modifiers: `final`, `override`, and `volatile`.

final and override

The `final` modifier indicates that a method cannot be overridden by a child class. It's effectively the opposite of `virtual`. Listing 9-1 attempts to override a `final` method and yields a compiler error.

```
#include <cstdio>

struct BostonCorbett {
  virtual void shoot() final❶ {
    printf("What a God we have...God avenged Abraham Lincoln");
  }
};

struct BostonCorbettJunior : BostonCorbett {
  void shoot() override❷ { } // Bang! shoot is final.
};

int main() {
  BostonCorbettJunior junior;
}
```

Listing 9-1: A class attempting to override a final method (This code doesn't compile.)

This listing marks the shoot method final ❶. Within BostonCorbettJunior, which inherits from BostonCorbett, you attempt to override the shoot method ❷. This causes a compiler error.

You can also apply the final keyword to an entire class, disallowing that class from becoming a parent entirely, as demonstrated in Listing 9-2.

```
#include <cstdio>

struct BostonCorbett final ❶ {
  void shoot()  {
    printf("What a God we have...God avenged Abraham Lincoln");
  }
};

struct BostonCorbettJunior : BostonCorbett ❷ { }; // Bang!

int main() {
  BostonCorbettJunior junior;
}
```

Listing 9-2: A program with a class attempting to inherit from a final class. (This code doesn't compile.)

The BostonCorbett class is marked as final ❶, and this causes a compiler error when you attempt to inherit from it in BostonCorbettJunior ❷.

NOTE *Neither final nor override is technically a language keyword; they are* identifiers. *Unlike keywords, identifiers gain special meaning only when used in a specific context. This means you can use final and override as symbol names elsewhere in your program, thereby leading to the insanity of constructions like virtual void final() override. Try not to do this.*

Whenever you're using interface inheritance, you should mark implementing classes final because the modifier can encourage the compiler to perform an optimization called *devirtualization*. When virtual calls are devirtualized, the compiler eliminates the runtime overhead associated with a virtual call.

volatile

Recall from Chapter 7 that a volatile object's value can change at any time, so the compiler must treat all accesses to volatile objects as visible side effects for optimization purposes. The volatile keyword indicates that a method can be invoked on volatile objects. This is analogous to how const methods can be applied to const objects. Together, these two keywords define a method's *const/volatile qualification* (or sometimes *cv qualification*), as demonstrated in Listing 9-3.

```
#include <cstdio>

struct Distillate {
```

```
  int apply() volatile ❶ {
    return ++applications;
  }
private:
  int applications{};
};

int main() {
  volatile ❷ Distillate ethanol;
  printf("%d Tequila\n", ethanol.apply()❸);
  printf("%d Tequila\n", ethanol.apply());
  printf("%d Tequila\n", ethanol.apply());
  printf("Floor!");
}
--------------------------------------------------------------------------
1 Tequila ❸
2 Tequila
3 Tequila
Floor!
```

Listing 9-3: Illustrating the use of a `volatile` method

In this listing, you declare the `apply` method on the `Distillate` class `volatile` ❶. You also create a `volatile` `Distillate` called `ethanol` within `main` ❷. Because the `apply` method is `volatile`, you can still invoke it ❸ (even though `ethanol` is `volatile`).

Had you not marked `apply` `volatile` ❶, the compiler would emit an error when you attempted to invoke it ❸. Just like you cannot invoke a non-`const` method on a `const` object, you cannot invoke a non-`volatile` method on a `volatile` object. Consider what would happen if you could perform such an operation: a non-`volatile` method is a candidate for all kinds of compiler optimizations for the reasons outlined in Chapter 7: many kinds of memory accesses can be optimized away without changing the observable side effects of your program.

How should the compiler treat a contradiction arising from you using a `volatile` object—which requires that all its memory accesses are treated as observable side effects—to invoke a non-`volatile` method? The compiler's answer is that it calls this contradiction an error.

auto Return Types

There are two ways to declare the return value of a function:

- (Primary) Lead a function declaration with its return type, as you've been doing all along.
- (Secondary) Have the compiler deduce the correct return type by using `auto`.

As with `auto` type deduction, the compiler deduces the return type, fixing the runtime type.

This feature should be used judiciously. Because function definitions are documentation, it's best to provide concrete return types when available.

auto and Function Templates

The primary use case for auto type deduction is with function templates, where a return type can depend (in potentially complicated ways) on the template parameters. Its usage is as follows:

```
auto my-function(arg1-type arg1, arg2-type arg2, ...) {
  // return any type and the
  // compiler will deduce what auto means
}
```

It's possible to extend the auto-return-type deduction syntax to provide the return type as a suffix with the arrow operator ->. This way, you can append an expression that evaluates to the function's return type. Its usage is as follows:

```
auto my-function(arg1-type arg1, arg2-type arg2, ...) -> type-expression {
  // return an object with type matching
  // the type-expression above
}
```

Usually, you wouldn't use this pedantic form, but in certain situations it's helpful. For example, this form of auto type deduction is commonly paired with a decltype type expression. A decltype type expression yields another expression's resultant type. Its usage is as follows:

```
decltype(expression)
```

This expression resolves to the resulting type of the expression. For example, the following decltype expression yields int, because the integer literal 100 has that type:

```
decltype(100)
```

Outside of generic programming with templates, decltype is rare.

You can combine auto-return-type deduction and decltype to document the return types of function templates. Consider the add function in Listing 9-4, which defines a function template add that adds two arguments together.

```
#include <cstdio>

template <typename X, typename Y>
auto add(X x, Y y) -> decltype(x + y) { ❶
  return x + y;
}
```

```
int main() {
  auto my_double = add(100., -10);
  printf("decltype(double + int) = double; %f\n", my_double); ❷

  auto my_uint = add(100U, -20);
  printf("decltype(uint + int) = uint; %u\n", my_uint); ❸

  auto my_ulonglong = add(char{ 100 }, 54'999'900ull);
  printf("decltype(char + ulonglong) = ulonglong; %llu\n", my_ulonglong); ❹
}
```

```
decltype(double + int) = double; 90.000000 ❷
decltype(uint + int) = uint; 80 ❸
decltype(char + ulonglong) = ulonglong; 55000000 ❹
```

Listing 9-4: Using `decltype` and auto-return-type deduction

The `add` function employs `auto` type deduction with the `decltype` type expression ❶. Each time you instantiate a template with two types `X` and `Y`, the compiler evaluates `decltype(X + Y)` and fixes the return type of `add`. Within `main`, you provide three instantiations. First, you add a `double` and an `int` ❷. The compiler determines that `decltype(double{ 100. } + int{ -10 })` is a `double`, which fixes the return type of this `add` instantiation. This, in turn, sets the type of `my_double` to `double` ❷. You have two other instantiations: one for an `unsigned int` and `int` (which results in an `unsigned int` ❸) and another for a `char` and an `unsigned long long` (which results in an `unsigned long long` ❹).

Overload Resolution

Overload resolution is the process that the compiler executes when matching a function invocation with its proper implementation.

Recall from Chapter 4 that function overloads allow you to specify functions with the same name but different types and possibly different arguments. The compiler selects among these function overloads by comparing the argument types within the function invocation with the types within each overload declaration. The compiler will choose the best among the possible options, and if it cannot select a best option, it will generate a compiler error.

Roughly, the matching process proceeds as follows:

1. The compiler will look for an exact type match.
2. The compiler will try using integral and floating-point promotions to get a suitable overload (for example, `int` to `long` or `float` to `double`).
3. The compiler will try to match using standard conversions like integral type to floating-point or casting a pointer-to-child into a pointer-to-parent.
4. The compiler will look for a user-defined conversion.
5. The compiler will look for a variadic function.

Variadic Functions

Variadic functions take a variable number of arguments. Typically, you specify the exact number of arguments a function takes by enumerating all of its parameters explicitly. With a variadic function, you can take any number of arguments. The variadic function printf is a canonical example: you provide a format specifier and an arbitrary number of parameters. Because printf is a variadic function, it accepts any number of parameters.

NOTE *The astute Pythonista will note an immediate conceptual relationship between variadic functions and *args/**kwargs.*

You declare variadic functions by placing ... as the final parameter in the function's argument list. When a variadic function is invoked, the compiler matches arguments against declared arguments. Any leftovers pack into the variadic arguments represented by the ... argument.

You cannot extract elements from the variadic arguments directly. Instead, you access individual arguments using the utility functions in the <cstdarg> header.

Table 9-1 lists these utility functions.

Table 9-1: Utility Functions in the <cstdarg> Header

Function	Description
va_list	Used to declare a local variable representing the variadic arguments
va_start	Enables access to the variadic arguments
va_end	Used to end iteration over the variadic arguments
va_arg	Used to iterate over each element in the variadic arguments
va_copy	Makes a copy of the variadic arguments

The utility functions' usage is a little convoluted and best presented in a cohesive example. Consider the variadic sum function in Listing 9-5, which contains a variadic argument.

```
#include <cstdio>
#include <cstdint>
#include <cstdarg>

int sum(size_t n, ...❶) {
  va_list args; ❷
  va_start(args, n); ❸
  int result{};
  while (n--) {
    auto next_element = va_arg(args, int); ❹
      result += next_element;
  }
  va_end(args); ❺
```

```
  return result;
}

int main() {
  printf("The answer is %d.", sum(6, 2, 4, 6, 8, 10, 12)); ❻
}
--------------------------------------------------------------------------
The answer is 42. ❻
```

Listing 9-5: A `sum` *function with a variadic argument list*

You declare `sum` as a variadic function ❶. All variadic functions must declare a `va_list`. You've named it `args` ❷. A `va_list` requires initialization with `va_start` ❸, which takes two arguments. The first argument is a `va_list`, and the second is the size of the variadic arguments. You iterate over each element in the variadic arguments using the `va_args` function. The first argument is the `va_list` argument, and the second is the argument type ❹. Once you've completed iterating, you call `va_list` with the `va_list` structure ❺.

You invoke `sum` with seven arguments: the first is the number of variadic arguments (six) followed by six numbers (2, 4, 6, 8, 10, 12) ❻.

Variadic functions are a holdover from C. Generally, variadic functions are unsafe and a common source of security vulnerabilities.

There are at least two major problems with variadic functions:

- Variadic arguments are not type-safe. (Notice that the second argument of `va_args` is a type.)
- The number of elements in the variadic arguments must be tracked separately.

The compiler cannot help you with either of these issues.

Fortunately, variadic templates provide a safer and more performant way to implement variadic functions.

Variadic Templates

The variadic template enables you to create function templates that accept variadic, same-typed arguments. They enable you to employ the considerable power of the template engine. To declare a variadic template, you add a special template parameter called a *template parameter pack*. Listing 9-6 demonstrates its usage.

```
template <typename...❶ Args>
return-type func-name(Args...❷ args) {
  // Use parameter pack semantics
  // within function body
}
```

Listing 9-6: A template function with a parameter pack

The template parameter pack is part of the template parameter list ❶. When you use Args within the function template ❷, it's called a *function parameter pack*. Some special operators are available for use with parameter packs:

- You can use `sizeof...(args)` to obtain the parameter pack's size.
- You can invoke a function (for example, `other_function`) with the special syntax `other_function(args...)`. This expands the parameter pack `args` and allows you to perform further processing on the arguments contained in the parameter pack.

Programming with Parameter Packs

Unfortunately, it's not possible to index into a parameter pack directly. You must invoke the function template from within itself—a process called *compile-time recursion*—to recursively iterate over the elements in a parameter pack.

Listing 9-7 demonstrates the pattern.

```
template <typename T, typename...Args>
void my_func(T x❶, Args...args) {
  // Use x, then recurse:
  my_func(args...); ❷
}
```

Listing 9-7: A template function illustrating compile-time recursion with parameter packs. Unlike other usage listings, the ellipses contained in this listing are literal.

The key is to add a regular template parameter before the parameter pack ❶. Each time you invoke `my_func`, `x` absorbs the first argument. The remainder packs into `args`. To invoke, you use the `args...` construct to expand the parameter pack ❷.

The recursion needs a stopping criteria, so you add a function template specialization without the parameter:

```
template <typename T>
void my_func(T x) {
  // Use x, but DON'T recurse
}
```

Revisiting the sum Function

Consider the (much improved) `sum` function implemented as a variadic template in Listing 9-8.

```
#include <cstdio>

template <typename T>
constexpr❶ T sum(T x) { ❷
    return x;
```

```
}

template <typename T, typename... Args>
constexpr❸ T sum(T x, Args... args) { ❹
    return x + sum(args...❺);
}

int main() {
  printf("The answer is %d.", sum(2, 4, 6, 8, 10, 12)); ❻
}
--------------------------------------------------------------------------
The answer is 42. ❻
```

Listing 9-8: A refactor of Listing 9-5 using a template parameter pack instead of va_args

The first function ❷ is the overload that handles the stopping condition; if the function has only a single argument, you simply return the argument `x`, because the sum of a single element is just the element. The variadic template ❹ follows the recursion pattern outlined in Listing 9-7. It peels a single argument `x` off the parameter pack `args` and then returns `x` plus the result of the recursive call to `sum` with the expanded parameter pack ❺. Because all of this generic programming can be computed at compile time, you mark these functions `constexpr` ❶❸. This compile-time computation is a *major* advantage over Listing 9-5, which has identical output but computes the result at runtime ❻. (Why pay runtime costs when you don't have to?)

When you just want to apply a single binary operator (like plus or minus) over a range of values (like Listing 9-5), you can use a fold expression instead of recursion.

Fold Expressions

A *fold expression* computes the result of using a binary operator over all the arguments of a parameter pack. Fold expressions are distinct from but related to variadic templates. Their usage is as follows:

```
(... binary-operator parameter-pack)
```

For example, you could employ the following fold expression to sum over all elements in a parameter pack called `pack`:

```
(... + args)
```

Listing 9-9 refactors 9-8 to use a fold expression instead of recursion.

```
#include <cstdio>

template <typename... T>
constexpr auto sum(T... args) {
  return (... + args); ❶
}
```

```
int main() {
  printf("The answer is %d.", sum(2, 4, 6, 8, 10, 12)); ❷
}
--------------------------------------------------------------------------
The answer is 42. ❷
```

Listing 9-9: A refactor of Listing 9-8 using a fold expression

You simplify the sum function by using a fold expression instead of the recursion approach ❶. The end result is identical ❷.

Function Pointers

Functional programming is a programming paradigm that emphasizes function evaluation and immutable data. One of the major concepts in functional programming is to pass a function as a parameter to another function.

One way you can achieve this is to pass a function pointer. Functions occupy memory, just like objects. You can refer to this memory address via usual pointer mechanisms. However, unlike objects, you cannot modify the pointed-to function. In this respect, functions are conceptually similar to const objects. You can take the address of functions and invoke them, and that's about it.

Declaring a Function Pointer

To declare a function pointer, use the following ugly syntax:

```
return-type (*pointer-name)(arg-type1, arg-type2, ...);
```

This has the same appearance as a function declaration where the function name is replaced (*pointer-name*).

As usual, you can employ the address-of operator & to take the address of a function. This is optional, however; you can simply use the function name as a pointer.

Listing 9-10 illustrates how you can obtain and use function pointers.

```
#include <cstdio>

float add(float a, int b) {
  return a + b;
}

float subtract(float a, int b) {
  return a - b;
}

int main() {
  const float first{ 100 };
  const int second{ 20 };

  float(*operation)(float, int) {}; ❶
  printf("operation initialized to 0x%p\n", operation); ❷
```

```
    operation = &add; ❸
    printf("&add = 0x%p\n", operation); ❹
    printf("%g + %d = %g\n", first, second, operation(first, second)); ❺

    operation = subtract; ❻
    printf("&subtract = 0x%p\n", operation); ❼
    printf("%g - %d = %g\n", first, second, operation(first, second)); ❽
}
--------------------------------------------------------------------------
operation initialized to 0x0000000000000000 ❷
&add = 0x00007FF6CDFE1070 ❹
100 + 20 = 120 ❺
&subtract = 0x00007FF6CDFE10A0 ❼
100 - 20 = 80 ❽
```

Listing 9-10: A program illustrating function pointers. (Due to address space layout randomization, the addresses ❹❼ will vary at runtime.)

This listing shows two functions with identical function signatures, `add` and `subtract`. Because the function signatures match, pointer types to these functions will also match. You initialize a function pointer `operation` accepting a `float` and an `int` as arguments and returning a `float` ❶. Next, you print the value of `operation`, which is `nullptr`, after initialization ❷.

You then assign the address of `add` to `operation` ❸ using the address-of operator and print its new address ❹. You invoke `operation` and print the result ❺.

To illustrate that you can reassign function pointers, you assign `operation` to `subtract` without using the address of operator ❻, print the new value of `operation` ❼, and finally print the result ❽.

Type Aliases and Function Pointers

Type aliases provide a neat way to program with function pointers. The usage is as follows:

```
using alias-name = return-type(*)(arg-type1, arg-type2, ...)
```

You could have defined an `operation_func` type alias in Listing 9-10, for example:

```
using operation_func = float(*)(float, int);
```

This is especially useful if you'll be using function pointers of the same type; it can really clean up the code.

The Function-Call Operator

You can make user-defined types callable or invocable by overloading the function-call operator `operator()()`. Such a type is called a *function type*, and instances of a function type are called *function objects*. The function-call operator permits any combination of argument types, return types, and modifiers (except static).

The primary reason you might want to make a user-defined type callable is to interoperate with code that expects function objects to use the function-call operator. You'll find that many libraries, such as the stdlib, use the function-call operator as the interface for function-like objects. For example, in Chapter 19, you'll learn how to create an asynchronous task with the std::async function, which accepts an arbitrary function object that can execute on a separate thread. It uses the function-call operator as the interface. The committee that invented std::async could have required you to expose, say, a run method, but they chose the function-call operator because it allows generic code to use identical notation to invoke a function or a function object.

Listing 9-11 illustrates the function-call operator's usage.

```
struct type-name {
  return-type❶ operator()❷(arg-type1 arg1, arg-type2 arg2, ...❸) {
    // Body of function-call operator
  }
}
```

Listing 9-11: The function-call operator's usage

The function-call operator has the special operator() method name ❷. You declare an arbitrary number of arguments ❸, and you also decide the appropriate return type ❶.

When the compiler evaluates a function-call expression, it will invoke the function-call operator on the first operand, passing the remaining operands as arguments. The result of the function-call expression is the result of invoking the corresponding function-call operator.

A Counting Example

Consider the function type CountIf in Listing 9-12, which computes the frequency of a particular char in a null-terminated string.

```
#include <cstdio>
#include <cstdint>

struct CountIf {
  CountIf(char x) : x{ x } { }❶
  size_t operator()(const char* str❷) const {
    size_t index{}❸, result{};
    while (str[index]) {
      if (str[index] == x) result++; ❹
      index++;
    }
    return result;
  }
private:
  const char x;
```

```
};

int main() {
  CountIf s_counter{ 's' }; ❺
  auto sally = s_counter("Sally sells seashells by the seashore."); ❻
  printf("Sally: %zd\n", sally);
  auto sailor = s_counter("Sailor went to sea to see what he could see.");
  printf("Sailor: %zd\n", sailor);
  auto buffalo = CountIf{ 'f' }("Buffalo buffalo Buffalo buffalo "
                                "buffalo buffalo Buffalo buffalo."); ❼
  printf("Buffalo: %zd\n", buffalo);
}
--------------------------------------------------------------------------
Sally: 7
Sailor: 3
Buffalo: 16
```

Listing 9-12: A function type that counts the number of characters appearing in a null-terminated string

You initialize CountIf objects using a constructor taking a char ❶. You can call the resulting function object as if it were a function taking a null-terminated string argument ❷, because you've implemented the function call operator. The function call operator iterates through each character in the argument str using an index variable ❸, incrementing the result variable whenever the character matches the x field ❹. Because calling the function doesn't modify the state of a CountIf object, you've marked it const.

Within main, you've initialized the CountIf function object s_counter, which will count the frequency of the letter s ❺. You can use s_counter as if it were a function ❻. You can even initialize a CountIf object and use the function operator directly as an rvalue object ❼. You might find this convenient to do in some settings where, for example, you might only need to invoke the object a single time.

You can employ function objects as partial applications. Listing 9-12 is conceptually similar to the count_if function in Listing 9-13.

```
#include <cstdio>
#include <cstdint>

size_t count_if(char x❶, const char* str) {
  size_t index{}, result{};
  while (str[index]) {
    if (str[index] == x) result++;
    index++;
  }
  return result;
}

int main() {
  auto sally = count_if('s', "Sally sells seashells by the seashore.");
  printf("Sally: %zd\n", sally);
  auto sailor = count_if('s', "Sailor went to sea to see what he could see.");
  printf("Sailor: %zd\n", sailor);
```

```
  auto buffalo = count_if('f', "Buffalo buffalo Buffalo buffalo "
                               "buffalo buffalo Buffalo buffalo.");
  printf("Buffalo: %zd\n", buffalo);
}
--------------------------------------------------------------------------
Sally: 7
Sailor: 3
Buffalo: 16
```

Listing 9-13: A free function emulating Listing 9-12

The `count_if` function has an extra argument `x` ❶, but otherwise it's almost identical to the function operator of `CountIf`.

NOTE *In functional programming parlance, the* `CountIf` *is the partial application of* `x` *to* `count_if`*. When you partially apply an argument to a function, you fix that argument's value. The product of such a partial application is another function taking one less argument.*

Declaring function types is verbose. You can often reduce the boilerplate substantially with lambda expressions.

Lambda Expressions

Lambda expressions construct unnamed function objects succinctly. The function object implies the function type, resulting in a quick way to declare a function object on the fly. Lambdas don't provide any additional functionality other than declaring function types the old-fashioned way. But they're extremely convenient when you need to initialize a function object in only a single context.

Usage

There are five components to a lambda expression:

- *captures*: The member variables of the function object (that is, the partially applied parameters)
- *parameters*: The arguments required to invoke the function object
- *body*: The function object's code
- *specifiers*: Elements like `constexpr`, `mutable`, `noexcept`, and `[[noreturn]]`
- *return type*: The type returned by the function object

Lambda expression usage is as follows:

```
[captures❶] (parameters❷) modifiers❺ -> return-type❹ { body❸ }
```

Only the captures and the body are required; everything else is optional. You'll learn about each of these components in depth in the next few sections.

Each lambda component has a direct analogue in a function object. To form a bridge between the function objects like CountIf and lambda expressions, look at Listing 9-14, which lists the CountIf function type from Listing 9-12 with annotations that correspond to the analogous portions of the lambda expression in the usage listing.

```
struct CountIf {
  CountIf(char x) : x{ x } { } ❶
  size_t❹ operator()(const char* str❷) const❺ {
    --snip--❸
  }
private:
  const char x; ❷
};
```

Listing 9-14: Comparing the CountIf type declaration with a lambda expression

The member variables you set in the constructor of CountIf are analogous to a lambda's capture ❶. The function-call operator's arguments ❷, body ❸, and return type ❹ are analogous to the lambda's parameters, body, and return type. Finally, modifiers can apply to the function-call operator ❺ and the lambda. (The numbers in the Lambda expession usage example and Listing 9-14 correspond.)

Lambda Parameters and Bodies

Lambda expressions produce function objects. As function objects, lambdas are callable. Most of the time, you'll want your function object to accept parameters upon invocation.

The lambda's body is just like a function body: all of the parameters have function scope.

You declare lambda parameters and bodies using essentially the same syntax that you use for functions.

For example, the following lambda expression yields a function object that will square its int argument:

```
[](int x) { return x*x; }
```

The lambda takes a single int x and uses it within the lambda's body to perform the squaring.

Listing 9-15 employs three different lambdas to transform the array 1, 2, 3.

```
#include <cstdio>
#include <cstdint>

template <typename Fn>
void transform(Fn fn, const int* in, int* out, size_t length) { ❶
  for(size_t i{}; i<length; i++) {
    out[i] = fn(in[i]); ❷
  }
```

```
}

int main() {
  const size_t len{ 3 };
  int base[]{ 1, 2, 3 }, a[len], b[len], c[len];
  transform([](int x) { return 1; }❸, base, a, len);
  transform([](int x) { return x; }❹, base, b, len);
  transform([](int x) { return 10*x+5; }❺, base, c, len);
  for (size_t i{}; i < len; i++) {
    printf("Element %zd: %d %d %d\n", i, a[i], b[i], c[i]);
  }
}
--------------------------------------------------------------------------
Element 0: 1 1 15
Element 1: 1 2 25
Element 2: 1 3 35
```

Listing 9-15: Three lambdas and a transform function

The `transform` template function ❶ accepts four arguments: a function object `fn`, an `in` array and an `out` array, and the corresponding `length` of those arrays. Within transform, you invoke `fn` on each element of `in` and assign the result to the corresponding element of `out` ❷.

Within `main`, you declare a `base` array `1, 2, 3` that will be used as the `in` array. In the same line you also declare three uninitialized arrays `a`, `b`, and `c`, which will be used as the `out` arrays. The first call to `transform` passes a lambda (`[](int x) { return 1; }`) that always returns 1 ❸, and the result is stored into `a`. (Notice that the lambda didn't need a name!) The second call to `transform` (`[](int x) { return x; }`) simply returns its argument ❹, and the result is stored into `b`. The third call to `transform` multiplies the argument by 10 and adds 5 ❺. The result is stored in `c`. You then print the output into a matrix where each column illustrates the transform that was applied to the different lambdas in each case.

Notice that you declared `transform` as a template function, allowing you to reuse it with any function object.

Default Arguments

You can provide default arguments to a lambda. Default lambda parameters behave just like default function parameters. The caller can specify values for default parameters, in which case the lambda uses the caller-provided values. If the caller doesn't specify a value, the lambda uses the default.

Listing 9-16 illustrates the default argument behavior.

```
#include <cstdio>

int main() {
  auto increment = [](auto x, int y = 1❶) { return x + y; };
  printf("increment(10)     = %d\n", increment(10)); ❷
  printf("increment(10, 5) = %d\n", increment(10, 5)); ❸
}
```

```
increment(10)     = 11 ❷
increment(10, 5) = 15 ❸
```

Listing 9-16: Using default lambda parameters

The increment lambda has two parameters, x and y. But the y parameter is optional because it has the default argument 1 ❶. If you don't specify an argument for y when you call the function ❷, increment returns 1 + x. If you do call the function with an argument for y ❸, that value is used instead.

Generic Lambdas

Generic lambdas are lambda expression templates. For one or more parameters, you specify auto rather than a concrete type. These auto types become template parameters, meaning the compiler will stamp out a custom instantiation of the lambda.

Listing 9-17 illustrates how to assign a generic lambda into a variable and then use the lambda in two different template instantiations.

```
#include <cstdio>
#include <cstdint>

template <typename Fn, typename T❶>
void transform(Fn fn, const T* in, T* out, size_t len) {
  for(size_t i{}; i<len; i++) {
    out[i] = fn(in[i]);
  }
}

int main() {
  constexpr size_t len{ 3 };
  int base_int[]{ 1, 2, 3 }, a[len]; ❷
  float base_float[]{ 10.f, 20.f, 30.f }, b[len]; ❸
  auto translate = [](auto x) { return 10 * x + 5; }; ❹
  transform(translate, base_int, a, l); ❺
  transform(translate, base_float, b, l); ❻

  for (size_t i{}; i < l; i++) {
    printf("Element %zd: %d %f\n", i, a[i], b[i]);
  }
}
```

```
Element 0: 15 105.000000
Element 1: 25 205.000000
Element 2: 35 305.000000
```

Listing 9-17: Using a generic lambda

You add a second template parameter to transform ❶, which you use as the pointed-to type of in and out. This allows you to apply transform to arrays of any type, not just of int types. To test out the upgraded transform template, you declare two arrays with different pointed-to types: int ❷ and float ❸. (Recall from Chapter 3 that the f in 10.f specifies a float literal.) Next, you assign a generic lambda expression to translate ❹. This allows you to use the same lambda for each instantiation of transform: when you instantiate with base_int ❺ and with base_float ❻.

Without a generic lambda, you'd have to declare the parameter types explicitly, like the following:

```
--snip-
  transform([](int x) { return 10 * x + 5; }, base_int, a, 1); ❺
  transform([](double x) { return 10 * x + 5; }, base_float, b, 1); ❻
```

So far, you've been leaning on the compiler to deduce the return types of your lambdas. This is especially useful for generic lambdas, because often the lambda's return type will depend on its parameter types. But you can explicitly state the return type if you want.

Lambda Return Types

The compiler deduces a lambda's return type for you. To take over from the compiler, you use the arrow -> syntax, as in the following:

```
[](int x, double y) -> double { return x + y; }
```

This lambda expression accepts an int and a double and returns a double.

You can also use decltype expressions, which can be useful with generic lambdas. For example, consider the following lambda:

```
[](auto x, double y) -> decltype(x+y) { return x + y; }
```

Here you've explicitly declared that the return type of the lambda is whatever type results from adding an x to a y.

You'll rarely need to specify a lambda's return type explicitly.

A far more common requirement is that you must inject an object into a lambda before invocation. This is the role of lambda captures.

Lambda Captures

Lambda captures inject objects into the lambda. The injected objects help to modify the behavior of the lambda.

Declare a lambda's capture by specifying a capture list within brackets []. The capture list goes before the parameter list, and it can contain any number of comma-separated arguments. You then use these arguments within the lambda's body.

A lambda can capture by reference or by value. By default, lambdas capture by value.

A lambda's capture list is analogous to a function type's constructor. Listing 9-18 reformulates CountIf from Listing 9-12 as the lambda s_counter.

```
#include <cstdio>
#include <cstdint>

int main() {
  char to_count{ 's' }; ❶
  auto s_counter = [to_count❷](const char* str) {
    size_t index{}, result{};
    while (str[index]) {
      if (str[index] == to_count❸) result++;
      index++;
    }
    return result;
  };
  auto sally = s_counter("Sally sells seashells by the seashore."❹);
  printf("Sally: %zd\n", sally);
  auto sailor = s_counter("Sailor went to sea to see what he could see.");
  printf("Sailor: %zd\n", sailor);
}
--------------------------------------------------------------------------
Sally: 7
Sailor: 3
```

Listing 9-18: Reformulating `CountIf` from Listing 9-12 as a lambda

You initialize a `char` called `to_count` to the letter `s` ❶. Next, you capture `to_count` within the lambda expression assigned to `s_counter` ❷. This makes `to_count` available within the body of the lambda expression ❸.

To capture an element by reference rather than by value, prefix the captured object's name with an ampersand `&`. Listing 9-19 adds a capture reference to `s_counter` that keeps a running tally across lambda invocations.

```
#include <cstdio>
#include <cstdint>

int main() {
  char to_count{ 's' };
  size_t tally{};❶
  auto s_counter = [to_count, &tally❷](const char* str) {
    size_t index{}, result{};
    while (str[index]) {
      if (str[index] == to_count) result++;
      index++;
    }
    tally += result;❸
    return result;
  };
  printf("Tally: %zd\n", tally); ❹
  auto sally = s_counter("Sally sells seashells by the seashore.");
  printf("Sally: %zd\n", sally);
  printf("Tally: %zd\n", tally); ❺
  auto sailor = s_counter("Sailor went to sea to see what he could see.");
  printf("Sailor: %zd\n", sailor);
```

```
  printf("Tally: %zd\n", tally); ❻
}
```

```
Tally: 0 ❹
Sally: 7
Tally: 7 ❺
Sailor: 3
Tally: 10 ❻
```

Listing 9-19: Using a capture reference in a lambda

You initialize the counter variable tally to zero ❶, and then the s_counter lambda captures tally by reference (note the ampersand &) ❷. Within the lambda's body, you add a statement to increment tally by an invocation's result before returning ❸. The result is that tally will track the total count no matter how many times you invoke the lambda. Before the first s_counter invocation, you print the value of tally ❹ (which is still zero). After you invoke s_counter with Sally sells seashells by the seashore., you have a tally of 7 ❺. The last invocation of s_counter with Sailor went to sea to see what he could see. returns 3, so the value of tally is 7 + 3 = 10 ❻.

Default Capture

So far, you've had to capture each element by name. Sometimes this style of capturing is called *named capture.* If you're lazy, you can capture all automatic variables used within a lambda using *default capture.* To specify a default capture by value within a capture list, use a lone equal sign =. To specify a default capture by reference, use a lone ampersand &.

For example, you could "simplify" the lambda expression in Listing 9-19 to perform a default capture by reference, as demonstrated in Listing 9-20.

```
--snip--
  auto s_counter = [&❶](const char* str) {
    size_t index{}, result{};
    while (str[index]) {
      if (str[index] == to_count❷) result++;
      index++;
    }
    tally❸ += result;
    return result;
  };
--snip--
```

Listing 9-20: Simplifying a lambda expression with a default capture by reference

You specify a default capture by reference ❶, which means any automatic variables in the body of the lambda expression get captured by reference. There are two: to_count ❷ and tally ❸.

If you compile and run the refactored listing, you'll obtain identical output. However, notice that to_count is now captured by reference. If you accidentally modify it within the lambda expression's body, the change will occur across lambda invocations as well as within main (where to_count is an automatic variable).

What would happen if you performed a default capture by value instead? You would only need to change the = to an & in the capture list, as demonstrated in Listing 9-21.

```
--snip--
  auto s_counter = [=❶](const char* str) {
    size_t index{}, result{};
    while (str[index]) {
      if (str[index] == to_count❷) result++;
      index++;
    }
    tally❸ += result;
    return result;
  };
--snip--
```

Listing 9-21: Modifying Listing 9-20 to capture by value instead of by reference (This code doesn't compile.)

You change the default capture to be by value ❶. The to_count capture is unaffected ❷, but attempting to modify tally results in a compiler error ❸. You're not allowed to modify variables captured by value unless you add the mutable keyword to the lambda expression. The mutable keyword allows you to modify value-captured variables. This includes calling non-const methods on that object.

Listing 9-22 adds the mutable modifier and has a default capture by value.

```
#include <cstdio>
#include <cstdint>

int main() {
  char to_count{ 's' };
  size_t tally{};
  auto s_counter = [=❶](const char* str) mutable❷ {
    size_t index{}, result{};
    while (str[index]) {
      if (str[index] == to_count) result++;
      index++;
    }
    tally += result;
    return result;
  };
  auto sally = s_counter("Sally sells seashells by the seashore.");
  printf("Tally: %zd\n", tally); ❸
  printf("Sally: %zd\n", sally);
  printf("Tally: %zd\n", tally); ❹
  auto sailor = s_counter("Sailor went to sea to see what he could see.");
  printf("Sailor: %zd\n", sailor);
```

```
  printf("Tally: %zd\n", tally); ❺
}
```

```
Tally: 0
Sally: 7
Tally: 0
Sailor: 3
Tally: 0
```

Listing 9-22: A `mutable` lambda expression with a default capture by value

You declare a default capture by value ❶, and you make the lambda `s_counter` `mutable` ❷. Each of the three times you print `tally` ❸❹❺, you get a zero value. Why?

Because `tally` gets copied by value (via the default capture), the version in the lambda is, in essence, an entirely different variable that just happens to have the same name. Modifications to the lambda's copy of `tally` don't affect the automatic `tally` variable of `main`. The `tally` in `main()` is initialized to zero and never gets modified.

It's also possible to mix a default capture with a named capture. You could, for example, default capture by reference and copy `to_count` by value using the following formulation:

```
auto s_counter = [&❶,to_count❷](const char* str) {
  --snip--
};
```

This specifies a default capture by reference ❶ and `to_count` ❷ capture by value.

Although performing a default capture might seem like an easy shortcut, refrain from using it. It's far better to declare captures explicitly. If you catch yourself saying "I'll just use a default capture because there are too many variables to list out," you probably need to refactor your code.

Initializer Expressions in Capture Lists

Sometimes you want to initialize a whole new variable within a capture list. Maybe renaming a captured variable would make a lambda expression's intent clearer. Or perhaps you want to move an object into a lambda and therefore need to initialize a variable.

To use an initializer expression, just declare the new variable's name followed by an equal sign and the value you want to initialize your variable with, as Listing 9-23 demonstrates.

```
auto s_counter = [&tally❶,my_char=to_count❷](const char* str) {
  size_t index{}, result{};
  while (str[index]) {
    if (str[index] == my_char❸) result++;
  --snip--
};
```

Listing 9-23: Using an initializer expression within a lambda capture

The capture list contains a simple named capture where you have tally by reference ❶. The lambda also captures to_count by value, but you've elected to use the variable name my_char instead ❷. Of course, you'll need to use the name my_char instead of to_count inside the lambda ❸.

NOTE *An initializer expression in a capture list is also called an* init capture.

Capturing this

Sometimes lambda expressions have an enclosing class. You can capture an enclosing object (pointed-to by this) by value or by reference using either [*this] or [this], respectively.

Listing 9-24 implements a LambdaFactory that generates counting lambdas and keeps track of a tally.

```
#include <cstdio>
#include <cstdint>

struct LambdaFactory {
  LambdaFactory(char in) : to_count{ in }, tally{} { }
  auto make_lambda() { ❶
    return [this❷](const char* str) {
      size_t index{}, result{};
      while (str[index]) {
        if (str[index] == to_count❸) result++;
        index++;
      }
      tally❹ += result;
      return result;
    };
  }
  const char to_count;
  size_t tally;
};

int main() {
  LambdaFactory factory{ 's' }; ❺
  auto lambda = factory.make_lambda(); ❻
  printf("Tally: %zd\n", factory.tally);
  printf("Sally: %zd\n", lambda("Sally sells seashells by the seashore."));
  printf("Tally: %zd\n", factory.tally);
  printf("Sailor: %zd\n", lambda("Sailor went to sea to see what he could
see."));
  printf("Tally: %zd\n", factory.tally);
}
```
```
Tally: 0
Sally: 7
Tally: 7
Sailor: 3
Tally: 10
```

Listing 9-24: A LambdaFactory illustrating the use of this capture

The LambdaFactory constructor takes a single character and initializes the to_count field with it. The make_lambda ❶ method illustrates how you can capture this by reference ❷ and use the to_count ❸ and tally ❹ member variables within the lambda expression.

Within main, you initialize a factory ❺ and make a lambda using the make_lambda method ❻. The output is identical to Listing 9-19, because you capture this by reference and state of tally persists across invocations of lambda.

Clarifying Examples

There are a lot of possibilities with capture lists, but once you have a command of the basics—capturing by value and by reference—there aren't many surprises. Table 9-2 provides short, clarifying examples that you can use for future reference.

Table 9-2: Clarifying Examples of Lambda Capture Lists

Capture list	Meaning
[&]	Default capture by reference
[&,i]	Default capture by reference; capture i by value
[=]	Default capture by value
[=,&i]	Default capture by value; capture i by reference
[i]	Capture i by value
[&i]	Capture i by reference
[i,&j]	Capture i by value; capture j by reference
[i=j,&k]	Capture j by value as i; capture k by reference
[this]	Capture enclosing object by reference
[*this]	Capture enclosing object by value
[=,*this,i,&j]	Default capture by value; capture this and i by value; capture j by reference

constexpr Lambda Expressions

All lambda expressions are constexpr as long as the lambda can be invoked at compile time. You can optionally make the constexpr declaration explicit, as in the following:

```
[] (int x) constexpr { return x * x; }
```

You should mark a lambda constexpr if you want to make sure that it meets all constexpr requirements. As of C++17, this means no dynamic memory allocations and no calling non-constexpr functions, among other restrictions. The standards committee plans to loosen these restrictions with each release, so if you write a lot of code using constexpr, be sure to brush up on the latest constexpr constraints.

std::function

Sometimes you just want a uniform container for storing callable objects. The `std::function` class template from the `<functional>` header is a polymorphic wrapper around a callable object. In other words, it's a generic function pointer. You can store a static function, a function object, or a lambda into a `std::function`.

NOTE *The* `function` *class is in the stdlib. We're presenting it a little ahead of schedule because it fits naturally.*

With `function`s, you can:

- Invoke without the caller knowing the function's implementation
- Assign, move, and copy
- Have an empty state, similar to a `nullptr`

Declaring a Function

To declare a `function`, you must provide a single template parameter containing the function prototype of the callable object:

```
std::function<return-type(arg-type-1, arg-type-2, etc.)>
```

The `std::function` class template has a number of constructors. The default constructor constructs a `std::function` in empty mode, meaning it contains no callable object.

Empty Functions

If you invoke a `std::function` with no contained object, `std::function` will throw a `std::bad_function_call` exception. Consider Listing 9-25.

```
#include <cstdio>
#include <functional>

int main() {
    std::function<void()> func; ❶
    try {
        func(); ❷
    } catch(const std::bad_function_call& e) {
        printf("Exception: %s", e.what()); ❸
    }
}
--------------------------------------------------------------------------
Exception: bad function call ❸
```

Listing 9-25: The default `std::function` *constructor and the* `std::bad_function_call` *exception*

You default-construct a std::function ❶. The template parameter void() denotes a function taking no arguments and returning void. Because you didn't fill func with a callable object, it's in an empty state. When you invoke func ❷, it throws a std::bad_function_call, which you catch and print ❸.

Assigning a Callable Object to a Function

To assign a callable object to a function, you can either use the constructor or assignment operator of function, as in Listing 9-26.

```
#include <cstdio>
#include <functional>

void static_func() { ❶
  printf("A static function.\n");
}

int main() {
  std::function<void()> func { [] { printf("A lambda.\n"); } }; ❷
  func(); ❸
  func = static_func; ❹
  func(); ❺
}
--------------------------------------------------------------------------
A lambda. ❸
A static function. ❺
```

Listing 9-26: Using the constructor and assignment operator of function

You declare the static function static_func that takes no arguments and returns void ❶. In main, you create a function called func ❷. The template parameter indicates that a callable object contained by func takes no arguments and returns void. You initialize func with a lambda that prints the message A lambda. You invoke func immediately afterward ❸, invoking the contained lambda and printing the expected message. Next, you assign static_func to func, which replaces the lambda you assigned upon construction ❹. You then invoke func, which invokes static_func rather than the lambda, so you see A static function. printed ❺.

An Extended Example

You can construct a function with callable objects, as long as that object supports the function semantics implied by the template parameter of function.

Listing 9-27 uses an array of std::function instances and fills it with a static function that counts spaces, a CountIf function object from Listing 9-12, and a lambda that computes string length.

```
#include <cstdio>
#include <cstdint>
#include <functional>

struct CountIf {
```

```
  --snip--
};

size_t count_spaces(const char* str) {
  size_t index{}, result{};
  while (str[index]) {
    if (str[index] == ' ') result++;
    index++;
  }
  return result;
}

std::function❶<size_t(const char*)❷> funcs[]{
  count_spaces, ❸
  CountIf{ 'e' }, ❹
  [](const char* str) { ❺
    size_t index{};
    while (str[index]) index++;
    return index;
  }
};

auto text = "Sailor went to sea to see what he could see.";

int main() {
  size_t index{};
  for(const auto& func : funcs❻) {
    printf("func #%zd: %zd\n", index++, func(text)❼);
  }
}
--------------------------------------------------------------------------
func #0: 9 ❸
func #1: 7 ❹
func #2: 44 ❺
```

Listing 9-27: Using a `std::function` array to iterate over a uniform collection of callable objects with varying underlying types

You declare a `std::function` array ❶ with static storage duration called `funcs`. The template argument is the function prototype for a function taking a `const char*` and returning a `size_t` ❷. In the `funcs` array, you pass in a static function pointer ❸, a function object ❹, and a lambda ❺. In `main`, you use a range-based `for` loop to iterate through each function in `funcs` ❻. You invoke each function `func` with the text `Sailor went to sea to see what he could see.` and print the result.

Notice that, from the perspective of `main`, all the elements in `funcs` are the same: you just invoke them with a null-terminated string and get back a `size_t` ❼.

NOTE *Using a `function` can incur runtime overhead. For technical reasons, `function` might need to make a dynamic allocation to store the callable object. The compiler also has difficulty optimizing away `function` invocations, so you'll often incur an indirect function call. Indirect function calls require additional pointer dereferences.*

The main Function and the Command Line

All C++ programs must contain a global function with the name `main`. This function is defined as the program's entry point, the function invoked at program startup. Programs can accept any number of environment-provided arguments called *command line parameters* upon startup.

Users pass command line parameters to programs to customize their behavior. You've probably used this feature when executing command line programs, as in the `copy` (on Linux: `cp`) command:

```
$ copy file_a.txt file_b.txt
```

When invoking this command, you instruct the program to copy `file_a.txt` into `file_b.txt` by passing these values as command line parameters. As with command line programs you might be used to, it's possible to pass values as command line parameters to your C++ programs.

You can choose whether your program handles command line parameters by how you declare `main`.

The Three main Overloads

You can access command line parameters within `main` by adding arguments to your `main` declaration.

There are three valid varieties of overload for `main`, as shown in Listing 9-28.

```
int main(); ❶
int main(int argc, char* argv[]); ❷
int main(int argc, char* argv[], impl-parameters); ❸
```

Listing 9-28: The valid overloads for `main`

The first overload ❶ takes no parameters, which is the way you've been using `main()` in this book so far. Use this form if you want to ignore any arguments provided to your program.

The second overload ❷ accepts two parameters, `argc` and `argv`. The first argument, `argc`, is a non-negative number corresponding to the number of elements in `argv`. The environment calculates this automatically: you don't have to provide the number of elements in `argc`. The second argument, `argv`, is an array of pointers to null-terminated strings that corresponds to an argument passed in from the execution environment.

The third overload ❸ is an extension of the second overload ❷: it accepts an arbitrary number of additional implementation parameters. This way, the target platform can offer some additional arguments to the program. Implementation parameters aren't common in modern desktop environments.

Usually, an operating system passes the full path to the program's executable as the first command line argument. This behavior depends on your operating environment. On macOS, Linux, and Windows, the executable's path is the first argument. The format of this path depends on the operating system. (Chapter 17 discusses filesystems in depth.)

Exploring Program Parameters

Let's build a program to explore how the operating system passes parameters to your program. Listing 9-29 prints the number of command line arguments and then prints the index and value of the arguments on each line.

```
#include <cstdio>
#include <cstdint>

int main(int argc, char** argv) { ❶
  printf("Arguments: %d\n", argc); ❷
  for(size_t i{}; i<argc; i++) {
    printf("%zd: %s\n", i, argv[i]); ❸
  }
}
```

Listing 9-29: A program that prints the command line arguments. Compile this program as `list_929`.

You declare main with the argc/argv overload, which makes command line parameters available to your program ❶. First, you print the number of command line arguments via argc ❷. Then you loop through each argument, printing its index and its value ❸.

Let's look at some sample output (on Windows 10 x64). Here is one program invocation:

```
$ list_929 ❶
Arguments: 1 ❷
0: list_929.exe ❸
```

Here, you provide no additional command line arguments aside from the name of the program, `list_929` ❶. (Depending on how you compiled the listing, you should replace this with the name of your executable.) On a Windows 10 x64 machine, the result is that your program receives a single argument ❷, the name of the executable ❸.

And here is another invocation:

```
$ list_929 Violence is the last refuge of the incompetent. ❶
Arguments: 9
0: list_929.exe
1: Violence
2: is
3: the
4: last
5: refuge
6: of
7: the
8: incompetent.
```

Here, you provide additional program arguments: `Violence is the last refuge of the incompetent.` ❶. You can see from the output that Windows has split the command line by spaces, resulting in a total of nine arguments.

In major desktop operating systems, you can force the operating system to treat such a phrase as a single argument by enclosing it within quotes, as in the following:

```
$ list_929 "Violence is the last refuge of the incompetent."
Arguments: 2
0: list_929.exe
1: Violence is the last refuge of the incompetent.
```

A More Involved Example

Now that you know how to process command line input, let's consider a more involved example. A *histogram* is an illustration that shows a distribution's relative frequency. Let's build a program that computes a histogram of the letter distribution of the command line arguments.

Start with two helper functions that determine whether a given `char` is an uppercase letter or a lowercase letter:

```
constexpr char pos_A{ 65 }, pos_Z{ 90 }, pos_a{ 97 }, pos_z{ 122 };
constexpr bool within_AZ(char x) { return pos_A <= x && pos_Z >= x; } ❶
constexpr bool within_az(char x) { return pos_a <= x && pos_z >= x; } ❷
```

The `pos_A`, `pos_Z`, `pos_a`, and `pos_z` constants contain the ASCII values of the letters A, Z, a, and z respectively (refer to the ASCII chart in Table 2-4). The `within_AZ` function determines whether some `char x` is an uppercase letter by determining whether its value is between `pos_A` and `pos_Z` inclusive ❶. The `within_az` function does the same for lowercase letters ❷.

Now that you have some elements for processing ASCII data from the command line, let's build an `AlphaHistogram` class that can ingest command line elements and store character frequencies, as shown in Listing 9-30.

```
struct AlphaHistogram {
  void ingest(const char* x); ❶
  void print() const; ❷
private:
  size_t counts[26]{}; ❸
};
```

Listing 9-30: An `AlphaHistogram` that ingests command line elements

An `AlphaHistogram` will store the frequency of each letter in the `counts` array ❸. This array initializes to zero whenever an `AlphaHistogram` is constructed. The `ingest` method will take a null-terminated string and update `counts` appropriately ❶. Then the `print` method will display the histogram information stored in `counts` ❷.

First, consider the implementation of ingest in Listing 9-31.

```
void AlphaHistogram::ingest(const char* x) {
  size_t index{}; ❶
  while(const auto c = x[index]) { ❷
    if (within_AZ(c)) counts[c - pos_A]++; ❸
    else if (within_az(c)) counts[c - pos_a]++; ❹
    index++; ❺
  }
}
```

Listing 9-31: An implementation of the `ingest` method

Because `x` is a null-terminated string, you don't know its length ahead of time. So, you initialize an `index` variable ❶ and use a `while` loop to extract a single `char c` at a time ❷. This loop will terminate if `c` is null, which is the end of the string. Within the loop, you use the `within_AZ` helper function to determine whether `c` is an uppercase letter ❸. If it is, you subtract `pos_A` from `c`. This normalizes an uppercase letter to the interval 0 to 25 to correspond with `counts`. You do the same check for lowercase letters using the `within_az` helper function ❹, and you update `counts` in case `c` is lowercase. If `c` is neither lowercase nor uppercase, `counts` is unaffected. Finally, you increment `index` before continuing to loop ❺.

Now, consider how to `print counts`, as shown in Listing 9-32.

```
void AlphaHistogram::print() const {
  for(auto index{ pos_A }; index <= pos_Z; index++) {  ❶
    printf("%c: ", index); ❷
    auto n_asterisks = counts[index - pos_A]; ❸
    while (n_asterisks--) printf("*"); ❹
    printf("\n"); ❺
  }
}
```

Listing 9-32: An implementation of the `print` method

To print the histogram, you loop over each letter from A to Z ❶. Within the loop, you first print the `index` letter ❷, and then determine how many asterisks to print by extracting the correct letter out of `counts` ❸. You print the correct number of asterisks using a `while` loop ❹, and then you print a terminating newline ❺.

Listing 9-33 shows `AlphaHistogram` in action.

```
#include <cstdio>
#include <cstdint>

constexpr char pos_A{ 65 }, pos_Z{ 90 }, pos_a{ 97 }, pos_z{ 122 };
constexpr bool within_AZ(char x) { return pos_A <= x && pos_Z >= x; }
constexpr bool within_az(char x) { return pos_a <= x && pos_z >= x; }

struct AlphaHistogram {
  --snip--
```

```
};

int main(int argc, char** argv) {
  AlphaHistogram hist;
  for(size_t i{ 1 }; i<argc; i++) { ❶
    hist.ingest(argv[i]); ❷
  }
  hist.print(); ❸
}
```

```
$ list_933 The quick brown fox jumps over the lazy dog
A: *
B: *
C: *
D: *
E: ***
F: *
G: *
H: **
I: *
J: *
K: *
L: *
M: *
N: *
O: ****
P: *
Q: *
R: **
S: *
T: **
U: **
V: *
W: *
X: *
Y: *
Z: *
```

Listing 9-33: A program illustrating `AlphaHistogram`

You iterate over each command line argument after the program name ❶, passing each into the `ingest` method of your `AlphaHistogram` object ❷. Once you've ingested them all, you print the `histogram` ❸. Each line corresponds to a letter, and the asterisks show the absolute frequency of the corresponding letter. As you can see, the phrase `The quick brown fox jumps over the lazy dog` contains each letter in the English alphabet.

Exit Status

The `main` function can return an `int` corresponding to the exit status of the program. What the values represent is environment defined. On modern desktop systems, for example, a zero return value corresponds with a successful program execution. If no `return` statement is explicitly given, an implicit `return 0` is added by the compiler.

Summary

This chapter took a deeper look at functions, including how to declare and define them, how to use the myriad keywords available to you to modify function behavior, how to specify return types, how overload resolution works, and how to take a variable number of arguments. After a discussion of how you take pointers to functions, you explored lambda expressions and their relationship to function objects. Then you learned about the entry point for your programs, the `main` function, and how to take command line arguments.

EXERCISES

9-1. Implement a `fold` function template with the following prototype:

```
template <typename Fn, typename In, typename Out>
constexpr Out fold(Fn function, In* input, size_t length, Out initial);
```

For example, your implementation must support the following usage:

```
int main() {
  int data[]{ 100, 200, 300, 400, 500 };
  size_t data_len = 5;
  auto sum = fold([](auto x, auto y) { return x + y; }, data, data_len,
0);
  print("Sum: %d\n", sum);
}
```

The value of `sum` should be 1,500. Use `fold` to calculate the following quantities: the `maximum`, the `minimum`, and the number of elements greater than 200.

9-2. Implement a program that accepts an arbitrary number of command line arguments, counts the length in characters of each argument, and prints a histogram of the argument length distribution.

9-3. Implement an `all` function with the following prototype:

```
template <typename Fn, typename In, typename Out>
constexpr bool all(Fn function, In* input, size_t length);
```

The `Fn` function type is a predicate that supports `bool operator()(In)`. Your `all` function must test whether `function` returns `true` for every element of `input`. If it does, return `true`. Otherwise, return `false`.

For example, your implementation must support the following usage:

```
int main() {
  int data[]{ 100, 200, 300, 400, 500 };
  size_t data_len = 5;
  auto all_gt100 = all([](auto x) { return x > 100; }, data, data_len);
  if(all_gt100) printf("All elements greater than 100.\n");
}
```

FURTHER READING

- *Functional Programming in C++: How to Improve Your C++ Programs Using Functional Techniques* by Ivan Čukić (Manning, 2019)
- *Clean Code: A Handbook of Agile Software Craftsmanship* by Robert C. Martin (Pearson Education, 2009)

PART II

C++ LIBRARIES AND FRAMEWORKS

NEO: Why do my eyes hurt?
MORPHEUS: You've never used them before.
—The Matrix

Part II exposes you to the world of C++ libraries and frameworks, including the C++ Standard Library (stdlib) and the Boost Libraries (Boost). The latter is an open source volunteer project to produce much-needed C++ libraries.

In Chapter 10, you'll tour several testing and mocking frameworks. In a major departure from Part I, most listings in Part II are unit tests. These provide you with practice in testing code, and unit tests are often more succinct and expressive than `printf`-based example programs.

Chapter 11 takes a broad look at smart pointers, which manage dynamic objects and facilitate the most powerful resource management model in any programming language.

Chapter 12 explores the many utilities that implement common programming tasks.

Chapter 13 delves into the massive suite of containers that can hold and manipulate objects.

Chapter 14 explains iterators, the common interface that all containers provide.

Chapter 15 reviews strings and string operations, which store and manipulate human-language data.

Chapter 16 discusses streams, a modern way to perform input and output operations.

Chapter 17 illuminates the filesystem library, which provides facilities for interacting with filesystems.

Chapter 18 surveys the dizzying array of algorithms that query and manipulate iterators.

Chapter 19 outlines the major approaches to concurrency, which allows your programs to run simultaneous threads of execution.

Chapter 20 reviews Boost ASIO, a cross-platform library for network and low-level input/output programming using an asynchronous approach.

Chapter 21 provides several application frameworks that implement standard structures required in everyday application programming.

Part II will function well as a quick reference, but your first reading should be sequential.

10

TESTING

"How could [the computer] pick up a picture of Ender's brother and put it into the graphics in this Fairyland routine?"
"Colonel Graff, I wasn't there when it was programmed. All I know is that the computer's never taken anyone to this place before."
—*Orson Scott Card,* Ender's Game

Many ways are available to you to test your software. The common thread running through all these testing methods is that each test provides some kind of input to your code and you evaluate the test's output for suitability. The nature of the environment, the scope of the investigation, and the form of the evaluation vary widely among testing types. This chapter covers how to perform testing with a few different frameworks, but the material is extensible to other testing varieties. Before diving in, let's take a quick survey of several kinds of testing.

Unit Tests

Unit tests verify that a focused, cohesive collection of code—a *unit*, such as a function or a class—behaves exactly as the programmer intended. Good unit tests isolate the unit being tested from its dependencies. Sometimes this can be hard to do: the unit might depend on other units. In such situations, you use mocks to stand in for these dependencies. *Mocks* are fake objects you use solely during testing to provide you with fine-grained control over how a unit's dependencies behave during the test. Mocks can also record how a unit interacted with them, so you can test whether a unit is interacting with its dependencies as expected. You can also use mocks to simulate rare events, such as a system running out of memory, by programming them to throw an exception.

Integration Tests

Testing a collection of units together is called an *integration test*. Integration tests can also refer to testing interactions between software and hardware, which system programmers deal with often. Integration tests are an important layer on top of unit tests, because they ensure that the software you've written works together as a system. These tests complement, but don't replace, unit tests.

Acceptance Tests

Acceptance tests ensure that your software meets all of your customers' requirements. High-performing software teams can use acceptance tests to guide development. Once all of the acceptance tests pass, your software is deliverable. Because these acceptance tests become part of the code base, there is built-in protection against refactoring or feature regression, where you break an existing feature in the process of adding a new one.

Performance Tests

Performance tests evaluate whether software meets effectiveness requirements, such as speed of execution or memory/power consumption. Optimizing code is a fundamentally empirical exercise. You can (and should) have ideas about which parts of your code are causing performance bottlenecks but can't know for sure unless you measure. Also, you cannot know whether the code changes you implement with the intent of optimizing are improving performance unless you measure again. You can use performance tests to instrument your code and provide relevant measures. *Instrumentation* is a technique for measuring product performance, detecting errors, and logging how a program executes. Sometimes customers have strict performance requirements (for example, computation cannot take more than 100 milliseconds or the system cannot allocate more than 1MB of memory). You can automate testing such requirements and make sure that future code changes don't violate them.

Code testing can be an abstract, dry subject. To avoid this, the next section introduces an extended example that lends context to the discussion.

An Extended Example: Taking a Brake

Suppose you're programming the software for an autonomous vehicle. Your team's software is very complicated and involves hundreds of thousands of code lines. The entire software solution is composed of several binaries. To deploy your software, you must upload the binaries into a car (using a relatively time-consuming process). Making a change to your code, compiling, uploading, and executing it in a live vehicle takes several hours per iteration.

The monumental task of writing all the vehicle's software is broken out into teams. Each team is responsible for a *service*, such as the steering wheel control, audio/video, or vehicle detection. Services interact with each other via a service bus, where each service publishes events. Other services subscribe to these events as needed. This design pattern is called a *service bus architecture*.

Your team is responsible for the autonomous braking service. The service must determine whether a collision is about to happen and, if so, tell the car to brake. Your service subscribes to two event types: the `SpeedUpdate` class, which tells you that the car's speed has changed, and the `CarDetected` class, which tells you that some other car has been detected in front of you. Your system is responsible for publishing a `BrakeCommand` to the service bus whenever an imminent collision is detected. These classes appear in Listing 10-1.

```
struct SpeedUpdate {
  double velocity_mps;
};

struct CarDetected {
  double distance_m;
  double velocity_mps;
};

struct BrakeCommand {
  double time_to_collision_s;
};
```

Listing 10-1: The POD classes that your service interacts with

You'll publish the `BrakeCommand` using a `ServiceBus` object that has a `publish` method:

```
struct ServiceBus {
  void publish(const BrakeCommand&);
  --snip--
};
```

The lead architect wants you to expose an observe method so you can subscribe to SpeedUpdate and CarDetected events on the service bus. You decide to build a class called AutoBrake that you'll initialize in the program's entry point. The AutoBrake class will keep a reference to the publish method of the service bus, and it will subscribe to SpeedUpdate and CarDetected events through its observe method, as in Listing 10-2.

```
template <typename T>
struct AutoBrake {
  AutoBrake(const T& publish);
  void observe(const SpeedUpdate&);
  void observe(const CarDetected&);
private:
  const T& publish;
  --snip--
};
```

Listing 10-2: The AutoBrake class, which provides the automatic braking service

Figure 10-1 summarizes the relationship between the service bus ServiceBus, the automatic braking system AutoBrake, and other services.

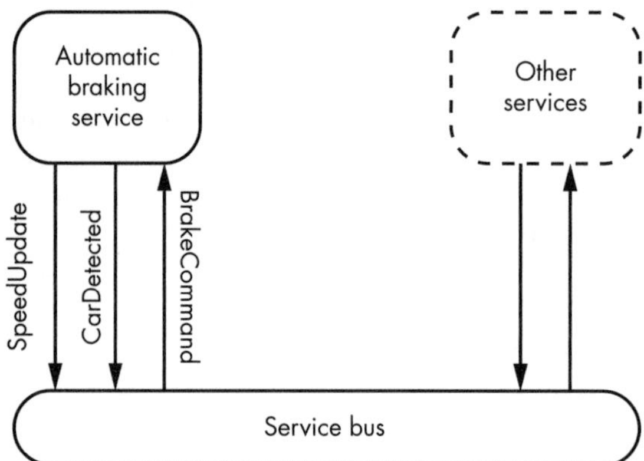

Figure 10-1: A high-level depiction of the interaction between services and the service bus

The service integrates into the car's software, yielding something like the code in Listing 10-3.

```
--snip--
int main() {
  ServiceBus bus;
  AutoBrake auto_brake{ [&bus❶] (const auto& cmd) {
                                bus.publish(cmd); ❷
                        }
  };
  while (true) {  // Service bus's event loop
    auto_brake.observe(SpeedUpdate{ 10L }); ❸
```

```
    auto_brake.observe(CarDetected{ 250L, 25L }); ❹
  }
}
```

Listing 10-3: A sample entry point using your `AutoBrake` *service*

You construct an `AutoBrake` with a lambda that captures a reference to a `ServiceBus` ❶. All the details of how `AutoBrake` decides when to brake are completely hidden from the other teams. The service bus mediates all interservice communication. You've simply passed any commands from the `AutoBrake` directly to the `ServiceBus` ❷. Within the event loop, a `ServiceBus` can pass `SpeedUpdate` ❸ and `CarDetected` objects ❹ to the `observe` method on your `auto_brake`.

Implementing AutoBrake

The conceptually simple way to implement `AutoBrake` is to iterate among writing some code, compiling the production binary, uploading it to a car, and testing functionality manually. This approach is likely to cause program (and car) crashes and to waste a whole lot of time. A better approach is to write code, compile a unit-test binary, and run it in your desktop development environment. You can iterate among these steps more quickly; once you're reasonably confident that the code you've written works as intended, you can do a manual test with a live car.

The *unit-test binary* will be a simple console application targeting the desktop operating system. In the unit-test binary, you'll run a suite of unit tests that pass specific inputs into an `AutoBrake` and assert that it produces the expected results.

After consulting with your management team, you've collected the following requirements:

- `AutoBrake` will consider the car's initial speed zero.
- `AutoBrake` should have a configurable sensitivity threshold based on how many seconds are forecast until a collision. The sensitivity must not be less than 1 second. The default sensitivity is 5 seconds.
- `AutoBrake` must save the car's speed in between `SpeedUpdate` observations.
- Each time `AutoBrake` observes a `CarDetected` event, it must publish a `BrakeCommand` if a collision is forecasted in less time than the configured sensitivity threshold.

Because you have such a pristine requirements list, the next step is to try implementing the automatic braking service using *test-driven development (TDD)*.

NOTE *Because this book is about C++ and not about physics, your* `AutoBrake` *only works when a car is directly in front of you.*

Test-Driven Development

At some point in the history of unit-testing adoption, some intrepid software engineers thought, "If I know I'm going to write a bunch of unit tests for this class, why not write the tests first?" This manner of writing software, known as TDD, underpins one of the great religious wars in the software engineering community. Vim or Emacs? Tabs or spaces? To use TDD or not to use TDD? This book humbly abstains from weighing in on these questions. But we'll use TDD because it fits so naturally into a unit-testing discussion.

Advantages of TDD

The process of writing a test that encodes a requirement *before* implementing the solution is the fundamental idea behind TDD. Proponents say that code written this way tends to be more modular, robust, clean, and well designed. Writing good tests is the best way to document your code for other developers. A good test suite is a fully working set of examples that never gets out of sync. It protects against regressions in functionality whenever you add new features.

Unit tests also serve as a fantastic way to submit bug reports by writing a unit test that fails. Once the bug is fixed, it will stay fixed because the unit test and the code that fixes the bug become part of the test suite.

Red-Green-Refactor

TDD practitioners have a mantra: *red, green, refactor.* Red is the first step, and it means to implement a failing test. This is done for several reasons, principal of which is to make sure you're actually testing something. You might be surprised how common it is to accidentally design a test that doesn't make any assertions. Next, you implement code that makes the test pass. No more, no less. This turns the test from red to green. Now that you have working code and a passing test, you can refactor your production code. To refactor means to restructure existing code without changing its functionality. For example, you might find a more elegant way to write the same code, replace your code with a third-party library, or rewrite your code to have better performance characteristics.

If you accidentally break something, you'll know immediately because your test suite will tell you. Then you continue to implement the remainder of the class using TDD. You can work on the collision threshold next.

Writing a Skeleton AutoBrake Class

Before you can write tests, you need to write a *skeleton class*, which implements an interface but provides no functionality. It's useful in TDD because you can't compile a test without a shell of the class you're testing.

Consider the skeleton `AutoBrake` class in Listing 10-4.

```
struct SpeedUpdate {
  double velocity_mps;
```

```
};

struct CarDetected {
  double distance_m;
  double velocity_mps;
};

struct BrakeCommand {
  double time_to_collision_s;
};

template <typename T>
struct AutoBrake {
  AutoBrake(const T& publish❶) : publish{ publish } { }
  void observe(const SpeedUpdate& cd) { } ❷
  void observe(const CarDetected& cd) { } ❸
  void set_collision_threshold_s(double x) { ❹
    collision_threshold_s = x;
  }
  double get_collision_threshold_s() const { ❺
    return collision_threshold_s;
  }
  double get_speed_mps() const { ❻
    return speed_mps;
  }
private:
  double collision_threshold_s;
  double speed_mps;
  const T& publish;
};
```

Listing 10-4: A skeleton `AutoBrake` class

The `AutoBrake` class has a single constructor that takes the template parameter `publish` ❶, which you save off into a `const` member. One of the requirements states that you'll invoke `publish` with a `BrakeCommand`. Using the template parameter `T` allows you to program generically against any type that supports invocation with a `BrakeCommand`. You provide two different observe functions: one for each kind of event you want to subscribe to ❷❸. Because this is just a skeleton class, no instructions are in the body. You just need a class that exposes the appropriate methods and compiles without error. Because the methods return `void`, you don't even need a return statement.

You implement a setter ❹ and getter ❺. These methods mediate interaction with the private member variable `collision_threshold_s`. One of the requirements implies a class invariant about valid values for `collision_threshold_s`. Because this value can change after construction, you can't just use the constructor to establish a class invariant. You need a way to enforce this class invariant throughout the object's lifetime. You can use the setter to perform validation before the class sets a member's value. The getter allows you to read the value of `collision_threshold_s` without permitting modification. It enforces a kind of *external constness*.

Finally, you have a getter for speed_mps ❻ with no corresponding setter. This is similar to making speed_mps a public member, with the important difference that it would be possible to modify speed_mps from an external class if it were public.

Assertions: The Building Blocks of Unit Tests

A unit test's most essential component is the *assertion*, which checks that some condition is met. If the condition isn't met, the enclosing test fails.

Listing 10-5 implements an assert_that function that throws an exception with an error message whenever some Boolean statement is false.

```
#include <stdexcept>
constexpr void assert_that(bool statement, const char* message) {
  if (!statement❶) throw std::runtime_error{ message }; ❷
}

int main() {
  assert_that(1 + 2 > 2, "Something is profoundly wrong with the universe."); ❸
  assert_that(24 == 42, "This assertion will generate an exception."); ❹
}
-----------------------------------------------------------------------------
terminate called after throwing an instance of 'std::runtime_error'
  what():  This assertion will generate an exception. ❹
```

Listing 10-5: A program illustrating assert_that (Output is from a binary compiled by GCC v7.1.1.)

The assert_that function checks whether the statement ❶ parameter is false, in which case it throws an exception with the message parameter ❷. The first assertion checks that 1 + 2 > 2, which passes ❸. The second assertion checks that 24 == 42, which fails and throws an uncaught exception ❹.

Requirement: Initial Speed Is Zero

Consider the first requirement that the car's initial speed is zero. Before implementing this functionality in AutoBrake, you need to write a unit test that encodes this requirement. You'll implement the unit test as a function that creates an AutoBrake, exercises the class, and makes assertions about the results. Listing 10-6 contains a unit test that encodes the requirement that the initial speed is zero.

```
void initial_speed_is_zero() {
  AutoBrake auto_brake{ [](const BrakeCommand&) {} }; ❶
  assert_that(auto_brake.get_speed_mps() == 0L, "speed not equal 0"); ❷
}
```

Listing 10-6: A unit test encoding the requirement that the initial speed be zero

You first construct an AutoBrake with an empty BrakeCommand publish function ❶. This unit test is only concerned with the initial value of AutoBrake for car speed. Because this unit test is not concerned with how or when AutoBrake publishes a BrakeCommand, you give it the simplest argument that will still compile.

NOTE *A subtle but important feature of unit tests is that if you don't care about some dependency of the unit under test, you can just provide an empty implementation that performs some innocuous, default behavior. This empty implementation is sometimes called a* stub.

In initial_speed_is_zero, you only want to assert that the initial speed of the car is zero and nothing else ❷. You use the getter get_speed_mps and compare the return value to 0. That's all you have to do; assert will throw an exception if the initial speed is zero.

Now you need a way to run the unit tests.

Test Harnesses

A *test harness* is code that executes unit tests. You can make a test harness that will invoke your unit test functions, like initial_speed_is_zero, and handle failed assertions gracefully. Consider the test harness run_test in Listing 10-7.

```
#include <exception>
--snip--
void run_test(void(*unit_test)(), const char* name) {
  try {
    unit_test(); ❶
    printf("[+] Test %s successful.\n", name); ❷
  } catch (const std::exception& e) {
    printf("[-] Test failure in %s. %s.\n", name, e.what()); ❸
  }
}
```

Listing 10-7: A test harness

The run_test harness accepts a unit test as a function pointer named unit_test and invokes it within a try-catch statement ❶. As long as unit_test doesn't throw an exception, run_test will print a friendly message stating that the unit test passed before returning ❷. If any exception is thrown, the test fails and prints a disapproving message ❸.

To make a *unit-test program* that will run all of your unit tests, you place the run_test test harness inside the main function of a new program. All together, the unit-test program looks like Listing 10-8.

```
#include <stdexcept>

struct SpeedUpdate {
  double velocity_mps;
};

struct CarDetected {
```

```
  double distance_m;
  double velocity_mps;
};

struct BrakeCommand {
  double time_to_collision_s;
};

template <typename T>
struct AutoBrake {
  --snip--
};

constexpr void assert_that(bool statement, const char* message) {
  if (!statement) throw std::runtime_error{ message };
}

void initial_speed_is_zero() {
  AutoBrake auto_brake{ [](const BrakeCommand&) {} };
  assert_that(auto_brake.get_speed_mps() == 0L, "speed not equal 0");
}

void run_test(void(*unit_test)(), const char* name) {
  try {
    unit_test();
    printf("[+] Test %s successful.\n", name);
  } catch (const std::exception& e) {
    printf("[-] Test failure in %s. %s.\n", name, e.what());
  }
}

int main() {
  run_test(initial_speed_is_zero, "initial speed is 0"); ❶
}
--------------------------------------------------------------------------
[-] Test failure in initial speed is 0. speed not equal 0. ❶
```

Listing 10-8: The unit-test program

When you compile and run this unit-test binary, you can see that the unit test initial_speed_is_zero fails with an informative message ❶.

NOTE *Because the AutoBrake member speed_mps is uninitialized in Listing 10-8, this program has undefined behavior. It's not actually certain that the test will fail. The solution, of course, is that you shouldn't write programs with undefined behavior.*

Getting the Test to Pass

To get initial_speed_is_zero to pass, all that's required is to initialize speed_mps to zero in the constructor of AutoBrake:

```
template <typename T>
struct AutoBrake {
```

```
  AutoBrake(const T& publish) : speed_mps{}❶, publish{ publish } { }
  --snip--
};
```

Simply add the initialization to zero ❶. Now, if you update, compile, and run the unit-test program in Listing 10-8, you're greeted with more pleasant output:

```
[+] Test initial speed is 0 successful.
```

Requirement: Default Collision Threshold Is Five

The default collision threshold needs to be 5. Consider the unit test in Listing 10-9.

```
void initial_sensitivity_is_five() {
  AutoBrake auto_brake{ [](const BrakeCommand&) {} };
  assert_that(auto_brake.get_collision_threshold_s() == 5L,
              "sensitivity is not 5");
}
```

Listing 10-9: A unit test encoding the requirement that the initial speed be zero

You can insert this test into the test program, as shown in Listing 10-10.

```
--snip--
int main() {
  run_test(initial_speed_is_zero, "initial speed is 0");
  run_test(initial_sensitivity_is_five, "initial sensitivity is 5");
}
```

```
[+] Test initial speed is 0 successful.
[-] Test failure in initial sensitivity is 5. sensitivity is not 5.
```

Listing 10-10: Adding the `initial-sensitivity-is-5` test to the test harness

As expected, Listing 10-10 reveals that `initial_speed_is_zero` still passes and the new test `initial_sensitivity_is_five` fails.

Now, make it pass. Add the appropriate member initializer to `AutoBrake`, as demonstrated in Listing 10-11.

```
template <typename T>
struct AutoBrake {
  AutoBrake(const T& publish)
    : collision_threshold_s{ 5 }, ❶
      speed_mps{},
      publish{ publish } { }
  --snip--
};
```

Listing 10-11: Updating `AutoBrake` to satisfy the collision threshold requirement

The new member initializer ❶ sets `collision_threshold_s` to 5. Recompiling the test program, you can see `initial_sensitivity_is_five` is now passing:

```
[+] Test initial speed is 0 successful.
[+] Test initial sensitivity is 5 successful.
```

Next, handle the class invariant that the sensitivity must be greater than 1.

Requirement: Sensitivity Must Always Be Greater Than One

To encode the sensitivity validation errors using exceptions, you can build a test that expects an exception to be thrown when `collision_threshold_s` is set to a value less than 1, as Listing 10-12 shows.

```
void sensitivity_greater_than_1() {
  AutoBrake auto_brake{ [](const BrakeCommand&) {} };
  try {
    auto_brake.set_collision_threshold_s(0.5L); ❶
  } catch (const std::exception&) {
    return; ❷
  }
  assert_that(false, "no exception thrown"); ❸
}
```

Listing 10-12: A test encoding the requirement that sensitivity is always greater than 1

You expect the `set_collision_threshold_s` method of `auto_brake` to throw an exception when called with a value of 0.5 ❶. If it does, you catch the exception and return immediately from the test ❷. If `set_collision_threshold_s` doesn't throw an exception, you fail an assertion with the message `no exception thrown` ❸.

Next, add `sensitivity_greater_than_1` to the test harness, as demonstrated in Listing 10-13.

```
--snip--
int main() {
  run_test(initial_speed_is_zero, "initial speed is 0");
  run_test(initial_sensitivity_is_five, "initial sensitivity is 5");
  run_test(sensitivity_greater_than_1, "sensitivity greater than 1"); ❶
}
--------------------------------------------------------------------------
[+] Test initial speed is 0 successful.
[+] Test initial sensitivity is 5 successful.
[-] Test failure in sensitivity greater than 1. no exception thrown. ❶
```

Listing 10-13: Adding `set_collision_threshold_s` to the test harness

As expected, the new unit test fails ❶.

You can implement validation that will make the test pass, as Listing 10-14 shows.

```
#include <exception>
--snip--
template <typename T>
struct AutoBrake {
  --snip--
  void set_collision_threshold_s(double x) {
    if (x < 1) throw std::exception{ "Collision less than 1." };
    collision_threshold_s = x;
  }
}
```

Listing 10-14: Updating the `set_collision_threshold` *method of* `AutoBrake` *to validate its input*

Recompiling and executing the unit-test suite turns the test green:

```
[+] Test initial speed is 0 successful.
[+] Test initial sensitivity is 5 successful.
[+] Test sensitivity greater than 1 successful.
```

Next, you want to make sure that an `AutoBrake` saves the car's speed in between each `SpeedUpdate`.

Requirement: Save the Car's Speed Between Updates

The unit test in Listing 10-15 encodes the requirement that an `AutoBrake` saves the car's speed.

```
void speed_is_saved() {
  AutoBrake auto_brake{ [](const BrakeCommand&) {} }; ❶
  auto_brake.observe(SpeedUpdate{ 100L }); ❷
  assert_that(100L == auto_brake.get_speed_mps(), "speed not saved to 100"); ❸
  auto_brake.observe(SpeedUpdate{ 50L });
  assert_that(50L == auto_brake.get_speed_mps(), "speed not saved to 50");
  auto_brake.observe(SpeedUpdate{ 0L });
  assert_that(0L == auto_brake.get_speed_mps(), "speed not saved to 0");
}
```

Listing 10-15: Encoding the requirement that an `AutoBrake` *saves the car's speed*

After constructing an `AutoBrake` ❶, you pass a `SpeedUpdate` with `velocity_mps` equal to 100 into its `observe` method ❷. Next, you get the speed back from `auto_brake` using the `get_speed_mps` method and expect it is equal to 100 ❸.

NOTE *As a general rule, you should have a single assertion per test. This test violates the strictest interpretation of this rule, but it's not violating its spirit. All of the assertions are examining the same, cohesive requirement, which is that the speed is saved whenever a* `SpeedUpdate` *is observed.*

You add the test in Listing 10-15 to the test harness in the usual way, as demonstrated in Listing 10-16.

```
--snip--
int main() {
  run_test(initial_speed_is_zero, "initial speed is 0");
  run_test(initial_sensitivity_is_five, "initial sensitivity is 5");
  run_test(sensitivity_greater_than_1, "sensitivity greater than 1");
  run_test(speed_is_saved, "speed is saved"); ❶
}
--------------------------------------------------------------------------
[+] Test initial speed is 0 successful.
[+] Test initial sensitivity is 5 successful.
[+] Test sensitivity greater than 1 successful.
[-] Test failure in speed is saved. speed not saved to 100. ❶
```

Listing 10-16: Adding the speed-saving unit test into the test harness

Unsurprisingly, the new test fails ❶. To make this test pass, you implement the appropriate `observe` function:

```
template <typename T>
struct AutoBrake {
  --snip--
  void observe(const SpeedUpdate& x) {
    speed_mps = x.velocity_mps; ❶
  }
};
```

You extract the `velocity_mps` from the `SpeedUpdate` and store it into the `speed_mps` member variable ❶. Recompiling the test binary shows that the unit test now passes:

```
[+] Test initial speed is 0 successful.
[+] Test initial sensitivity is 5 successful.
[+] Test sensitivity greater than 1 successful.
[+] Test speed is saved successful.
```

Finally, you require that `AutoBrake` can compute the correct time to collision and, if appropriate, publish a `BrakeCommand` using the `publish` function.

Requirement: AutoBrake Publishes a BrakeCommand When Collision Detected

The relevant equations for computing times to collision come directly from high school physics. First, you calculate your car's relative velocity to the detected car:

$$\text{Velocity}_{\text{Relative}} = \text{Velocity}_{\text{OurCar}} - \text{Velocity}_{\text{OtherCar}}$$

If your relative velocity is constant and positive, the cars will eventually collide. You can compute the time to such a collision as follows:

$$\text{Time}_{\text{Collision}} = \text{Distance} \,/\, \text{Velocity}_{\text{Relative}}$$

If $Time_{Collision}$ is greater than zero and less than or equal to `collision_threshold_s`, you invoke `publish` with a `BrakeCommand`. The unit test in Listing 10-17 sets the collision threshold to 10 seconds and then observes events that indicate a crash.

```
void alert_when_imminent() {
  int brake_commands_published{}; ❶
  AutoBrake auto_brake{
    [&brake_commands_published❷](const BrakeCommand&) {
      brake_commands_published++; ❸
  } };
  auto_brake.set_collision_threshold_s(10L); ❹
  auto_brake.observe(SpeedUpdate{ 100L }); ❺
  auto_brake.observe(CarDetected{ 100L, 0L }); ❻
  assert_that(brake_commands_published == 1, "brake commands published not
one"); ❼
}
```

Listing 10-17: Unit testing for brake events

Here, you initialize the local variable `brake_commands_published` to zero ❶. This will keep track of the number of times that the `publish` callback is invoked. You pass this local variable by reference into the lambda used to construct your `auto_brake` ❷. Notice that you increment `brake_commands_published` ❸. Because the lambda captures by reference, you can inspect the value of `brake_commands_published` later in the unit test. Next, you set `set_collision_threshold` to 10 ❹. You update the car's speed to 100 meters per second ❺, and then you detect a car 100 meters away traveling at 0 meters per second (it is stopped) ❻. The `AutoBrake` class should determine that a collision will occur in 1 second. This should trigger a callback, which will increment `brake_commands_published`. The assertion ❼ ensures that the callback happens exactly once.

After adding to `main`, compile and run to yield a new red test:

```
[+] Test initial speed is 0 successful.
[+] Test initial sensitivity is 5 successful.
[+] Test sensitivity greater than 1 successful.
[+] Test speed is saved successful.
[-] Test failure in alert when imminent. brake commands published not one.
```

You can implement the code to make this test pass. Listing 10-18 provides all the code needed to issue brake commands.

```
template <typename T>
struct AutoBrake {
  --snip--
  void observe(const CarDetected& cd) {
    const auto relative_velocity_mps = speed_mps - cd.velocity_mps; ❶
    const auto time_to_collision_s = cd.distance_m / relative_velocity_mps; ❷
    if (time_to_collision_s > 0 && ❸
        time_to_collision_s <= collision_threshold_s ❹) {
```

```
      publish(BrakeCommand{ time_to_collision_s }); ❺
    }
  }
};
```

Listing 10-18: Code implementing the braking functionality

First, you calculate the relative velocity ❶. Next, you use this value to compute the time to collision ❷. If this value is positive ❸ and less than or equal to the collision threshold ❹, you publish a `BrakeCommand` ❺.

Recompiling and running the unit-test suite yields success:

```
[+] Test initial speed is 0 successful.
[+] Test initial sensitivity is 5 successful.
[+] Test sensitivity greater than 1 successful.
[+] Test speed is saved successful.
[+] Test alert when imminent successful.
```

Finally, you need to check that the `AutoBrake` will not invoke `publish` with a `BrakeCommand` if a collision will occur later than `collision_threshold_s`. You can repurpose the `alert_when_imminent` unit test, as in Listing 10-19.

```
void no_alert_when_not_imminent() {
  int brake_commands_published{};
  AutoBrake auto_brake{
    [&brake_commands_published](const BrakeCommand&) {
      brake_commands_published++;
  } };
  auto_brake.set_collision_threshold_s(2L);
  auto_brake.observe(SpeedUpdate{ 100L });
  auto_brake.observe(CarDetected{ 1000L, 50L });
  assert_that(brake_commands_published == 0 ❶, "brake command published");
}
```

Listing 10-19: Testing that the car doesn't issue a `BrakeCommand` if a collision isn't anticipated within the collision threshold

This changes the setup. Your car's threshold is set to 2 seconds with a speed of 100 meters per second. A car is detected 1,000 meters away traveling 50 meters per second. The `AutoBrake` class should forecast a collision in 20 seconds, which is more than the 2-second threshold. You also change the assertion ❶.

After adding this test to `main` and running the unit-test suite, you have the following:

```
[+] Test initial speed is 0 successful.
[+] Test initial sensitivity is 5 successful.
[+] Test sensitivity greater than 1 successful.
[+] Test speed is saved successful.
[+] Test alert when imminent successful.
[+] Test no alert when not imminent successful. ❶
```

For this test case, you already have all the code needed for this test to pass ❶. Not having a failing test at the outset bends the red, green, refactor mantra, but that's okay. This test case is closely related to `alert_when_imminent`. The point of TDD is not dogmatic adherence to strict rules. TDD is a set of reasonably loose guidelines that helps you write better software.

Adding a Service-Bus Interface

The `AutoBrake` class has a few dependencies: `CarDetected`, `SpeedUpdated`, and a generic dependency on some `publish` object callable with a single `BrakeCommand` parameter. The `CarDetected` and `SpeedUpdated` classes are plain-old-data types that are easy to use directly in your unit tests. The `publish` object is a little more complicated to initialize, but thanks to lambdas, it's really not bad.

Suppose you want to refactor the service bus. You want to accept a `std::function` to subscribe to each service, as in the new `IServiceBus` interface in Listing 10-20.

```
#include <functional>

using SpeedUpdateCallback = std::function<void(const SpeedUpdate&)>;
using CarDetectedCallback = std::function<void(const CarDetected&)>;

struct IServiceBus {
  virtual ~IServiceBus() = default;
  virtual void publish(const BrakeCommand&) = 0;
  virtual void subscribe(SpeedUpdateCallback) = 0;
  virtual void subscribe(CarDetectedCallback) = 0;
};
```

Listing 10-20: The `IServiceBus` interface

Because `IServiceBus` is an interface, you don't need to know the implementation details. It's a nice solution because it allows you to do your own wiring into the service bus. But there's a problem. How do you test `AutoBrake` in isolation? If you try to use the production bus, you're firmly in integration-test territory, and you want easy-to-configure, isolated unit tests.

Mocking Dependencies

Fortunately, you don't depend on the implementation: you depend on the interface. You can create a mock class that implements the `IServiceBus` interface and use this within `AutoBrake`. A mock is a special implementation that you generate for the express purpose of testing a class that depends on the mock.

Now when you exercise `AutoBrake` in your unit tests, `AutoBrake` interacts with the mock rather than the production service bus. Because you have complete control over the mock's implementation and the mock is a unit-test-specific class, you have major flexibility in how you can test classes that depend on the interface:

- You can capture arbitrarily detailed information about how the mock gets called. This can include information about the parameters and the number of times the mock was called, for example.
- You can perform arbitrary computation in the mock.

In other words, you have complete control over the inputs and the outputs of the dependency of `AutoBrake`. How does `AutoBrake` handle the case where the service bus throws an out-of-memory exception inside of a `publish` invocation? You can unit test that. How many times did `AutoBrake` register a callback for `SpeedUpdates`? Again, you can unit test that.

Listing 10-21 presents a simple mock class you can use for your unit tests.

```
struct MockServiceBus : IServiceBus {
  void publish(const BrakeCommand& cmd) override {
    commands_published++; ❶
    last_command = cmd; ❷
  }
  void subscribe(SpeedUpdateCallback callback) override {
    speed_update_callback = callback; ❸
  }
  void subscribe(CarDetectedCallback callback) override {
    car_detected_callback = callback; ❹
  }
  BrakeCommand last_command{};
  int commands_published{};
  SpeedUpdateCallback speed_update_callback{};
  CarDetectedCallback car_detected_callback{};
};
```

Listing 10-21: A definition of `MockServiceBus`

The `publish` method records the number of times a `BrakeCommand` is published ❶ and the `last_command` that was published ❷. Each time `AutoBrake` publishes a command to the service bus, you'll see updates to the members of `MockServiceBus`. You'll see in a moment that this allows for some very powerful assertions about how `AutoBrake` behaved during a test. You save the callback functions used to subscribe to the service bus ❸❹. This allows you to simulate events by manually invoking these callbacks on the mock object.

Now, you can turn your attention to refactoring `AutoBrake`.

Refactoring AutoBrake

Listing 10-22 updates `AutoBrake` with the minimum changes necessary to get the unit-test binary compiling again (but not necessarily passing!).

```
#include <exception>
--snip--
struct AutoBrake { ❶
```

```
  AutoBrake(IServiceBus& bus) ❷
    : collision_threshold_s{ 5 },
      speed_mps{} {
  }
  void set_collision_threshold_s(double x) {
    if (x < 1) throw std::exception{ "Collision less than 1." };
    collision_threshold_s = x;
  }
  double get_collision_threshold_s() const {
    return collision_threshold_s;
  }
  double get_speed_mps() const {
    return speed_mps;
  }
private:
  double collision_threshold_s;
  double speed_mps;
};
```

Listing 10-22: A refactored `AutoBrake` skeleton taking an `IServiceBus` reference

Notice that all the `observe` functions have been removed. Additionally, `AutoBrake` is no longer a template ❶. Rather, it accepts an `IServiceBus` reference in its constructor ❷.

You'll also need to update your unit tests to get the test suite compiling again. One TDD-inspired approach is to comment out all the tests that are not compiling and update `AutoBrake` so all the failing unit tests pass. Then, one by one, uncomment each unit test. You reimplement each unit test using the new `IServiceBus` mock, then update `AutoBrake` so the tests pass.

Let's give it a try.

Refactoring the Unit Tests

Because you've changed the way to construct an `AutoBrake` object, you'll need to reimplement every test. The first three are easy: Listing 10-23 just plops the mock into the `AutoBrake` constructor.

```
void initial_speed_is_zero() {
  MockServiceBus bus{}; ❶
  AutoBrake auto_brake{ bus }; ❷
  assert_that(auto_brake.get_speed_mps() == 0L, "speed not equal 0");
}

void initial_sensitivity_is_five() {
  MockServiceBus bus{}; ❶
  AutoBrake auto_brake{ bus }; ❷
  assert_that(auto_brake.get_collision_threshold_s() == 5,
              "sensitivity is not 5");
}

void sensitivity_greater_than_1() {
  MockServiceBus bus{}; ❶
  AutoBrake auto_brake{ bus }; ❷
```

```
  try {
    auto_brake.set_collision_threshold_s(0.5L);
  } catch (const std::exception&) {
    return;
  }
  assert_that(false, "no exception thrown");
}
```

Listing 10-23: Reimplemented unit-test functions using the `MockServiceBus`

Because these three tests deal with functionality not related to the service bus, it's unsurprising that you didn't need to make any major changes to `AutoBrake`. All you need to do is create a `MockServiceBus` ❶ and pass it into the `AutoBrake` constructor ❷. Running the unit-test suite, you have the following:

```
[+] Test initial speed is 0 successful.
[+] Test initial sensitivity is 5 successful.
[+] Test sensitivity greater than 1 successful.
```

Next, look at the `speed_is_saved` test. The `AutoBrake` class no longer exposes an `observe` function, but because you've saved the `SpeedUpdateCallback` on the mock service bus, you can invoke the callback directly. If `AutoBrake` subscribed properly, this callback will update the car's speed, and you'll see the effects when you call the `get_speed_mps` method. Listing 10-24 contains the refactor.

```
void speed_is_saved() {
  MockServiceBus bus{};
  AutoBrake auto_brake{ bus };

  bus.speed_update_callback(SpeedUpdate{ 100L }); ❶
  assert_that(100L == auto_brake.get_speed_mps(), "speed not saved to 100"); ❷
  bus.speed_update_callback(SpeedUpdate{ 50L });
  assert_that(50L == auto_brake.get_speed_mps(), "speed not saved to 50");
  bus.speed_update_callback(SpeedUpdate{ 0L });
  assert_that(0L == auto_brake.get_speed_mps(), "speed not saved to 0");
}
```

Listing 10-24: Reimplemented `speed_is_saved` *unit-test function using the* `MockServiceBus`

The test didn't change too much from the previous implementation. You invoke the `speed_update_callback` function stored on the mock bus ❶. You make sure that the `AutoBrake` object updated the car's speed correctly ❷. Compiling and running the resulting unit-test suite results in the following output:

```
[+] Test initial speed is 0 successful.
[+] Test initial sensitivity is 5 successful.
[+] Test sensitivity greater than 1 successful.
[-] Test failure in speed is saved. bad function call.
```

Recall that the bad function call message comes from the std::bad_function_call exception. This is expected: you still need to subscribe from AutoBrake, so std::function throws an exception when you invoke it.

Consider the approach in Listing 10-25.

```
struct AutoBrake {
  AutoBrake(IServiceBus& bus)
    : collision_threshold_s{ 5 },
    speed_mps{} {
    bus.subscribe([this](const SpeedUpdate& update) {
      speed_mps = update.velocity_mps;
    });
  }
  --snip--
}
```

Listing 10-25: Subscribing the AutoBrake *to speed updates from the* IServiceBus

Thanks to std::function, you can pass your callback into the subscribe method of bus as a lambda that captures speed_mps. (Notice that you don't need to save a copy of bus.) Recompiling and running the unit-test suite yields the following:

```
[+] Test initial speed is 0 successful.
[+] Test initial sensitivity is 5 successful.
[+] Test sensitivity greater than 1 successful.
[+] Test speed is saved successful.
```

Next, you have the first of the alert-related unit tests, no_alert_when_not_imminent. Listing 10-26 highlights one way to update this test with the new architecture.

```
void no_alert_when_not_imminent() {
  MockServiceBus bus{};
  AutoBrake auto_brake{ bus };
  auto_brake.set_collision_threshold_s(2L);
  bus.speed_update_callback(SpeedUpdate{ 100L }); ❶
  bus.car_detected_callback(CarDetected{ 1000L, 50L }); ❷
  assert_that(bus.commands_published == 0, "brake commands were published");
}
```

Listing 10-26: Updating the no_alert_when_not_imminent *test with the* IServiceBus

As in the speed_is_saved test, you invoke the callbacks on the bus mock to simulate events on the service bus ❶❷. Recompiling and running the unit-test suite results in an expected failure.

```
[+] Test initial speed is 0 successful.
[+] Test initial sensitivity is 5 successful.
[+] Test sensitivity greater than 1 successful.
[+] Test speed is saved successful.
[-] Test failure in no alert when not imminent. bad function call.
```

You need to subscribe with `CarDetectedCallback`. You can add this into the `AutoBus` constructor, as demonstrated in Listing 10-27.

```
struct AutoBrake {
  AutoBrake(IServiceBus& bus)
    : collision_threshold_s{ 5 },
    speed_mps{} {
    bus.subscribe([this](const SpeedUpdate& update) {
      speed_mps = update.velocity_mps;
    });
    bus.subscribe([this❶, &bus❷](const CarDetected& cd) {
      const auto relative_velocity_mps = speed_mps - cd.velocity_mps;
      const auto time_to_collision_s = cd.distance_m / relative_velocity_mps;
      if (time_to_collision_s > 0 &&
          time_to_collision_s <= collision_threshold_s) {
        bus.publish(BrakeCommand{ time_to_collision_s }); ❸
      }
    });
  }
  --snip--
}
```

Listing 10-27: An updated `AutoBrake` constructor that wires itself into the service bus

All you've done is port over the original `observe` method corresponding to `CarDetected` events. The lambda captures `this` ❶ and `bus` ❷ by reference in the callback. Capturing `this` allows you to compute collision times, whereas capturing `bus` allows you to publish a `BrakeCommand` ❸ if the conditions are satisfied. Now the unit-test binary outputs the following:

```
[+] Test initial speed is 0 successful.
[+] Test initial sensitivity is 5 successful.
[+] Test sensitivity greater than 1 successful.
[+] Test speed is saved successful.
[+] Test no alert when not imminent successful.
```

Finally, turn on the last test, `alert_when_imminent`, as displayed in Listing 10-28.

```
void alert_when_imminent() {
  MockServiceBus bus{};
  AutoBrake auto_brake{ bus };
  auto_brake.set_collision_threshold_s(10L);
  bus.speed_update_callback(SpeedUpdate{ 100L });
  bus.car_detected_callback(CarDetected{ 100L, 0L });
  assert_that(bus.commands_published == 1, "1 brake command was not published");
  assert_that(bus.last_command.time_to_collision_s == 1L,
            "time to collision not computed correctly."); ❶
}
```

Listing 10-28: Refactoring the `alert_when_imminent` unit test

In MockServiceBus, you actually saved the last BrakeCommand published to the bus into a member. In the test, you can use this member to verify that the time to collision was computed correctly. If a car is going 100 meters per second, it will take 1 second to hit a stationary car parked 100 meters away. You check that the BrakeCommand has the correct time to collision recorded by referring to the time_to_collision_s field on our mock bus ❶.

Recompiling and rerunning, you finally have the test suite fully green again:

```
[+] Test initial speed is 0 successful.
[+] Test initial sensitivity is 5 successful.
[+] Test sensitivity greater than 1 successful.
[+] Test speed is saved successful.
[+] Test no alert when not imminent successful.
[+] Test alert when imminent successful.
```

Refactoring is now complete.

Reevaluating the Unit-Testing Solution

Looking back at the unit-testing solution, you can identify several components that have nothing to do with AutoBrake. These are general purpose unit-testing components that you could reuse in future unit tests. Recall the two helper functions created in Listing 10-29.

```
#include <stdexcept>
#include <cstdio>

void assert_that(bool statement, const char* message) {
  if (!statement) throw std::runtime_error{ message };
}

void run_test(void(*unit_test)(), const char* name) {
  try {
    unit_test();
    printf("[+] Test %s successful.\n", name);
    return;
  } catch (const std::exception& e) {
    printf("[-] Test failure in %s. %s.\n", name, e.what());
  }
}
```

Listing 10-29: An austere unit-testing framework

These two functions reflect two fundamental aspects of unit testing: making assertions and running tests. Rolling your own simple assert_that function and run_test harness works, but this approach doesn't scale very well. You can do a lot better by leaning on a unit-testing framework.

Unit-Testing and Mocking Frameworks

Unit-testing frameworks provide commonly used functions and the scaffolding you need to tie your tests together into a user-friendly program. These frameworks provide a wealth of functionality that helps you create concise, expressive tests. This section offers a tour of several popular unit-testing and mocking frameworks.

The Catch Unit-Testing Framework

One of the most straightforward unit-testing frameworks, Catch by Phil Nash, is available at *https://github.com/catchorg/Catch2/*. Because it's a header-only library, you can set up Catch by downloading the single-header version and including it in each translation unit that contains unit-testing code.

NOTE *At press time, Catch's latest version is 2.9.1.*

Defining an Entry Point

Tell Catch to provide your test binary's entry point with `#define CATCH_CONFIG_MAIN`. Together, the Catch unit-test suite starts as follows:

```
#define CATCH_CONFIG_MAIN
#include "catch.hpp"
```

That's it. Within the `catch.hpp` header, it looks for the `CATCH_CONFIG_MAIN` preprocessor definition. When present, Catch will add in a `main` function so you don't have to. It will automatically grab all the unit tests you've defined and wrap them with a nice harness.

Defining Test Cases

Earlier, in "Unit Tests" on page 282, you defined a separate function for each unit test. Then you would pass a pointer to this function as the first parameter to `run_test`. You passed the name of the test as the second parameter, which is a bit redundant because you've already provided a descriptive name for the function pointed to by the first argument. Finally, you had to implement your own assert function. Catch handles all of this ceremony implicitly. For each unit test, you use the `TEST_CASE` macro, and Catch handles all the integration for you.

Listing 10-30 illustrates how to build a trivial Catch unit test program.

```
#define CATCH_CONFIG_MAIN
#include "catch.hpp"

TEST_CASE("AutoBrake") { ❶
  // Unit test here
}
```

```
-------------------------------------------------------------------------------
===============================================================================
test cases: 1 | 1 passed ❶
assertions: - none - ❷
```

Listing 10-30: A simple Catch unit-test program

The Catch entry point detects that you declared one test called `AutoBrake` ❶. It also provides a warning that you haven't made any assertions ❷.

Making Assertions

Catch comes with a built-in assertion that features two distinct families of assertion macros: `REQUIRE` and `CHECK`. The difference between them is that `REQUIRE` will fail a test immediately, whereas `CHECK` will allow the test to run to completion (but still cause a failure). `CHECK` can be useful sometimes when groups of related assertions that fail lead the programmer down the right path of debugging problems. Also included are `REQUIRE_FALSE` and `CHECK_FALSE`, which check that the contained statement evaluates to false rather than true. In some situations, you might find this a more natural way to represent a requirement.

All you need to do is wrap a Boolean expression with the `REQUIRE` macro. If the expression evaluates to false, the assertion fails. You provide an *assertion expression* that evaluates to true if the assertion passes and false if it fails:

```
REQUIRE(assertion-expression);
```

Let's look at how to combine `REQUIRE` with a `TEST_CASE` to build a unit test.

NOTE *Because it's by far the most common Catch assertion, we'll use* `REQUIRE` *here. Refer to the Catch documentation for more information.*

Refactoring the initial_speed_is_zero Test to Catch

Listing 10-31 shows the `initial_speed_is_zero` test refactored to use Catch.

```
#define CATCH_CONFIG_MAIN
#include "catch.hpp"
#include <functional>

struct IServiceBus {
  --snip--
};

struct MockServiceBus : IServiceBus {
  --snip--
};

struct AutoBrake {
  --snip--
};
```

```
TEST_CASE❶("initial car speed is zero"❷) {
  MockServiceBus bus{};
  AutoBrake auto_brake{ bus };
  REQUIRE(auto_brake.get_speed_mps() == 0); ❸
}
```

Listing 10-31: An `initial_speed_is_zero` unit test refactored to use Catch

You use the `TEST_CASE` macro to define a new unit test ❶. The test is described by its sole parameter ❷. Inside the body of the `TEST_CASE` macro, you proceed with the unit test. You also see the `REQUIRE` macro in action ❸. To see how Catch handles failed tests, comment out the `speed_mps` member initializer to cause a failing test and observe the program's output, as shown in Listing 10-32.

```
struct AutoBrake {
  AutoBrake(IServiceBus& bus)
    : collision_threshold_s{ 5 }/*,
    speed_mps{} */{ ❶
  --snip--
};
```

Listing 10-32: Intentionally commenting out the `speed_mps` member initializer to cause test failures (using Catch)

The appropriate member initializer ❶ is commented out, resulting in a test failure. Rerunning the Catch test suite in Listing 10-31 yields the output in Listing 10-33.

```
~~~~~~~~~~~~~~~~~~~~~~~~~~~~~~~~~~~~~~~~~~~~~~~~~~~~~~~~~~~~~~~~~~~~~~~~~~~~~~~
catch_example.exe is a Catch v2.0.1 host application.
Run with -? for options

-------------------------------------------------------------------------------
initial car speed is zero
-------------------------------------------------------------------------------
c:\users\jalospinoso\catch-test\main.cpp(82)
...............................................................................

c:\users\jalospinoso\catch-test\main.cpp(85):❶ FAILED:
  REQUIRE( auto_brake.get_speed_mps()L == 0 ) ❷
with expansion:
  -92559631349317830736831783200707727132248687965119994463780864.0 ❸
  ==
  0

===============================================================================
test cases: 1 | 1 failed
assertions: 1 | 1 failed
```

Listing 10-33: The output from running the test suite after implementing Listing 10-31

This is vastly superior output to what you had produced in the home-grown unit-test suite. Catch tells you the exact line where the unit test failed ❶ and then prints this line for you ❷. Next, it expands this line into the actual values encountered at runtime. You can see that the grotesque (uninitialized) value returned by `get_speed_mps()` is clearly not `0` ❸. Compare this output to the output of the home-grown unit test; I think you'll agree that there's immediate value to using Catch.

Assertions and Exceptions

Catch also provides a special assertion called `REQUIRE_THROWS`. This macro requires that the contained expression throw an exception. To achieve similar functionality in the home-grown unit-test framework, consider this multiline monstrosity:

```
try {
  auto_brake.set_collision_threshold_s(0.5L);
} catch (const std::exception&) {
  return;
}
assert_that(false, "no exception thrown");
```

Other exception-aware macros are available as well. You can require that some expression evaluation not throw an exception using the `REQUIRE_NOTHROW` and `CHECK_NOTHROW` macros. You can also be specific about the type of the exception you expect to be thrown by using the `REQUIRE_THROWS_AS` and `CHECK_THROWS_AS` macros. These expect a second parameter describing the expected type. Their usages are similar to `REQUIRE`; you simply provide some expression that must throw an exception for the assertion to pass:

```
REQUIRE_THROWS(expression-to-evaluate);
```

If the *expression-to-evaluate* doesn't throw an exception, the assertion fails.

Floating-Point Assertions

The `AutoBrake` class involves floating-point arithmetic, and we've been glossing over a potentially very serious problem with the assertions. Because floating-point numbers entail rounding errors, it's not a good idea to check for equality using `operator==`. The more robust approach is to test whether the difference between floating-point numbers is arbitrarily small. With Catch, you can handle these situations effortlessly using the `Approx` class, as shown in Listing 10-34.

```
TEST_CASE("AutoBrake") {
  MockServiceBus bus{};
  AutoBrake auto_brake{ bus };
  REQUIRE(auto_brake.get_collision_threshold_s() == Approx(5L));
}
```

Listing 10-34: A refactor of the "initializes sensitivity to five" test using the `Approx` class

The Approx class helps Catch perform tolerant comparisons of floating-point values. It can exist on either side of a comparison expression. It has sensible defaults for how tolerant it is, but you have fine-grained control over the specifics (see the Catch documentation on epsilon, margin, and scale).

Fail

You can cause a Catch test to fail using the FAIL() macro. This can sometimes be useful when combined with conditional statements, as in the following:

```
if (something-bad) FAIL("Something bad happened.")
```

Use a REQUIRE statement if a suitable one is available.

Test Cases and Sections

Catch supports the idea of test cases and sections, which make common setup and teardown in your unit tests far easier. Notice that each of the tests has some repeated ceremony each time you construct an AutoBrake:

```
  MockServiceBus bus{};
  AutoBrake auto_brake{ bus };
```

There's no need to repeat this code over and over again. Catch's solution to this common setup is to use nested SECTION macros. You can nest SECTION macros within a TEST_CASE in the basic usage pattern, as demonstrated in Listing 10-35.

```
TEST_CASE("MyTestGroup") {
  // Setup code goes here ❶
  SECTION("MyTestA") { ❷
    // Code for Test A
  }
  SECTION("MyTestB") { ❸
    // Code for Test B
  }
}
```

Listing 10-35: An example Catch setup with nested macros

You can perform all of the setup once at the beginning of a TEST_CASE ❶. When Catch sees SECTION macros nested within a TEST_CASE, it (conceptually) copies and pastes all the setup into each SECTION ❷❸. Each SECTION runs independently of the others, so generally any side effects on objects created in the TEST_CASE aren't observed across SECTION macros. Further, you can embed a SECTION macro within another SECTION macro. This might be useful if you have a lot of setup code for a suite of closely related tests (although it may just make sense to split this suite into its own TEST_CASE).

Let's look at how this approach simplifies the AutoBrake unit-test suite.

Refactoring the AutoBrake Unit Tests to Catch

Listing 10-36 refactors all the unit tests into a Catch style.

```
#define CATCH_CONFIG_MAIN
#include "catch.hpp"
#include <functional>
#include <stdexcept>

struct IServiceBus {
  --snip--
};

struct MockServiceBus : IServiceBus {
  --snip--
};

struct AutoBrake {
  --snip--
};

TEST_CASE("AutoBrake"❶) {
  MockServiceBus bus{}; ❷
  AutoBrake auto_brake{ bus }; ❸

  SECTION❹("initializes speed to zero"❺) {
    REQUIRE(auto_brake.get_speed_mps() == Approx(0));
  }

  SECTION("initializes sensitivity to five") {
    REQUIRE(auto_brake.get_collision_threshold_s() == Approx(5));
  }

  SECTION("throws when sensitivity less than one") {
    REQUIRE_THROWS(auto_brake.set_collision_threshold_s(0.5L));
  }

  SECTION("saves speed after update") {
    bus.speed_update_callback(SpeedUpdate{ 100L });
    REQUIRE(100L == auto_brake.get_speed_mps());
    bus.speed_update_callback(SpeedUpdate{ 50L });
    REQUIRE(50L == auto_brake.get_speed_mps());
    bus.speed_update_callback(SpeedUpdate{ 0L });
    REQUIRE(0L == auto_brake.get_speed_mps());
  }

  SECTION("no alert when not imminent") {
    auto_brake.set_collision_threshold_s(2L);
    bus.speed_update_callback(SpeedUpdate{ 100L });
    bus.car_detected_callback(CarDetected{ 1000L, 50L });
    REQUIRE(bus.commands_published == 0);
  }

  SECTION("alert when imminent") {
    auto_brake.set_collision_threshold_s(10L);
```

```
    bus.speed_update_callback(SpeedUpdate{ 100L });
    bus.car_detected_callback(CarDetected{ 100L, 0L });
    REQUIRE(bus.commands_published == 1);
    REQUIRE(bus.last_command.time_to_collision_s == Approx(1));
  }
}
--------------------------------------------------------------------------------
================================================================================
All tests passed (9 assertions in 1 test case)
```

Listing 10-36: Using the Catch framework to implement the unit tests

Here, `TEST_CASE` is renamed to `AutoBrake` to reflect its more generic purpose ❶. Next, the body of the `TEST_CASE` begins with the common setup code that all the `AutoBrake` unit tests share ❷❸. Each of the unit tests has been converted into a `SECTION` macro ❹. You name each of the sections ❺ and then place the test-specific code within the `SECTION` body. Catch will do all the work of stitching together the setup code with each of the `SECTION` bodies. In other words, you get a fresh `AutoBrake` each time: the order of the `SECTIONS` doesn't matter here, and they're totally independent.

Google Test

Google Test is another extremely popular unit-testing framework. Google Test follows the xUnit unit-testing framework tradition, so if you're familiar with, for example, junit for Java or nunit for .NET, you'll feel right at home using Google Test. One nice feature when you're using Google Test is that the mocking framework Google Mocks was merged in some time ago.

Configuring Google Test

Google Test takes some time to get up and running. Unlike Catch, Google Test is not a header-only library. You must download it from *https://github.com/google/googletest/*, compile it into a set of libraries, and link those libraries into your test project as appropriate. If you use a popular desktop build system, such as GNU Make, Mac Xcode, or Visual Studio, some templates are available that you can use to start building the relevant libraries.

For more information about getting Google Test up and running, refer to the Primer available in the repository's `docs` directory.

NOTE *At press time, Google Test's latest version is 1.8.1. See this book's companion source, available at* https://ccc.codes, *for one method of integrating Google Test into a Cmake build.*

Within your unit-test project, you must perform two operations to set up Google Test. First, you must ensure that the included directory of your Google Test installation is in the header search path of your unit-test project. This allows you to use `#include "gtest/gtest.h"` within your tests. Second, you must instruct your linker to include `gtest` and `gtest_main` static libraries from your Google Test installation. Make sure that you link in the correct architecture and configuration settings for your computer.

NOTE *A common gotcha getting Google Test set up in Visual Studio is that the C/C++ > Code Generation > Runtime Library option for Google Test must match your project's option. By default, Google Test compiles the runtime statically (that is, with the* `/MT` *or* `/MTd` *options). This choice is different from the default, which is to compile the runtime dynamically (for example, with the* `/MD` *or* `/MDd` *options in Visual Studio).*

Defining an Entry Point

Google Test will supply a `main()` function for you when you link `gtest_main` into your unit-test project. Think of this as Google Test's analogy for Catch's `#define CATCH_CONFIG_MAIN`; it will locate all the unit tests you've defined and roll them together into a nice test harness.

Defining Test Cases

To define test cases, all you need to do is provide unit tests using the `TEST` macro, which is quite similar to Catch's `TEST_CASE`. Listing 10-37 illustrates the basic setup of a Google Test unit test.

```
#include "gtest/gtest.h" ❶

TEST❷(AutoBrake❸, UnitTestName❹) {
  // Unit test here ❺
}
```

```
Running main() from gtest_main.cc ❻
[==========] Running 1 test from 1 test case.
[----------] Global test environment set-up.
[----------] 1 test from AutoBrake
[ RUN      ] AutoBrake.UnitTestName
[       OK ] AutoBrake.UnitTestName (0 ms)
[----------] 1 test from AutoBrake (0 ms total)

[----------] Global test environment tear-down
[==========] 1 test from 1 test case ran. (1 ms total)
[  PASSED  ] 1 test. ❼
```

Listing 10-37: An example Google Test unit test

First, you include the `gtest/gtest.h` header ❶. This pulls in all the definitions you need to define your unit tests. Each unit test starts with the `TEST` macro ❷. You define each unit test with two labels: a *test case name*, which is `AutoBrake` ❸ and a *test name*, which is `UnitTestName` ❹. These are roughly analogous to the `TEST_CASE` and `SECTION` names (respectively) in Catch. A test case contains one or many tests. Usually, you place tests together that share some a common theme. The framework will group the tests together, which can be useful for some of the more advanced uses. Different test cases can have tests with the same name.

You would put the code for your unit test within the braces ❺. When you run the resulting unit-test binary, you can see that Google Test provides an entry point for you ❻. Because you provided no assertions (or code that could throw an exception), your unit tests pass with flying colors ❼.

Making Assertions

Assertions in Google Test are less magical than in Catch's `REQUIRE`. Although they're also macros, the Google Test assertions require a lot more work on the programmer's part. Where `REQUIRE` will parse the Boolean expression and determine whether you're testing for equality, a greater-than relationship, and so on, Google Test's assertions don't. You must pass in each component of the assertion separately.

There are many other options for formulating assertions in Google Test. Table 10-1 summarizes them.

Table 10-1: Google Test Assertions

Assertion	Verifies that . . .
`ASSERT_TRUE(`*condition*`)`	*condition* is true.
`ASSERT_FALSE(`*condition*`)`	*condition* is false.
`ASSERT_EQ(`*val1*`, `*val2*`)`	*val1* `==` *val2* is true.
`ASSERT_FLOAT_EQ(`*val1*`, `*val2*`)`	*val1* `-` *val2* is a rounding error (`float`).
`ASSERT_DOUBLE_EQ(`*val1*`, `*val2*`)`	*val1* `-` *val2* is a rounding error (`double`).
`ASSERT_NE(`*val1*`, `*val2*`)`	*val1* `!=` *val2* is true.
`ASSERT_LT(`*val1*`, `*val2*`)`	*val1* `<` *val2* is true.
`ASSERT_LE(`*val1*`, `*val2*`)`	*val1* `<=` *val2* is true.
`ASSERT_GT(`*val1*`, `*val2*`)`	*val1* `>` *val2* is true.
`ASSERT_GE(`*val1*`, `*val2*`)`	*val1* `>=` *val2* is true.
`ASSERT_STREQ(`*str1*`, `*str2*`)`	The two C-style strings *str1* and *str2* have the same content.
`ASSERT_STRNE(`*str1*`, `*str2*`)`	The two C-style strings *str1* and *str2* have different content.
`ASSERT_STRCASEEQ(`*str1*`, `*str2*`)`	The two C-style strings *str1* and *str2* have the same content, ignoring case.
`ASSERT_STRCASENE(`*str1*`, `*str2*`)`	The two C-style strings *str1* and *str2* have different content, ignoring case.
`ASSERT_THROW(`*statement*`, `*ex_type*`)`	The evaluating *statement* causes an exception of type *ex_type* to be thrown.
`ASSERT_ANY_THROW(`*statement*`)`	The evaluating *statement* causes an exception of any type to be thrown.
`ASSERT_NO_THROW(`*statement*`)`	The evaluating *statement* causes no exception to be thrown.
`ASSERT_HRESULT_SUCCEEDED(`*statement*`)`	The `HRESULT` returned by *statement* corresponds with a success (Win32 API only).
`ASSERT_HRESULT_FAILED(`*statement*`)`	The `HRESULT` returned by *statement* corresponds with a failure (Win32 API only).

Let's combine a unit-test definition with an assertion to see Google Test in action.

Refactoring the initial_car_speed_is_zero Test to Google Test

With the intentionally broken AutoBrake in Listing 10-32, you can run the following unit test to see what the test harness's failure messages look like. (Recall that you commented out the member initializer for speed_mps.) Listing 10-38 uses ASSERT_FLOAT_EQ to assert that the car's initial speed is zero.

```
#include "gtest/gtest.h"
#include <functional>

struct IServiceBus {
  --snip--
};

struct MockServiceBus : IServiceBus {
  --snip--
};

struct AutoBrake {
  AutoBrake(IServiceBus& bus)
    : collision_threshold_s{ 5 }/*,
    speed_mps{} */ {
  --snip--
};

TEST❶(AutoBrakeTest❷, InitialCarSpeedIsZero❸) {
  MockServiceBus bus{};
  AutoBrake auto_brake{ bus };
  ASSERT_FLOAT_EQ❹(0❺, auto_brake.get_speed_mps()❻);
}
--------------------------------------------------------------------------------
Running main() from gtest_main.cc
[==========] Running 1 test from 1 test case.
[----------] Global test environment set-up.
[----------] 1 test from AutoBrakeTest
[ RUN      ] AutoBrakeTest.InitialCarSpeedIsZero
C:\Users\josh\AutoBrake\gtest.cpp(80): error: Expected equality of these
values:
  0 ❺
  auto_brake.get_speed_mps()❻
    Which is: -inf
[  FAILED  ] AutoBrakeTest❷.InitialCarSpeedIsZero❸ (5 ms)
[----------] 1 test from AutoBrakeTest (5 ms total)

[----------] Global test environment tear-down
[==========] 1 test from 1 test case ran. (7 ms total)
[  PASSED  ] 0 tests.
[  FAILED  ] 1 test, listed below:
[  FAILED  ] AutoBrakeTest.InitialCarSpeedIsZero

 1 FAILED TEST
```

Listing 10-38: Intentionally commenting out the `collision_threshold_s` member initializer to cause test failures (using Google Test)

You declare a unit test ❶ with the test case name `AutoBrakeTest` ❷ and test name `InitialCarSpeedIsZero` ❸. Within the test, you set up the `auto_brake` and assert ❹ that the car's initial speed is zero ❺. Notice that the constant value is the first parameter and the quantity you're testing is the second parameter ❻.

Like the Catch output in Listing 10-33, the Google Test output in Listing 10-38 is very clear. It tells you that a test failed, identifies the failed assertion, and gives a good indication of how you might fix the issue.

Test Fixtures

Unlike Catch's `TEST_CASE` and `SECTION` approach, Google Test's approach is to formulate *test fixture classes* when a common setup is involved. These fixtures are classes that inherit from the `::testing::Test` class that the framework provides.

Any members you plan to use inside tests you should mark as `public` or `protected`. If you want some setup or teardown computation, you can put it inside the (default) constructor or destructor (respectively).

NOTE *You can also place such setup and teardown logic in overridden* `SetUp()` *and* `TearDown()` *functions, although it's rare that you would need to. One case is if the teardown computation might throw an exception. Because you generally shouldn't allow an uncaught exception to throw from a destructor, you would have to put such code in a* `TearDown()` *function. (Recall from "Throwing in Destructors" on page 106 that throwing an uncaught exception in a destructor when another exception is already in flight calls* `std::terminate`*.)*

If a test fixture is like a Catch `TEST_CASE`, then `TEST_F` is like a Catch `SECTION`. Like `TEST`, `TEST_F` takes two parameters. The first *must* be the exact name of the test fixture class. The second is the name of the unit test. Listing 10-39 illustrates the basic usage of Google Test's test fixtures.

```
#include "gtest/gtest.h"

struct MyTestFixture❶ : ::testing::Test❷ { };

TEST_F(MyTestFixture❸, MyTestA❹) {
  // Test A here
}

TEST_F(MyTestFixture, MyTestB❺) {
  // Test B here
}
```

```
Running main() from gtest_main.cc
[==========] Running 2 tests from 1 test case.
[----------] Global test environment set-up.
[----------] 2 tests from MyTestFixture
[ RUN      ] MyTestFixture.MyTestA
[       OK ] MyTestFixture.MyTestA (0 ms)
[ RUN      ] MyTestFixture.MyTestB
```

```
[       OK ] MyTestFixture.MyTestB (0 ms)
[----------] 2 tests from MyTestFixture (1 ms total)

[----------] Global test environment tear-down
[==========] 2 tests from 1 test case ran. (3 ms total)
[  PASSED  ] 2 tests.
```

Listing 10-39: The basic setup of Google Test's test fixtures

You declare a class `MyTestFixture` ❶ that inherits from the `::testing::Test` class that Google Test provides ❷. You use the class's name as the first parameter to the `TEST_F` macro ❸. The unit test then has access to any public or protected methods inside `MyTestFixture`, and you can use the constructor and destructor of `MyTestFixture` to perform any common test setup/teardown. The second argument is the name of the unit test ❹❺.

Next, let's look at how to use Google Test Fixtures to reimplement the `AutoBrake` unit tests.

Refactoring AutoBrake Unit Tests with Google Test

Listing 10-40 reimplements all the `AutoBrake` unit tests into Google Test's test-fixture framework.

```
#include "gtest/gtest.h"
#include <functional>

struct IServiceBus {
  --snip--
};

struct MockServiceBus : IServiceBus {
  --snip--
};

struct AutoBrake {
  --snip--
};

struct AutoBrakeTest : ::testing::Test { ❶
  MockServiceBus bus{};
  AutoBrake auto_brake { bus };
};

TEST_F❷(AutoBrakeTest❸, InitialCarSpeedIsZero❹) {
  ASSERT_DOUBLE_EQ(0, auto_brake.get_speed_mps()); ❺
}

TEST_F(AutoBrakeTest, InitialSensitivityIsFive) {
  ASSERT_DOUBLE_EQ(5, auto_brake.get_collision_threshold_s());
}

TEST_F(AutoBrakeTest, SensitivityGreaterThanOne) {
  ASSERT_ANY_THROW(auto_brake.set_collision_threshold_s(0.5L)); ❻
}
```

```
TEST_F(AutoBrakeTest, SpeedIsSaved) {
  bus.speed_update_callback(SpeedUpdate{ 100L });
  ASSERT_EQ(100, auto_brake.get_speed_mps());
  bus.speed_update_callback(SpeedUpdate{ 50L });
  ASSERT_EQ(50, auto_brake.get_speed_mps());
  bus.speed_update_callback(SpeedUpdate{ 0L });
  ASSERT_DOUBLE_EQ(0, auto_brake.get_speed_mps());
}

TEST_F(AutoBrakeTest, NoAlertWhenNotImminent) {
  auto_brake.set_collision_threshold_s(2L);
  bus.speed_update_callback(SpeedUpdate{ 100L });
  bus.car_detected_callback(CarDetected{ 1000L, 50L });
  ASSERT_EQ(0, bus.commands_published);
}

TEST_F(AutoBrakeTest, AlertWhenImminent) {
  auto_brake.set_collision_threshold_s(10L);
  bus.speed_update_callback(SpeedUpdate{ 100L });
  bus.car_detected_callback(CarDetected{ 100L, 0L });
  ASSERT_EQ(1, bus.commands_published);
  ASSERT_DOUBLE_EQ(1L, bus.last_command.time_to_collision_s);
}
```

```
Running main() from gtest_main.cc
[==========] Running 6 tests from 1 test case.
[----------] Global test environment set-up.
[----------] 6 tests from AutoBrakeTest
[ RUN      ] AutoBrakeTest.InitialCarSpeedIsZero
[       OK ] AutoBrakeTest.InitialCarSpeedIsZero (0 ms)
[ RUN      ] AutoBrakeTest.InitialSensitivityIsFive
[       OK ] AutoBrakeTest.InitialSensitivityIsFive (0 ms)
[ RUN      ] AutoBrakeTest.SensitivityGreaterThanOne
[       OK ] AutoBrakeTest.SensitivityGreaterThanOne (1 ms)
[ RUN      ] AutoBrakeTest.SpeedIsSaved
[       OK ] AutoBrakeTest.SpeedIsSaved (0 ms)
[ RUN      ] AutoBrakeTest.NoAlertWhenNotImminent
[       OK ] AutoBrakeTest.NoAlertWhenNotImminent (1 ms)
[ RUN      ] AutoBrakeTest.AlertWhenImminent
[       OK ] AutoBrakeTest.AlertWhenImminent (0 ms)
[----------] 6 tests from AutoBrakeTest (3 ms total)

[----------] Global test environment tear-down
[==========] 6 tests from 1 test case ran. (4 ms total)
[  PASSED  ] 6 tests.
```

Listing 10-40: Using Google Test to implement the `AutoBrake` unit tests

First, you implement the test fixture `AutoBrakeTest` ❶. This class encapsulates the common setup code across all the unit tests: to construct a `MockServiceBus` and use it to construct an `AutoBrake`. Each of the unit tests is represented by a `TEST_F` macro ❷. These macros take two parameters: the test fixture, such as `AutoBrakeTest` ❸, and the name of the test, such as

InitialCarSpeedIsZero ❹. Within the body of the unit tests, you have the correct invocations for each of the assertions, such as ASSERT_DOUBLE_EQ ❺ and ASSERT_ANY_THROW ❻.

Comparing Google Test and Catch

As you've seen, several major differences exist between Google Test and Catch. The most striking initial impression should be your investment in installing Google Test and making it work correctly in your solution. Catch is on the opposite end of this spectrum: as a header-only library, it's trivial to make it work in your project.

Another major difference is the assertions. To a newcomer, REQUIRE is a lot simpler to use than the Google Test assertion style. To a seasoned user of another xUnit framework, Google Test might seem more natural. The failure messages are also a bit different. It's really up to you to determine which of these styles is more sensible.

Finally, there's performance. Theoretically, Google Test will compile more quickly than Catch because all of Catch must be compiled for each translation unit in your unit-test suite. This is the trade-off for header-only libraries; the setup investment you make when setting up Google Test pays you back later with faster compilation. This might or might not be perceptible depending on the size of your unit-test suite.

Boost Test

Boost Test is a unit-testing framework that ships as part of the *Boost C++ libraries* (or simply *Boost*). Boost is an excellent collection of open source C++ libraries. It has a history of incubating many ideas that are eventually incorporated into the C++ standard, although not all Boost libraries aim for eventual inclusion. You'll see mention of a number of Boost libraries throughout the remainder of this book, and Boost Test is the first. For help installing boost into your environment, see Boost's home page *https://www.boost.org* or have a look at this book's companion code.

NOTE *At press time, the latest version of the Boost libraries is 1.70.0.*

You can use Boost Test in three modes: as a header-only library (like Catch), as a static library (like Google Test), or as a shared library, which will link the Boost Test module at runtime. The dynamic library usage can save quite a bit of disk space in the event you have multiple unit-test binaries. Rather than baking the unit-test framework into each of the unit-test binaries, you can build a single shared library (like a *.so* or *.dll*) and load it at runtime.

As you've discovered while exploring Catch and Google Test, trade-offs are involved with each of these approaches. A major advantage of Boost Test is that it allows you to choose the best mode as you see fit. It's not terribly difficult to switch modes should a project evolve, so one possible approach is to begin using Boost Test as a header-only library and transition into another mode as requirements change.

Setting Up Boost Test

To set up Boost Test in the header-only mode (what Boost documentation calls the "single-header variant"), you simply include the `<boost/test/included/unit_test.hpp>` header. For this header to compile, you need to define `BOOST_TEST_MODULE` with a user-defined name. For example:

```
#define BOOST_TEST_MODULE test_module_name
#include <boost/test/included/unit_test.hpp>
```

Unfortunately, you cannot take this approach if you have more than one translation unit. For such situations, Boost Test contains prebuilt static libraries that you can use. By linking these in, you avoid having to compile the same code for every translation unit. When taking this approach, you include the `boost/test/unit_test.hpp` header for each translation unit in the unit-test suite:

```
#include <boost/test/unit_test.hpp>
```

In exactly *one* translation unit, you also include the `BOOST_TEST_MODULE` definition:

```
#define BOOST_TEST_MODULE AutoBrake
#include <boost/test/unit_test.hpp>
```

You must also configure the linker to include the appropriate Boost Test static library that comes with the Boost Test installation. The compiler and architecture corresponding to the selected static library must match the rest of your unit-test project.

Setting Up Shared Library Mode

To set up Boost Test in shared library mode, you must add the following lines to each translation unit of the unit-test suite:

```
#define BOOST_TEST_DYN_LINK
#include <boost/test/unit_test.hpp>
```

In exactly *one* translation unit, you must also define `BOOST_TEST_MODULE`:

```
#define BOOST_TEST_MODULE AutoBrake
#define BOOST_TEST_DYN_LINK
#include <boost/test/unit_test.hpp>
```

As with the static library usage, you must instruct the linker to include Boost Test. At runtime, the unit-test shared library must be available as well.

Defining Test Cases

You can define a unit test in Boost Test with the `BOOST_AUTO_TEST_CASE` macro, which takes a single parameter corresponding to the name of the test. Listing 10-41 shows the basic usage.

```
#define BOOST_TEST_MODULE TestModuleName ❶
#include <boost/test/unit_test.hpp> ❷

BOOST_AUTO_TEST_CASE❸(TestA❹) {
  // Unit Test A here ❺
}
```

```
Running 1 test case...

*** No errors detected
```

Listing 10-41: Using Google Test to implement the `AutoBrake` *unit tests*

The test module's name is `TestModuleName` ❶, which you define as the `BOOST_TEST_MODULE`. You include the `boost/test/unit_test.hpp` header ❷, which provides you with access to all the components you need from Boost Test. The `BOOST_AUTO_TEST_CASE` declaration ❸ denotes a unit test called `TestA` ❹. The body of the unit test goes between the braces ❺.

Making Assertions

Assertions in Boost are very similar to the assertions in Catch. The `BOOST_TEST` macro is like the `REQUIRE` macro in Catch. You simply provide an expression that evaluates to true if the assertion passes and false if it fails:

```
BOOST_TEST(assertion-expression)
```

To require an expression to throw an exception upon evaluation, use the `BOOST_REQUIRE_THROW` macro, which is similar to Catch's `REQUIRE_THROWS` macro, except you must also provide the type of the exception you want thrown. Its usage is as follows:

```
BOOST_REQUIRE_THROW(expression, desired-exception-type);
```

If the *`expression`* doesn't throw an exception of type *`desired-exception-type`*, the assertion will fail.

Let's examine what the `AutoBrake` unit-test suite looks like using Boost Test.

Refactoring the initial_car_speed_is_zero Test to Boost Test

You'll use the intentionally broken `AutoBrake` in Listing 10-32 with the missing member initializer for `speed_mps`. Listing 10-42 causes Boost Test to deal with a failed unit test.

```
#define BOOST_TEST_MODULE AutoBrakeTest ❶
#include <boost/test/unit_test.hpp>
#include <functional>

struct IServiceBus {
  --snip--
};

struct MockServiceBus : IServiceBus {
  --snip--
};

struct AutoBrake {
  AutoBrake(IServiceBus& bus)
    : collision_threshold_s{ 5 }/*,
      speed_mps{} */❷ {
  --snip--
};

BOOST_AUTO_TEST_CASE(InitialCarSpeedIsZero❸) {
  MockServiceBus bus{};
  AutoBrake auto_brake{ bus };
  BOOST_TEST(0 == auto_brake.get_speed_mps()); ❹
}
```

```
Running 1 test case...
C:/Users/josh/projects/cpp-book/manuscript/part_2/10-testing/samples/boost/
minimal.cpp(80): error: in "InitialCarSpeedIsZero": check 0 == auto_brake.
get_speed_mps() has failed [0 != -9.2559631349317831e+61] ❺
*** 1 failure is detected in the test module "AutoBrakeTest"
```

Listing 10-42: Intentionally commenting out the speed_mps member initializer to cause test failures (using Boost Test)

The test module name is `AutoBrakeTest` ❶. After commenting out the `speed_mps` member initializer ❷, you have the `InitialCarSpeedIsZero` test ❸. The `BOOST_TEST` assertion tests whether `speed_mps` is zero ❹. As with Catch and Google Test, you have an informative error message that tells you what went wrong ❺.

Test Fixtures

Like Google Test, Boost Test deals with common setup code using the notion of test fixtures. Using them is as simple as declaring an RAII object where the setup logic for the test is contained in that class's constructor and the teardown logic is contained in the destructor. Unlike Google Test, you don't have to derive from a parent class in your test fixture. The test fixtures work with any user-defined structure.

To use the test fixture in a unit test, you employ the `BOOST_FIXTURE_TEST_CASE` macro, which takes two parameters. The first parameter is the name of the unit test, and the second parameter is the test fixture class. Within the body of the macro, you implement a unit test as if it were a method of the test fixture class, as demonstrated in Listing 10-43.

```
#define BOOST_TEST_MODULE TestModuleName
#include <boost/test/unit_test.hpp>

struct MyTestFixture { }; ❶

BOOST_FIXTURE_TEST_CASE❷(MyTestA❸, MyTestFixture) {
  // Test A here
}

BOOST_FIXTURE_TEST_CASE(MyTestB❹, MyTestFixture) {
  // Test B here
}
--------------------------------------------------------------------------
Running 2 test cases...

*** No errors detected
```

Listing 10-43: Illustrating Boost test fixture usage

Here, you define a class called `MyTestFixture` ❶ and use it as the second parameter for each instance of `BOOST_FIXTURE_TEST_CASE` ❷. You declare two unit tests: `MyTestA` ❸ and `MyTestB` ❹. Any setup you perform within `MyTestFixture` affects each `BOOST_FIXTURE_TEST_CASE`.

Next, you'll use Boost Test fixtures to reimplement the `AutoBrake` test suite.

Refactoring AutoBrake Unit Tests with Boost Test

Listing 10-44 implements the `AutoBrake` unit-test suite using Boost Test's test fixture.

```
#define BOOST_TEST_MODULE AutoBrakeTest
#include <boost/test/unit_test.hpp>
#include <functional>

struct IServiceBus {
  --snip--
};

struct MockServiceBus : IServiceBus {
  --snip--
};

struct AutoBrakeTest { ❶
  MockServiceBus bus{};
  AutoBrake auto_brake{ bus };
};

BOOST_FIXTURE_TEST_CASE❷(InitialCarSpeedIsZero, AutoBrakeTest) {
  BOOST_TEST(0 == auto_brake.get_speed_mps());
}
```

```
BOOST_FIXTURE_TEST_CASE(InitialSensitivityIsFive, AutoBrakeTest) {
  BOOST_TEST(5 == auto_brake.get_collision_threshold_s());
}

BOOST_FIXTURE_TEST_CASE(SensitivityGreaterThanOne, AutoBrakeTest) {
  BOOST_REQUIRE_THROW(auto_brake.set_collision_threshold_s(0.5L),
                      std::exception);
}

BOOST_FIXTURE_TEST_CASE(SpeedIsSaved, AutoBrakeTest) {
  bus.speed_update_callback(SpeedUpdate{ 100L });
  BOOST_TEST(100 == auto_brake.get_speed_mps());
  bus.speed_update_callback(SpeedUpdate{ 50L });
  BOOST_TEST(50 == auto_brake.get_speed_mps());
  bus.speed_update_callback(SpeedUpdate{ 0L });
  BOOST_TEST(0 == auto_brake.get_speed_mps());
}

BOOST_FIXTURE_TEST_CASE(NoAlertWhenNotImminent, AutoBrakeTest) {
  auto_brake.set_collision_threshold_s(2L);
  bus.speed_update_callback(SpeedUpdate{ 100L });
  bus.car_detected_callback(CarDetected{ 1000L, 50L });
  BOOST_TEST(0 == bus.commands_published);
}

BOOST_FIXTURE_TEST_CASE(AlertWhenImminent, AutoBrakeTest) {
  auto_brake.set_collision_threshold_s(10L);
  bus.speed_update_callback(SpeedUpdate{ 100L });
  bus.car_detected_callback(CarDetected{ 100L, 0L });
  BOOST_TEST(1 == bus.commands_published);
  BOOST_TEST(1L == bus.last_command.time_to_collision_s);
}
```

```
Running 6 test cases...

*** No errors detected
```

Listing 10-44: Using Boost Test to implement your unit tests

You define the test fixture class `AutoBrakeTest` to perform the setup of the `AutoBrake` and `MockServiceBus` ❶. It's identical to the Google Test test fixture except you didn't need to inherit from any framework-issued parent classes. You represent each unit test with a `BOOST_FIXTURE_TEST_CASE` macro ❷. The rest of the tests use the `BOOST_TEST` and `BOOST_REQUIRE_THROW` assertion macros; otherwise, the tests look very similar to Catch tests. Instead of `TEST_CASE` and `SECTION` elements, you have a test fixture class and `BOOST_FIXTURE_TEST_CASE`.

Summary: Testing Frameworks

Although three different unit-testing frameworks were presented in this section, dozens of high-quality options are available. None of them is universally superior. Most frameworks support the same basic set of features, whereas some of the more advanced features will have heterogeneous support. Mainly, you should select a unit-testing framework based on the style that makes you comfortable and productive.

Mocking Frameworks

The unit-testing frameworks you just explored will work in a wide range of settings. It would be totally feasible to build integration tests, acceptance tests, unit tests, and even performance tests using Google Test, for example. The testing frameworks support a broad range of programming styles, and their creators have only modest opinions about how you must design your software to make them testable.

Mocking frameworks are a bit more opinionated than unit-testing frameworks. Depending on the mocking framework, you must follow certain design guidelines for how classes depend on each other. The AutoBrake class used a modern design pattern called *dependency injection*. The AutoBrake class depends on an IServiceBus, which you injected using the constructor of AutoBrake. You also made IServiceBus an interface. Other methods for achieving polymorphic behavior exist (like templates), and each involves trade-offs.

All the mocking frameworks discussed in this section work extremely well with dependency injection. To varying degrees, the mocking frameworks remove the need to define your own mocks. Recall that you implemented a MockServiceBus to allow you to unit test AutoBrake, as displayed in Listing 10-45.

```
struct MockServiceBus : IServiceBus {
  void publish(const BrakeCommand& cmd) override {
    commands_published++;
    last_command = cmd;
  };
  void subscribe(SpeedUpdateCallback callback) override {
    speed_update_callback = callback;
  };
  void subscribe(CarDetectedCallback callback) override {
    car_detected_callback = callback;
  };
  BrakeCommand last_command{};
  int commands_published{};
  SpeedUpdateCallback speed_update_callback{};
  CarDetectedCallback car_detected_callback{};
};
```

Listing 10-45: Your hand-rolled MockServiceBus

Each time you want to add a unit test involving some new kind of interaction with IServiceBus, you'll likely need to update your MockServiceBus class. This is tedious and error prone. Additionally, it's not clear that you can share this mock class with other teams: you've implemented a lot of your own logic in it that won't be very useful to, say, the tire-pressure-sensor team. Also, each test might have different requirements. Mocking frameworks enables you to define mock classes, often using macro or template voodoo. Within each unit test, you can customize the mock specifically for that test. This would be extremely difficult to do with a single mock definition.

This decoupling of the mock's declaration from the mock's test-specific definition is extremely powerful for two reasons. First, you can define different kinds of behavior for each unit test. This allows you to, for example, simulate exceptional conditions for some unit tests but not for others. Second, it makes the unit tests far more specific. By placing the custom mock's behavior within a unit test rather than in a separate source file, it's much clearer to the developer what the test is trying to achieve.

The net effect of using a mocking framework is that it makes mocking much less problematic. When mocking is easy, it makes good unit testing (and TDD) possible. Without mocking, unit testing can be very difficult; tests can be slow, unreliable, and brittle due to slow or error-prone dependencies. It's generally preferable, for example, to use a mock database connection instead of a full-blown production instance while you're trying to use TDD to implement new features into a class.

This section provides a tour of two mocking frameworks, Google Mock and HippoMocks, and includes a brief mention of two others, FakeIt and Trompeloeil. For technical reasons having to do with a lack of compile time code generation, creating a mocking framework is much harder in C++ than in most other languages, especially those with type reflection, a language feature that allows code to programmatically reason about type information. Consequently, there are a lot of high-quality mocking frameworks, each with their own trade-offs resulting from the fundamental difficulties associated with mocking C++.

Google Mock

One of the most popular mocking frameworks is the Google C++ Mocking Framework (or Google Mock), which is included as part of Google Test. It's one of the oldest and most feature-rich mocking frameworks. If you've already installed Google Test, incorporating Google Mock is easy. First, make sure you include the `gmock` static library in your linker, as you did for `gtest` and `gtest_main`. Next, add `#include "gmock/gmock.h"`.

If you're using Google Test as your unit-testing framework, that's all the setup you'll need to do. Google Mock will work seamlessly with its sister library. If you're using another unit-testing framework, you'll need to provide the initialization code in the entry point of the binary, as shown in Listing 10-46.

```
#include "gmock/gmock.h"

int main(int argc, char** argv) {
  ::testing::GTEST_FLAG(throw_on_failure) = true; ❶
  ::testing::InitGoogleMock(&argc, argv); ❷
  // Unit test as usual, Google Mock is initialized
}
```

Listing 10-46: Adding Google Mock to a third-party unit-testing framework

The GTEST_FLAG throw_on_failure ❶ causes Google Mock to throw an exception when some mock-related assertion fails. The call to InitGoogleMock ❷ consumes the command line arguments to make any necessary customization (refer to the Google Mock documentation for more details).

Mocking an Interface

For each interface you need to mock, there is some unfortunate ceremony. You need to take each virtual function of the interface and transmute it into a macro. For non-const methods, you use MOCK_METHOD*, and for const methods, you use MOCK_CONST_METHOD*, replacing * with the number of parameters that the function takes. The first parameter of MOCK_METHOD is the name of the virtual function. The second parameter is the function prototype. For example, to make a mock IServiceBus, you would build the definition shown in Listing 10-47.

```
struct MockServiceBus : IServiceBus { ❶
  MOCK_METHOD1❷(publish❸, void(const BrakeCommand& cmd)❹);
  MOCK_METHOD1(subscribe, void(SpeedUpdateCallback callback));
  MOCK_METHOD1(subscribe, void(CarDetectedCallback callback));
};
```

Listing 10-47: A Google Mock MockServiceBus

The beginning of the definition of MockServiceBus is identical to the definition of any other IServiceBus implementation ❶. You then employ MOCK_METHOD three times ❷. The first parameter ❸ is the name of the virtual function, and the second parameter ❹ is the prototype of the function.

It's a bit tedious to have to generate these definitions on your own. There's no additional information in the MockServiceBus definition that isn't already available in the IServiceBus. For better or worse, this is one of the costs of using Google Mock. You can take the sting out of generating this boilerplate by using the gmock_gen.py tool included in the scripts/generator folder of the Google Mock distribution. You'll need Python 2 installed, and it's not guaranteed to work in all situations. See the Google Mock documentation for more information.

Now that you've defined a MockServiceBus, you can use it in your unit tests. Unlike the mock you defined on your own, you can configure a Google Mock specifically for each unit test. You have an incredible amount of flexibility in this configuration. The key to successful mock configuration is the use of appropriate expectations.

Expectations

An *expectation* is like an assertion for a mock object; it expresses the circumstances in which the mock expects to be called and what it should do in response. The "circumstances" are specified using objects called *matchers*. The "what it should do in response" part is called an *action*. The sections that follow will introduce each of these concepts.

Expectations are declared with the EXPECT_CALL macro. The first parameter to this macro is the mock object, and the second is the expected method call. This method call can optionally contain matchers for each parameter. These matchers help Google Mock decide whether a particular method invocation qualifies as an expected call. The format is as follows:

```
EXPECT_CALL(mock_object, method(matchers))
```

There are several ways to formulate assertions about expectations, and which you choose depends on how strict your requirements are for how the unit being tested interacts with the mock. Do you care whether your code calls mocked functions that you didn't expect? It really depends on the application. That's why there are three options: naggy, nice, and strict.

A *naggy mock* is the default. If a naggy mock's function is called and no EXPECT_CALL matches the call, Google Mock will print a warning about an "uninteresting call," but the test won't fail just because of the uninteresting call. You can just add an EXPECT_CALL into the test as a quick fix to suppress the uninteresting call warning, because the call then ceases to be unexpected.

In some situations, there might be too many uninteresting calls. In such cases, you should use a *nice mock*. The nice mock won't produce a warning about uninteresting calls.

If you're very concerned about any interaction with the mock that you haven't accounted for, you might use a *strict mock*. Strict mocks will fail the test if any call is made to the mock for which you don't have a corresponding EXPECT_CALL.

Each of these types of mocks is a class template. The way to instantiate these classes is straightforward, as outlined in Listing 10-48.

```
MockServiceBus naggy_mock❶;
::testing::NiceMock<MockServiceBus> nice_mock❷;
::testing::StrictMock<MockServiceBus> strict_mock❸;
```

Listing 10-48: Three different styles of Google Mock

Naggy mocks ❶ are the default. Every ::testing::NiceMock ❷ and ::testing::StrictMock ❸ takes a single template parameter, the class of the underlying mock. All three of these options are perfectly valid first parameters to an EXPECT_CALL.

As a general rule, you should use nice mocks. Using naggy and strict mocks can lead to very brittle tests. When you're using a strict mock, consider whether it's really necessary to be so restrictive about the way the unit under test collaborates with the mock.

The second parameter to EXPECT_CALL is the name of the method you expect to be called followed by the parameters you expect the method to be called with. Sometimes, this is easy. Other times, there are more complicated conditions you want to express for what invocations match and don't match. In such situations, you use matchers.

Matchers

When a mock's method takes arguments, you have broad discretion over whether an invocation matches the expectation. In simple cases, you can use literal values. If the mock method is invoked with exactly the specified literal value, the invocation matches the expectation; otherwise, it doesn't. On the other extreme, you can use Google Mock's `::testing::_` object, which tells Google Mock that *any* value matches.

Suppose, for example, that you want to invoke `publish`, and you don't care what the argument is. The `EXPECT_CALL` in Listing 10-49 would be appropriate.

```
--snip--
using ::testing::_; ❶

TEST(AutoBrakeTest, PublishIsCalled) {
  MockServiceBus bus;
  EXPECT_CALL(bus, publish(_❷));
  --snip--
}
```

Listing 10-49: Using the `::testing::_` matcher in an expectation

To make the unit test nice and tidy, you employ a `using` for `::testing::_` ❶. You use `_` to tell Google Mock that *any* invocation of `publish` with a single argument will match ❷.

A slightly more selective matcher is the class template `::testing::A`, which will match only if a method is invoked with a particular type of parameter. This type is expressed as the template parameter to `A`, so `A<MyType>` will match only a parameter of type `MyType`. In Listing 10-50, the modification to Listing 10-49 illustrates a more restrictive expectation that requires a `BrakeCommand` as the parameter to `publish`.

```
--snip--
using ::testing::A; ❶

TEST(AutoBrakeTest, PublishIsCalled) {
  MockServiceBus bus;
  EXPECT_CALL(bus, publish(A<BrakeCommand>❷));
  --snip--
}
```

Listing 10-50: Using the `::testing::A` matcher in an expectation

Again, you employ `using` ❶ and use `A<BrakeCommand>` to specify that only a `BrakeCommand` will match this expectation.

Another matcher, `::testing::Field`, allows you to inspect fields on arguments passed to the mock. The `Field` matcher takes two parameters: a pointer to the field you want to expect and then another matcher to express whether the pointed-to field meets the criteria. Suppose you want to be even more specific about the call to `publish` ❷: you want to specify that the `time_to_collision_s` is equal to 1 second. You can accomplish this task with the refactor of Listing 10-49 shown in Listing 10-51.

```
--snip--
using ::testing::Field; ❶
using ::testing::DoubleEq; ❷

TEST(AutoBrakeTest, PublishIsCalled) {
  MockServiceBus bus;
  EXPECT_CALL(bus, publish(Field(&BrakeCommand::time_to_collision_s❸,
                                 DoubleEq(1L)❹)));
  --snip--
}
```

Listing 10-51: Using the `Field` matcher in an expectation

You employ `using` for `Field` ❶ and `DoubleEq` ❷ to clean up the expectation code a bit. The `Field` matcher takes a pointer to the field you're interested in `time_to_collision_s` ❸ and the matcher that decides whether the field meets the criteria `DoubleEq` ❹.

Many other matchers are available, and they're summarized in Table 10-2. But refer to the Google Mock documentation for all the details about their usages.

Table 10-2: Google Mock Matchers

Matcher	Matches when argument is . . .
`_`	Any value of the correct type
`A<`*type*`>)()`	Of the given *type*
`An<`*type*`>)()`	Of the given *type*
`Ge(`*value*`)`	Greater than or equal to *value*
`Gt(`*value*`)`	Greater than *value*
`Le(`*value*`)`	Less than or equal to *value*
`Lt(`*value*`)`	Less than *value*
`Ne(`*value*`)`	Not equal to *value*
`IsNull()`	Null
`NotNull()`	Not null
`Ref(`*variable*`)`	A reference to *variable*
`DoubleEq(`*variable*`)`	A `double` value approximately equal to *variable*
`FloatEq(`*variable*`)`	A `float` value approximately equal to *variable*
`EndsWith(`*str*`)`	A string ending with *str*
`HasSubstr(`*str*`)`	A string containing the substring *str*
`StartsWith(`*str*`)`	A string starting with *str*
`StrCaseEq(`*str*`)`	A string equal to *str* (ignoring case)
`StrCaseNe(`*str*`)`	A string not equal to *str* (ignoring case)
`StrEq(`*str*`)`	A string equal to *str*
`StrNeq(`*string*`)`	A string not equal to *str*

NOTE *One beneficial feature of matchers is that you can use them as an alternate kind of assertion for your unit tests. The alternate macro is one of* `EXPECT_THAT(value, matcher)` *or* `ASSERT_THAT(value, matcher)`. *For example, you could replace the assertion*

```
ASSERT_GT(power_level, 9000);
```

with the more syntactically pleasing

```
ASSERT_THAT(power_level, Gt(9000));
```

You can use `EXPECT_CALL` with `StrictMock` to enforce how the unit under test interacts with the mock. But you might also want to specify how many times the mock should respond to calls. This is called the expectation's *cardinality*.

Cardinality

Perhaps the most common method for specifying cardinality is `Times`, which specifies the number of times that a mock should expect to be called. The `Times` method takes a single parameter, which can be an integer literal or one of the functions listed in Table 10-3.

Table 10-3: A Listing of the Cardinality Specifiers in Google Mock

Cardinality	Specifies that a method will be called . . .
`AnyNumber()`	Any number of times
`AtLeast(n)`	At least *n* times
`AtMost(n)`	At most *n* times
`Between(m, n)`	Between *m* and *n* times
`Exactly(n)`	Exactly *n* times

Listing 10-52 elaborates Listing 10-51 to indicate that `publish` must be called only once.

```
--snip--
using ::testing::Field;
using ::testing::DoubleEq;

TEST(AutoBrakeTest, PublishIsCalled) {
  MockServiceBus bus;
  EXPECT_CALL(bus, publish(Field(&BrakeCommand::time_to_collision_s,
                                 DoubleEq(1L)))).Times(1)❶;
  --snip--
}
```

Listing 10-52: Using the `Times` *cardinality specifier in an expectation*

The `Times` call ❶ ensures that `publish` gets called exactly once (regardless of whether you use a nice, strict, or naggy mock).

NOTE *Equivalently, you could have specified* `Times(Exactly(1))`.

Now that you have some tools to specify the criteria and cardinality for an expected invocation, you can customize how the mock should respond to expectations. For this, you employ actions.

Actions

Like cardinalities, all actions are chained off `EXPECT_CALL` statements. These statements can help clarify how many times a mock expects to be called, what values to return each time it's called, and any side effects (like throwing an exception) it should perform. The `WillOnce` and `WillRepeatedly` actions specify what a mock should do in response to a query. These actions can get quite complicated, but for brevity's sake, this section covers two usages. First, you can use the `Return` construct to return values to the caller:

```
EXPECT_CALL(jenny_mock, get_your_number()) ❶
  .WillOnce(Return(8675309)) ❷
  .WillRepeatedly(Return(911))❸;
```

You set up an `EXPECT_CALL` the usual way and then tag on some actions that specify what value the `jenny_mock` will return each time `get_your_number` is called ❶. These are read sequentially from left to right, so the first action, `WillOnce` ❷, specifies that the first time `get_your_number` is called, the value `8675309` is returned by `jenny_mock`. The next action, `WillRepeatedly` ❸, specifies that for all subsequent calls, the value `911` will be returned.

Because `IServiceBus` doesn't return any values, you'll need the action to be a little more involved. For highly customizable behavior, you can use the `Invoke` construct, which enables you to pass an `Invocable` that will get called with the exact arguments passed into the mock's method. Let's say you want to save off a reference to the callback function that the `AutoBrake` registers via `subscribe`. You can do this easily with an `Invoke`, as illustrated in Listing 10-53.

```
CarDetectedCallback callback; ❶
EXPECT_CALL(bus, subscribe(A<CarDetectedCallback>()))
    .Times(1)
    .WillOnce(Invoke([&callback❷](const auto& callback_in❸) {
      callback = callback_in; ❹
    }));
```

Listing 10-53: Using `Invoke` *to save off a reference to the* `subscribe` *callback registered by an* `AutoBrake`

The first (and only) time that `subscribe` is called with a `CarDetectedCallback`, the `WillOnce(Invoke(...))` action will call the lambda that's been passed in as a parameter. This lambda captures the `CarDetectedCallback` declared ❶ by reference ❷. By definition, the lambda has the same function prototype as the `subscribe` function, so you can use auto-type deduction ❸ to determine the correct type for `callback_in` (it's `CarDetectedCallback`). Finally, you assign `callback_in` to `callback` ❹. Now, you can pass events off to whoever `subscribes` simply by invoking your `callback` ❶. The `Invoke` construct is the Swiss Army Knife of actions, because you get to execute arbitrary code with full information about the invocation parameters. *Invocation parameters* are the parameters that the mocked method received at runtime.

Putting It All Together

Reconsidering our `AutoBrake` testing suite, you can reimplement the Google Test unit-test binary to use Google Mock rather than the hand-rolled mock, as demonstrated in Listing 10-54.

```
#include "gtest/gtest.h"
#include "gmock/gmock.h"
#include <functional>

using ::testing::_;
using ::testing::A;
using ::testing::Field;
using ::testing::DoubleEq;
using ::testing::NiceMock;
using ::testing::StrictMock;
using ::testing::Invoke;

struct NiceAutoBrakeTest : ::testing::Test { ❶
  NiceMock<MockServiceBus> bus;
  AutoBrake auto_brake{ bus };
};

struct StrictAutoBrakeTest : ::testing::Test { ❷
  StrictAutoBrakeTest() {
    EXPECT_CALL(bus, subscribe(A<CarDetectedCallback>())) ❸
      .Times(1)
      .WillOnce(Invoke([this](const auto& x) {
        car_detected_callback = x;
      }));
    EXPECT_CALL(bus, subscribe(A<SpeedUpdateCallback>())) ❹
      .Times(1)
      .WillOnce(Invoke([this](const auto& x) {
        speed_update_callback = x;
      }));;
  }
  CarDetectedCallback car_detected_callback;
  SpeedUpdateCallback speed_update_callback;
  StrictMock<MockServiceBus> bus;
};

TEST_F(NiceAutoBrakeTest, InitialCarSpeedIsZero) {
  ASSERT_DOUBLE_EQ(0, auto_brake.get_speed_mps());
}

TEST_F(NiceAutoBrakeTest, InitialSensitivityIsFive) {
  ASSERT_DOUBLE_EQ(5, auto_brake.get_collision_threshold_s());
}
```

```
TEST_F(NiceAutoBrakeTest, SensitivityGreaterThanOne) {
  ASSERT_ANY_THROW(auto_brake.set_collision_threshold_s(0.5L));
}

TEST_F(StrictAutoBrakeTest, NoAlertWhenNotImminent) {
  AutoBrake auto_brake{ bus };

  auto_brake.set_collision_threshold_s(2L);
  speed_update_callback(SpeedUpdate{ 100L });
  car_detected_callback(CarDetected{ 1000L, 50L });
}

TEST_F(StrictAutoBrakeTest, AlertWhenImminent) {
  EXPECT_CALL(bus, publish(
                     Field(&BrakeCommand::time_to_collision_s, DoubleEq{ 1L
}))
                 ).Times(1);
  AutoBrake auto_brake{ bus };

  auto_brake.set_collision_threshold_s(10L);
  speed_update_callback(SpeedUpdate{ 100L });
  car_detected_callback(CarDetected{ 100L, 0L });
}
```

Listing 10-54: Reimplementing your unit tests using a Google Mock rather than a roll-your-own mock

Here, you actually have two different test fixtures: `NiceAutoBrakeTest` ❶ and `StrictAutoBrakeTest` ❷. The `NiceAutoBrakeTest` test instantiates a `NiceMock`. This is useful for `InitialCarSpeedIsZero`, `InitialSensitivityIsFive`, and `SensitivityGreaterThanOne`, because you don't want to test any meaningful interactions with the mock; it's not the focus of these tests. But you do want to focus on `AlertWhenImminent` and `NoAlertWhenNotImminent`. Each time an event is published or a type is subscribed to, it could have potentially major ramifications on your system. The paranoia of a `StrictMock` here is warranted.

In the `StrictAutoBrakeTest` definition, you can see the `WillOnce`/`Invoke` approach to saving off the callbacks for each subscription ❸❹. These are used in `AlertWhenImminent` and `NoAlertWhenNotImminent` to simulate events coming off the service bus. It gives the unit tests a nice, clean, succinct feel, even though there's a lot of mocking logic going on behind the scenes. Remember, you don't even require a working service bus to do all this testing!

HippoMocks

Google Mock is one of the original C++ mocking frameworks, and it's still a mainstream choice today. HippoMocks is an alternative mocking framework created by Peter Bindels. As a header-only library, HippoMocks is trivial to install. Simply pull down the latest version from GitHub (*https://github.com/dascandy/hippomocks/*). You must include the `"hippomocks.h"` header in your tests. HippoMocks will work with any testing framework.

NOTE *At press time, the latest version of HippoMocks is v5.0.*

To create a mock using HippoMocks, you start by instantiating a `MockRespository` object. By default, all the mocks derived from this `MockRepository` will require *strict ordering* of expectations. Strictly ordered expectations cause a test to fail if each of the expectations is not invoked in the exact order you've specified. Usually, this is not what you want. To modify this default behavior, set the `autoExpect` field on `MockRepository` to `false`:

```
MockRepository mocks;
mocks.autoExpect = false;
```

Now you can use `MockRepository` to generate a mock of `IServiceBus`. This is done through the (member) function template `Mock`. This function will return a pointer to your newly minted mock:

```
auto* bus = mocks.Mock<IServiceBus>();
```

A major selling point of `HippoMocks` is illustrated here: notice that you didn't need to generate any macro-laden boilerplate for the mock `IServiceBus` like you did for Google Mock. The framework can handle vanilla interfaces without any further effort on your part.

Setting up expectations is very straightforward as well. For this, use the `ExpectCall` macro on `MockRespository`. The `ExpectCall` macro takes two parameters: a pointer to your mock and a pointer to the method you're expecting:

```
mocks.ExpectCall(bus, IServiceBus::subscribe_to_speed)
```

This example adds an expectation that `bus.subscribe_to_speed` will be invoked. You have several matchers you can add to this expectation, as summarized in Table 10-4.

Table 10-4: HippoMocks Matchers

Matcher	Specifies that an expectation matches when . . .
`With(`*`args`*`)`	The invocation parameters match *`args`*
`Match(`*`predicate`*`)`	*`predicate`* invoked with the invocation parameters returns `true`
`After(`*`expectation`*`)`	*`expectation`* has already been satisfied (This is useful for referring to a previously registered call.)

You can define actions to perform in response to `ExpectCall`, as summarized in Table 10-5.

Table 10-5: HippoMocks Actions

Action	Does the following upon invocation:
`Return(value)`	Returns *value* to the caller
`Throw(exception)`	Throws *exception*
`Do(callable)`	Executes *callable* with the invocation parameters

By default, HippoMocks requires an expectation to be met exactly once (like Google Mock's `.Times(1)` cardinality).

For example, you can express the expectation that `publish` is called with a `BrakeCommand` having a `time_to_collision_s` of `1.0` in the following way:

```
mocks.ExpectCall➊(bus, IServiceBus::publish)
  .Match➋([](const BrakeCommand& cmd) {
    return cmd.time_to_collision_s == Approx(1); ➌
  });
```

You use `ExpectCall` to specify that `bus` should be called with the `publish` method ➊. You refine this expectation with the `Match` matcher ➋, which takes a predicate accepting the same arguments as the `publish` method—a single `const BrakeCommand` reference. You return `true` if the `time_to_collision_s` field of the `BrakeCommand` is 1.0; otherwise, you return `false` ➌, which is fully compatible.

NOTE *As of v5.0, HippoMocks doesn't have built-in support for approximate matchers. Instead, Catch's* `Approx` ➌ *was used.*

HippoMocks supports function overloads for free functions. It also supports overloads for methods, but the syntax is not very pleasing to the eye. If you are using HippoMocks, it is best to avoid method overloads in your interface, so it would be better to refactor `IServiceBus` along the following lines:

```
struct IServiceBus {
  virtual ~IServiceBus() = default;
  virtual void publish(const BrakeCommand&) = 0;
  virtual void subscribe_to_speed(SpeedUpdateCallback) = 0;
  virtual void subscribe_to_car_detected(CarDetectedCallback) = 0;
};
```

NOTE *One design philosophy states that it's undesirable to have an overloaded method in an interface, so if you subscribe to that philosophy, the lack of support in HippoMocks is a moot point.*

Now `subscribe` is no longer overloaded, and it's possible to use HippoMocks. Listing 10-55 refactors the test suite to use HippoMocks with Catch.

```
#include "hippomocks.h"
--snip--
TEST_CASE("AutoBrake") {
  MockRepository mocks; ❶
  mocks.autoExpect = false;
  CarDetectedCallback car_detected_callback;
  SpeedUpdateCallback speed_update_callback;
  auto* bus = mocks.Mock<IServiceBus>();
  mocks.ExpectCall(bus, IServiceBus::subscribe_to_speed) ❷
    .Do([&](const auto& x) {
      speed_update_callback = x;
    });
  mocks.ExpectCall(bus, IServiceBus::subscribe_to_car_detected) ❸
    .Do([&](const auto& x) {
    car_detected_callback = x;
  });
  AutoBrake auto_brake{ *bus };

  SECTION("initializes speed to zero") {
    REQUIRE(auto_brake.get_speed_mps() == Approx(0));
  }

  SECTION("initializes sensitivity to five") {
    REQUIRE(auto_brake.get_collision_threshold_s() == Approx(5));
  }

  SECTION("throws when sensitivity less than one") {
    REQUIRE_THROWS(auto_brake.set_collision_threshold_s(0.5L));
  }

  SECTION("saves speed after update") {
    speed_update_callback(SpeedUpdate{ 100L }); ❹
    REQUIRE(100L == auto_brake.get_speed_mps());
    speed_update_callback(SpeedUpdate{ 50L });
    REQUIRE(50L == auto_brake.get_speed_mps());
    speed_update_callback(SpeedUpdate{ 0L });
    REQUIRE(0L == auto_brake.get_speed_mps());
  }

  SECTION("no alert when not imminent") {
    auto_brake.set_collision_threshold_s(2L);
    speed_update_callback(SpeedUpdate{ 100L }); ❺
    car_detected_callback(CarDetected{ 1000L, 50L });
  }

  SECTION("alert when imminent") {
    mocks.ExpectCall(bus, IServiceBus::publish) ❻
      .Match([](const auto& cmd) {
        return cmd.time_to_collision_s == Approx(1);
      });

    auto_brake.set_collision_threshold_s(10L);
    speed_update_callback(SpeedUpdate{ 100L });
```

```
        car_detected_callback(CarDetected{ 100L, 0L });
    }
}
```

Listing 10-55: Reimplementing Listing 10-54 to use HippoMocks and Catch rather than Google Mock and Google Test.

NOTE *This section couples HippoMocks with Catch for demonstration purposes, but HippoMocks works with all the unit-testing frameworks discussed in this chapter.*

You create the `MockRepository` ❶ and relax the strict ordering requirements by setting `autoExpect` to `false`. After declaring the two callbacks, you create an `IServiceBusMock` (without having to define a mock class!), and then set expectations ❷❸ that will hook up your callback functions with `AutoBrake`. Finally, you create `auto_brake` using a reference to the mock bus.

The `initializes speed to zero`, `initializes sensitivity to five`, and `throws when sensitivity less than one` tests require no further interaction with the mock. In fact, as a strict mock, `bus` won't let any further interactions happen without complaining. Because HippoMocks doesn't allow nice mocks like Google Mock, this is actually a fundamental difference between Listing 10-54 and Listing 10-55.

In the `saves speed after update` test ❹, you issue a series of `speed_update` callbacks and assert that the speeds are saved off correctly as before. Because `bus` is a strict mock, you're also implicitly asserting that no further interaction happens with the service bus here.

In the `no alert when not imminent` test, no changes are needed to `speed_update_callback` ❺. Because the mock is strict (and you don't expect a `BrakeCommand` to get published), no further expectations are needed.

NOTE *HippoMocks offers the* `NeverCall` *method on its mocks, which will improve the clarity of your tests and errors if it's called.*

However, in the `alert when imminent` test, you expect that your program will invoke `publish` on a `BrakeCommand`, so you set up this expectation ❻. You use the `Match` matcher to provide a predicate that checks for `time_to_collision_s` to equal approximately `1`. The rest of the test is as before: you send `AutoBrake` a `SpeedUpdate` event and a subsequent `CarDetected` event that should cause a collision to be detected.

HippoMocks is a more streamlined mocking framework than Google Mock is. It requires far less ceremony, but it's a little less flexible.

NOTE *One area where HippoMocks is* more *flexible than Google Mock is in mocking free functions. HippoMocks can mock free functions and static class functions directly, whereas Google Mock requires you to rewrite the code to use an interface.*

A Note on Other Mocking Options: FakeIt and Trompeloeil

A number of other excellent mocking frameworks are available. But for the sake of keeping an already long chapter from getting much longer, let's briefly look at two more frameworks: FakeIt (by Eran Pe'er, available at *https://github.com/eranpeer/FakeIt/*) and Trompeloeil (by Björn Fahller, available at *https://github.com/rollbear/trompeloeil/*).

FakeIt is similar to HippoMocks in its succinct usage patterns, and it's a header-only library. It differs in that it follows the record-by-default pattern in building expectations. Rather than specifying expectations up front, FakeIt verifies that a mock's methods were invoked correctly at the *end* of the test. Actions, of course, are still specified at the beginning.

Although this is a totally valid approach, I prefer the Google Mock/ HippoMocks approach of specifying expectations—and their associated actions—all up front in one concise location.

Trompeloeil (from the French *trompe-l'œil* for "deceive the eye") can be considered a modern replacement for Google Mock. Like Google Mock, it requires some macro-laden boilerplate for each of the interfaces you want to mock. In exchange for this extra effort, you gain many powerful features, including actions, such as setting test variables, returning values based on invocation parameters, and forbidding particular invocations. Like Google Mock and HippoMocks, Trompeloeil requires you to specify your expectations and actions up front (see the documentation for more details).

Summary

This chapter used an extended example of building the automatic braking system for an autonomous vehicle to explore the basics of TDD. You rolled your own testing and mocking framework, then learned about the many benefits of using available testing and mocking frameworks. You toured Catch, Google Test, and Boost Test as possible testing frameworks. For mocking frameworks, you dove into Google Mock and HippoMocks (with a brief mention of FakeIt and Trompeloeil). Each of these frameworks has strengths and weaknesses. Which you choose should be driven principally by which frameworks make you most efficient and productive.

NOTE *For the remainder of the book, examples will be couched in terms of unit tests. Accordingly, I had to choose a framework for the examples. I've chosen Catch for a few reasons. First, Catch's syntax is the most succinct, and it lends itself well to book form. In header-only mode, Catch compiles much quicker than Boost Test. This might be considered an endorsement of the framework (and it is), but it's not my intention to discourage the use of Google Test, Boost Test, or any other testing framework. You should make such decisions after careful consideration (and hopefully some experimentation.)*

EXERCISES

10-1. Your car company has completed work on a service that detects speed limits based on signage it observes on the side of the road. The speed-limit-detection team will publish objects of the following type to the event bus periodically:

```
struct SpeedLimitDetected {
  unsigned short speed_mps;
}
```

The service bus has been extended to incorporate this new type:

```
#include <functional>
--snip--
using SpeedUpdateCallback = std::function<void(const SpeedUpdate&)>;
using CarDetectedCallback = std::function<void(const CarDetected&)>;
using SpeedLimitCallback = std::function<void(const SpeedLimitDetected&)>;

struct IServiceBus {
  virtual ~IServiceBus() = default;
  virtual void publish(const BrakeCommand&) = 0;
  virtual void subscribe(SpeedUpdateCallback) = 0;
  virtual void subscribe(CarDetectedCallback) = 0;
  virtual void subscribe(SpeedLimitCallback) = 0;
};
```

Update the service with the new interface and make sure the tests still pass.

10-2. Add a private field for the last known speed limit. Implement a getter method for this field.

10-3. The product owner wants you to initialize the last known speed limit to 39 meters per second. Implement a unit test that checks a newly constructed AutoBrake that has a last known speed limit of 39.

10-4. Make unit tests pass.

10-5. Implement a unit test where you publish three different `SpeedLimitDetected` objects using the same callback technique you used for `SpeedUpdate` and `CarDetected`. After invoking each of the callbacks, check the last known speed limit on the `AutoBrake` object to ensure it matches.

10-6. Make all unit tests pass.

10-7. Implement a unit test where the last known speed limit is 35 meters per second, and you're traveling at 34 meters per second. Ensure that no `BrakeCommand` is published by `AutoBrake`.

10-8. Make all unit tests pass.

10-9. Implement a unit test where the last known speed limit is 35 meters per second and then publish a `SpeedUpdate` at 40 meters per second. Ensure that exactly one `BrakeCommand` is issued. The `time_to_collision_s` field should equal 0.

10-10. Make all unit tests pass.

10-11. Implement a new unit test where the last known speed limit is 35 meters per second and then publish a `SpeedUpdate` at 30 meters per second. Then issue a `SpeedLimitDetected` with a `speed_mps` of 25 meters per second. Ensure that exactly one `BrakeCommand` is issued. The `time_to_collision_s` field should equal 0.

10-12. Make all unit tests pass.

FURTHER READING

- *Specification by Example* by Gojko Adzic (Manning, 2011)
- *BDD in Action* by John Ferguson Smart (Manning, 2014)
- *Optimized C++: Proven Techniques for Heightened Performance* by Kurt Guntheroth (O'Reilly, 2016)
- *Agile Software Development and Agile Principles, Patterns, and Practices in C#* by Robert C. Martin (Prentice Hall, 2006)
- *Test-Driven Development: By Example* by Kent Beck (Pearson, 2002)
- *Growing Object-Oriented Software, Guided by Tests* by Steve Freeman and Nat Pryce (Addison-Wesley, 2009)
- "Editor war." *https://en.wikipedia.org/wiki/Editor_war*
- "Tabs versus Spaces: An Eternal Holy War" by Jamie Zawinski. *https://www.jwz.org/doc/tabs-vs-spaces.html*
- "Is TDD dead?" by Martin Fowler. *https://martinfowler.com/articles/is-tdd-dead/*

11

SMART POINTERS

If you want to do a few small things right, do them yourself. If you want to do great things and make a big impact, learn to delegate.
—*John C. Maxwell*

In this chapter, you'll explore stdlib and Boost libraries. These libraries contain a collection of smart pointers, which manage dynamic objects with the RAII paradigm you learned in Chapter 4. They also facilitate the most powerful resource management model in any programming language. Because some smart pointers use *allocators* to customize dynamic memory allocation, the chapter also outlines how to provide a user-defined allocator.

Smart Pointers

Dynamic objects have the most flexible lifetimes. With great flexibility comes great responsibility, so you must make sure each dynamic object gets destructed *exactly* once. This might not look daunting with small programs, but looks can be deceiving. Just consider how exceptions factor into dynamic memory management. Each time an error or an exception could occur, you need to keep track of which allocations you've made successfully and be sure to release them in the correct order.

Fortunately, you can use RAII to handle such tedium. By acquiring dynamic storage in the constructor of the RAII object and releasing dynamic storage in the destructor, it's relatively difficult to leak (or double free) dynamic memory. This enables you to manage dynamic object lifetimes using move and copy semantics.

You could write these RAII objects yourself, but you can also use some excellent prewritten implementations called *smart pointers*. Smart pointers are class templates that behave like pointers and implement RAII for dynamic objects.

This section delves into five available options included in stdlib and Boost: scoped, unique, shared, weak, and intrusive pointers. Their ownership models differentiate these five smart pointer categories.

Smart Pointer Ownership

Every smart pointer has an *ownership* model that specifies its relationship with a dynamically allocated object. When a smart pointer owns an object, the smart pointer's lifetime is guaranteed to be at least as long as the object's. Put another way, when you use a smart pointer, you can rest assured that the pointed-to object is alive and that the pointed-to object won't leak. The smart pointer manages the object it owns, so you can't forget to destroy it thanks to RAII.

When considering which smart pointer to use, your ownership requirements drive your choice.

Scoped Pointers

A *scoped pointer* expresses *non-transferable, exclusive ownership* over a single dynamic object. Non-transferable means that the scoped pointers cannot be moved from one scope to another. Exclusive ownership means that they can't be copied, so no other smart pointers can have ownership of a scoped pointer's dynamic object. (Recall from "Memory Management" on page 90 that an object's scope is where it's visible to the program.)

The `boost::scoped_ptr` is defined in the `<boost/smart_ptr/scoped_ptr.hpp>` header.

NOTE *There is no stdlib scoped pointer.*

Constructing

The `boost::scoped_ptr` takes a single template parameter corresponding to the pointed-to type, as in `boost::scoped_ptr<int>` for a "scoped pointer to `int`" type.

All smart pointers, including scoped pointers, have two modes: *empty* and *full*. An empty smart pointer owns no object and is roughly analogous to a `nullptr`. When a smart pointer is default constructed, it begins life empty.

The scoped pointer provides a constructor taking a raw pointer. (The pointed-to type must match the template parameter.) This creates a full-scoped pointer. The usual idiom is to create a dynamic object with `new` and pass the result to the constructor, like this:

```
boost::scoped_ptr<PointedToType> my_ptr{ new PointedToType };
```

This line dynamically allocates a `PointedToType` and passes its pointer to the scoped pointer constructor.

Bring in the Oath Breakers

To explore scoped pointers, let's create a Catch unit-test suite and a `DeadMenOfDunharrow` class that keeps track of how many objects are alive, as shown in Listing 11-1.

```
#define CATCH_CONFIG_MAIN ❶
#include "catch.hpp" ❷
#include <boost/smart_ptr/scoped_ptr.hpp> ❸

struct DeadMenOfDunharrow { ❹
  DeadMenOfDunharrow(const char* m="") ❺
    : message{ m } {
    oaths_to_fulfill++; ❻
  }
  ~DeadMenOfDunharrow() {
    oaths_to_fulfill--; ❼
  }
  const char* message;
  static int oaths_to_fulfill;
};
int DeadMenOfDunharrow::oaths_to_fulfill{};
using ScopedOathbreakers = boost::scoped_ptr<DeadMenOfDunharrow>; ❽
```

Listing 11-1: Setting up a Catch unit-test suite with a `DeadMenOfDunharrow` class to investigate scoped pointers

First, you declare `CATCH_CONFIG_MAIN` so Catch will provide an entry point ❶ and include the Catch header ❷ and then the Boost scoped pointer's header ❸. Next, you declare the `DeadMenOfDunharrow` class ❹, which takes an optional null-terminated string that you save into the `message` field ❺. The `static int` field called `oaths_to_fulfill` tracks how many `DeadMenOfDunharrow` objects have been constructed. Accordingly, you increment in the constructor ❻, and you decrement in the destructor ❼. Finally, you declare the `ScopedOathbreakers` type alias for convenience ❽.

CATCH LISTINGS

You'll use Catch unit tests in most listings from now on. For conciseness, the listings omit the following Catch ceremony:

```
#define CATCH_CONFIG_MAIN
#include "catch.hpp"
```

All listings containing TEST_CASE require this preamble.

Also, every test case in each listing passes unless a comment indicates otherwise. Again, for conciseness, the listings omit the All tests pass output from the listings.

Finally, tests that employ user-defined types, functions, and variables from a previous listing will omit them for brevity.

Implicit bool Conversion Based on Ownership

Sometimes you need to determine whether a scoped pointer owns an object or whether it's empty. Conveniently, scoped_ptr casts implicitly to bool depending on its ownership status: true if it owns an object; false otherwise. Listing 11-2 illustrates how this implicit casting behavior works.

```
TEST_CASE("ScopedPtr evaluates to") {
  SECTION("true when full") {
    ScopedOathbreakers aragorn{ new DeadMenOfDunharrow{} }; ❶
    REQUIRE(aragorn); ❷
  }
  SECTION("false when empty") {
    ScopedOathbreakers aragorn; ❸
    REQUIRE_FALSE(aragorn); ❹
  }
}
```

Listing 11-2: The boost::scoped_ptr casts implicitly to bool.

When you use the constructor taking a pointer ❶, the scoped_ptr converts to true ❷. When you use the default constructor ❸, the scoped_ptr converts to false ❹.

RAII Wrapper

When a scoped_ptr owns a dynamic object, it ensures proper dynamic object management. In the scoped_ptr destructor, it checks whether it owns an object. If it does, the scoped_ptr destructor deletes the dynamic object.

Listing 11-3 illustrates this behavior by investigating the static oaths_to_fulfill variable between scoped pointer initializations.

```
TEST_CASE("ScopedPtr is an RAII wrapper.") {
  REQUIRE(DeadMenOfDunharrow::oaths_to_fulfill == 0); ❶
  ScopedOathbreakers aragorn{ new DeadMenOfDunharrow{} }; ❷
  REQUIRE(DeadMenOfDunharrow::oaths_to_fulfill == 1); ❸
  {
    ScopedOathbreakers legolas{ new DeadMenOfDunharrow{} }; ❹
    REQUIRE(DeadMenOfDunharrow::oaths_to_fulfill == 2); ❺
  } ❻
  REQUIRE(DeadMenOfDunharrow::oaths_to_fulfill == 1); ❼
}
```

Listing 11-3: The `boost::scoped_ptr` is an RAII wrapper.

At the beginning of the test, `oaths_to_fulfill` is 0 because you haven't constructed any `DeadMenOfDunharrow` yet ❶. You construct the scoped pointer `aragorn` and pass in a pointer to the dynamic `DeadMenOfDunharrow` object ❷. This increments the `oaths_to_fulfill` to 1 ❸. Within a nested scope, you declare another scoped pointer `legolas` ❹. Because `aragorn` is still alive, `oaths_to_fulfill` is now 2 ❺. Once the inner scope closes, `legolas` falls out of scope and destructs, taking a `DeadMenOfDunharrow` with it ❻. This decrements `DeadMenOfDunharrow` to 1 ❼.

Pointer Semantics

For convenience, `scoped_ptr` implements the dereference `operator*` and the member dereference `operator->`, which simply delegate the calls to the owned dynamic object. You can even extract a raw pointer from a `scoped_ptr` with the get method, as demonstrated in Listing 11-4.

```
TEST_CASE("ScopedPtr supports pointer semantics, like") {
  auto message = "The way is shut";
  ScopedOathbreakers aragorn{ new DeadMenOfDunharrow{ message } }; ❶
  SECTION("operator*") {
    REQUIRE((*aragorn).message == message); ❷
  }
  SECTION("operator->") {
    REQUIRE(aragorn->message == message); ❸
  }
  SECTION("get(), which returns a raw pointer") {
    REQUIRE(aragorn.get() != nullptr); ❹
  }
}
```

Listing 11-4: The `boost::scoped_ptr` supports pointer semantics.

You construct the scoped pointer `aragorn` with a `message` of `The way is shut` ❶, which you use in three separate scenarios to test pointer semantics. First, you can use `operator*` to dereference the underlying, pointed-to dynamic object. In the example, you dereference `aragorn` and extract the `message` to verify that it matches ❷. You can also use `operator->` to perform member dereference ❸. Finally, if you want a raw pointer to the dynamic object, you can use the get method to extract it ❹.

Comparison with nullptr

The `scoped_ptr` class template implements the comparison operators `operator==` and `operator!=`, which are only defined when comparing a `scoped_ptr` with a `nullptr`. Functionally, this is essentially identical to implicit `bool` conversion, as Listing 11-5 illustrates.

```
TEST_CASE("ScopedPtr supports comparison with nullptr") {
  SECTION("operator==") {
    ScopedOathbreakers legolas{};
    REQUIRE(legolas == nullptr); ❶
  }
  SECTION("operator!=") {
    ScopedOathbreakers aragorn{ new DeadMenOfDunharrow{} };
    REQUIRE(aragorn != nullptr); ❷
  }
}
```

Listing 11-5: The `boost::scoped_ptr` supports comparison with `nullptr`.

An empty scoped pointer equals (`==`) `nullptr` ❶, whereas a full scoped pointer doesn't equal (`!=`) `nullptr` ❷.

Swapping

Sometimes you want to switch the dynamic object owned by a `scoped_ptr` with the dynamic object owned by another `scoped_ptr`. This is called an *object swap*, and `scoped_ptr` contains a `swap` method that implements this behavior, as shown in Listing 11-6.

```
TEST_CASE("ScopedPtr supports swap") {
  auto message1 = "The way is shut.";
  auto message2 = "Until the time comes.";
  ScopedOathbreakers aragorn {
    new DeadMenOfDunharrow{ message1 } ❶
  };
  ScopedOathbreakers legolas {
    new DeadMenOfDunharrow{ message2 } ❷
  };
  aragorn.swap(legolas); ❸
  REQUIRE(legolas->message == message1); ❹
  REQUIRE(aragorn->message == message2); ❺
}
```

Listing 11-6: The `boost::scoped_ptr` supports `swap`.

You construct two `scoped_ptr` objects, `aragorn` ❶ and `legolas` ❷, each with a different message. After you perform a swap between `aragorn` and `legolas` ❸, they exchange dynamic objects. When you pull out their messages after the swap, you find that they've switched ❹❺.

Resetting and Replacing a scoped_ptr

Rarely do you want to destruct an object owned by scoped_ptr before the scoped_ptr dies. For example, you might want to replace its owned object with a new dynamic object. You can handle both of these tasks with the overloaded reset method of scoped_ptr.

If you provide no argument, reset simply destroys the owned object.

If you instead provide a new dynamic object as a parameter, reset will first destroy the currently owned object and then gain ownership of the parameter. Listing 11-7 illustrates such behavior with one test for each scenario.

```
TEST_CASE("ScopedPtr reset") {
  ScopedOathbreakers aragorn{ new DeadMenOfDunharrow{} }; ❶
  SECTION("destructs owned object.") {
    aragorn.reset(); ❷
    REQUIRE(DeadMenOfDunharrow::oaths_to_fulfill == 0); ❸
  }
  SECTION("can replace an owned object.") {
    auto message = "It was made by those who are Dead.";
    auto new_dead_men = new DeadMenOfDunharrow{ message }; ❹
    REQUIRE(DeadMenOfDunharrow::oaths_to_fulfill == 2); ❺
    aragorn.reset(new_dead_men); ❻
    REQUIRE(DeadMenOfDunharrow::oaths_to_fulfill == 1); ❼
    REQUIRE(aragorn->message == new_dead_men->message); ❽
    REQUIRE(aragorn.get() == new_dead_men); ❾
  }
}
```

Listing 11-7: The boost::scoped_ptr supports reset.

The first step in both tests is to construct the scoped pointer aragorn owning a DeadMenOfDunharrow ❶. In the first test, you call reset without an argument ❷. This causes the scoped pointer to destruct its owned object, and oaths_to_fulfill decrements to 0 ❸.

In the second test, you create the new, dynamically allocated new_dead_men with a custom message ❹. This increases the oaths_to_fill to 2, because aragorn is also still alive ❺. Next, you invoke reset with new_dead_men as the argument ❻, which does two things:

- It causes the original DeadMenOfDunharrow owned by aragorn to get destructed, which decrements oaths_to_fulfill to 1 ❼.
- It emplaces new_dead_men as the dynamically allocated object owned by aragorn. When you dereference the message field, notice that it matches the message held by new_dead_men ❽. (Equivalently, aragorn.get() yields new_dead_men ❾.)

Non-transferability

You cannot move or copy a scoped_ptr, making it non-transferable. Listing 11-8 illustrates how attempting to move or copy a scoped_ptr results in an invalid program.

```
void by_ref(const ScopedOathbreakers&) { } ❶
void by_val(ScopedOathbreakers) { } ❷

TEST_CASE("ScopedPtr can") {
  ScopedOathbreakers aragorn{ new DeadMenOfDunharrow };
  SECTION("be passed by reference") {
    by_ref(aragorn); ❸
  }
  SECTION("not be copied") {
    // DOES NOT COMPILE:
    by_val(aragorn); ❹
    auto son_of_arathorn = aragorn; ❺
  }
  SECTION("not be moved") {
    // DOES NOT COMPILE:
    by_val(std::move(aragorn)); ❻
    auto son_of_arathorn = std::move(aragorn); ❼
  }
}
```

Listing 11-8: The boost::scoped_ptr is non-transferable. (This code doesn't compile.)

First, you declare dummy functions that take a scoped_ptr by reference ❶ and by value ❷. You can still pass a scoped_ptr by reference ❸, but attempting to pass one by value will fail to compile ❹. Also, attempting to use the scoped_ptr copy constructor or a copy assignment operator ❺ will fail to compile. In addition, if you try to move a scoped_ptr with std::move, your code won't compile ❻❼.

NOTE *Generally, using a boost::scoped_ptr incurs no overhead compared with using a raw pointer.*

boost::scoped_array

The boost::scoped_array is a scoped pointer for dynamic arrays. It supports the same usages as a boost::scoped_ptr, but it also implements an operator[] so you can interact with elements of the scoped array in the same way as you can with a raw array. Listing 11-9 illustrates this additional feature.

```
TEST_CASE("ScopedArray supports operator[]") {
  boost::scoped_array<int❶> squares{
    new int❷[5] { 0, 4, 9, 16, 25 }
  };
  squares[0] = 1; ❸
  REQUIRE(squares[0] == 1); ❹
```

```
  REQUIRE(squares[1] == 4);
  REQUIRE(squares[2] == 9);
}
```

Listing 11-9: The `boost::scoped_array` implements `operator[]`.

You declare a `scoped_array` the same way you declare a `scoped_ptr`, by using a single template parameter ❶. In the case of `scoped_array`, the template parameter is the type contained by the array ❷, not the type of the array. You pass in a dynamic array to the constructor of `squares`, making the dynamic array `squares` the array's owner. You can use `operator[]` to write ❸ and read ❹ elements.

A Partial List of Supported Operations

So far, you've learned about the major features of scoped pointers. For reference, Table 11-1 enumerates all the operators discussed, plus a few that haven't been covered yet. In the table, `ptr` is a raw pointer and `s_ptr` is a scoped pointer. See the Boost documentation for more information.

Table 11-1: All of the Supported `boost::scoped_ptr` Operations

Operation	Notes
`scoped_ptr<...>{ }` or `scoped_ptr <...>{ nullptr }`	Creates an empty scoped pointer.
`scoped_ptr <...>{ ptr }`	Creates a scoped pointer owning the dynamic object pointed to by **`ptr`**.
`~scoped_ptr<...>()`	Calls **`delete`** on the owned object if full.
`s_ptr1``.swap(`**`s_ptr2`**`)`	Exchanges owned objects between **`s_ptr1`** and **`s_ptr2`**.
`swap(`**`s_ptr1, s_ptr2`**`)`	A free function identical to the `swap` method.
`s_ptr``.reset()`	If full, calls `delete` on object owned by **`s_ptr`**.
`s_ptr``.reset(`**`ptr`**`)`	Deletes currently owned object and then takes ownership of **`ptr`**.
`ptr` `=` **`s_ptr`**`.get()`	Returns the raw pointer **`ptr`**; **`s_ptr`** retains ownership.
`*s_ptr`	Dereferences operator on owned object.
`s_ptr->`	Member dereferences operator on owned object.
`bool{` **`s_ptr`** `}`	`bool` conversion: `true` if full, `false` if empty.

Unique Pointers

A *unique pointer* has transferable, exclusive ownership over a single dynamic object. You *can* move unique pointers, which makes them transferable. They also have exclusive ownership, so they *cannot* be copied. The stdlib has a `unique_ptr` available in the `<memory>` header.

NOTE *Boost doesn't offer a unique pointer.*

Constructing

The std::unique_ptr takes a single template parameter corresponding to the pointed-to type, as in std::unique_ptr<int> for a "unique pointer to int" type.

As with a scoped pointer, the unique pointer has a default constructor that initializes the unique pointer to empty. It also provides a constructor taking a raw pointer that takes ownership of the pointed-to dynamic object. One construction method is to create a dynamic object with new and pass the result to the constructor, like this:

```
std::unique_ptr<int> my_ptr{ new int{ 808 } };
```

Another method is to use the std::make_unique function. The make_unique function is a template that takes all the arguments and forwards them to the appropriate constructor of the template parameter. This obviates the need for new. Using std::make_unique, you could rewrite the preceding object initialization as:

```
auto my_ptr = make_unique<int>(808);
```

The make_unique function was created to avoid some devilishly subtle memory leaks that used to occur when you used new with previous versions of C++. However, in the latest version of C++, these memory leaks no longer occur. Which constructor you use mainly depends on your preference.

Supported Operations

The std::unique_ptr function supports every operation that boost::scoped_ptr supports. For example, you can use the following type alias as a drop-in replacement for ScopedOathbreakers in Listings 11-1 to 11-7:

```
using UniqueOathbreakers = std::unique_ptr<DeadMenOfDunharrow>;
```

One of the major differences between unique and scoped pointers is that you can move unique pointers because they're *transferable.*

Transferable, Exclusive Ownership

Not only are unique pointers transferable, but they have exclusive ownership (you *cannot* copy them). Listing 11-10 illustrates how you can use the move semantics of unique_ptr.

```
TEST_CASE("UniquePtr can be used in move") {
  auto aragorn = std::make_unique<DeadMenOfDunharrow>(); ❶
  SECTION("construction") {
    auto son_of_arathorn{ std::move(aragorn) }; ❷
    REQUIRE(DeadMenOfDunharrow::oaths_to_fulfill == 1); ❸
  }
  SECTION("assignment") {
    auto son_of_arathorn = std::make_unique<DeadMenOfDunharrow>(); ❹
```

```
    REQUIRE(DeadMenOfDunharrow::oaths_to_fulfill == 2); ❺
    son_of_arathorn = std::move(aragorn); ❻
    REQUIRE(DeadMenOfDunharrow::oaths_to_fulfill == 1); ❼
  }
}
```

Listing 11-10: The `std::unique_ptr` supports move semantics for transferring ownership.

This listing creates a `unique_ptr` called `aragorn` ❶ that you use in two separate tests.

In the first test, you move `aragorn` with `std::move` into the move constructor of `son_of_arathorn` ❷. Because `aragorn` transfers ownership of its `DeadMenOfDunharrow` to `son_of_arathorn`, the `oaths_to_fulfill` object still only has value 1 ❸.

The second test constructs `son_of_arathorn` via `make_unique` ❹, which pushes the `oaths_to_fulfill` to 2 ❺. Next, you use the move assignment operator to move `aragorn` into `son_of_arathorn` ❻. Again, `aragorn` transfers ownership to `son_of_aragorn`. Because `son_of_aragorn` can own only one dynamic object at a time, the move assignment operator destroys the currently owned object before emptying the dynamic object of `aragorn`. This results in `oaths_to_fulfill` decrementing to 1 ❼.

Unique Arrays

Unlike `boost::scoped_ptr`, `std::unique_ptr` has built-in dynamic array support. You just use the array type as the template parameter in the unique pointer's type, as in `std::unique_ptr<int[]>`.

It's *very important* that you don't initialize a `std::unique_ptr<T>` with a dynamic array `T[]`. Doing so will cause undefined behavior, because you'll be causing a `delete` of an array (rather than `delete[]`). The compiler cannot save you, because `operator new[]` returns a pointer that is indistinguishable from the kind returned by `operator new`.

Like `scoped_array`, a `unique_ptr` to array type offers `operator[]` for accessing elements. Listing 11-11 demonstrates this concept.

```
TEST_CASE("UniquePtr to array supports operator[]") {
  std::unique_ptr<int[]❶> squares{
    new int[5]{ 1, 4, 9, 16, 25 } ❷
  };
  squares[0] = 1; ❸
  REQUIRE(squares[0] == 1); ❹
  REQUIRE(squares[1] == 4);
  REQUIRE(squares[2] == 9);
}
```

Listing 11-11: The `std::unique_ptr` to an array type supports `operator[]`.

The template parameter `int[]` ❶ indicates to `std::unique_ptr` that it owns a dynamic array. You pass in a newly minted dynamic array ❷ and then use `operator[]` to set the first element ❸; then you use `operator[]` to retrieve elements ❹.

Deleters

The `std::unique_ptr` has a second, optional template parameter called its deleter type. A unique pointer's *deleter* is what gets called when the unique pointer needs to destroy its owned object.

A `unique_ptr` instantiation contains the following template parameters:

```
std::unique_ptr<T, Deleter=std::default_delete<T>>
```

The two template parameters are `T`, the type of the owned dynamic object, and `Deleter`, the type of the object responsible for freeing an owned object. By default, `Deleter` is `std::default_delete<T>`, which calls `delete` or `delete[]` on the dynamic object.

To write a custom deleter, all you need is a function-like object that is invokable with a `T*`. (The unique pointer will ignore the deleter's return value.) You pass this deleter as the second parameter to the unique pointer's constructor, as shown in Listing 11-12.

```
#include <cstdio>

auto my_deleter = [](int* x) { ❶
  printf("Deleting an int at %p.", x);
  delete x;
};
std::unique_ptr<int❷, decltype(my_deleter)❸> my_up{
  new int,
  my_deleter
};
```

Listing 11-12: Passing a custom deleter to a unique pointer

The owned object type is `int` ❷, so you declare a `my_deleter` function object that takes an `int*` ❶. You use `decltype` to set the deleter template parameter ❸.

Custom Deleters and System Programming

You use a custom deleter whenever `delete` doesn't provide the resource-releasing behavior you require. In some settings, you'll never need a custom deleter. In others, like system programming, you might find them quite useful. Consider a simple example where you manage a file using the low-level APIs `fopen`, `fprintf`, and `fclose` in the `<cstdio>` header.

The `fopen` function opens a file and has the following signature:

```
FILE*❶ fopen(const char *filename❷, const char *mode❸);
```

On success, `fopen` returns a non-`nullptr`-valued `FILE*` ❶. On failure, `fopen` returns `nullptr` and it sets the static `int` variable `errno` equal to an error code, like access denied (`EACCES = 13`) or no such file (`ENOENT = 2`).

NOTE *See the* `errno.h` *header for a listing of all error conditions and their corresponding* `int` *values.*

The `FILE*` file handle is a reference to a file the operating system manages. A *handle* is an opaque, abstract reference to some resource in an operating system. The `fopen` function takes two arguments: `filename` ❷ is the path to the file you want to open, and `mode` ❸ is one of the six options shown in Table 11-2.

Table 11-2: All Six `mode` Options for `fopen`

String	Operations	File exists:	File doesn't exist:	Notes
`r`	Read		`fopen` fails	
`w`	Write	Overwrite	Create it	If the file exists, all contents are discarded.
`a`	Append		Create it	Always write to the end of the file.
`r+`	Read/Write		`fopen` fails	
`w+`	Read/Write	Overwrite	Create it	If the file exists, all contents are discarded.
`a+`	Read/Write		Create it	Always write to the end of the file.

You must close the file manually with `fclose` once you're done using it. Failure to close file handles is a common source of resource leakages, like so:

```
void fclose(FILE* file);
```

To write to a file, you can use the `fprintf` function, which is like a `printf` that prints to a file instead of the console. The `fprintf` function has identical usage to `printf` except you provide a file handle as the first argument before the format string:

```
int❶ fprintf(FILE* file❷, const char* format_string❸, ...❹);
```

On success, `fprintf` returns the number of characters ❶ written to the open file ❷. The `format_string` is the same as the format string for `printf` ❸, as are the variadic arguments ❹.

You can use a `std::unique_ptr` to a `FILE`. Obviously, you don't want to call `delete` on the `FILE*` file handle when you're ready to close the file. Instead, you need to close with `fclose`. Because `fclose` is a function-like object accepting a `FILE*`, it's a suitable deleter.

The program in Listing 11-13 writes the string `HELLO, DAVE.` to the file `HAL9000` and uses a unique pointer to perform resource management over the open file.

```
#include <cstdio>
#include <memory>

using FileGuard = std::unique_ptr<FILE, int(*)(FILE*)>; ❶

void say_hello(FileGuard file❷) {
  fprintf(file.get(), "HELLO DAVE"); ❸
}

int main() {
  auto file = fopen("HAL9000", "w"); ❹
  if (!file) return errno; ❺
  FileGuard file_guard{ file, fclose }; ❻
  // File open here
  say_hello(std::move(file_guard)); ❼
  // File closed here
  return 0;
}
```

Listing 11-13: A program using a `std::unique_ptr` and a custom deleter to manage a file handle

This listing makes the `FileGuard` type alias ❶ for brevity. (Notice the deleter type matches the type of `fclose`.) Next is a `say_hello` function that takes a `FileGuard` by value ❷. Within `say_hello`, you `fprintf` `HELLO DAVE` to the `file` ❸. Because the lifetime of `file` is bound to `say_hello`, the file gets closed once `say_hello` returns. Within `main`, you open the file `HAL9000` in `w` mode, which will create or overwrite the file, and you save the raw `FILE*` file handle into `file` ❹. You check whether `file` is `nullptr`, indicating an error occurred, and return with `errno` if `HAL9000` couldn't be opened ❺. Next, you construct a `FileGuard` by passing the file handle `file` and the custom deleter `fclose` ❻. At this point, the file is open, and thanks to its custom deleter, `file_guard` manages the file's lifetime automatically.

To call `say_hello`, you need to transfer ownership into that function (because it takes a `FileGuard` by value) ❼. Recall from "Value Categories" on page 124 that variables like `file_guard` are lvalues. This means you must move it into `say_hello` with `std::move`, which writes `HELLO DAVE` to the file. If you omit `std::move`, the compiler would attempt to copy it into `say_hello`. Because `unique_ptr` has a deleted copy constructor, this would generate a compiler error.

When `say_hello` returns, its `FileGuard` argument destructs and the custom deleter calls `fclose` on the file handle. Basically, it's impossible to leak the file handle. You've tied it to the lifetime of `FileGuard`.

A Partial List of Supported Operations

Table 11-3 enumerates all the supported `std::unique_ptr` operations. In this table, `ptr` is a raw pointer, `u_ptr` is a unique pointer, and `del` is a deleter.

Table 11-3: All of the Supported `std::unique_ptr` Operations

Operation	Notes
`unique_ptr<...>{ }` or `unique_ptr<...>{ nullptr }`	Creates an empty unique pointer with a `std::default_delete<...>` deleter.
`unique_ptr<...>{ ptr }`	Creates a unique pointer owning the dynamic object pointed to by **`ptr`**. Uses a `std::default_delete<...>` deleter.
`unique_ptr<...>{ ptr, del }`	Creates a unique pointer owning the dynamic object pointed to by **`ptr`**. Uses **`del`** as deleter.
`unique_ptr<...>{ move(u_ptr) }`	Creates a unique pointer owning the dynamic object pointed to by the unique pointer **`u_ptr`**. Transfers ownership from **`u_ptr`** to the newly created unique pointer. Also moves the deleter of **`u_ptr`**.
`~unique_ptr<...>()`	Calls deleter on the owned object if full.
`u_ptr1 = move(u_ptr2)`	Transfers ownership of owned object and deleter from **`u_ptr2`** to **`u_ptr1`**. Destroys currently owned object if full.
`u_ptr1.swap(u_ptr2)`	Exchanges owned objects and deleters between **`u_ptr1`** and **`u_ptr2`**.
`swap(u_ptr1, u_ptr2)`	A free function identical to the swap method.
`u_ptr.reset()`	If full, calls deleter on object owned by **`u_ptr`**.
`u_ptr.reset(ptr)`	Deletes currently owned object; then takes ownership of **`ptr`**.
`ptr = u_ptr.release()`	Returns the raw pointer **`ptr`**; **`u_ptr`** becomes empty. Deleter is not called.
`ptr = u_ptr.get()`	Returns the raw pointer **`ptr`**; **`u_ptr`** retains ownership.
`*u_ptr`	Dereference operator on owned object.
`u_ptr->`	Member dereference operator on owned object.
`u_ptr[index]`	References the element at **`index`** (arrays only).
`bool{ u_ptr }`	`bool` conversion: `true` if full, `false` if empty.

`u_ptr1 == u_ptr2`
`u_ptr1 != u_ptr2`
`u_ptr1 > u_ptr2`
`u_ptr1 >= u_ptr2`
`u_ptr1 < u_ptr2`
`u_ptr1 <= u_ptr2`
	Comparison operators; equivalent to evaluating comparison operators on raw pointers.

`u_ptr.get_deleter()`	Returns a reference to the deleter.

Shared Pointers

A *shared pointer* has transferable, non-exclusive ownership over a single dynamic object. You can move shared pointers, which makes them transferable, and you *can* copy them, which makes their ownership non-exclusive.

Non-exclusive ownership means that a shared_ptr checks whether any other shared_ptr objects also own the object before destroying it. This way, the last owner is the one to release the owned object.

The stdlib has a std::shared_ptr available in the <memory> header, and Boost has a boost::shared_ptr available in the <boost/smart_ptr/shared_ptr.hpp> header. You'll use the stdlib version here.

NOTE *Both the stdlib and Boost shared_ptr are essentially identical, with the notable exception that Boost's shared pointer doesn't support arrays and requires you to use the boost::shared_array class in <boost/smart_ptr/shared_array.hpp>. Boost offers a shared pointer for legacy reasons, but you should use the stdlib shared pointer.*

Constructing

The std::shared_ptr pointer supports all the same constructors as std::unique_ptr. The default constructor yields an empty shared pointer. To instead establish ownership over a dynamic object, you can pass a pointer to the shared_ptr constructor, like so:

```
std::shared_ptr<int> my_ptr{ new int{ 808 } };
```

You also have a corollary std::make_shared template function that forwards arguments to the pointed-to type's constructor:

```
auto my_ptr = std::make_shared<int>(808);
```

You should generally use make_shared. Shared pointers require a *control block*, which keeps track of several quantities, including the number of shared owners. When you use make_shared, you can allocate the control block and the owned dynamic object simultaneously. If you first use operator new and then allocate a shared pointer, you're making two allocations instead of one.

NOTE *Sometimes you might want to avoid using make_shared. For example, if you'll be using a weak_ptr, you'll still need the control block even if you can deallocate the object. In such a situation, you might prefer to have two allocations.*

Because a control block is a dynamic object, shared_ptr objects sometimes need to allocate dynamic objects. If you wanted to take control over how shared_ptr allocates, you could override operator new. But this is shooting a sparrow with a cannon. A more tailored approach is to provide an optional template parameter called an *allocator type*.

Specifying an Allocator

The allocator is responsible for allocating, creating, destroying, and deallocating objects. The default allocator, std::allocator, is a template class defined in the <memory> header. The default allocator allocates memory from dynamic storage and takes a template parameter. (You'll learn about customizing this behavior with a user-defined allocator in "Allocators" on page 365).

Both the shared_ptr constructor and make_shared have an allocator type template parameter, making three total template parameters: the pointed-to type, the deleter type, and the allocator type. For complicated reasons, you only ever need to declare the *pointed-to type* parameter. You can think of the other parameter types as being deduced from the pointed-to type.

For example, here's a fully adorned make_shared invocation including a constructor argument, a custom deleter, and an explicit std::allocator:

```
std::shared_ptr<int❶> sh_ptr{
  new int{ 10 }❷,
  [](int* x) { delete x; } ❸,
  std::allocator<int>{} ❹
};
```

Here, you specify a single template parameter, int, for the pointed-to type ❶. In the first argument, you allocate and initialize an int ❷. Next is a custom deleter ❸, and as a third argument you pass a std::allocator ❹.

For technical reasons, you can't use a custom deleter or custom allocator with make_shared. If you want a custom allocator, you can use the sister function of make_shared, which is std::allocate_shared. The std::allocate_shared function takes an allocator as the first argument and forwards the remainder of the arguments to the owned object's constructor:

```
auto sh_ptr = std::allocate_shared<int❶>(std::allocator<int>{}❷, 10❸);
```

As with make_shared, you specify the owned type as a template parameter ❶, but you pass an allocator as the first argument ❷. The rest of the arguments forward to the constructor of int ❸.

NOTE *For the curious, here are two reasons why you can't use a custom deleter with* make_shared*. First,* make_shared *uses* new *to allocate space for the owned object and the control block. The appropriate deleter for* new *is* delete*, so generally a custom deleter wouldn't be appropriate. Second, the custom deleter can't generally know how to deal with the control block, only with the owned object.*

It isn't possible to specify a custom deleter with either make_shared or allocate_shared. If you want to use a custom deleter with shared pointers, you must use one of the appropriate shared_ptr constructors directly.

Supported Operations

The std::shared_ptr supports every operation that std::unique_ptr and boost::scoped_ptr support. You could use the following type alias as a drop-in replacement for ScopedOathbreakers in Listings 11-1 to 11-7 and UniqueOathbreakers from Listings 11-10 to 11-13:

```
using SharedOathbreakers = std::shared_ptr<DeadMenOfDunharrow>;
```

The major functional difference between a shared pointer and a unique pointer is that you can copy shared pointers.

Transferable, Non-Exclusive Ownership

Shared pointers are transferable (you *can* move them), and they have non-exclusive ownership (you *can* copy them). Listing 11-10, which illustrates a unique pointer's move semantics, works the same for a shared pointer. Listing 11-14 demonstrates that shared pointers also support copy semantics.

```
TEST_CASE("SharedPtr can be used in copy") {
  auto aragorn = std::make_shared<DeadMenOfDunharrow>();
  SECTION("construction") {
    auto son_of_arathorn{ aragorn }; ❶
    REQUIRE(DeadMenOfDunharrow::oaths_to_fulfill == 1); ❷
  }
  SECTION("assignment") {
    SharedOathbreakers son_of_arathorn; ❸
    son_of_arathorn = aragorn; ❹
    REQUIRE(DeadMenOfDunharrow::oaths_to_fulfill == 1); ❺
  }
  SECTION("assignment, and original gets discarded") {
    auto son_of_arathorn = std::make_shared<DeadMenOfDunharrow>(); ❻
    REQUIRE(DeadMenOfDunharrow::oaths_to_fulfill == 2);  ❼
    son_of_arathorn = aragorn; ❽
    REQUIRE(DeadMenOfDunharrow::oaths_to_fulfill == 1); ❾
  }
}
```

Listing 11-14: The `std::shared_ptr` supports copy.

After constructing the shared pointer `aragorn`, you have three tests. The first test illustrates that the copy constructor that you use to build `son_of_arathorn` ❶ shares ownership over the same `DeadMenOfDunharrow` ❷.

In the second test, you construct an empty shared pointer `son_of_arathorn` ❸ and then show that copy assignment ❹ also doesn't change the number of `DeadMenOfDunharrow` ❺.

The third test illustrates that when you construct the full shared pointer `son_of_arathorn` ❻, the number of `DeadMenOfDunharrow` increases to 2 ❼. When you copy assign `aragorn` to `son_of_arathorn` ❽, the `son_of_arathorn` deletes its `DeadMenOfDunharrow` because it has sole ownership. It then increments the reference count of the `DeadMenOfDunharrow` owned by `aragorn`. Because both shared pointers own the same `DeadMenOfDunharrow`, the `oaths_to_fulfill` decrements from 2 to 1 ❾.

Shared Arrays

A *shared array* is a shared pointer that owns a dynamic array and supports `operator[]`. It works just like a unique array except it has non-exclusive ownership.

Deleters

Deleters work the same way for shared pointers as they do for unique pointers except you don't need to provide a template parameter with the deleter's type. Simply pass the deleter as the second constructor argument. For example, to convert Listing 11-12 to use a shared pointer, you simply drop in the following type alias:

```
using FileGuard = std::shared_ptr<FILE>;
```

Now, you're managing `FILE*` file handles with shared ownership.

A Partial List of Supported Operations

Table 11-4 provides a mostly complete listing of the supported constructors of `shared_ptr`. In this table, `ptr` is a raw pointer, `sh_ptr` is a shared pointer, `u_ptr` is a unique pointer, `del` is a deleter, and `alc` is an allocator.

Table 11-4: All of the Supported `std::shared_ptr` Constructors

Operation	Notes
`shared_ptr<...>{ }` or `shared_ptr<...>{ nullptr }`	Creates an empty shared pointer with a `std::default_delete<T>` and a `std::allocator<T>`.
`shared_ptr<...>{` **`ptr, [del], [alc]`** `}`	Creates a shared pointer owning the dynamic object pointed to by **`ptr`**. Uses a `std::default_delete<T>` and a `std::allocator<T>` by default; otherwise, **`del`** as deleter, **`alc`** as allocator if supplied.
`shared_ptr<...>{` **`sh_ptr`** `}`	Creates a shared pointer owning the dynamic object pointed to by the shared pointer **`sh_ptr`**. Copies ownership from **`sh_ptr`** to the newly created shared pointer. Also copies the deleter and allocator of **`sh_ptr`**.
`shared_ptr<...>{` **`sh_ptr , ptr`** `}`	An aliasing constructor: the resulting shared pointer holds an unmanaged reference to **`ptr`** but participates in **`sh_ptr`** reference counting.
`shared_ptr<...>{ move(`**`sh_ptr`**`) }`	Creates a shared pointer owning the dynamic object pointed to by the shared pointer **`sh_ptr`**. Transfers ownership from **`sh_ptr`** to the newly created shared pointer. Also moves the deleter of **`sh_ptr`**.
`shared_ptr<...>{ move(`**`u_ptr`**`) }`	Creates a shared pointer owning the dynamic object pointed to by the unique pointer **`u_ptr`**. Transfers ownership from **`u_ptr`** to the newly created shared pointer. Also moves the deleter of **`u_ptr`**.

Table 11-5 provides a listing of most of the supported operations of `std::shared_ptr`. In this table, `ptr` is a raw pointer, `sh_ptr` is a shared pointer, `u_ptr` is a unique pointer, `del` is a deleter, and `alc` is an allocator.

Table 11-5: Most of the Supported `std::shared_ptr` Operations

Operation	Notes
`~shared_ptr<...>()`	Calls deleter on the owned object if no other owners exist.
`sh_ptr1 = sh_ptr2`	Copies ownership of owned object and deleter from `sh_ptr2` to `sh_ptr1`. Increments number of owners by 1. Destroys currently owned object if no other owners exist.
`sh_ptr = move(u_ptr)`	Transfers ownership of owned object and deleter from `u_ptr` to `sh_ptr`. Destroys currently owned object if no other owners exist.
`sh_ptr1 = move(sh_ptr2)`	Transfers ownership of owned object and deleter from `sh_ptr2` to `sh_ptr1`. Destroys currently owned object if no other owners exist.
`sh_ptr1.swap(sh_ptr2)`	Exchanges owned objects and deleters between `sh_ptr1` and `sh_ptr2`.
`swap(sh_ptr1, sh_ptr2)`	A free function identical to the `swap` method.
`sh_ptr.reset()`	If full, calls deleter on object owned by `sh_ptr` if no other owners exist.
`sh_ptr.reset(ptr, [del], [alc])`	Deletes currently owned object if no other owners exist; then takes ownership of `ptr`. Can optionally provide deleter `del` and allocator `alc`. These default to `std::default_delete<T>` and `std::allocator<T>`.
`ptr = sh_ptr.get()`	Returns the raw pointer `ptr`; `sh_ptr` retains ownership.
`*sh_ptr`	Dereference operator on owned object.
`sh_ptr->`	Member dereference operator on owned object.
`sh_ptr.use_count()`	References the total number of shared pointers owning the owned object; zero if empty.
`sh_ptr[index]`	Returns the element at `index` (arrays only).
`bool{ sh_ptr }`	`bool` conversion: `true` if full, `false` if empty.

`sh_ptr1 == sh_ptr2`
`sh_ptr1 != sh_ptr2`
`sh_ptr1 > sh_ptr2`
`sh_ptr1 >= sh_ptr2`
`sh_ptr1 < sh_ptr2`
`sh_ptr1 <= sh_ptr2`
	Comparison operators; equivalent to evaluating comparison operators on raw pointers.

`sh_ptr.get_deleter()`	Returns a reference to the deleter.

Weak Pointers

A *weak pointer* is a special kind of smart pointer that has no ownership over the object to which it refers. Weak pointers allow you to track an object and to convert the weak pointer into a shared pointer *only if the tracked object still exists*. This allows you to generate temporary ownership over an object. Like shared pointers, weak pointers are movable and copyable.

A common usage for weak pointers is *caches*. In software engineering, a cache is a data structure that stores data temporarily so it can be retrieved faster. A cache could keep weak pointers to objects so they destruct once all other owners release them. Periodically, the cache can scan its stored weak pointers and trim those with no other owners.

The stdlib has a `std::weak_ptr`, and Boost has a `boost::weak_ptr`. These are essentially identical and are only meant to be used with their respective shared pointers, `std::shared_ptr` and `boost::shared_ptr`.

Constructing

Weak pointer constructors are completely different from scoped, unique, and shared pointers because weak pointers don't directly own dynamic objects. The default constructor constructs an empty weak pointer. To construct a weak pointer that tracks a dynamic object, you must construct it using either a shared pointer or another weak pointer.

For example, the following passes a shared pointer into the weak pointer's constructor:

```
auto sp = std::make_shared<int>(808);
std::weak_ptr<int> wp{ sp };
```

Now the weak pointer `wp` will track the object owned by the shared pointer `sp`.

Obtaining Temporary Ownership

Weak pointers invoke their `lock` method to get temporary ownership of their tracked object. The lock method always creates a shared pointer. If the tracked object is alive, the returned shared pointer owns the tracked object. If the tracked object is no longer alive, the returned shared pointer is empty. Consider the example in Listing 11-15.

```
TEST_CASE("WeakPtr lock() yields") {
  auto message = "The way is shut.";
  SECTION("a shared pointer when tracked object is alive") {
    auto aragorn = std::make_shared<DeadMenOfDunharrow>(message); ❶
    std::weak_ptr<DeadMenOfDunharrow> legolas{ aragorn }; ❷
    auto sh_ptr = legolas.lock(); ❸
    REQUIRE(sh_ptr->message == message); ❹
    REQUIRE(sh_ptr.use_count() == 2); ❺
  }
  SECTION("empty when shared pointer empty") {
    std::weak_ptr<DeadMenOfDunharrow> legolas;
    {
      auto aragorn = std::make_shared<DeadMenOfDunharrow>(message); ❻
      legolas = aragorn; ❼
    }
```

```
    auto sh_ptr = legolas.lock(); ❽
    REQUIRE(nullptr == sh_ptr); ❾
  }
}
```

Listing 11-15: The `std::weak_ptr` exposes a `lock` method for obtaining temporary ownership.

In the first test, you create the shared pointer `aragorn` ❶ with a message. Next, you construct a weak pointer `legolas` using `aragorn` ❷. This sets up `legolas` to track the dynamic object owned by `aragorn`. When you call `lock` on the weak pointer ❸, `aragorn` is still alive, so you obtain the shared pointer `sh_ptr`, which also owns the same `DeadMenOfDunharrow`. You confirm this by asserting that the `message` is the same ❹ and that the *use count* is 2 ❺.

In the second test, you also create an `aragorn` shared pointer ❻, but this time you use the assignment operator ❼, so the previously empty weak pointer `legolas` now tracks the dynamic object owned by `aragorn`. Next, `aragorn` falls out of block scope and dies. This leaves `legolas` tracking a dead object. When you call `lock` at this point ❽, you obtain an empty shared pointer ❾.

Advanced Patterns

In some advanced usages of shared pointers, you might want to create a class that allows instances to create shared pointers referring to themselves. The `std::enable_shared_from_this` class template implements this behavior. All that's required from a user perspective is to inherit from `enable_shared_from_this` in the class definition. This exposes the `shared_from_this` and `weak_from_this` methods, which produce either a `shared_ptr` or a `weak_ptr` referring to the current object. This is a niche case, but if you want to see more details, refer to [util.smartptr.enab].

Supported Operations

Table 11-6 lists most of the supported weak pointer operations. In this table, `w_ptr` is a weak pointer, and `sh_ptr` is a shared pointer.

Table 11-6: Most of the Supported `std::shared_ptr` Operations

Operation	Notes
`weak_ptr<...>{ }`	Creates an empty weak pointer.
`weak_ptr<...>{ w_ptr }` or `weak_ptr<...>{ sh_ptr }`	Tracks the object referred to by weak pointer **`w_ptr`** or shared pointer **`sh_ptr`**.
`weak_ptr<...>{ move(w_ptr) }`	Tracks the object referred to by **`w_ptr`**; then empties **`w_ptr`**.
`~weak_ptr<...>()`	Has no effect on the tracked object.
`w_ptr1 = sh_ptr` or `w_ptr1 = w_ptr2`	Replaces currently tracked object with the object owned by **`sh_ptr`** or tracked by **`w_ptr2`**.
`w_ptr1 = move(w_ptr2)`	Replaces currently tracked object with object tracked by **`w_ptr2`**. Empties **`w_ptr2`**.

Operation	Notes
`sh_ptr = w_ptr.lock()`	Creates the shared pointer **sh_ptr** owning the object tracked by **w_ptr**. If the tracked object has expired, **sh_ptr** is empty.
`w_ptr1.swap(w_ptr2)`	Exchanges tracked objects between **w_ptr1** and **w_ptr2**.
`swap(w_ptr1, w_ptr2)`	A free function identical to the swap method.
`w_ptr.reset()`	Empties the weak pointer.
`w_ptr.use_count()`	Returns the number of shared pointers owning the tracked object.
`w_ptr.expired()`	Returns `true` if the tracked object has expired, `false` if it hasn't.
`sh_ptr.use_count()`	Returns the total number of shared pointers owning the owned object; zero if empty.

Intrusive Pointers

An *intrusive pointer* is a shared pointer to an object with an embedded reference count. Because shared pointers usually keep reference counts, they're not suitable for owning such objects. Boost provides an implementation called `boost::intrusive_ptr` in the `<boost/smart_ptr/intrusive_ptr.hpp>` header.

It's rare that a situation calls for an intrusive pointer. But sometimes you'll use an operating system or a framework that contains embedded references. For example, in Windows COM programming an intrusive pointer can be very useful: COM objects that inherit from the `IUnknown` interface have an `AddRef` and a `Release` method, which increment and decrement an embedded reference count (respectively).

Each time an `intrusive_ptr` is created, it calls the function `intrusive_ptr_add_ref`. When an `intrusive_ptr` is destroyed, it calls the `intrusive_ptr_release` free function. You're responsible for freeing appropriate resources in `intrusive_ptr_release` when the reference count falls to zero. To use `intrusive_ptr`, you must provide a suitable implementation of these functions.

Listing 11-16 demonstrates intrusive pointers using the `DeadMenOfDunharrow` class. Consider the implementations of `intrusive_ptr_add_ref` and `intrusive_ptr_release` in this listing.

```
#include <boost/smart_ptr/intrusive_ptr.hpp>

using IntrusivePtr = boost::intrusive_ptr<DeadMenOfDunharrow>; ❶
size_t ref_count{}; ❷

void intrusive_ptr_add_ref(DeadMenOfDunharrow* d) {
  ref_count++; ❸
}

void intrusive_ptr_release(DeadMenOfDunharrow* d) {
```

```
  ref_count--; ❹
  if (ref_count == 0) delete d; ❺
}
```

Listing 11-16: Implementations of `intrusive_ptr_add_ref` *and* `intrusive_ptr_release`

Using the type alias `IntrusivePtr` saves some typing ❶. Next, you declare a `ref_count` with static storage duration ❷. This variable keeps track of the number of living intrusive pointers. In `intrusive_ptr_add_ref`, you increment `ref_count` ❸. In `intrusive_ptr_release`, you decrement `ref_count` ❹. When `ref_count` drops to zero, you delete the `DeadMenOfDunharrow` argument ❺.

NOTE *It's absolutely critical that you use only a single* `DeadMenOfDunharrow` *dynamic object with intrusive pointers when using the setup in Listing 11-16. The* `ref_count` *approach will correctly track only a single object. If you have multiple dynamic objects owned by different intrusive pointers, the* `ref_count` *will become invalid, and you'll get incorrect* `delete` *behavior* ❺.

Listing 11-17 shows how to use the setup in Listing 11-16 with intrusive pointers.

```
TEST_CASE("IntrusivePtr uses an embedded reference counter.") {
  REQUIRE(ref_count == 0); ❶
  IntrusivePtr aragorn{ new DeadMenOfDunharrow{} }; ❷
  REQUIRE(ref_count == 1); ❸
  {
    IntrusivePtr legolas{ aragorn }; ❹
    REQUIRE(ref_count == 2); ❺
  }
  REQUIRE(DeadMenOfDunharrow::oaths_to_fulfill == 1); ❻
}
```

Listing 11-17: Using a `boost::intrusive_ptr`

This test begins by checking that `ref_count` is zero ❶. Next, you construct an intrusive pointer by passing a dynamically allocated `DeadMenOfDunharrow` ❷. This increases `ref_count` to 1, because creating an intrusive pointer invokes `intrusive_ptr_add_ref` ❸. Within a block scope, you construct another intrusive pointer `legolas` that shares ownership with `aragorn` ❹. This increases the `ref_count` to 2 ❺, because creating an intrusive pointer invokes `intrusive_ptr_add_ref`. When `legolas` falls out of block scope, it destructs, causing `intrusive_ptr_release` to invoke. This decrements `ref_count` to 1 but doesn't cause the owned object to delete ❻.

Summary of Smart Pointer Options

Table 11-7 summarizes all the smart pointer options available to use in stdlib and Boost.

Table 11-7: Smart Pointers in stdlib and Boost

Type name	stdlib header	Boost header	Movable/ transferable ownership	Copyable/ non-exclusive ownership
scoped_ptr		<boost/smart_ptr/scoped_ptr.hpp>		
scoped_array		<boost/smart_ptr/scoped_array.hpp>		
unique_ptr	<memory>		✓	
shared_ptr	<memory>	<boost/smart_ptr/shared_ptr.hpp>	✓	✓
shared_array		<boost/smart_ptr/shared_array.hpp>	✓	✓
weak_ptr	<memory>	<boost/smart_ptr/weak_ptr.hpp>	✓	✓
intrusive_ptr		<boost/smart_ptr/intrusive_ptr.hpp>	✓	✓

Allocators

Allocators are low-level objects that service requests for memory. The stdlib and Boost libraries enable you to provide allocators to customize how a library allocates dynamic memory.

In the majority of cases, the default allocator `std::allocate` is totally sufficient. It allocates memory using `operator new(size_t)`, which allocates raw memory from the free store, also known as the heap. It deallocates memory using `operator delete(void*)`, which deallocates the raw memory from the free store. (Recall from "Overloading Operator `new`" on page 189 that `operator new` and `operator delete` are defined in the `<new>` header.)

In some settings, such as gaming, high-frequency trading, scientific analyses, and embedded applications, the memory and computational overhead associated with the default free store operations is unacceptable. In such settings, it's relatively easy to implement your own allocator. Note that you really shouldn't implement a custom allocator unless you've conducted some performance testing that indicates that the default allocator is a bottleneck. The idea behind a custom allocator is that you know a lot more about your specific program than the designers of the default allocator model, so you can make improvements that will increase allocation performance.

At a minimum, you need to provide a template class with the following characteristics for it to work as an allocator:

- An appropriate default constructor
- A `value_type` member corresponding to the template parameter
- A template constructor that can copy an allocator's internal state while dealing with a change in `value_type`
- An `allocate` method
- A `deallocate` method
- An `operator==` and an `operator!=`

The MyAllocator class in Listing 11-18 implements a simple, pedagogical variant of std::allocate that keeps track of how many allocations and deallocations you've made.

```
#include <new>

static size_t n_allocated, n_deallocated;

template <typename T>
struct MyAllocator {
  using value_type = T; ❶
  MyAllocator() noexcept{ } ❷
  template <typename U>
  MyAllocator(const MyAllocator<U>&) noexcept { } ❸
  T* allocate(size_t n) { ❹
    auto p = operator new(sizeof(T) * n);
    ++n_allocated;
    return static_cast<T*>(p);
  }
  void deallocate(T* p, size_t n) { ❺
    operator delete(p);
    ++n_deallocated;
  }
};

template <typename T1, typename T2>
bool operator==(const MyAllocator<T1>&, const MyAllocator<T2>&) {
  return true; ❻
}
template <typename T1, typename T2>
bool operator!=(const MyAllocator<T1>&, const MyAllocator<T2>&) {
  return false; ❼
}
```

Listing 11-18: A `MyAllocator` class modeled after `std::allocate`

First, you declare the value_type type alias for T, one of the requirements for implementing an allocator ❶. Next is a default constructor ❷ and a template constructor ❸. Both of these are empty because the allocator doesn't have state to pass on.

The allocate method ❹ models std::allocate by allocating the requisite number of bytes, sizeof(T) * n, using operator new. Next, it increments the static variable n_allocated so you can keep track of the number of allocations for testing purposes. The allocate method then returns a pointer to the newly allocated memory after casting void* to the relevant pointer type.

The deallocate method ❺ also models std::allocate by calling operator delete. As an analogy to allocate, it increments the n_deallocated static variable for testing and returns.

The final task is to implement an `operator==` and an `operator!=` taking the new class template. Because the allocator has no state, any instance is the same as any other instance, so `operator==` returns `true` ❻ and `operator!=` returns `true` ❼.

NOTE *Listing 11-18 is a teaching tool and doesn't actually make allocations any more efficient. It simply wraps the call to* `new` *and* `delete`*.*

So far, the only class you know about that uses an allocator is `std::shared_ptr`. Consider how Listing 11-19 uses `MyAllocator` with `std::allocate shared`.

```
TEST_CASE("Allocator") {
  auto message = "The way is shut.";
  MyAllocator<DeadMenOfDunharrow> alloc; ❶
  {
    auto aragorn = std::allocate_shared<DeadMenOfDunharrow>(my_alloc❷,
                                                            message❸);
    REQUIRE(aragorn->message == message); ❹
    REQUIRE(n_allocated == 1); ❺
    REQUIRE(n_deallocated == 0); ❻
  }
  REQUIRE(n_allocated == 1); ❼
  REQUIRE(n_deallocated == 1); ❽
}
```

Listing 11-19: Using `MyAllocator` *with* `std::shared_ptr`

You create a `MyAllocator` instance called `alloc` ❶. Within a block, you pass `alloc` as the first argument to `allocate_shared` ❷, which creates the shared pointer `aragorn` containing a custom `message` ❸. Next, you confirm that `aragorn` contains the correct `message` ❹, `n_allocated` is 1 ❺, and `n_deallocated` is 0 ❻.

After `aragorn` falls out of block scope and destructs, you verify that `n_allocated` is still 1 ❼ and `n_deallocated` is now 1 ❽.

NOTE *Because allocators handle low-level details, you can really get down into the weeds when specifying their behavior. See [allocator.requirements] in the ISO C++ 17 Standard for a thorough treatment.*

Summary

Smart pointers manage dynamic objects via RAII, and you can provide allocators to customize dynamic memory allocation. Depending on which smart pointer you choose, you can encode different ownership patterns onto the dynamic object.

EXERCISES

11-1. Reimplement Listing 11-12 to use a `std::shared_ptr` rather than a `std::unique_ptr`. Notice that although you've relaxed the ownership requirements from exclusive to non-exclusive, you're still transferring ownership to the `say_hello` function.

11-2. Remove the `std::move` from the call to `say_hello`. Then make an additional call to `say_hello`. Notice that the ownership of `file_guard` is no longer *transferred* to `say_hello`. This permits multiple calls.

11-3. Implement a `Hal` class that accepts a `std::shared_ptr<FILE>` in its constructor. In Hal's destructor, write the phrase `Stop, Dave.` to the file handle held by your shared pointer. Implement a `write_status` function that writes the phrase `I'm completely operational.` to the file handle. Here's a class declaration you can work from:

```
struct Hal {
  Hal(std::shared_ptr<FILE> file);
  ~Hal();
  void write_status();
  std::shared_ptr<FILE> file;
};
```

11-4. Create several `Hal` instances and invoke `write_status` on them. Notice that you don't need to keep track of how many `Hal` instances are open: file management gets handled via the shared pointer's shared ownership model.

FURTHER READING

- *ISO International Standard ISO/IEC (2017) — Programming Language C++* (International Organization for Standardization; Geneva, Switzerland; *https://isocpp.org/std/the-standard/*)
- *The C++ Programming Language*, 4th Edition, by Bjarne Stroustrup (Pearson Education, 2013)
- *The Boost C++ Libraries*, 2nd Edition, by Boris Schäling (XML Press, 2014)
- *The C++ Standard Library: A Tutorial and Reference*, 2nd Edition, by Nicolai M. Josuttis (Addison-Wesley Professional, 2012)

12

UTILITIES

"See, the world is full of things more powerful than us. But if you know how to catch a ride, you can go places," Raven says.
"Right. I'm totally hip to what you're saying."
—Neal Stephenson, Snow Crash

The stdlib and Boost libraries provide a throng of types, classes, and functions that satisfy common programming needs. Together, this motley collection of tools is called *utilities*. Aside from their small, uncomplicated, and focused nature, utilities vary functionally.

In this chapter, you'll learn about several simple data structures that handle many routine situations where you need objects to contain other objects. A discussion of dates and times follows, including coverage of several provisions for encoding calendars and clocks and for measuring elapsed time. The chapter wraps up with a trek through many numerical and mathematical tools available to you.

NOTE *The discussions of dates/times and numerics/math will be of great interest to certain readers and of only passing interest to others. If you are in the latter category, feel free to skim these sections.*

Data Structures

Between them, the stdlib and Boost libraries provide a venerable collection of useful data structures. A *data structure* is a type that stores objects and permits some set of operations over those stored objects. There is no magic compiler pixie dust that makes the utility data structures in this section work; you could implement your own versions with sufficient time and effort. But why reinvent the wheel?

tribool

The *tribool* is a bool-like type that supports three states rather than two: true, false, and indeterminate. Boost offers boost::logic::tribool in the <boost/logic/tribool.hpp> header. Listing 12-1 demonstrates how to initialize Boost a tribool using true, false, and the boost::logic::indeterminate type.

```
#include <boost/logic/tribool.hpp>

using boost::logic::indeterminate; ❶
boost::logic::tribool t = true❷, f = false❸, i = indeterminate❹;
```

Listing 12-1: Initializing Boost tribool

For convenience, a using declaration pulls in indeterminate from boost::logic ❶. Then you initialize the tribool t equal to true ❷, f equal to false ❸, and i equal to indeterminate ❹.

The tribool class implicitly converts to bool. If a tribool is true, it converts to true; otherwise, it converts to false. The tribool class also supports operator!, which returns true if tribool is false; otherwise, it returns false. Finally, indeterminate supports operator(), which takes a single tribool argument and returns true if that argument is indeterminate; otherwise, it returns false.

Listing 12-2 samples these Boolean conversions.

```
TEST_CASE("Boost tribool converts to bool") {
  REQUIRE(t); ❶
  REQUIRE_FALSE(f); ❷
  REQUIRE(!f); ❸
  REQUIRE_FALSE(!t); ❹
  REQUIRE(indeterminate(i)); ❺
  REQUIRE_FALSE(indeterminate(t)); ❻
}
```

Listing 12-2: Converting a tribool to a bool

This test demonstrates the basic results from bool conversion ❶❷, operator! ❸❹, and indeterminate ❺❻.

Boolean Operations

The tribool class supports all the Boolean operators. Whenever a tribool expression doesn't involve an indeterminate value, the result is the same as the equivalent Boolean expression. Whenever an indeterminate is involved, the result can be indeterminate, as Listing 12-3 illustrates.

```
TEST_CASE("Boost Tribool supports Boolean operations") {
  auto t_or_f = t || f;
  REQUIRE(t_or_f); ❶
  REQUIRE(indeterminate(t && indeterminate)); ❷
  REQUIRE(indeterminate(f || indeterminate)); ❸
  REQUIRE(indeterminate(!i)); ❹
}
```

Listing 12-3: The `boost::tribool` supports Boolean operations.

Because neither t nor f is indeterminate, t || f evaluates just like an ordinary Boolean expression, so t_or_f is true ❶. Boolean expressions that involve an indeterminate can be indeterminate. Boolean AND ❷, OR ❸, and NOT ❹ evaluate to indeterminate if there isn't enough information.

When to Use tribool

Aside from describing the vital status of Schrödinger's cat, you can use tribool in settings in which operations can take a long time. In such settings, a tribool could describe whether the operation was successful. An indeterminate value could model that the operation is still pending.

The tribool class makes for neat, concise if statements, as shown in Listing 12-4.

```
TEST_CASE("Boost Tribool works nicely with if statements") {
  if (i) FAIL("Indeterminate is true."); ❶
  else if (!i) FAIL("Indeterminate is false."); ❷
  else {} // OK, indeterminate ❸
}
```

Listing 12-4: Using an `if` statement with `tribool`

The first expression ❶ evaluates only if the tribool is true, the second expression ❷ evaluates only if it's false, and the third only executes in the indeterminate case ❸.

NOTE *The mere mention of a `tribool` might have caused you to scrunch up your face in disgust. Why, you might ask, couldn't you just use an integer where 0 is false, 1 is true, and any other value is indeterminate? You could, but consider that the `tribool` type supports all the usual Boolean operations while correctly propagating indeterminate values. Again, why reinvent the wheel?*

A Partial List of Supported Operations

Table 12-1 provides a list of the most supported boost::tribool operations. In this table, tb is a boost::tribool.

Table 12-1: The Most Supported boost::tribool Operations

Operation	Notes
tribool{} tribool{ false }	Constructs a tribool with value false.
tribool{ true }	Constructs a tribool with value true.
tribool{ indeterminate }	Constructs a tribool with value indeterminate.
tb.safe_bool()	Evaluates to true if **tb** is true, else false.
indeterminate(**tb**)	Evaluates to true if **tb** is indeterminate, else false.
!**tb**	Evaluates to true if **tb** is false, else false.
tb1 && **tb2**	Evaluates to true if **tb1** and **tb2** are true; evaluates to false if **tb1** or **tb2** are false; otherwise, indeterminate.
tb1 || **tb2**	Evaluates to true if **tb1** or **tb2** are true; evaluates to false if **tb1** and **tb2** are false; otherwise, indeterminate.
bool{ **tb** }	Evaluates to true if **tb** is true, else false.

optional

An *optional* is a class template that contains a value that might or might not be present. The primary use case for an optional is the return type of a function that might fail. Rather than throwing an exception or returning multiple values, a function can instead return an optional that will contain a value if the function succeeded.

The stdlib has std::optional in the <optional> header, and Boost has boost::optional in the <boost/optional.hpp> header.

Consider the setup in Listing 12-5. The function take wants to return an instance of TheMatrix only if you take a Pill::Blue; otherwise, take returns a std::nullopt, which is a stdlib-provided constant std::optional type with uninitialized state.

```
#include <optional>

struct TheMatrix { ❶
  TheMatrix(int x) : iteration { x } { }
  const int iteration;
};

enum Pill { Red, Blue }; ❷

std::optional<TheMatrix>❸ take(Pill pill❹) {
  if(pill == Pill::Blue) return TheMatrix{ 6 }; ❺
  return std::nullopt; ❻
}
```

Listing 12-5: A take function returning a std::optional

The TheMatrix type takes a single int constructor argument and stores it into the iteration member ❶. The enum called Pill takes the values Red and

Blue ❷. The take function returns a std::optional<TheMatrix> ❸ and accepts a single Pill argument ❹. If you pass Pill::Blue to the take function, it returns a TheMatrix instance ❺; otherwise, it returns a std::nullopt ❻.

First, consider Listing 12-6, where you take the blue pill.

```
TEST_CASE("std::optional contains types") {
  if (auto matrix_opt = take(Pill::Blue)) { ❶
    REQUIRE(matrix_opt->iteration == 6); ❷
    auto& matrix = matrix_opt.value();
    REQUIRE(matrix.iteration == 6); ❸
  } else {
    FAIL("The optional evaluated to false.");
  }
}
```

Listing 12-6: A test exploring the std::optional type with Pill::Blue

You take the blue pill, which results in the std::optional result containing an initialized TheMatrix, so the if statement's conditional expression evaluates to true ❶. Listing 12-6 also demonstrates the use of operator-> ❷ and value() ❸ to access the underlying value.

What happens when you take the red pill? Consider Listing 12-7.

```
TEST_CASE("std::optional can be empty") {
  auto matrix_opt = take(Pill::Red); ❶
  if (matrix_opt) FAIL("The Matrix is not empty."); ❷
  REQUIRE_FALSE(matrix_opt.has_value()); ❸
}
```

Listing 12-7: A test exploring the std::optional type with Pill::Red

You take the red pill ❶, and the resulting matrix_opt is empty. This means matrix_opt converts to false ❷ and has_value() also returns false ❸.

A Partial List of Supported Operations

Table 12-2 provides a list of the most supported std::optional operations. In this table, opt is a std::optional<T> and t is an object of type T.

Table 12-2: The Most Supported std::optional Operations

Operation	Notes
optional<T>{} optional<T>{std::nullopt}	Constructs an empty optional.
optional<T>{ **opt** }	Copy constructs an optional from **opt**.
optional<T>{ move(**opt**) }	Move constructs an optional from **opt**, which is empty after the constructor completes.
optional<T>{ **t** } **opt** = **t**	Copies **t** into optional.
optional<T>{ move(**t**) } **opt** = move(**t**)	Moves **t** into optional.

(continued)

Table 12-2: The Most Supported std::optional Operations (continued)

Operation	Notes
opt->mbr	Member dereference; accesses the mbr member of object contained by opt.
*opt opt.value()	Returns a reference to the object contained by opt; value() checks for empty and throws bad_optional_access.
opt.value_or(T{ ... })	If opt contains an object, returns a copy; else returns the argument.
bool{ opt } opt.has_value()	Returns true if opt contains an object, else false.
opt1.swap(opt2) swap(opt1, opt2)	Swaps the objects contained by opt1 and opt2.
opt.reset()	Destroys object contained by opt, which is empty after reset.
opt.emplace(...)	Constructs a type in place, forwarding all arguments to the appropriate constructor.
make_optional<T>(...)	Convenience function for constructing an optional; forwards arguments to the appropriate constructor.
opt1 == opt2 opt1 != opt2 opt1 > opt2 opt1 >= opt2 opt1 < opt2 opt1 <= opt2	When evaluating equality of two optional objects, true if both are empty or if both contain objects and those objects are equal; else false. For comparison, an empty optional is always less than an optional containing a value. Otherwise, the result is the comparison of the contained types.

pair

A *pair* is a class template that contains two objects of different types in a single object. The objects are ordered, and you can access them via the members first and second. A pair supports comparison operators, has defaulted copy/move constructors, and works with structured binding syntax.

The stdlib has std::pair in the <utility> header, and Boost has boost::pair in the <boost/pair.hpp> header.

NOTE *Boost also has boost::compressed_pair available in the <boost/compressed_pair.hpp> header. It's slightly more efficient when one of the members is empty.*

First, you create some simple types to make a pair out of, such as the simple Socialite and Valet classes in Listing 12-8.

```
#include <utility>

struct Socialite { const char* birthname; };
struct Valet { const char* surname; };
Socialite bertie{ "Wilberforce" };
Valet reginald{ "Jeeves" };
```

Listing 12-8: The Socialite and Valet classes

Now that you have a Socialite and a Valet, bertie and reginald, you can construct a std::pair and experiment with extracting elements. Listing 12-9 uses the first and second members to access the contained types.

```
TEST_CASE("std::pair permits access to members") {
  std::pair<Socialite, Valet> inimitable_duo{ bertie, reginald }; ❶
  REQUIRE(inimitable_duo.first.birthname == bertie.birthname); ❷
  REQUIRE(inimitable_duo.second.surname == reginald.surname); ❸
}
```

Listing 12-9: The std::pair supports member extraction.

You construct a std::pair by passing in the objects you want to copy ❶. You use the first and second members of std::pair to extract the Socialite ❷ and Valet ❸ out of inimitable_duo. Then you can compare the birthname and surname members of these to their originals.

Listing 12-10 shows std::pair member extraction and structured binding syntax.

```
TEST_CASE("std::pair works with structured binding") {
  std::pair<Socialite, Valet> inimitable_duo{ bertie, reginald };
  auto& [idle_rich, butler] = inimitable_duo; ❶
  REQUIRE(idle_rich.birthname == bertie.birthname); ❷
  REQUIRE(butler.surname == reginald.surname); ❸
}
```

Listing 12-10: The std::pair supports structured binding syntax.

Here you use the structured binding syntax ❶ to extract references to the first and second members of inimitable_duo into idle_rich and butler. As in Listing 12-9, you ensure that the birthname ❷ and surname ❸ match the originals.

A Partial List of Supported Operations

Table 12-3 provides a list of the most supported std::pair operations. In this table, pr is a std::pair<A, B>, a is an object of type A, and b is an object of type B.

Table 12-3: The Most Supported std::pair Operations

Operation	Notes
pair<...>{}	Constructs an empty pair.
pair<...>{ **pr** }	Copy constructs from **pr**.
pair<...>{ move(**pr**) }	Move constructs from **pr**.
pair<...>{ **a**, **b** }	Constructs a pair by copying **a** and **b**.
pair<...>{ move(**a**), move(**b**) }	Constructs a pair by moving **a** and **b**.
pr1 = **pr2**	Copy assigns from **pr2**.
pr1 = move(**pr2**)	Move assigns from **pr2**.

(continued)

Table 12-3: The Most Supported std::pair Operations (continued)

Operation	Notes
pr.first get<0>(pr)	Returns a reference to the first element.
pr.second get<1>(pr)	Returns a reference to the second element.
get<T>(pr)	If first and second have different types, returns a reference to the element of type T.
pr1.swap(pr2) swap(pr1, pr2)	Swaps the objects contained by pr1 and pr2.
make_pair<...>(a, b)	Convenience function for constructing a pair.
pr1 == pr2 pr1 != pr2 pr1 > pr2 pr1 >= pr2 pr1 < pr2 pr1 <= pr2	Equal if both first and second are equal. Greater than/less than comparisons begin with first. If first members are equal, compare second members.

tuple

A *tuple* is a class template that takes an arbitrary number of heterogeneous elements. It's a generalization of pair, but a tuple doesn't expose its members as first, second, and so on like a pair. Instead, you use the non-member function template get to extract elements.

The stdlib has std::tuple and std::get in the <tuple> header, and Boost has boost::tuple and boost::get in the <boost/tuple/tuple.hpp> header.

Let's add a third class, Acquaintance, to test a tuple:

```
struct Acquaintance { const char* nickname; };
Acquaintance hildebrand{ "Tuppy" };
```

To extract these elements, you have two modes of using get. In the primary case, you can always provide a template parameter corresponding to the zero-based index of the element you want to extract. In the event the tuple doesn't contain elements with the same types, you can alternatively provide a template parameter corresponding to the type of the element you want to extract, as Listing 12-11 illustrates.

```
TEST_CASE("std::tuple permits access to members with std::get") {
  using Trio = std::tuple<Socialite, Valet, Acquaintance>;
  Trio truculent_trio{ bertie, reginald, hildebrand };
  auto& bertie_ref = std::get<0>(truculent_trio); ❶
  REQUIRE(bertie_ref.birthname == bertie.birthname);

  auto& tuppy_ref = std::get<Acquaintance>(truculent_trio); ❷
  REQUIRE(tuppy_ref.nickname == hildebrand.nickname);
}
```

Listing 12-11: A std::tuple supports member extraction and structured binding syntax.

You can build a std::tuple in an analogous way to how you built a std::pair. First, you extract the Socialite member with get<0> ❶. Because Socialite is the first template parameter, you use 0 for the std::get template parameter. Then you extract the Acquaintance member with std::get<Acquaintance> ❷. Because there's only one element of type Acquaintance, you're permitted to use this mode of get access.

Like pair, tuple also allows structured binding syntax.

A Partial List of Supported Operations

Table 12-4 provides a list of the most supported std::tuple operations. In this table, tp is a std::tuple<A, B>, a is an object of type A, and b is an object of type B.

Table 12-4: The Most Supported std::tuple Operations

Operation	Notes
tuple<...>{ [alc] }	Constructs an empty tuple. Uses std::allocate as default allocator alc.
tuple<...>{ [alc], tp }	Copy constructs from tp. Uses std::allocate as default allocator alc.
tuple<...>{ [alc],move(tp) }	Move constructs from tp. Uses std::allocate as default allocator alc.
tuple<...>{ [alc], a, b }	Constructs a tuple by copying a and b. Uses std::allocate as default allocator alc.
tuple<...>{ [alc], move(a), move(b) }	Constructs a tuple by moving a and b. Uses std::allocate as default allocator alc.
tp1 = tp2	Copy assigns from tp2.
tp1 = move(tp2)	Move assigns from tp2.
get<i>(tp)	Returns a reference to the ith element (zero-based).
get<T>(tp)	Returns a reference to the element of type T. Fails to compile if more than one element share this type.
tp1.swap(tp2) swap(tp1, tp2)	Swaps the objects contained by tp1 and tp2.
make_tuple<...>(a, b)	Convenience function for constructing a tuple.
tuple_cat<...>(tp1, tp2)	Concatenates all the tuples passed in as arguments.
tp1 == tp2 tp1 != tp2 tp1 > tp2 tp1 >= tp2 tp1 < tp2 tp1 <= tp2	Equal if all elements are equal. Greater than/less than comparisons proceed from first element to last.

any

An *any* is a class that stores single values of any type. It is *not* a class template. To convert an any into a concrete type, you use an *any cast*, which is a nonmember function template. Any cast conversions are type safe; if you attempt to cast an any and the type doesn't match, you get an exception. With any, you can perform some kinds of generic programming *without templates*.

The stdlib has std::any in the <any> header, and Boost has boost::any in the <boost/any.hpp> header.

To store a value into an any, you use the emplace method template. It takes a single template parameter corresponding to the type you want to store into any (the *storage type*). Any arguments you pass into emplace get forwarded to an appropriate constructor for the given storage type. To extract the value, you use any_cast, which takes a template parameter corresponding to the current storage type of any (called the *state* of any). You pass the any as the sole parameter to any_cast. As long as the state of any matches the template parameter, you get the desired type out. If the state doesn't match, you get a bad_any_cast exception.

Listing 12-12 illustrates these basic interactions with a std::any.

```
#include <any>

struct EscapeCapsule {
  EscapeCapsule(int x) : weight_kg{ x } { }
  int weight_kg;
}; ❶

TEST_CASE("std::any allows us to std::any_cast into a type") {
  std::any hagunemnon; ❷
  hagunemnon.emplace<EscapeCapsule>(600); ❸
  auto capsule = std::any_cast<EscapeCapsule>(hagunemnon); ❹
  REQUIRE(capsule.weight_kg == 600);
  REQUIRE_THROWS_AS(std::any_cast<float>(hagunemnon), std::bad_any_cast); ❺
}
```

Listing 12-12: The std::any and std::any_cast allow you to extract concrete types.

You declare the EscapeCapsule class ❶. Within the test, you construct an empty std::any called hagunemnon ❷. Next, you use emplace to store an EscapeCapsule with weight_kg = 600 ❸. You can extract the EscapeCapsule back out using std::any_cast ❹, which you store into a new EscapeCapsule called capsule. Finally, you show that attempting to invoke any_cast to cast the hagunemnon into a float results in a std::bad_any_cast exception ❺.

A Partial List of Supported Operations

Table 12-5 provides a list of the most supported std::any operations. In this table, ay is a std::any and t is an object of type T.

Table 12-5: The Most Supported std::any Operations

Operation	Notes
any{}	Constructs an empty any object.
any{ **ay** }	Copy constructs from **ay**.
any{ move(**ay**) }	Move constructs from **ay**.
any{ move(**t**) }	Constructs an any object containing an in-place constructed object from **t**.
ay = **t**	Destructs the object currently contained by **ay**; copies **t**.
ay = move(**t**)	Destructs the object currently contained by **ay**; moves **t**.
ay1 = **ay2**	Copy assigns from **ay2**.
ay1 = move(**ay2**)	Move assigns from **ay2**.
ay.emplace<T>(...)	Destructs the object currently contained by **ay**; constructs a T in place, forwarding the arguments ... to the appropriate constructor.
ay.reset()	Destroys the currently contained object.
ay1.swap(**ay2**) swap(**ay1**, **ay2**)	Swaps the objects contained by **ay1** and **ay2**.
make_any<T>(...)	Convenience function for constructing an any constructs a T in place, forwarding the arguments ... to the appropriate constructor.
t = any_cast<T>(**ay**)	Casts **ay** into type T. Throws a std::bad_any_cast if the type T doesn't match the contained object's type.

variant

A *variant* is a class template that stores single values whose types are restricted to the user-defined list provided as template parameters. The variant is a type-safe union (refer to "Unions" on page 53). It shares a lot of functionality with the any type, but variant requires that you explicitly enumerate all the types that you'll store.

The stdlib has std::variant in the <variant> header, and Boost has boost::variant in the <boost/variant.hpp> header.

Listing 12-13 demonstrates creating another type called BugblatterBeast for variant to contain alongside EscapeCapsule.

```
#include <variant>

struct BugblatterBeast {
  BugblatterBeast() : is_ravenous{ true }, weight_kg{ 20000 } { }
  bool is_ravenous;
  int weight_kg; ❶
};
```

Listing 12-13: The std::variant can hold an object from one of a list of predefined types.

Aside from also containing a weight_kg member ❶, BugblatterBeast is totally independent from EscapeCapsule.

Constructing a variant

A variant can only be default constructed if one of two conditions is met:

- The first template parameter is default constructible.
- It is monostate, a type intended to communicate that a variant can have an empty state.

Because BugblatterBeast is default constructible (meaning it has a default constructor), make it the first type in the template parameter list so your variant is also default constructible, like so:

```
std::variant<BugblatterBeast, EscapeCapsule> hagunemnon;
```

To store a value into a variant, you use the emplace method template. As with any, a variant takes a single template parameter corresponding to the type you want to store. This template parameter must be contained in the list of template parameters for the variant. To extract a value, you use either of the non-member function templates get or get_if. These accept either the desired type or the index into the template parameter list corresponding to the desired type. If get fails, it throws a bad_variant_access exception, while get_if returns a nullptr.

You can determine which type corresponds with the current state of variant using the index() member, which returns the index of the current object's type within the template parameter list.

Listing 12-14 illustrates how to use emplace to change the state of a variant and index to determine the type of the contained object.

```
TEST_CASE("std::variant") {
  std::variant<BugblatterBeast, EscapeCapsule> hagunemnon;
  REQUIRE(hagunemnon.index() == 0); ❶

  hagunemnon.emplace<EscapeCapsule>(600); ❷
  REQUIRE(hagunemnon.index() == 1); ❸

  REQUIRE(std::get<EscapeCapsule>(hagunemnon).weight_kg == 600); ❹
  REQUIRE(std::get<1>(hagunemnon).weight_kg == 600); ❺
  REQUIRE_THROWS_AS(std::get<0>(hagunemnon), std::bad_variant_access); ❻
}
```

Listing 12-14: A std::get allows you to extract concrete types from std::variant.

After default constructing hagunemnon, invoking index yields 0 because this is the index of the correct template parameter ❶. Next, you emplace an EscapeCapsule ❷, which causes index to return 1 instead ❸. Both std::get<EscapeCapsule> ❹ and std::get<1> ❺ illustrate identical ways of extracting the contained type. Finally, attempting to invoke std::get to obtain a type that doesn't correspond with the current state of variant results in a bad_variant_access ❻.

You can use the non-member function std::visit to apply a callable object to a variant. This has the advantage of dispatching the correct function to handle whatever the contained object is without having to specify it explicitly with std::get. Listing 12-15 illustrates the basic usage.

```
TEST_CASE("std::variant") {
  std::variant<BugblatterBeast, EscapeCapsule> hagunemnon;
  hagunemnon.emplace<EscapeCapsule>(600); ❶
  auto lbs = std::visit([](auto& x) { return 2.2*x.weight_kg; }, hagunemnon); ❷
  REQUIRE(lbs == 1320); ❸
}
```

Listing 12-15: The std::visit allows you to apply a callable object to a contained type of std::variant.

First, you invoke emplace to store the value 600 into hagunemnon ❶. Because both BugblatterBeast and EscapeCapsule have a weight_kg member, you can use std::visit on hagunemnon with a lambda that performs the correct conversion (2.2 lbs per kg) to the weight_kg field ❷ and returns the result ❸ (notice that you don't have to include any type information).

Comparing variant and any

The universe is big enough to accommodate both any and variant. It's not possible to recommend one over the other generally, because each has its strengths and weaknesses.

An any is more flexible; it can take *any* type, whereas variant is only allowed to contain an object of a predetermined type. It also mostly avoids templates, so it's generally easier to program with.

A variant is less flexible, making it safer. Using the visit function, you can check for the safety of operations at compile time. With any, you would need to build your own visit-like functionality, and it would require runtime checking (for example, of the result of any_cast).

Finally, variant can be more performant than any. Although any is allowed to perform dynamic allocation if the contained type is too large, variant is not.

A Partial List of Supported Operations

Table 12-6 provides a list of the most supported std::variant operations. In this table, vt is a std::variant and t is an object of type T.

Table 12-6: The Most Supported `std::variant` Operations

Operation	Notes
`variant<...>{}`	Constructs an empty variant object. First template parameter must be default constructible.
`variant<...>{ vt }`	Copy constructs from `vt`.
`variant<...>{ move(vt) }`	Move constructs from `vt`.
`variant<...>{ move(t) }`	Constructs an `variant` object containing an in-place constructed object.
`vt = t`	Destructs the object currently contained by `vt`; copies `t`.
`vt = move(t)`	Destructs the object currently contained by `vt`; moves `t`.
`vt1 = vt2`	Copy assigns from `vt2`.
`vt1 = move(vt2)`	Move assigns from `vt2`.
`vt.emplace<T>(...)`	Destructs the object currently contained by `vt`; constructs a `T` in place, forwarding the arguments `...` to the appropriate constructor.
`vt.reset()`	Destroys the currently contained object.
`vt.index()`	Returns the zero-based index of the type of the currently contained object. (Order determined by template parameters of the `std::variant`.)
`vt1.swap(vt2)` `swap(vt1, vt2)`	Swaps the objects contained by `vt1` and `vt2`.
`make_variant<T>(...)`	Convenience function for constructing a `tuple`; constructs a `T` in place, forwarding the arguments `...` to the appropriate constructor.
`std::visit(vt, callable)`	Invokes `callable` with contained object.
`std::holds_alternative<T>(vt)`	Returns `true` if the contained object's type is `T`.
`std::get<I>(vt)` `std::get<T>(vt)`	Returns contained object if its type is `T` or the `i`th type. Otherwise, throws `std::bad_variant_access` exception.
`std::get_if<I>(&vt)` `std::get_if<T>(&vt)`	Returns a pointer to the contained object if its type is `T` or the `i`th type. Otherwise, returns `nullptr`.

`vt1 == vt2`
`vt1 != vt2`
`vt1 > vt2`
`vt1 >= vt2`
`vt1 < vt2`
`vt1 <= vt2`
	Compares the contained objects of `vt1` and `vt2`.

Date and Time

Between stdlib and Boost, a number of libraries are available that handle dates and times. When handling calendar dates and times, look to Boost's DateTime library. When you're trying get the current time or measure elapsed time, look to Boost's or stdlib's Chrono libraries and to Boost's Timer library.

Boost DateTime

Boost DateTime library supports date programming with a rich system based on the Gregorian calendar, which is the most widely used civil calendar internationally. Calendars are more complicated than they might seem at first glance. For example, consider the following excerpt from the US Naval Observatory's Introduction to Calendars, which describes the basics of leap years:

> Every year that is exactly divisible by four is a leap year, except for years that are exactly divisible by 100, but these centurial years are leap years if they are exactly divisible by 400. For example, the years 1700, 1800, and 1900 are not leap years, but the year 2000 is.

Rather than attempting to build your own solar calendar functions, just include DateTime's date-programming facilities with the following header:

```
#include <boost/date_time/gregorian/gregorian.hpp>
```

The principal type you'll use is the `boost::gregorian::date`, which is the primary interface for date-programming.

Constructing a date

Several options are available for constructing a `date`. You can default construct a `date`, which sets its value to the special date `boost::gregorian::not_a_date_time`. To construct a `date` with a valid date, you can use a constructor that accepts three arguments: a year, a month, and a date. The following statement constructs a `date` `d` with the date September 15, 1986:

```
boost::gregorian::date d{ 1986, 9, 15 };
```

Alternatively, you can construct a date from a string using the `boost::gregorian::from_string` utility function, like this:

```
auto d = boost::gregorian::from_string("1986/9/15");
```

If you pass an invalid date, the `date` constructor will throw an exception, such as `bad_year`, `bad_day_of_month`, or `bad_month`. For example, Listing 12-16 attempts to construct a date with September 32, 1986.

```
TEST_CASE("Invalid boost::Gregorian::dates throw exceptions") {
  using boost::gregorian::date;
  using boost::gregorian::bad_day_of_month;

  REQUIRE_THROWS_AS(date(1986, 9, 32), bad_day_of_month); ❶
}
```

Listing 12-16: The `boost::gregorian::date` constructor throws exceptions for bad dates.

Because September 32 isn't a valid day of the month, the `date` constructor throws a `bad_day_of_month` exception ❶.

NOTE *Due to a limitation in Catch, you cannot use braced initialization for* `date` *in the* `REQUIRE_THROWS_AS` *macro* ❶.

You can obtain the current day from the environment using the nonmember function `boost::gregorian::day_clock::local_day` or `boost::gregorian::day_clock::universal_day` to obtain the local day based on the system's time zone settings and the UTC day, respectively:

```
auto d_local = boost::gregorian::day_clock::local_day();
auto d_univ = boost::gregorian::day_clock::universal_day();
```

Once you construct a date, you can't change its value (it's *immutable*). However, dates support copy construction and copy assignment.

Accessing Date Members

You can inspect the features of a `date` through its many `const` methods. Table 12-7 provides a partial list. In this table, `d` is a `date`.

Table 12-7: The Most Supported `boost::gregorian::date` Accessors

Accessor	Notes
`d.year()`	Returns the year portion of the date.
`d.month()`	Returns the month portion of the date.
`d.day()`	Returns the day portion of the date.
`d.day_of_week()`	Returns the day of the week as an enum of type `greg_day_of_week`.
`d.day_of_year()`	Returns the day of the year (from 1 to 366 inclusive).
`d.end_of_month()`	Returns a date object set to the last day of the month of `d`.
`d.is_not_a_date()`	Returns true if `d` is not a date.
`d.week_number()`	Returns the ISO 8601 week number.

Listing 12-17 illustrates how to construct a `date` and use the accessors in Table 12-7.

```
TEST_CASE("boost::gregorian::date supports basic calendar functions") {
  boost::gregorian::date d{ 1986, 9, 15 }; ❶
  REQUIRE(d.year() == 1986); ❷
  REQUIRE(d.month() == 9); ❸
  REQUIRE(d.day() == 15); ❹
  REQUIRE(d.day_of_year() == 258); ❺
  REQUIRE(d.day_of_week() == boost::date_time::Monday); ❻
}
```

Listing 12-17: The `boost::gregorian::date` *supports basic calendar functions.*

Here, you construct a `date` from September 15, 1986 ❶. From there, you extract the year ❷, month ❸, day ❹, day of the year ❺, and day of the week ❻.

Calendar Math

You can perform simple calendar math on dates. When you subtract one date from another, you get a boost::gregorian::date_duration. The main functionality of date_duration is storing an integral number of days, which you can extract using the days method. Listing 12-18 illustrates how to compute the number of days elapsed between two date objects.

```
TEST_CASE("boost::gregorian::date supports calendar arithmetic") {
  boost::gregorian::date d1{ 1986, 9, 15 }; ❶
  boost::gregorian::date d2{ 2019, 8, 1 }; ❷
  auto duration = d2 - d1; ❸
  REQUIRE(duration.days() == 12008); ❹
}
```

Listing 12-18: Subtracting boost::gregorian::date objects yields a boost::gregorian::date_duration.

Here, you construct a date for September 15, 1986 ❶ and for August 1, 2019 ❷. You subtract these two dates to yield a date_duration ❸. Using the days method, you can extract the number of days between the two dates ❹.

You can also construct a date_duration using a long argument corresponding to the number of days. You can add a date_duration to a date to obtain another date, as Listing 12-19 illustrates.

```
TEST_CASE("date and date_duration support addition") {
  boost::gregorian::date d1{ 1986, 9, 15 }; ❶
  boost::gregorian::date_duration dur{ 12008 }; ❷
  auto d2 = d1 + dur; ❸
  REQUIRE(d2 == boost::gregorian::from_string("2019/8/1")); ❹
}
```

Listing 12-19: Adding a date_duration to a date yields another date.

You construct a date for September 15, 1986 ❶ and 12,008 days for duration ❷. From Listing 12-18, you know that this day plus 12008 yields August 1, 2019. So after adding them ❸, the resulting day is as you expect ❹.

Date Periods

A *date period* represents the interval between two dates. DateTime provides a boost::gregorian::date_period class, which has three constructors, as described in Table 12-8. In this table, constructors d1 and d2 are date arguments and dp is a date_period.

Table 12-8: Supported boost::gregorian::date_period Constructors

Accessor	Notes
date_period{ **d1, d2** }	Creates a period including **d1** but not **d2**; invalid if **d2 <= d1**.
date_period{ **d, n_days** }	Returns the month portion of the date.
date_period{ **dp** }	Copy constructor.

The date_period class supports many operations, such as the contain method, which takes a date argument and returns true if the argument is contained in the period. Listing 12-20 illustrates this operation.

```
TEST_CASE("boost::gregorian::date supports periods") {
  boost::gregorian::date d1{ 1986, 9, 15 }; ❶
  boost::gregorian::date d2{ 2019, 8, 1 }; ❷
  boost::gregorian::date_period p{ d1, d2 }; ❸
  REQUIRE(p.contains(boost::gregorian::date{ 1987, 10, 27 })); ❹
}
```

Listing 12-20: Using the contains method on a boost::gregorian::date_period to determine whether a date falls within a particular time interval

Here, you construct two dates, September 15, 1986 ❶ and August 1, 2019 ❷, which you use to construct a date_period ❸. Using the contains method, you can determine that the date_period contains the date October 27, 1987 ❹.

Table 12-9 contains a partial list of other date_period operations. In this table, p, p1, and p2 are date_period classes and d is a date.

Table 12-9: Supported boost::gregorian::date_period Operations

Accessor	Notes
p.begin()	Returns the first day.
p.last()	Returns the last day.
p.length()	Returns the number of days contained.
p.is_null()	Returns true if the period is invalid (for example, end is before start).
p.contains(d)	Returns true if d falls within p.
p1.contains(p2)	Returns true if all of p2 falls within p1.
p1.intersects(p2)	Returns true if any of p2 falls within p1.
p.is_after(d)	Returns true if p falls after d.
p.is_before(d)	Returns true if p falls before d.

Other DateTime Features

The Boost DateTime library contains three broad categories of programming:

Date Date programming is the calendar-based programming you just toured.

Time Time programming, which allows you to work with clocks with microsecond resolution, is available in the <boost/date_time/posix_time/posix_time.hpp> header. The mechanics are similar to date programming, but you work with clocks instead of Gregorian calendars.

Local-time Local-time programming is simply time-zone-aware time programming. It's available in the <boost/date_time/time_zone_base.hpp> header.

NOTE *For brevity, this chapter won't go into detail about time and local-time programming. See the Boost documentation for information and examples.*

Chrono

The stdlib Chrono library provides a variety of clocks in the `<chrono>` header. You typically use these when you need to program something that depends on time or for timing your code.

NOTE *Boost also offers a Chrono library in the* `<boost/chrono.hpp>` *header. It's a superset of stdlib's Chrono library, which includes, for example, process- and thread-specific clocks and user-defined output formats for time.*

Clocks

Three clocks are available in Chrono library; each provides a different guarantee, and all reside in the `std::chrono` namespace:

- The `std::chrono::system_clock` is the system-wide, real-time clock. It's sometimes also called the *wall clock*, the elapsed real time since an implementation-specific start date. Most implementations specify the Unix start date of January 1, 1970, at midnight.
- The `std::chrono::steady_clock` guarantees that its value will never decrease. This might seem absurd to guarantee, but measuring time is more complicated than it seems. For example, a system might have to contend with leap seconds or inaccurate clocks.
- The `std::chrono::high_resolution_clock` has the shortest *tick* period available: a tick is the smallest atomic change that the clock can measure.

Each of these three clocks supports the static member function `now`, which returns a time point corresponding to the current value of the clock.

Time Points

A *time point* represents a moment in time, and Chrono encodes time points using the `std::chrono::time_point` type. From a user perspective, `time_point` objects are very simple. They provide a `time_since_epoch` method that returns the amount of time elapsed between the time point and the clock's *epoch*. This elapsed time is called a *duration*.

An epoch is an implementation-defined reference time point denoting the beginning of a clock. The Unix Epoch (or POSIX time) begins on January 1, 1970, whereas the Windows Epoch begins on January 1, 1601 (corresponding with the beginning of a 400-year, Gregorian-calendar cycle).

The `time_since_epoch` method is not the only way to obtain a duration from a `time_point`. You can obtain the duration between two `time_point` objects by subtracting them.

Durations

A std::chrono::duration represents the time between the two time_point objects. Durations expose a count method, which returns the number of clock ticks in the duration.

Listing 12-21 shows how to obtain the current time from each of the three available clocks, extract the time since each clock's epoch as a duration, and then convert them to ticks.

```
TEST_CASE("std::chrono supports several clocks") {
  auto sys_now = std::chrono::system_clock::now(); ❶
  auto hires_now = std::chrono::high_resolution_clock::now(); ❷
  auto steady_now = std::chrono::steady_clock::now(); ❸


  REQUIRE(sys_now.time_since_epoch().count() > 0); ❹
  REQUIRE(hires_now.time_since_epoch().count() > 0); ❺
  REQUIRE(steady_now.time_since_epoch().count() > 0); ❻
}
```

Listing 12-21: The std::chrono *supports several kinds of clocks.*

You obtain the current time from the system_clock ❶, the high_resolution_clock ❷, and the steady_clock ❸. For each clock, you convert the time point into a duration since the clock's epoch using the time_since_epoch method. You immediately call count on the resulting duration to yield a tick count, which should be greater than zero ❹❺❻.

In addition to deriving durations from time points, you can construct them directly. The std::chrono namespace contains helper functions to generate durations. For convenience, Chrono offers a number of user-defined duration literals in the std::literals::chrono_literals namespace. These provide some syntactic sugar, convenient language syntax that makes life easier for the developer, for defining duration literals.

Table 12-10 shows the helper functions and their literal equivalents, where each expression corresponds to an hour's duration.

Table 12-10: std::chrono Helper Functions and User-Defined Literals for Creating Durations

Helper function	Literal equivalent
nanoseconds(3600000000000)	3600000000000ns
microseconds(3600000000)	3600000000us
milliseconds(3600000)	3600000ms
seconds(3600)	3600s
minutes(60)	60m
hours(1)	1h

For example, Listing 12-22 illustrates how to construct a duration of 1 second with `std::chrono::seconds` and another duration of 1,000 milliseconds using the `ms` duration literal.

```
#include <chrono>
TEST_CASE("std::chrono supports several units of measurement") {
  using namespace std::literals::chrono_literals; ❶
  auto one_s = std::chrono::seconds(1); ❷
  auto thousand_ms = 1000ms; ❸
  REQUIRE(one_s == thousand_ms); ❹
}
```

Listing 12-22: The `std::chrono` supports many units of measurement, which are comparable.

Here, you bring in the `std::literals::chrono_literals` namespace so you have access to the duration literals ❶. You construct a duration called `one_s` from the `seconds` helper function ❷ and another called `thousand_ms` from the `ms` duration literal ❸. These are equivalent because a second contains a thousand milliseconds ❹.

Chrono provides the function template `std::chrono::duration_cast` to cast a duration from one unit to another. As with other cast-related function templates, such as `static_cast`, `duration_cast` takes a single template parameter corresponding to the target duration and a single argument corresponding to the duration you want to cast.

Listing 12-23 illustrates how to cast a `nanosecond` duration into a `second` duration.

```
TEST_CASE("std::chrono supports duration_cast") {
  using namespace std::chrono; ❶
  auto billion_ns_as_s = duration_cast<seconds❷>(1'000'000'000ns❸);
  REQUIRE(billion_ns_as_s.count() == 1); ❹
}
```

Listing 12-23: The `std::chrono` supports `std::chrono::duration_cast`.

First, you bring in the `std::chrono` namespace for easy access to `duration_cast`, the duration helper functions, and the duration literals ❶. Next, you use the `ns` duration literal to specify a billion-nanosecond duration ❸, which you pass as the argument to `duration_cast`. You specify the template parameter of `duration_cast` as seconds ❷, so the resulting duration, `billion_ns_as_s`, equals 1 second ❹.

Waiting

Sometimes, you'll use durations to specify some period of time for your program to wait. The stdlib provides concurrency primitives in the `<thread>` header, which contains the non-member function `std::this_thread::sleep_for`. The `sleep_for` function accepts a `duration` argument corresponding to how long you want the current thread of execution to wait or "sleep."

Listing 12-24 shows how to employ `sleep_for`.

```
#include <thread>
#include <chrono>

TEST_CASE("std::chrono used to sleep") {
  using namespace std::literals::chrono_literals; ❶
  auto start = std::chrono::system_clock::now(); ❷
  std::this_thread::sleep_for(100ms); ❸
  auto end = std::chrono::system_clock::now(); ❹
  REQUIRE(end - start >= 100ms); ❺
}
```

Listing 12-24: The `std::chrono` works with `<thread>` to put the current thread to sleep.

As before, you bring in the `chrono_literals` namespace so you have access to the duration literals ❶. You record the current time according to `system_clock`, saving the resulting `time_point` into the `start` variable ❷. Next, you invoke `sleep_for` with a 100-millisecond duration (a tenth of a second) ❸. You then record the current time again, saving the resulting `time_point` into `end` ❹. Because the program slept for 100 milliseconds between calls to `std::chrono::system_clock`, the duration resulting from subtracting `start` from `end` should be at least `100ms` ❺.

Timing

To optimize code, you absolutely need accurate measurements. You can use Chrono to measure how long a series of operations takes. This enables you to establish that a particular code path is actually responsible for observed performance issues. It also enables you to establish an objective measure for the progress of your optimization efforts.

Boost's Timer library contains the `boost::timer::auto_cpu_timer` class in the `<boost/timer/timer.hpp>` header, which is an RAII object that begins timing in its constructor and stops timing in its destructor.

You can build your own makeshift `Stopwatch` class using just the stdlib Chrono library. The `Stopwatch` class can keep a reference to a `duration` object. In the `Stopwatch` destructor, you can set the `duration` via its reference. Listing 12-25 provides an implementation.

```
#include <chrono>

struct Stopwatch {
  Stopwatch(std::chrono::nanoseconds& result❶)
    : result{ result }, ❷
    start{ std::chrono::high_resolution_clock::now() } { } ❸
  ~Stopwatch() {
    result = std::chrono::high_resolution_clock::now() - start; ❹
  }
private:
  std::chrono::nanoseconds& result;
```

```
  const std::chrono::time_point<std::chrono::high_resolution_clock> start;
};
```

Listing 12-25: A simple `Stopwatch` *class that computes the duration of its lifetime*

The `Stopwatch` constructor requires a single `nanoseconds` reference ❶, which you store into the `result` field with a member initializer ❷. You also save the current time of the `high_resolution_clock` by setting the `start` field to the result of `now()` ❸. In the `Stopwatch` destructor, you again invoke `now()` on the `high_resolution_clock` and subtract `start` to obtain the duration of the lifetime of `Stopwatch`. You use the `result` reference to write the `duration` ❹.

Listing 12-26 shows the `Stopwatch` in action, performing a million floating-point divisions within a loop and computing the average time elapsed per iteration.

```
#include <cstdio>
#include <cstdint>
#include <chrono>

struct Stopwatch {
--snip--
};

int main() {
  const size_t n = 1'000'000; ❶
  std::chrono::nanoseconds elapsed; ❷
  {
    Stopwatch stopwatch{ elapsed }; ❸
    volatile double result{ 1.23e45 }; ❹
    for (double i = 1; i < n; i++) {
      result /= i; ❺
    }
  }
  auto time_per_division = elapsed.count() / double{ n }; ❻
  printf("Took %gns per division.", time_per_division); ❼
}
-----------------------------------------------------------------------
Took 6.49622ns per division. ❼
```

Listing 12-26: Using the `Stopwatch` *to estimate the time taken for* `double` *division*

First, you initialize a variable `n` to a million, which stores the total number of iterations your program will make ❶. You declare the `elapsed` variable, which will store the time elapsed across all the iterations ❷. Within a block, you declare a `Stopwatch` and pass an `elapsed` reference to the constructor ❸. Next, you declare a `double` called `result` with a junk value in it ❹. You declare this variable `volatile` so the compiler doesn't try to optimize the loop away. Within the loop, you do some arbitrary, floating-point division ❺.

Once the block completes, `stopwatch` destructs. This writes the duration of `stopwatch` to `elapsed`, which you use to compute the average number of nanoseconds per loop iteration and store into the `time_per_addition` variable ❻. You conclude the program by printing `time_per_division` with `printf` ❼.

Numerics

This section discusses handling numbers with a focus on common mathematical functions and constants; handling complex numbers; generating random numbers, numeric limits, and conversions; and computing ratios.

Numeric Functions

The stdlib Numerics and Boost Math libraries provide a profusion of numeric/mathematical functions. For the sake of brevity, this chapter presents only quick references. For detailed treatment, see [numerics] in the ISO C++ 17 Standard and the Boost Math documentation.

Table 12-11 provides a partial list of many common, non-member mathematical functions available in the stdlib's Math library.

Table 12-11: A Partial List of Common Math Functions in the stdlib

Function	Computes the . . .	Ints	Floats	Header
abs(x)	Absolute value of x.	✓		<cstdlib>
div(x, y)	Quotient and remainder of x divided by y.	✓		<cstdlib>
abs(x)	Absolute value of x.		✓	<cmath>
fmod(x, y)	Remainder of floating-point division of x by y.		✓	<cmath>
remainder(x, y)	Signed remainder of dividing x by y.	✓	✓	<cmath>
fma(x, y, z)	Multiply the first two arguments and add their product to the third argument; also called fused multiplication addition; that is, x * y + z.	✓	✓	<cmath>
max(x, y)	Maximum of x and y.	✓	✓	<algorithm>
min(x, y)	Minimum of x and y.	✓	✓	<algorithm>
exp(x)	Value of e^x.	✓	✓	<cmath>
exp2(x)	Value of 2^x.	✓	✓	<cmath>
log(x)	Natural log of x; that is, ln x.	✓	✓	<cmath>
log10(x)	Common log of x; that is, log10 x.	✓	✓	<cmath>
log2(x)	Base 2 log of x; that is, log10 x.	✓	✓	<cmath>
gcd(x, y)	Greatest common denominator of x and y.	✓		<numeric>
lcm(x, y)	Least common multiple of x and y.	✓		<numeric>
erf(x)	Gauss error function of x.	✓	✓	<cmath>
pow(x, y)	Value of x^y.	✓	✓	<cmath>
sqrt(x)	Square root of x.	✓	✓	<cmath>
cbrt(x)	Cube root of x.	✓	✓	<cmath>
hypot(x, y)	Square root of $x^2 + y^2$.	✓	✓	<cmath>
sin(x) cos(x) tan(x) asin(x) acos(x) atan(x)	Associated trigonometric function value.	✓	✓	<cmath>

Function	Computes the . . .	Ints	Floats	Header
sinh(x) cosh(x) tanh(x) asinh(x) acosh(x) atanh(x)	Associated hyperbolic function value.	✓	✓	<cmath>
ceil(x)	Nearest integer greater than or equal to x.	✓	✓	<cmath>
floor(x)	Nearest integer less than or equal to x.	✓	✓	<cmath>
round(x)	Nearest integer equal to x; rounds away from zero in midpoint cases.	✓	✓	<cmath>
isfinite(x)	Value true if x is a finite number.	✓	✓	<cmath>
isinf(x)	Value true if x is an infinite number.	✓	✓	<cmath>

NOTE *Other specialized mathematical functions are in the* `<cmath>` *header. For example, functions to compute Laguerre and Hermite polynomials, elliptic integrals, cylindrical Bessel and Neumann functions, and the Riemann zeta function appear in the header.*

Complex Numbers

A *complex number* is of the form `a+bi`, where `i` is an *imaginary number* that, when multiplied by itself, equals negative one; that is, `i*i=-1`. Imaginary numbers have applications in control theory, fluid dynamics, electrical engineering, signal analysis, number theory, and quantum physics, among other fields. The `a` portion of a complex number is called its *real component*, and the `b` portion is called the *imaginary component*.

The stdlib offers the `std::complex` class template in the `<complex>` header. It accepts a template parameter for the underlying type of the real and imaginary component. This template parameter must be one of the fundamental floating-point types.

To construct a `complex`, you can pass in two arguments: the real and the imaginary components. The `complex` class also supports copy construction and copy assignment.

The non-member functions `std::real` and `std::imag` can extract the real and imaginary components from a `complex`, respectively, as Listing 12-27 illustrates.

```
#include <complex>

TEST_CASE("std::complex has a real and imaginary component") {
  std::complex<double> a{0.5, 14.13}; ❶
  REQUIRE(std::real(a) == Approx(0.5)); ❷
  REQUIRE(std::imag(a) == Approx(14.13)); ❸
}
```

Listing 12-27: Constructing a `std::complex` *and extracting its components*

You construct a `std::complex` with a real component of 0.5 and an imaginary component of 14.13 ❶. You use `std::real` to extract the real component ❷ and `std::imag` to extract the imaginary component ❸.

Table 12-12 contains a partial list of supported operations with `std::complex`.

Table 12-12: A Partial List of `std::complex` Operations

Operation	Notes

`c1+c2`
`c1-c2`
`c1*c2`
`c1/c2`
	Performs addition, subtraction, multiplication, and division.

`c+s`
`c-s`
`c*s`
`c/s`
	Converts the scalar `s` into a complex number with the real component equal to the scalar value and the imaginary component equal to zero. This conversion supports the corresponding complex operation (addition, subtraction, multiplication, or division) in the preceding row.

`real(c)`	Extracts real component.
`imag(c)`	Extracts imaginary component.
`abs(c)`	Computes magnitude.
`arg(c)`	Computes the phase angle.
`norm(c)`	Computes the squared magnitude.
`conj(c)`	Computes the complex conjugate.
`proj(c)`	Computes Riemann sphere projection.
`sin(c)`	Computes the sine.
`cos(c)`	Computes the cosine.
`tan(c)`	Computes the tangent.
`asin(c)`	Computes the arcsine.
`acos(c)`	Computes the arccosine.
`atan(c)`	Computes the arctangent.
`c = polar(m, a)`	Computes complex number determined by magnitude `m` and angle `a`.

Mathematical Constants

Boost offers a suite of commonly used mathematical constants in the `<boost/math/constants/constants.hpp>` header. More than 70 constants are available, and you can obtain them in `float`, `double`, or `long double` form by obtaining the relevant global variable from the `boost::math::float_constants`, `boost::math::double_constants`, and `boost::math::long_double_constants` respectively.

One of the many constants available is `four_thirds_pi`, which approximates $4\pi/3$. The formula for computing the volume of a sphere of radius r is $4\pi r^3/3$, so you could pull in this constant to make computing such a volume easy. Listing 12-28 illustrates how to compute the volume of a sphere with radius 10.

```
#include <cmath>
#include <boost/math/constants/constants.hpp>

TEST_CASE("boost::math offers constants") {
  using namespace boost::math::double_constants; ❶
  auto sphere_volume = four_thirds_pi * std::pow(10, 3); ❷
  REQUIRE(sphere_volume == Approx(4188.7902047));
}
```

Listing 12-28: The `boost::math` namespace offers constants

Here, you pull in the namespace `boost::math::double_constants`, which brings all the `double` versions of the Boost Math constants ❶. Next, you calculate the `sphere_volume` by computing `four_thirds_pi` times 10^3 ❷.

Table 12-13 provides some of the more commonly used constants in Boost Math.

Table 12-13: Some of the Most Common Boost Math Constants

Constant	Value	Approx.	Note
`half`	1/2	0.5	
`third`	1/3	0.333333	
`two_thirds`	2/3	0.66667	
`three_quarters`	3/4	0.75	
`root_two`	√2	1.41421	
`root_three`	√3	1.73205	
`half_root_two`	√2 / 2	0.707106	
`ln_two`	ln(2)	0.693147	
`ln_ten`	ln(10)	2.30258	
`pi`	π	3.14159	Archimedes' constant
`two_pi`	2π	6.28318	Circumference of unit circle
`four_thirds_pi`	4π/3	4.18879	Volume of unit sphere
`one_div_two_pi`	1/(2π)	1.59155	Gaussian integrals
`root_pi`	√π	1.77245	
`e`	e	2.71828	Euler's constant e
`e_pow_pi`	e^π	23.14069	Gelfond's constant
`root_e`	√e	1.64872	
`log10_e`	log10(e)	0.434294	
`degree`	π / 180	0.017453	Number of radians per degree
`radian`	180 / π	57.2957	Number of degrees per radian
`sin_one`	sin(1)	0.84147	
`cos_one`	cos(1)	0.5403	
`phi`	(1 + √5) / 2	1.61803	Phidias' golden ratio φ
`ln_phi`	ln(φ)	0.48121	

Random Numbers

In some settings, it's often necessary to generate random numbers. In scientific computing, you might need to run large numbers of simulations based on random numbers. Such numbers need to emulate draws from random processes with certain characteristics, such as coming from a Poisson or normal distribution. In addition, you usually want these simulations to be repeatable, so the code responsible for generating randomness—the *random number engine*—should produce the same output given the same input. Such random number engines are sometimes called *pseudo*-random number engines.

In cryptography, you might require random numbers to instead secure information. In such settings, it must be virtually impossible for someone to obtain a similar stream of random numbers; so accidental use of pseudorandom number engines often seriously compromises an otherwise secure cryptosystem.

For these reasons and others, *you should never attempt to build your own random number generator.* Building a correct random number generator is surprisingly difficult. It's too easy to introduce patterns into your random number generator, which can have nasty and hard to diagnose side effects on systems that use your random numbers as input.

NOTE *If you're interested in random number generation, refer to Chapter 2 of* Stochastic Simulation *by Brian D. Ripley for scientific applications and Chapter 2 of* Serious Cryptography *by Jean-Philippe Aumasson for cryptographic applications.*

If you're in the market for random numbers, look no further than the Random libraries available in the stdlib in the `<random>` header or in Boost in the `<boost/math/...>` headers.

Random Number Engines

Random number engines generate random bits. Between Boost and stdlib, there is a dizzying array of candidates. Here's a general rule: if you need repeatable pseudo-random numbers, consider using the Mersenne Twister engine `std::mtt19937_64`. If you need cryptographically secure random numbers, consider using `std::random_device`.

The Mersenne Twister has some desirable statistical properties for simulations. You provide its constructor with an integer seed value, which completely determines the sequence of random numbers. All random engines are function objects; to obtain a random number, use the function call `operator()`. Listing 12-29 shows how to construct a Mersenne Twister engine with the seed 91586 and invoke the resulting engine three times.

```
#include <random>
TEST_CASE("mt19937_64 is pseudorandom") {
  std::mt19937_64 mt_engine{ 91586 }; ❶
```

```
  REQUIRE(mt_engine() == 8346843996631475880); ❷
  REQUIRE(mt_engine() == 2237671392849523263); ❸
  REQUIRE(mt_engine() == 7333164488732543658); ❹
}
```

Listing 12-29: The `mt19937_64` *is a pseudo-random number engine.*

Here, you construct an `mt19937_64` Mersenne Twister engine with the seed 91586 ❶. Because it's a pseudo-random engine, you're guaranteed to get the same sequence of random numbers ❷❸❹ each time. This sequence is determined entirely by the seed.

Listing 12-30 illustrates how to construct a `random_device` and invoke it to obtain a cryptographically secure random value.

```
TEST_CASE("std::random_device is invocable") {
  std::random_device rd_engine{}; ❶
  REQUIRE_NOTHROW(rd_engine()); ❷
}
```

Listing 12-30: The `random_device` *is a function object.*

You construct a `random_device` using the default constructor ❶. The resulting object `rd_engine` ❷ is invokable, but you should treat the object as opaque. Unlike the Mersenne Twister in Listing 12-29, `random_device` is unpredictable by design.

NOTE *Because computers are deterministic by design, the* `std::random_device` *cannot make any strong guarantees about cryptographic security.*

Random Number Distributions

A *random number distribution* is a mathematical function that maps a number to a probability density. Roughly, the idea is that if you take infinite samples from a random variable that has a particular distribution and you plot the relative frequencies of your sample values, that plot would look like the distribution.

Distributions break out into two broad categories: *discrete* and *continuous*. A simple analogy is that discrete distributions map integral values, and continuous distributions map floating-point values.

Most distributions accept customization parameters. For example, the normal distribution is a continuous distribution that accepts two parameters: a mean and a variance. Its density has a familiar bell shape centered around the mean, as shown in Figure 12-1. The discrete uniform distribution is a random number distribution that assigns equal probability to the numbers between some minimum and maximum. Its density looks perfectly flat across its range from minimum to maximum, as shown in Figure 12-2.

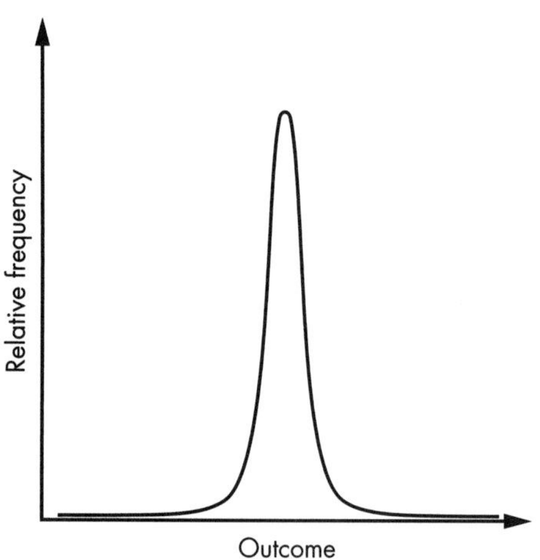

Figure 12-1: A representation of the normal distribution's probability density function

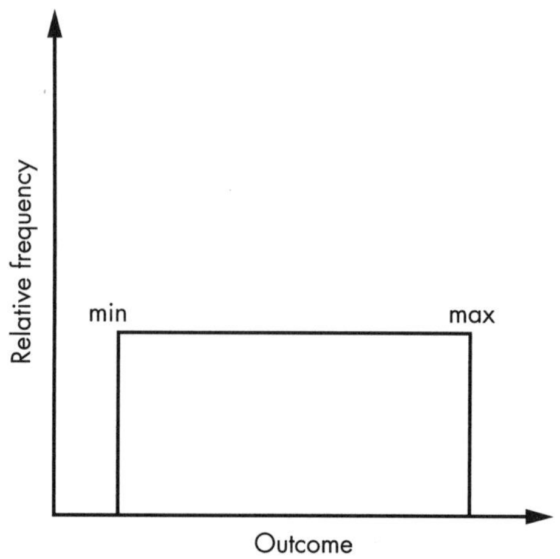

Figure 12-2: A representation of the uniform distribution's probability density function

You can easily generate random numbers from common statistical distributions, such as the uniform and the normal, using the same stdlib Random library. Each distribution accepts some parameters in its constructor, corresponding to the underlying distribution's parameters. To draw a random variable from the distribution, you use the function call `operator()` and pass in an instance of a random number engine, such as a Mersenne Twister.

The `std::uniform_int_distribution` is a class template available in the `<random>` header that takes a single template parameter corresponding to the type you want returned by draws from the distribution, like an `int`. You specify the uniform distribution's minimum and maximum by passing them in as constructor parameters. Each number in the range has equal probability. It's perhaps the most common distribution to arise in general software engineering contexts.

Listing 12-31 illustrates how to take a million draws from a uniform distribution with a minimum of 1 and a maximum of 10 and compute the sample mean.

```
TEST_CASE("std::uniform_int_distribution produces uniform ints") {
  std::mt19937_64 mt_engine{ 102787 }; ❶
  std::uniform_int_distribution<int> int_d{ 0, 10 }; ❷
  const size_t n{ 1'000'000 }; ❸
  int sum{}; ❹
  for (size_t i{}; i < n; i++)
    sum += int_d(mt_engine); ❺
  const auto sample_mean = sum / double{ n }; ❻
  REQUIRE(sample_mean == Approx(5).epsilon(.1)); ❼
}
```

Listing 12-31: The `uniform_int_distribution` simulates draws from the discrete uniform distribution.

You construct a Mersenne Twister with the seed 102787 ❶ and then construct a `uniform_int_distribution` with a minimum of 0 and a maximum of 10 ❷. Then you initialize a variable `n` to hold the number of iterations ❸ and initialize a variable to hold the `sum` of all the uniform random variables ❹. In the loop, you draw random variables from the uniform distribution with `operator()`, passing in the Mersenne Twister instance ❺.

The mean of a discrete uniform distribution is the minimum plus the maximum divided by 2. Here, `int_d` has a mean of 5. You can compute a sample mean by dividing `sum` by the number of samples `n` ❻. With high confidence, you assert that this `sample_mean` is approximately 5 ❼.

A Partial List of Random Number Distributions

Table 12-14 contains a partial list of the random number distributions in `<random>`, their default template parameters, and their constructor parameters.

Table 12-14: Random Number Distributions in `<random>`

Distribution	Notes
`uniform_int_distribution<int>{ min, max }`	Discrete uniform distribution with minimum **`min`** and maximum **`max`**.
`uniform_real_distribution<double>{ min, max }`	Continuous uniform distribution with minimum **`min`** and maximum **`max`**.
`normal_distribution<double>{ m, s }`	Normal distribution with mean **`m`** and standard deviation **`s`**. Commonly used to model the additive product of many independent random variables. Also called the Gaussian distribution.
`lognormal_distribution<double>{ m, s }`	Log-normal distribution with mean **`m`** and standard deviation **`s`**. Commonly used to model the multiplicative product of many independent random variables. Also called Galton's distribution.
`chi_squared_distribution<double>{ n }`	Chi-squared distribution with degrees of freedom **`n`**. Commonly used in inferential statistics.
`cauchy_distribution<double>{ a, b }`	Cauchy distribution with location parameter **`a`** and scale parameter **`b`**. Used in physics. Also called the Lorentz distribution.
`fisher_f_distribution<double>{ m, n }`	F distribution with degrees of freedom **`m`** and **`n`**. Commonly used in inferential statistics. Also called the Snedecor distribution.
`student_t_distribution<double>{ n }`	T distribution with degrees of freedom **`n`**. Commonly used in inferential statistics. Also called the Student's T distribution.

(continued)

Table 12-14: Random Number Distributions in <random> (continued)

Distribution	Notes
`bernoulli_distribution{ p }`	Bernoulli distribution with success probability **p**. Commonly used to model the result of a single, Boolean-valued outcome.
`binomial_distribution<int>{ n, p }`	Binomial distribution with **n** trials and success probability **p**. Commonly used to model the number of successes when sampling with replacement in a series of Bernoulli experiments.
`geometric_distribution<int>{ p }`	Geometric distribution with success probability **p**. Commonly used to model the number of failures occurring before the first success in a series of Bernoulli experiments.
`poisson_distribution<int>{ m }`	Poisson distribution with mean **m**. Commonly used to model the number of events occurring in a fixed interval of time.
`exponential_distribution<double>{ l }`	Exponential distribution with mean 1/**l**, where **l** is known as the lambda parameter. Commonly used to model the amount of time between events in a Poisson process.
`gamma_distribution<double>{ a, b }`	Gamma distribution with shape parameter **a** and scale parameter **b**. Generalization of the exponential distribution and chi-squared distribution.
`weibull_distribution<double>{ k, l }`	Weibull distribution with shape parameter **k** and scale parameter **l**. Commonly used to model time to failure.
`extreme_value_distribution<double>{ a, b }`	Extreme value distribution with location parameter **a** and scale parameter **b**. Commonly used to model maxima of independent random variables. Also called the Gumbel type-I distribution.

NOTE *Boost Math offers more random number distributions in the* `<boost/math/...>` *series of headers, for example, the beta, hypergeometric, logistic, and inverse normal distributions.*

Numeric Limits

The stdlib offers the class template `std::numeric_limits` in the `<limits>` header to provide you with compile time information about various properties for arithmetic types. For example, if you want to identify the smallest finite value for a given type `T`, you can use the static member function `std::numeric_limits<T>::min()` to obtain it.

Listing 12-32 illustrates how to use `min` to facilitate an underflow.

```
#include <limits>
TEST_CASE("std::numeric_limits::min provides the smallest finite value.") {
  auto my_cup = std::numeric_limits<int>::min(); ❶
  auto underfloweth = my_cup - 1; ❷
  REQUIRE(my_cup < underfloweth); ❸
}
```

Listing 12-32: Using `std::numeric_limits<T>::min()` to facilitate an `int` underflow. Although at press time the major compilers produce code that passes the test, this program contains undefined behavior.

First, you set the `my_cup` variable equal to the smallest possible `int` value by using `std::numeric_limits<int>::min()` ❶. Next, you intentionally cause an underflow by subtracting 1 from `my_cup` ❷. Because `my_cup` is the minimum value an `int` can take, `my_cup` runneth under, as the saying goes. This causes the deranged situation that `underfloweth` is greater than `my_cup` ❸, even though you initialized `underfloweth` by subtracting from `my_cup`.

NOTE *Such silent underflows have been the cause of untold numbers of software security vulnerabilities. Don't rely on this undefined behavior!*

Many static member functions and member constants are available on `std::numeric_limits`. Table 12-15 lists some of the most common.

Table 12-15: Some Common Member Constants in `std::numeric_limits`

Operation	Notes
`numeric_limits<T>::is_signed`	`true` if `T` is signed.
`numeric_limits<T>::is_integer`	`true` if `T` is an integer.
`numeric_limits<T>::has_infinity`	Identifies whether `T` can encode an infinite value. (Usually, all floating-point types have an infinite value, whereas integral types don't.)
`numeric_limits<T>::digits10`	Identifies the number of digits `T` can represent.
`numeric_limits<T>::min()`	Returns the smallest value of `T`.
`numeric_limits<T>::max()`	Returns the largest value of `T`.

NOTE *Boost Integer provides some additional facilities for introspecting integer types, such as determining the fastest or smallest integer, or the smallest integer with at least* N *bits.*

Boost Numeric Conversion

Boost provides the Numeric Conversion library, which contains a collection of tools to convert between numeric objects. The `boost::converter` class template in the `<boost/numeric/conversion/converter.hpp>` header encapsulates code to perform a specific numeric conversion from one type to another. You must provide two template parameters: the target type T and the source type S. You can specify a numeric converter that takes a double and converts it to an int with the simple type alias double_to_int:

```
#include <boost/numeric/conversion/converter.hpp>
using double_to_int = boost::numeric::converter<int❶, double❷>;
```

To convert with your new type alias double_to_int, you have several options. First, you can use its static method convert, which accepts a double ❷ and returns an int ❶, as Listing 12-33 illustrates.

```
TEST_CASE("boost::converter offers the static method convert") {
  REQUIRE(double_to_int::convert(3.14159) == 3);
}
```

Listing 12-33: The boost::converter offers the static method convert.

Here, you simply invoke the convert method with the value 3.14159, which boost::convert converts to 3.

Because boost::convert provides the function call operator(), you can construct a function object double_to_int and use it to convert, as in Listing 12-34.

```
TEST_CASE("boost::numeric::converter implements operator()") {
  double_to_int dti; ❶
  REQUIRE(dti(3.14159) == 3); ❷
  REQUIRE(double_to_int{}(3.14159) == 3); ❸
}
```

Listing 12-34: The boost::converter implements operator().

You construct a double_to_int function object called dti ❶, which you invoke with the same argument, 3.14159 ❷, as in Listing 12-33. The result is the same. You also have the option of constructing a temporary function object and using operator() directly, which yields identical results ❸.

A major advantage of using boost::converter instead of alternatives like static_cast is runtime bounds checking. If a conversion would cause an overflow, boost::converter will throw a boost::numeric::positive_overflow or boost::numeric::negative_overflow. Listing 12-35 illustrates this behavior when you attempt to convert a very large double into an int.

```
#include <limits>
TEST_CASE("boost::numeric::converter checks for overflow") {
  auto yuge = std::numeric_limits<double>::max(); ❶
  double_to_int dti; ❷
  REQUIRE_THROWS_AS(dti(yuge)❸, boost::numeric::positive_overflow❹);
}
```

Listing 12-35: The boost::converter checks for overflow.

You use numeric_limits to obtain a yuge value ❶. You construct a double_to_int converter ❷, which you use to attempt a conversion of yuge to an int ❸. This throws a positive_overflow exception because the value is too large to store ❹.

It's possible to customize the conversion behavior of boost::converter using template parameters. For example, you can customize the overflow handling to throw a custom exception or perform some other operation. You can also customize rounding behavior so that rather than truncating off the decimal from a floating-point value, you perform custom rounding. See the Boost Numeric Conversion documentation for details.

If you're happy with the default boost::converter behavior, you can use the boost::numeric_cast function template as a shortcut. This function template accepts a single template parameter corresponding to the target type of the conversion and a single argument corresponding to the source number. Listing 12-36 provides an update to Listing 12-35 that uses boost::numeric_cast instead.

```
#include <limits>
#include <boost/numeric/conversion/cast.hpp>

TEST_CASE("boost::boost::numeric_cast checks overflow") {
  auto yuge = std::numeric_limits<double>::max(); ❶
  REQUIRE_THROWS_AS(boost::numeric_cast<int>(yuge), ❷
                    boost::numeric::positive_overflow ❸);
}
```

Listing 12-36: The boost::numeric_cast function template also performs runtime bounds checking.

As before, you use numeric_limits to obtain a yuge value ❶. When you try to numeric_cast yuge into an int ❷, you get a positive_overflow exception because the value is too large to store ❸.

NOTE *The boost::numeric_cast function template is a suitable replacement for the narrow_cast you hand-rolled in Listing 6-6 on page 154.*

Compile-Time Rational Arithmetic

The stdlib std::ratio in the <ratio> header is a class template that enables you to compute rational arithmetic at compile time. You provide two template parameters to std::ratio: a numerator and a denominator. This defines a new type that you can use to compute rational expressions.

The way you perform compile-time computation with std::ratio is by using template metaprogramming techniques. For example, to multiply two ratio types, you can use the std::ratio_multiply type, which takes the two ratio types as template parameters. You can extract the numerator and denominator of the result using static member variables on the resulting type.

Listing 12-37 illustrates how to multiply 10 by 2/3 at compile time.

```
#include <ratio>

TEST_CASE("std::ratio") {
  using ten = std::ratio<10, 1>; ❶
  using two_thirds = std::ratio<2, 3>; ❷
  using result = std::ratio_multiply<ten, two_thirds>; ❸
  REQUIRE(result::num == 20); ❹
  REQUIRE(result::den == 3); ❺
}
```

Listing 12-37: Compile time rational arithmetic with `std::ratio`

You declare the `std::ratio` types `ten` ❶ and `two_thirds` ❷ as type aliases. To compute the product of `ten` and `two_thirds`, you again declare another type, `result`, using the `std::ratio_multiply` template ❸. Using the static members `num` and `den`, you can extract the result, 20/3 ❹❺.

Of course, it's always better to do computation at compile time rather than at runtime when you can. Your programs will be more efficient because they'll need to do less computation when they run.

A Partial List of Random Number Distributions

Table 12-16 contains a partial list of the operations provided by stdlib's `<ratio>` library.

Table 12-16: A Partial List of Operations Available in `<ratio>`

Distribution	Notes
`ratio_add<r1, r2>`	Adds `r1` and `r2`
`ratio_subtract<r1, r2>`	Subtracts `r2` from `r1`
`ratio_multiply<r1, r2>`	Multiplies `r1` and `r2`
`ratio_divide<r1, r2>`	Divides `r1` by `r2`
`ratio_equal<r1, r2>`	Tests whether `r1` equals `r2`
`ratio_not_equal<r1, r2>`	Tests whether `r1` is not equal to `r2`
`ratio_less<r1, r2>`	Tests whether `r1` is less than `r2`
`ratio_greater<r1, r2>`	Tests whether `r1` is greater than `r2`
`ratio_less_equal<r1, r2>`	Tests whether `r1` is less than or equal to `r2`
`ratio_greater_equal<r1, r2>`	Tests whether `r1` is greater than or equal to `r2`
`micro`	Literal: `ratio<1, 1000000>`
`milli`	Literal: `ratio<1, 1000>`
`centi`	Literal: `ratio<1, 100>`
`deci`	Literal: `ratio<1, 10>`
`deca`	Literal: `ratio<10, 1>`

Distribution	Notes
`hecto`	Literal: `ratio<100, 1>`
`kilo`	Literal: `ratio<1000, 1>`
`mega`	Literal: `ratio<1000000, 1>`
`giga`	Literal: `ratio<1000000000, 1>`

Summary

In this chapter, you examined a potpourri of small, simple, focused utilities that service common programming needs. Data structures, such as `tribool`, `optional`, `pair`, `tuple`, `any`, and `variant` handle many commonplace scenarios in which you need to contain objects within a common structure. In the coming chapters, a few of these data structures will make repeat appearances throughout the stdlib. You also learned about date/time and numerics/math facilities. These libraries implement very specific functionality, but when you have such requirements, these libraries are invaluable.

EXERCISES

12-1. Reimplement the `narrow_cast` in Listing 6-6 to return a `std::optional`. If the cast would result in a narrowing conversion, return an empty optional rather than throwing an exception. Write a unit test that ensures your solution works.

12-2. Implement a program that generates random alphanumeric passwords and writes them to the console. You can store the alphabet of possible characters into a `char[]` and use the discrete uniform distribution with a minimum of zero and a maximum of the last index of your alphabet array. Use a cryptographically secure random number engine.

FURTHER READING

- *ISO International Standard ISO/IEC (2017) — Programming Language C++* (International Organization for Standardization; Geneva, Switzerland; *https://isocpp.org/std/the-standard/*)
- *The Boost C++ Libraries*, 2nd Edition, by Boris Schäling (XML Press, 2014)
- *The C++ Standard Library: A Tutorial and Reference*, 2nd Edition, by Nicolai M. Josuttis (Addison-Wesley Professional, 2012)

13

CONTAINERS

Fixing bugs in `std::vector` *is equal parts delight (it is the bestest data structure) and terror (if I mess it up, the world explodes).*
—Stephan T. Lavavej (Principal Developer, Visual C++ Libraries). Tweet dated 3:11 AM on August 22, 2016.

The *standard template library (STL)* is the portion of the stdlib that provides containers and the algorithms to manipulate them, with iterators serving as the interface between the two. In the next three chapters, you'll learn more about each of these components.

A *container* is a special data structure that stores objects in an organized way that follows specific access rules. There are three kinds of containers:

- Sequence containers store elements consecutively, as in an array.
- Associative containers store sorted elements.
- Unordered associative containers store hashed objects.

Associative and unordered associative containers offer rapid search for individual elements. All containers are RAII wrappers around their contained objects, so they manage the storage durations and lifetimes of the elements they own. Additionally, each container provides some set of member functions that perform various operations on the object collection.

Modern C++ programs use containers all the time. Which container you choose for a particular application depends on the required operations, the contained objects' characteristics, and efficiencies under particular access patterns. This chapter surveys the vast container landscape covered between the STL and Boost. Because there are so many containers in these libraries, you'll explore the most popular ones.

Sequence Containers

Sequence containers are STL containers that allow sequential member access. That is, you can start from one end of the container and iterate through to the other end. But except for this commonality, sequence containers are a varied and motley crew. Some containers have a fixed length; others can shrink and grow as program needs dictate. Some allow indexing directly into the container, whereas you can only access others sequentially. Additionally, each sequence container has unique performance characteristics that make it desirable in some situations and undesirable in others.

Working with sequence containers should feel intuitive because you've been acquainted with a primitive one since "Arrays" on page 42, where you saw the built-in or "C-style" array `T[]`. You'll begin the survey of sequence containers by looking at the built-in array's more sophisticated, cooler younger brother `std::array`.

Arrays

The STL provides `std::array` in the `<array>` header. An `array` is a sequential container that holds a fixed-size, contiguous series of elements. It combines the sheer performance and efficiency of built-in arrays with the modern conveniences of supporting copy/move construction/assignment, knowing its own size, providing bounds-checked member access, and other advanced features.

You should use `array` instead of built-in arrays in virtually all situations. It supports almost all the same usage patterns as `operator[]` to access elements, so there aren't many situations in which you'll need a built-in array instead.

NOTE *Boost also offers a `boost::array` in Boost Array's `<boost/array.hpp>`. You shouldn't need to use the Boost version unless you have a very old C++ tool chain.*

Constructing

The `array<T, S>` class template takes two template parameters:

- The contained type `T`
- The fixed size of the array `S`

You can construct an array and built-in arrays using the same rules. To summarize these rules from "Arrays" on page 42, the preferred method is to use braced initialization to construct an array. Braced initialization fills the array with the values contained in the braces and fills the remaining elements with zeros. If you omit initialization braces, the array contains uninitialized values depending on its storage duration. Listing 13-1 illustrates braced initialization with several array declarations.

```
#include <array>

std::array<int, 10> static_array; ❶

TEST_CASE("std::array") {
  REQUIRE(static_array[0] == 0); ❷

  SECTION("uninitialized without braced initializers") {
    std::array<int, 10> local_array; ❸
    REQUIRE(local_array[0] != 0); ❹
  }

  SECTION("initialized with braced initializers") {
    std::array<int, 10> local_array{ 1, 1, 2, 3 }; ❺
    REQUIRE(local_array[0] == 1);
    REQUIRE(local_array[1] == 1);
    REQUIRE(local_array[2] == 2);
    REQUIRE(local_array[3] == 3);
    REQUIRE(local_array[4] == 0); ❻
  }
}
```

Listing 13-1: Initializing a `std::array`*. You might get compiler warnings from* `REQUIRE(local_array[0] != 0);` *❹, since* `local_array` *has uninitialized elements.*

You declare an array of 10 `int` objects called `static_array` with static storage duration ❶. You haven't used braced initialization, but its elements initialize to zero anyway ❷, thanks to the initialization rules covered in "Arrays" on page 42.

Next, you try declaring another array of 10 `int` objects, this time with automatic storage duration ❸. Because you haven't used braced initialization, `local_array` contains uninitialized elements (that have an extremely low probability of equaling zero ❹).

Finally, you use braced initialization to declare another array and to fill the first four elements ❺. All remaining elements get set to zero ❻.

Element Access

The three main methods by which you can access arbitrary array elements are:

- `operator[]`
- `at`
- `get`

The operator[] and at methods take a single size_t argument corresponding to the index of the desired element. The difference between these two lies in bounds checking: if the index argument is out of bounds, at will throw a std::out_of_range exception, whereas operator[] will cause undefined behavior. The function template get takes a template parameter of the same specification. Because it's a template, the index must be known at compile time.

NOTE *Recall from "The size_t Type" on page 41 that a size_t object guarantees that its maximum value is sufficient to represent the maximum size in bytes of all objects. It is for this reason that operator[] and at take a size_t rather than an int, which makes no such guarantee.*

A major bonus of using get is that you get compile-time bounds checking, as illustrated in Listing 13-2.

```
TEST_CASE("std::array access") {
   std::array<int, 4> fib{ 1, 1, 0, 3}; ❶

  SECTION("operator[] can get and set elements") {
    fib[2] = 2; ❷
    REQUIRE(fib[2] == 2); ❸
    // fib[4] = 5; ❹
  }

  SECTION("at() can get and set elements") {
    fib.at(2) = 2; ❺
    REQUIRE(fib.at(2) == 2); ❻
    REQUIRE_THROWS_AS(fib.at(4), std::out_of_range); ❼
  }
  SECTION("get can get and set elements") {
    std::get<2>(fib) = 2; ❽
    REQUIRE(std::get<2>(fib) == 2); ❾
    // std::get<4>(fib); ❿
  }
}
```

Listing 13-2: Accessing elements of an array. Uncommenting // fib[4] = 5; ❹ will cause undefined behavior, whereas uncommenting // std::get<4>(fib); ❿ will cause compilation failure.

You declare an array of length 4 called fib ❶. Using operator[] ❷ you can set elements and retrieve them ❸. The out of bounds write you've commented out would cause undefined behavior; there is no bounds checking with operator[] ❹.

You can use at for the same read ❺ and write ❻ operations, and you can safely perform an out-of-bounds operation thanks to bounds checking ❼.

Finally, you can use std::get to set ❽ and get ❾ elements. The get element also performs bounds checking, so // std::get<4>(fib); ❿ will fail to compile if uncommented.

You've also have a front and a back method, which return references to the first and last elements of the array. You'll get undefined behavior if you call one of these methods if the array has zero length, as Listing 13-3 illustrates.

```
TEST_CASE("std::array has convenience methods") {
  std::array<int, 4> fib{ 0, 1, 2, 0 };

  SECTION("front") {
    fib.front() = 1; ❶
    REQUIRE(fib.front() == 1); ❷
    REQUIRE(fib.front() == fib[0]); ❸
  }

  SECTION("back") {
    fib.back() = 3; ❹
    REQUIRE(fib.back() == 3); ❺
    REQUIRE(fib.back() == fib[3]); ❻
  }
}
```

Listing 13-3: Using the convenience methods `front` and `back` on a `std::array`

You can use the `front` and `back` methods to set ❶❹ and get ❷❺ the first and last elements of an `array`. Of course, `fib[0]` is identical to `fib.front()` ❸, and `fib[3]` is identical to `fib.back()` ❻. The `front()` and `back()` methods are simply convenience methods. Additionally, if you're writing generic code, some containers will offer `front` and `back` but not `operator[]`, so it's best to use the `front` and `back` methods.

Storage Model

An `array` doesn't make allocations; rather, like a built-in array, it contains all of its elements. This means copies will generally be expensive, because each constituent element needs to be copied. Moves can be expensive, depending on whether the underlying type of the `array` also has move construction and move assignment, which are relatively inexpensive.

Each `array` is just a built-in array underneath. In fact, you can extract a pointer to the first element of an `array` using four distinct methods:

- The go-to method is to use the `data` method. As advertised, this returns a pointer to the first element.
- The other three methods involve using the address-of operator `&` on the first element, which you can obtain using `operator[]`, `at`, and `front`.

You should use `data`. If the `array` is empty, the address-of-based approaches will return undefined behavior.

Listing 13-4 illustrates how to obtain a pointer using these four methods.

```
TEST_CASE("We can obtain a pointer to the first element using") {
  std::array<char, 9> color{ 'o', 'c', 't', 'a', 'r', 'i', 'n', 'e' };
  const auto* color_ptr = color.data(); ❶

  SECTION("data") {
    REQUIRE(*color_ptr == 'o'); ❷
  }
  SECTION("address-of front") {
    REQUIRE(&color.front() == color_ptr); ❸
  }
  SECTION("address-of at(0)") {
    REQUIRE(&color.at(0) == color_ptr); ❹
  }
  SECTION("address-of [0]") {
    REQUIRE(&color[0] == color_ptr); ❺
  }
}
```

Listing 13-4: Obtaining a pointer to the first element of a `std::array`

After initializing the array `color`, you obtain a pointer to the first element, the letter `o`, using the `data` method ❶. When you dereference the resulting `color_ptr`, you obtain the letter `o` as expected ❷. This pointer is identical to the pointer obtained from the `address-of-plus-front` ❸, `-at` ❹, and `-operator[]` ❺ approaches.

To conclude arrays, you can query the size of an array using either the `size` or `max_size` methods. (These are identical for an `array`.) Because an `array` has a fixed size, these method's values are static and known at compile time.

A Crash Course in Iterators

The interface between containers and algorithms is the iterator. An iterator is a type that knows the internal structure of a container and exposes simple, pointer-like operations to a container's elements. Chapter 14 is dedicated entirely to iterators, but you need to know the very basics here so you can explore how to use iterators to manipulate containers and how containers expose iterators to users.

Iterators come in various flavors, but they all support at least the following operations:

1. Get the current element (`operator*`)
2. Go to the next element (`operator++`)
3. Assign an iterator equal to another iterator (`operator=`)

You can extract iterators from all STL containers (including `array`) using their `begin` and `end` methods. The `begin` method returns an iterator pointing to the first element, and the `end` method returns a pointer to one element past the last element. Figure 13-1 illustrates where the `begin` and `end` iterators point in an array of three elements.

Figure 13-1: A half-open range over an array of three elements

The arrangement in Figure 13-1, where end() points after the last element, is called a *half-open range*. It might seem counterintuitive at first—why not have a closed range where end() points to the last element—but a half-open range has some advantages. For example, if a container is empty, begin() will return the same value as end(). This allows you to know that, regardless of whether the container is empty, if the iterator equals end(), you've traversed the container.

Listing 13-5 illustrates what happens with half-open range iterators and empty containers.

```
TEST_CASE("std::array begin/end form a half-open range") {
  std::array<int, 0> e{}; ❶
  REQUIRE(e.begin()❷ == e.end()❸);
}
```

Listing 13-5: With an empty array, the begin iterator equals the end iterator.

Here, you construct an empty array e ❶, and the begin ❷ and end ❸ iterators are equal.

Listing 13-6 examines how to use iterators to perform pointer-like operations over a non-empty array.

```
TEST_CASE("std::array iterators are pointer-like") {
  std::array<int, 3> easy_as{ 1, 2, 3 }; ❶
  auto iter = easy_as.begin(); ❷
  REQUIRE(*iter == 1); ❸
  ++iter; ❹
  REQUIRE(*iter == 2);
  ++iter;
  REQUIRE(*iter == 3); ❺
  ++iter; ❻
  REQUIRE(iter == easy_as.end()); ❼
}
```

Listing 13-6: Basic array iterator operations

The array easy_as contains the elements 1, 2, and 3 ❶. You invoke begin on easy_as to obtain an iterator iter pointing to the first element ❷. The dereference operator yields the first element 1, because this is the first element in the array ❸. Next, you increment iter so it points to the next element ❹. You continue in this fashion until you reach the last element ❺. Incrementing the pointer one last time puts you 1 past the last element ❻, so iter equals easy_as.end(), indicating that you've traversed the array ❼.

Recall from "Range Expressions" on page 235 that you can build your own types for use in range expressions by exposing a begin and an end method, as implemented in the FibonacciIterator in Listing 8-29. Well, containers already do all this work for you, meaning you can use any STL container as a range expression. Listing 13-7 illustrates by iterating over an array.

```
TEST_CASE("std::array can be used as a range expression") {
  std::array<int, 5> fib{ 1, 1, 2, 3, 5 }; ❶
  int sum{}; ❷
  for (const auto element : fib) ❸
    sum += element; ❹
  REQUIRE(sum == 12);
}
```

Listing 13-7: Range-based for loops and arrays

You initialize an array ❶ and a sum variable ❷. Because array is a valid range, you can use it in a ranged-based for loop ❸. This enables you to accumulate the sum of each element ❹.

A Partial List of Supported Operations

Table 13-1 provides a partial list of array operations. In this table, a, a1, and a2 are of type std::array<T, S>, t is of type T, S is the fixed length of the array, and i is of type size_t.

Table 13-1: A Partial List of std::array Operations

Operation	Notes
array<T, S>{ ... }	Performs braced initialization of a newly constructed array.
~array	Destructs all elements contained by the array.
a1 = a2	Copy-assigns all the members of a1 with the members of a2.
a.at(i)	Returns a reference to element i of a. Throws std::out_of_range if out of bounds.
a[i]	Returns a reference to element i of a. Undefined behavior if out of bounds.
get<i>(a)	Returns a reference to element i of a. Fails to compile if out of bounds.
a.front()	Returns a reference to first element.
a.back()	Returns a reference to last element.
a.data()	Returns a raw pointer to the first element if the array is non-empty. For empty arrays, returns a valid but non-dereferencable pointer.
a.empty()	Returns true if the array's size is zero; otherwise false.
a.size()	Returns the size of the array.
a.max_size()	Identical to a.size().
a.fill(t)	Copy-assigns t to every element of a.

Operation	Notes
`a1.swap(a2)` `swap(a1, a2)`	Exchanges each element of `a1` with those of `a2`.
`a.begin()`	Returns an iterator pointing to the first element.
`a.cbegin()`	Returns a `const` iterator pointing to the first element.
`a.end()`	Returns an iterator pointing to 1 past the last element.
`a.cend()`	Returns a `const` iterator pointing to 1 past the last element.

`a1 == a2`
`a1 != a2`
`a1 > a2`
`a1 >= a2`
`a1 < a2`
`a1 <= a2`
	Equal if all elements are equal.
	Greater than/less than comparisons proceed from first element to last.

NOTE *The partial operations in Table 13-1 function as quick, reasonably comprehensive references. For gritty details, refer to the freely available online references* https://cppreference.com/ *and* http://cplusplus.com/, *as well as Chapter 31 of* The C++ Programming Language, *4th Edition, by Bjarne Stroustrup and Chapters 7, 8, and 12 of* The C++ Standard Library, *2nd Edition, by Nicolai M. Josuttis.*

Vectors

The `std::vector` available in the STL's `<vector>` header is a sequential container that holds a dynamically sized, contiguous series of elements. A `vector` manages its storage dynamically, requiring no outside help from the programmer.

The `vector` is the workhorse of the sequential-data-structure stable. For a very modest overhead, you gain substantial flexibility over the array. Plus, `vector` supports almost all of the same operations as an `array` and adds a slew of others. If you have a fixed number of elements on hand, you should strongly consider an `array` because you'll get some small reductions in overhead versus a `vector`. In all other situations, your go-to sequential container is the `vector`.

NOTE *The Boost Container library also contains a* `boost::container::vector` *in the* `<boost/container/vector.hpp>` *header.*

Constructing

The class template `std::vector<T, Allocator>` takes two template parameters. The first is the contained type `T`, and the second is the allocator type `Allocator`, which is optional and defaults to `std::allocator<T>`.

You have much more flexibility in constructing `vector`s than you do with arrays. A `vector` supports user-defined allocators because `vector`s need to allocate dynamic memory. You can default construct a `vector` so it contains no elements. You might want to construct an empty `vector` so you can fill it with a variable number of elements depending on what happens during runtime. Listing 13-8 illustrates default constructing a vector and checking that it contains no elements.

```
#include <vector>
TEST_CASE("std::vector supports default construction") {
  std::vector<const char*❶> vec; ❷
  REQUIRE(vec.empty()); ❸
}
```

Listing 13-8: A vector supports default construction.

You declare a vector containing elements of type `const char*` ❶ called `vec`. Because it's been default constructed ❷, the `vector` contains no elements, and the `empty` method returns `true` ❸.

You can use braced initialization with a `vector`. Similar to how you brace initialize an array, this fills the vector with the specified elements, as Listing 13-9 illustrates.

```
TEST_CASE("std::vector supports braced initialization ") {
    std::vector<int> fib{ 1, 1, 2, 3, 5 }; ❶
    REQUIRE(fib[4] == 5); ❷
}
```

Listing 13-9: A vector supports braced initializers.

Here, you construct a `vector` called `fib` and use braced initializers ❶. After initialization, the `vector` contains the five elements 1, 1, 2, 3, and 5 ❷.

If you want to populate a `vector` with many identical values, you can use one of the *fill constructors*. To fill construct a `vector`, you first pass a `size_t` corresponding to the number of elements you want to fill. Optionally, you can pass a `const` reference to an object to copy. Sometimes you want to initialize all your elements to the same value, for example, to keep track of counts related to particular indices. You might also have a `vector` of some user-defined type that keeps track of program state, and you might need to keep track of such state by index.

Unfortunately, the general rule to use braced initialization to construct objects breaks down here. With `vector`, you must use parentheses to invoke these constructors. To the compiler, `std::vector<int>{ 99, 100 }` specifies an initialization list with the elements 99 and 100, which will construct a vector with the two elements 99 and 100. What if you want a vector with 99 copies of the number 100?

In general, the compiler will try very hard to treat the initializer list as elements to fill the vector with. You can try to memorize the rules (refer to Item 7 of *Effective Modern C++* by Scott Meyers) or just commit to using parentheses for stdlib container constructors.

Listing 13-10 highlights the initializer list/braced initialization general rule for STL containers.

```
TEST_CASE("std::vector supports") {
  SECTION("braced initialization") {
    std::vector<int> five_nine{ 5, 9 }; ❶
```

```
    REQUIRE(five_nine[0] == 5); ❷
    REQUIRE(five_nine[1] == 9); ❸
  }
  SECTION("fill constructor") {
    std::vector<int> five_nines(5, 9); ❹
    REQUIRE(five_nines[0] == 9); ❺
    REQUIRE(five_nines[4] == 9); ❻
  }
}
```

Listing 13-10: A vector supports braced initializers and fill constructors.

The first example uses braced initialization to construct a vector with two elements ❶: 5 at index 0 ❷ and 9 at index 1 ❸. The second example uses parentheses to invoke the fill constructor ❹, which fills the vector with five copies of the number 9, so the first ❺ and last ❻ elements are both 9.

NOTE *This notational clash is unfortunate and isn't the result of some well-thought-out trade-off. The reasons are purely historical and related to backward compatibility.*

You can also construct vectors from a half-open range by passing in the begin and end iterators of the range you want to copy. In various programming contexts, you might want to splice out a subset of some range and copy it into a vector for further processing. For example, you could construct a vector that copies all the elements contained by an array, as in Listing 13-11.

```
TEST_CASE("std::vector supports construction from iterators") {
  std::array<int, 5> fib_arr{ 1, 1, 2, 3, 5 }; ❶
  std::vector<int> fib_vec(fib_arr.begin(), fib_arr.end()); ❷
  REQUIRE(fib_vec[4] == 5); ❸
  REQUIRE(fib_vec.size() == fib_arr.size()); ❹
}
```

Listing 13-11: Constructing a vector from a range

You construct the array fib_arr with five elements ❶. To construct the vector fib_vec with the elements contained in fib_arr, you invoke the begin and end methods on fib_arr ❷. The resulting vector has copies of the array's elements ❸ and has the same size ❹.

At a high level, you can think of this constructor as taking pointers to the beginning and the end of some target sequence. It will then copy that target sequence.

Move and Copy Semantics

With vectors, you have full copy/move construction/assignment support. Any vector copy operation is potentially very expensive, because these are element-wise or deep copies. Move operations, on the other hand, are usually very fast, because the contained elements reside in dynamic memory and the moved-from vector can simply pass ownership to the moved-into vector; there's no need to move the contained elements.

Element Access

A vector supports most of the same element access operations as array: at, operator[], front, back, and data.

As with an array, you can query the number of contained elements in a vector using the size method. This method's return value can vary at runtime. You can also determine whether a vector contains any elements with the empty method, which returns true if the vector contains no elements; otherwise, it returns false.

Adding Elements

You can use various methods to insert elements into a vector. If you want to replace all the elements in a vector, you can use the assign method, which takes an initialization list and replaces all the existing elements. If needed, the vector will resize to accommodate a larger list of elements, as Listing 13-12 illustrates.

```
TEST_CASE("std::vector assign replaces existing elements") {
  std::vector<int> message{ 13, 80, 110, 114, 102, 110, 101 }; ➊
  REQUIRE(message.size() == 7); ➋
  message.assign({ 67, 97, 101, 115, 97, 114 }); ➌
  REQUIRE(message[5] == 114); ➍
  REQUIRE(message.size() == 6); ➎
}
```

Listing 13-12: The assign method of a vector

Here, you construct a vector ➊ with seven elements ➋. When you assign a new, smaller initializer list ➌, all the elements get replaced ➍, and the vector's size updates to reflect the new contents ➎.

If you want to insert a single new element into a vector, you can use the insert method, which expects two arguments: an iterator and an element to insert. It will insert a copy of the given element just before the existing element pointed to by the iterator, as shown in Listing 13-13.

```
TEST_CASE("std::vector insert places new elements") {
  std::vector<int> zeros(3, 0); ➊
  auto third_element = zeros.begin() + 2; ➋
  zeros.insert(third_element, 10); ➌
  REQUIRE(zeros[2] == 10); ➍
  REQUIRE(zeros.size() == 4); ➎
}
```

Listing 13-13: The insert method of a vector

You initialize a vector with three zeros ➊ and generate an iterator pointing to the third element of zeros ➋. Next, you insert the value 10 immediately before the third element by passing the iterator and the value 10 ➌. The third element of zeros is now 10 ➍. The zeros vector now contains four elements ➎.

Any time you use insert, existing iterators become invalid. For example, in Listing 13-13 you must not reuse third_element: the vector could have resized and relocated in memory, leaving the old iterator dangling in garbage memory.

To insert an element to the end of a vector, you use the push_back method. Unlike insert, push_back doesn't require an iterator argument. You simply provide the element to copy into the vector, as shown in Listing 13-14.

```
TEST_CASE("std::vector push_back places new elements") {
  std::vector<int> zeros(3, 0); ❶
  zeros.push_back(10); ❷
  REQUIRE(zeros[3] == 10); ❸
}
```

Listing 13-14: The push_back method of a vector

Again, you initialize a vector with three zeros ❶, but this time you insert the element 10 to the back of the vector using the push_back method ❷. The vector now contains four elements, the last of which equals 10 ❸.

You can construct new elements in place using the emplace and emplace_back methods. The emplace method is a variadic template that, like insert, accepts an iterator as its first argument. The remaining arguments get forwarded to the appropriate constructor. The emplace_back method is also a variadic template, but like push_back, it doesn't require an iterator. It accepts any number of arguments and forwards those to the appropriate constructor. Listing 13-15 illustrates these two methods by emplacing a few pairs into a vector.

```
#include <utility>

TEST_CASE("std::vector emplace methods forward arguments") {
  std::vector<std::pair<int, int>> factors; ❶
  factors.emplace_back(2, 30); ❷
  factors.emplace_back(3, 20); ❸
  factors.emplace_back(4, 15); ❹
  factors.emplace(factors.begin()❺, 1, 60);
  REQUIRE(factors[0].first == 1); ❻
  REQUIRE(factors[0].second == 60); ❼
}
```

Listing 13-15: The emplace_back and emplace methods of a vector

Here, you default construct a vector containing pairs of ints ❶. Using the emplace_back method, you push three pairs onto the vector: 2, 30 ❷; 3, 20 ❸; and 4, 15 ❹. These values get forwarded directly to the constructor of pair, which gets constructed in place. Next, you use emplace to insert a new pair at the beginning of the vector by passing the result of factors.begin() as the first argument ❺. This causes all the elements in the vector to shift down to make room for the new pair (1 ❻, 60 ❼).

NOTE *There's absolutely nothing special about a* `std::vector<std::pair<int, int>>`*. It's just like any other* `vector`*. The individual elements in this sequential container just happen to be a* `pair`*. Because* `pair` *has a constructor that accepts two arguments, one for* `first` *and one for* `second`*,* `emplace_back` *can add a new element by simply passing the two values it should write into the newly created* `pair`*.*

Because the emplacement methods can construct elements in place, it seems they should be more efficient than the insertion methods. This intuition is often correct, but for complicated and unsatisfying reasons it's not always faster. As a general rule, use the emplacement methods. If you determine a performance bottleneck, also try the insertion methods. See Item 42 of *Effective Modern C++* by Scott Meyers for a treatise.

Storage Model

Although `vector` elements are contiguous in memory, like an `array`, the similarities stop there. A `vector` has dynamic size, so it must be able to resize. The allocator of a `vector` manages the dynamic memory underpinning the `vector`.

Because allocations are expensive, a `vector` will request more memory than it needs to contain the current number of elements. Once it can no longer add any more elements, it will request additional memory. The memory for a `vector` is always contiguous, so if there isn't enough space at the end of the existing vector, it will allocate a whole new region of memory and move all the elements of the `vector` into the new region. The number of elements a `vector` holds is called its *size*, and the number of elements it could theoretically hold before having to resize is called its *capacity*. Figure 13-2 illustrates a `vector` containing three elements with additional capacity for three more.

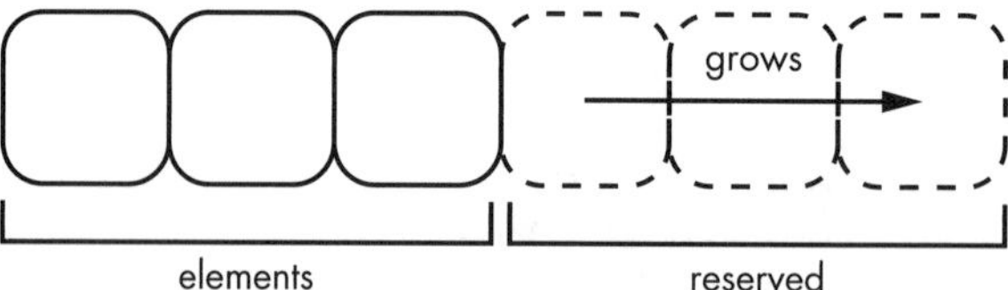

Figure 13-2: The `vector` *storage model*

As Figure 13-2 shows, the `vector` continues past the last element. The capacity determines how many elements the `vector` could hold in this space. In this figure, the size is three and the capacity is six. You can think of the memory in a `vector` as an auditorium: it might have a capacity of 500 but a crowd size of only 250.

The upshot of this design is that inserting at the end of a `vector` is extremely fast (unless the `vector` needs to resize). Inserting anywhere else incurs additional cost, because the `vector` needs to move elements around to make room.

You can obtain the vector's current capacity via the capacity method, and you can obtain the absolute maximum capacity that a vector could resize to with the max_size method.

If you know ahead of time that you'll need a certain capacity, you can use the reserve method, which takes a single size_t argument corresponding to the number of elements you want capacity for. On the other hand, if you've just removed several elements and want to return memory to the allocator, you can use the shrink_to_fit method, which declares that you have excess capacity. The allocator can decide to reduce capacity or not (it's a non-binding call).

Additionally, you can delete all the elements in a vector and set its size to zero using the clear method.

Listing 13-16 demonstrates all these storage-related methods in a cohesive story: you create an empty vector, reserve a bunch of space, add some elements, release excess capacity, and finally empty the vector.

```
#include <cstdint>
#include <array>

TEST_CASE("std::vector exposes size management methods") {
  std::vector<std::array<uint8_t, 1024>> kb_store; ❶
  REQUIRE(kb_store.max_size() > 0);
  REQUIRE(kb_store.empty()); ❷

  size_t elements{ 1024 };
  kb_store.reserve(elements); ❸
  REQUIRE(kb_store.empty());
  REQUIRE(kb_store.capacity() == elements); ❹

  kb_store.emplace_back();
  kb_store.emplace_back();
  kb_store.emplace_back();
  REQUIRE(kb_store.size() == 3); ❺

  kb_store.shrink_to_fit();
  REQUIRE(kb_store.capacity() >= 3); ❻

  kb_store.clear(); ❼
  REQUIRE(kb_store.empty());
  REQUIRE(kb_store.capacity() >= 3); ❽
}
```

Listing 13-16: The storage management functions of a vector. (Strictly speaking, kb_store .capacity() >= 3 ❻❽ is not guaranteed because the call is non-binding.)

You construct a vector of array objects called kb_store, which stores 1 KiB chunks ❶. Unless you're using a peculiar platform with no dynamic memory, kb_store.max_size() will be greater than zero; because you default initialize the vector, it's empty ❷.

Next, you reserve 1,024 elements ❸, which doesn't change the vector's empty status but increases its capacity to match ❹. The vector now has 1,024 × 1 KiB = 1 MiB of contiguous space reserved. After reserving space, you emplace three arrays and check that `kb_store.size()` increased accordingly ❺.

You've reserved space for 1,024 elements. To release the 1,024 – 3 = 1,021 elements you aren't using back to the allocator, you call `shrink_to_fit`, which reduces the capacity to 3 ❻.

Finally, you invoke `clear` on the `vector` ❼, which destructs all elements and reduces its size to zero. However, the capacity remains unchanged because you haven't made another call to `shrink_to_fit` ❽. This is significant because the vector doesn't want to do extra work if you're going to add elements again.

A Partial List of Supported Operations

Table 13-2 provides a partial list of `vector` operations. In this table, `v`, `v1`, and `v2` are of type `std::vector<T>`, `t` is of type `T`, `alc` is an appropriate allocator, and `itr` is an iterator. An asterisk (*) indicates that this operation invalidates raw pointers and iterators to v's elements in at least some circumstances.

Table 13-2: A Partial List of `std::vector` Operations

Operation	Notes
`vector<T>{ ..., [alc]}`	Performs braced initialization of a newly constructed vector. Uses `alc=std::allocator<T>` by default.
`vector<T>(s,[t], [alc])`	Fills the newly constructed vector with `s` number of copies of `t`. If no `t` is provided, default constructs `T` instances.
`vector<T>(v)`	Deep copy of `v`; allocates new memory.
`vector<T>(move(v))`	Takes ownership of memory, elements in `v`. No allocations.
`~vector`	Destructs all elements contained by the vector and releases dynamic memory.
`v.begin()`	Returns an iterator pointing to the first element.
`v.cbegin()`	Returns a `const` iterator pointing to the first element.
`v.end()`	Returns an iterator pointing to 1 past the last element.
`v.cend()`	Returns a `const` iterator pointing to 1 past the last element.
`v1 = v2`	`v1` destructs its elements; copies each `v2` element. Only allocates if it needs to resize to fit `v2`'s elements.*
`v1 = move(v2)`	`v1` destructs its elements; moves each `v2` element. Only allocates if it needs to resize to fit `v2`'s elements.*
`v.at(0)`	Accesses element `0` of `v`. Throws `std::out_of_range` if out of bounds.
`v[0]`	Accesses element `0` of `v`. Undefined behavior if out of bounds.
`v.front()`	Accesses first element.
`v.back()`	Accesses last element.

Operation	Notes
`v.data()`	Returns a raw pointer to the first element if array is non-empty. For empty arrays, returns a valid but non-dereferencable pointer.
`v.assign({ ... })`	Replaces the contents of `v` with the elements `...`.*
`v.assign(s, t)`	Replaces the contents of `v` with `s` number of copies of `t`.*
`v.empty()`	Returns `true` if vector's size is zero; otherwise `false`.
`v.size()`	Returns the number of elements in the vector.
`v.capacity()`	Returns the maximum number of elements the vector could hold without having to resize.
`v.shrink_to_fit()`	Might reduce the vector's storage so `capacity()` equals `size()`.*
`v.resize(s, [t])`	Resizes `v` to contain `s` elements. If this shrinks `v`, destructs elements at the end. If this grows `v`, inserts default constructed `T`s or copies of `t` if provided.*
`v.reserve(s)`	Increases the vector's storage so it can contain at least `s` elements.*
`v.max_size()`	Returns the maximum possible size the vector can resize to.
`v.clear()`	Removes all elements in `v`, but capacity remains.*
`v.insert(itr, t)`	Inserts a copy of `t` just before the element pointed to by `itr`; `v`'s range must contain `itr`.*
`v.push_back(t)`	Inserts a copy of `t` at the end of `v`.*
`v.emplace(itr, ...)`	Constructs a `T` in place by forwarding the arguments `...` to the appropriate constructor. Element inserted just before the element pointed to by `itr`.*
`v.emplace_back(...)`	Constructs a `T` in place by forwarding the arguments `...` to the appropriate constructor. Element inserted at the end of `v`.*
`v1.swap(v2)` `swap(v1, v2)`	Exchanges each element of `v1` with those of `v2`.*

`v1 == v2`
`v1 != v2`
`v1 > v2`
`v1 >= v2`
`v1 < v2`
`v1 <= v2`
	Equal if all elements are equal.
	Greater than/less than comparisons proceed from first element to last.

Niche Sequential Containers

The `vector` and `array` containers are the clear choice in most situations in which you need a sequential data structure. If you know the number of elements you'll need ahead of time, use an `array`. If you don't, use a `vector`.

You might find yourself in a niche situation where `vector` and `array` don't have the performance characteristics you desire. This section highlights a number of alternative sequential containers that might offer superior performance characteristics in such a situation.

Deque

A *deque* (pronounced "deck") is a sequential container with fast insert and remove operations from the front and back. Deque is a portmanteau of **d**ouble-**e**nded **que**ue. The STL implementation `std::deque` is available from the `<deque>` header.

NOTE *The Boost Container library also contains a* `boost::container::deque` *in the* `<boost/container/deque.hpp>` *header.*

A `vector` and a `deque` have very similar interfaces, but internally their storage models are totally different. A `vector` guarantees that all elements are sequential in memory, whereas a `deque`'s memory is usually scattered about, like a hybrid between a `vector` and a `list`. This makes large resizing operations more efficient and enables fast element insertion/deletion at the container's front.

Constructing and accessing members are identical operations for `vector`s and `deque`s.

Because the internal structure of `deque` is complex, it doesn't expose a `data` method. In exchange, you gain access to `push_front` and `emplace_front`, which mirror the `push_back` and `emplace_back` that you're familiar with from `vector`. Listing 13-17 illustrates how to use `push_back` and `push_front` to insert values into a `deque` of `char`s.

```
#include <deque>

TEST_CASE("std::deque supports front insertion") {
  std::deque<char> deckard;
  deckard.push_front('a'); ❶ //  a
  deckard.push_back('i'); ❷ //  ai
  deckard.push_front('c');   // cai
  deckard.push_back('n');    // cain
  REQUIRE(deckard[0] == 'c'); ❸
  REQUIRE(deckard[1] == 'a');
  REQUIRE(deckard[2] == 'i');
  REQUIRE(deckard[3] == 'n');
}
```

Listing 13-17: A deque supports `push_front` and `push_back`.

After constructing an empty `deque`, you push alternating letters to the front ❶ and back ❷ of the `deque` so it contains the elements `c`, `a`, `i`, and `n` ❸.

NOTE *It would be a very bad idea to attempt to extract a string here, for example,* `&deckard[0]`*, because* `deque` *makes no guarantees about internal layout.*

The `vector` methods not implemented by `deque`, along with an explanation for their absence, are as follows:

`capacity`, `reserve` Because the internal structure is complicated, it might not be efficient to compute capacity. Also, `deque` allocations are relatively fast because a deque doesn't relocate existing elements, so reserving memory ahead of time is unnecessary.

data The elements of deque are not contiguous.

Table 13-3 summarizes the additional operators offered by a deque but not by a vector. In this table, d is of type std::deque<T> and t is of type T. An asterisk (*) indicates that this operation invalidates iterators to v's elements in at least some circumstances. (Pointers to existing elements remain valid.)

Table 13-3: A Partial List of std::deque Operations

Operation	Notes
d.emplace_front(...)	Constructs an element in place at the front of the d by forwarding all arguments to the appropriate constructor.*
d.push_front(t)	Constructs an element in place at the front of the d by copying t.*
d.pop_front()	Removes the element at the front of d.*

List

A *list* is a sequence container with fast insert/remove operations everywhere but with no random element access. The STL implementation std::list is available from the <list> header.

NOTE *The Boost Container library also contains a* boost::container::list *in the* <boost/container/list.hpp> *header.*

The list is implemented as a doubly linked list, a data structure composed of *nodes*. Each node contains an element, a forward link ("flink"), and a backward link ("blink"). This is completely different from a vector, which stores elements in contiguous memory. As a result, you cannot use operator[] or at to access arbitrary elements in a list, because such operations would be very inefficient. (These methods are simply not available in list because of their horrible performance characteristics.) The trade-off is that inserting and removing elements in a list is much faster. All you need to update are the flinks and blinks of an element's neighbors rather than shuffling potentially large, contiguous element ranges.

The list container supports the same constructor patterns as vector.

You can perform special operations on lists, such as splicing elements from one list into another using the splice method, removing consecutive duplicate elements using the unique method, and even sorting the elements of a container using the sort method. Consider, for example, the remove_if method. The remove_if method accepts a function object as a parameter, and it traverses the list while invoking the function object on each element. If the result is true, remove_if removes the element. Listing 13-18 illustrates how to use the remove_if method to eliminate all the even numbers of a list with a lambda predicate.

```
#include <list>

TEST_CASE("std::list supports front insertion") {
  std::list<int> odds{ 11, 22, 33, 44, 55 }; ❶
  odds.remove_if([](int x) { return x % 2 == 0; }); ❷
  auto odds_iter = odds.begin(); ❸
  REQUIRE(*odds_iter == 11); ❹
  ++odds_iter; ❺
  REQUIRE(*odds_iter == 33);
  ++odds_iter;
  REQUIRE(*odds_iter == 55);
  ++odds_iter;
  REQUIRE(odds_iter == odds.end()); ❻
}
```

Listing 13-18: A `list` supports `remove_if`.

Here, you use braced initialization to fill a `list` of `int` objects ❶. Next, you use the `remove_if` method to remove all the even numbers ❷. Because only even numbers modulo 2 equal zero, this lambda tests whether a number is even. To establish that `remove_if` has extracted the even elements 22 and 44, you create an iterator pointing at the beginning of the list ❸, check its value ❹, and increment ❺ until you reach the end of the list ❻.

All the `vector` methods not implemented by `list`, along with an explanation for their absence, are as follows:

`capacity, reserve, shrink_to_fit` Because `list` acquires memory incrementally, it doesn't require periodic resizing.

`operator[], at` Random element access is prohibitively expensive on `lists`.

`data` Unneeded because `list` elements are not contiguous.

Table 13-4 summarizes the additional operators offered by a `list` but not by a `vector`. In this table, `lst`, `lst1`, and `lst2` are of type `std::list<T>`, and `t` is of type `T`. The arguments `itr1`, `itr2a`, and `itr2b` are `list` iterators. An asterisk (*) indicates that the operation invalidates iterators to `v`'s elements in at least some circumstances. (Pointers to existing elements remain valid.)

Table 13-4: A Partial List of `std::list` Operations

Operation	Notes
`lst.emplace_front(...)`	Constructs an element in place at the front of the **d** by forwarding all arguments to the appropriate constructor.
`lst.push_front(t)`	Constructs an element in place at the front of **d** by copying **t**.
`lst.pop_front()`	Removes the element at the front of **d**.
`lst.push_back(t)`	Constructs an element in place at the back of **d** by copying **t**.
`lst.pop_back()`	Removes the element at the back of **d**.
`lst1.splice(itr1,lst2, [itr2a], [itr2b])`	Transfers items from **lst2** into **lst1** at position **itr1**. Optionally, only transfer the element at **itr2a** or the elements within the half-open range **itr2a** to **itr2b**.

Operation	Notes
`lst.remove(t)`	Removes all elements in `lst` equal to `t`.
`lst.remove_if(pred)`	Eliminates elements in `lst` where `pred` returns true; `pred` accepts a single `T` argument.
`lst.unique(pred)`	Eliminates duplicate consecutive elements in `lst` according to the function object `pred`, which accepts two `T` arguments and returns `t1 == t2`.
`lst1.merge(lst2, comp)`	Merges `lst1` and `lst2` according to the function object `comp`, which accepts two `T` arguments and returns `t1 < t2`.
`lst.sort(comp)`	Sorts `lst` according to the function object `comp`.
`lst.reverse()`	Reverses the order of `lst`'s elements (mutates `lst`).

NOTE *The STL also offers a `std::forward_list` in the `<forward_list>` header, which is a singly linked list that only allows iteration in one direction. The `forward_list` is slightly more efficient than `list`, and it's optimized for situations in which you need to store very few (or no) elements.*

Stacks

The STL provides three *container adapters* that encapsulate other STL containers and expose special interfaces for tailored situations. The adapters are the stack, the queue, and the priority queue.

A *stack* is a data structure with two fundamental operations: push and pop. When you *push* an element onto a stack, you insert the element onto the stack's end. When you *pop* an element off a stack, you remove the element from the stack's end. This arrangement is called *last-in, first-out*: the last element to be pushed onto a stack is the first to be popped off.

The STL offers the `std::stack` in the `<stack>` header. The class template `stack` takes two template parameters. The first is the underlying type of the wrapped container, such as `int`, and the second is the type of the wrapped container, such as `deque` or `vector`. This second argument is optional and defaults to `deque`.

To construct a `stack`, you can pass a reference to a `deque`, a `vector`, or a `list` to encapsulate. This way, the `stack` translates its operations, such as `push` and `pop`, into methods that the underlying container understands, like `push_back` and `pop_back`. If you provide no constructor argument, the `stack` uses a `deque` by default. The second template parameter must match this container's type.

To obtain a reference to the element on top of a `stack`, you use the `top` method.

Listing 13-19 illustrates how to use a `stack` to wrap a `vector`.

```
#include <stack>

TEST_CASE("std::stack supports push/pop/top operations") {
  std::vector<int> vec{ 1, 3 }; ❶ // 1 3
  std::stack<int, decltype(vec)> easy_as(vec); ❷
```

```
  REQUIRE(easy_as.top() == 3); ❸
  easy_as.pop(); ❹                // 1
  easy_as.push(2); ❺              // 1 2
  REQUIRE(easy_as.top() == 2); ❻
  easy_as.pop();                 // 1
  REQUIRE(easy_as.top() == 1);
  easy_as.pop();                 //
  REQUIRE(easy_as.empty()); ❼
}
```

Listing 13-19: Using a stack to wrap a vector

You construct a vector of ints called vec containing the elements 1 and 3 ❶. Next, you pass vec into the constructor of a new stack, making sure to supply the second template parameter decltype(vec) ❷. The top element in stack is now 3, because this is the last element in vec ❸. After the first pop ❹, you push a new element 2 onto the stack ❺. Now, the top element is 2 ❻. After another pop-top-pop series, the stack is empty ❼.

Table 13-5 summarizes the operations of stack. In this table, s, s1, and s2 are of type std::stack<T>; t is of type T; and ctr is a container of type ctr_type<T>.

Table 13-5: A Summary of std::stack Operations

Operation	Notes
stack<T, [ctr_type<T>]>([ctr])	Constructs a stack of Ts using ctr as its internal container reference. If no container is provided, constructs an empty deque.
s.empty()	Returns true if container is empty.
s.size()	Returns number of elements in container.
s.top()	Returns a reference to the element on top of the stack.
s.push(t)	Puts a copy of t onto the end of the container.
s.emplace(...)	Constructs a T in place by forwarding ... to the appropriate constructor.
s.pop()	Removes the element at the end of the container.
s1.swap(s2) swap(s1, s2)	Exchanges the contents of s2 with s1.

Queues

A *queue* is a data structure that, like a stack, has push and pop as its fundamental operations. Unlike a stack, a queue is *first-in, first-out*. When you push an element into a queue, you insert onto the queue's end. When you pop an element off the queue, you remove from the queue's beginning. This way, the element that has been in the queue the longest is the one to get popped off.

The STL offers the std::queue in the <queue> header. Like stack, queue takes two template parameters. The first parameter is the underlying type of the wrapped container, and the optional second parameter is the type of the wrapped container, which also defaults to deque.

Among STL containers, you can only use deque or list as the underlying container for a queue, because pushing and popping from the front of a vector is inefficient.

You can access the element at the front or back of a queue using the front and back methods.

Listing 13-20 shows how to use a queue to wrap a deque.

```
#include <queue>

TEST_CASE("std::queue supports push/pop/front/back") {
  std::deque<int> deq{ 1, 2 }; ❶
  std::queue<int> easy_as(deq); ❷ // 1 2

  REQUIRE(easy_as.front() == 1); ❸
  REQUIRE(easy_as.back() == 2); ❹
  easy_as.pop(); ❺                // 2
  easy_as.push(3); ❻              // 2 3
  REQUIRE(easy_as.front() == 2); ❼
  REQUIRE(easy_as.back() == 3); ❽
  easy_as.pop();                  // 3
  REQUIRE(easy_as.front() == 3);
  easy_as.pop();                  //
  REQUIRE(easy_as.empty()); ❾
}
```

Listing 13-20: Using a queue to wrap a deque

You start with a deque containing the elements 1 and 2 ❶, which you pass into a queue called easy_as ❷. Using the front and back methods, you can validate that the queue begins with a 1 ❸ and ends with a 2 ❹. When you pop the first element, 1, you're left with a queue containing just the single element 2 ❺. You then push 3 ❻, so the method front yields 2 ❼ and back yields 3 ❽. After two more iterations of pop-front, you're left with an empty queue ❾.

Table 13-6 summarizes the operations of queue. In this table, q, q1, and q2 are of type std::queue<T>; t is of type T; and ctr is a container of type ctr_type<T>.

Table 13-6: A Summary of std::queue Operations

Operation	Notes
queue<T, [ctr_type<T>]>([ctr])	Constructs a queue of Ts using ctr as its internal container. If no container is provided, constructs an empty deque.
q.empty()	Returns true if container is empty.
q.size()	Returns number of elements in container.

(continued)

Table 13-6: A Summary of std::queue Operations (continued)

Operation	Notes
q.front()	Returns a reference to the element in front of the queue.
q.back()	Returns a reference to the element in back of the queue.
q.push(**t**)	Puts a copy of **t** onto the end of the container.
q.emplace(**...**)	Constructs a T in place by forwarding **...** to the appropriate constructor.
q.pop()	Removes the element at the front of the container.
q1.swap(**q2**) swap(**q1**, **q2**)	Exchanges the contents of **q2** with **q1**.

Priority Queues (Heaps)

A *priority queue* (also called a heap) is a data structure that supports push and pop operations and keeps elements sorted according to some user-specified *comparator object*. The comparator object is a function object invokable with two parameters, returning true if the first argument is less than the second. When you pop an element from a priority queue, you remove the element that is greatest, according to the comparator object.

The STL offers the std::priority_queue in the <queue> header. A priority_queue has three template parameters:

- The underlying type of the wrapped container
- The type of the wrapped container
- The type of the comparator object

Only the underlying type is mandatory. The wrapped container type defaults to vector (probably because it's the most widely used sequential container), and the comparator object type defaults to std::less.

NOTE *The* std::less *class template is available from the* <functional> *header, and it returns* true *if the first argument is less than the second.*

The priority_queue has an identical interface to a stack. The only difference is that stacks pop elements according to the last-in, first-out arrangement, whereas priority queues pop elements according to the comparator object criteria.

Listing 13-21 illustrates the basic usage of priority_queue.

```
#include <queue>

TEST_CASE("std::priority_queue supports push/pop") {
  std::priority_queue<double> prique; ❶
  prique.push(1.0); // 1.0
  prique.push(2.0); // 2.0 1.0
  prique.push(1.5); // 2.0 1.5 1.0
```

```
  REQUIRE(prique.top() == Approx(2.0)); ❷
  prique.pop();      // 1.5 1.0
  prique.push(1.0); // 1.5 1.0 1.0
  REQUIRE(prique.top() == Approx(1.5)); ❸
  prique.pop();      // 1.0 1.0
  REQUIRE(prique.top() == Approx(1.0)); ❹
  prique.pop();      // 1.0
  REQUIRE(prique.top() == Approx(1.0)); ❺
  prique.pop();      //
  REQUIRE(prique.empty()); ❻
}
```

Listing 13-21: Basic priority_queue usage

Here, you default construct a priority_queue ❶, which internally initializes an empty vector to hold its elements. You push the elements 1.0, 2.0, and 1.5 into the priority_queue, which sorts the elements in descending order so the container represents them in the order 2.0 1.5 1.0.

You assert that top yields 2.0 ❷, pop this element off the priority_queue, and then invoke push with the new element 1.0. The container now represents them in the order 1.5 ❸ 1.0 ❹ 1.0 ❺, which you verify with a series of top-pop operations until the container is empty ❻.

NOTE *A priority_queue holds its elements in a tree structure, so if you peered into its underlying container, the memory ordering wouldn't match the orders implied by Listing 13-21.*

Table 13-7 summarizes the operations of priority_queue. In this table, pq, pq1, and pq2 are of type std::priority_queue<T>; t is of type T; ctr is a container of type ctr_type<T>; and **srt** is a container of type srt_type<T>.

Table 13-7: A Summary of std::priority_queue Operations

Operation	Notes
priority_queue <**T**, [**ctr_type<T>**], [**cmp_type**]>([**cmp**], [**ctr**])	Constructs a priority_queue of **T**s using **ctr** as its internal container and **srt** as its comparator object. If no container is provided, constructs an empty deque. Uses std::less as default sorter.
pq.empty()	Returns true if container is empty.
pq.size()	Returns number of elements in container.
pq.top()	Returns a reference to the greatest element in the container.
pq.push(**t**)	Puts a copy of **t** onto the end of the container.
pq.emplace(**...**)	Constructs a **T** in place by forwarding **...** to the appropriate constructor.
pq.pop()	Removes the element at the end of the container.
pq1.swap(**pq2**) swap(**pq1**, **pq2**)	Exchanges the contents of **s2** with **s1**.

Bitsets

A *bitset* is a data structure that stores a fixed-size bit sequence. You can manipulate each bit.

The STL offers the `std::bitset` in the `<bitset>` header. The class template `bitset` takes a single template parameter corresponding to the desired size. You could achieve similar functionality using a `bool array`, but `bitset` is optimized for space efficiency and provides some special convenience operations.

> **NOTE** *The STL specializes* `std::vector<bool>`*, so it might benefit from the same space efficiencies as* `bitset`*. (Recall from "Template Specialization" on page 178 that template specialization is the process of making certain kinds of template instantiations more efficient.) Boost offers* `boost::dynamic_bitset`*, which provides dynamic sizing at runtime.*

A default constructed `bitset` contains all zero (false) bits. To initialize bitsets with other contents, you can provide an `unsigned long long` value. This integer's bitwise representation sets the value of `bitset`. You can access individual bits in the `bitset` using `operator[]`. Listing 13-22 demonstrates how to initialize a `bitset` with an integer literal and extract its elements.

```
#include <bitset>

TEST_CASE("std::bitset supports integer initialization") {
  std::bitset<4> bs(0b0101); ❶
  REQUIRE_FALSE(bs[0]); ❷
  REQUIRE(bs[1]); ❸
  REQUIRE_FALSE(bs[2]); ❹
  REQUIRE(bs[3]); ❺
}
```

Listing 13-22: Initializing a `bitset` *with an integer*

You initialize a `bitset` with the 4-bit *nybble* `0101` ❶. So, the first ❷ and third ❹ elements are zero, and the second ❸ and fourth ❺ elements are 1.

You can also provide a string representation of the desired `bitset`, as shown in Listing 13-23.

```
TEST_CASE("std::bitset supports string initialization") {
  std::bitset<4> bs1(0b0110); ❶
  std::bitset<4> bs2("0110"); ❷
  REQUIRE(bs1 == bs2); ❸
}
```

Listing 13-23: Initializing a `bitset` *with a string*

Here, you construct a bitset called bs1 using the same integer nybble 0b0110 ❶ and another bitset called bs2 using the string literal 0110 ❷. Both of these initialization approaches produce identical bitset objects ❸.

Table 13-8 summarizes the operations of bitset. In this table, bs, bs 1, and bs 2 are of type std::bitset<N>, and i is a size_t.

Table 13-8: A Summary of std::bitset Operations

Operation	Notes
bitset<N>([val])	Constructs a bitset with initial value val, which can be either a string of 0s and 1s or an unsigned long long. Default constructor initializes all bits to zero.
bs[i]	Returns the value of the i-th bit: 1 returns true; 0 returns false.
bs.test(i)	Returns the value of the i-th bit: 1 returns true; 0 returns false. Performs bounds checking; throws std::out_of_range.
bs.set()	Sets all bits to 1.
bs.set(i, val)	Sets the i-th bit to val. Performs bounds checking; throws std::out_of_range.
bs.reset()	Sets all bits to 0.
bs.reset(i)	Sets the i-th bit to zero. Performs bounds checking; throws std::out_of_range.
bs.flip()	Flips all the bits: (0 becomes 1; 1 becomes 0).
bs.flip(i)	Flips the i-th bit to zero. Performs bounds checking; throws std::out_of_range.
bs.count()	Returns the number of bits set to 1.
bs.size()	Returns the size N of the bitset.
bs.any()	Returns true if any bits are set to 1.
bs.none()	Returns true if all bits are set to 0.
bs.all()	Returns true if all bits are set to 1.
bs.to_string()	Returns the string representation of the bitset.
bs.to_ulong()	Returns the unsigned long representation of the bitset.
bs.to_ullong()	Returns the unsigned long long representation of the bitset.

Special Sequential Boost Containers

Boost provides an abundance of special containers, and there simply isn't enough room to explore all their features here. Table 13-9 provides the names, headers, and brief descriptions of a number of them.

NOTE *Refer to the Boost Container documentation for more information.*

Table 13-9: Special Boost Containers

Class/Header	Description
`boost::intrusive::*` `<boost/intrusive/*.hpp>`	Intrusive containers impose requirements on the elements they contain (such as inheriting from a particular base class). In exchange, they offer substantial performance gains.
`boost::container::stable_vector` `<boost/container/stable_vector.hpp>`	A vector without contiguous elements but guarantees that iterators and references to elements remain valid as long as the element isn't erased (as with `list`).
`boost::container::slist` `<boost/container/slist.hpp>`	A `forward_list` with a fast `size` method.
`boost::container::static_vector` `<boost/container/static_vector.hpp>`	A hybrid between array and vector that stores a dynamic number of elements up to a fixed size. Elements are stored within the memory of `stable_vector`, like an `array`.
`boost::container::small_vector` `<boost/container/small_vector.hpp>`	A vector-like container optimized for holding a small number of elements. Contains some preallocated space, avoiding dynamic allocation.
`boost::circular_buffer` `<boost/circular_buffer.hpp>`	A fixed-capacity, queue-like container that fills elements in a circular fashion; a new element overwrites the oldest element once capacity is reached.
`boost::multi_array` `<boost/multi_array.hpp>`	An array-like container that accepts multiple dimensions. Rather than having, for example, an array of arrays of arrays, you can specify a three-dimensional `multi_array` **x** that allows element access, such as **x**`[5][1][2]`.
`boost::ptr_vector` `boost::ptr_list` `<boost/ptr_container/*.hpp>`	Having a collection of smart pointers can be suboptimal. Pointer vectors manage a collection of dynamic objects in a more efficient and user-friendly way.

NOTE *Boost Intrusive also contains some specialized containers that provide performance benefits in certain situations. These are primarily useful for library implementers.*

Associative Containers

Associative containers allow for very fast element search. Sequential containers have some natural ordering that allows you to iterate from the beginning of the container to the end in a well-specified order. Associative containers are a bit different. This container family splits along three axes:

- Whether elements contain keys (a set) or key-value pairs (a map)
- Whether elements are ordered
- Whether keys are *unique*

Sets

The std::set available in the STL's <set> header is an associative container that contains sorted, unique elements called *keys*. Because set stores sorted elements, you can insert, remove, and search efficiently. In addition, set supports sorted iteration over its elements, and you have complete control over how keys sort using comparator objects.

NOTE *Boost also provides a* boost::container::set *in the* <boost/container/set.hpp> *header.*

Constructing

The class template set<T, Comparator, Allocator> takes three template parameters:

- The key type T
- The comparator type that defaults to std::less
- The allocator type that defaults to std::allocator<T>

You have a lot of flexibility when constructing sets. Each of the following constructors accepts an optional comparator and allocator (whose types must match their corresponding template parameters):

- A default constructor that initializes an empty set
- Move and copy constructors with the usual behavior
- A range constructor that copies the elements from the range into the set
- A braced initializer

Listing 13-24 showcases each of these constructors.

```
#include <set>

TEST_CASE("std::set supports") {
  std::set<int> emp; ❶
  std::set<int> fib{ 1, 1, 2, 3, 5 }; ❷
  SECTION("default construction") {
    REQUIRE(emp.empty()); ❸
  }
  SECTION("braced initialization") {
    REQUIRE(fib.size() == 4); ❹
  }
  SECTION("copy construction") {
    auto fib_copy(fib);
    REQUIRE(fib.size() == 4); ❺
    REQUIRE(fib_copy.size() == 4); ❻
  }
  SECTION("move construction") {
    auto fib_moved(std::move(fib));
    REQUIRE(fib.empty()); ❼
    REQUIRE(fib_moved.size() == 4); ❽
```

```
  }
  SECTION("range construction") {
    std::array<int, 5> fib_array{ 1, 1, 2, 3, 5 };
    std::set<int> fib_set(fib_array.cbegin(), fib_array.cend());
    REQUIRE(fib_set.size() == 4); ❾
  }
}
```

Listing 13-24: The constructors of a set

You default construct ❶ and brace initialize ❷ two different sets. The default constructed set called emp is empty ❸, and the braced initialized set called fib has four elements ❹. You include five elements in the braced initializer, so why only four elements? Recall that set elements are unique, so the 1 enters only once.

Next, you copy construct fib, which results in two sets with size 4 ❺❻. On the other hand, the move constructor empties the moved-from set ❼ and transfers the elements to the new set ❽.

Then you can initialize a set from a range. You construct an array with five elements and then pass it as a range to a set constructor using the cbegin and cend methods. As with the braced initialization earlier in the code, the set contains only four elements because duplicates are discarded ❾.

Move and Copy Semantics

In addition to move/copy constructors, move/copy assignment operators are also available. As with other container copy operations, set copies are potentially very slow because each element needs to get copied, and move operations are usually fast because elements reside in dynamic memory. A set can simply pass ownership without disturbing the elements.

Element Access

You have several options for extracting elements from a set. The basic method is find, which takes a const reference to a key and returns an iterator. If the set contains an element-matching key, find will return an iterator pointing to the found element. If the set does not, it will return an iterator pointing to end. The lower_bound method returns an iterator to the first element *not less than* the key argument, whereas the upper_bound method returns the first element *greater than* the given key.

The set class supports two additional lookup methods, mainly for compatibility of non-unique associative containers:

- The count method returns the number of elements matching the key. Because set elements are unique, count returns either 0 or 1.
- The equal_range method returns a half-open range containing all the elements matching the given key. The range returns a std::pair of iterators with first pointing to the matching element and second pointing to

the element after first. If equal_range finds no matching element, first and second both point to the first element greater than the given key. In other words, the pair returned by equal_range is equivalent to a pair of lower_bound as first and upper_bound as second.

Listing 13-25 illustrates these two access methods.

```
TEST_CASE("std::set allows access") {
  std::set<int> fib{ 1, 1, 2, 3, 5 }; ❶
  SECTION("with find") { ❷
    REQUIRE(*fib.find(3) == 3);
    REQUIRE(fib.find(100) == fib.end());
  }
  SECTION("with count") { ❸
    REQUIRE(fib.count(3) == 1);
    REQUIRE(fib.count(100) == 0);
  }
  SECTION("with lower_bound") { ❹
    auto itr = fib.lower_bound(3);
    REQUIRE(*itr == 3);
  }
  SECTION("with upper_bound") { ❺
    auto itr = fib.upper_bound(3);
    REQUIRE(*itr == 5);
  }
  SECTION("with equal_range") { ❻
    auto pair_itr = fib.equal_range(3);
    REQUIRE(*pair_itr.first == 3);
    REQUIRE(*pair_itr.second == 5);
  }
}
```

Listing 13-25: A set member access

First, you construct a set with the four elements 1 2 3 5 ❶. Using find, you can extract an iterator to the element 3. You can also determine that 8 isn't in the set, because find returns an iterator pointing to end ❷. You can determine similar information with count, which returns 1 when you give the key 3 and 0 when you give the key 8 ❸. When you pass 3 to the lower_bound method, it returns an iterator pointing to 3 because this is the first element that's not less than the argument ❹. When you pass this to upper_bound, on the other hand, you obtain a pointer to the element 5, because this is the first element greater than the argument ❺. Finally, when you pass 3 to the equal_range method, you obtain a pair of iterators. The first iterator points to 3, and the second iterator points to 5, the element just after 3 ❻.

A set also exposes iterators through its begin and end methods, so you can use range-based for loops to iterate through the set from least element to greatest.

Adding Elements

You have three options when adding elements to a set:

- insert to copy an existing element into the set
- emplace to in-place construct a new element into the set
- emplace_hint to in-place construct a new element, just like emplace (because adding an element requires sorting). The difference is the emplace_hint method takes an iterator as its first argument. This iterator is the search's starting point (a hint). If the iterator is close to the correct position for the newly inserted element, this can provide a substantial speedup.

Listing 13-26 illustrates the several ways to insert elements into a set.

```
TEST_CASE("std::set allows insertion") {
  std::set<int> fib{ 1, 1, 2, 3, 5 };
  SECTION("with insert") { ❶
    fib.insert(8);
    REQUIRE(fib.find(8) != fib.end());
  }
  SECTION("with emplace") { ❷
    fib.emplace(8);
    REQUIRE(fib.find(8) != fib.end());
  }
  SECTION("with emplace_hint") { ❸
    fib.emplace_hint(fib.end(), 8);
    REQUIRE(fib.find(8) != fib.end());
  }
}
```

Listing 13-26: Inserting into a set

Both insert ❶ and emplace ❷ add the element 8 into fib, so when you invoke find with 8, you get an iterator pointing to the new element. You can achieve the same effect a bit more efficiently with emplace_hint ❸. Because you know ahead of time that the new element 8 is greater than all the other elements in the set, you can use end as the hint.

If you attempt to insert, emplace, or emplace_hint a key that's already present in the set, the operation has no effect. All three of these methods return a std::pair<Iterator, bool> where the second element indicates whether the operation resulted in insertion (true) or not (false). The iterator at first points to either the newly inserted element or the existing element that prevented insertion.

Removing Elements

You can remove elements from a set using erase, which is overloaded to accept a key, an iterator, or a half-open range, as shown in Listing 13-27.

```
TEST_CASE("std::set allows removal") {
  std::set<int> fib{ 1, 1, 2, 3, 5 };
  SECTION("with erase") { ❶
```

```
    fib.erase(3);
    REQUIRE(fib.find(3) == fib.end());
  }
  SECTION("with clear") { ❷
    fib.clear();
    REQUIRE(fib.empty());
  }
}
```

Listing 13-27: Removing from a set

In the first test, you call erase with the key 3, which removes the corresponding element from the set. When you invoke find on 3, you get an iterator pointing to the end, indicating that no matching element was found ❶. In the second test, you invoke clear, which eliminates all the elements from the set ❷.

Storage Model

Set operations are fast because sets are typically implemented as *red-black trees.* These structures treat each element as a node. Each node has one parent and up to two children, its left and right legs. Each node's children are sorted so all children to the left are less than the children to the right. This way, you can perform searches much quicker than with linear iteration, as long as a tree's branches are roughly balanced (equal in length). Red-black trees have additional facilities for rebalancing branches after insertions and deletions.

NOTE *For details on red-black trees, refer to* Data Structures and Algorithms in C++ *by Adam Drozdek.*

A Partial List of Supported Operations

Table 13-10 summarizes the operations of set. Operations s, s1, and s2 are of type std::set<T,[cmp_type<T>]>. T is the contained element/key type, and itr, beg, and end are set iterators. The variable t is a T. A dagger (†) denotes a method that returns a std::pair<Iterator, bool>, where the iterator points to the resulting element and the bool equals true if the method inserted an element and false if the element already existed.

Table 13-10: A Summary of std::set

Operation	Notes
set<T>{ ..., [cmp], [alc] }	Performs braced initialization of a newly constructed set. Uses **cmp**=std::less<T> and **alc**=std::allocator<T> by default.
set<T>{ **beg**, **end**, [**cmp**], [**alc**] }	Range constructor that copies elements from the half-open range **beg** to **end**. Uses **cmp**=std::less<T> and **alc**=std::allocator<T> by default.
set<T>(**s**)	Deep copy of **s**; allocates new memory.

(continued)

Table 13-10: A Summary of std::set *(continued)*

Operation	Notes
`set<T>(move(s))`	Takes ownership of memory; elements in **s**. No allocations.
`~set`	Destructs all elements contained by the set and releases dynamic memory.
`s1 = s2`	**s1** destructs its elements; copies each **s2** element. Only allocates if it needs to resize to fit **s2**'s elements.
`s1 = move(s2)`	**s1** destructs its elements; moves each **s2** element. Only allocates if it needs to resize to fit **s2**'s elements.
`s.begin()`	Returns an iterator pointing to the first element.
`s.cbegin()`	Returns a const iterator pointing to the first element.
`s.end()`	Returns an iterator pointing to 1 past the last element.
`s.cend()`	Returns a const iterator pointing to 1 past the last element.
`s.find(t)`	Returns an iterator pointing to the element matching **t** or **s**.end() if no such element exists.
`s.count(t)`	Returns 1 if set contains **t**; otherwise 0.
`s.equal_range(t)`	Returns a pair of iterators corresponding to the half-open range of elements matching **t**.
`s.lower_bound(t)`	Returns an iterator pointing to the first element not less than **t** or **s**.end() if no such element exists.
`s.upper_bound(t)`	Returns an iterator pointing to the first element greater than **t** or **s**.end() if no such element exists.
`s.clear()`	Removes all elements from the set.
`s.erase(t)`	Removes the element equal to **t**.
`s.erase(itr)`	Removes the element pointed to by **itr**.
`s.erase(beg, end)`	Removes all elements on the half-open range from **beg** to **end**.
`s.insert(t)`	Inserts a copy of **t** into the set.†
`s.emplace(...)`	Constructs a T in place by forwarding the arguments **...**.†
`s.emplace_hint(itr, ...)`	Constructs a T in place by forwarding the arguments **...**. Uses **itr** as a hint for where to insert the new element.†
`s.empty()`	Returns true if set's size is zero; otherwise false.
`s.size()`	Returns the number of elements in the set.
`s.max_size()`	Returns the maximum number of elements in the set.
`s.extract(t)` `s.extract(itr)`	Obtains a node handle that owns the element matching **t** or pointed to by **itr**. (This is the only way to remove a move-only element.)
`s1.merge(s2)` `s1.merge(move(s2))`	Splices each element of **s2** into **s1**. If argument is an rvalue, will move the elements into **s1**.
`s1.swap(s2)` `swap(s1, s2)`	Exchanges each element of **s1** with those of **s2**.

Multisets

The std::multiset available in the STL's <set> header is an associative container that contains sorted, *non-unique* keys. A multiset supports the same operations as a set, but it will store redundant elements. This has important ramifications for two methods:

- The method count can return values other than 0 or 1. The count method of multiset will tell you how many elements matched the given key.
- The method equal_range can return half-open ranges containing more than one element. The equal_range method of multiset will return a range containing all the elements matching the given key.

You might want to use a multiset rather than a set if it's important that you store multiple elements with the same key. For example, you could store all of an address's occupants by treating the address as a key and each member of the house as an element. If you used a set, you'd be stuck having only a single occupant.

Listing 13-28 illustrates using a multiset.

```
TEST_CASE("std::multiset handles non-unique elements") {
  std::multiset<int> fib{ 1, 1, 2, 3, 5 };
  SECTION("as reflected by size") {
    REQUIRE(fib.size() == 5); ❶
  }
  SECTION("and count returns values greater than 1") {
    REQUIRE(fib.count(1) == 2); ❷
  }
  SECTION("and equal_range returns non-trivial ranges") {
    auto [begin, end] = fib.equal_range(1); ❸
    REQUIRE(*begin == 1); ❹
    ++begin;
    REQUIRE(*begin == 1); ❺
    ++begin;
    REQUIRE(begin == end); ❻
  }
}
```

Listing 13-28: Accessing multiset elements

Unlike set in Listing 13-24, multiset permits multiple 1s, so size returns 5, the number of elements you provided in the braced initializers ❶. When you count the number of 1s, you get 2 ❷. You can use equal_range to iterate over these elements. Using structured binding syntax, you obtain a begin and end iterator ❸. You iterate over the two 1s ❹❺ and arrive at the end of the half-open range ❻.

Every operation in Table 13-10 works for multiset.

NOTE *Boost also provides a boost::container::multiset in the <boost/container/set.hpp> header.*

Unordered Sets

The `std::unordered_set` available in the STL's `<unordered_set>` header is an associative container that contains *unsorted*, unique keys. The `unordered_set` supports most of the same operations as set and `multiset`, but its internal storage model is completely different.

NOTE *Boost also provides a* `boost::unordered_set` *in the* `<boost/unordered_set.hpp>` *header.*

Rather than using a comparator to sort elements into a red-black tree, an `unordered_set` is usually implemented as a hash table. You might want to use an `unordered_set` in a situation in which there is no natural ordering among the keys and you don't need to iterate through the collection in such an order. You might find that in many situations, you could use either a `set` or an `unordered_set`. Although they appear quite similar, their internal representations are fundamentally different, so they'll have different performance characteristics. If performance is an issue, measure how both perform and use the one that's more appropriate.

Storage Model: Hash Tables

A hash function, or a *hasher*, is a function that accepts a key and returns a unique `size_t` value called a hash code. The `unordered_set` organizes its elements into a hash table, which associates a hash code with a collection of one or more elements called a *bucket*. To find an element, an `unordered_set` computes its hash code and then searches through the corresponding bucket in the hash table.

If you've never seen a hash table before, this information might be a lot to take in, so let's look at an example. Imagine you had a large group of people that you needed to sort into some kind of sensible groups to find an individual easily. You could group people by birthday, which would give you 365 groups (well, 366 if you count February 29 for leap years). The birthday is like a hash function that returns one of 365 values for each person. Each value forms a bucket, and all people in the same bucket have the same birthday. In this example, to find a person, you first determine their birthday, which gives you the correct bucket. Then you can search through the bucket to find the person you're looking for.

As long as the hash function is quick and there aren't too many elements per bucket, `unordered_sets` have even more impressive performance than their ordered counterparts: the contained element count doesn't increase insertion, search, and deletion times. When two different keys have the same hash code, it's called a *hash collision*. When you have a hash collision, it means that the two keys will reside in the same bucket. In the preceding birthday example, many people will have the same birthday, so there will be a lot of hash collisions. The more hash collisions there are, the larger the buckets will be, and the more time you'll spend searching through a bucket for the correct element.

A hash function has several requirements:

- It accepts a Key and returns a size_t hash code.
- It doesn't throw exceptions.
- Equal keys yield equal hash codes.
- Unequal keys yield unequal hash codes with high probability. (There is a low probability of a hash collision.)

The STL provides the hasher class template std::hash<T> in the <functional> header, which contains specializations for fundamental types, enumeration types, pointer types, optional, variant, smart pointers, and more. As an example, Listing 13-29 illustrates how std::hash<long> meets the equivalence criteria.

```
#include <functional>
TEST_CASE("std::hash<long> returns") {
  std::hash<long> hasher; ❶
  auto hash_code_42 = hasher(42); ❷
  SECTION("equal hash codes for equal keys") {
    REQUIRE(hash_code_42 == hasher(42)); ❸
  }
  SECTION("unequal hash codes for unequal keys") {
    REQUIRE(hash_code_42 != hasher(43)); ❹
  }
}
```

Listing 13-29: The std::hash<long> returns equal hash codes for equal keys and unequal hash codes for unequal keys.

You construct a hasher of type std::hash<long> ❶ and use it to compute the hash code of 42, storing the result into size_t hash_code_42 ❷. When you invoke hasher with 42 again, you obtain the same value ❸. When you invoke hasher with 43 instead, you obtain a different value ❹.

Once an unordered_set hashes a key, it can obtain a bucket. Because the bucket is a list of possible matching elements, you need a function object that determines equality between a key and a bucket element. The STL provides the class template std::equal_to<T> in the <functional> header, which simply invokes operator== on its arguments, as Listing 13-30 illustrates.

```
#include <functional>
TEST_CASE("std::equal_to<long> returns") {
  std::equal_to<long> long_equal_to; ❶
  SECTION("true when arguments equal") {
    REQUIRE(long_equal_to(42, 42)); ❷
  }
  SECTION("false when arguments unequal") {
    REQUIRE_FALSE(long_equal_to(42, 43)); ❸
  }
}
```

Listing 13-30: The std::equal_to<long> calls operator== on its arguments to determine equality.

Here, you've initialized an equal_to<long> called long_equal_to ❶. When you invoke long_equal_to with equal arguments, it returns true ❷. When you invoke it with unequal arguments, it returns false ❸.

NOTE *For brevity, this chapter won't cover implementing your own hashing and equivalence functions, which you'll need if you want to construct unordered containers given user-defined key types. See Chapter 7 of* The C++ Standard Library, *2nd Edition, by Nicolai Josuttis.*

Constructing

The class template std::unordered_set<T, Hash, KeyEqual, Allocator> takes four template parameters:

- Key type T
- The Hash hash function type, which defaults to std::hash<T>
- The KeyEqual equality function type, which defaults to std::equal_to<T>
- The Allocator allocator type, which defaults to std::allocator<T>

An unordered_set supports equivalent constructors to set with adjustments for the different template parameters (set needs a Comparator, whereas unordered_set needs a Hash and a KeyEqual). For example, you can use unordered_set as a drop-in replacement for set in Listing 13-24, because unordered_set has range constructors and copy/move constructors and supports braced initialization.

Supported set Operations

An unordered_set supports all set operations in Table 13-10 except for lower_bound and upper_bound, because unordered_set doesn't sort its elements.

Bucket Management

Generally, the reason you reach for an unordered_set is its high performance. Unfortunately, this performance comes at a cost: unordered_set objects have a somewhat complicated interior structure. You have various knobs and dials you can use to inspect and modify this internal structure at runtime.

The first control measure you have is to customize the bucket count of the unordered_set (that is, the number of buckets, not the number of elements in a particular bucket). Each unordered_set constructor takes a size_t bucket_count as its first argument, which defaults to some implementation-defined value. Table 13-11 lists the main unordered_set constructors.

Table 13-11: The unordered_set Constructors

Operation	Notes
unordered_set<T>([bck], [hsh], [keq], [alc])	Bucket size **bck** has an implementation-defined default value. Uses **hsh**=std::hash<T>, **keq**=std::equal_to<T>, and **alc**=std::allocator<T> by default.

Operation	Notes
unordered_set<T>(..., [**bck**], [**hsh**], [**keq**], [**alc**])	Performs braced initialization of a newly constructed unordered set.
unordered_set<T>(**beg**, **end** [**bck**], [**hsh**], [**keq**], [**alc**])	Constructs an unordered set with the elements on the half-open range from **beg** to **end**.
unordered_set<T>(**s**)	Deep copy of **s**; allocates new memory.
unordered_set<T>(move(**s**))	Takes ownership of memory; elements in **s**. No allocations.

You can inspect the number of buckets in an `unordered_set` using the `bucket_count` method. You can also obtain the maximum bucket count using the `max_bucket_count` method.

An important concept in the runtime performance of `unordered_set` is its *load factor*, the average number of elements per bucket. You can obtain the load factor of an `unordered_set` using the `load_factor` method, which is equivalent to `size()` divided by `bucket_count()`. Each `unordered_set` has a maximum load factor, which triggers an increase in the bucket count and a potentially expensive rehashing of all the contained elements. A *rehashing* is an operation where elements get reorganized into new buckets. This requires that you generate new hashes for each element, which can be a relatively computationally expensive operation.

You can obtain the maximum load factor using the `max_load_factor`, which is overloaded, so you can set a new maximum load factor (it defaults to 1.0).

To avoid expensive rehashing at inopportune times, you can manually trigger a rehashing using the `rehash` method, which accepts a `size_t` argument for the desired bucket count. You can also use the `reserve` method, which instead accepts a `size_t` argument for the desired *element* count.

Listing 13-31 illustrates some of these basic bucket management operations.

```
#include <unordered_set>
TEST_CASE("std::unordered_set") {
  std::unordered_set<unsigned long> sheep(100); ❶
  SECTION("allows bucket count specification on construction") {
    REQUIRE(sheep.bucket_count() >= 100); ❷
    REQUIRE(sheep.bucket_count() <= sheep.max_bucket_count()); ❸
    REQUIRE(sheep.max_load_factor() == Approx(1.0)); ❹
  }
  SECTION("allows us to reserve space for elements") {
    sheep.reserve(100'000); ❺
    sheep.insert(0);
    REQUIRE(sheep.load_factor() <= 0.00001); ❻

    while(sheep.size() < 100'000)
      sheep.insert(sheep.size()); ❼
    REQUIRE(sheep.load_factor() <= 1.0); ❽
  }
}
```

Listing 13-31: The `unordered_set` bucket management

You construct an unordered_set and specify a bucket count of 100 ❶. This results in a bucket_count of at least 100 ❷, which must be less than or equal to the max_bucket_count ❸. By default, the max_load_factor is 1.0 ❹.

In the next test, you invoke reserve with enough space for a hundred thousand elements ❺. After inserting an element, the load_factor should be less than or equal to one one-hundred-thousandth (0.00001) ❻ because you've reserved enough space for a hundred thousand elements. As long as you stay below this threshold, you won't need a rehashing. After inserting a hundred thousand elements ❼, the load_factor should still be less than or equal to 1 ❽. This demonstrates that you needed no rehashing, thanks to reserve.

Unordered Multisets

The std::unordered_multiset available in the STL's <unordered_set> header is an associative container that contains unsorted, *non-unique* keys. An unordered_multiset supports all the same constructors and operations as an unordered_set, but it will store redundant elements. This relationship is analogous to unordered_sets and sets: both equal_range and count have slightly different behavior to account for the non-uniqueness of keys.

NOTE *Boost also provides a boost::unordered_multiset in the <boost/unordered_set.hpp> header.*

Maps

The std::map available in the STL's <map> header is an associative container that contains key-value pairs. The keys of a map are sorted and unique, and map supports all the same operations as set. In fact, you can think of a set as a special kind of map containing keys and empty values. Accordingly, map supports efficient insertion, removal, and search, and you have control over sorting with comparator objects.

The major advantage of working with a map instead of a set of pairs is that map works as an *associative array*. An associative array takes a key rather than an integer-valued index. Think of how you use the at and operator[] methods to access indices in sequential containers. Because sequential containers have a natural ordering of elements, you use an integer to refer to them. The associative array allows you to use types other than integers to refer to elements. For example, you could use a string or a float as a key.

To enable associative array operations, map supports a number of useful operations; for example, allowing you to insert, modify, and retrieve values by their associated keys.

Constructing

The class template map<Key, Value, Comparator, Allocator> takes four template parameters. The first is the key type Key. The second is the value type Value. The third is the comparator type, which defaults to std::less. The fourth parameter is the allocator type, which defaults to std::allocator<T>.

The map constructors are direct analogues to the constructors of set: a default constructor that initializes an empty map; move and copy constructors with the usual behavior; a range constructor that copies the elements from the range into the map; and a braced initializer. The main difference is in the braced initializer, because you need to initialize key-value pairs instead of just keys. To achieve this nested initialization, you use nested initializer lists, as Listing 13-32 illustrates.

```
#include <map>

auto colour_of_magic = "Colour of Magic";
auto the_light_fantastic = "The Light Fantastic";
auto equal_rites = "Equal Rites";
auto mort = "Mort";

TEST_CASE("std::map supports") {
  SECTION("default construction") {
    std::map<const char*, int> emp; ❶
    REQUIRE(emp.empty()); ❷
  }
  SECTION("braced initialization") {
    std::map<const char*, int> pub_year { ❸
      { colour_of_magic, 1983 }, ❹
      { the_light_fantastic, 1986 },
      { equal_rites, 1987 },
      { mort, 1987 },
    };
    REQUIRE(pub_year.size() == 4); ❺
  }
}
```

Listing 13-32: A `std::map` supports default construction and braced initialization.

Here, you default construct a map with keys of type const char* and values of type int ❶. This results in an empty map ❷. In the second test, you again have a map with keys of type const char* and values of type int ❸, but this time you use braced initialization ❹ to pack four elements into the map ❺.

Move and Copy Semantics

The move and copy semantics of map are identical to those of set.

Storage Model

Both map and set use the same red-black tree internal structure.

Element Access

The major advantage to using a map instead of a set of pair objects is that map offers two associative array operations: operator[] and at. Unlike the sequential containers supporting these operations, like vector and array, which take a size_t index argument, map takes a Key argument and returns a reference to the corresponding value. As with sequential containers, at will throw a std::out_of_range exception if the given key doesn't exist in the map. Unlike with sequential containers, operator[] won't cause undefined behavior if the key doesn't exist; instead, it will (silently) default construct a Value and insert the corresponding key-value pair into the map, even if you only intended to perform a read, as Listing 13-33 illustrates.

```
TEST_CASE("std::map is an associative array with") {
  std::map<const char*, int> pub_year { ❶
    { colour_of_magic, 1983 },
    { the_light_fantastic, 1986 },
  };
  SECTION("operator[]") {
    REQUIRE(pub_year[colour_of_magic] == 1983); ❷

    pub_year[equal_rites] = 1987; ❸
    REQUIRE(pub_year[equal_rites] == 1987); ❹

    REQUIRE(pub_year[mort] == 0); ❺
  }
  SECTION("an at method") {
    REQUIRE(pub_year.at(colour_of_magic) == 1983); ❻

    REQUIRE_THROWS_AS(pub_year.at(equal_rites), std::out_of_range); ❼
  }
}
```

Listing 13-33: A std::map is an associative array with several access methods.

You construct a map called pub_year containing two elements ❶. Next, you use operator[] to extract the value corresponding to the key colour_of_magic ❷. You also use operator[] to insert the new key-value pair equal_rites, 1987 ❸ and then retrieve it ❹. Notice that when you attempt to retrieve an element with the key mort (which doesn't exist), the map has silently default-initialized an int for you ❺.

Using at, you can still set and retrieve ❻ elements, but if you attempt to access a key that doesn't exist, you get a std::out_of_range exception ❼.

A map supports all the set-like, element-retrieval operations. For example, map supports find, which accepts a key argument and returns an iterator pointing to the key-value pair or, if no matching key is found, to the end of map. Also similarly supported are count, equal_range, lower_bound, and upper_bound.

Adding Elements

In addition to the element access methods operator[] and at, you also have all the insert and emplace methods available from set. You simply need to treat each key-value pair as a std::pair<Key, Value>. As with set, insert returns a pair containing an iterator and a bool. The iterator points to the inserted element, and the bool answers whether insert added a new element (true) or not (false), as Listing 13-34 illustrates.

```
TEST_CASE("std::map supports insert") {
  std::map<const char*, int> pub_year; ❶
  pub_year.insert({ colour_of_magic, 1983 }); ❷
  REQUIRE(pub_year.size() == 1); ❸

  std::pair<const char*, int> tlfp{ the_light_fantastic, 1986 }; ❹
  pub_year.insert(tlfp); ❺
  REQUIRE(pub_year.size() == 2); ❻

  auto [itr, is_new] = pub_year.insert({ the_light_fantastic, 9999 }); ❼
  REQUIRE(itr->first == the_light_fantastic);
  REQUIRE(itr->second == 1986); ❽
  REQUIRE_FALSE(is_new); ❾
  REQUIRE(pub_year.size() == 2); ❿
}
```

Listing 13-34: A `std::map` supports `insert` to add new elements.

You default construct a `map` ❶ and use the `insert` method with a braced initializer for a `pair` ❷. This construction is roughly equivalent to the following:

```
pub_year.insert(std::pair<const char*, int>{ colour_of_magic, 1983 });
```

After insertion, the `map` now contains one element ❸. Next, you create a stand-alone `pair` ❹ and then pass it as an argument to `insert` ❺. This inserts a copy into the `map`, so it now contains two elements ❻.

When you attempt to invoke `insert` with a new element with the same `the_light_fantastic` key ❼, you get an iterator pointing to the element you already inserted ❺. The key (`first`) and the value (`second`) match ❽. The return value `is_new` indicates that no new element was inserted ❾, and you still have two elements ❿. This behavior mirrors the `insert` behavior of `set`.

A `map` also offers an `insert_or_assign` method, which, unlike `insert`, will overwrite an existing value. Also unlike `insert`, `insert_or_assign` accepts separate key and value arguments, as Listing 13-35 illustrates.

```
TEST_CASE("std::map supports insert_or_assign") {
  std::map<const char*, int> pub_year{ ❶
    { the_light_fantastic, 9999 }
  };
  auto [itr, is_new] = pub_year.insert_or_assign(the_light_fantastic, 1986); ❷
  REQUIRE(itr->second == 1986); ❸
  REQUIRE_FALSE(is_new); ❹
}
```

Listing 13-35: A `std::map` supports `insert_or_assign` to overwrite existing elements.

You construct a `map` with a single element ❶ and then call `insert_or_assign` to reassign the value associated with the key `the_light_fantastic` to 1986 ❷. The iterator points to the existing element, and when you query the corresponding value with `second`, you see the value updated to 1986 ❸. The `is_new` return value also indicates that you've updated an existing element rather than inserting a new one ❹.

Removing Elements

Like set, map supports erase and clear to remove elements, as shown in Listing 13-36.

```
TEST_CASE("We can remove std::map elements using") {
    std::map<const char*, int> pub_year {
      { colour_of_magic, 1983 },
      { mort, 1987 },
    }; ❶
  SECTION("erase") {
    pub_year.erase(mort); ❷
    REQUIRE(pub_year.find(mort) == pub_year.end()); ❸
  }
  SECTION("clear") {
    pub_year.clear(); ❹
    REQUIRE(pub_year.empty()); ❺
  }
}
```

Listing 13-36: A `std::map` *supports element removal.*

You construct a map with two elements ❶. In the first test, you invoke erase on the element with key mort ❷, so when you try to find it, you get back end ❸. In the second test, you clear map ❹, which causes empty to return true ❺.

List of Supported Operations

Table 13-12 summarizes the supported operations of map. A key k has type K. A value v has type V. P is the type pair<K, V>, and p is of type P. The map m is map<K, V>. A dagger (†) denotes a method that returns a std::pair<Iterator, bool>, where the iterator points to the resulting element and the bool equals true if the method inserted an element and false if the element already existed.

Table 13-12: A Partial List of Supported map Operations

Operation	Notes
map<T>{ ..., [**cmp**], [**alc**] }	Performs braced initialization of a newly constructed map. Uses **cmp**=std::less<T> and **alc**=std::allocator<T> by default.
map<T>{ **beg**, **end**, [**cmp**], [**alc**] }	Range constructor that copies elements from the half-open range **beg** to **end**. Uses **cmp**=std::less<T> and **alc**=std::allocator<T> by default.
map<T>(**m**)	Deep copy of **m**; allocates new memory.
map<T>(move(**m**))	Takes ownership of memory; elements in **m**. No allocations.
~map	Destructs all elements contained by the map and releases dynamic memory.
m1 = **m2**	**m1** destructs its elements; copies each **m2** element. Only allocates if it needs to resize to fit **m2**'s elements.

Operation	Notes
`m1 = move(m2)`	m1 destructs its elements; moves each m2 element. Only allocates if it needs to resize to fit m2's elements.
`m.at(k)`	Accesses the value corresponding to the key k. Throws std::out_of_bounds if key not found.
`m[k]`	Accesses the value corresponding to the key k. If the key is not found, inserts a new key-value pair using k and a default initialized value.
`m.begin()`	Returns an iterator pointing to the first element.
`m.cbegin()`	Returns a const iterator pointing to the first element.
`m.end()`	Returns an iterator pointing to 1 past the last element.
`m.cend()`	Returns a const iterator pointing to 1 past the last element.
`m.find(k)`	Returns an iterator pointing to the element matching k, or m.end() if no such element exists.
`m.count(k)`	Returns 1 if the map contains k; otherwise 0.
`m.equal_range(k)`	Returns a pair of iterators corresponding to the half-open range of elements matching k.
`m.lower_bound(k)`	Returns an iterator pointing to the first element not less than k, or t.end() if no such element exists.
`m.upper_bound(k)`	Returns an iterator pointing to the first element greater than k, or t.end() if no such element exists.
`m.clear()`	Removes all elements from the map.
`m.erase(k)`	Removes the element with key k.
`m.erase(itr)`	Removes the element pointed to by itr.
`m.erase(beg, end)`	Removes all elements on the half-open range from beg to end.
`m.insert(p)`	Inserts a copy of the pair p into the map.†
`m.insert_or_assign(k, v)`	If k exists, overwrites the corresponding value with v. If k doesn't exist, inserts the pair k, v into the map.†
`m.emplace(...)`	Constructs a P in place by forwarding the arguments ....†
`m.emplace_hint(k, ...)`	Constructs a P in place by forwarding the arguments .... Uses itr as a hint for where to insert the new element.†
`m.try_emplace(itr, ...)`	If key k exists, does nothing. If k doesn't exist, constructs a V in place by forwarding the arguments ....
`m.empty()`	Returns true if map's size is zero; otherwise false.
`m.size()`	Returns the number of elements in the map.
`m.max_size()`	Returns the maximum number of elements in the map.

(continued)

Table 13-12: A Partial List of Supported map Operation (continued)

Operation	Notes
m.extract(k) m.extract(itr)	Obtains a node handle that owns the element matching **k** or pointed to by **itr**. (This is the only way to remove a move-only element.)
m1.merge(m2) m1.merge(move(m2))	Splices each element of **m2** into **m1**. If argument is an rvalue, will move the elements into **m1**.
m1.swap(m2) swap(m1, m2)	Exchanges each element of **m1** with those of **m2**.

Multimaps

The std::multimap available in the STL's <map> header is an associative container that contains key-value pairs with *non-unique* keys. Because the keys are not unique, multimap doesn't support the associative array features that map does. Namely, operator[] and at aren't supported. As with multiset, multimap offers element access primarily through the equal_range method, as Listing 13-37 illustrates.

```
TEST_CASE("std::multimap supports non-unique keys") {
  std::array<char, 64> far_out {
    "Far out in the uncharted backwaters of the unfashionable end..."
  }; ❶
  std::multimap<char, size_t> indices; ❷
  for(size_t index{}; index<far_out.size(); index++)
    indices.emplace(far_out[index], index); ❸

  REQUIRE(indices.count('a') == 6); ❹

  auto [itr, end] = indices.equal_range('d'); ❺
  REQUIRE(itr->second == 23); ❻
  itr++;
  REQUIRE(itr->second == 59); ❼
  itr++;
  REQUIRE(itr == end);
}
```

Listing 13-37: A std::multimap supports non-unique keys.

You construct an array containing a message ❶. You also default construct a multimap<char, size_t> called indices that you'll use to store the index of every character in the message ❷. By looping through the array, you can store each character in the message along with its index as a new element in multimap ❸. Because you're allowed to have non-unique keys, you can use the count method to reveal how many indices you insert with the key a ❹. You can also use the equal_range method to obtain the half-open range of indices with the key d ❺. Using the resulting begin and end iterators, you can see that the message has the letter d at indices 23 ❻ and 59 ❼.

Aside from operator[] and at, every operation in Table 13-12 works for multimap as well. (Note that the count method can take on values other than 0 and 1.)

Unordered Maps and Unordered Multimaps

Unordered maps and unordered multimaps are completely analogous to unordered sets and unordered multisets. The std::unordered_map and std::unordered_multimap are available in the STL's <unordered_map> header. These associative containers typically use a red-black tree like their set counterparts. They also require a hash function and an equivalence function, and they support the bucket interface.

NOTE *Boost offers the boost::unordered_map and boost::unordered_multimap in the <boost/unordered_map.hpp> header.*

Niche Associative Containers

Use set, map, and their associated non-unique and unordered counterparts as the default choices when you need associative data structures. When special needs arise, Boost libraries offer a number of specialized associative containers, as highlighted in Table 13-13.

Table 13-13: Special Boost Containers

Class/Header	Description
boost::container::flat_map <boost/container/flat_map.hpp>	Similar to an STL map, but it's implemented like an ordered vector. This means fast random element access.
boost::container::flat_set <boost/container/flat_set.hpp>	Similar to an STL set, but it's implemented like an ordered vector. This means fast random element access.
boost::intrusive::* <boost/intrusive/*.hpp>	Intrusive containers impose requirements on the elements they contain (such as inheriting from a particular base class). In exchange, they offer substantial performance gains.
boost::multi_index_container <boost/multi_index_container.hpp>	Permits you to create associative arrays taking multiple indices rather than just one (like a map).
boost::ptr_map boost::ptr_set boost::ptr_unordered_map boost::ptr_unordered_set <boost/ptr_container/*.hpp>	Having a collection of smart pointers can be suboptimal. Pointer vectors manage a collection of dynamic objects in a more efficient and user-friendly way.
boost::bimap < boost/bimap.hpp>	A bimap is an associative container that allows both types to be used as a key.
boost::heap::binomial_heap boost::heap::d_ary_heap boost::heap::fibonacci_heap boost::heap::pairing_heap boost::heap::priority_queue boost::heap::skew_heap <boost/heap/*.hpp>	The Boost Heap containers implement more advanced, featureful versions of priority_queue.

Graphs and Property Trees

This section discusses two specialized Boost libraries that serve niche but valuable purposes: modeling graphs and property trees. A *graph* is a set of objects in which some have a pairwise relation. The objects are called *vertices,* and their relations are called *edges.* Figure 13-3 illustrates a graph containing four vertices and five edges.

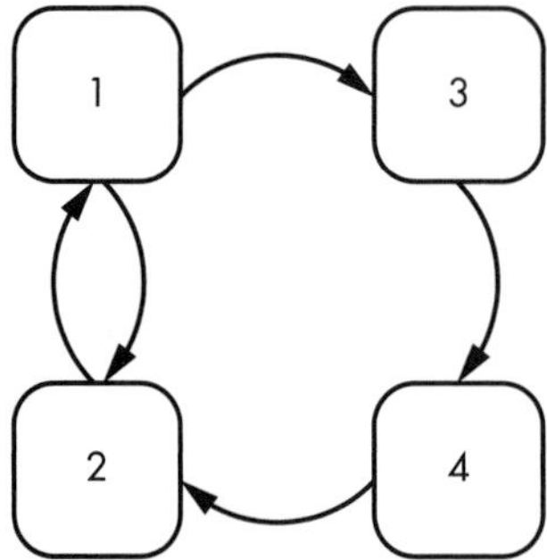

Figure 13-3: A graph containing four vertices and five edges

Each square represents a vertex, and each arrow represents an edge.

A *property tree* is a tree structure storing nested key-value pairs. The hierarchical nature of a property tree's key-value pairs makes it a hybrid between a map and a graph; each key-value pair has a relation to other key-value pairs. Figure 13-4 illustrates an example property tree containing nested key-value pairs.

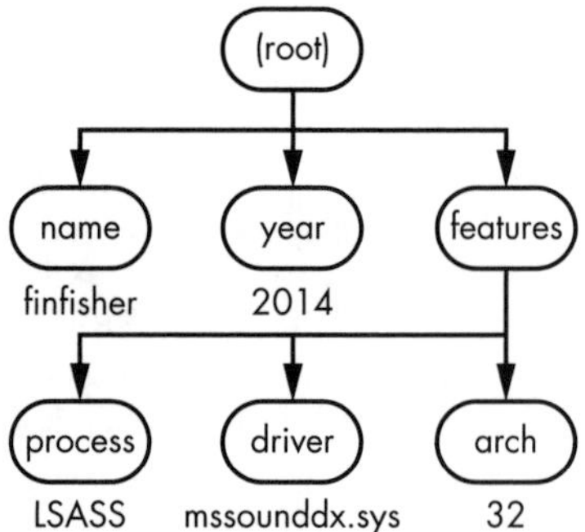

Figure 13-4: An example property tree

The root element has three children: name, year, and features. In Figure 13-4, name has a value finfisher, year has a value 2014, and features has three children: process with value LSASS, driver with value mssounddx .sys, and arch with value 32.

The Boost Graph Library

The *Boost Graph Library* (BGL) is a set of collections and algorithms for storing and manipulating graphs. The BGL offers three containers that represent graphs:

- The `boost::adjacency_list` in the `<boost/graph/adjacency_list.hpp>` header
- The `boost::adjacency_matrix` in the `<boost/graph/adjacency_matrix.hpp>` header
- The `boost::edge_list` in the `<boost/graph/ edge_list.hpp>` header

You use two non-member functions to build graphs: `boost::add_vertex` and `boost::add_edge`. To add a vertex to one of the BGL graph containers, you pass the graph object to `add_vertex`, which will return reference to the new vertex object. To add an edge, we pass the source vertex, the destination vertex, then the graph to `add_edge`.

BGL contains a number of graph-specific algorithms. You can count the number of vertices in a graph object by passing it to the non-member function `boost::num_vertices` and the number of edges using `boost::num_edges`. You can also query a graph for adjacent vertices. Two vertices are *adjacent* if they share an edge. To get the vertices adjacent to a particular vertex, you can pass it and the graph object to the non-member function `boost::adjacent_vertices`. This returns a half-open range as a `std::pair` of iterators.

Listing 13-38 illustrates how you can build the graph represented in Figure 13-3, count its vertices and edges, and compute adjacent vertices.

```
#include <set>
#include <boost/graph/adjacency_list.hpp>

TEST_CASE("boost::adjacency_list stores graph data") {
  boost::adjacency_list<> graph{}; ❶
  auto vertex_1 = boost::add_vertex(graph);
  auto vertex_2 = boost::add_vertex(graph);
  auto vertex_3 = boost::add_vertex(graph);
  auto vertex_4 = boost::add_vertex(graph); ❷
  auto edge_12 = boost::add_edge(vertex_1, vertex_2, graph);
  auto edge_13 = boost::add_edge(vertex_1, vertex_3, graph);
  auto edge_21 = boost::add_edge(vertex_2, vertex_1, graph);
  auto edge_24 = boost::add_edge(vertex_2, vertex_4, graph);
  auto edge_43 = boost::add_edge(vertex_4, vertex_3, graph); ❸

  REQUIRE(boost::num_vertices(graph) == 4); ❹
  REQUIRE(boost::num_edges(graph) == 5); ❺

  auto [begin, end] = boost::adjacent_vertices(vertex_1, graph); ❻
  std::set<decltype(vertex_1)> neighboors_1 { begin, end }; ❼
  REQUIRE(neighboors_1.count(vertex_2) == 1); ❽
  REQUIRE(neighboors_1.count(vertex_3) == 1); ❾
  REQUIRE(neighboors_1.count(vertex_4) == 0); ❿
}
```

Listing 13-38: The `boost::adjacency_list` stores graph data.

Here, you've constructed an adjacency_list called graph ❶, then added four vertices using add_vertex ❷. Next, you add all the edges represented in Figure 13-3 using add_edge ❸. Then num_vertices shows you that you've added four vertices ❹, and num_edges tells you that you've added five edges ❺.

Finally, you've determined the adjacent_vertices to vertex_1, which you unpack into the iterators begin and end ❻. You use these iterators to construct a std::set ❼, which you use to show that vertex_2 ❽ and vertex_3 ❾ are adjacent, but vertex_4 is not ❿.

Boost Property Trees

Boost offers the boost::property_tree::ptree in the <boost/property_tree/ptree.hpp> header. This is a property tree that permits us to build and query property trees, as well as some limited serialization into various formats.

The tree ptree is default constructible. Default constructing will build an empty ptree.

You can insert elements into a ptree using its put method, which takes a path and a value argument. A *path* is a sequence of one or more nested keys separated by a period (.), and a *value* is an arbitrarily typed object.

You can remove subtrees from a ptree using the get_child method, which takes the path of the desired subtree. If the subtree does not have any children (a so-called *leaf node*), you can also use the method template get_value to extract the corresponding value from the key-value pair; get_value takes a single template parameter corresponding to the desired output type.

Finally, ptree supports serialization and deserialization to several formats including Javascript object notation (JSON), the Windows initialization file (INI) format, the extensible markup language (XML), and a custom, ptree-specific format called INFO. For example, to write a ptree into a file in JSON format, you could use the boost::property_tree::write_json function from the <boost/property_tree/json_parser.hpp> header. The function write_json accepts two arguments: the path to the desired output file and a ptree reference.

Listing 13-39 highlights these basic ptree functions by building a ptree representing the property tree in Figure 13-4, writing the ptree to file as JSON, and reading it back.

```
#include <boost/property_tree/ptree.hpp>
#include <boost/property_tree/json_parser.hpp>

TEST_CASE("boost::property_tree::ptree stores tree data") {
  using namespace boost::property_tree;
  ptree p; ❶
  p.put("name", "finfisher");
  p.put("year", 2014);
  p.put("features.process", "LSASS");
  p.put("features.driver", "mssounddx.sys");
  p.put("features.arch", 32); ❷
```

```
  REQUIRE(p.get_child("year").get_value<int>() == 2014); ❸

  const auto file_name = "rootkit.json";
  write_json(file_name, p); ❹

  ptree p_copy;
  read_json(file_name, p_copy); ❺
  REQUIRE(p_copy == p); ❻
}
```

```
{
    "name": "finfisher",
    "year": "2014",
    "features": {
        "process": "LSASS",
        "driver": "mssounddx.sys",
        "arch": "32"
    }
} ❹
```

Listing 13-39: The `boost::property_tree::ptree` *method stores tree data. Output shows the contents of* `rootkit.json`*.*

Here, you've default constructed a `ptree` ❶, which you populate with the key values shown in Figure 13-4. Keys with parents, such as `arch` ❷, use periods to show the appropriate path. Using `get_child`, you've extracted the subtree for key `year`. Because it's a leaf node (having no children), you also invoke `get_value`, specifying the output type as `int` ❸.

Next, you write the `ptree`'s JSON representation to the file `rootkit.json` ❹. To ensure that you get the same property tree back, you default construct another `ptree` called `p_copy` and pass it into `read_json` ❺. This copy is equivalent to the original ❻, illustrating that the serialization-deserialization operation is successful.

Initializer Lists

You can accept initializer lists in your user-defined types by incorporating the `std::initializer_list` container available in the STL's `<initializer_list>` header. The `initializer_list` is a class template that takes a single template parameter corresponding to the underlying type contained in the initializer list. This template serves as a simple proxy for accessing the elements of an initializer list.

The `initializer_list` is immutable and supports three operations:

- The `size` method returns the number of elements in the `initializer_list`.
- The `begin` and `end` methods return the usual half-open-range iterators.

Generally, you should design functions to accept an `initializer_list` by value.

Listing 13-40 implements a SquareMatrix class that stores a matrix with equal numbers of rows and columns. Internally, the class will hold elements in a vector of vectors.

```
#include <cmath>
#include <stdexcept>
#include <initializer_list>
#include <vector>

size_t square_root(size_t x) { ❶
  const auto result = static_cast<size_t>(sqrt(x));
  if (result * result != x) throw std::logic_error{ "Not a perfect square." };
  return result;
}

template <typename T>
struct SquareMatrix {
  SquareMatrix(std::initializer_list<T> val) ❷
    : dim{ square_root(val.size()) }, ❸
      data(dim, std::vector<T>{}) { ❹
    auto itr = val.begin(); ❺
    for(size_t row{}; row<dim; row++){
      data[row].assign(itr, itr+dim); ❻
      itr += dim; ❼
    }
  }
  T& at(size_t row, size_t col) {
    if (row >= dim || col >= dim)
      throw std::out_of_range{ "Index invalid." }; ❽
    return data[row][col]; ❾
  }
  const size_t dim;
private:
  std::vector<std::vector<T>> data;
};
```

Listing 13-40: An implementation of a `SquareMatrix`

Here, you declare a convenience `square_root` function that finds the square root of a `size_t`, throwing an exception if the argument isn't a perfect square ❶. The `SquareMatrix` class template defines a single constructor that accepts a `std::initializer` called `val` ❷. This permits braced initialization.

First, you need to determine the dimensions of `SquareMatrix`. Use the `square_root` function to compute the square root of `val.size()` ❸ and store this into the `dim` field, which represents the number of rows and columns of the `SquareMatrix` instance. You can then use `dim` to initialize the vector of vectors `data` using its fill constructor ❹. Each of these `vectors` will correspond to a row in `SquareMatrix`. Next, you extract an iterator pointing to the first element in `initializer_list` ❺. You iterate over each row in `SquareMatrix`, assigning the corresponding `vector` to the appropriate half-open range ❻. You increment the iterator on each iteration to point to the next row ❼.

Finally, you implement an at method to permit element access. You perform bounds checking ❽ and then return a reference to the desired element by extracting the appropriate vector and element ❾.

Listing 13-41 illustrates how to use braced initialization to generate a SquareMatrix object.

```
TEST_CASE("SquareMatrix and std::initializer_list") {
  SquareMatrix<int> mat { ❶
     1,  2,  3,  4,
     5,  0,  7,  8,
     9, 10, 11, 12,
    13, 14, 15, 16
  };
  REQUIRE(mat.dim == 4); ❷
  mat.at(1, 1) = 6; ❸
  REQUIRE(mat.at(1, 1) == 6); ❹
  REQUIRE(mat.at(0, 2) ==  3); ❺
}
```

Listing 13-41: Using braced initializers with a SquareMatrix

You use braced initializers to set up SquareMatrix ❶. Because the initializer list contains 16 elements, you end up with a dim of 4 ❷. You can use at to obtain a reference to any element, meaning you can set ❸ and get ❹❺ elements.

Summary

This chapter began with a discussion of the two go-to sequence containers, array and vector, which offer you a great balance between performance and features in a wide range of applications. Next, you learned about several sequence containers—deque, list, stack, queue, priority_queue, and bitset—that fill in when vector doesn't meet the demands of a particular application. Then you explored the major associative containers, set and map, and their unordered/multipermutations. You also learned about two niche Boost containers, graph and ptree. The chapter wrapped up with a brief discussion of incorporating initializer_lists into user-defined types.

EXERCISES

13-1. Write a program that default constructs a std::vector of unsigned longs. Print the capacity of vector and then reserve 10 elements. Next, append the first 20 elements of the Fibonacci series to the vector. Print capacity again. Does capacity match the number of elements in the vector? Why or why not? Print the elements of vector using a range-based for loop.

(continued)

13-2. Rewrite Listings 2-9, 2-10, and 2-11 in Chapter 2 using `std::array`.

13-3. Write a program that accepts any number of command line arguments and prints them in alphanumerically sorted order. Use a `std::set<const char*>` to store the elements, then iterate over the set to obtain the sorted result. You'll need to implement a custom comparator that compares two C-style strings.

13-4. Write a program that default constructs a `std::vector` of unsigned longs. Print the `capacity` of `vector` and then `reserve` 10 elements. Next, append the first 20 elements of the Fibonacci series to the vector. Print `capacity` again. Does `capacity` match the number of elements in the vector? Why or why not? Print the elements of `vector` using a range-based `for` loop.

13-5. Consider the following program that profiles the performance of a function summing a Fibonacci series:

```
#include <chrono>
#include <cstdio>
#include <random>

long fib_sum(size_t n) { ❶
  // TODO: Adapt code from Exercise 12.1
  return 0;
}

long random() { ❷
  static std::mt19937_64 mt_engine{ 102787 };
  static std::uniform_int_distribution<long> int_d{ 1000, 2000 };
  return int_d(mt_engine);
}

struct Stopwatch { ❸
  Stopwatch(std::chrono::nanoseconds& result)
    : result{ result },
    start{ std::chrono::system_clock::now() } { }
  ~Stopwatch() {
    result = std::chrono::system_clock::now() - start;
  }
private:
  std::chrono::nanoseconds& result;
  const std::chrono::time_point<std::chrono::system_clock> start;
};

long cached_fib_sum(const size_t& n) { ❹
  static std::map<long, long> cache;
  // TODO: Implement me
  return 0;
}

int main() {

  size_t samples{ 1'000'000 };
  std::chrono::nanoseconds elapsed;
```

```
  {
    Stopwatch stopwatch{elapsed};
    volatile double answer;
    while(samples--) {
      answer = fib_sum(random()); ❺
      //answer = cached_fib_sum(random()); ❻
    }
  }
  printf("Elapsed: %g s.\n", elapsed.count() / 1'000'000'000.); ❼
}
```

This program contains a computationally intensive function `fib_sum` ❶ that computes the sum of a Fibonacci series with a given length. Adapt your code from Exercise 13-1 by (a) generating the appropriate vector and (b) summing over the result with a range-based `for` loop. The `random` function ❷ returns a random number between 1,000 and 2,000, and the `Stopwatch` class ❸ adopted from Listing 12-25 in Chapter 12 helps you determine elapsed time. In the program's `main`, you perform a million evaluations of the `fib_sum` function using random input ❺. You time how long this takes and print the result before exiting the program ❼. Compile the program and run it a few times to get an idea of how long your program takes to run. (This is called a *baseline*.)

13-6. Next, comment out ❺ and uncomment ❻. Implement the function `cached_fib_sum` ❹ so you first check whether you've computed `fib_sum` for the given length yet. (Treat the length n as a key into the cache.) If the key is present in the cache, simply return the result. If the key isn't present, compute the correct answer with `fib_sum`, store the new key-value entry into cache, and return the result. Run the program again. Is it faster? Try `unordered_map` instead of `map`. Could you use a `vector` instead? How fast can you get the program to run?

13-7. Implement a `Matrix` class like `SquareMatrix` in Listing 13-38. Your `Matrix` should allow unequal numbers of rows and columns. Accept as your constructor's first argument the number of rows in `Matrix`.

FURTHER READING

- *ISO International Standard ISO/IEC (2017) — Programming Language C++* (International Organization for Standardization; Geneva, Switzerland; *https://isocpp.org/std/the-standard/*)
- *The Boost C++ Libraries*, 2nd Edition, by Boris Schäling (XML Press, 2014)
- *The C++ Standard Library: A Tutorial and Reference*, 2nd Edition, by Nicolai M. Josuttis (Addison-Wesley Professional, 2012)

14

ITERATORS

Say "friend" and enter.
—J.R.R. Tolkein, The Lord of the Rings

Iterators are the STL component that provides the interface between containers and algorithms to manipulate them. An iterator is an interface to a type that knows how to traverse a particular sequence and exposes simple, pointer-like operations to elements.

Every iterator supports at least the following operations:

- Access the current element (`operator*`) for reading and/or writing
- Go to the next element (`operator++`)
- Copy construct

Iterators are categorized based on which additional operations they support. These categories determine which algorithms are available and what you can do with an iterator in your generic code. In this chapter, you'll learn about these iterator categories, convenience functions, and adapters.

Iterator Categories

An iterator's category determines the operations it supports. These operations include reading and writing elements, iterating forward and backward, reading multiple times, and accessing random elements.

Because code that accepts an iterator is usually generic, the iterator's type is typically a template parameter that you can encode with concepts, which you learned about in "Concepts" on page 163. Although you probably won't have to interact with iterators directly (unless you're writing a library), you'll still need to know the iterator categories so you don't try to apply an algorithm to inappropriate iterators. If you do, you're likely to get cryptic compiler errors. Recall from "Type Checking in Templates" on page 161 that because of how templates instantiate, error messages generated from inappropriate type arguments are usually inscrutable.

Output Iterators

You can use an *output iterator* to write into and increment but nothing else. Think of an output iterator as a bottomless pit that you throw data into.

When using an output iterator, you write, then increment, then write, then increment, ad nauseam. Once you've written to an output iterator, you cannot write again until you've incremented at least once. Likewise, once you've incremented an output iterator, you cannot increment again before writing.

To write to an output iterator, dereference the iterator using the dereference operator (*) and assign a value to the resulting reference. To increment an output iterator, use `operator++` or `operator++(int)`.

Again, unless you're writing a C++ library, it's unlikely that you'll have to *implement* your own output iterator types; however, you'll *use* them quite a lot.

One prominent usage is writing into containers as if they were output iterators. For this, you use insert iterators.

Insert Iterators

An *insert iterator* (or *inserter*) is an output iterator that wraps a container and transforms writes (assignments) into insertions. Three insert iterators exist in the STL's `<iterator>` header as class templates:

- `std::back_insert_iterator`
- `std::front_insert_iterator`
- `std::insert_iterator`

The STL also offers three convenience functions for building these iterators:

- `std::back_inserter`
- `std::front_inserter`
- `std::inserter`

The back_insert_iterator transforms iterator writes into calls to the container's push_back, whereas front_insert_iterator calls to push_front. Both of these insert iterators expose a single constructor that accepts a container reference, and their corresponding convenience functions take a single argument. Obviously, the wrapped container must implement the appropriate method. For example, a vector won't work with a front_insert_iterator, and a set won't work with either of them.

The insert_iterator takes two constructor arguments: a container to wrap and an iterator pointing into a position in that container. The insert_iterator then transforms writes into calls to the container's insert method, and it will pass the position you provided on construction as the first argument. For example, you use the insert_iterator to insert into the middle of a sequential container or to add elements into a set with a hint.

NOTE *Internally, all the insert iterators completely ignore* operator++, operator++(int), *and* operator*. *Containers don't need this intermediate step between insertions, but it's generally a requirement for output iterators.*

Listing 14-1 illustrates the basic usages of the three insert iterators by adding elements to a deque.

```
#include <deque>
#include <iterator>

TEST_CASE("Insert iterators convert writes into container insertions.") {
  std::deque<int> dq;
  auto back_instr = std::back_inserter(dq); ❶
  *back_instr = 2; ❷ // 2
  ++back_instr; ❸
  *back_instr = 4; ❹ // 2 4
  ++back_instr;

  auto front_instr = std::front_inserter(dq); ❺
  *front_instr = 1; ❻ // 1 2 4
  ++front_instr;

  auto instr = std::inserter(dq, dq.begin()+2); ❼
  *instr = 3; ❽ // 1 2 3 4
  instr++;

  REQUIRE(dq[0] == 1);
  REQUIRE(dq[1] == 2);
  REQUIRE(dq[2] == 3);
  REQUIRE(dq[3] == 4); ❾
}
```

Listing 14-1: Insert iterators convert writes into container insertions.

First, you build a back_insert_iterator with back_inserter to wrap a deque called dq ❶. When you write into the back_insert_iterator, it translates the write into a push_back, so the deque contains a single element, 2 ❷. Because output iterators require incrementing before you can write again, you follow with an increment ❸. When you write 4 to the `back_insert_iterator`, it again translates the write into a `push_back` so the `deque` contains the elements `2 4` ❹.

Next, you build a `front_insert_iterator` with `front_inserter` to wrap `dq` ❺. Writing `1` into this newly constructed inserter results in a call to `push_front`, so the deque contains the elements `1 2 4` ❻.

Finally, you build an `insert_iterator` with `inserter` by passing `dq` and an iterator pointing to its third element (`4`). When you write 3 into this inserter ❽, it inserts just before the element pointed to by the iterator you passed at construction ❼. This results in `dq` containing the elements `1 2 3 4` ❾.

Table 14-1 summarizes the insert iterators.

Table 14-1: Summary of Insert Iterators

Class	Convenience function	Delegated function	Example containers
`back_insert_iterator`	`back_inserter`	`push_back`	vectors, deques, lists
`front_insert_iterator`	`front_inserter`	`push_front`	deques, lists
`insert_iterator`	`inserter`	`insert`	vectors, deques, lists, sets

List of Supported Output Iterator Operations

Table 14-2 summarizes the output iterator's supported operations.

Table 14-2: Output Iterator's Supported Operations

Operation	Notes
`*itr=t`	Writes into the output iterator. After operation, iterator is incrementable but not necessarily dereferencable.
`++itr` `itr++`	Increments the iterator. After operation, iterator is either dereferencable or exhausted (past the end) but is not necessarily incrementable.
`iterator-type``{ itr }`	Copy-constructs an iterator from `itr`.

Input Iterators

You can use an *input iterator* to read from, increment, and check for equality. It's the foil to the output iterator. You can only iterate through an input iterator once.

The usual pattern when reading from an input iterator is to obtain a half-open range with a *begin* and an *end* iterator. To read through the range, you read the `begin` iterator using `operator*` followed by an increment with `operator++`. Next, you evaluate whether the iterator equals `end`. If it does, you've exhausted the range. If it doesn't, you can continue reading/incrementing.

NOTE *Input iterators are the magic that makes the range expressions discussed in "Range-Based for Loops" on page 234 work.*

A canonical usage of an input iterator is to wrap a program's standard input (usually the keyboard). Once you've read a value from standard input, it's gone. You cannot go back to the beginning and replay. This behavior matches an input iterator's supported operations really well.

In "A Crash Course in Iterators" on page 412, you learned that every container exposes iterators with begin/cbegin/end/cend methods. All of these methods are *at least* input iterators (and they might support additional functionality). For example, Listing 14-2 illustrates how to extract a range from a forward_list and manipulate the iterators manually for reading.

```
#include <forward_list>

TEST_CASE("std::forward_list begin and end provide input iterators") {
  const std::forward_list<int> easy_as{ 1, 2, 3 }; ❶
  auto itr = easy_as.begin(); ❷
  REQUIRE(*itr == 1); ❸
  itr++; ❹
  REQUIRE(*itr == 2);
  itr++;
  REQUIRE(*itr == 3);
  itr++;
  REQUIRE(itr == easy_as.end()); ❺
}
```

Listing 14-2: Interacting with input iterators from a forward_list

You create a forward_list containing three elements ❶. The container's constness means the elements are immutable, so the iterators support only read operations. You extract an iterator with the begin method of forward_list ❷. Using operator*, you extract the element pointed to by itr ❸ and follow up with the obligatory incrementation ❹. Once you've exhausted the range by reading/incrementing, itr equals the end of the forward_list ❺.

Table 14-3 summarizes the input iterator's supported operations.

Table 14-3: Input Iterator's Supported Operations

Operation	Notes
`*itr`	Dereferences the pointed-to member. Might or might not be read-only.
`itr->mbr`	Dereferences the member **mbr** of the object pointed-to by **itr**.
`++itr` `itr++`	Increments the iterator. After operation, iterator is either dereferencable or exhausted (past the end).
`itr1 == itr2` `itr1 != itr2`	Compares whether the iterators are equal (pointing to the same element).
iterator-type`{ itr }`	Copy-constructs an iterator from **itr**.

Forward Iterators

A *forward iterator* is an input iterator with additional features: a forward iterator can also traverse multiple times, default construct, and copy assign. You can use a forward iterator in place of an input iterator in all cases.

All STL containers provide forward iterators. Accordingly, the forward _list used in Listing 14-2 actually provides a forward iterator (which is also an input iterator).

Listing 14-3 updates Listing 14-2 to iterate over the forward_list multiple times.

```
TEST_CASE("std::forward_list's begin and end provide forward iterators") {
  const std::forward_list<int> easy_as{ 1, 2, 3 }; ❶
  auto itr1 = easy_as.begin(); ❷
  auto itr2{ itr1 }; ❸
  int double_sum{};
  while (itr1 != easy_as.end()) ❹
    double_sum += *(itr1++);
  while (itr2 != easy_as.end()) ❺
    double_sum += *(itr2++);
  REQUIRE(double_sum == 12); ❻
}
```

Listing 14-3: Traversing a forward iterator twice

Again you create a forward_list containing three elements ❶. You extract an iterator called itr1 with the begin method of forward_list ❷, then create a copy called itr2 ❸. You exhaust itr1 ❹ and itr2 ❺, iterating over the range twice while summing both times. The resulting double_sum equals 12 ❻.

Table 14-4 summarizes the forward iterator's supported operations.

Table 14-4: Forward Iterator's Supported Operations

Operation	Notes
`*itr`	Dereferences the pointed-to member. Might or might not be read-only.
`itr->mbr`	Dereferences the member `mbr` of the object pointed-to by `itr`.
`++itr` `itr++`	Increments the iterator so it points to the next element.
`itr1 == itr2` `itr1 != itr2`	Compares whether the iterators are equal (pointing to the same element).
iterator-type`{}`	Default constructs an iterator.
iterator-type`{ itr }`	Copy-constructs an iterator from `itr`.
`itr1 = itr2`	Assigns an iterator `itr1` from `itr2`.

Bidirectional Iterators

A *bidirectional iterator* is a forward iterator that can also iterate backward. You can use a bidirectional iterator in place of a forward or input iterator in all cases.

Bidirectional iterators permit backward iteration with operator-- and operator–(int). The STL containers that provide bidirectional iterators are array, list, deque, vector, and all of the ordered associative containers.

Listing 14-4 illustrates how to iterate in both directions using the bidirectional iterator of list.

```
#include <list>

TEST_CASE("std::list begin and end provide bidirectional iterators") {
  const std::list<int> easy_as{ 1, 2, 3 }; ❶
  auto itr = easy_as.begin(); ❷
  REQUIRE(*itr == 1); ❸
  itr++; ❹
  REQUIRE(*itr == 2);
  itr--; ❺
  REQUIRE(*itr == 1); ❻
  REQUIRE(itr == easy_as.cbegin());
}
```

Listing 14-4: The `std::list` methods `begin` and `end` provide bidirectional iterators.

Here, you create a list containing three elements ❶. You extract an iterator called itr with the begin method of list ❷. As with the input and forward iterators, you can dereference ❸ and increment ❹ the iterator. Additionally, you can decrement the iterator ❺ so you can go back to elements you've already iterated over ❻.

Table 14-5 summarizes a bidirectional iterator's supported operations.

Table 14-5: Bidirectional Iterator's Supported Operations

Operation	Notes
`*itr`	Dereferences the pointed-to member. Might or might not be read-only.
`itr->mbr`	Dereferences the member `mbr` of the object pointed to by `itr`.
`++itr` `itr++`	Increments the iterator so it points to the next element.
`--itr` `itr--`	Decrements the iterator so it points to the previous element.
`itr1 == itr2` `itr1 != itr2`	Compares whether the iterators are equal (pointing to the same element).
`iterator-type``{}`	Default constructs an iterator.
`iterator-type``{ itr }`	Copy-constructs an iterator from `itr`.
`itr1 = itr2`	Assigns an iterator `itr1` from `itr2`.

Random-Access Iterators

A *random-access iterator* is a bidirectional iterator that supports random element access. You can use a random-access iterator in place of bidirectional, forward, and input iterators in all cases.

Random-access iterators permit random access with operator[] and also iterator arithmetic, such as adding or subtracting integer values and subtracting other iterators to find distances. The STL containers that provide random-access iterators are array, vector, and deque. Listing 14-5 illustrates how to access arbitrary elements using a random-access iterator from a vector.

```
#include <vector>

TEST_CASE("std::vector begin and end provide random-access iterators") {
  const std::vector<int> easy_as{ 1, 2, 3 }; ❶
  auto itr = easy_as.begin(); ❷
  REQUIRE(itr[0] == 1); ❸
  itr++; ❹
  REQUIRE(*(easy_as.cbegin() + 2) == 3); ❺
  REQUIRE(easy_as.cend() - itr == 2); ❻
}
```

Listing 14-5: Interacting with a random-access iterator

You create a vector containing three elements ❶. You extract an iterator called itr with the begin method of vector ❷. Because this is a random-access iterator, you can use operator[] to dereference arbitrary elements ❸. Of course, you can still increment the iterator using operator++ ❹. You can also add to or subtract from an iterator to access elements at a given offset ❺❻.

List of Supported Random-Access Iterator Operations

Table 14-6 summarizes the random-access iterator's supported operations.

Table 14-6: Random-Access Iterator's Supported Operations

Operation	Notes
`itr[n]`	Dereferences the element with index **n**.
`itr+n` `itr-n`	Returns the iterator at offset **n** from **itr**.
`itr2-itr1`	Computes the distance between **itr1** and **itr2**.
`*itr`	Dereferences the pointed-to member. Might or might not be read-only.
`itr->mbr`	Dereferences the member **mbr** of the object pointed to by **itr**.
`++itr` `itr++`	Increments the iterator so it points to the next element.
`--itr` `itr--`	Decrements the iterator so it points to the previous element.
`itr1 == itr2` `itr1 != itr2`	Compares whether the iterators are equal (pointing to the same element).
iterator-type`{}`	Default constructs an iterator.
iterator-type`{ itr }`	Copy-constructs an iterator from **itr**.

`itr1 < itr2`
`itr1 > itr2`
`itr1 <= itr2`
`itr1 >= itr2`
	Performs the corresponding comparison to the iterators' positions.

Contiguous Iterators

A *contiguous iterator* is a random-access iterator with elements adjacent in memory. For a contiguous iterator `itr`, all elements `itr[n]` and `itr[n+1]` satisfy the following relation for all valid selections of indices `n` and offsets `i`:

```
&itr[n] + i == &itr[n+i]
```

The `vector` and `array` containers provide contiguous iterators, but `list` and `deque` don't.

Mutable Iterators

All forward iterators, bidirectional iterators, random-access iterators, and contiguous iterators can support read-only or read-and-write modes. If an iterator supports read and write, you can assign values to the references returned by dereferencing an iterator. Such iterators are called *mutable iterators*. For example, a bidirectional iterator that supports reading and writing is called a mutable bidirectional iterator.

In each of the examples so far, the containers used to underpin the iterators have been `const`. This produces iterators to `const` objects, which are of course not writable. Listing 14-6 extracts a mutable, random-access iterator from a (non-`const`) `deque`, allowing you to write into arbitrary elements of the container.

```
#include <deque>

TEST_CASE("Mutable random-access iterators support writing.") {
  std::deque<int> easy_as{ 1, 0, 3 }; ❶
  auto itr = easy_as.begin(); ❷
  itr[1] = 2; ❸
  itr++; ❹
  REQUIRE(*itr == 2); ❺
}
```

Listing 14-6: A mutable random-access iterator permits writing.

You construct a `deque` containing three elements ❶ and then obtain an iterator pointing to the first element ❷. Next, you write the value 2 to the second element ❸. Then, you increment the iterator so it points to the element you just modified ❹. When you dereference the pointed-to element, you get back the value you wrote in ❺.

Figure 14-1 illustrates the relationship between the input iterator and all its more featureful descendants.

Iterator category					Supported operations
Contiguous	Random access	Bidirectional	Forward	Input	Read and increment
					Multi-pass
					Decrement
					Random access
					Contiguous elements

Figure 14-1: Input iterator categories and their nested relationships

To summarize, the input iterator supports only read and increment. Forward iterators are also input iterators, so they also support read and increment but additionally allow you to iterate over their range multiple times ("multi-pass"). Bidirectional iterators are also forward iterators, but they additionally permit decrement operations. Random access iterators are also bidirectional iterators, but you can access arbitrary elements in the sequence directly. Finally, contiguous iterators are random-access iterators that guarantee their elements are contiguous in memory.

Auxiliary Iterator Functions

If you write generic code dealing with iterators, you should use *auxiliary iterator functions* from the `<iterator>` header to manipulate iterators rather than using the supported operations directly. These iterator functions perform common tasks of traversing, swapping, and computing distances between iterators. The major advantage of using the auxiliary functions instead of direct iterator manipulation is that the auxiliary functions will inspect an iterator's type traits and determine the most efficient method for performing the desired operation. Additionally, auxiliary iterator functions make generic code even more generic because it will work with the widest range of iterators.

std::advance

The `std::advance` auxiliary iterator function allows you to increment or decrement by the desired amount. This function template accepts an iterator reference and an integer value corresponding to the distance you want to move the iterator:

```
void std::advance(InputIterator&❶ itr, Distance❷ d);
```

The `InputIterator` template parameter must be at least an input iterator ❶, and the `Distance` template parameter is usually an integer ❷.

The advance function doesn't perform bounds checking, so you must ensure that you've not exceeded the valid range for the iterator's position.

Depending on the iterator's category, advance will perform the most efficient operation that achieves the desired effect:

Input iterator The advance function will invoke itr++ the correct number of times; dist cannot be negative.

Bidirectional iterator The function will invoke itr++ or itr-- the correct number of times.

Random access iterator It will invoke itr+=dist; dist can be negative.

NOTE *Random-access iterators will be more efficient than lesser iterators with* advance*, so you might want to use* operator+= *instead of* advance *if you want to forbid the worst-case (linear-time) performance.*

Listing 14-7 illustrates how to use advance to manipulate a random-access iterator.

```
#include <iterator>

TEST_CASE("advance modifies input iterators") {
  std::vector<unsigned char> mission{ ❶
    0x9e, 0xc4, 0xc1, 0x29,
    0x49, 0xa4, 0xf3, 0x14,
    0x74, 0xf2, 0x99, 0x05,
    0x8c, 0xe2, 0xb2, 0x2a
  };
  auto itr = mission.begin(); ❷
  std::advance(itr, 4); ❸
  REQUIRE(*itr == 0x49);
  std::advance(itr, 4); ❹
  REQUIRE(*itr == 0x74);
  std::advance(itr, -8); ❺
  REQUIRE(*itr == 0x9e);
}
```

Listing 14-7: Using advance to manipulate a contiguous iterator

Here, you initialize a vector called mission with 16 unsigned char objects ❶. Next, you extract an iterator called itr using the begin method of mission ❷ and invoke advance on itr to advance four elements so it points at the fourth element (with value 0x49) ❸. You advance again four elements to the eighth element (with value 0x74) ❹. Finally, you invoke advance with –8 to retreat eight values, so the iterator again points to the first element (with value 0x9e) ❺.

std::next and std::prev

The std::next and std::prev auxiliary iterator functions are function templates that compute offsets from a given iterator. They return a new iterator pointing to the desired element without modifying the original iterator, as demonstrated here:

```
ForwardIterator std::next(ForwardIterator& itr❶, Distance d=1❷);
BidirectionalIterator std::prev(BidirectionalIterator& itr❸, Distance d=1❹);
```

The function next accepts at least a forward iterator ❶ and optionally a distance ❷, and it returns an iterator pointing to the corresponding offset. This offset can be negative if itr is bidirectional. The prev function template works like next in reverse: it accepts at least a bidirectional iterator ❸ and optionally a distance ❹ (which can be negative).

Neither next nor prev performs bounds checking. This means you must be absolutely sure that your math is correct and that you're staying within the sequence; otherwise, you'll get undefined behavior.

NOTE *For both next and prev, itr remains unchanged unless it's an rvalue, in which case advance is used for efficiency.*

Listing 14-8 illustrates how to use next to obtain a new iterator pointing to the element at a given offset.

```
#include <iterator>

TEST_CASE("next returns iterators at given offsets") {
  std::vector<unsigned char> mission{
    0x9e, 0xc4, 0xc1, 0x29,
    0x49, 0xa4, 0xf3, 0x14,
    0x74, 0xf2, 0x99, 0x05,
    0x8c, 0xe2, 0xb2, 0x2a
  };
  auto itr1 = mission.begin(); ❶
  std::advance(itr1, 4); ❷
  REQUIRE(*itr1 == 0x49); ❸

  auto itr2 = std::next(itr1); ❹
  REQUIRE(*itr2 == 0xa4); ❺

  auto itr3 = std::next(itr1, 4); ❻
  REQUIRE(*itr3 == 0x74); ❼

  REQUIRE(*itr1 == 0x49); ❽
}
```

Listing 14-8: Using next to obtain offsets from an iterator

As in Listing 14-7, you initialize a vector containing 16 unsigned chars and extract an iterator itr1 pointing to the first element ❶. You use advance to increment the iterator four elements ❷ so it points to the element with the value 0x49 ❸. The first use of next omits a distance argument, which defaults to 1 ❹. This produces a new iterator, itr2, which is one past itr1 ❺.

You invoke next a second time with a distance argument of 4 ❻. This produces another new iterator, itr3, which points to four past the element of itr1 ❼. Neither of these invocations affects the original iterator itr1 ❽.

std::distance

The std::distance auxiliary iterator function enables you to compute the distance between two input iterators itr1 and itr2:

```
Distance std::distance(InputIterator itr1, InputIterator itr2);
```

If the iterators are not random access, itr2 must refer to an element after itr1. It's a good idea to ensure that itr2 comes after itr1, because you'll get undefined behavior if you accidentally violate this requirement and the iterators are not random access.

Listing 14-9 illustrates how to compute the distance between two random access iterators.

```
#include <iterator>

TEST_CASE("distance returns the number of elements between iterators") {
  std::vector<unsigned char> mission{ ❶
    0x9e, 0xc4, 0xc1, 0x29,
    0x49, 0xa4, 0xf3, 0x14,
    0x74, 0xf2, 0x99, 0x05,
    0x8c, 0xe2, 0xb2, 0x2a
  };
  auto eighth = std::next(mission.begin(), 8); ❷
  auto fifth = std::prev(eighth, 3); ❸
  REQUIRE(std::distance(fifth, eighth) == 3); ❹
}
```

Listing 14-9: Using distance to obtain the distance between iterators

After initializing your vector ❶, you create an iterator pointing to the eighth element using std::next ❷. You use std::prev on eighth to obtain an iterator to the fifth element by passing 3 as the second argument ❸. When you pass fifth and eighth as the arguments to distance, you get 3 ❹.

std::iter_swap

The std::iter_swap auxiliary iterator function allows you to swap the values pointed to by two forward iterators itr1 and itr2:

```
Distance std::iter_swap(ForwardIterator itr1, ForwardIterator itr2);
```

The iterators don't need to have the same type, as long as their pointed-to types are assignable to one another. Listing 14-10 illustrates how to use iter_swap to exchange two vector elements.

```
#include <iterator>

TEST_CASE("iter_swap swaps pointed-to elements") {
  std::vector<long> easy_as{ 3, 2, 1 }; ❶
  std::iter_swap(easy_as.begin()❷, std::next(easy_as.begin(), 2)❸);
  REQUIRE(easy_as[0] == 1); ❹
  REQUIRE(easy_as[1] == 2);
  REQUIRE(easy_as[2] == 3);
}
```

Listing 14-10: Using `iter_swap` to exchange pointed-to elements

After you construct a vector with the elements `3 2 1` ❶, you invoke `iter_swap` on the first element ❷ and the last element ❸. After the exchange, the vector contains the elements `1 2 3` ❹.

Additional Iterator Adapters

In addition to insert iterators, the STL provides move iterator adapters and reverse iterator adapters to modify iterator behavior.

NOTE *The STL also provides stream iterator adapters, which you'll learn about in Chapter 16 alongside streams.*

Move Iterator Adapters

A *move iterator adapter* is a class template that converts all iterator accesses into move operations. The convenience function template `std::make_move_iterator` in the `<iterator>` header accepts a single iterator argument and returns a move iterator adapter.

The canonical use of a move iterator adapter is to move a range of objects into a new container. Consider the toy class `Movable` in Listing 14-11, which stores an `int` value called `id`.

```
struct Movable{
  Movable(int id) : id{ id } { } ❶
  Movable(Movable&& m) {
    id = m.id; ❷
    m.id = -1; ❸
  }
  int id;
};
```

Listing 14-11: The `Movable` class stores an `int`.

The `Movable` constructor takes an `int` and stores it into its `id` field ❶. Movable is also move constructible; it will steal the `id` from its move-constructor argument ❷, replacing it with –1 ❸.

Listing 14-12 constructs a `vector` of `Movable` objects called `donor` and moves them into a `vector` called `recipient`.

```
#include <iterator>

TEST_CASE("move iterators convert accesses into move operations") {
  std::vector<Movable> donor; ❶
  donor.emplace_back(1); ❷
  donor.emplace_back(2);
  donor.emplace_back(3);
  std::vector<Movable> recipient{
    std::make_move_iterator(donor.begin()), ❸
    std::make_move_iterator(donor.end()),
  };
  REQUIRE(donor[0].id == -1); ❹
  REQUIRE(donor[1].id == -1);
  REQUIRE(donor[2].id == -1);
  REQUIRE(recipient[0].id == 1); ❺
  REQUIRE(recipient[1].id == 2);
  REQUIRE(recipient[2].id == 3);
}
```

Listing 14-12: Using the move iterator adapter to convert iterator operations into move operations

Here, you default construct a vector called donor ❶, which you use to emplace_back three Movable objects with id fields 1, 2, and 3 ❷. You then use the range constructor of vector with the begin and end iterators of donor, which you pass to make_move_iterator ❸. This converts all iterator operations into move operations, so the move constructor of Movable gets called. As a result, all the elements of donor are in a moved-from state ❹, and all the elements of recipient match the previous elements of donor ❺.

Reverse Iterator Adapters

A *reverse iterator adapter* is a class template that swaps an iterator's increment and decrement operators. The net effect is that you can reverse the input to an algorithm by applying a reverse iterator adapter. One common scenario where you might want to use a reverse iterator is when searching backward from the end of a container. For example, perhaps you've been pushing logs onto the end of a deque and want to find the latest entry that meets some criterion.

Almost all containers in Chapter 13 expose reverse iterators with rbegin/rend/crbegin/crend methods. For example, you can create a container with the reverse sequence of another container, as shown in Listing 14-13.

```
TEST_CASE("reverse iterators can initialize containers") {
  std::list<int> original{ 3, 2, 1 }; ❶
  std::vector<int> easy_as{ original.crbegin(), original.crend() }; ❷
  REQUIRE(easy_as[0] == 1); ❸
  REQUIRE(easy_as[1] == 2);
  REQUIRE(easy_as[2] == 3);
}
```

Listing 14-13: Creating a container with the reverse of another container's elements

Here, you create a list containing the elements 3 2 1 ❶. Next, you construct a vector with the reverse of the sequence by using the crbegin and crend methods ❷. The vector contains 1 2 3, the reverse of the list elements ❸.

Although containers usually expose reverse iterators directly, you can also convert a normal iterator into a reverse iterator manually. The convenience function template std::make_reverse_iterator in the <iterator> header accepts a single iterator argument and returns a reverse iterator adapter.

Reverse iterators are designed to work with half-open ranges that are exactly opposite of normal half-open ranges. Internally, a *reverse half-open range* has an rbegin iterator that refers to 1 past a half-open range's end and an rend iterator that refers to the half-open range's begin, as shown in Figure 14-2.

Figure 14-2: A reverse half-open range

However, these implementation details are all transparent to the user. The iterators dereference as you would expect. As long as the range isn't empty, you can dereference the reverse-begin iterator, and it will return the first element. But you *cannot* dereference the reverse-end iterator.

Why introduce this representational complication? With this design, you can easily swap the begin and end iterators of a half-open range to produce a reverse half-open range. For example, Listing 14-14 uses std::make_reverse_iterator to convert normal iterators to reverse iterators, accomplishing the same task as Listing 14-13.

```
TEST_CASE("make_reverse_iterator converts a normal iterator") {
  std::list<int> original{ 3, 2, 1 };
  auto begin = std::make_reverse_iterator(original.cend()); ❶
  auto end = std::make_reverse_iterator(original.cbegin()); ❷
  std::vector<int> easy_as{ begin, end }; ❸
  REQUIRE(easy_as[0] == 1);
  REQUIRE(easy_as[1] == 2);
  REQUIRE(easy_as[2] == 3);
}
```

Listing 14-14: The make_reverse_iterator function converts a normal iterator to a reverse iterator

Pay special attention to the iterators you're extracting from original. To create the begin iterator, you extract an end iterator from original and pass it to make_reverse_iterator ❶. The reverse iterator adapter will swap increment and decrement operators, but it needs to start in the right place. Likewise, you need to terminate at the original's beginning, so you pass the result of cbegin to make_reverse_iterator to produce the correct end ❷. Passing these to the range constructor of easy_as ❸ produces identical results to Listing 14-13.

NOTE *All reverse iterators expose a* base *method, which will convert the reverse iterator back into a normal iterator.*

Summary

In this short chapter, you learned all the iterator categories: output, input, forward, bidirectional, random-access, and contiguous. Knowing the basic properties of each category provides you with a framework for understanding how containers connect with algorithms. The chapter also surveyed iterator adapters, which enable you to customize iterator behavior, and the auxiliary iterator functions, which help you write generic code with iterators.

EXERCISES

14-1. Create a corollary to Listing 14-8 using `std::prev` rather than `std::next`.

14-2. Write a function template called `sum` that accepts a half-open range of `int` objects and returns the sum of the sequence.

14-3. Write a program that uses the `Stopwatch` class in Listing 12-25 to determine the runtime performance of `std::advance` when given a forward iterator from a large `std::forward_list` and a large `std::vector`. How does the runtime change with the number of elements in the container? (Try hundreds of thousands or millions of elements.)

FURTHER READING

- *The C++ Standard Library: A Tutorial and Reference*, 2nd Edition, by Nicolai M. Josuttis (Addison-Wesley Professional, 2012)
- *C++ Templates: The Complete Guide*, 2nd Edition, by David Vandevoorde et al. (Addison-Wesley, 2017)

15

STRINGS

If you talk to a man in a language he understands, that goes to his head. If you talk to him in his language, that goes to his heart.
—Nelson Mandela

The STL provides a special *string container* for human-language data, such as words, sentences, and markup languages. Available in the `<string>` header, the `std::basic_string` is a class template that you can specialize on a string's underlying character type. As a sequential container, `basic_string` is essentially similar to a `vector` but with some special facilities for manipulating language.

STL `basic_string` provides major safety and feature improvements over C-style or null-terminated strings, and because human-language data inundates most modern programs, you'll probably find `basic_string` indispensable.

std::string

The STL provides four `basic_string` specializations in the `<string>` header. Each specialization implements a string using one of the fundamental character types that you learned about in Chapter 2:

- `std::string` for `char` is used for character sets like ASCII.
- `std::wstring` for `wchar_t` is large enough to contain the largest character of the implementation's locale.
- `std::u16string` for `char16_t` is used for character sets like UTF-16.
- `std::u32string` for `char32_t` is used for character sets like UTF-32.

You'll use the specialization with the appropriate underlying type. Because these specializations have the same interface, all the examples in this chapter will use `std::string`.

Constructing

The `basic_string` container takes three template parameters:

- The underlying character type, `T`
- The underlying type's traits, `Traits`
- An allocator, `Alloc`

Of these, only `T` is required. The STL's `std::char_traits` template class in the `<string>` header abstracts character and string operations from the underlying character type. Also, unless you plan on supporting a custom character type, you won't need to implement your own type traits, because `char_traits` has specializations available for `char`, `wchar_t`, `char16_t`, and `char32_t`. When the stdlib provides specializations for a type, you won't need to provide it yourself unless you require some kind of exotic behavior.

Together, a `basic_string` specialization looks like this, where `T` is a character type:

```
std::basic_string<T, Traits=std::char_traits<T>, Alloc=std::allocator<T>>
```

NOTE *In most cases, you'll be dealing with one of the predefined specializations, especially* `string` *or* `wstring`*. However, if you need a custom allocator, you'll need to specialize* `basic_string` *appropriately.*

The `basic_string<T>` container supports the same constructors as `vector<T>`, plus additional convenience constructors for converting a C-style string. In other words, a `string` supports the constructors of `vector<char>`, a `wstring` supports the constructors of `vector<wchar_t>`, and so on. As with `vector`, use parentheses for all `basic_string` constructors except when you actually want an initializer list.

You can default construct an empty string, or if you want to fill a string with a repeating character, you can use the fill constructor by passing a size_t and a char, as Listing 15-1 illustrates.

```
#include <string>
TEST_CASE("std::string supports constructing") {
  SECTION("empty strings") {
    std::string cheese; ❶
    REQUIRE(cheese.empty()); ❷
  }
  SECTION("repeated characters") {
    std::string roadside_assistance(3, 'A'); ❸
    REQUIRE(roadside_assistance == "AAA"); ❹
  }
}
```

Listing 15-1: The default and fill constructors of `string`

After you default construct a string ❶, it contains no elements ❷. If you want to fill the string with repeating characters, you can use the fill constructor by passing in the number of elements you want to fill and their value ❸. The example fills a string with three A characters ❹.

NOTE *You'll learn about* `std::string` *comparisons with* `operator==` *later in the chapter. Because you generally handle C-style strings with raw pointers or raw arrays,* `operator==` *returns true only when given the same object. However, for* `std::string`, `operator==` *returns true if the contents are equivalent. As you can see in Listing 15-1, the comparison works even when one of the operands is a C-style string literal.*

The string constructor also offers two const char*-based constructors. If the argument points to a null-terminated string, the string constructor can determine the input's length on its own. If the pointer does *not* point to a null-terminated string or if you only want to use the first part of a string, you can pass a length argument that informs the string constructor of how many elements to copy, as Listing 15-2 illustrates.

```
TEST_CASE("std::string supports constructing substrings ") {
  auto word = "gobbledygook"; ❶
  REQUIRE(std::string(word) == "gobbledygook"); ❷
  REQUIRE(std::string(word, 6) == "gobble"); ❸
}
```

Listing 15-2: Constructing a `string` *from C-style strings*

You create a const char* called word pointing to the C-style string literal gobbledygook ❶. Next, you construct a string by passing word. As expected, the resulting string contains gobbledygook ❷. In the next test, you pass the number 6 as a second argument. This causes string to only take the first six characters of word, resulting in the string containing gobble ❸.

Additionally, you can construct strings from other strings. As an STL container, string fully supports copy and move semantics. You can also construct a string from a *substring*—a contiguous subset of another string. Listing 15-3 illustrates these three constructors.

```
TEST_CASE("std::string supports") {
  std::string word("catawampus"); ❶
  SECTION("copy constructing") {
    REQUIRE(std::string(word) == "catawampus"); ❷
  }
  SECTION("move constructing") {
    REQUIRE(std::string(move(word)) == "catawampus"); ❸
  }
  SECTION("constructing from substrings") {
    REQUIRE(std::string(word, 0, 3) == "cat"); ❹
    REQUIRE(std::string(word, 4) == "wampus"); ❺
  }
}
```

Listing 15-3: Copy, move, and substring construction of `string` *objects*

NOTE *In Listing 15-3,* `word` *is in a moved-from state, which, you'll recall from "Move Semantics" on page 122, means it can only be reassigned or destructed.*

Here, you construct a string called `word` containing the characters `catawampus` ❶. Copy construction yields another string containing a copy of the characters of `word` ❷. Move construction steals the characters of `word`, resulting in a new string containing `catawampus` ❸. Finally, you can construct a new string based on substrings. By passing `word`, a starting position of 0, and a length of 3, you construct a new string containing the characters `cat` ❹. If you instead pass `word` and a starting position of 4 (without a length), you get all the characters from the fourth to the end of the original string, resulting in `wampus` ❺.

The string class also supports literal construction with `std::string_literals::operator""s`. The major benefit is notational convenience, but you can also use `operator""s` to embed null characters within a string easily, as Listing 15-4 illustrates.

```
TEST_CASE("constructing a string with") {
  SECTION("std::string(char*) stops at embedded nulls") {
    std::string str("idioglossia\0ellohay!"); ❶
    REQUIRE(str.length() == 11); ❷
  }
  SECTION("operator\"\"s incorporates embedded nulls") {
    using namespace std::string_literals; ❸
    auto str_lit = "idioglossia\0ellohay!"s; ❹
    REQUIRE(str_lit.length() == 20); ❺
  }
}
```

Listing 15-4: Constructing a `string`

In the first test, you construct a string using the literal idioglossia\0ellohay! ❶, which results in a string containing idioglossia ❷. The remainder of the literal didn't get copied into the string due to embedded nulls. In the second test, you bring in the std::string_literals namespace ❸ so you can use operator""s to construct a string from a literal directly ❹. Unlike the std::string constructor ❶, operator""s yields a string containing the entire literal—embedded null bytes and all ❺.

Table 15-1 summarizes the options for constructing a string. In this table, c is a char, n and pos are size_t, str is a string or a C-style string, c_str is a C-style string, and beg and end are input iterators.

Table 15-1: Supported std::string Constructors

Constructor	Produces a string containing
string()	No characters.
string(**n**, **c**)	**c** repeated **n** times.
string(**str**, **pos**, [**n**])	The half-open range **pos** to **pos+n** of **str**. Substring extends from **pos** to **str**'s end if **n** is omitted.
string(**c_str**, [**n**])	A copy of **c_str**, which has length **n**. If **c_str** is null terminated, **n** defaults to the null-terminated string's length.
string(**beg**, **end**)	A copy of the elements in the half-open range from **beg** to **end**.
string(**str**)	A copy of **str**.
string(move(**str**))	The contents of **str**, which is in a moved-from state after construction.
string{ **c1**, **c2**, **c3** }	The characters **c1**, **c2**, and **c3**.
"**my string literal**"s	A string containing the characters my string literal.

String Storage and Small String Optimizations

Exactly like vector, string uses dynamic storage to store its constituent elements contiguously. Accordingly, vector and string have very similar copy/move-construction/assignment semantics. For example, copy operations are potentially more expensive than move operations because the contained elements reside in dynamic memory.

The most popular STL implementations have *small string optimizations (SSO)*. The SSO places the contents of a string within the object's storage (rather than dynamic storage) if the contents are small enough. As a general rule, a string with fewer than 24 bytes is an SSO candidate. Implementers make this optimization because in many modern programs, most strings are short. (A vector doesn't have any small optimizations.)

NOTE *Practically, SSO affects moves in two ways. First, any references to the elements of a string will invalidate if the string moves. Second, moves are potentially slower for strings than vectors because strings need to check for SSO.*

A string has a *size* (or *length*) and a *capacity*. The size is the number of characters contained in the string, and the capacity is the number of characters that the string can hold before needing to resize.

Table 15-2 contains methods for reading and manipulating the size and capacity of a string. In this table, n is a size_t. An asterisk (*) indicates that this operation invalidates raw pointers and iterators to the elements of s in at least some circumstances.

Table 15-2: Supported std::string Storage and Length Methods

Method	Returns
s.empty()	true if s contains no characters; otherwise false.
s.size()	The number of characters in s.
s.length()	Identical to s.size()
s.max_size()	The maximum possible size of s (due to system/runtime limitations).
s.capacity()	The number of characters s can hold before needing to resize.
s.shrink_to_fit()	void; issues a non-binding request to reduce s.capacity() to s.size().*
s.reserve([n])	void; if n > s.capacity(), resizes so s can hold at least n elements; otherwise, issues a non-binding request* to reduce s.capacity() to n or s.size(), whichever is greater.

NOTE *At press time, the draft C++20 standard changes the behavior of the* reserve *method when its argument is less than the size of the* string*. This will match the behavior of* vector*, where there is no effect rather than being equivalent to invoking* shrink_to_fit*.*

Note that the size and capacity methods of string match those of vector very closely. This is a direct result of the closeness of their storage models.

Element and Iterator Access

Because string offers random-access iterators to contiguous elements, it accordingly exposes similar element- and iterator-access methods to vector.

For interoperation with C-style APIs, string also exposes a c_str method, which returns a non-modifiable, null-terminated version of the string as a const char*, as Listing 15-5 illustrates.

```
TEST_CASE("string's c_str method makes null-terminated strings") {
  std::string word("horripilation"); ❶
  auto as_cstr = word.c_str(); ❷
  REQUIRE(as_cstr[0] ==  'h'); ❸
  REQUIRE(as_cstr[1] ==  'o');
  REQUIRE(as_cstr[11] == 'o');
  REQUIRE(as_cstr[12] == 'n');
  REQUIRE(as_cstr[13] == '\0'); ❹
}
```

Listing 15-5: Extracting a null-terminated string from a string

You construct a string called word containing the characters horripilation ❶ and use its c_str method to extract a null-terminated string called as_cstr ❷. Because as_cstr is a const char*, you can use operator[] to illustrate that it contains the same characters as word ❸ and that it is null terminated ❹.

NOTE *The std::string class also supports operator[], which has the same behavior as with a C-style string.*

Generally, c_str and data produce identical results except that references returned by data can be non-const. Whenever you manipulate a string, implementations usually ensure that the contiguous memory backing the string ends with a null terminator. The program in Listing 15-6 illustrates this behavior by printing the results of calling data and c_str alongside their addresses.

```
#include <string>
#include <cstdio>

int main() {
  std::string word("pulchritudinous");
  printf("c_str: %s at 0x%p\n", word.c_str(), word.c_str()); ❶
  printf("data:  %s at 0x%p\n", word.data(), word.data()); ❷
}
--------------------------------------------------------------------------
c_str: pulchritudinous at 0x0000002FAE6FF8D0 ❶
data:  pulchritudinous at 0x0000002FAE6FF8D0 ❷
```

Listing 15-6: Illustrating that c_str and data return equivalent addresses

Both c_str and data produce identical results because they point to the same addresses ❶❷. Because the address is the beginning of a null-terminated string, printf yields identical output for both invocations.

Table 15-3 lists the access methods of string. Note that n is a size_t in the table.

Table 15-3: Supported std::string Element and Iterator Access Methods

Method	Returns
s.begin()	An iterator pointing to the first element.
s.cbegin()	A const iterator pointing to the first element.
s.end()	An iterator pointing to one past the last element.
s.cend()	A const iterator pointing to one past the last element.
s.at(n)	A reference to element n of s. Throws std::out_of_range if out of bounds.
s[n]	A reference to element n of s. Undefined behavior if n > s.size(). Also s[s.size()] must be 0, so writing a non-zero value into this character is undefined behavior.
s.front()	A reference to first element.
s.back()	A reference to last element.

(continued)

Table 15-3: Supported `std::string` Element and Iterator Access Methods (continued)

Method	Returns
`s.data()`	A raw pointer to the first element if string is non-empty. For an empty string, returns a pointer to a null character.
`s.c_str()`	Returns a non-modifiable, null-terminated version of the contents of `s`.

String Comparisons

Note that `string` supports comparisons with other strings and with raw C-style strings using the usual comparison operators. For example, the equality `operator==` returns `true` if the size and contents of the left and right size are equal, whereas the inequality `operator!=` returns the opposite. The remaining comparison operators perform *lexicographical comparison*, meaning they sort alphabetically where $A < Z < a < z$ and where, if all else is equal, shorter words are less than longer words (for example, *pal* < *palindrome*). Listing 15-7 illustrates comparisons.

NOTE *Technically, lexicographical comparison depends on the encoding of the* `string`*. It's theoretically possible that a system could use a default encoding where the alphabet is in some completely jumbled order (such as the nearly obsolete EBCDIC encoding, which put lowercase letters before uppercase letters), which would affect* `string` *comparison. For ASCII-compatible encodings, you don't need to worry since they imply the expected lexicographical behavior.*

```
TEST_CASE("std::string supports comparison with") {
  using namespace std::literals::string_literals; ❶
  std::string word("allusion"); ❷
  SECTION("operator== and !=") {
    REQUIRE(word == "allusion"); ❸
    REQUIRE(word == "allusion"s); ❹
    REQUIRE(word != "Allusion"s); ❺
    REQUIRE(word != "illusion"s); ❻
    REQUIRE_FALSE(word == "illusion"s); ❼
  }
  SECTION("operator<") {
    REQUIRE(word < "illusion"); ❽
    REQUIRE(word < "illusion"s); ❾
    REQUIRE(word > "Illusion"s); ❿
  }
}
```

Listing 15-7: The `string` *class supports comparison*

Here, you bring in the `std::literals::string_literals` namespace so you can easily construct a `string` with `operator""s` ❶. You also construct a `string` called `word` containing the characters `allusion` ❷. In the first set of tests, you examine `operator==` and `operator!=`.

You can see that word equals (==) allusion as both a C-style string ❸ and a string ❹, but it doesn't equal (!=) strings containing Allusion ❺ or illusion ❻. As usual, operator== and operator!= always return opposite results ❼.

The next set of tests uses operator< to show that allusion is less than illusion ❽, because *a* is lexicographically less than *i*. Comparisons work with C-style strings and strings ❾. Listing 15-7 also shows that Allusion is less than allusion ❿ because *A* is lexicographically less than *a*.

Table 15-4 lists the comparison methods of string. Note that other is a string or char* C-style string in the table.

Table 15-4: Supported std::string Comparison Operators

Method	Returns
s == other	true if s and other have identical characters and lengths; otherwise false
s != other	The opposite of operator==
s.compare(other)	Returns 0 if s == other, a negative number if s < other, and a positive number if s > other
s < other s > other s <= other s >= other	The result of the corresponding comparison operation, according to lexicographical sort

Manipulating Elements

For manipulating elements, string has *a lot* of methods. It supports all the methods of vector<char> plus many others useful to manipulating human-language data.

Adding Elements

To add elements to a string, you can use push_back, which inserts a single character at the end. When you want to insert more than one character to the end of a string, you can use operator+= to append a character, a null-terminated char* string, or a string. You can also use the append method, which has three overloads. First, you can pass a string or a null-terminated char* string, an optional offset into that string, and an optional number of characters to append. Second, you can pass a length and a char, which will append that number of chars to the string. Third, you can append a half-open range. Listing 15-8 illustrates all of these operations.

```
TEST_CASE("std::string supports appending with") {
  std::string word("butt"); ❶
  SECTION("push_back") {
    word.push_back('e'); ❷
    REQUIRE(word == "butte");
  }
  SECTION("operator+=") {
    word += "erfinger"; ❸
```

```
    REQUIRE(word == "butterfinger");
  }
  SECTION("append char") {
    word.append(1, 's'); ❹
    REQUIRE(word == "butts");
  }
  SECTION("append char*") {
    word.append("stockings", 5); ❺
    REQUIRE(word == "buttstock");
  }
  SECTION("append (half-open range)") {
    std::string other("onomatopoeia"); ❻
    word.append(other.begin(), other.begin()+2); ❼
    REQUIRE(word == "button");
  }
}
```

Listing 15-8: Appending to a string

To begin, you initialize a string called word containing the characters butt ❶. In the first test, you invoke push_back with the letter e ❷, which yields butte. Next, you add erfinger to word using operator+= ❸, yielding butterfinger. In the first invocation of append, you append a single s ❹ to yield butts. (This setup works just like push_back.) A second overload of append allows you to provide a char* and a length. By providing stockings and length 5, you add stock to word to yield buttstock ❺. Because append works with half-open ranges, you can also construct a string called other containing the characters onomatopoeia ❻ and append the first two characters via a half-open range to yield button ❼.

NOTE *Recall from "Test Cases and Sections" on page 308 that each SECTION of a Catch unit test runs independently, so modifications to word are independent of each other: the setup code resets word for each test.*

Removing Elements

To remove elements from a string, you have several options. The simplest method is to use pop_back, which follows vector in removing the last character from a string. If you want to instead remove all the characters (to yield an empty string), use the clear method. When you need more precision in removing elements, use the erase method, which provides several overloads. You can provide an index and a length, which removes the corresponding characters. You can also provide an iterator to remove a single element or a half-open range to remove many. Listing 15-9 illustrates removing elements from a string.

```
TEST_CASE("std::string supports removal with") {
  std::string word("therein"); ❶
  SECTION("pop_back") {
    word.pop_back();
    word.pop_back(); ❷
    REQUIRE(word == "there");
  }
```

```
  SECTION("clear") {
    word.clear(); ❸
    REQUIRE(word.empty());
  }
  SECTION("erase using half-open range") {
    word.erase(word.begin(), word.begin()+3); ❹
    REQUIRE(word == "rein");
  }
  SECTION("erase using an index and length") {
    word.erase(5, 2);
    REQUIRE(word == "there"); ❺
  }
}
```

Listing 15-9: Removing elements from a `string`

You construct a `string` called `word` containing the characters `therein` ❶. In the first test, you call `pop_back` twice to first remove the letter `n` followed by the letter `i` so `word` contains the characters `there` ❷. Next, you invoke `clear`, which removes all the characters from `word` so it's `empty` ❸. The last two tests use `erase` to remove some subset of the characters in `word`. In the first usage, you remove the first three characters with a half-open range so `word` contains `rein` ❹. In the second, you remove the characters starting at index 5 (`i` in `therein`) and extending two characters ❺. Like the first test, this yields the characters `there`.

Replacing Elements

To insert and remove elements simultaneously, use `string` to expose the `replace` method, which has many overloads.

First, you can provide a half-open range and a null-terminated `char*` or a `string`, and `replace` will perform a simultaneous `erase` of all the elements within the half-open range and an `insert` of the provided `string` where the range used to be. Second, you can provide two half-open ranges, and `replace` will insert the second range instead of a `string`.

Instead of replacing a range, you can use either an index or a single iterator and a length. You can supply a new half-open range, a character and a size, or a `string`, and `replace` will substitute new elements over the implied range. Listing 15-10 demonstrates some of these possibilities.

```
TEST_CASE("std::string replace works with") {
  std::string word("substitution"); ❶
  SECTION("a range and a char*") {
    word.replace(word.begin()+9, word.end(), "e"); ❷
    REQUIRE(word == "substitute");
  }
  SECTION("two ranges") {
    std::string other("innuendo");
    word.replace(word.begin(), word.begin()+3,
                 other.begin(), other.begin()+2); ❸
    REQUIRE(word == "institution");
  }
```

```
  SECTION("an index/length and a string") {
    std::string other("vers");
    word.replace(3, 6, other); ❹
    REQUIRE(word == "subversion");
  }
}
```

Listing 15-10: Replacing elements of a `string`

Here, you construct a `string` called `word` containing `substitution` ❶. In the first test, you replace all the characters from index 9 to the end with the letter `e`, resulting in the word `substitute` ❷. Next, you replace the first three letters of `word` with the first two letters of a `string` containing `innuendo` ❸, resulting in `institution`. Finally, you use an alternate way of specifying the target sequence with an index and a length to replace the characters `stitut` with the characters `vers`, yielding `subversion` ❹.

The `string` class offers a `resize` method to manually set the length of `string`. The `resize` method takes two arguments: a new length and an optional `char`. If the new length of `string` is smaller, `resize` ignores the `char`. If the new length of `string` is larger, `resize` appends the `char` the implied number of times to achieve the desired length. Listing 15-11 illustrates the `resize` method.

```
TEST_CASE("std::string resize") {
  std::string word("shamp"); ❶
  SECTION("can remove elements") {
    word.resize(4); ❷
    REQUIRE(word == "sham");
  }
  SECTION("can add elements") {
    word.resize(7, 'o'); ❸
    REQUIRE(word == "shampoo");
  }
}
```

Listing 15-11: Resizing a `string`

You construct a `string` called `word` containing the characters `shamp` ❶. In the first test, you resize `word` to length `4` so it contains `sham` ❷. In the second, you `resize` to a length of 7 and provide the optional character `o` as the value to extend `word` with ❸. This results in `word` containing `shampoo`.

The "Constructing" section on page 482 explained a substring constructor that can extract contiguous sequences of characters to create a new `string`. You can also generate substrings using the `substr` method, which takes two optional arguments: a position argument and a length. The position defaults to 0 (the beginning of the `string`), and the length defaults to the remainder of the `string`. Listing 15-12 illustrates how to use `substr`.

```
TEST_CASE("std::string substr with") {
  std::string word("hobbits"); ❶
  SECTION("no arguments copies the string") {
```

```
    REQUIRE(word.substr() == "hobbits"); ❷
  }
  SECTION("position takes the remainder") {
    REQUIRE(word.substr(3) == "bits"); ❸
  }
  SECTION("position/index takes a substring") {
    REQUIRE(word.substr(3, 3) == "bit"); ❹
  }
}
```

Listing 15-12: Extracting substrings from a string

You declare a string called word containing hobbits ❶. If you invoke substr with no arguments, you simply copy the string ❷. When you provide the position argument 3, substr extracts the substring beginning at element 3 and extending to the end of the string, yielding bits ❸. Finally, when you provide a position (3) and a length (3), you instead get bit ❹.

Summary of string Manipulation Methods

Table 15-5 lists many of the insertion and deletion methods of string. In this table, str is a string or a C-style char* string, p and n are size_t, ind is a size_t index or an iterator into s, n and i are a size_t, c is a char, and beg and end are iterators. An asterisk (*) indicates that this operation invalidates raw pointers and iterators to v's elements in at least some circumstances.

Table 15-5: Supported std::string Element Manipulation Methods

Method	Description
s.insert(**ind**, **str**, [**p**], [**n**])	Inserts the **n** elements of **str**, starting at **p**, into **s** just before **ind**. If no **n** supplied, inserts the entire string or up to the first null of a char*; **p** defaults to 0.*
s.insert(**ind**, **n**, **c**)	Inserts **n** copies of **c** just before **ind**.*
s.insert(**ind**, **beg**, **end**)	Inserts the half-open range from **beg** to **end** just before **ind**. *
s.append(**str**, [**p**], [**n**])	Equivalent to **s**.insert(**s**.end(), **str**, [**p**], [**n**]).*
s.append(**n**, **c**)	Equivalent to **s**.insert(**s**.end(), **n**, **c**).*
s.append(**beg**, **end**)	Appends the half-open range from **beg** to **end** to the end of **s**.*
s += **c** s += **str**	Appends **c** or **str** to the end of **s**.*
s.push_back(**c**)	Appends **c** to the end of **s**.*
s.clear()	Removes all characters from **s**.*
s.erase([**i**], [**n**])	Removes **n** characters starting at position **i**; **i** defaults to 0, and **n** defaults to the remainder of **s**.*
s.erase(**itr**)	Erases the element pointed to by **itr**.*
s.erase(**beg**, **end**)	Erases the elements on the half-open range from **beg** to **end**.*
s.pop_back()	Removes the last element of **s**.*

(continued)

Table 15-5: Supported std::string Element Manipulation Methods (continued)

Method	Description
s.resize(n,[c])	Resizes the string so it contains **n** characters. If this operation increases the string's length, it adds copies of **c**, which defaults to 0.*
s.replace(i, n1, str, [p], [n2])	Replaces the **n1** characters starting at index **i** with the **n2** elements in **str** starting at **p**. By default, **p** is 0 and **n2** is **str**.length().*
s.replace(beg, end, str)	Replaces the half-open range **beg** to **end** with **str**.*
s.replace(p, n, str)	Replaces from index **p** to **p+n** with **str**.*
s.replace(beg1, end1, beg2, end2)	Replaces the half-open range **beg1** to **end1** with the half-open range **beg2** to **end2**.*
s.replace(ind, c, [n])	Replaces **n** elements starting at **ind** with **c**s.*
s.replace(ind, beg, end)	Replaces elements starting at **ind** with the half-open range **beg** to **end**.*
s.substr([p], [c])	Returns the substring starting at **p** with length **c**. By default, **p** is 0 and **c** is the remainder of the string.
s1.swap(s2) swap(s1, s2)	Exchanges the contents of **s1** and **s2**.*

Search

In addition to the preceding methods, string offers several *search methods*, which enable you to locate substrings and characters that you're interested in. Each method performs a particular kind of search, so which you choose depends on the particulars of the application.

find

The first method string offers is find, which accepts a string, a C-style string, or a char as its first argument. This argument is an element that you want to locate within this. Optionally, you can provide a second size_t position argument that tells find where to start looking. If find fails to locate the substring, it returns the special size_t-valued, constant, static member std::string::npos. Listing 15-13 illustrates the find method.

```
TEST_CASE("std::string find") {
  using namespace std::literals::string_literals;
  std::string word("pizzazz"); ❶
  SECTION("locates substrings from strings") {
    REQUIRE(word.find("zz"s) == 2); // pi(z)zazz ❷
  }
  SECTION("accepts a position argument") {
    REQUIRE(word.find("zz"s, 3) == 5); // pizza(z)z ❸
  }
  SECTION("locates substrings from char*") {
    REQUIRE(word.find("zaz") == 3); // piz(z)azz ❹
  }
```

```
  SECTION("returns npos when not found") {
    REQUIRE(word.find('x') == std::string::npos); ❺
  }
}
```

Listing 15-13: Finding substrings within a string

Here, you construct the string called word containing pizzazz ❶. In the first test, you invoke find with a string containing zz, which returns 2 ❷, the index of the first *z* in pizzazz. When you provide a position argument of 3 corresponding to the second *z* in pizzazz, find locates the second *zz* beginning at 5 ❸. In the third test, you use the C-style string zaz, and find returns 3, again corresponding to the second *z* in pizzazz ❹. Finally, you attempt to find the character *x*, which doesn't appear in pizzazz, so find returns std::string::npos ❺.

rfind

The rfind method is an alternative to find that takes the same arguments but searches *in reverse*. You might want to use this functionality if, for example, you were looking for particular punctuation at the end of a string, as Listing 15-14 illustrates.

```
TEST_CASE("std::string rfind") {
  using namespace std::literals::string_literals;
  std::string word("pizzazz"); ❶
  SECTION("locates substrings from strings") {
    REQUIRE(word.rfind("zz"s) == 5); // pizza(z)z ❷
  }
  SECTION("accepts a position argument") {
    REQUIRE(word.rfind("zz"s, 3) == 2); // pi(z)zazz ❸
  }
  SECTION("locates substrings from char*") {
    REQUIRE(word.rfind("zaz") == 3); // piz(z)azz ❹
  }
  SECTION("returns npos when not found") {
    REQUIRE(word.rfind('x') == std::string::npos); ❺
  }
}
```

Listing 15-14: Finding substrings in reverse within a string

Using the same word ❶, you use the same arguments as in Listing 15-13 to test rfind. Given zz, rfind returns 5, the second to last *z* in pizzazz ❷. When you provide the positional argument 3, rfind instead returns the first *z* in pizzazz ❸. Because there's only one occurrence of the substring zaz, rfind returns the same position as find ❹. Also like find, rfind returns std::string::npos when given x ❺.

find_*_of

Whereas find and rfind locate exact subsequences in a string, a family of related functions finds the first character contained in a given argument.

The find_first_of function accepts a string and locates the first character in this contained in the argument. Optionally, you can provide a size_t position argument to indicate to find_first_of where to start in the string. If find _first_of cannot find a matching character, it will return std::string::npos. Listing 15-15 illustrates the find_first_of function.

```
TEST_CASE("std::string find_first_of") {
  using namespace std::literals::string_literals;
  std::string sentence("I am a Zizzer-Zazzer-Zuzz as you can plainly see."); ❶
  SECTION("locates characters within another string") {
    REQUIRE(sentence.find_first_of("Zz"s) == 7); // (Z)izzer ❷
  }
  SECTION("accepts a position argument") {
    REQUIRE(sentence.find_first_of("Zz"s, 11) == 14); // (Z)azzer ❸
  }
  SECTION("returns npos when not found") {
    REQUIRE(sentence.find_first_of("Xx"s) == std::string::npos); ❹
  }
}
```

Listing 15-15: Finding the first element from a set within a string

The string called sentence contains I am a Zizzer-Zazzer-Zuzz as you can plainly see. ❶. Here, you invoke find_first_of with the string Zz, which matches both lowercase and uppercase *z*. This returns 7, which corresponds to the first Z in sentence, **Z**izzer ❷. In the second test, you again provide the string Zz but also pass the position argument 11, which corresponds to the e in Zizz**e**r. This results in 14, which corresponds to the Z in **Z**azzer ❸. Finally, you invoke find_first_of with Xx, which results in std::string::npos because sentence doesn't contain an x (or an X) ❹.

A string offers three find_first_of variations:

- find_first_not_of returns the first character *not* contained in the string argument. Rather than providing a string containing the elements you want to find, you provide a string of characters you *don't* want to find.
- find_last_of performs matching in reverse; rather than searching from the beginning of the string or from the position argument and proceeding to the end, find_last_of begins at the end of the string or from the position argument and proceeds to the beginning.
- find_last_not_of combines the two prior variations: you pass a string containing elements you don't want to find, and find_last_not_of searches in reverse.

Your choice of find function boils down to what your algorithmic requirements are. Do you need to search from the back of a string, say for a punctuation mark? If so, use find_last_of. Are you looking for the first space in a string? If so, use find_first_of. Do you want to invert your search and look for the first element that is not a member of some set? Then use the alternatives find_first_not_of and find_last_not_of, depending on whether you want to start from the beginning or end of the string.

Listing 15-16 illustrates these three find_first_of variations.

```
TEST_CASE("std::string") {
  using namespace std::literals::string_literals;
  std::string sentence("I am a Zizzer-Zazzer-Zuzz as you can plainly see."); ❶
  SECTION("find_last_of finds last element within another string") {
    REQUIRE(sentence.find_last_of("Zz"s) == 24); // Zuz(z) ❷
  }
  SECTION("find_first_not_of finds first element not within another string") {
    REQUIRE(sentence.find_first_not_of(" -IZaeimrz"s) == 22); // Z(u)zz ❸
  }
  SECTION("find_last_not_of finds last element not within another string") {
    REQUIRE(sentence.find_last_not_of(" .es"s) == 43); // plainl(y) ❹
  }
}
```

Listing 15-16: Alternatives to the `find_first_of` method of `string`

Here, you initialize the same sentence as in Listing 15-15 ❶. In the first test, you use find_last_of on Zz, which searches in reverse for any *z* or *Z* and returns 24, the last *z* in the sentence **Zuzz** ❷. Next, you use find_first_not_of and pass a farrago of characters (not including the letter *u*), which results in 22, the position of the first *u* in **Zuzz** ❸. Finally, you use find_last_not_of to find the last character not equal to space, period, *e*, or *s*. This results in 43, the position of *y* in **plainly** ❹.

Summary of string Search Methods

Table 15-6 lists many of the search methods for string. Note that s2 is a string; cstr is a C-style char* string; c is a char; and n, l, and pos are size_t in the table.

Table 15-6: Supported std::string Search Algorithms

Method	Searches s starting at p and returns the position of the . . .
s.find(**s2**, [**p**])	First substring equal to **s2**; **p** defaults to 0.
s.find(**cstr**, [**p**], [**l**])	First substring equal to the first **l** characters of **cstr**; **p** defaults to 0; **l** defaults to **cstr**'s length per null termination.
s.find(**c**, [**p**])	First character equal to **c**; **p** defaults to 0.
s.rfind(**s2**, [**p**])	Last substring equal to **s2**; **p** defaults to npos.
s.rfind(**cstr**, [**p**], [**l**])	Last substring equal to the first **l** characters of **cstr**; **p** defaults to npos; **l** defaults to **cstr**'s length per null termination.
s.rfind(**c**, [**p**])	Last character equal to **c**; **p** defaults to npos.
s.find_first_of(**s2**, [**p**])	First character contained in **s2**; **p** defaults to 0.
s.find_first_of(**cstr**, [**p**], [**l**])	First character contained in the first **l** characters of **cstr**; **p** defaults to 0; **l** defaults to **cstr**'s length per null termination.

(continued)

Table 15-6: Supported std::string Search Algorithms (continued)

Method	Searches s starting at p and returns the position of the . . .
s.find_first_of(**c**, [**p**])	First character equal to **c**; **p** defaults to 0.
s.find_last_of(**s2**, [**p**])	Last character contained in **s2**; **p** defaults to 0.
s.find_last_of(**cstr**, [**p**], [**l**])	Last character contained in the first **l** characters of **cstr**; **p** defaults to 0; **l** defaults to **cstr**'s length per null termination.
s.find_last_of(**c**, [**p**])	Last character equal to **c**; **p** defaults to 0.
s.find_first_not_of(**s2**, [**p**])	First character not contained in **s2**; **p** defaults to 0.
s.find_first_not_of(**cstr**, [**p**], [**l**])	First character not contained in the first **l** characters of **cstr**; **p** defaults to 0; **l** defaults to **cstr**'s length per null termination.
s.find_first_not_of(**c**, [**p**])	First character not equal to **c**; **p** defaults to 0.
s.find_last_not_of(**s2**, [**p**])	Last character not contained in **s2**; **p** defaults to 0.
s.find_last_not_of(**cstr**, [**p**], [**l**])	Last character not contained in the first **l** characters of **cstr**; **p** defaults to 0; **l** defaults to **cstr**'s length per null termination.
s.find_last_not_of(**c**, [**p**])	Last character not equal to **c**; **p** defaults to 0.

Numeric Conversions

The STL provides functions for converting between string or wstring and the fundamental numeric types. Given a numeric type, you can use the std::to_string and std::to_wstring functions to generate its string or wstring representation. Both functions have overloads for all the numeric types. Listing 15-17 illustrates string and wstring.

```
TEST_CASE("STL string conversion function") {
  using namespace std::literals::string_literals;
  SECTION("to_string") {
    REQUIRE("8675309"s == std::to_string(8675309)); ❶
  }
  SECTION("to_wstring") {
    REQUIRE(L"109951.1627776"s == std::to_wstring(109951.1627776)); ❷
  }
}
```

Listing 15-17: Numeric conversion functions of string

NOTE *Thanks to the inherent inaccuracy of the double type, the second unit test ❷ might fail on your system.*

The first example uses to_string to convert the int 8675309 into a string ❶; the second example uses to_wstring to convert the double 109951.1627776 into a wstring ❷.

You can also convert the other way, going from a string or wstring to a numeric type. Each numeric conversion function accepts a string or wstring containing a string-encoded number as its first argument. Next, you can provide an optional pointer to a size_t. If provided, the conversion function will write the index of the last character it was able to convert (or the length of the input string if it decoded all characters). By default, this index argument is nullptr, in which case the conversion function doesn't write the index. When the target type is integral, you can provide a third argument: an int corresponding to the base of the encoded string. This base argument is optional and defaults to 10.

Each conversion function throws std::invalid_argument if no conversion could be performed and throws std::out_of_range if the converted value is out of range for the corresponding type.

Table 15-7 lists each of these conversion functions along with its target type. In this table, s is a string. If p is not nullptr, the conversion function will write the position of the first unconverted character in s to the memory pointed to by p. If all characters are encoded, returns the length of s. Here, b is the number's base representation in s. Note that p defaults to nullptr, and b defaults to 10.

Table 15-7: Supported Numeric Conversion Functions for std::string and std::wstring

Function	Converts s to
stoi(s, [p], [b])	An int
stol(s, [p], [b])	A long
stoll(s, [p], [b])	A long long
stoul(s, [p], [b])	An unsigned long
stoull(s, [p], [b])	An unsigned long long
stof(s, [p])	A float
stod(s, [p])	A double
stold(s, [p])	A long double
to_string(n)	A string
to_wstring(n)	A wstring

Listing 15-18 illustrates several numeric conversion functions.

```
TEST_CASE("STL string conversion function") {
  using namespace std::literals::string_literals;
  SECTION("stoi") {
    REQUIRE(std::stoi("8675309"s) == 8675309); ❶
  }
  SECTION("stoi") {
    REQUIRE_THROWS_AS(std::stoi("1099511627776"s), std::out_of_range); ❷
  }
  SECTION("stoul with all valid characters") {
    size_t last_character{};
    const auto result = std::stoul("0xD3C34C3D"s, &last_character, 16); ❸
```

```
    REQUIRE(result == 0xD3C34C3D);
    REQUIRE(last_character == 10);
  }
  SECTION("stoul") {
    size_t last_character{};
    const auto result = std::stoul("42six"s, &last_character); ❹
    REQUIRE(result == 42);
    REQUIRE(last_character == 2);
  }
  SECTION("stod") {
    REQUIRE(std::stod("2.7182818"s) == Approx(2.7182818)); ❺
  }
}
```

Listing 15-18: String conversion functions of `string`

First, you use `stoi` to convert `8675309` to an integer ❶. In the second test, you attempt to use `stoi` to convert the `string` `1099511627776` into an integer. Because this value is too large for an `int`, `stoi` throws `std::out_of_range` ❷. Next, you convert `0xD3C34C3D` with `stoi`, but you provide the two optional arguments: a pointer to a `size_t` called `last_character` and a hexadecimal base ❸. The `last_character` object is `10`, the length of `0xD3C34C3D`, because `stoi` can parse every character. The `string` in the next test, `42six`, contains the unparsable characters `six`. When you invoke `stoul` this time, the `result` is `42` and `last_character` equals `2`, the position of `s` in `six` ❹. Finally, you use `stod` to convert the `string` `2.7182818` to a `double` ❺.

NOTE *Boost's Lexical Cast provides an alternative, template-based approach to numeric conversions. Refer to the documentation for* `boost::lexical_cast` *available in the* `<boost/lexical_cast.hpp>` *header.*

String View

A *string view* is an object that represents a constant, contiguous sequence of characters. It's very similar to a `const string` reference. In fact, string view classes are often implemented as a pointer to a character sequence and a length.

The STL offers the class template `std::basic_string_view` in the `<string_view>` header, which is analogous to `std::basic_string`. The template `std::basic_string_view` has a specialization for each of the four commonly used character types:

- `char` has `string_view`
- `wchar_t` has `wstring_view`
- `char16_t` has `u16string_view`
- `char32_t` has `u32string_view`

This section discusses the string_view specialization for demonstration purposes, but the discussion generalizes to the other three specializations.

The string_view class supports most of the same methods as string; in fact, it's designed to be a drop-in replacement for a const string&.

Constructing

The string_view class supports default construction, so it has zero length and points to nullptr. Importantly, string_view supports implicit construction from a const string& or a C-style string. You can construct string_view from a char* and a size_t, so you can manually specify the desired length in case you want a substring or you have embedded nulls. Listing 15-19 illustrates the use of string_view.

```
TEST_CASE("std::string_view supports") {
  SECTION("default construction") {
    std::string_view view; ❶
    REQUIRE(view.data() == nullptr);
    REQUIRE(view.size() == 0);
    REQUIRE(view.empty());
  }
  SECTION("construction from string") {
    std::string word("sacrosanct");
    std::string_view view(word); ❷
    REQUIRE(view == "sacrosanct");
  }
  SECTION("construction from C-string") {
    auto word = "viewership";
    std::string_view view(word); ❸
    REQUIRE(view == "viewership");
  }
  SECTION("construction from C-string and length") {
    auto word = "viewership";
    std::string_view view(word, 4); ❹
    REQUIRE(view == "view");
  }
}
```

Listing 15-19: The constructors of string_view

The default-constructed string_view points to nullptr and is empty ❶. When you construct a string_view from a string ❷ or a C-style string ❸, it points to the original's contents. The final test provides the optional length argument 4, which means the string_view refers to only the first four characters instead ❹.

Although string_view also supports copy construction and assignment, it doesn't support move construction or assignment. This design makes sense when you consider that string_view doesn't own the sequence to which it points.

Supported string_view Operations

The string_view class supports many of the same operations as a const string& with identical semantics. The following lists all the shared methods between string and string_view:

Iterators begin, end, rbegin, rend, cbegin, cend, crbegin, crend

Element Access operator[], at, front, back, data

Capacity size, length, max_size, empty

Search find, rfind, find_first_of, find_last_of, find_first_not_of, find_last_not_of

Extraction copy, substr

Comparison compare, operator==, operator!= , operator<, operator>, operator<=, operator>=

In addition to these shared methods, string_view supports the remove _prefix method, which removes the given number of characters from the beginning of the string_view, and the remove_suffix method, which instead removes characters from the end. Listing 15-20 illustrates both methods.

```
TEST_CASE("std::string_view is modifiable with") {
  std::string_view view("previewing"); ❶
  SECTION("remove_prefix") {
    view.remove_prefix(3); ❷
    REQUIRE(view == "viewing");
  }
  SECTION("remove_suffix") {
    view.remove_suffix(3); ❸
    REQUIRE(view == "preview");
  }
}
```

Listing 15-20: Modifying a string_view with remove_prefix and remove_suffix

Here, you declare a string_view referring to the string literal previewing ❶. The first test invokes remove_prefix with 3 ❷, which removes three characters from the front of string_view so it now refers to viewing. The second test instead invokes remove_suffix with 3 ❸, which removes three characters from the back of the string_view and results in preview.

Ownership, Usage, and Efficiency

Because string_view doesn't own the sequence to which it refers, it's up to you to ensure that the lifetime of the string_view is a subset of the referred-to sequence's lifetime.

Perhaps the most common usage of string_view is as a function parameter. When you need to interact with an immutable sequence of characters, it's the first port of call. Consider the count_vees function in Listing 15-21, which counts the frequency of the letter v in a sequence of characters.

```
#include <string_view>

size_t count_vees(std::string_view my_view❶) {
  size_t result{};
  for(auto letter : my_view) ❷
    if (letter == 'v') result++; ❸
  return result; ❹
}
```

Listing 15-21: The count_vees function

The count_vees function takes a string_view called my_view ❶, which you iterate over using a range-based for loop ❷. Each time a character in my_view equals v, you increment a result variable ❸, which you return after exhausting the sequence ❹.

You could reimplement Listing 15-21 by simply replacing string_view with const string&, as demonstrated in Listing 15-22.

```
#include <string>

size_t count_vees(const std::string& my_view) {
--snip--
}
```

Listing 15-22: The count_vees function reimplemented to use a const string& instead of a string_view

If string_view is just a drop-in replacement for a const string&, why bother having it? Well, if you invoke count_vees with a std::string, there's no difference: modern compilers will emit the same code.

If you instead invoke count_vees with a string literal, there's a big difference: when you pass a string literal for a const string&, you construct a string. When you pass a string literal for a string_view, you construct a string_view. Constructing a string is probably more expensive, because it might have to allocate dynamic memory and it definitely has to copy characters. A string_view is just a pointer and a length (no copying or allocating is required).

Regular Expressions

A *regular expression*, also called a *regex*, is a string that defines a search pattern. Regexes have a long history in computer science and form a sort of mini-language for searching, replacing, and extracting language data. The STL offers regular expression support in the <regex> header.

When used judiciously, regular expressions can be tremendously powerful, declarative, and concise; however, it's also easy to write regexes that are totally inscrutable. Use regexes deliberately.

Patterns

You build regular expressions using strings called *patterns*. Patterns represent a desired set of strings using a particular regular expression grammar that sets the syntax for building patterns. In other words, a pattern defines the subset of all possible strings that you're interested in. The STL supports a handful of grammars, but the focus here will be on the very basics of the default grammar, the modified ECMAScript regular expression grammar (see [re.grammar] for details).

Character Classes

In the ECMAScript grammar, you intermix literal characters with special markup to describe your desired strings. Perhaps the most common markup is a *character class*, which stands in for a set of possible characters: `\d` matches any digit, `\s` matches any whitespace, and `\w` matches any alphanumeric ("word") character.

Table 15-8 lists a few example regular expressions and possible interpretations.

Table 15-8: Regular Expression Patterns Using Only Character Classes and Literals

Regex pattern	Possibly describes
`\d\d\d-\d\d\d-\d\d\d\d`	An American phone number, such as 202-456-1414
`\d\d:\d\d \wM`	A time in HH:MM AM/PM format, such as 08:49 PM
`\w\w\d\d\d\d\d`	An American ZIP code including a prepended state code, such as NJ07932
`\w\d-\w\d`	An astromech droid identifier, such as R2-D2
`c\wt`	A three-letter word starting with c and ending with t, such as cat or cot

You can also invert a character class by capitalizing the *d*, *s*, or *w* to give the opposite: `\D` matches any non-digit, `\S` matches any non-whitespace, and `\W` matches any non-word character.

In addition, you can build your own character classes by explicitly enumerating them between square brackets `[]`. For example, the character class `[02468]` includes even digits. You can also use hyphens as shortcuts to include implied ranges, so the character class `[0-9a-fA-F]` includes any hexadecimal digit whether the letter is capitalized or not. Finally, you can invert a custom character class by prepending the list with a caret `^`. For example, the character class `[^aeiou]` includes all non-vowel characters.

Quantifiers

You can save some typing by using *quantifiers*, which specify that the character directly to the left should be repeated some number of times. Table 15-9 lists the regex quantifiers.

Table 15-9: Regular Expression Quantifiers

Regex quantifier	Specifies a quantity of
*	0 or more
+	1 or more
?	0 or 1
{n}	Exactly n
{n,m}	Between n and m, inclusive
{n,}	At least n

Using quantifiers, you can specify all words beginning with *c* and ending with *t* using the pattern `c\w*t`, because `\w*` matches any number of word characters.

Groups

A *group* is a collection of characters. You can specify a group by placing it within parentheses. Groups are useful in several ways, including specifying a particular collection for eventual extraction and for quantification.

For example, you could improve the ZIP pattern in Table 15-8 to use quantifiers and groups, like this:

```
(\w{2})?❶(\d{5})❷(-\d{4})?❸
```

Now you have three groups: the optional state ❶, the ZIP code ❷, and an optional four-digit suffix ❸. As you'll see later on, these groups make parsing from regexes much easier.

Other Special Characters

Table 15-10 lists several other special characters available for use in regex patterns.

Table 15-10: Example Special Characters

Character	Specifies
X|Y	Character X or Y
\Y	The special character Y as a literal (in other words, escape it)
\n	Newline
\r	Carriage return
\t	Tab
\0	Null
\xYY	The hexadecimal character corresponding to YY

basic_regex

The STL's std::basic_regex class template in the <regex> header represents a regular expression constructed from a pattern. The basic_regex class accepts two template parameters, a character type and an optional traits class. You'll almost always want to use one of the convenience specializations: std::regex for std::basic_regex<char> or std::wregex for std::basic_regex<wchar_t>.

The primary means of constructing a regex is by passing a string literal containing your regex pattern. Because patterns will require a lot of escaped characters—especially the backslash \—it's a good idea to use raw string literals, such as R"()". The constructor accepts a second, optional parameter for specifying syntax flags like the regex grammar.

Although regex is used primarily as input into regular expression algorithms, it does offer a few methods that users can interact with. It supports the usual copy and move construction and assignment suite and swap, plus the following:

- assign(**s**) reassigns the pattern to **s**
- mark_count() returns the number of groups in the pattern
- flags() returns the syntax flags issued at construction

Listing 15-23 illustrates how you could construct a ZIP code regex and inspect its subgroups.

```
#include <regex>

TEST_CASE("std::basic_regex constructs from a string literal") {
  std::regex zip_regex{ R"((\w{2})?(\d{5})(-\d{4})?)" }; ❶
  REQUIRE(zip_regex.mark_count() == 3); ❷
}
```

Listing 15-23: Constructing a regex using a raw string literal and extracting its group count

Here, you construct a regex called zip_regex using the pattern (\w{2})?(\d{5})(-\d{4})? ❶. Using the mark_count method, you see that zip_regex contains three groups ❷.

Algorithms

The <regex> class contains three algorithms for applying std::basic_regex to a target string: matching, searching, or replacing. Which you choose depends on the task at hand.

Matching

Matching attempts to marry a regular expression to an *entire* string. The STL provides the std::regex_match function for matching, which has four overloads.

First, you can provide regex_match a string, a C-string, or a begin and end iterator forming a half-open range. The next parameter is an optional reference to a `std::match_results` object that receives details about the match. The next parameter is a `std::basic_regex` that defines the matching, and the final parameter is an optional `std::regex_constants::match_flag_type` that specifies additional matching options for advanced use cases. The `regex_match` function returns a `bool`, which is `true` if it found a match; otherwise, it's `false`.

To summarize, you can invoke `regex_match` in the following ways:

```
regex_match(beg, end, [mr], rgx, [flg])
regex_match(str, [mr], rgx, [flg])
```

Either provide a half-open range from `beg` to `end` or a `string`/C-string `str` to search. Optionally, you can provide a `match_results` called `mr` to store all the details of any matches found. You obviously have to provide a regex `rgx`. Finally, the flags `flg` are seldom used.

NOTE *For details on match flags* **`flg`**, *refer to [re.alg.match].*

A *submatch* is a subsequence of the matched string that corresponds to a group. The ZIP code–matching regular expression `(\w{2})(\d{5})(-\d{4})?` can produce two or three submatches depending on the string. For example, TX78209 contains the two submatches TX and 78209, and NJ07936-3173 contains the three submatches NJ, 07936, and -3173.

The `match_results` class stores zero or more `std::sub_match` instances. A `sub_match` is a simple class template that exposes a `length` method to return the length of a submatch and a `str` method to build a `string` from the `sub_match`.

Somewhat confusingly, if `regex_match` successfully matches a string, `match_results` stores the entire matched string as its first element and then stores any submatches as subsequent elements.

The `match_results` class provides the operations listed in Table 15-11.

Table 15-11: Supported Operations of `match_results`

Operation	Description
`mr.empty()`	Checks whether the match was successful.
`mr.size()`	Returns the number of submatches.
`mr.max_size()`	Returns the maximum number of submatches.
`mr.length([i])`	Returns the length of the submatch `i`, which defaults to 0.
`mr.position([i])`	Returns the character of the first position of submatch `i`, which defaults to 0.
`mr.str([i])`	Returns the string representing submatch `i`, which defaults to 0.
`mr[i]`	Returns a reference to a `std::sub_match` class corresponding to submatch `i`, which defaults to 0.
`mr.prefix()`	Returns a reference to a `std::sub_match` class corresponding to the sequence before the match.

(continued)

Table 15-11: Supported Operations of `match_results` (continued)

Operation	Description
`mr.suffix()`	Returns a reference to a `std::sub_match` class corresponding to the sequence after the match.
`mr.format(str)`	Returns a `string` with contents according to the format string **`str`**. There are three special sequences: `$'` for the characters before a match, `$'` for the characters after the match, and `$&` for the matched characters.

`mr.begin()`
`mr.end()`
`mr.cbegin()`
`mr.cend()`
	Returns the corresponding iterator to the sequence of submatches.

The `std::sub_match` class template has predefined specializations to work with common string types:

- `std::csub_match` for a `const char*`
- `std::wcsub_match` for a `const wchar_t*`
- `std::ssub_match` for a `std::string`
- `std::wssub_match` for a `std::wstring`

Unfortunately, you'll have to keep track of all these specializations manually due to the design of `std::regex_match`. This design generally befuddles newcomers, so let's look at an example. Listing 15-24 uses the ZIP code regular expression `(\w{2})(\d{5})(-\d{4})?` to match against the strings `NJ07936-3173` and `Iomega Zip 100`.

```
#include <regex>
#include <string>

TEST_CASE("std::sub_match") {
  std::regex regex{ R"((\w{2})(\d{5})(-\d{4})?)" }; ❶
  std::smatch results; ❷
  SECTION("returns true given matching string") {
    std::string zip("NJ07936-3173");
    const auto matched = std::regex_match(zip, results, regex); ❸
    REQUIRE(matched); ❹
    REQUIRE(results[0] == "NJ07936-3173"); ❺
    REQUIRE(results[1] == "NJ"); ❻
    REQUIRE(results[2] == "07936");
    REQUIRE(results[3] == "-3173");
  }
  SECTION("returns false given non-matching string") {
    std::string zip("Iomega Zip 100");
    const auto matched = std::regex_match(zip, results, regex); ❼
    REQUIRE_FALSE(matched); ❽
    }
}
```

Listing 15-24: A `regex_match` attempts to match a `regex` to a `string`.

You construct a regex with the raw literal `R"((\w{2})(\d{5})(-\d{4})?)"` ❶ and default construct an `smatch` ❷. In the first test, you `regex_match` the valid ZIP code `NJ07936-3173` ❸, which returns the `true` value `matched` to indicate success ❹. Because you provide an `smatch` to `regex_match`, it contains the valid ZIP code as the first element ❺, followed by each of the three subgroups ❻.

In the second test, you `regex_match` the invalid ZIP code `Iomega Zip 100` ❼, which fails to match and returns `false` ❽.

Searching

Searching attempts to match a regular expression to a *part* of a string. The STL provides the `std::regex_search` function for searching, which is essentially a replacement for `regex_match` that succeeds even when only a part of a string matches a regex.

For example, `The string NJ07936-3173 is a ZIP Code.` contains a ZIP code. But applying the ZIP regular expression to it using `std::regex_match` will return `false` because the regex doesn't match the *entire* string. However, applying `std::regex_search` instead would yield `true` because the string embeds a valid ZIP code. Listing 15-25 illustrates `regex_match` and `regex_search`.

```
TEST_CASE("when only part of a string matches a regex, std::regex_ ") {
  std::regex regex{ R"((\w{2})(\d{5})(-\d{4})?)" }; ❶
  std::string sentence("The string NJ07936-3173 is a ZIP Code."); ❷
  SECTION("match returns false") {
    REQUIRE_FALSE(std::regex_match(sentence, regex)); ❸
  }
  SECTION("search returns true") {
    REQUIRE(std::regex_search(sentence, regex)); ❹
  }
}
```

Listing 15-25: Comparing `regex_match` and `regex_search`

As before, you construct the ZIP regex ❶. You also construct the example string `sentence`, which embeds a valid ZIP code ❷. The first test calls `regex_match` with `sentence` and `regex`, which returns `false` ❸. The second test instead calls `regex_search` with the same arguments and returns `true` ❹.

Replacing

Replacing substitutes regular expression occurrences with replacement text. The STL provides the `std::regex_replace` function for replacing.

In its most basic usage, you pass `regex_replace` three arguments:

- A source string/C-string/half-open range to search
- A regular expression
- A replacement string

As an example, Listing 15-26 replaces all the vowels in the phrase `queueing and cooeeing in eutopia` with underscores (`_`).

```
TEST_CASE("std::regex_replace") {
  std::regex regex{ "[aeoiu]" }; ❶
  std::string phrase("queueing and cooeeing in eutopia"); ❷
  const auto result = std::regex_replace(phrase, regex, "_"); ❸
  REQUIRE(result == "q_____ng _nd c_____ng _n __t_p_"); ❹
}
```

Listing 15-26: Using `std::regex_replace` to substitute underscores for vowels in a `string`

You construct a `std::regex` that contains the set of all vowels ❶ and a `string` called `phrase` containing the vowel-rich contents `queueing and cooeeing in eutopia` ❷. Next, you invoke `std::regex_replace` with `phrase`, the regex, and the string literal `_` ❸, which replaces all vowels with underscores ❹.

NOTE *Boost Regex provides regular expression support mirroring the STL's in the `<boost/regex.hpp>` header. Another Boost library, Xpressive, offers an alternative approach with regular expressions that you can express directly in C++ code. It has some major advantages, such as expressiveness and compile-time syntax checking, but the syntax necessarily diverges from standard regular expression syntaxes like POSIX, Perl, and ECMAScript.*

Boost String Algorithms

Boost's String Algorithms library offers a bounty of `string` manipulation functions. It contains functions for common tasks related to `string`, such as trimming, case conversion, finding/replacing, and evaluating characteristics. You can access all the Boost String Algorithms functions in the `boost::algorithm` namespace and in the `<boost/algorithm/string.hpp>` convenience header.

Boost Range

Range is a concept (in the Chapter 6 compile-time polymorphism sense of the word) that has a beginning and an end that allow you to iterate over constituent elements. The range aims to improve the practice of passing a half-open range as a pair of iterators. By replacing the pair with a single object, you can *compose* algorithms together by using the range result of one algorithm as the input to another. For example, if you wanted to transform a range of strings to all uppercase and sort them, you could pass the results of one operation directly into the other. This is not generally possible to do with iterators alone.

Ranges are not currently part of the C++ standard, but several experimental implementations exist. One such implementation is Boost Range, and because Boost String Algorithms uses Boost Range extensively, let's look at it now.

The Boost Range concept is like the STL container concept. It provides the usual complement of `begin`/`end` methods to expose iterators over the elements in the range. Each range has a *traversal category*, which indicates the range's supported operations:

- A *single-pass range* allows one-time, forward iteration.
- A *forward range* allows (unlimited) forward iteration and satisfies single-pass range.
- A *bidirectional range* allows forward and backward iteration and satisfies forward range.
- A *random-access range* allows arbitrary element access and satisfies bidirectional range.

Boost String Algorithms is designed for `std::string`, which satisfies the random-access range concept. For the most part, the fact that Boost String Algorithms accepts Boost Range rather than `std::string` is a totally transparent abstraction to users. When reading the documentation, you can mentally substitute `Range` with `string`.

Predicates

Boost String Algorithms incorporates predicates extensively. You can use them directly by bringing in the `<boost/algorithm/string/predicate.hpp>` header. Most of the predicates contained in this header accept two ranges, `r1` and `r2`, and return a `bool` based on their relationship. The predicate `starts_with`, for example, returns `true` if `r1` begins with `r2`.

Each predicate has a case-insensitive version, which you can use by prepending the letter `i` to the method name, such as `istarts_with`. Listing 15-27 illustrates `starts_with` and `istarts_with`.

```
#include <string>
#include <boost/algorithm/string/predicate.hpp>

TEST_CASE("boost::algorithm") {
  using namespace boost::algorithm;
  using namespace std::literals::string_literals;
  std::string word("cymotrichous"); ❶
  SECTION("starts_with tests a string's beginning") {
    REQUIRE(starts_with(word, "cymo"s)); ❷
  }
  SECTION("istarts_with is case insensitive") {
    REQUIRE(istarts_with(word, "cYmO"s)); ❸
  }
}
```

Listing 15-27: Both `starts_with` and `istarts_with` check a range's beginning characters.

You initialize a string containing `cymotrichous` ❶. The first test shows that `starts_with` returns `true` when with `word` and `cymo` ❷. The case-insensitive version `istarts_with` also returns `true` given `word` and `cYmO` ❸.

Note that <boost/algorithm/string/predicate.hpp> also contains an all predicate, which accepts a single range r and a predicate p. It returns true if p evaluates to true for all elements of r, as Listing 15-28 illustrates.

```
TEST_CASE("boost::algorithm::all evaluates a predicate for all elements") {
  using namespace boost::algorithm;
  std::string word("juju"); ❶
  REQUIRE(all(word❷, [](auto c) { return c == 'j' || c =='u'; }❸));
}
```

Listing 15-28: The all predicate evaluates if all elements in a range satisfy a predicate.

You initialize a string containing juju ❶, which you pass to all as the range ❷. You pass a lambda predicate, which returns true for the letters j and u ❸. Because juju contains only these letters, all returns true.

Table 15-12 lists the predicates available in <boost/algorithm/string/predicate.hpp>.In this table, r, r1, and r2 are string ranges, and p is an element comparison predicate.

Table 15-12: Predicates in the Boost String Algorithms Library

Predicate	Returns true if
starts_with(**r1**, **r2**, [**p**]) istarts_with(**r1**, **r2**)	**r1** starts with **r2**; **p** used for character-wise comparison.
ends_with(**r1**, **r2**, [**p**]) iends_with(**r1**, **r2**)	**r1** ends with **r2**; **p** used for character-wise comparison.
contains(**r1**, **r2**, [**p**]) icontains(**r1**, **r2**)	**r1** contains **r2**; **p** used for character-wise comparison.
equals(**r1**, **r2**, [**p**]) iequals(**r1**, **r2**)	**r1** equals **r2**; **p** used for character-wise comparison.
lexicographical_compare(**r1**, **r2**, [**p**]) ilexicographical_compare(**r1**, **r2**)	**r1** lexicographically less than **r2**; **p** used for character-wise comparison.
all(**r**, [**p**])	All elements of **r** return true for **p**.

Function permutations beginning with i are case-insensitive.

Classifiers

Classifiers are predicates that evaluate some characteristics about a character. The <boost/algorithm/string/classification.hpp> header offers generators for creating classifiers. A *generator* is a non-member function that acts like a constructor. Some generators accept arguments for customizing the classifier.

NOTE *Of course, you can create your own predicates just as easily with your own function objects, like lambdas, but Boost provides a menu of premade classifiers for convenience.*

The is_alnum generator, for example, creates a classifier that determines whether a character is alphanumeric. Listing 15-29 illustrates how to use this classifier independently or in conjunction with all.

```
#include <boost/algorithm/string/classification.hpp>

TEST_CASE("boost::algorithm::is_alnum") {
  using namespace boost::algorithm;
  const auto classifier = is_alnum(); ❶
  SECTION("evaluates alphanumeric characters") {
    REQUIRE(classifier('a')); ❷
    REQUIRE_FALSE(classifier('$')); ❸
  }
  SECTION("works with all") {
    REQUIRE(all("nostarch", classifier)); ❹
    REQUIRE_FALSE(all("@nostarch", classifier)); ❺
  }
}
```

Listing 15-29: The is_alum generator determines whether a character is alphanumeric.

Here, you construct a classifier from the is_alnum generator ❶. The first test uses the classifier to evaluate that a is alphanumeric ❷ and $ is not ❸. Because all classifiers are predicates that operate on characters, you can use them in conjunction with the all predicate discussed in the previous section to determine that nostarch contains all alphanumeric characters ❹ and @nostarch doesn't ❺.

Table 15-13 lists the character classifications available in <boost/algorithm/string/classification.hpp>. In this table, r is a string range, and beg and end are element comparison predicates.

Table 15-13: Character Predicates in the Boost String Algorithms Library

Predicate	Returns true if element is . . .
is_space	A space
is_alnum	An alphanumeric character
is_alpha	An alphabetical character
is_cntrl	A control character
is_digit	A decimal digit
is_graph	A graphical character
is_lower	A lowercase character
is_print	A printable character
is_punct	A punctuation character
is_upper	An uppercase character
is_xdigit	A hexadecimal digit
is_any_of(**r**)	Contained in **r**
is_from_range(**beg**, **end**)	Contained in the half-open range from **beg** to **end**

Finders

A *finder* is a concept that determines a position in a range corresponding to some specified criteria, usually a predicate or a regular expression. Boost String Algorithms provides some generators for producing finders in the <boost/algorithm/string/finder.hpp> header.

For example, the nth_finder generator accepts a range r and an index n, and it creates a finder that will search a range (taken as a begin and an end iterator) for the nth occurrence of r, as Listing 15-30 illustrates.

```
#include <boost/algorithm/string/finder.hpp>

TEST_CASE("boost::algorithm::nth_finder finds the nth occurrence") {
  const auto finder = boost::algorithm::nth_finder("na", 1); ❶
  std::string name("Carl Brutananadilewski"); ❷
  const auto result = finder(name.begin(), name.end()); ❸
  REQUIRE(result.begin() == name.begin() + 12); ❹ // Brutana(n)adilewski
  REQUIRE(result.end() == name.begin() + 14); ❺ // Brutanana(d)ilewski
}
```

Listing 15-30: The nth_finder generator creates a finder that locates the nth occurrence of a sequence.

You use the nth_finder generator to create finder, which will locate the second instance of na in a range (n is zero based) ❶. Next, you construct name containing Carl Brutananadilewski ❷ and invoke finder with the begin and end iterators of name ❸. The result is a range whose begin points to the second *n* in Brutana**n**adilewski ❹ and whose end points to the first *d* in Brutanana**d**ilewski ❺.

Table 15-14 lists the finders available in <boost/algorithm/string/finder.hpp>. In this table, s is a string, p is an element comparison predicate, n is an integral value, beg and end are iterators, rgx is a regular expression, and r is a string range.

Table 15-14: Finders in the Boost String Algorithms Library

Generator	Creates a finder that, when invoked, returns . . .
first_finder(**s**, **p**)	The first element matching **s** using **p**
last_finder(**s**, **p**)	The last element matching **s** using **p**
nth_finder(**s**, **p**, **n**)	The **n**th element matching **s** using **p**
head_finder(**n**)	The first **n** elements
tail_finder(**n**)	the last **n** elements
token_finder(**p**)	The character matching **p**
range_finder(**r**) range_finder(**beg**, **end**)	**r** regardless of input
regex_finder(**rgx**)	The first substring matching **rgx**

NOTE *Boost String Algorithms specifies a formatter concept, which presents the results of a finder to a replace algorithm. Only an advanced user will need these algorithms. Refer to the documentation for the `find_format` algorithms in the `<boost/algorithm/string/find_format.hpp>` header for more information.*

Modifying Algorithms

Boost contains a *lot* of algorithms for modifying a string (range). Between the `<boost/algorithm/string/case_conv.hpp>`, `<boost/algorithm/string/trim.hpp>`, and `<boost/algorithm/string/replace.hpp>` headers, algorithms exist to convert case, trim, replace, and erase many different ways.

For example, the `to_upper` function will convert all of a string's letters to uppercase. If you want to keep the original unmodified, you can use the `to_upper_copy` function, which will return a new object. Listing 15-31 illustrates `to_upper` and `to_upper_copy`.

```
#include <boost/algorithm/string/case_conv.hpp>

TEST_CASE("boost::algorithm::to_upper") {
  std::string powers("difficulty controlling the volume of my voice"); ❶
  SECTION("upper-cases a string") {
    boost::algorithm::to_upper(powers); ❷
    REQUIRE(powers == "DIFFICULTY CONTROLLING THE VOLUME OF MY VOICE"); ❸
  }
  SECTION("_copy leaves the original unmodified") {
    auto result = boost::algorithm::to_upper_copy(powers); ❹
    REQUIRE(powers == "difficulty controlling the volume of my voice"); ❺
    REQUIRE(result == "DIFFICULTY CONTROLLING THE VOLUME OF MY VOICE"); ❻
  }
}
```

Listing 15-31: Both `to_upper` and `to_upper_copy` convert the case of a `string`.

You create a string called `powers` ❶. The first test invokes `to_upper` on `powers` ❷, which modifies it in place to contain all uppercase letters ❸. The second test uses the `_copy` variant to create a new string called `result` ❹. The `powers` string is unaffected ❺, whereas `result` contains an all uppercase version ❻.

Some Boost String Algorithms, such as `replace_first`, also have case-insensitive versions. Just prepend an `i`, and matching will proceed regardless of case. For algorithms like `replace_first` that also have `_copy` variants, any permutation will work (`replace_first`, `ireplace_first`, `replace_first_copy`, and `ireplace_first_copy`).

The `replace_first` algorithm and its variants accept an input range `s`, a match range `m`, and a replace range `r`, and replaces the first instance of `m` in `s` with `r`. Listing 15-32 illustrates `replace_first` and `i_replace_first`.

```
#include <boost/algorithm/string/replace.hpp>

TEST_CASE("boost::algorithm::replace_first") {
  using namespace boost::algorithm;
  std::string publisher("No Starch Press"); ❶
  SECTION("replaces the first occurrence of a string") {
    replace_first(publisher, "No", "Medium"); ❷
    REQUIRE(publisher == "Medium Starch Press"); ❸
  }
  SECTION("has a case-insensitive variant") {
    auto result = ireplace_first_copy(publisher, "NO", "MEDIUM"); ❹
    REQUIRE(publisher == "No Starch Press"); ❺
    REQUIRE(result == "MEDIUM Starch Press"); ❻
  }}
```

Listing 15-32: Both `replace_first` and `i_replace_first` replace matching string sequences.

Here, you construct a string called `publisher` containing `No Starch Press` ❶. The first test invokes `replace_first` with `publisher` as the input string, `No` as the match string, and `Medium` as the replacement string ❷. Afterward, `publisher` contains `Medium Starch Press` ❸. The second test uses the `ireplace_first_copy` variant, which is case insensitive and performs a copy. You pass `NO` and `MEDIUM` as the match and replace strings ❹, respectively, and the result contains `MEDIUM Starch Press` ❻, whereas `publisher` is unaffected ❺.

Table 15-15 lists many of the modifying algorithms available in Boost String Algorithms. In this table, `r`, `s`, `s1`, and `s2` are strings; `p` is an element comparison predicate; `n` is an integral value; and `rgx` is a regular expression.

Table 15-15: Modifying Algorithms in the Boost String Algorithms Library

Algorithm	Description
`to_upper(s)` `to_upper_copy(s)`	Converts **s** to all uppercase
`to_lower(s)` `to_lower_copy(s)`	Converts **s** to all lowercase

`trim_left_copy_if(s, [p])`
`trim_left_if(s, [p])`
`trim_left_copy(s)`
`trim_left(s)`
	Removes leading spaces from **s**

`trim_right_copy_if(s, [p])`
`trim_right_if(s, [p])`
`trim_right_copy(s)`
`trim_right(s)`
	Removes trailing spaces from **s**

`trim_copy_if(s, [p])`
`trim_if(s, [p])`
`trim_copy(s)`
`trim(s)`
	Removes leading and trailing spaces from **s**

`replace_first(s1, s2, r)`
`replace_first_copy(s1, s2, r)`
`ireplace_first(s1, s2, r)`
`ireplace_first_copy(s1, s2, r)`
	Replaces the first occurrence of **s2** in **s1** with **r**

Algorithm	Description
erase_first(s1, s2) erase_first_copy(s1, s2) ierase_first(s1, s2) ierase_first_copy(s1, s2)	Erases the first occurrence of s2 in s1
replace_last(s1, s2, r) replace_last_copy(s1, s2, r) ireplace_last(s1, s2, r) ireplace_last_copy(s1, s2, r)	Replaces the last occurrence of s2 in s1 with r
erase_last(s1, s2) erase_last_copy(s1, s2) ierase_last(s1, s2) ierase_last_copy(s1, s2)	Erases the last occurrence of s2 in s1
replace_nth(s1, s2, n, r) replace_nth_copy(s1, s2, n, r) ireplace_nth(s1, s2, n, r) ireplace_nth_copy(s1, s2, n, r)	Replaces the nth occurrence of s2 in s1 with r
erase_nth(s1, s2, n) erase_nth_copy(s1, s2, n) ierase_nth(s1, s2, n) ierase_nth_copy(s1, s2, n)	Erases the nth occurrence of s2 in s1
replace_all(s1, s2, r) replace_all_copy(s1, s2, r) ireplace_all(s1, s2, r) ireplace_all_copy(s1, s2, r)	Replaces all occurrences of s2 in s1 with r
erase_all(s1, s2) erase_all_copy(s1, s2) ierase_all(s1, s2) ierase_all_copy(s1, s2)	Erases all occurrences of s2 in s1
replace_head(s, n, r) replace_head_copy(s, n, r)	Replaces the first n characters of s with r
erase_head(s, n) erase_head_copy(s, n)	Erases the first n characters of s
replace_tail(s, n, r) replace_tail_copy(s, n, r)	Replaces the last n characters of s with r
erase_tail(s, n) erase_tail_copy(s, n)	Erases the last n characters of s
replace_regex(s, rgx, r) replace_regex_copy(s, rgx, r)	Replaces the first instance of rgx in s with r
erase_regex(s, rgx) erase_regex_copy(s, rgx)	Erases the first instance of rgx in s
replace_all_regex(s, rgx, r) replace_all_regex_copy(s, rgx, r)	Replaces all instances of rgx in s with r
erase_all_regex(s, rgx) erase_all_regex_copy(s, rgx)	Erases all instances of rgx in s

Splitting and Joining

Boost String Algorithms contains functions for splitting and joining strings in the `<boost/algorithm/string/split.hpp>` and `<boost/algorithm/string/join.hpp>` headers.

To split a string, you provide the split function with an STL container res, a range s, and a predicate p. It will tokenize the range s using the predicate p to determine delimiters and insert the results into res. Listing 15-33 illustrates the split function.

```
#include <vector>
#include <boost/algorithm/string/split.hpp>
#include <boost/algorithm/string/classification.hpp>

TEST_CASE("boost::algorithm::split splits a range based on a predicate") {
  using namespace boost::algorithm;
  std::string publisher("No Starch Press"); ❶
  std::vector<std::string> tokens; ❷
  split(tokens, publisher, is_space()); ❸
  REQUIRE(tokens[0] == "No"); ❹
  REQUIRE(tokens[1] == "Starch");
  REQUIRE(tokens[2] == "Press");
}
```

Listing 15-33: The split function tokenizes a string.

Armed again with publisher ❶, you create a vector called tokens to contain the results ❷. You invoke split with tokens as the results container, publisher as the range, and an is_space as your predicate ❸. This splits the publisher into pieces by spaces. Afterward, tokens contains No, Starch, and Press as expected ❹.

You can perform the inverse operation with join, which accepts an STL container seq and a separator string sep. The join function will bind each element of seq together with sep between each.

Listing 15-34 illustrates the utility of join and the indispensability of the Oxford comma.

```
#include <vector>
#include <boost/algorithm/string/join.hpp>

TEST_CASE("boost::algorithm::join staples tokens together") {
  std::vector<std::string> tokens{ "We invited the strippers",
                                   "JFK", "and Stalin." }; ❶
  auto result = boost::algorithm::join(tokens, ", "); ❷
  REQUIRE(result == "We invited the strippers, JFK, and Stalin."); ❸
}
```

Listing 15-34: The join function attaches string tokens together with a separator.

You instantiate a vector called tokens with three string objects ❶. Next, you use join to bind token's constituent elements together with a comma followed by a space ❷. The result is a single string containing the constituent elements bound together with commas and spaces ❸.

Table 15-16 lists many of the split/join algorithms available in <boost/algorithm/string/split.hpp> and <boost/algorithm/string/join.hpp>. In this table, res, s, s1, s2, and sep are strings; seq is a range of strings; p is an element comparison predicate; and rgx is a regular expression.

Table 15-16: split and join Algorithms in the Boost String Algorithms Library

Function	Description
find_all(**res**, **s1**, **s2**) ifind_all(**res**, **s1**, **s2**) find_all_regex(**res**, **s1**, **rgx**) iter_find(**res**, **s1**, **s2**)	Finds all instances of **s2** or **rgx** in **s1**, writing each into **res**
split(**res**, **s**, **p**) split_regex(**res**, **s**, **rgx**) iter_split(**res**, **s**, **s2**)	Split **s** using **p**, **rgx**, or **s2**, writing tokens into **res**
join(**seq**, **sep**)	Returns a string joining **seq** using **sep** as a separator
join_if(**seq**, **sep**, **p**)	Returns a string joining all elements of **seq** matching **p** using **sep** as a separator

Searching

Boost String Algorithms offers a handful of functions for searching ranges in the <boost/algorithm/string/find.hpp> header. These are essentially convenient wrappers around the finders in Table 15-8.

For example, the find_head function accepts a range s and a length n, and it returns a range containing the first n elements of s. Listing 15-35 illustrates the find_head function.

```
#include <boost/algorithm/string/find.hpp>

TEST_CASE("boost::algorithm::find_head computes the head") {
  std::string word("blandishment"); ❶
  const auto result = boost::algorithm::find_head(word, 5); ❷
  REQUIRE(result.begin() == word.begin()); ❸ // (b)landishment
  REQUIRE(result.end() == word.begin()+5); ❹ // bland(i)shment
}
```

Listing 15-35: The find_head function creates a range from the beginning of a string.

You construct a string called word containing blandishment ❶. You pass it into find_head along with the length argument 5 ❷. The begin of result points to the beginning of word ❸, and its end points to 1 past the fifth element ❹.

Table 15-17 lists many of the find algorithms available in <boost/algorithm/string/find.hpp>. In this table, s, s1, and s2 are strings; p is an element comparison predicate; rgx is a regular expression; and n is an integral value.

Table 15-17: Find Algorithms in the Boost String Algorithms Library

Predicate	Finds the . . .
`find_first(s1, s2)` `ifind_first(s1, s2)`	First instance of **s2** in **s1**
`find_last(s1, s2)` `ifind_last(s1, s2)`	First instance of **s2** in **s1**
`find_nth(s1, s2, n)` `ifind_nth(s1, s2, n)`	nth instance of **s2** in **s1**
`find_head(s, n)`	First **n** characters of **s**
`find_tail(s, n)`	Last **n** characters of **s**
`find_token(s, p)`	First character matching **p** in **s**
`find_regex(s, rgx)`	First substring matching **rgx** in **s**
`find(s, fnd)`	Result of applying **fnd** to **s**

Boost Tokenizer

Boost Tokenizer's `boost::tokenizer` is a class template that provides a view of a series of tokens contained in a `string`. A `tokenizer` takes three optional template parameters: a tokenizer function, an iterator type, and a string type.

The *tokenizer function* is a predicate that determines whether a character is a delimiter (returns `true`) or not (returns `false`). The default tokenizer function interprets spaces and punctuation marks as separators. If you want to specify the delimiters explicitly, you can use the `boost::char_separator<char>` class, which accepts a C-string containing all the delimiting characters. For example, a `boost::char_separator<char>(";|,")` would separate on semicolons (`;`), pipes (`|`), and commas (`,`).

The iterator type and string type correspond with the type of `string` you want to split. By default, these are `std::string::const_iterator` and `std::string`, respectively.

Because `tokenizer` doesn't allocate memory and `boost::algorithm::split` does, you should strongly consider using the former whenever you only need to iterate over the tokens of a `string` once.

A `tokenizer` exposes `begin` and `end` methods that return input iterators, so you can treat it as a range of values corresponding to the underlying token sequence.

Listing 15-36 tokenizes the iconic palindrome `A man, a plan, a canal, Panama!` by comma.

```
#include<boost/tokenizer.hpp>
#include<string>

TEST_CASE("boost::tokenizer splits token-delimited strings") {
  std::string palindrome("A man, a plan, a canal, Panama!"); ❶
  boost::char_separator<char> comma{ "," }; ❷
  boost::tokenizer<boost::char_separator<char>> tokens{ palindrome, comma }; ❸
  auto itr = tokens.begin(); ❹
```

```
  REQUIRE(*itr == "A man"); ❺
  itr++; ❻
  REQUIRE(*itr == " a plan");
  itr++;
  REQUIRE(*itr == " a canal");
  itr++;
  REQUIRE(*itr == " Panama!");
}
```

Listing 15-36: The `boost::tokenizer` splits strings by specified delimiters.

Here, you construct `palindrome` ❶, `char_separator` ❷, and the corresponding `tokenizer` ❸. Next, you extract an iterator from the tokenizer using its `begin` method ❹. You can treat the resulting iterator as usual, dereferencing its value ❺ and incrementing to the next element ❻.

Localizations

A *locale* is a class for encoding cultural preferences. The locale concept is typically encoded in whatever operating environment your application runs within. It also controls many preferences, such as string comparison; date and time, money, and numeric formatting; postal and ZIP codes; and phone numbers.

The STL offers the `std::locale` class and many helper functions and classes in the `<locale>` header.

Mainly for brevity (and partially because English speakers are the primary intended audience for this book), this chapter won't explore locales any further.

Summary

This chapter covered `std::string` and its ecosystem in detail. After exploring its similarities to `std::vector`, you learned about its built-in methods for handling human-language data, such as comparing, adding, removing, replacing, and searching. You looked at how the numeric conversion functions allow you to convert between numbers and strings, and you examined the role that `std::string_view` plays in passing strings around your programs. You also learned how to employ regular expressions to perform intricate match, search, and replacement based on potentially complicated patterns. Finally, you trekked through the Boost String Algorithms library, which complements and extends the built-in methods of `std::string` with additional methods for searching, replacing, trimming, erasing, splitting, and joining.

EXERCISES

15-1. Refactor the histogram calculator in Listings 9-30 and 9-31 to use `std::string`. Construct a string from the program's input and modify `AlphaHistogram` to accept a `string_view` or a `const string&` in its `ingest` method. Use a range-based `for` loop to iterate over the ingested elements of `string`. Replace the `counts` field's type with an associative container.

15-2. Implement a program that determines whether the user's input is a palindrome.

15-3. Implement a program that counts the number of vowels in the user's input.

15-4. Implement a calculator program that supports addition, subtraction, multiplication, and division of any two numbers. Consider using the `find` method of `std::string` and the numeric conversion functions.

15-5. Extend your calculator program in some of the following ways: permit multiple operations or the modulo operator and accept floating-point numbers or parentheses.

15-6. Optional: Read more about locales in [localization].

FURTHER READING

- *ISO International Standard ISO/IEC (2017) — Programming Language C++* (International Organization for Standardization; Geneva, Switzerland; *https://isocpp.org/std/the-standard/*)
- *The C++ Programming Language*, 4th Edition, by Bjarne Stroustrup (Pearson Education, 2013)
- *The Boost C++ Libraries*, 2nd Edition, by Boris Schäling (XML Press, 2014)
- *The C++ Standard Library: A Tutorial and Reference*, 2nd Edition, by Nicolai M. Josuttis (Addison-Wesley Professional, 2012)

16

STREAMS

Either write something worth reading or
do something worth writing.
—Benjamin Franklin

This chapter introduces streams, the major concept that enables you to connect inputs from any kind of source and outputs to any kind of destination using a common framework. You'll learn about the classes that form the base elements of this common framework, several built-in facilities, and how to incorporate streams into user-defined types.

Streams

A *stream* models a *stream of data*. In a stream, data flows between objects, and those objects can perform arbitrary processing on the data. When you're working with streams, output is data going into the stream and input is data coming out of the stream. These terms reflect the streams as viewed from the user's perspective.

In C++, streams are the primary mechanism for performing input and output (I/O). Regardless of the source or destination, you can use streams as the common language to connect inputs to outputs. The STL uses class inheritance to encode the relationships between various stream types. The primary types in this hierarchy are:

- The `std::basic_ostream` class template in the `<ostream>` header that represents an output device
- The `std::basic_istream` class template in the `<istream>` header that represents an input device
- The `std::basic_iostream` class template in the `<iostream>` header for devices that are input and output

All three stream types require two template parameters. The first corresponds to the stream's underlying data type and the second to a traits type.

This section covers streams from a user's perspective rather than from a library implementer's perspective. You'll understand the streams interface and know how to interact with standard I/O, files, and strings using the STL's built-in stream support. If you must implement a new kind of stream (for example, for a new library or framework), you'll need a copy of the ISO C++ 17 Standard, some working examples, and an ample supply of coffee. I/O is complicated, and you'll see this difficulty reflected in a stream implementation's internal complexity. Fortunately, a well-designed stream class hides much of this complexity from users.

Stream Classes

All STL stream classes that users interact with derive from `basic_istream`, `basic_ostream`, or both via `basic_iostream`. The headers that declare each type also provide `char` and `wchar_t` specializations for those templates, as outlined in Table 16-1. These heavily used specializations are particularly useful when you're working with human-language data input and output.

Table 16-1: Template Specializations for the Primary Stream Templates

Template	Parameter	Specialization	Header
basic_istream	char	istream	<istream>
basic_ostream	char	ostream	<ostream>
basic_iostream	char	iostream	<iostream>
basic_istream	wchar_t	wistream	<istream>
basic_ostream	wchar_t	wostream	<ostream>
basic_iostream	wchar_t	wiostream	<iostream>

The objects in Table 16-1 are abstractions that you can use in your programs to write generic code. Do you want to write a function that logs output to an arbitrary source? If so, you can accept an `ostream` reference parameter and not deal with all the nasty implementation details. (Later in the "Output File Streams" on page 542, you'll learn how to do this.)

Often, you'll want to perform I/O with the user (or the program's environment). Global stream objects provide a convenient, stream-based wrapper for you to work against.

Global Stream Objects

The STL provides several *global stream objects* in the `<iostream>` header that wrap the input, output, and error streams stdin, stdout, and stderr. These implementation-defined standard streams are preconnected channels between your program and its executing environment. For example, in a desktop environment, stdin typically binds to the keyboard and stdout and stderr bind to the console.

NOTE *Recall that in Part I you saw extensive use of* `printf` *to write to stdout.*

Table 16-2 lists the global stream objects, all of which reside in the `std` namespace.

Table 16-2: The Global Stream Objects

Object	Type	Purpose
`cout` `wcout`	`ostream` `wostream`	Output, like a screen
`cin` `wcin`	`istream` `wistream`	Input, like a keyboard
`cerr` `wcerr`	`ostream` `wostream`	Error output (unbuffered)
`clog` `wclog`	`ostream` `wostream`	Error output (buffered)

So how do you use these objects? Well, stream classes support operations that you can partition into two categories:

Formatted operations Might perform some preprocessing on their input parameters before performing I/O

Unformatted operations Perform I/O directly

The following sections explain each of these categories in turn.

Formatted Operations

All formatted I/O passes through two functions: the *standard stream operators*, `operator<<` and `operator>>`. You'll recognize these as the left and right shift operators from "Logical Operators" on page 182. Somewhat confusingly, streams overload the left and right shift operators with completely unrelated functionality. The semantic meaning of the expression `i << 5` depends entirely on the type of `i`. If `i` is an integral type, this expression means *take i and shift the bits to the left by five binary digits*. If i is not an integral type, it means *write the value 5 into* i. Although this notational collision is unfortunate, in practice it doesn't cause too much trouble. Just pay attention to the types you're using and test your code well.

Output streams overload operator<<, which is referred to as the *output operator* or the *inserter*. The basic_ostream class template overloads the output operator for all fundamental types (except void and nullptr_t) and some STL containers, such as basic_string, complex, and bitset. As an ostream user, you need not worry about how these overloads translate objects into readable output.

Listing 16-1 illustrates how to use the output operator to write various types into cout.

```
#include <iostream>
#include <string>
#include <bitset>

using namespace std;

int main() {
  bitset<8> s{ "01110011" };
  string str("Crying zeros and I'm hearing ");
  size_t num{ 111 };
  cout << s; ❶
  cout << '\n'; ❷
  cout << str; ❸
  cout << num; ❹
  cout << "s\n"; ❺
}
--------------------------------------------------------------------------------
01110011 ❶❷
Crying zeros and I'm hearing 111s ❸❹❺
```

Listing 16-1: Using cout and operator<< to write into stdout

You use the output operator<< to write a bitset ❶, a char ❷, a string ❸, a size_t ❹, and a null-terminated string literal ❺ to stdout via cout. Even though you write five distinct types to the console, you never deal with serialization issues. (Consider the hoops you would have had to jump through to get printf to yield similar output given these types.)

One very nice feature of the standard stream operators is that they generally return a reference to the stream. Conceptually, overloads are typically defined along the following lines:

```
ostream& operator<<(ostream&, char);
```

This means you can chain output operators together. Using this technique, you can refactor Listing 16-1 so cout appears only once, as Listing 16-2 illustrates.

```
#include <iostream>
#include <string>
#include <bitset>

using namespace std;

int main() {
  bitset<8> s{ "01110011" };
  string str("Crying zeros and I'm hearing ");
  size_t num{ 111 };
  cout << s << '\n' << str << num << "s\n"; ❶
}
--------------------------------------------------------------------------
01110011
Crying zeros and I'm hearing 111s ❶
```

Listing 16-2: Refactoring Listing 16-1 by chaining output operators together

Because each invocation of `operator<<` returns a reference to the output stream (here, `cout`), you simply chain the calls together to obtain identical output ❶.

Input streams overload `operator>>`, which is referred to as the *input operator* or the *extractor*. The `basic_istream` class has corresponding overloads for the input operator for all the same types as `basic_ostream`, and again as a user, you can largely ignore the deserialization details.

Listing 16-3 illustrates how to use the input operator to read two `double` objects and a `string` from `cin`, then print the implied mathematical operation's result to stdout.

```
#include <iostream>
#include <string>

using namespace std;

int main() {
  double x, y;
  cout << "X: ";
  cin >> x; ❶
  cout << "Y: ";
  cin >> y; ❷

  string op;
  cout << "Operation: ";
  cin >> op; ❸
  if (op == "+") {
    cout << x + y; ❹
  } else if (op == "-") {
    cout << x - y; ❺
  } else if (op == "*") {
    cout << x * y; ❻
  } else if (op == "/") {
```

```
    cout << x / y; ❼
  } else {
    cout << "Unknown operation " << op; ❽
  }
}
```

Listing 16-3: A primitive calculator program using `cin` and `operator<<` to collect input

Here, you collect two `doubles` `x` ❶ and `y` ❷ followed by the `string` `op` ❸, which encodes the desired operation. Using an `if` statement, you can output the specified operation's result for addition ❹, subtraction ❺, multiplication ❻, and division ❼, or indicate to the user that `op` is unknown ❽.

To use the program, you type the requested values into the console when directed. A newline will send the input (as stdin) to `cin`, as Listing 16-4 illustrates.

```
X: 3959 ❶
Y: 6.283185 ❷
Operation: * ❸
24875.1 ❹
```

Listing 16-4: A sample run of the program in Listing 16-3 that calculates the circumference of Earth in miles

You input the two `double` objects: the radius of Earth in miles, **`3959`** ❶ and 2π, **`6.283185`** ❷, and you specify multiplication `*` ❸. The result is Earth's circumference in miles ❹. Note that you don't need to provide a decimal point for an integral value ❶; the stream is smart enough to know that there's an implicit decimal.

NOTE *You might wonder what happens in Listing 16-4 if you input a non-numeric string for `X` ❶ or `Y` ❷. The stream enters an error state, which you'll learn about later in this chapter in the "Stream State" section on page 530. In an error state, the stream ceases to accept input, and the program won't accept any more input.*

Unformatted Operations

When you're working with text-based streams, you'll usually want to use formatted operators; however, if you're working with binary data or if you're writing code that needs low-level access to streams, you'll want to know about the unformatted operations. Unformatted I/O involves a lot of detail. For brevity, this section provides a summary of the relevant methods, so if you need to use unformatted operations, refer to [input.output].

The `istream` class has many unformatted input methods. These methods manipulate streams at the byte level and are summarized in Table 16-3. In this table, `is` is of type `std::istream <T>`, `s` is a `char*`, `n` is a stream size, `pos` is a position type, and `d` is a delimiter of type `T`.

Table 16-3: Unformatted Read Operations for istream

Method	Description
`is.get([c])`	Returns next character or writes to character reference **c** if provided.
`is.get(s, n, [d])` `is.getline(s, n, [d])`	The operation get reads up to **n** characters into the buffer **s**, stopping if it encounters a newline, or **d** if provided. The operation getline is the same except it reads the newline character as well. Both write a terminating null character to **s**. You must ensure **s** has enough space.
`is.read(s, n)` `is.readsome(s, n)`	The operation read reads up to **n** characters into the buffer **s**; encountering end of file is an error. The operation readsome is the same except it doesn't consider end of file an error.
`is.gcount()`	Returns the number of characters read by **is**'s last unformatted read operation.
`is.ignore()`	Extracts and discards a single character.
`is.ignore(n, [d])`	Extracts and discards up to **n** characters. If **d** is provided, ignore stops if **d** is found.
`is.peek()`	Returns the next character to be read without extracting.
`is.unget()`	Puts the last extracted character back into the string.
`is.putback(c)`	If **c** is the last character extracted, executes unget. Otherwise, sets the badbit. Explained in the "Stream State" section.

Output streams have corollary unformatted write operations, which manipulate streams at a very low level, as summarized in Table 16-4. In this table, `os` is of type `std::ostream <T>`, `s` is a `char*`, and `n` is a stream size.

Table 16-4: Unformatted Write Operations for ostream

Method	Description
`os.put(c)`	Writes **c** to the stream
`os.write(s, n)`	Writes **n** characters from **s** to the stream
`os.flush()`	Writes all buffered data to the underlying device

Special Formatting for Fundamental Types

All fundamental types, in addition to `void` and `nullptr`, have input and output operator overloads, but some have special rules:

`char` and `wchar_t` The input operator skips whitespace when assigning character types.

`char*` and `wchar_t*` The input operator first skips whitespace and then reads the string until it encounters another whitespace or an end-of-file (EOF). You must reserve enough space for the input.

`void*` Address formats are implementation dependent for input and output operators. On desktop systems, addresses take hexadecimal literal form, such as `0x01234567` for 32-bit or `0x0123456789abcdef` for 64-bit.

`bool` The input and output operators treat Boolean values as numbers: 1 for `true` and 0 for `false`.

Numeric types The input operator requires that input begin with at least one digit. Badly formed input numbers yield a zero-valued result.

These rules might seem a bit strange at first, but they're fairly straightforward once you get used to them.

NOTE *Avoid reading into C-style strings, because it's up to you to ensure that you've allocated enough space for the input data. Failure to perform adequate checking results in undefined behavior and possibly major security vulnerabilities. Use* `std::string` *instead.*

Stream State

A stream's state indicates whether I/O failed. Each stream type exposes the constant static members referred to collectively as its *bits*, which indicate a possible stream state: `goodbit`, `badbit`, `eofbit`, and `failbit`. To determine whether a stream is in a particular state, you invoke member functions that return a `bool` indicating whether the stream is in the corresponding state. Table 16-5 lists these member functions, the stream state corresponding to a `true` result, and the state's meaning.

Table 16-5: The Possible Stream States, Their Accessor Methods, and Their Meanings

Method	State	Meaning
`good()`	`goodbit`	The stream is in a good working state.
`eof()`	`eofbit`	The stream encountered an EOF.
`fail()`	`failbit`	An input or output operation failed, but the stream might still be in a good working state.
`bad()`	`badbit`	A catastrophic error occurred, and the stream is not in a good state.

NOTE *To reset a stream's status to indicate a good working state, you can invoke its* `clear()` *method.*

Streams implement an implicit bool conversion (`operator bool`), so you can check whether a stream is in a good working state simply and directly. For example, you can read input from stdin word by word until it encounters an EOF (or some other failure condition) using a simple `while` loop. Listing 16-5 illustrates a simple program that uses this technique to generate word counts from stdin.

```
#include <iostream>
#include <string>
```

```
int main() {
  std::string word; ❶
  size_t count{}; ❷
  while (std::cin >> word) ❸
    count++; ❹
  std::cout << "Discovered " << count << " words.\n"; ❺
}
```

Listing 16-5: A program that counts words from stdin

You declare a string called word to receive words from stdin ❶, and you initialize a count variable to zero ❷. Within the while loop's Boolean expression, you attempt to assign new input into word ❸. When this succeeds, you increment count ❹. Once it fails—for example, due to encountering an EOF—you cease incrementing and print the final tally ❺.

You can try two methods to test Listing 16-5. First, you can simply invoke the program, enter some input, and provide an EOF. How to send EOF depends on your operating system. In the Windows command line, you can enter EOF by pressing CTRL-Z and pressing enter. In Linux bash or in the OS X shell, you press CTRL-D. Listing 16-6 demonstrates how to invoke Listing 16-5 from the Windows command line.

```
$ listing_16_5.exe ❶
Size matters not. Look at me. Judge me by my size, do you? Hmm? Hmm. And well
you should not. For my ally is the Force, and a powerful ally it is. Life
creates it, makes it grow. Its energy surrounds us and binds us. Luminous
beings are we, not this crude matter. You must feel the Force around you;
here, between you, me, the tree, the rock, everywhere, yes. ❷
^Z ❸
Discovered 70 words. ❹
```

Listing 16-6: Invoking the program in Listing 16-5 by typing input into the console

First, you invoke your program ❶. Next, enter some arbitrary text followed by a new line ❷. Then issue EOF. The Windows command line shows the somewhat cryptic sequence **^Z** on the command line, after which you must press ENTER. This causes std::cin to enter the eofbit state, ending the while loop in Listing 16-5 ❸. The program indicates that you've sent 70 words into stdin ❹.

On Linux and Mac and in Windows PowerShell, you have another option. Rather than entering the input directly into the console, you can save the text to a file, say *yoda.txt*. The trick is to use cat to read the text file and then use the pipe operator | to send the contents to your program. The pipe operator "pipes" the stdout of the program to its left into the stdin of the program on the right. The following command illustrates this process:

```
$ cat yoda.txt❶ |❷ ./listing_15_4❸
Discovered 70 words.
```

The cat command reads the contents of *yoda.txt* ❶. The pipe operator ❷ pipes the stdout of cat into stdin of listing_15_4 ❸. Because cat sends EOF when it encounters the end of *yoda.txt*, you don't need to enter it manually.

Sometimes you'll want streams to throw an exception when certain fail bits occur. You can do this easily with a stream's exceptions method, which accepts a single argument corresponding to the bit you want to throw exceptions. If you desire multiple bits, you can simply join them together using Boolean OR (|).

Listing 16-7 illustrates how to refactor Listing 16-5 so it handles the badbit with exceptions and eofbit/failbit with the default handling.

```
#include <iostream>
#include <string>

using namespace std;

int main() {
  cin.exceptions(istream::badbit); ❶
  string word;
  size_t count{};
  try { ❷
    while(cin >> word) ❸
      count++;
    cout << "Discovered " << count << " words.\n"; ❹
  } catch (const std::exception& e) { ❺
    cerr << "Error occurred reading from stdin: " << e.what(); ❻
  }
}
```

Listing 16-7: Refactoring Listing 16-5 to handle badbit with exceptions

You start the program by invoking the exceptions method on std::cin ❶. Because cin is an istream, you pass istream::badbit as the argument of exception, indicating that you want cin to throw an exception any time it gets into a catastrophic state. To account for possible exceptions, you wrap the existing code in a try-catch block ❷, so if cin sets badbit while it's reading input ❸, the user never receives a message about the word count ❹. Instead, the program catches the resulting exception ❺ and prints the error message ❻.

Buffering and Flushing

Many ostream class templates involve operating system calls under the hood, for example, to write to a console, a file, or a network socket. Relative to other function calls, system calls are usually slow. Rather than invoking a system call for each output element, an application can wait for multiple elements and then send them all together to improve performance.

The queuing behavior is called *buffering*. When the stream empties the buffered output, it's called *flushing*. Usually, this behavior is completely transparent to the user, but sometimes you want to manually flush the ostream. For this (and other tasks), you turn to manipulators.

Manipulators

Manipulators are special objects that modify how streams interpret input or format output. Manipulators exist to perform many kinds of stream alterations. For example, `std::ws` modifies an `istream` to skip over whitespace. Here are some other manipulators that work on `ostreams`:

- `std::flush` empties any buffered output directly to an `ostream`.
- `std::ends` sends a null byte.
- `std::endl` is like `std::flush` except it sends a newline before flushing.

Table 16-6 summarizes the manipulators in the `<istream>` and `<ostream>` headers.

Table 16-6: Four Manipulators in the `<istream>` and `<ostream>` Headers

Manipulator	Class	Behavior
`ws`	`istream`	Skips over all whitespaces
`flush`	`ostream`	Writes any buffered data to the stream by invoking its `flush` method
`ends`	`ostream`	Sends a null byte
`endl`	`ostream`	Sends a newline and flushes

For example, you could replace ❹ in Listing 16-7 with the following:

```
cout << "Discovered " << count << " words." << endl;
```

This will print a newline and also flush output.

NOTE *As a general rule, use* `std::endl` *when your program has finished outputting text to the stream for a while and* `\n` *when you know your program will output more text soon.*

The stdlib provides many other manipulators in the `<ios>` header. You can, for example, determine whether an `ostream` will represent Boolean values textually (`boolalpha`) or numerically (`noboolalpha`); integral values as octal (`oct`), decimal (`dec`), or hexadecimal (`hex`); and floating-point numbers as decimal notation (`fixed`) or scientific notation (`scientific`). Simply pass one of these manipulators to an `ostream` using `operator<<` and *all* subsequent insertions of the corresponding type will be manipulated (not just an immediately preceding operand).

You can also set a stream's width parameter using the `setw` manipulator. A stream's width parameter has varied effects, depending on the stream. For example, with `std::cout`, `setw` will fix the number of output characters allocated to the next output object. Additionally, for floating-point output, `setprecision` will set the following numbers' precision.

Listing 16-8 illustrates how these manipulators perform functions similar to those of the various `printf` format specifiers.

```
#include <iostream>
#include <iomanip>

using namespace std;

int main() {
  cout << "Gotham needs its " << boolalpha << true << " hero."; ❶
  cout << "\nMark it " << noboolalpha << false << "!"; ❷
  cout << "\nThere are " << 69 << "," << oct << 105 << " leaves in here."; ❸
  cout << "\nYabba " << hex << 3669732608 << "!"; ❹
  cout << "\nAvogadro's number: " << scientific << 6.0221415e-23; ❺
  cout << "\nthe Hogwarts platform: " << fixed << setprecision(2) << 9.750123; ❻
  cout << "\nAlways eliminate " << 3735929054; ❼
  cout << setw(4) << "\n"
       << 0x1 << "\n"
       << 0x10 << "\n"
       << 0x100 << "\n"
       << 0x1000 << endl; ❽
}
```

```
Gotham needs its true hero. ❶
Mark it 0! ❷
There are 69,151 leaves in here. ❸
Yabba dabbad00! ❹
Avogadro's Number: 6.022142e-23 ❺
the Hogwarts platform: 9.75 ❻
Always eliminate deadc0de ❼
1
10
100
1000 ❽
```

Listing 16-8: A program illustrating some of the manipulators available in the `<iomanip>` header

The `boolalpha` manipulator in the first line causes Boolean values to print textually as `true` and `false` ❶, whereas `noboolalpha` causes them to print as 1 and 0 instead ❷. For integral values, you can print as octal with `oct` ❸ or hexadecimal with `hex` ❹. For floating-point values, you can specify scientific notation with `scientific` ❺, and you can set the number of digits to print with `setprecision` and specify decimal notation with `fixed` ❻. Because manipulators apply to all subsequent objects you insert into a stream, when you print another integral value at the end of the program, the last integral manipulator (`hex`) applies, so you get a hexadecimal representation ❼. Finally, you employ `setw` to set the field width for output to 4, and you print some integral values ❽.

Table 16-7 summarizes this sampling of common manipulators.

Table 16-7: Many of the Manipulators Available in the <iomanip> Header

Manipulator	Behavior
`boolalpha`	Represents Booleans textually rather than numerically.
`noboolalpha`	Represents Booleans numerically rather than textually.
`oct`	Represents integral values as octal.
`dec`	Represents integral values as decimal.
`hex`	Represents integral values as hexadecimal.
`setw(n)`	Sets the width parameter of a stream to **n**. The exact effect depends on the stream.
`setprecision(p)`	Specifies floating-point precision as **p**.
`fixed`	Represents floating-point numbers in decimal notation.
`scientific`	Represents floating-point numbers in scientific notation.

NOTE *Refer to Chapter 15 in* The C++ Standard Library, *2nd Edition, by Nicolai M. Josuttis or [iostream.format].*

User-Defined Types

You can make user-defined types work with streams by implementing certain non-member functions. To implement the output operator for type `YourType`, the following function declaration serves most purposes:

```
ostream&❶ operator<<(ostream&❷ s, const YourType& m ❸);
```

For most cases, you'll simply return ❶ the same `ostream` you receive ❷. It's up to you how to send output into the `ostream`. But typically, this involves accessing fields on `YourType` ❸, optionally performing some formatting and transformations, and then using the output operator. For example, Listing 16-9 shows how to implement an output operator for `std::vector` to print its size, capacity, and elements.

```
#include <iostream>
#include <vector>
#include <string>

using namespace std;

template <typename T>
ostream& operator<<(ostream& s, vector<T> v) { ❶
  s << "Size: " << v.size()
    << "\nCapacity: " << v.capacity()
    << "\nElements:\n"; ❷
  for (const auto& element : v)
    s << "\t" << element << "\n"; ❸
  return s; ❹
}
```

```
int main() {
  const vector<string> characters {
    "Bobby Shaftoe",
    "Lawrence Waterhouse",
    "Gunter Bischoff",
    "Earl Comstock"
  }; ❺
  cout << characters << endl; ❻

  const vector<bool> bits { true, false, true, false }; ❼
  cout << boolalpha << bits << endl; ❽
}
--------------------------------------------------------------------------------
Size: 4
Capacity: 4
Elements: ❷
        Bobby Shaftoe ❸
        Lawrence Waterhouse ❸
        Gunter Bischoff ❸
        Earl Comstock ❸

Size: 4
Capacity: 32
Elements: ❷
        true ❸
        false ❸
        true ❸
        false ❸
```

Listing 16-9: A program illustrating how to implement an output operator for a vector

First, you define a custom output operator as a template, using the template parameter as the template parameter of `std::vector` ❶. This allows you to use the output operator for many kinds of `vector`s (as long as the type `T` also supports the output operator). The first three lines of output give the size and capacity of `vector`, as well as the title `Elements` indicating that the elements of the `vector` follow ❷. The following `for` loop iterates over each element in the `vector`, sending each on a separate line to the `ostream` ❸. Finally, you return the stream reference `s` ❹.

Within `main`, you initialize a `vector` called `characters` containing four `strings` ❺. Thanks to your user-defined output operator, you can simply send `characters` to `cout` as if it were a fundamental type ❻. The second example uses a `vector<bool>` called `bits`, which you also initialize with four elements ❼ and print to stdout ❽. Notice that you use the `boolalpha` manipulator, so when your user-defined output operator runs, the `bool` elements print textually ❸.

You can also provide user-defined input operators, which work similarly. A simple corollary is as follows:

```
istream&❶ operator>>(istream&❷ s, YourType& m ❸);
```

As with the output operator, the input operator typically returns ❶ the same stream it receives ❷. However, unlike with the output operator, the `YourType` reference will generally not be `const`, because you'll want to modify the corresponding object using input from the stream ❸.

Listing 16-10 illustrates how to specify an input operator for `deque` so it pushes elements into the container until an insertion fails (for example, due to an EOF character).

```
#include <iostream>
#include <deque>

using namespace std;

template <typename T>
istream& operator>>(istream& s, deque<T>& t) { ❶
  T element; ❷
  while (s >> element) ❸
    t.emplace_back(move(element)); ❹
  return s; ❺
}

int main() {
  cout << "Give me numbers: "; ❻
  deque<int> numbers;
  cin >> numbers; ❼
  int sum{};
  cout << "Cumulative sum:\n";
  for(const auto& element : numbers) {
    sum += element;
    cout << sum << "\n"; ❽
  }
}
```

```
Give me numbers: ❻ 1 2 3 4 5 ❼
Cumulative sum:
1  ❽
3  ❽
6  ❽
10 ❽
15 ❽
```

Listing 16-10: A program illustrating how to implement an input operator for a deque

Your user-defined input operator is a function template so you can accept any `deque` containing a type that supports the input operator ❶. First, you construct an element of type `T` so you can store input from the `istream` ❷. Next, you use the familiar `while` construct to accept input from the `istream` until the input operation fails ❸. (Recall from the "Stream State" section that streams can get into failed states in many ways, including reaching an EOF or encountering an I/O error.) After each insertion, you `move` the result into `emplace_back` on the `deque` to avoid unnecessary copies ❹. Once you're done inserting, you simply return the `istream` reference ❺.

Within main, you prompt the user for numbers ❻ and then use the insertion operator on a newly initialized deque to insert elements from stdin. In this sample program run, you input the numbers 1 to 5 ❼. For a bit of fun, you compute a cumulative sum by keeping a tally and iterating over each element, printing that iteration's result ❽.

NOTE *The preceding examples are simple user-defined implementations of input and output operators. You might want to elaborate these implementations in production code. For example, the implementations only work with* `ostream` *classes, which implies that they won't work with any non-*`char` *sequences.*

String Streams

The *string stream classes* provide facilities for reading from and writing to character sequences. These classes are useful in several situations. Input strings are especially useful if you want to parse string data into types. Because you can use the input operator, all the standard manipulator facilities are available to you. Output strings are excellent for building up strings from variable-length input.

Output String Streams

Output string streams provide output-stream semantics for character sequences, and they all derive from the class template `std::basic_ostringstream` in the `<sstream>` header, which provides the following specializations:

```
using ostringstream = basic_ostringstream<char>;
using wostringstream = basic_ostringstream<wchar_t>;
```

The output string streams support all the same features as an `ostream`. Whenever you send input to the string stream, the stream stores this input into an internal buffer. You can think of this as functionally equivalent to the `append` operation of `string` (except that string streams are potentially more efficient).

Output string streams also support the `str()` method, which has two modes of operation. Given no argument, `str` returns a copy of the internal buffer as a `basic_string` (so `ostringstream` returns a `string`; `wostringstream` returns a `wstring`). Given a single `basic_string` argument, the string stream will replace its buffer's current contents with the contents of the argument. Listing 16-11 illustrates how to use an `ostringstream`, send character data to it, build a `string`, reset its contents, and repeat.

```
#include <string>
#include <sstream>

TEST_CASE("ostringstream produces strings with str") {
  std::ostringstream ss; ❶
  ss << "By Grabthar's hammer, ";
  ss << "by the suns of Worvan. ";
```

```
  ss << "You shall be avenged."; ❷
  const auto lazarus = ss.str(); ❸

  ss.str("I am Groot."); ❹
  const auto groot = ss.str(); ❺

  REQUIRE(lazarus == "By Grabthar's hammer, by the suns"
                     " of Worvan. You shall be avenged.");
  REQUIRE(groot == "I am Groot.");
}
```

Listing 16-11: Using an `ostringstream` *to build strings*

After declaring an `ostringstream` ❶, you treat it just like any other `ostream` and use the output operator to send it three separate character sequences ❷. Next, you invoke `str` without an argument, which produces a `string` called `lazarus` ❸. Then you invoke `str` with the string literal `I am Groot` ❹, which replaces the contents of `ostringstream` ❺.

NOTE *Recall from "C-Style Strings" on page 45 that you can place multiple string literals on consecutive lines and the compiler will treat them as one. This is done purely for source code–formatting purposes.*

Input String Streams

Input string streams provide input stream semantics for character sequences, and they all derive from the class template `std::basic_istringstream` in the `<sstream>` header, which provides the following specializations:

```
using istringstream = basic_istringstream<char>;
using wistringstream = basic_istringstream<wchar_t>;
```

These are analogous to the `basic_ostringstream` specializations. You can construct input string streams by passing a `basic_string` with appropriate specialization (`string` for an `istringstream` and `wstring` for a `wistringstream`). Listing 16-12 illustrates by constructing an input string stream with a string containing three numbers and using the input operator to extract them. (Recall from "Formatted Operations" on page 525 that whitespace is the appropriate delimiter for string data.)

```
TEST_CASE("istringstream supports construction from a string") {
  std::string numbers("1 2.23606 2"); ❶
  std::istringstream ss{ numbers }; ❷
  int a;
  float b, c, d;
  ss >> a; ❸
  ss >> b; ❹
  ss >> c;
  REQUIRE(a == 1);
  REQUIRE(b == Approx(2.23606));
  REQUIRE(c == Approx(2));
```

```
  REQUIRE_FALSE(ss >> d); ❺
}
```

Listing 16-12: Using a string to build istringstream objects and extract numeric types

You construct a string from the literal `1 2.23606 2` ❶, which you pass into the constructor of an istringstream called ss ❷. This allows you to use the input operator to parse out int objects ❸ and float objects ❹ just like any other input stream. Once you've exhausted the stream and the output operator fails, ss converts to false ❺.

String Streams Supporting Input and Output

Additionally, if you want a string stream that supports input and output operations, you can use the basic_stringstream, which has the following specializations:

```
using stringstream = basic_stringstream<char>;
using wstringstream = basic_stringstream<wchar_t>;
```

This class supports the input and output operators, the str method, and construction from a string. Listing 16-13 illustrates how to use a combination of input and output operators to extract tokens from a string.

```
TEST_CASE("stringstream supports all string stream operations") {
  std::stringstream ss;
  ss << "Zed's DEAD"; ❶

  std::string who;
  ss >> who; ❷
  int what;
  ss >> std::hex >> what; ❸

  REQUIRE(who == "Zed's");
  REQUIRE(what == 0xdead);
}
```

Listing 16-13: Using a stringstream for input and output

You create a stringstream and sent the `Zed's DEAD` with the output operator ❶. Next, you parse `Zed's` out of the stringstream using the input operator ❷. Because DEAD is a valid hexadecimal integer, you use the input operator and the std::hex manipulator to extract it into an int ❸.

NOTE *All string streams are moveable.*

Summary of String Stream Operations

Table 16-8 provides a partial list of basic_stringstream operations. In this table, ss, ss1, and ss2 are of type std::basic_stringstream<T>; s is a std::basic_string<T>; obj is a formatted object; pos is a position type; dir is a std::ios_base::seekdir; and flg is a std::ios_base::iostate.

Table 16-8: A Partial List of std::basic_stringstream Operations

Operation	Notes
basic_stringstream<T> { [s], [om] }	Performs braced initialization of a newly constructed string stream. Defaults to empty string **s** and in|out open mode **om**.
basic_stringstream<T> { move(**ss**) }	Takes ownership of **ss**'s internal buffer.
~basic_stringstream	Destructs internal buffer.
ss.rdbuf()	Returns raw string device object.
ss.str()	Gets the contents of the string device object.
ss.str(**s**)	Sets the contents of the string device object to **s**.
ss >> **obj**	Extracts formatted data from the string stream.
ss << **obj**	Inserts formatted data into the string stream.
ss.tellg()	Returns the input position index.
ss.seekg(**pos**) **ss**.seekg(**pos**, **dir**)	Sets the input position indicator.
ss.flush()	Synchronizes the underlying device.
ss.good() **ss**.eof() **ss**.bad() !**ss**	Inspects the string stream's bits.
ss.exceptions(**flg**)	Configures the string stream to throw an exception whenever a bit in **flg** gets set.
ss1.swap(**ss2**) swap(**ss1**, **ss2**)	Exchanges each element of **ss1** with those of **ss2**.

File Streams

The *file stream classes* provide facilities for reading from and writing to character sequences. The file stream class structure follows that of the string stream classes. File stream class templates are available for input, output, and both.

File stream classes provide the following major benefits over using native system calls to interact with file contents:

- You get the usual stream interfaces, which provide a rich set of features for formatting and manipulating output.
- The file stream classes are RAII wrappers around the files, meaning it's impossible to leak resources, such as files.
- File stream classes support move semantics, so you can have tight control over where files are in scope.

Opening Files with Streams

You have two options for opening a file with any file stream. The first option is the `open` method, which accepts a `const char* filename` and an optional `std::ios_base::openmode` bitmask argument. The `openmode` argument can be one of the many possible combinations of values listed in Table 16-9.

Table 16-9: Possible Stream States, Their Accessor Methods, and Their Meanings

Flag (in `std::ios`)	File	Meaning
`in`	Must exist	Read
`out`	Created if doesn't exist	Erase the file; then write
`app`	Created if doesn't exist	Append
`in|out`	Must exist	Read and write from beginning
`in|app`	Created if doesn't exist	Update at end
`out|app`	Created if doesn't exist	Append
`out|trunc`	Created if doesn't exist	Erase the file; then read and write
`in|out|app`	Created if doesn't exist	Update at end
`in|out|trunc`	Created if doesn't exist	Erase the file; then read and write

Additionally, you can add the `binary` flag to any of these combinations to put the file in *binary mode*. In binary mode, the stream won't convert special character sequences, like end of line (for example, a carriage return plus a line feed on Windows) or EOF.

The second option for specifying a file to open is to use the stream's constructor. Each file stream provides a constructor taking the same arguments as the `open` method. All file stream classes are RAII wrappers around the file handles they own, so the files will be automatically cleaned up when the file stream destructs. You can also manually invoke the `close` method, which takes no arguments. You might want to do this if you know you're done with the file but your code is written in such a way that the file stream class object won't destruct for a while.

File streams also have default constructors, which don't open any files. To check whether a file is open, invoke the `is_open` method, which takes no arguments and returns a Boolean.

Output File Streams

Output file streams provide output stream semantics for character sequences, and they all derive from the class template `std::basic_ofstream` in the `<fstream>` header, which provides the following specializations:

```
using ofstream = basic_ofstream<char>;
using wofstream = basic_ofstream<wchar_t>;
```

The default basic_ofstream constructor doesn't open a file, and the non-default constructor's second optional argument defaults to ios::out.

Whenever you send input to the file stream, the stream writes the data to the corresponding file. Listing 16-14 illustrates how to use ofstream to write a simple message to a text file.

```
#include <fstream>

using namespace std;

int main() {
  ofstream file{ "lunchtime.txt", ios::out|ios::app }; ❶
  file << "Time is an illusion." << endl; ❷
  file << "Lunch time, " << 2 << "x so." << endl; ❸
}
--------------------------------------------------------------------------------
lunchtime.txt:
Time is an illusion. ❷
Lunch time, 2x so. ❸
```

Listing 16-14: A program opening the file lunchtime.txt *and appending a message to it. (The output corresponds to the contents of* lunchtime.txt *after a single program execution.)*

You initialize an ofstream called file with the path lunchtime.txt and the flags out and app ❶. Because this combination of flags appends output, any data you send through the output operator into this file stream gets appended to the end of the file. As expected, the file contains the message you passed to the output operator ❷❸.

Thanks to the ios::app flag, the program will append output to *lunchtime.txt* if it exists. For example, if you run the program again, you'll get the following output:

```
Time is an illusion.
Lunch time, 2x so.
Time is an illusion.
Lunch time, 2x so.
```

The second iteration of the program added the same phrase to the end of the file.

Input File Streams

Input file streams provide input stream semantics for character sequences, and they all derive from the class template std::basic_ifstream in the <fstream> header, which provides the following specializations:

```
using ifstream = basic_ifstream<char>;
using wifstream = basic_ifstream<wchar_t>;
```

The default `basic_ifstream` constructor doesn't open a file, and the non-default constructor's second optional argument defaults to `ios::in`.

Whenever you read from the file stream, the stream reads data from the corresponding file. Consider the following sample file, *numbers.txt*:

```
-54
203
9000
0
99
-789
400
```

Listing 16-15 contains a program that uses an `ifstream` to read from a text file containing integers and return the maximum. The output corresponds with invoking the program and passing the path of the file *numbers.txt*.

```
#include <iostream>
#include <fstream>
#include <limits>

using namespace std;

int main() {
  ifstream file{ "numbers.txt" }; ❶
  auto maximum = numeric_limits<int>::min(); ❷
  int value;
  while (file >> value) ❸
    maximum = maximum < value ? value : maximum; ❹
  cout << "Maximum found was " << maximum << endl; ❺
}
--------------------------------------------------------------------------
Maximum found was 9000 ❺
```

Listing 16-15: A program that reads the text file numbers.txt *and prints its maximum integer*

You first initialize an `istream` to open the *numbers.txt* text file ❶. Next, you initialize the maximum variable with the minimum value an `int` can take ❷. Using the idiomatic input stream and `while`-loop combination ❸, you cycle through each integer in the file, updating the maximum as you find higher values ❹. Once the file stream cannot parse any more integers, you print the result to stdout ❺.

Handling Failure

As with other streams, file streams fail silently. If you use a file stream constructor to open a file, you must check the `is_open` method to determine whether the stream successfully opened the file. This design differs from most other stdlib objects where invariants are enforced by exceptions. It's hard to say why the library implementors chose this approach, but the fact is that you can opt into an exception-based approach fairly easily.

You can make your own factory functions to handle file-opening failures with exceptions. Listing 16-16 illustrates how to implement an `ifstream` factory called `open`.

```
#include <fstream>
#include <string>

using namespace std;

ifstream❶ open(const char* path❷, ios_base::openmode mode = ios_base::in❸) {
  ifstream file{ path, mode }; ❹
  if(!file.is_open()) { ❺
    string err{ "Unable to open file " };
    err.append(path);
    throw runtime_error{ err }; ❻
  }
  file.exceptions(ifstream::badbit);
  return file; ❼
}
```

Listing 16-16: A factory function for generating `ifstream`s that handle errors with exceptions rather than failing silently

Your factory function returns an `ifstream` ❶ and accepts the same arguments as a file stream's constructor (and `open` method): a file `path` ❷ and an `openmode` ❸. You pass these two arguments into the constructor of `ifstream` ❹ and then determine whether the file opened successfully ❺. If it didn't, you throw a `runtime_error` ❻. If it did, you tell the resulting `ifstream` to throw an exception whenever its `badbit` gets set in the future ❼.

Summary of File Stream Operations

Table 16-10 provides a partial list of `basic_fstream` operations. In this table, `fs`, `fs1`, and `fs2` are of type `std:: basic_fstream <T>`; `p` is a C-style string, `std::string`, or a `std::filesystem::path`; `om` is an `std::ios_base::openmode`; `s` is a `std::basic_string<T>`; `obj` is a formatted object; `pos` is a position type; `dir` is a `std::ios_base::seekdir`; and `flg` is a `std::ios_base::iostate`.

Table 16-10: A Partial List of `std::basic_fstream` Operations

Operation	Notes
`basic_fstream<T> { [p], [om] }`	Performs braced initialization of a newly constructed file stream. If **p** is provided, attempts to open file at path **p**. Defaults to not opened and in|out open mode.
`basic_fstream<T> { move(fs) }`	Takes ownership of the internal buffer of **fs**.
`~basic_fstream`	Destructs internal buffer.
`fs.rdbuf()`	Returns raw string device object.
`fs.str()`	Gets the contents of the file device object.
`fs.str(s)`	Puts the contents of the file device object into **s**.

(continued)

Table 16-10: A Partial List of `std::basic_fstream` Operations (continued)

Operation	Notes
`fs >> obj`	Extracts formatted data from the file stream.
`fs << obj`	Inserts formatted data into the file stream.
`fs.tellg()`	Returns the input position index.
`fs.seekg(pos)` `fs.seekg(pos, dir)`	Sets the input position indicator.
`fs.flush()`	Synchronizes the underlying device.

`fs.good()`
`fs.eof()`
`fs.bad()`
`!fs`
	Inspects the file stream's bits.

`fs.exceptions(flg)`	Configures the file stream to throw an exception whenever a bit in `flg` gets set.
`fs1.swap(fs2)` `swap(fs1, fs2)`	Exchanges each element of `fs1` with one of `fs2`.

Stream Buffers

Streams don't read and write directly. Under the covers, they use stream buffer classes. At a high level, *stream buffer classes* are templates that send or extract characters. The implementation details aren't important unless you're planning on implementing your own stream library, but it's important to know that they exist in several contexts. The way you obtain stream buffers is by using a stream's `rdbuf` method, which all streams provide.

Writing Files to sdout

Sometimes you just want to write the contents of an input file stream directly into an output stream. To do this, you can extract the stream buffer pointer from the file stream and pass it to the output operator. For example, you can dump the contents of a file to stdout using `cout` in the following way:

```
cout << my_ifstream.rdbuf()
```

It's that easy.

Output Stream Buffer Iterators

Output stream buffer iterators are template classes that expose an output iterator interface that translates writes into output operations on the underlying stream buffer. In other words, these are adapters that allow you to use output streams as if they were output iterators.

To construct an output stream buffer iterator, use the `ostreambuf_iterator` template class in the `<iterator>` header. Its constructor takes a single output stream argument and a single template parameter corresponding to the constructor argument's template parameter (the character type). Listing 16-17 shows how to construct an output stream buffer iterator from `cout`.

```
#include <iostream>
#include <iterator>

using namespace std;

int main() {
  ostreambuf_iterator<char> itr{ cout }; ❶
  *itr = 'H'; ❷
  ++itr; ❸
  *itr = 'i'; ❹
}
--------------------------------------------------------------------------
H❷i❹
```

Listing 16-17: Writing the message `Hi` *to stdout using the* `ostreambuf_iterator` *class*

Here, you construct an output stream buffer iterator from `cout` ❶, which you write to in the usual way for an output operator: assign ❷, increment ❸, assign ❹, and so on. The result is character-by-character output to stdout. (Recall the procedures for handling output operators in "Output Iterators" on page 464.)

Input Stream Buffer Iterators

Input stream buffer iterators are template classes that expose an input iterator interface that translates reads into read operations on the underlying stream buffer. These are entirely analogous to output stream buffer iterators.

To construct an input stream buffer iterator, use the `istreambuf_iterator` template class in the `<iterator>` header. Unlike `ostreambuf_iterator`, it takes a stream buffer argument, so you must call `rdbuf()` on whichever input stream you want to adapt. This argument is optional: the default constructor of `istreambuf_iterator` corresponds to the end-of-range iterator of input iterator. For example, Listing 16-18 illustrates how to construct a string from `std::cin` using the range-based constructor of `string`.

```
#include <iostream>
#include <iterator>
#include <string>

using namespace std;

int main() {
  istreambuf_iterator<char> cin_itr{ cin.rdbuf() } ❶, end{} ❷;
  cout << "What is your name? "; ❸
  const string name{ cin_itr, end }; ❹
  cout << "\nGoodbye, " << name; ❺
}
--------------------------------------------------------------------------
What is your name? ❸josh ❹
Goodbye, josh❺
```

Listing 16-18: Constructing a string from `cin` *using input stream buffer iterators*

You construct an `istreambuf_iterator` from the stream buffer of `cin` ❶ as well as the end-of-range iterator ❷. After sending a prompt to the program's user ❸, you construct the `string name` using its range-based constructor ❹. When the user sends input (terminated by EOF), the string's constructor copies it. You then bid the user farewell using their `name` ❺. (Recall from "Stream State" on page 530 that methods for sending EOF to the console differ by operating system.)

Random Access

Sometimes you'll want random access into a stream (especially a file stream). The input and output operators clearly don't support this use case, so `basic_istream` and `basic_ostream` offer separate methods for random access. These methods keep track of the cursor or position, the index of the stream's current character. The position indicates the next byte that an input stream will read or an output stream will write.

For input streams, you can use the two methods `tellg` and `seekg`. The `tellg` method takes no arguments and returns the position. The `seekg` method allows you to set the cursor position, and it has two overloads. Your first option is to provide a `pos_type` position argument, which sets the read position. The second is to provide an `off_type` offset argument plus an `ios_base::seekdir` direction argument. The `pos_type` and `off_type` are determined by the template arguments to the `basic_istream` or `basic_ostream`, but usually these convert to/from integer types. The `seekdir` type takes one of the following three values:

- `ios_base::beg` specifies that the position argument is relative to the beginning.
- `ios_base::cur` specifies that the position argument is relative to the current position.
- `ios_base::end` specifies that the position argument is relative to the end.

For output streams, you can use the two methods `tellp` and `seekp`. These are roughly analogous to the `tellg` and `seekg` methods of input streams: the `p` stands for put and the `g` stands for get.

Consider a file *introspection.txt* with the following contents:

```
The problem with introspection is that it has no end.
```

Listing 16-19 illustrates how to employ random access methods to reset the file cursor.

```
#include <fstream>
#include <exception>
#include <iostream>

using namespace std;
```

```
ifstream open(const char* path, ios_base::openmode mode = ios_base::in) { ❶
--snip--
}

int main() {
  try {
    auto intro = open("introspection.txt"); ❷
    cout << "Contents: " << intro.rdbuf() << endl; ❸
    intro.seekg(0); ❹
    cout << "Contents after seekg(0): " << intro.rdbuf() << endl; ❺
    intro.seekg(-4, ios_base::end); ❻
    cout << "tellg() after seekg(-4, ios_base::end): "
                                                  << intro.tellg() << endl; ❼
    cout << "Contents after seekg(-4, ios_base::end): "
                                                  << intro.rdbuf() << endl; ❽
  }
  catch (const exception& e) {
    cerr << e.what();
  }
}
-----------------------------------------------------------------------------
Contents: The problem with introspection is that it has no end. ❸
Contents after seekg(0): The problem with introspection is that it has no end. ❺
tellg() after seekg(-4, ios_base::end): 49 ❼
Contents after seekg(-4, ios_base::end): end. ❽
```

Listing 16-19: A program using random access methods to read arbitrary characters in a text file

Using the factory function in Listing 16-16 ❶, you open the text file *introspection.txt* ❷. Next, you print the contents to stdout using the rdbuf method ❸, rewind the cursor to the first character ❹, and print the contents again. Notice that these yield identical output (because the file hasn't changed) ❺. You then use the relative offset overload of seekg to navigate to the fourth character from the end ❻. Using tellg, you learn that this is the 49th character (with zero-base indexing) ❼. When you print the input file to stdout, the output is only end., because these are the last four characters in the file ❽.

NOTE *Boost offers an IOStream library with a rich set of additional features that stdlib doesn't have, including facilities for memory mapped file I/O, compression, and filtering.*

Summary

In this chapter, you learned about streams, the major concept that provides a common abstraction for performing I/O. You also learned about files as a primary source and destination for I/O. You first learned about the fundamental stream classes in the stdlib and how to perform formatted and unformatted operations, inspect stream state, and handle errors with exceptions. You learned about manipulators and how to incorporate streams into user-defined types, string streams, and file streams. This chapter culminated with stream buffer iterators, which allow you to adapt a stream to an iterator.

EXERCISES

16-1. Implement an output operator that prints information about the `AutoBrake` from "An Extended Example: Taking a Brake" on page 283. Include the vehicle's current collision threshold and speed.

16-2. Write a program that takes output from stdin, capitalizes it, and writes the result to stdout.

16-3. Read the introductory documentation for Boost IOStream.

16-4. Write a program that accepts a file path, opens the file, and prints summary information about the contents, including word count, average word length, and a histogram of the characters.

FURTHER READING

- *Standard C++ IOStreams and Locales: Advanced Programmer's Guide and Reference* by Angelika Langer (Addison-Wesley Professional, 2000)
- *ISO International Standard ISO/IEC (2017) — Programming Language C++* (International Organization for Standardization; Geneva, Switzerland; *https://isocpp.org/std/the-standard/*)
- *The Boost C++ Libraries*, 2nd Edition, by Boris Schäling (XML Press, 2014)

17

FILESYSTEMS

"So, you're the UNIX guru." At the time, Randy was still stupid enough to be flattered by this attention, when he should have recognized them as bone-chilling words.
—Neal Stephenson, Cryptonomicon

This chapter teaches you how to use the stdlib's Filesystem library to perform operations on filesystems, such as manipulating and inspecting files, enumerating directories, and interoperating with file streams.

The stdlib and Boost contain Filesystem libraries. The stdlib's Filesystem library grew out of Boost's, and accordingly they're largely interchangeable. This chapter focuses on the stdlib implementation. If you're interested in learning more about Boost, refer to the Boost Filesystem documentation. Boost and stdlib's implementations are mostly identical.

NOTE *The C++ Standard has a history of subsuming Boost libraries. This allows the C++ community to gain experience with new features in Boost before going through the more arduous process of including the features in the C++ Standard.*

Filesystem Concepts

Filesystems model several important concepts. The central entity is the file. A *file* is a filesystem object that supports input and output and holds data. Files exist in containers called *directories*, which can be nested within other directories. For simplicity, directories are considered files. The directory containing a file is called that file's *parent directory*.

A path is a string that identifies a specific file. Paths begin with an optional *root name*, which is an implementation-specific string, such as *C:* or *//localhost* on Windows followed by an optional root directory, which is another implementation-specific string, such as / on Unix-like systems. The remainder of the path is a sequence of directories separated by implementation-defined separators. Optionally, paths terminate in a non-directory file. Paths can contain the special names "." and "..", which mean current directory and parent directory, respectively.

A *hard link* is a directory entry that assigns a name to an existing file, and a *symbolic link* (or *symlink*) assigns a name to a path (which might or might not exist). A path whose location is specified in relation to another path (usually the current directory) is called a *relative path*, and a *canonical path* unambiguously identifies a file's location, doesn't contain the special names "." and "..", and doesn't contain any symbolic links. An *absolute path* is any path that unambiguously identifies a file's location. A major difference between a canonical path and an absolute path is that a canonical path cannot contain the special names "." and "..".

WARNING *The stdlib filesystem might not be available if the target platform doesn't offer a hierarchical filesystem.*

std::filesystem::path

The `std::filesystem::path` is the Filesystem library's class for modeling a path, and you have many options for constructing paths. Perhaps the two most common are the default constructor, which constructs an empty path, and the constructor taking a string type, which creates the path indicated by the characters in the string. Like all other filesystem classes and functions, the `path` class resides in the `<filesystem>` header.

In this section, you'll learn how to construct a path from a `string` representation, decompose it into constituent parts, and modify it. In many common system- and application-programming contexts, you'll need to interact with files. Because each operating system has a unique representation for filesystems, the stdlib's Filesystem library is a welcome abstraction that allows you to write cross-platform code easily.

Constructing Paths

The `path` class supports comparison with other `path` objects and with `string` objects using the `operator==`. But if you just want to check whether the `path` is empty, it offers an empty method that returns a Boolean. Listing 17-1 illustrates how to construct two paths (one empty and one non-empty) and test them.

```
#include <string>
#include <filesystem>

TEST_CASE("std::filesystem::path supports == and .empty()") {
  std::filesystem::path empty_path; ❶
  std::filesystem::path shadow_path{ "/etc/shadow" }; ❷
  REQUIRE(empty_path.empty()); ❸
  REQUIRE(shadow_path == std::string{ "/etc/shadow" }); ❹
}
```

Listing 17-1: Constructing std::filesystem::path

You construct two paths: one with the default constructor ❶ and one referring to /etc/shadow ❷. Because you default construct it, the empty method of empty_path returns true ❸. The shadow_path equals a string containing /etc /shadow, because you construct it with the same contents ❹.

Decomposing Paths

The path class contains some decomposition methods that are, in effect, specialized string manipulators that allow you to extract components of the path, for example:

- root_name() returns the root name.
- root_directory() returns the root directory.
- root_path() returns the root path.
- relative_path() returns a path relative to the root.
- parent_path() returns the parent path.
- filename() returns the filename component.
- stem() returns the filename stripped of its extension.
- extension() returns the extension.

Listing 17-2 provides the values returned by each of these methods for a path pointing to a very important Windows system library, kernel32.dll.

```
#include <iostream>
#include <filesystem>

using namespace std;

int main() {
  const filesystem::path kernel32{ R"(C:\Windows\System32\kernel32.dll)" }; ❶
  cout << "Root name: " << kernel32.root_name() ❷
    << "\nRoot directory: " << kernel32.root_directory() ❸
    << "\nRoot path: " << kernel32.root_path() ❹
    << "\nRelative path: " << kernel32.relative_path() ❺
    << "\nParent path: " << kernel32.parent_path() ❻
```

```
    << "\nFilename: " << kernel32.filename() ❼
    << "\nStem: " << kernel32.stem() ❽
    << "\nExtension: " << kernel32.extension() ❾
    << endl;
}
--------------------------------------------------------------------------
Root name: "C:" ❷
Root directory: "\\" ❸
Root path: "C:\\" ❹
Relative path: "Windows\\System32\\kernel32.dll" ❺
Parent path: "C:\\Windows\\System32" ❻
Filename: "kernel32.dll" ❼
Stem: "kernel32" ❽
Extension: ".dll" ❾
```

Listing 17-2: A program printing various decompositions of a path

You construct a path to kernel32 using a raw string literal to avoid having to escape the backslashes ❶. You extract the root name ❷, the root directory ❸, and the root path of kernel32 ❹ and output them to stdout. Next, you extract the relative path, which displays the path relative to the root `C:\` ❺. The parent path is the path of `kernel32.dll`'s parent, which is simply the directory containing it ❻. Finally, you extract the filename ❼, its stem ❽, and its extension ❾.

Notice that you don't need to run Listing 17-2 on any particular operating system. None of the decomposition methods require that the path actually point to an existing file. You simply extract components of the path's contents, not the pointed-to file. Of course, different operating systems will yield different results, especially with respect to the delimiters (which are, for example, forward slashes on Linux).

NOTE *Listing 17-2 illustrates that `std::filesystem::path` has an `operator<<` that prints quotation marks at the beginning and end of its path. Internally, it uses `std::quoted`, a class template in the `<iomanip>` header that facilitates the insertion and extraction of quoted strings. Also, recall that you must escape the backslash in a string literal, which is why you see two rather than one in the paths embedded in the source code.*

Modifying Paths

In addition to decomposition methods, `path` offers several *modifier methods*, which allow you to modify various characteristics of a path:

- `clear()` empties the `path`.
- `make_preferred()` converts all the directory separators to the implementation-preferred directory separator. For example, on Windows this converts the generic separator / to the system-preferred separator \.
- `remove_filename()` removes the filename portion of the path.
- `replace_filename(p)` replaces the `path`'s filename with that of another `path p`.

- replace_extension(p) replaces the path's extension with that of another path p.
- remove_extension() removes the extension portion of the path.

Listing 17-3 illustrates how to manipulate a path using several modifier methods.

```
#include <iostream>
#include <filesystem>

using namespace std;

int main() {
  filesystem::path path{ R"(C:/Windows/System32/kernel32.dll)" };
  cout << path << endl; ❶

  path.make_preferred();
  cout << path << endl; ❷

  path.replace_filename("win32kfull.sys");
  cout << path << endl; ❸

  path.remove_filename();
  cout << path << endl; ❹

  path.clear();
  cout << "Is empty: " << boolalpha << path.empty() << endl; ❺
}
--------------------------------------------------------------------------------
"C:/Windows/System32/kernel32.dll" ❶
"C:\\Windows\\System32\\kernel32.dll" ❷
"C:\\Windows\\System32\\win32kfull.sys" ❸
"C:\\Windows\\System32\\" ❹
Is empty: true ❺
```

Listing 17-3: Manipulating a path using modifier methods. (Output is from a Windows 10 x64 system.)

As in Listing 17-2, you construct a path to kernel32, although this one is non-const because you're about to modify it ❶. Next, you convert all the directory separators to the system's preferred directory separator using make_preferred. Listing 17-3 shows output from a Windows 10 x64 system, so it has converted from slashes (/) to backslashes (\) ❷. Using replace_filename, you replace the filename from kernel32.dll to win32kfull.sys ❸. Notice again that the file described by this path doesn't need to exist on your system; you're just manipulating the path. Finally, you remove the filename using the remove_filename method ❹ and then empty the path's contents entirely using clear ❺.

Summary of Filesystem Path Methods

Table 17-1 contains a partial listing of the available methods of path. Note that p, p1, and p2 are path objects and s is a stream in the table.

Table 17-1: A Summary of std::filesystem::path Operations

Operation	Notes
path{}	Constructs an empty path.
Path{ s, [f] }	Constructs a path from the string type s; f is an optional path::format type that defaults to the implementation-defined pathname format.
Path{ p } p1 = p2	Copy construction/assignment.
Path{ move(p) } p1 = move(p2)	Move construction/assignment.
p.assign(s)	Assigns p to s, discarding current contents.
p.append(s) p / s	Appends s to p, including the appropriate separator, path::preferred_separator.
p.concat(s) p + s	Appends s to p without including a separator.
p.clear()	Erases the contents.
p.empty()	Returns true if p is empty.
p.make_preferred()	Converts all the directory separators to the implementation-preferred directory separator.
p.remove_filename()	Removes the filename portion.
p1.replace_filename(p2)	Replaces the filename of p1 with that of p2.
p1.replace_extension(p2)	Replaces the extension of p1 with that of p2.
p.root_name()	Returns the root name.
p.root_directory()	Returns the root directory.
p.root_path()	Returns the root path.
p.relative_path()	Returns the relative path.
p.parent_path()	Returns the parent path.
p.filename()	Returns the filename.
p.stem()	Returns the stem.
p.extension()	Returns the extension.
p.has_root_name()	Returns true if p has a root name.
p.has_root_directory()	Returns true if p has a root directory.
p.has_root_path()	Returns true if p has a root path.
p.has_relative_path()	Returns true if p has a relative path.
p.has_parent_path()	Returns true if p has a parent path.
p.has_filename()	Returns true if p has a filename.
p.has_stem()	Returns true if p has a stem.
p.has_extension()	Returns true if p has an extension.

Operation	Notes
`p.c_str()` `p.native()`	Returns the native-string representation of `p`.
`p.begin()` `p.end()`	Accesses the elements of a path sequentially as a half-open range.
`s << p`	Writes `p` into `s`.
`s >> p`	Reads `s` into `p`.
`p1.swap(p2)` `swap(p1, p2)`	Exchanges each element of `p1` with the elements of `p2`.

`p1 == p2`
`p1 != p2`
`p1 > p2`
`p1 >= p2`
`p1 < p2`
`p1 <= p2`
	Lexicographically compares two paths `p1` and `p2`.

Files and Directories

The `path` class is the central element of the Filesystem library, but none of its methods actually interact with the filesystem. Instead, the `<filesystem>` header contains non-member functions to do this. Think of `path` objects as the way you declare which filesystem components you want to interact with and think of the `<filesystem>` header as containing the functions that perform work on those components.

These functions have friendly error-handling interfaces and allow you to break paths into, for example, directory name, filename, and extension. Using these functions, you have many tools for interacting with the files in your environment without having to use an operating-specific application programming interface.

Error Handling

Interacting with the environment's filesystem involves the potential for errors, such as files not found, insufficient permissions, or unsupported operations. Therefore, each non-member function in the Filesystem library that interacts with the filesystem must convey error conditions to the caller. These non-member functions provide two options: throw an exception or set an error variable.

Each function has two overloads: one that allows you to pass a reference to a `std::system_error` and one that omits this parameter. If you provide the reference, the function will set the `system_error` equal to an error condition, should one occur. If you don't provide this reference, the function will throw a `std::filesystem::filesystem_error` (an exception type inheriting from `std::system_error`) instead.

Path-Composing Functions

As an alternative to using the constructor of path, you can construct various kinds of paths:

- absolute(**p**, [**ec**]) returns an absolute path referencing the same location as **p** but where is_absolute() is true.
- canonical(**p**, [**ec**]) returns a canonical path referencing the same location as **p**.
- current_path([**ec**]) returns the current path.
- relative(**p**, [**base**], [**ec**]) returns a path where **p** is made relative to **base**.
- temp_directory_path([**ec**]) returns a directory for temporary files. The result is guaranteed to be an existing directory.

Note that current_path supports an overload so you can set the current directory (as in **cd** or **chdir** on Posix). Simply provide a path argument, as in current_path(**p**, [**ec**]).

Listing 17-4 illustrates several of these functions in action.

```
#include <filesystem>
#include <iostream>

using namespace std;

int main() {
  try {
    const auto temp_path = filesystem::temp_directory_path(); ❶
    const auto relative = filesystem::relative(temp_path); ❷
    cout << boolalpha
      << "Temporary directory path: " << temp_path ❸
      << "\nTemporary directory absolute: " << temp_path.is_absolute() ❹
      << "\nCurrent path: " << filesystem::current_path() ❺
      << "\nTemporary directory's relative path: " << relative ❻
      << "\nRelative directory absolute: " << relative.is_absolute() ❼
      << "\nChanging current directory to temp.";

    filesystem::current_path(temp_path); ❽
    cout << "\nCurrent directory: " << filesystem::current_path(); ❾
  } catch(const exception& e) {
    cerr << "Error: " << e.what(); ❿
  }
}
```

```
Temporary directory path: "C:\\Users\\lospi\\AppData\\Local\\Temp\\" ❸
Temporary directory absolute: true ❹
Current path: "c:\\Users\\lospi\\Desktop" ❺
Temporary directory's relative path: "..\\AppData\\Local\\Temp" ❻
Relative directory absolute: false ❼
Changing current directory to temp. ❽
Current directory: "C:\\Users\\lospi\\AppData\\Local\\Temp" ❾
```

Listing 17-4: A program using several path composing functions. (Output is from a Windows 10 x64 system.)

You construct a path using `temp_directory_path`, which returns the system's directory for temporary files ➊, and then use `relative` to determine its relative path ➋. After printing the temporary path ➌, `is_absolute` illustrates that this path is absolute ➍. Next, you print the current path ➎ and the temporary directory's path relative to the current path ➏. Because this path is relative, `is_absolute` returns `false` ➐. Once you change the path to the temporary path ➑, you then print the current directory ➒. Of course, your output will look different from the output in Listing 17-4, and you might even get an `exception` if your system doesn't support certain operations ➓. (Recall the warning at the beginning of the chapter: the C++ Standard allows that some environments might not support some or all of the filesystem library.)

Inspecting File Types

You can inspect a file's attributes given a path by using the following functions:

- `is_block_file(p, [ec])` determines if `p` is a *block file*, a special file in some operating systems (for example, block devices in Linux that allow you to transfer randomly accessible data in fixed-size blocks).
- `is_character_file(p, [ec])` determines if `p` is a *character file*, a special file in some operating systems (for example, character devices in Linux that allow you to send and receive single characters).
- `is_regular_file(p, [ec])` determines if `p` is a regular file.
- `is_symlink(p, [ec])` determines if `p` is a symlink, which is a reference to another file or directory.
- `is_empty(p, [ec])` determines if `p` is either an empty file or an empty directory.
- `is_directory(p, [ec])` determines if `p` is a directory.
- `is_fifo(p, [ec])` determines if `p` is a *named pipe*, a special kind of interprocess communication mechanism in many operating systems.
- `is_socket(p, [ec])` determines if `p` is a *socket*, another special kind of interprocess communication mechanism in many operating systems.
- `is_other(p, [ec])` determines if `p` is some kind of file other than a regular file, a directory, or a symlink.

Listing 17-5 uses `is_directory` and `is_regular_file` to inspect four different paths.

```
#include <iostream>
#include <filesystem>

using namespace std;

void describe(const filesystem::path& p) { ➊
  cout << boolalpha << "Path: " << p << endl;
  try {
    cout << "Is directory: " << filesystem::is_directory(p) << endl; ➋
```

```
    cout << "Is regular file: " << filesystem::is_regular_file(p) << endl; ❸
  } catch (const exception& e) {
    cerr << "Exception: " << e.what() << endl;
  }
}

int main() {
  filesystem::path win_path{ R"(C:/Windows/System32/kernel32.dll)" };
  describe(win_path); ❹
  win_path.remove_filename();
  describe(win_path); ❺

  filesystem::path nix_path{ R"(/bin/bash)" };
  describe(nix_path); ❻
  nix_path.remove_filename();
  describe(nix_path); ❼
}
```

Listing 17-5: A program inspecting four iconic Windows and Linux paths with `is_directory` and `is_regular_file`.

On a Windows 10 x64 machine, running the program in Listing 17-5 yielded the following output:

```
Path: "C:/Windows/System32/kernel32.dll" ❹
Is directory: false ❹
Is regular file: true ❹
Path: "C:/Windows/System32/" ❺
Is directory: true ❺
Is regular file: false ❺
Path: "/bin/bash" ❻
Is directory: false ❻
Is regular file: false ❻
Path: "/bin/" ❼
Is directory: false ❼
Is regular file: false ❼
```

And on an Ubuntu 18.04 x64 machine, running the program in Listing 17-5 yielded the following output:

```
Path: "C:/Windows/System32/kernel32.dll" ❹
Is directory: false ❹
Is regular file: false ❹
Path: "C:/Windows/System32/" ❺
Is directory: false ❺
Is regular file: false ❺
Path: "/bin/bash" ❻
Is directory: false ❻
Is regular file: true ❻
Path: "/bin/" ❼
Is directory: true ❼
Is regular file: false ❼
```

First, you define the describe function, which takes a single path ❶. After printing the path, you also print whether the path is a directory ❷ or a regular file ❸. Within main, you pass four different paths to describe:

- C:/Windows/System32/kernel32.dll ❹
- C:/Windows/System32/ ❺
- /bin/bash ❻
- /bin/ ❼

Note that the result is operating system specific.

Inspecting Files and Directories

You can inspect various filesystem attributes using the following functions:

- current_path([p], [ec]), which, if p is provided, sets the program's current path to p; otherwise, it returns the program's current path.
- exists(p, [ec]) returns whether a file or directory exists at p.
- equivalent(p1, p2, [ec]) returns whether p1 and p2 refer to the same file or directory.
- file_size(p, [ec]) returns the size in bytes of the regular file at p.
- hard_link_count(p, [ec]) returns the number of hard links for p.
- last_write_time(p, [t] [ec]), which, if t is provided, sets p's last modified time to t; otherwise, it returns the last time p was modified. (t is a std::chrono::time_point.)
- permissions(p, prm, [ec]) sets p's permissions. prm is of type std::filesystem::perms, which is an enum class modeled after POSIX permission bits. (Refer to [fs.enum.perms].)
- read_symlink(p, [ec]) returns the target of the symlink p.
- space(p, [ec]) returns space information about the filesystem p occupies in the form of a std::filesystem::space_info. This POD contains three fields: capacity (the total size), free (the free space), and available (the free space available to a non-privileged process). All are an unsigned integer type, measured in bytes.
- status(p, [ec]) returns the type and attributes of the file or directory p in the form of a std::filesystem::file_status. This class contains a type method that accepts no parameters and returns an object of type std::filesystem::file_type, which is an enum class that takes values describing a file's type, such as not_found, regular, directory. The symlink file_status class also offers a permissions method that accepts no parameters and returns an object of type std::filesystem::perms. (Refer to [fs.class.file_status] for details.)
- symlink_status(p, [ec]) is like a status that won't follow symlinks.

If you're familiar with Unix-like operating systems, you've no doubt used the ls (short for "list") program many times to enumerate files and directories. On DOS-like operating systems (including Windows), you have the analogous dir command. You'll use several of these functions later in the chapter (in Listing 17-7) to build your own simple listing program.

Now that you know how to inspect files and directories, let's turn to how you can manipulate the files and directories your paths refer to.

Manipulating Files and Directories

Additionally, the Filesystem library contains a number of methods for manipulating files and directories:

- copy(**p1**, **p2**, [**opt**], [**ec**]) copies files or directories from **p1** to **p2**. You can provide a std::filesystem::copy_options **opt** to customize the behavior of copy_file. This enum class can take several values, including none (report an error if the destination already exists), skip_existing (to keep existing), overwrite_existing (to overwrite), and update_existing (to overwrite if **p1** is newer). (Refer to [fs.enum.copy.opts] for details.)
- copy_file(**p1**, **p2**, [**opt**], [**ec**]) is like copy except it will generate an error if **p1** is anything but a regular file.
- create_directory(**p**, [**ec**]) creates the directory **p**.
- create_directories(**p**, [**ec**]) is like calling create_directory recursively, so if a nested path contains parents that don't exist, use this form.
- create_hard_link(**tgt**, **lnk**, [**ec**]) creates a hard link to **tgt** at **lnk**.
- create_symlink(**tgt**, **lnk**, [**ec**]) creates a symlink to **tgt** at **lnk**.
- create_directory_symlink(**tgt**, **lnk**, [**ec**]) should be used for directories instead of create_symlink.
- remove(**p**, [**ec**]) removes a file or empty directory **p** (without following symlinks).
- remove_all(**p**, [**ec**]) removes a file or directory recursively **p** (without following symlinks).
- rename(**p1**, **p2**, [**ec**]) renames **p1** to **p2**.
- resize_file(**p**, **new_size**, [**ec**]) changes the size of **p** (if it's a regular file) to **new_size**. If this operation grows the file, zeros fill the new space. Otherwise, the operation trims **p** from the end.

You can create a program that copies, resizes, and deletes a file using several of these methods. Listing 17-6 illustrates this by defining a function that prints file size and modification time. In main, the program creates and modifies two path objects, and it invokes that function after each modification.

```
#include <iostream>
#include <filesystem>

using namespace std;
using namespace std::filesystem;
using namespace std::chrono;
```

```
void write_info(const path& p) {
  if (!exists(p)) { ❶
    cout << p << " does not exist." << endl;
    return;
  }
  const auto last_write = last_write_time(p).time_since_epoch();
  const auto in_hours = duration_cast<hours>(last_write).count();
  cout << p << "\t" << in_hours << "\t" << file_size(p) << "\n"; ❷
}

int main() {
  const path win_path{ R"(C:/Windows/System32/kernel32.dll)" }; ❸
  const auto reamde_path = temp_directory_path() / "REAMDE"; ❹
  try {
    write_info(win_path); ❺
    write_info(reamde_path); ❻

    cout << "Copying " << win_path.filename()
         << " to " << reamde_path.filename() << "\n";
    copy_file(win_path, reamde_path);
    write_info(reamde_path); ❼

    cout << "Resizing " << reamde_path.filename() << "\n";
    resize_file(reamde_path, 1024);
    write_info(reamde_path); ❽

    cout << "Removing " << reamde_path.filename() << "\n";
    remove(reamde_path);
    write_info(reamde_path); ❾
  } catch(const exception& e) {
    cerr << "Exception: " << e.what() << endl;
  }
}
--------------------------------------------------------------------------
"C:/Windows/System32/kernel32.dll"      3657767 720632 ❺
"C:\\Users\\lospi\\AppData\\Local\\Temp\\REAMDE" does not exist. ❻
Copying "kernel32.dll" to "REAMDE"
"C:\\Users\\lospi\\AppData\\Local\\Temp\\REAMDE"        3657767 720632 ❼
Resizing "REAMDE"
"C:\\Users\\lospi\\AppData\\Local\\Temp\\REAMDE"        3659294 1024 ❽
Removing "REAMDE"
"C:\\Users\\lospi\\AppData\\Local\\Temp\\REAMDE" does not exist. ❾
```

Listing 17-6: A program illustrating several methods for interacting with the filesystem. (Output is from a Windows 10 x64 system.)

The write_info function takes a single path parameter. You check whether this path exists ❶, printing an error message and returning immediately if it doesn't. If the path does exist, you print a message indicating its last modification time (in hours since epoch) and its file size ❷.

Within main, you create a path win_path to kernel32.dll ❸ and a path to a nonexistent file called REAMDE in the filesystem's temporary file directory at reamde_path ❹. (Recall from Table 17-1 that you can use operator/ to concatenate two path objects.) Within a try-catch block, you invoke write_info on both paths ❺❻. (If you're using a non-Windows machine, you'll get different output. You can modify win_path to an existing file on your system to follow along.)

Next, you copy the file at win_path to reamde_path and invoke write_info on it ❼. Notice that, as opposed to earlier ❻, the file at reamde_path exists and it has the same last write time and file size as kernel32.dll.

You then resize the file at reamde_path to 1024 bytes and invoke write_info ❽. Notice that the last write time increased from 3657767 to 3659294 and the file size decreased from 720632 to 1024.

Finally, you remove the file at reamde_path and invoke write_info ❾, which tells you that the file again no longer exists.

NOTE *How filesystems resize files behind the scenes varies by operating system and is beyond the scope of this book. But you can think of how a resize operation might work conceptually as the* resize *operation on a* std::vector*. All the data at the end of the file that doesn't fit into the file's new size is discarded by the operating system.*

Directory Iterators

The Filesystem library provides two classes for iterating over the elements of a directory: std::filesystem::directory_iterator and std::filesystem::recursive_directory_iterator. A directory_iterator won't enter subdirectories, but the recursive_directory_iterator will. This section introduces the directory_iterator, but the recursive_directory_iterator is a drop-in replacement and supports all the following operations.

Constructing

The default constructor of directory_iterator produces the end iterator. (Recall that an input end iterator indicates when an input range is exhausted.) Another constructor accepts path, which indicates the directory you want to enumerate. Optionally, you can provide std::filesystem::directory_options, which is an enum class bitmask with the following constants:

- none directs the iterator to skip directory symlinks. If the iterator encounters a permission denial, it produces an error.
- follow_directory_symlink follows symlinks.
- skip_permission_denied skips directories if the iterator encounters a permission denial.

Additionally, you can provide a std::error_code, which, like all other Filesystem library functions that accept an error_code, will set this parameter rather than throwing an exception if an error occurs during construction.

Table 17-2 summarizes these options for constructing a directory_iterator. Note that p is path and d is directory, op is directory_options, and ec is error_code in the table.

Table 17-2: A Summary of `std::filesystem::directory_iterator` Operations

Operation	Notes
`directory_iterator{}`	Constructs the end iterator.
`directory_iterator{ p, [op], [ec] }`	Constructs a directory iterator referring to the directory **p**. The argument **op** defaults to none. If provided, **ec** receives error conditions rather than throwing an exception.
`directory_iterator { d }` `d1 = d2`	Copies construction/assignment.
`directory_iterator { move(d) }` `d1 = move(d2)`	Moves construction/assignment.

Directory Entries

The input iterators `directory_iterator` and `recursive_directory_iterator` produce a `std::filesystem::directory_entry` element for each entry they encounter. The `directory_entry` class stores a `path`, as well as some attributes about that `path` exposed as methods. Table 17-3 lists these methods. Note that `de` is a `directory_entry` in the table.

Table 17-3: A Summary of `std::filesystem::directory_entry` Operations

Operation	Description
`de.path()`	Returns the referenced path.
`de.exists()`	Returns `true` if the referenced path exists on the filesystem.
`de.is_block_file()`	Returns `true` if the referenced path is a block device.
`de.is_character_file()`	Returns `true` if the referenced path is a character device.
`de.is_directory()`	Returns `true` if the referenced path is a directory.
`de.is_fifo()`	Returns `true` if the referenced path is a named pipe.
`de.is_regular_file()`	Returns `true` if the referenced path is a regular file.
`de.is_socket()`	Returns `true` if the referenced path is a socket.
`de.is_symlink()`	Returns `true` if the referenced path is a symlink
`de.is_other()`	Returns `true` if the referenced path is something else.
`de.file_size()`	Returns the size of the referenced path.
`de.hard_link_count()`	Returns the number of hard links to the referenced path.
`de.last_write_time([t])`	If **t** is provided, sets the last modified time of the referenced path; otherwise, it returns the last modified time.
`de.status()` `de.symlink_status()`	Returns a `std::filesystem::file_status` for the referenced path.

You can employ `directory_iterator` and several of the operations in Table 17-3 to create a simple directory-listing program, as Listing 17-7 illustrates.

```
#include <iostream>
#include <filesystem>
#include <iomanip>

using namespace std;
using namespace std::filesystem;
using namespace std::chrono;

void describe(const directory_entry& entry) { ❶
  try {
    if (entry.is_directory()) { ❷
      cout << "           *";
    } else {
      cout << setw(12) << entry.file_size();
    }
    const auto lw_time =
      duration_cast<seconds>(entry.last_write_time().time_since_epoch());
    cout << setw(12) << lw_time.count()
      << " " << entry.path().filename().string()
      << "\n"; ❸
  } catch (const exception& e) {
    cout << "Error accessing " << entry.path().string()
         << ": " << e.what() << endl; ❹
  }
}

int main(int argc, const char** argv) {
  if (argc != 2) {
    cerr << "Usage: listdir PATH";
    return -1; ❺
  }
  const path sys_path{ argv[1] }; ❻
  cout << "Size         Last Write  Name\n";
  cout << "------------ ----------- ------------\n"; ❼
  for (const auto& entry : directory_iterator{ sys_path }) ❽
    describe(entry); ❾
}
```

```
> listdir c:\Windows
Size         Last Write  Name
------------ ----------- ------------
           * 13177963504 addins
           * 13171360979 appcompat
--snip--
           * 13173551028 WinSxS
      316640 13167963236 WMSysPr9.prx
       11264 13167963259 write.exe
```

Listing 17-7: A file- and directory-listing program that uses `std::filesystem::directory_iterator` to enumerate a given directory. (Output is from a Windows 10 x64 system.)

NOTE *You should modify the program's name from `listdir` to whatever value matches your compiler's output.*

You first define a describe function that takes a path reference ❶, which checks whether the path is a directory ❷ and prints an asterisk for a directory and a corresponding size for a file. Next, you determine the entry's last modification in seconds since epoch and print it along with the entry's associated filename ❸. If any exception occurs, you print an error message and return ❹.

Within main, you first check that the user invoked your program with a single argument and return with a negative number if not ❺. Next, you construct a path using the single argument ❻, print some fancy headers for your output ❼, iterate over each entry in the directory ❽, and pass it to describe ❾.

Recursive Directory Iteration

The recursive_directory_iterator is a drop-in replacement for directory_iterator in the sense that it supports all the same operations but will enumerate subdirectories. You can use these iterators in combination to build a program that computes the size and quantity of files and subdirectories for a given directory. Listing 17-8 illustrates how.

```
#include <iostream>
#include <filesystem>

using namespace std;
using namespace std::filesystem;

struct Attributes {
  Attributes& operator+=(const Attributes& other) {
    this->size_bytes += other.size_bytes;
    this->n_directories += other.n_directories;
    this->n_files += other.n_files;
    return *this;
  }
  size_t size_bytes;
  size_t n_directories;
  size_t n_files;
}; ❶

void print_line(const Attributes& attributes, string_view path) {
  cout << setw(14) << attributes.size_bytes
       << setw(7) << attributes.n_files
       << setw(7) << attributes.n_directories
       << " " << path << "\n"; ❷
}

Attributes explore(const directory_entry& directory) {
  Attributes attributes{};
  for(const auto& entry : recursive_directory_iterator{ directory.path() }) { ❸
      if (entry.is_directory()) {
        attributes.n_directories++; ❹
      } else {
        attributes.n_files++;
```

```
        attributes.size_bytes += entry.file_size(); ❺
      }
  }
  return attributes;
}

int main(int argc, const char** argv) {
  if (argc != 2) {
    cerr << "Usage: treedir PATH";
    return -1; ❻
  }
  const path sys_path{ argv[1] };
  cout << "Size           Files  Dirs   Name\n";
  cout << "-------------- ------ ------ ------------\n";
  Attributes root_attributes{};
  for (const auto& entry : directory_iterator{ sys_path }) { ❼
    try {
      if (entry.is_directory()) {
        const auto attributes = explore(entry); ❽
        root_attributes += attributes;
        print_line(attributes, entry.path().string());
        root_attributes.n_directories++;
      } else {
        root_attributes.n_files++;
        error_code ec;
        root_attributes.size_bytes += entry.file_size(ec); ❾
        if (ec) cerr << "Error reading file size: "
                     << entry.path().string() << endl;
      }
    } catch(const exception&) {
    }
  }
  print_line(root_attributes, argv[1]); ❿
}
```

```
> treedir C:\Windows
Size         Files  Dirs Name
------------ ----- ----- ------------
         802     1     0 C:\Windows\addins
     8267330     9     5 C:\Windows\apppatch
--snip--
  11396916465  73383  20480 C:\Windows\WinSxS
  21038460348 110950  26513 C:\Windows ❿
```

Listing 17-8: A file- and directory-listing program that uses `std::filesystem::recursive_directory_iterator` *to list the number of files and total size of a given path's subdirectory. (Output is from a Windows 10 x64 system.)*

NOTE *You should modify the program's name from* `treedir` *to whatever value matches your compiler's output.*

After declaring the `Attributes` class for storing accounting data ❶, you define a `print_line` function that presents an `Attributes` instance in a user-friendly way alongside a path string ❷. Next, you define an `explore` function that accepts a directory_entry reference and iterates over it recursively ❸. If the resulting entry is a directory, you increment the directory count ❹; otherwise, you increment the file count and total size ❺.

Within main, you check that the program invoked with exactly two arguments. If not, you return with an error code -1 ❻. You employ a (non-recursive) directory_iterator to enumerate the contents of the target path referred by sys_path ❼. If an entry is a directory, you invoke explore to determine its attributes ❽, which you subsequently print to the console. You also increment the n_directories member of root_attributes to keep account. If the entry isn't a directory, you add to the n_files and size_bytes members of root_attributes accordingly ❾.

Once you've completed iterating over all sys_path subelements, you print root_attributes as the final line ❿. The final line of output in Listing 17-8, for example, shows that this particular Windows directory contains 110,950 files occupying 21,038,460,348 bytes (about 21GB) and 26,513 subdirectories.

fstream Interoperation

You can construct file streams (basic_ifstream, basic_ofstream, or basic_fstream) using std::filesystem::path or std::filesystem::directory_entry in addition to string types.

For example, you can iterate over a directory and construct an ifstream to read each file you encounter. Listing 17-9 illustrates how to check for the magic MZ bytes at the beginning of each Windows portable executable file (a *.sys*, a *.dll*, a *.exe*, and so on) and report any file that violates this rule.

```
#include <iostream>
#include <fstream>
#include <filesystem>
#include <unordered_set>

using namespace std;
using namespace std::filesystem;

int main(int argc, const char** argv) {
  if (argc != 2) {
    cerr << "Usage: pecheck PATH";
    return -1; ❶
  }
  const unordered_set<string> pe_extensions{
    ".acm", ".ax",  ".cpl", ".dll", ".drv",
    ".efi", ".exe", ".mui", ".ocx", ".scr",
    ".sys", ".tsp"
  }; ❷
  const path sys_path{ argv[1] };
  cout << "Searching " << sys_path << " recursively.\n";
  size_t n_searched{};
  auto iterator = recursive_directory_iterator{ sys_path,
                               directory_options::skip_permission_denied }; ❸
  for (const auto& entry : iterator) { ❹
    try {
```

```
      if (!entry.is_regular_file()) continue;
      const auto& extension = entry.path().extension().string();
      const auto is_pe = pe_extensions.find(extension) != pe_extensions.end();
      if (!is_pe) continue; ❺
      ifstream file{ entry.path() }; ❻
      char first{}, second{};
      if (file) file >> first;
      if (file) file >> second; ❼
      if (first != 'M' || second != 'Z')
        cout << "Invalid PE found: " << entry.path().string() << "\n"; ❽
      ++n_searched;
    } catch(const exception& e) {
      cerr << "Error reading " << entry.path().string()
           << ": " << e.what() << endl;
    }
  }
  cout << "Searched " << n_searched << " PEs for magic bytes." << endl; ❾
}
```

```
listing_17_9.exe c:\Windows\System32
Searching "c:\\Windows\\System32" recursively.
Searched 8231 PEs for magic bytes.
```

Listing 17-9: Searching the Windows System32 directory for Windows portable executable files

In `main`, you check for exactly two arguments and return an error code as appropriate ❶. You construct an `unordered_set` containing all the extensions associated with portable executable files ❷, which you'll use to check file extensions. You use a `recursive_directory_iterator` with the `directory_options::skip_permission_denied` option to enumerate all the files in the specified path ❸. You iterate over each entry ❹, skipping over anything that's not a regular file, and you determine whether the entry is a portable executable by attempting to `find` it in `pe_extensions`. If the entry doesn't have such an extension, you skip over the file ❺.

To open the file, you simply pass the path of the `entry` into the constructor of `ifstream` ❻. You then use the resulting input file stream to read the first two bytes of the file into `first` and `second` ❼. If these first two characters aren't `MZ`, you print a message to the console ❽. Either way, you increment a counter called `n_searched`. After exhausting the directory iterator, you print a message indicating `n_searched` to the user before returning from `main` ❾.

Summary

In this chapter, you learned about the stdlib filesystem facilities, including paths, files, directories, and error handling. These facilities enable you to write cross-platform code that interacts with the files in your environment. The chapter culminated with some important operations, directory iterators, and interoperation with file streams.

EXERCISES

17-1. Implement a program that takes two arguments: a path and an extension. The program should search the given path recursively and print any file with the specified extension.

17-2. Improve the program in Listing 17-8 so it can take an optional second argument. If the first argument begins with a hyphen (-), the program reads all contiguous letters immediately following the hyphen and parses each letter as an option. The second argument then becomes the path to search. If the list of options contains an *R*, perform a recursive directory. Otherwise, don't use a recursive directory iterator.

17-3. Refer to the documentation for the *dir* or *ls* command and implement as many of the options as possible in your new, improved version of Listing 17-8.

FURTHER READING

- *Windows NT File System Internals: A Developer's Guide* by Rajeev Nagar (O'Reilly, 1997)
- *The Boost C++ Libraries*, 2nd Edition, by Boris Schäling (XML Press, 2014)
- *The Linux Programming Interface: A Linux and UNIX System Programming Handbook* by Michael Kerrisk (No Starch Press, 2010)

18

ALGORITHMS

And that's really the essence of programming. By the time you've sorted out a complicated idea into little steps that even a stupid machine can deal with, you've learned something about it yourself.
—*Douglas Adams,* Dirk Gently's Holistic Detective Agency

An *algorithm* is a procedure for solving a class of problems. The stdlib and Boost libraries contain a multitude of algorithms that you can use in your programs. Because many very smart people have put a lot of time into ensuring these algorithms are correct and efficient, you should usually not attempt to, for example, write your own sorting algorithm.

Because this chapter covers almost the entire stdlib algorithm suite, it's lengthy; however, the individual algorithm presentations are succinct. On first reading, you should skim through each section to survey the wide range of algorithms available to you. Don't try to memorize them. Instead, focus on getting insight into the kinds of problems you can solve with them as you write code in the future. That way, when you need to use an algorithm, you can say, "Wait, didn't someone already invent this wheel?"

Before you begin working with the algorithms, you'll need some grounding in complexity and parallelism. These two algorithmic characteristics are the main drivers behind how your code will perform.

Algorithmic Complexity

Algorithmic complexity describes the difficulty of a computational task. One way to quantify this complexity is with *Bachmann-Landau* or *"Big O" notation*. Big O notation characterizes functions according to how computation grows with respect to the size of input. This notation only includes the leading term of the complexity function. The *leading term* is the one that grows most quickly as input size increases.

For example, an algorithm whose complexity increases by roughly a fixed amount for each additional input element has a Big O notation of **O(N)**, whereas an algorithm whose complexity doesn't change given additional input has a Big O notation of **O(1)**.

This chapter characterizes the stdlib's algorithms that fall into five complexity classes, as outlined in the list that follows. To give you some idea of how these algorithms scale, each class is listed with its Big O notation and an idea of roughly how many additional operations would be required due to the leading term when input increases from 1,000 elements to 10,000 elements. Each example provides an operation with the given complexity class, where *N* is the number of elements involved in the operation:

Constant time O(1) No additional computation. An example is determining the size of a `std::vector`.

Logarithmic time O(log *N*) About one additional computation. An example is finding an element in a `std::set`.

Linear time O(*N*) About 9,000 additional computations. An example is summing all the elements in a collection.

Quasilinear time O(*N* log *N*) About 37,000 additional computations. An example is quicksort, a commonly used sorting algorithm.

Polynomial (or quadratic) time O(N^2) About 99,000,000 additional computations. An example is comparing all the elements in a collection with all the elements in another collection.

An entire field of computer science is dedicated to classifying computational problems according to their difficulty, so this is an involved topic. This chapter mentions each algorithm's complexity according to how the size of the target sequence affects the amount of required work. In practice, you should profile performance to determine whether an algorithm has suitable scaling properties. But these complexity classes can give you a sense of how expensive a particular algorithm is.

Execution Policies

Some algorithms, those that are commonly called *parallel algorithms*, can divide an algorithm so that independent entities can work on different parts of the problem simultaneously. Many stdlib algorithms allow you to specify parallelism with an *execution policy*. An execution policy indicates the allowed parallelism for an algorithm. From the stdlib's perspective, an algorithm can be executed either *sequentially* or *in parallel*. A sequential algorithm can have only a single entity working on the problem at a time; a parallel algorithm can have many entities working in concert to resolve the problem.

In addition, parallel algorithms can either be *vectorized* or *non-vectorized*. Vectorized algorithms allow entities to perform work in an unspecified order, even allowing a single entity to work on multiple portions of the problem simultaneously. For example, an algorithm that requires synchronization among entities is usually non-vectorizable because the same entity could attempt to acquire a lock multiple times, resulting in a deadlock.

Three execution policies exist in the `<execution>` header:

- `std::execution::seq` specifies sequential (not parallel) execution.
- `std::execution::par` specifies parallel execution.
- `std::execution::par_unseq` specifies parallel *and* vectorized execution.

For those algorithms that support an execution policy, the default is `seq`, meaning you have to opt into parallelism and the associated performance benefits. Note that the C++ Standard doesn't specify the precise meaning of these execution policies because different platforms handle parallelism differently. When you provide a non-sequential execution policy, you're simply declaring that "this algorithm is safe to parallelize."

In Chapter 19, you'll explore execution policies in greater detail. For now, just note that some algorithms permit parallelism.

WARNING *The algorithm descriptions in this chapter aren't complete. They contain enough information to give you a good background on many algorithms available to you in the Standard library. I suggest that, once you've identified an algorithm that fits your needs, you look at one of the resources in the "Further Reading" section at the end of this chapter. Algorithms that accept an optional execution policy often have different requirements when non-default policies are provided, especially where iterators are concerned. For example, if an algorithm normally takes an input iterator, using an execution policy will typically cause the algorithm to require forward iterators instead. Listing these differences would lengthen an already prodigious chapter, so the descriptions omit them.*

HOW TO USE THIS CHAPTER

This chapter is a quick reference that contains more than 50 algorithms. Coverage of each algorithm is necessarily succinct. Each algorithm begins with a terse description. A shorthand representation of the algorithm's function declaration follows along with an explanation of each argument. The declaration depicts optional arguments in brackets. Next, the listing displays the algorithmic complexity. The listing concludes with a non-exhaustive but illustrative example that employs the algorithm. Almost all examples in this chapter are unit tests and implicitly include the following frontmatter:

```
#include "catch.hpp"
#include <vector>
#include <string>

using namespace std;
```

Refer to the relevant subsection [algorithms] for algorithm details should you need them.

Non-Modifying Sequence Operations

A *non-modifying sequence operation* is an algorithm that performs computation over a sequence but doesn't modify the sequence in any way. You can think of these as `const` algorithms. Each algorithm explained in this section is in the `<algorithm>` header.

all_of

The `all_of` algorithm determines whether each element in a sequence meets some user-specified criteria.

The algorithm returns `true` if the target sequence is empty or if `pred` is `true` for *all* elements in the sequence; otherwise, it returns `false`.

```
bool all_of([ep], ipt_begin, ipt_end, pred);
```

Arguments

- An optional `std::execution` execution policy, `ep` (default: `std::execution::seq`)
- A pair of `InputIterator` objects, `ipt_begin` and `ipt_end`, representing the target sequence
- A unary predicate, `pred`, that accepts an element from the target sequence

Complexity

Linear The algorithm invokes pred at most distance(ipt_begin, ipt_end) times.

Examples

```
#include <algorithm>

TEST_CASE("all_of") {
  vector<string> words{ "Auntie", "Anne's", "alligator" }; ❶
  const auto starts_with_a =
    [](const auto& word❷) {
      if (word.empty()) return false; ❸
      return word[0] == 'A' || word[0] == 'a'; ❹
    };
  REQUIRE(all_of(words.cbegin(), words.cend(), starts_with_a)); ❺
  const auto has_length_six = [](const auto& word) {
    return word.length() == 6; ❻
  };
  REQUIRE_FALSE(all_of(words.cbegin(), words.cend(), has_length_six)); ❼
}
```

After constructing a vector containing string objects called words ❶, you construct the lambda predicate starts_with_a, which takes a single object called word ❷. If word is empty, starts_with_a returns false ❸; otherwise, it returns true if word starts with either a or A ❹. Because all of the word elements start with either a or A, all_of returns true when it applies starts_with_a ❺.

In the second example, you construct the predicate has_length_six, which returns true only if word has length six ❻. Because alligator doesn't have length six, all_of returns false when it applies has_length_six to words ❼.

any_of

The any_of algorithm determines whether any element in a sequence meets some user-specified criteria.

The algorithm returns false if the target sequence is empty or if pred is true for *any* element in the sequence; otherwise, it returns false.

```
bool any_of([ep], ipt_begin, ipt_end, pred);
```

Arguments

- An optional std::execution execution policy, ep (default: std::execution ::seq)
- A pair of InputIterator objects, ipt_begin and ipt_end, representing the target sequence
- A unary predicate, pred, that accepts an element from the target sequence

Complexity

Linear The algorithm invokes pred at most distance(ipt_begin, ipt_end) times.

Examples

```
#include <algorithm>

TEST_CASE("any_of") {
  vector<string> words{ "Barber", "baby", "bubbles" }; ❶
  const auto contains_bar = [](const auto& word) {
    return word.find("Bar") != string::npos;
  }; ❷
  REQUIRE(any_of(words.cbegin(), words.cend(), contains_bar)); ❸

  const auto is_empty = [](const auto& word) { return word.empty(); }; ❹
  REQUIRE_FALSE(any_of(words.cbegin(), words.cend(), is_empty)); ❺
}
```

After constructing a vector containing string objects called words ❶, you construct the lambda predicate contains_bar that takes a single object called word ❷. If word contains the substring Bar, it returns true; otherwise, it returns false. Because Barber contains Bar, any_of returns true when it applies contains_bar ❸.

In the second example, you construct the predicate is_empty, which returns true only if a word is empty ❹. Because none of the words are empty, any_of returns false when it applies is_empty to words ❺.

none_of

The none_of algorithm determines whether no element in a sequence meets some user-specified criteria.

The algorithm returns true if the target sequence is empty or if pred is true for *no* element in the sequence; otherwise, it returns false.

```
bool none_of([ep], ipt_begin, ipt_end, pred);
```

Arguments

- An optional std::execution execution policy, ep (default: std::execution ::seq)
- A pair of InputIterator objects, ipt_begin and ipt_end, representing the target sequence
- A unary predicate, pred, that accepts an element from the target sequence

Complexity

Linear The algorithm invokes pred at most distance(ipt_begin, ipt_end) times.

Examples

```
#include <algorithm>

TEST_CASE("none_of") {
  vector<string> words{ "Camel", "on", "the", "ceiling" }; ❶
  const auto is_hump_day = [](const auto& word) {
    return word == "hump day";
  }; ❷
  REQUIRE(none_of(words.cbegin(), words.cend(), is_hump_day)); ❸

  const auto is_definite_article = [](const auto& word) {
    return word == "the" || word == "ye";
  }; ❹
  REQUIRE_FALSE(none_of(words.cbegin(), words.cend(), is_definite_article)); ❺
}
```

After constructing a vector containing string objects called `words` ❶, you construct the lambda predicate `is_hump_day` that takes a single object called `word` ❷. If `word` equals `hump day`, it returns `true`; otherwise, it returns `false`. Because `words` doesn't contain `hump day`, `none_of` returns `true` when it applies `is_hump_day` ❸.

In the second example, you construct the predicate `is_definite_article`, which returns `true` only if `word` is a definite article ❹. Because `the` is a definite article, `none_of` returns `false` when it applies `is_definite_article` to `words` ❺.

for_each

The `for_each` algorithm applies some user-defined function to each element in a sequence.

The algorithm applies `fn` to each element of the target sequence. Although `for_each` is considered a non-modifying sequence operation, if `ipt_begin` is a mutable iterator, `fn` can accept a non-`const` argument. Any values that `fn` returns are ignored.

If you omit `ep`, `for_each` will return `fn`. Otherwise, `for_each` returns `void`.

```
for_each([ep], ipt_begin, ipt_end, fn);
```

Arguments

- An optional `std::execution` execution policy, `ep` (default: `std::execution::seq`)
- A pair of `InputIterator` objects, `ipt_begin` and `ipt_end`, representing the target sequence
- A unary function, `fn`, that accepts an element from the target sequence

Complexity

Linear The algorithm invokes `fn` exactly `distance(ipt_begin, ipt_end)` times.

Additional Requirements

- `fn` must be movable if you omit `ep`.
- `fn` must be copyable if you provide `ep`.

Example

```
#include <algorithm>

TEST_CASE("for_each") {
  vector<string> words{ "David", "Donald", "Doo" }; ❶
  size_t number_of_Ds{}; ❷
  const auto count_Ds = [&number_of_Ds❸](const auto& word❹) {
    if (word.empty()) return; ❺
    if (word[0] == 'D') ++number_of_Ds; ❻
  };
  for_each(words.cbegin(), words.cend(), count_Ds); ❼
  REQUIRE(3 == number_of_Ds); ❽
}
```

After constructing a `vector` containing `string` objects called `words` ❶ and a counter variable `number_of_Ds` ❷, you construct the lambda predicate `count_Ds` that captures a reference to `number_of_Ds` ❸ and takes a single object called `word` ❹. If `word` is empty, you return ❺; otherwise, if the first letter of `word` is `D`, you increment `number_of_Ds` ❻.

Next, you use `for_each` to iterate over every word, passing each to `count_Ds` ❼. The result is that `number_of_Ds` is three ❽.

for_each_n

The `for_each_n` algorithm applies some user-defined function to each element in a sequence.

The algorithm applies `fn` to each element of the target sequence. Although `for_each_n` is considered a non-modifying sequence operation, if `ipt_begin` is a mutable iterator, `fn` can accept a non-`const` argument. Any values that `fn` returns are ignored. It returns `ipt_begin+n`.

```
InputIterator for_each_n([ep], ipt_begin, n, fn);
```

Arguments

- An optional `std::execution` execution policy, `ep` (default: `std::execution ::seq`)
- An `InputIterator ipt_begin` representing the target sequence's first element

- An integer n representing the desired number of iterations so that the half-open range representing the target sequence is ipt_begin to ipt_begin+n (Size is the templated type of n.)
- A unary function fn that accepts an element from the target sequence

Complexity

Linear The algorithm invokes fn exactly n times.

Additional Requirements

- fn must be movable if you omit ep.
- fn must copyable if you provide ep.
- n must be non-negative.

Example

```
#include <algorithm>

TEST_CASE("for_each_n") {
  vector<string> words{ "ear", "egg", "elephant" }; ❶
  size_t characters{}; ❷
  const auto count_characters = [&characters❸](const auto& word❹) {
    characters += word.size(); ❺
  };
  for_each_n(words.cbegin(), words.size(), count_characters); ❻
  REQUIRE(14 == characters); ❼
}}
```

After constructing a vector containing string objects called words ❶ and a counter variable characters ❷, you construct the lambda predicate count_characters that captures a reference to characters ❸ and takes a single object called word ❹. The lambda adds the length of word to characters ❺.

Next, you use for_each_n to iterate over every word, passing each to count_characters ❻. The result is that characters is 14 ❼.

find, find_if, and find_if_not

The find, find_if , and find_if_not algorithms find the first element in a sequence matching some user-defined criteria.

These algorithms return the InputIterator pointing to the target sequence's first element matching value (find), resulting in a true result when invoked with pred (find_if), or resulting in a false result when invoked with pred (find_if_not).

If the algorithm finds no match, it returns ipt_end.

```
InputIterator find([ep], ipt_begin, ipt_end, value);
InputIterator find_if([ep], ipt_begin, ipt_end, pred);
InputIterator find_if_not([ep], ipt_begin, ipt_end, pred);
```

Arguments

- An optional `std::execution` execution policy, `ep` (default: `std::execution::seq`)
- A pair of `InputIterator` objects, `ipt_begin` and `ipt_end`, representing the target sequence
- A `const` reference `value` that is equality comparable to the target sequence's underlying type (`find`) or a predicate that accepts a single argument with the target sequence's underlying type (`find_if` and `find_if_not`)

Complexity

Linear The algorithm makes at most `distance(ipt_begin, ipt_end)` comparisons (`find`) or invocations of `pred` (`find_if` and `find_if_not`).

Examples

```
#include <algorithm>

TEST_CASE("find find_if find_if_not") {
  vector<string> words{ "fiffer", "feffer", "feff" }; ❶
  const auto find_result = find(words.cbegin(), words.cend(), "feff"); ❷
  REQUIRE(*find_result == words.back()); ❸

  const auto defends_digital_privacy = [](const auto& word) {
    return string::npos != word.find("eff"); ❹
  };
  const auto find_if_result = find_if(words.cbegin(), words.cend(),
                                      defends_digital_privacy); ❺
  REQUIRE(*find_if_result == "feffer"); ❻

  const auto find_if_not_result = find_if_not(words.cbegin(), words.cend(),
                                              defends_digital_privacy); ❼
  REQUIRE(*find_if_not_result == words.front()); ❽
}
```

After constructing a `vector` containing `string` objects called `words` ❶, you use `find` to locate `feff` ❷, which is at the end of `words` ❸. Next, you construct the predicate `defends_digital_privacy`, which returns `true` if `word` contains the letters `eff` ❹. You then use `find_if` to locate the first string in `words` that contains `eff` ❺, `feffer` ❻. Finally, you use `find_if_not` to apply `defends_digital_privacy` to `words` ❼, which returns the first element `fiffer` (because it doesn't contain `eff`) ❽.

find_end

The `find_end` algorithm finds the last occurrence of a subsequence.

If the algorithm finds no such sequence, it returns `fwd_end1`. If `find_end` does find a subsequence, it returns a `ForwardIterator` pointing to the first element of the last matching subsequence.

```
InputIterator find_end([ep], fwd_begin1, fwd_end1,
                       fwd_begin2, fwd_end2, [pred]);
```

Arguments

- An optional `std::execution` execution policy, `ep` (default: `std::execution::seq`)
- Two pairs of `ForwardIterator`s, `fwd_begin1` / `fwd_end1` and `fwd_begin2` / `fwd_end2`, representing the target sequences 1 and 2
- An optional binary predicate `pred` to compare whether two elements are equal

Complexity

Quadratic The algorithm makes at most the following number of comparisons or invocations of `pred`:

```
distance(fwd_begin2, fwd_end2) * (distance(fwd_begin1, fwd_end1) -
                                  distance(fwd_begin2, fwd_end2) + 1)
```

Examples

```
#include <algorithm>

TEST_CASE("find_end") {
  vector<string> words1{ "Goat", "girl", "googoo", "goggles" }; ❶
  vector<string> words2{ "girl", "googoo" }; ❷
  const auto find_end_result1 = find_end(words1.cbegin(), words1.cend(),
                                         words2.cbegin(), words2.cend()); ❸
  REQUIRE(*find_end_result1 == words1[1]); ❹

  const auto has_length = [](const auto& word, const auto& len) {
    return word.length() == len; ❺
  };
  vector<size_t> sizes{ 4, 6 }; ❻
  const auto find_end_result2 = find_end(words1.cbegin(), words1.cend(),
                                         sizes.cbegin(), sizes.cend(),
                                         has_length); ❼
  REQUIRE(*find_end_result2 == words1[1]); ❽
}
```

After constructing a `vector` containing `string` objects called `words1` ❶ and another called `words2` ❷, you invoke `find_end` to determine which element in `words1` begins the subsequence equal to `words2` ❸. The result is `find_end_result1`, which equals the element `girl` ❹.

Next, you construct the lambda `has_length`, which takes two arguments, `word` and `len`, and returns `true` if `word.length()` equals `len` ❺. You construct a `vector` of `size_t` objects called `sizes` ❻ and invoke `find_end` with `words1`, `sizes`, and has_length ❼. The result, find_end_result2, points to the first element in words1 that has length 4 with the subsequent word having length 6. Because girl has length 4 and googoo has length 6, find_end_result2 points to girl ❽.

find_first

The find_first_of algorithm finds the first occurrence in sequence 1 equal to some element in sequence 2.

If you provide pred, the algorithm finds the first occurrence **i** in sequence 1 where, for some **j** in sequence 2, pred **(i, j)** is true.

If find_first_of finds no such sequence, it returns ipt_end1. If find_first_of does find a subsequence, it returns an InputIterator pointing to the first element of the first matching subsequence. (Note that if ipt_begin1 is also a ForwardIterator, find_first_of instead returns a ForwardIterator.)

```
InputIterator find_first_of([ep], ipt_begin1, ipt_end1,
                            fwd_begin2, fwd_end2, [pred]);
```

Arguments

- An optional std::execution execution policy, ep (default: std::execution ::seq)
- A pair of InputIterator objects, ipt_begin1 / ipt_end1, representing the target sequence 1
- A pair of ForwardIterators, fwd_begin2 / fwd_end2, representing the target sequence 2
- An optional binary predicate, pred, to compare whether two elements are equal

Complexity

Quadratic The algorithm makes at most the following number of comparisons or invocations of pred:

```
distance(ipt_begin1, ipt_end1) * distance(fwd_begin2, fwd_end2)
```

Example

```
#include <algorithm>

TEST_CASE("find_first_of") {
  vector<string> words{ "Hen", "in", "a", "hat" }; ❶
  vector<string> indefinite_articles{ "a", "an" }; ❷
  const auto find_first_of_result = find_first_of(words.cbegin(),
                                                  words.cend(),
                                                  indefinite_articles.cbegin(),
                                                  indefinite_articles.cend()); ❸
  REQUIRE(*find_first_of_result == words[2]); ❹
}
```

After constructing a vector containing string objects called words ❶ and another called indefinite_articles ❷, you invoke find_first_of to determine which element in words begins the subsequence equal to indefinite_articles ❸. The result is find_first_of_result, which equals the element a ❹.

adjacent_find

The adjacent_find algorithm finds the first repeat in a sequence.

The algorithm finds the first occurrence in the target sequence where two adjacent elements are equal or where, if you provide pred, the algorithm finds the first occurrence element **i** in the sequence where pred (**i**, **i**+1) is true.

If adjacent_find finds no such element, it returns fwd_end. If adjacent_find does find such an element, it returns a ForwardIterator pointing to it.

```
ForwardIterator adjacent_find([ep], fwd_begin, fwd_end, [pred]);
```

Arguments

- An optional std::execution execution policy, ep (default: std::execution ::seq)
- A pair of ForwardIterators, fwd_begin / fwd_end, representing the target sequence
- An optional binary predicate pred to compare whether two elements are equal

Complexity

Linear When no execution policy is given, the algorithm makes at most the following number of comparisons or invocations of pred:

```
min(distance(fwd_begin, i)+1, distance(fwd_begin, fwd_end)-1)
```

where **i** is the index of the return value.

Example

```
#include <algorithm>
TEST_CASE("adjacent_find") {
  vector<string> words{ "Icabod", "is", "itchy" }; ❶
  const auto first_letters_match = [](const auto& word1, const auto& word2) { ❷
    if (word1.empty() || word2.empty()) return false;
    return word1.front() == word2.front();
  };
  const auto adjacent_find_result = adjacent_find(words.cbegin(), words.cend(),
                                                   first_letters_match); ❸
  REQUIRE(*adjacent_find_result == words[1]); ❹
}
```

After constructing a vector containing string objects called words ❶, you construct a lambda called first_letters_match, which takes two words and evaluates whether they start with the first letter ❷. You invoke adjacent_find to determine which element has the same first letter as the subsequent letter ❸. The result, adjacent_find_result ❹, equals is because it shares a first letter with itchy ❹.

count

The count algorithm counts the elements in a sequence matching some user-defined criteria.

The algorithm returns the number of elements **i** in the target sequence where pred (**i**) is true or where value == **i**. Usually, DifferenceType is size_t, but it depends on the implementation of InputIterator. You use count when you want to count the occurrences of a particular value, and you use count_if when you have a more complicated predicate you want to use for comparison.

```
DifferenceType count([ep], ipt_begin, ipt_end, value);
DifferenceType count_if([ep], ipt_begin, ipt_end, pred);
```

Arguments

- An optional std::execution execution policy, ep (default: std::execution ::seq)
- A pair of InputIterator objects, ipt_begin / ipt_end, representing the target sequence
- Either a value or a unary predicate pred to evaluate whether an element x in the target sequence should be counted

Complexity

Linear When no execution policy is given, the algorithm makes distance (ipt_begin, ipt_end) comparisons or invocations of pred.

Examples

```
#include <algorithm>
TEST_CASE("count") {
  vector<string> words{ "jelly", "jar", "and", "jam" }; ❶
  const auto n_ands = count(words.cbegin(), words.cend(), "and"); ❷
  REQUIRE(n_ands == 1); ❸

  const auto contains_a = [](const auto& word) { ❹
    return word.find('a') != string::npos;
  };
  const auto count_if_result = count_if(words.cbegin(), words.cend(),
                                        contains_a); ❺
  REQUIRE(count_if_result == 3); ❻
}
```

After constructing a vector containing string objects called words ❶, you use it to invoke count with the value and ❷. This returns 1, because a single element equals and ❸. Next, you construct a lambda called contains_a, which takes a word and evaluates whether it contains a ❹. You invoke count_if to determine how many words contain a ❺. The result equals 3 because three elements contain a ❻.

mismatch

The mismatch algorithm finds the first mismatch in two sequences.

The algorithm finds the first mismatched element pair **i**, **j** from sequence 1 and sequence 2. Specifically, it finds the first index **n** such that **i** = (ipt_begin1 + **n**); **j** = (ipt_begin2 + **n**); and **i** != **j** or pred(**i**, **j**) == false.

The types of the iterators in the returned pair equal the types of ipt_begin1 and ipt_begin2.

```
pair<Itr, Itr> mismatch([ep], ipt_begin1, ipt_end1,
                        ipt_begin2, [ipt_end2], [pred]);
```

Arguments

- An optional std::execution execution policy, ep (default: std::execution ::seq).
- Two pairs of InputIterators, ipt_begin1 / ipt_end1 and ipt_begin2 / ipt _end2, representing the target sequences 1 and 2. If you don't provide ipt_end2, sequence 1's length implies sequence 2's length.
- An optional binary predicate pred to compare whether two elements are equal.

Complexity

Linear When no execution policy is given, at worst the algorithm makes the following number of comparisons or invocations of pred:

```
min(distance(ipt_begin1, ipt_end1), distance(ipt_begin2, ipt_end2))
```

Examples

```
#include <algorithm>

TEST_CASE("mismatch") {
  vector<string> words1{ "Kitten", "Kangaroo", "Kick" }; ❶
  vector<string> words2{ "Kitten", "bandicoot", "roundhouse" }; ❷
  const auto mismatch_result1 = mismatch(words1.cbegin(), words1.cend(),
                                         words2.cbegin()); ❸
  REQUIRE(*mismatch_result1.first == "Kangaroo"); ❹
  REQUIRE(*mismatch_result1.second == "bandicoot"); ❺

  const auto second_letter_matches = [](const auto& word1,
                                        const auto& word2) { ❻
```

```
    if (word1.size() < 2) return false;
    if (word2.size() < 2) return false;
    return word1[1] == word2[1];
  };
  const auto mismatch_result2 = mismatch(words1.cbegin(), words1.cend(),
                                         words2.cbegin(), second_letter_matches); ❼
  REQUIRE(*mismatch_result2.first == "Kick"); ❽
  REQUIRE(*mismatch_result2.second == "roundhouse"); ❾
}
```

After constructing two vectors of strings called `words1` ❶ and `words2` ❷, you use them as the target sequences for `mismatch` ❸. This returns a `pair` pointing to the elements `Kangaroo` and `bandicoot` ❹❺. Next, you construct a lambda called `second_letter_matches`, which takes two words and evaluates whether their second letters match ❻. You invoke `mismatch` to determine the first pair of elements with mismatched second letters ❼. The result is the pair `Kick` ❽ and `roundhouse` ❾.

equal

The `equal` algorithm determines whether two sequences are equal.

The algorithm determines whether sequence 1's elements equal sequence 2's.

```
bool equal([ep], ipt_begin1, ipt_end1, ipt_begin2, [ipt_end2], [pred]);
```

Arguments

- An optional `std::execution` execution policy, `ep` (default: `std::execution ::seq`) .
- Two pairs of `InputIterator`s, `ipt_begin1` / `ipt_end1` and `ipt_begin2` / `ipt_end2`, representing the target sequences `1` and `2`. If you don't provide `ipt_end2`, sequence 1's length implies sequence 2's length.
- An optional binary predicate `pred` to compare whether two elements are equal.

Complexity

Linear When no execution policy is given, at worst the algorithm makes the following number of comparisons or invocations of `pred`:

```
min(distance(ipt_begin1, ipt_end1), distance(ipt_begin2, ipt_end2))
```

Examples

```
#include <algorithm>

TEST_CASE("equal") {
  vector<string> words1{ "Lazy", "lion", "licks" }; ❶
  vector<string> words2{ "Lazy", "lion", "kicks" }; ❷
```

```
  const auto equal_result1 = equal(words1.cbegin(), words1.cend(),
                                   words2.cbegin()); ❸
  REQUIRE_FALSE(equal_result1); ❹

  words2[2] = words1[2]; ❺
  const auto equal_result2 = equal(words1.cbegin(), words1.cend(),
                                   words2.cbegin()); ❻
  REQUIRE(equal_result2); ❼
}
```

After constructing two vectors of strings called `words1` and `words2` ❶❷, you use them as the target sequences for `equal` ❸. Because their last elements, `lick` and `kick`, aren't equal, `equal_result1` is `false` ❹. After setting the third element of `words2` to the third element of `words1` ❺, you again invoke `equal` with the same arguments ❻. Because the sequences are now identical, `equal_result2` is `true` ❼.

is_permutation

The `is_permutation` algorithm determines whether two sequences are permutations, meaning they contain the same elements but potentially in a different order.

The algorithm determines whether some permutation of sequence 2 exists such that sequence 1's elements equal the permutation's.

```
bool is_permutation([ep], fwd_begin1, fwd_end1, fwd_begin2, [fwd_end2], [pred]);
```

Arguments

- An optional `std::execution` execution policy, `ep` (default: `std::execution ::seq`) .
- Two pairs of `ForwardIterator`s, `fwd_begin1` / `fwd_end1` and `fwd_begin2` / `fwd_end2`, representing the target sequences 1 and 2. If you don't provide `fwd_end2`, sequence 1's length implies sequence 2's length.
- An optional binary predicate `pred` to compare whether two elements are equal.

Complexity

Quadratic When no execution policy is given, at worst the algorithm makes the following number of comparisons or invocations of `pred`:

```
distance(fwd_begin1, fwd_end1) * distance(fwd_begin2, fwd_end2)
```

Example

```
#include <algorithm>

TEST_CASE("is_permutation") {
  vector<string> words1{ "moonlight", "mighty", "nice" }; ❶
```

```
  vector<string> words2{ "nice", "moonlight", "mighty" }; ❷
  const auto result = is_permutation(words1.cbegin(), words1.cend(),
                                     words2.cbegin()); ❸
  REQUIRE(result); ❹
}
```

After constructing two vectors of strings called `words1` and `words2` ❶❷, you use them as the target sequences for `is_permutation` ❸. Because `words2` is a permutation of `words1`, `is_permutation` returns `true` ❹.

NOTE *The `<algorithm>` header also contains `next_permutation` and `prev_permutation` for manipulating a range of elements so you can generate permutations. See [alg.permutation.generators].*

search

The `search` algorithm locates a subsequence.

The algorithm locates sequence 2 within sequence 1. In other words, it returns the first iterator **i** in sequence 1 such that for each non-negative integer `n`, `*(i + n)` equals `*(ipt_begin2 + n)`, or if you provide a predicate `pred(*(i + n), *(ipt_begin2 + n))` is `true`. The `search` algorithm returns `ipt_begin1` if sequence 2 is empty or `ipt_begin2` if no subsequence is found. This is different from `find` because it locates a subsequence rather than a single element.

```
ForwardIterator search([ep], fwd_begin1, fwd_end1,
                             fwd_begin2, fwd_end2, [pred]);
```

Arguments

- An optional `std::execution` execution policy, `ep` (default: `std::execution::seq`)
- Two pairs of `ForwardIterators`, `fwd_begin1` / `fwd_end1` and `fwd_begin2` / `fwd_end2`, representing the target sequences 1 and 2
- An optional binary predicate `pred` to compare whether two elements are equal

Complexity

Quadratic When no execution policy is given, at worst the algorithm makes the following number of comparisons or invocations of `pred`:

```
distance(fwd_begin1, fwd_end1) * distance(fwd_begin2, fwd_end2)
```

Examples

```
#include <algorithm>

TEST_CASE("search") {
```

```
  vector<string> words1{ "Nine", "new", "neckties", "and",
                         "a", "nightshirt" }; ❶
  vector<string> words2{ "and", "a", "nightshirt" }; ❷
  const auto search_result_1 = search(words1.cbegin(), words1.cend(),
                                      words2.cbegin(), words2.cend()); ❸
  REQUIRE(*search_result_1 == "and"); ❹

  vector<string> words3{ "and", "a", "nightpant" }; ❺
  const auto search_result_2 = search(words1.cbegin(), words1.cend(),
                                      words3.cbegin(), words3.cend()); ❻
  REQUIRE(search_result_2 == words1.cend()); ❼
}
```

After constructing two vectors of strings called words1 ❶ and words2 ❷, you use them as the target sequences for search ❸. Because words2 is a subsequence of words1, search returns an iterator pointing to and ❹. The vector containing string objects words3 ❺ contains the word nightpant instead of nightshirt, so invoking search with it instead of words2 ❻ yields the end iterator of words1 ❼.

search_n

The search_n algorithm locates a subsequence containing identical, consecutive values.

The algorithm searches for count consecutive values in the sequence and returns an iterator pointing to the first value, or it returns fwd_end if no such subsequence is found. This is different from adjacent_find because it locates a subsequence rather than a single element.

```
ForwardIterator search([ep], fwd_begin, fwd_end, count, value, [pred]);
```

Arguments

- An optional std::execution execution policy, ep (default: std::execution ::seq)
- A pair of ForwardIterators, fwd_begin / fwd_end, representing the target sequence
- An integral count value representing the number of consecutive matches you want to find
- A value representing the element you want to find
- An optional binary predicate pred to compare whether two elements are equal

Complexity

Linear When no execution policy is given, at worst the algorithm makes distance(fwd_begin, fwd_end) comparisons or invocations of pred.

Example

```
#include <algorithm>

TEST_CASE("search_n") {
  vector<string> words{ "an", "orange", "owl", "owl", "owl", "today" }; ❶
  const auto result = search_n(words.cbegin(), words.cend(), 3, "owl"); ❷
  REQUIRE(result == words.cbegin() + 2); ❸
}
```

After constructing a vector of strings called words ❶, you use it as the target sequence for search_n ❷. Because words contains three instances of the word owl, it returns an iterator pointing to the first instance ❸.

Mutating Sequence Operations

A *mutating sequence operation* is an algorithm that performs computation over a sequence and is allowed to modify the sequence in some way. Each algorithm explained in this section is in the <algorithm> header.

copy

The copy algorithm copies one sequence into another.

The algorithm copies the target sequence into result and returns the receiving sequence's end iterator. It's your responsibility to ensure that result represents a sequence with enough space to store the target sequence.

```
OutputIterator copy([ep], ipt_begin, ipt_end, result);
```

Arguments

- An optional std::execution execution policy, ep (default: std::execution ::seq)
- A pair of InputIterator objects, ipt_begin and ipt_end, representing the target sequence
- An OutputIterator, result, that receives the copied sequence

Complexity

Linear The algorithm copies elements from the target sequence exactly distance(ipt_begin, ipt_end) times.

Additional Requirements

Sequences 1 and 2 must not overlap unless the operation is a *copy to the left.* For example, for a vector v with 10 elements, std::copy(v.begin()+3, v.end(), v.begin()) is well defined, but std::copy(v.begin(), v.begin()+7, v.begin()+3) is not.

NOTE *Recall the* back_inserter *in "Insert Iterators" on page 464, which returns an output iterator that converts write operations into insert operations on the underlying container.*

Example

```
#include <algorithm>

TEST_CASE("copy") {
  vector<string> words1{ "and", "prosper" }; ❶
  vector<string> words2{ "Live", "long" }; ❷
  copy(words1.cbegin(), words1.cend(), ❸
       back_inserter(words2)❹);
  REQUIRE(words2 == vector<string>{ "Live", "long", "and", "prosper" }); ❺
}
```

After constructing two vectors of string objects ❶❷, you invoke copy with words1 as the sequence to copy ❸ and words2 as the destination sequence ❹. The result is that words2 contains the contents of words1 appended to the original contents ❺.

copy_n

The copy_n algorithm copies one sequence into another.

The algorithm copies the target sequence into result and returns the receiving sequence's end iterator. It's your responsibility to ensure that result represents a sequence with enough space to store the target sequence and that n represents the correct length of the target sequence.

```
OutputIterator copy_n([ep], ipt_begin, n, result);
```

Arguments

- An optional std::execution execution policy, ep (default: std::execution ::seq)
- A begin iterator, ipt_begin, representing the beginning of the target sequence
- The size of the target sequence, n
- An OutputIterator result that receives the copied sequence

Complexity

Linear The algorithm copies elements from the target sequence exactly distance(ipt_begin, ipt_end) times.

Additional Requirements

Sequences 1 and 2 must not contain the same objects unless the operation is a *copy to the left*.

Example

```
#include <algorithm>

TEST_CASE("copy_n") {
  vector<string> words1{ "on", "the", "wind" }; ❶
  vector<string> words2{ "I'm", "a", "leaf" }; ❷
  copy_n(words1.cbegin(), words1.size(), ❸
         back_inserter(words2)); ❹
  REQUIRE(words2 == vector<string>{ "I'm", "a", "leaf",
                                    "on", "the", "wind" }); ❺
}
```

After constructing two vectors of string objects ❶❷, you invoke copy_n with words1 as the sequence to copy_n ❸ and words2 as the destination sequence ❹. The result is that words2 contains the contents of words1 appended to the original contents ❺.

copy_backward

The copy_backward algorithm copies the reverse of one sequence into another.

The algorithm copies sequence 1 into sequence 2 and returns the receiving sequence's end iterator. Elements copy backward but will appear in the target sequence in the original order. It's your responsibility to ensure that sequence 1 represents a sequence with enough space to store sequence 2.

```
OutputIterator copy_backward([ep], ipt_begin1, ipt_end1, ipt_end2);
```

Arguments

- An optional std::execution execution policy, ep (default: std::execution ::seq)
- A pair of InputIterator objects, ipt_begin1 and ipt_end1, representing sequence 1
- An InputIterator, ipt_end2, representing 1 past the end of sequence 2

Complexity

Linear The algorithm copies elements from the target sequence exactly distance(ipt_begin1, ipt_end1) times.

Additional Requirements

Sequences 1 and 2 must not overlap.

Example

```
#include <algorithm>

TEST_CASE("copy_backward") {
```

```
  vector<string> words1{ "A", "man", "a", "plan", "a", "bran", "muffin" }; ❶
  vector<string> words2{ "a", "canal", "Panama" }; ❷
  const auto result = copy_backward(words2.cbegin(), words2.cend(), ❸
                                    words1.end()); ❹
  REQUIRE(words1 == vector<string>{ "A", "man", "a", "plan",
                                    "a", "canal", "Panama" }); ❺
}
```

After constructing two vectors of strings ❶❷, you invoke copy_backward with words2 as the sequence to copy ❸ and words1 as the destination sequence ❹. The result is that the contents of word2 replace the last three words of words1 ❺.

move

The move algorithm moves one sequence into another.

The algorithm moves the target sequence and returns the receiving sequence's end iterator. It's your responsibility to ensure that the target sequence represents a sequence with at least as many elements as the source sequence.

```
OutputIterator move([ep], ipt_begin, ipt_end, result);
```

Arguments

- An optional std::execution execution policy, ep (default: std::execution ::seq)
- A pair of InputIterator objects, ipt_begin and ipt_end, representing the target sequence
- An InputIterator, result, representing the beginning of the sequence to move into

Complexity

Linear The algorithm moves elements from the target sequence exactly distance(ipt_begin, ipt_end) times.

Additional Requirements

- Sequences must not overlap unless *moving to the left.*
- Types must be moveable but not necessarily copyable.

Example

```
#include <algorithm>

struct MoveDetector { ❶
  MoveDetector() : owner{ true } {} ❷
  MoveDetector(const MoveDetector&) = delete;
  MoveDetector& operator=(const MoveDetector&) = delete;
  MoveDetector(MoveDetector&& o) = delete;
  MoveDetector& operator=(MoveDetector&&) { ❸
    o.owner = false;
```

```
    owner = true;
    return *this;
  }
  bool owner;
};

TEST_CASE("move") {
  vector<MoveDetector> detectors1(2); ❹
  vector<MoveDetector> detectors2(2); ❺
  move(detectors1.begin(), detectors1.end(), detectors2.begin()); ❻
  REQUIRE_FALSE(detectors1[0].owner); ❼
  REQUIRE_FALSE(detectors1[1].owner); ❽
  REQUIRE(detectors2[0].owner); ❾
  REQUIRE(detectors2[1].owner); ❿
}
```

First, you declare the MoveDetector's class ❶, which defines a default constructor setting its only member owner to true ❷. It deletes the copy and move constructor and the copy assignment operator but defines a move assignment operator that swaps owner ❸.

After constructing two vectors of MoveDetector objects ❹❺, you invoke move with detectors1 as the sequence to move and detectors2 as the destination sequence ❻. The result is that the elements of detector1 are in a *moved from* state ❼❽ and the elements of detector2 are moved into detectors2 ❾❿.

move_backward

The move_backward algorithm moves the reverse of one sequence into another.

The algorithm moves sequence 1 into sequence 2 and returns an iterator pointing to the last moved element. Elements move backward but will appear in the target sequence in the original order. It's your responsibility to ensure that the target sequence represents a sequence with at least as many elements as the source sequence.

```
OutputIterator move_backward([ep], ipt_begin, ipt_end, result);
```

Arguments

- An optional std::execution execution policy, ep (default: std::execution ::seq)
- A pair of InputIterator objects, ipt_begin and ipt_end, representing the target sequence
- An InputIterator, result, representing the sequence to move into

Complexity

Linear The algorithm moves elements from the target sequence exactly distance(ipt_begin, ipt_end) times.

Additional Requirements

- Sequences must not overlap.
- Types must be moveable but not necessarily copyable.

Example

```
#include <algorithm>

struct MoveDetector { ❶
--snip--
};

TEST_CASE("move_backward") {
  vector<MoveDetector> detectors1(2); ❷
  vector<MoveDetector> detectors2(2); ❸
  move_backward(detectors1.begin(), detectors1.end(), detectors2.end()); ❹
  REQUIRE_FALSE(detectors1[0].owner); ❺
  REQUIRE_FALSE(detectors1[1].owner); ❻
  REQUIRE(detectors2[0].owner); ❼
  REQUIRE(detectors2[1].owner); ❽
}
```

First, you declare the `MoveDetector` class ❶ (see "move" back on page 595 for the implementation).

After constructing two `vectors` of `MoveDetector` objects ❷❸, you invoke `move` with `detectors1` as the sequence to `move` and `detectors2` as the destination sequence ❹. The result is that the elements of `detector1` are in a *moved from* state ❺❻ and the elements of `detector2` are *moved into* ❼❽.

swap_ranges

The `swap_ranges` algorithm exchanges elements from one sequence into another.

The algorithm calls `swap` on each element of sequence 1 and sequence 2, and it returns the receiving sequence's end iterator. It's your responsibility to ensure that the target sequence represents a sequence with at least as many elements as the source sequence.

```
OutputIterator swap_ranges([ep], ipt_begin1, ipt_end1, ipt_begin2);
```

Arguments

- An optional `std::execution` execution policy, `ep` (default: `std::execution ::seq`)
- A pair of `ForwardIterators`, `ipt_begin1` and `ipt_end1`, representing sequence 1
- A `ForwardIterator`, `ipt_begin2`, representing the beginning of sequence 2

Complexity

Linear The algorithm calls swap exactly `distance(ipt_begin1, ipt_end1)` times.

Additional Requirements

The elements contained in each sequence must be swappable.

Example

```
#include <algorithm>

TEST_CASE("swap_ranges") {
  vector<string> words1{ "The", "king", "is", "dead." }; ❶
  vector<string> words2{ "Long", "live", "the", "king." }; ❷
  swap_ranges(words1.begin(), words1.end(), words2.begin()); ❸
  REQUIRE(words1 == vector<string>{ "Long", "live", "the", "king." }); ❹
  REQUIRE(words2 == vector<string>{ "The", "king", "is", "dead." }); ❺
}
```

After constructing two `vector`s of `string`s ❶❷, you invoke `swap` with `words1` and `words2` as the sequences to swap ❸. The result is that `words1` and `words2` swap contents ❹❺.

transform

The `transform` algorithm modifies the elements of one sequence and writes them into another.

The algorithm invokes `unary_op` on each element of the target sequence and outputs it into the output sequence, or it invokes `binary_op` on corresponding elements of each target sequence.

```
OutputIterator transform([ep], ipt_begin1, ipt_end1, result, unary_op);
OutputIterator transform([ep], ipt_begin1, ipt_end1, ipt_begin2,
                         result, binary_op);
```

Arguments

- An optional `std::execution` execution policy, `ep` (default: `std::execution::seq`).
- A pair of `InputIterator` objects, `ipt_begin1` and `ipt_end1`, representing the target sequence.
- An optional `InputIterator`, `ipt_begin2`, representing a second target sequence. You must ensure that this second target sequence has at least as many elements as the first target sequence.
- An `OutputIterator`, `result`, representing the beginning of the output sequence.
- A unary operation, `unary_op`, that transforms elements of the target sequence into elements of the output sequence. If you supply two

target sequences, you instead provide a binary operation, binary_op, which accepts an element from each target sequence and transforms each into an element of the output sequence.

Complexity

Linear The algorithm invokes unary_op or binary_op exactly distance(ipt _begin1, ipt_end1) times.

Examples

```
#include <algorithm>
#include <boost/algorithm/string/case_conv.hpp>

TEST_CASE("transform") {
  vector<string> words1{ "farewell", "hello", "farewell", "hello" }; ❶
  vector<string> result1;
  auto upper = [](string x) { ❷
    boost::algorithm::to_upper(x);
    return x;
  };
  transform(words1.begin(), words1.end(), back_inserter(result1), upper); ❸
  REQUIRE(result1 == vector<string>{ "FAREWELL", "HELLO",
                                     "FAREWELL", "HELLO" }); ❹

  vector<string> words2{ "light", "human", "bro", "quantum" }; ❺
  vector<string> words3{ "radar", "robot", "pony", "bit" }; ❻
  vector<string> result2;
  auto portmantize = [](const auto &x, const auto &y) { ❼
    const auto x_letters = min(size_t{ 2 }, x.size());
    string result{ x.begin(), x.begin() + x_letters };
    const auto y_letters = min(size_t{ 3 }, y.size());
    result.insert(result.end(), y.end() - y_letters, y.end() );
    return result;
  };
  transform(words2.begin(), words2.end(), words3.begin(),
            back_inserter(result2), portmantize); ❽
  REQUIRE(result2 == vector<string>{ "lidar", "hubot", "brony", "qubit" }); ❾
}
```

After constructing a vector containing string objects ❶, you construct a lambda called upper, which takes a string by value and converts it to uppercase using the Boost to_upper algorithm discussed in Chapter 15 ❷. You invoke transform with words1 as the target sequence, a back_inserter for an empty results1 vector, and upper as the unary operation ❸. After transform, results1 contains the uppercase version of words1 ❹.

In the second example, you construct two vectors of string objects ❺❻. You also construct a lambda called portmantize that accepts two string objects ❼. The lambda returns a new string containing up to two letters from the beginning of the first argument and up to three letters from the end of the second argument. You pass the two target sequences, a back_inserter to an empty vector called results2 and portmantize ❽. The result2 contains portmanteaus of the contents of words1 and words2 ❾.

replace

The replace algorithm replaces certain elements of a sequence with some new element.

The algorithm searches for target sequence elements **x** for which either **x** == old_ref or pred(**x**) == true and assigns them to new_ref.

```
void replace([ep], fwd_begin, fwd_end, old_ref, new_ref);
void replace_if([ep], fwd_begin, fwd_end, pred, new_ref);
void replace_copy([ep], fwd_begin, fwd_end, result, old_ref, new_ref);
void replace_copy_if([ep], fwd_begin, fwd_end, result, pred, new_ref);
```

Arguments

- An optional std::execution execution policy, ep (default: std::execution ::seq)
- A pair of ForwardIterators, fwd_begin and fwd_end, representing the target sequence
- An OutputIterator, result, representing the beginning of the output sequence
- An old const reference representing the element to find
- A unary predicate, pred, that determines whether an element meets the criteria for replacement
- A new_ref const reference that represents the element to replace

Complexity

Linear The algorithm invokes pred exactly distance(fwd_begin, fwd_end) times.

Additional Requirements

The elements contained in each sequence must be comparable to old_ref and assignable to new_ref.

Examples

```
#include <algorithm>
#include <string_view>

TEST_CASE("replace") {
  using namespace std::literals; ❶
  vector<string> words1{ "There", "is", "no", "try" }; ❷
  replace(words1.begin(), words1.end(), "try"sv, "spoon"sv); ❸
  REQUIRE(words1 == vector<string>{ "There", "is", "no", "spoon" }); ❹

  const vector<string> words2{ "There", "is", "no", "spoon" }; ❺
```

```
  vector<string> words3{ "There", "is", "no", "spoon" }; ❻
  auto has_two_os = [](const auto& x) { ❼
    return count(x.begin(), x.end(), 'o') == 2;
  };
  replace_copy_if(words2.begin(), words2.end(), words3.begin(), ❽
                  has_two_os, "try"sv);
  REQUIRE(words3 == vector<string>{ "There", "is", "no", "try" }); ❾
}
```

You first bring in the `std::literals` namespace ❶ so you can employ the `string_view` literal later on. After constructing a `vector` containing `string` objects ❷, you invoke `replace` with the `vector` ❸ to replace all instances of `try` with `spoon` ❹.

In the second example, you construct two `vectors` of `string` objects ❺❻ and a lambda called `has_two_os`, which accepts a string and returns `true` if it contains exactly two `os` ❼. You then pass `words2` as the target sequence and `words3` as the destination sequence to `replace_copy_if`, which applies `has_two_os` to each element of `words2` and replaces elements that evaluate to `true` with `try` ❽. The result is that `words2` is unaffected and `words3` has the element `spoon` replaced with `try` ❾.

fill

The `fill` algorithm fills a sequence with some value.

The algorithm writes a value into each element of the target sequence. The `fill_n` function returns `opt_begin+n`.

```
void fill([ep], fwd_begin, fwd_end, value);
OutputIterator fill_n([ep], opt_begin, n, value);
```

Arguments

- An optional `std::execution` execution policy, `ep` (default: `std::execution ::seq`)
- A `ForwardIterator`, `fwd_begin`, representing the target sequence's beginning
- A `ForwardIterator`, `fwd_end`, representing one past the sequence's end
- A `Size` `n` representing the number of elements
- A `value` to write into each element of the target sequence

Complexity

Linear The algorithm assigns `value` exactly `distance(fwd_begin, fwd_end)` or `n` times.

Additional Requirements

- The `value` parameter must be writable into the sequence.
- Objects of type `Size` must be convertible into an integral type.

Examples

```
#include <algorithm>

// If police police police police, who polices the police police?
TEST_CASE("fill") {
  vector<string> answer1(6); ❶
  fill(answer1.begin(), answer1.end(), "police"); ❷
  REQUIRE(answer1 == vector<string>{ "police", "police", "police",
                                     "police", "police", "police" }); ❸

  vector<string> answer2; ❹
  fill_n(back_inserter(answer2), 6, "police"); ❺
  REQUIRE(answer2 == vector<string>{ "police", "police", "police",
                                     "police", "police", "police" }); ❻
}
```

You first initialize a vector containing string objects containing six empty elements ❶. Next, you invoke fill using this vector as the target sequence and police as the value ❷. The result is that your vector contains six police ❸.

In the second example, you initialize an empty vector containing string objects ❹. You then invoke fill_n with a back_inserter pointing to the empty vector, a length of 6, and police as the value ❺. The result is the same as before: your vector contains six police ❻.

generate

The generate algorithm fills a sequence by invoking a function object.

The algorithm invokes generator and assigns the result into the target sequence. The generate_n function returns opt_begin+n.

```
void generate([ep], fwd_begin, fwd_end, generator);
OutputIterator generate_n([ep], opt_begin, n, generator);
```

Arguments

- An optional std::execution execution policy, ep (default: std::execution ::seq)
- A ForwardIterator, fwd_begin, representing the target sequence's beginning
- A ForwardIterator, fwd_end, representing 1 past the sequence's end
- A Size n representing the number of elements
- A generator that, when invoked with no arguments, produces an element to write into the target sequence

Complexity

Linear The algorithm invokes generator exactly distance(fwd_begin, fwd_end) or n times.

Additional Requirements

- The value parameter must be writable into the sequence.
- Objects of type Size must be convertible into an integral type.

Examples

```
#include <algorithm>

TEST_CASE("generate") {
  auto i{ 1 }; ❶
  auto pow_of_2 = [&i]() { ❷
    const auto tmp = i;
    i *= 2;
    return tmp;
  };
  vector<int> series1(6); ❸
  generate(series1.begin(), series1.end(), pow_of_2); ❹
  REQUIRE(series1 == vector<int>{ 1, 2, 4, 8, 16, 32 }); ❺

  vector<int> series2; ❻
  generate_n(back_inserter(series2), 6, pow_of_2); ❼
  REQUIRE(series2 == vector<int>{ 64, 128, 256, 512, 1024, 2048 }); ❽
}
```

You first initialize an int called i to 1 ❶. Next, you create a lambda called pow_of_2, which takes i by reference ❷. Each time you invoke pow_of_2, it doubles i and returns its value just before the doubling. Next, you initialize a vector of int objects with six elements ❸. You then invoke generate with the vector as the target sequence and pow_of_2 as the generator ❹. The result is that the vector contains the first six powers of two ❺.

In the second example, you initialize an empty vector of int objects ❻. Next, you invoke generate_n using a back_inserter to your empty vector, a size of 6, and pow_of_2 as your generator ❼. The result is the next six powers of two ❽. Notice that pow_of_2 has state because it captures i by reference.

remove

The remove algorithm removes certain elements from a sequence.

The algorithm moves all elements where pred evaluates to true or where the element equals value in such a way that the remaining elements' order is preserved, and it returns an iterator pointing to the first moved element. This iterator is called the resulting sequence's *logical end*. The sequence's physical size remains unchanged, and a call to remove is typically followed by a call to a container's erase method.

```
ForwardIterator remove([ep], fwd_begin, fwd_end, value);
ForwardIterator remove_if([ep], fwd_begin, fwd_end, pred);
ForwardIterator remove_copy([ep], fwd_begin, fwd_end, result, value);
ForwardIterator remove_copy_if([ep], fwd_begin, fwd_end, result, pred);
```

Arguments

- An optional `std::execution` execution policy, `ep` (default: `std::execution::seq`)
- A pair of `ForwardIterator`s, `fwd_begin` and `fwd_end`, representing the target sequence
- An `OutputIterator`, `result`, representing the destination sequence (if copying)
- A `value` representing the element to remove
- A unary predicate, `pred`, that determines whether an element meets the criteria for removal

Complexity

Linear The algorithm invokes `pred` or compares with `value` exactly `distance(fwd_begin, fwd_end)` times.

Additional Requirements

- The elements of the target sequence must be moveable.
- If copying, the elements must be copyable, and the target and destination sequences must not overlap.

Examples

```
#include <algorithm>

TEST_CASE("remove") {
  auto is_vowel = [](char x) { ❶
    const static string vowels{ "aeiouAEIOU" };
    return vowels.find(x) != string::npos;
  };
  string pilgrim = "Among the things Billy Pilgrim could not change "
                   "were the past, the present, and the future."; ❷
  const auto new_end = remove_if(pilgrim.begin(), pilgrim.end(), is_vowel); ❸

  REQUIRE(pilgrim == "mng th thngs Blly Plgrm cld nt chng wr th pst, "
                     "th prsnt, nd th ftr.present, and the future."); ❹

  pilgrim.erase(new_end, pilgrim.end()); ❺
  REQUIRE(pilgrim == "mng th thngs Blly Plgrm cld nt chng wr th "
                     "pst, th prsnt, nd th ftr."); ❻
}
```

You first create a lambda called `is_vowel` that returns true if the given `char` is a vowel ❶. Next, you construct a `string` called `pilgrim` containing a sentence ❷. You then invoke `remove_if` with `pilgrim` as the target sentence and `is_vowel` as the predicate ❸. This eliminates all the vowels in the sentence by shifting the remaining characters to the left each time `remove_if` encounters a vowel. The result is that pilgrim contains the original sentence with vowels removed plus the phrase `present, and the future.` ❹. This phrase contains 24 characters, which is exactly the number of vowels that remove_if removed from the original sentence. The phrase `present, and the future.` is the detritus from shifting the remaining string during removal.

To eliminate these leftovers, you save the iterator new_end, which remove_if returns. This points to 1 past the last character in the new target sequence, the p in `present, and the future.` To eliminate, you simply use the erase method on pilgrim, which has an overload that accepts a half-open range. You pass the logical end returned by remove_if, new_end, as the begin iterator. You also pass pilgrim.end() as the end iterator ❺. The result is that pilgrim is now equal to the original sentence with vowels removed ❻.

This combination of remove (or remove_if) and the erase method, which is called the *erase-remove idiom*, is widely used.

unique

The unique algorithm removes redundant elements from a sequence.

The algorithm moves all repeat elements where pred evaluates to true or where the elements are equal such that the remaining elements are unique from their neighbors and original ordering is preserved. It returns an iterator pointing to the new logical end. As with std::remove, the physical storage doesn't change.

```
ForwardIterator unique([ep], fwd_begin, fwd_end, [pred]);
ForwardIterator unique_copy([ep], fwd_begin, fwd_end, result, [pred]);
```

Arguments

- An optional std::execution execution policy, ep (default: std::execution ::seq)
- A pair of ForwardIterators, fwd_begin and fwd_end, representing the target sequence
- An OutputIterator, result, representing the destination sequence (if copying)
- A binary predicate, pred, that determines whether two elements are equal

Complexity

Linear The algorithm invokes pred exactly distance(fwd_begin, fwd_end) - 1 times.

Additional Requirements

- The elements of the target sequence must be moveable.
- If copying, elements of the target sequence must by copyable, and the target and destination ranges cannot overlap.

Example

```
#include <algorithm>

TEST_CASE("unique") {
  string without_walls = "Wallless"; ❶
  const auto new_end = unique(without_walls.begin(), without_walls.end()); ❷
  without_walls.erase(new_end, without_walls.end()); ❸
  REQUIRE(without_walls == "Wales"); ❹
}
```

You first construct a string containing a word with multiple repeated characters ❶. You then invoke unique with the string as the target sequence ❷. This returns the logical end, which you assign to new_end. Next, you erase the range beginning with new_end and ending with without_walls.end() ❸. This is a corollary to the erase-remove idiom: you're left with the contents Wales, which contains consecutively unique characters ❹.

reverse

The reverse algorithm reverses the order of a sequence.

The algorithm reverses a sequence by either swapping its elements or copying them into a target sequence.

```
void reverse([ep], bi_begin, bi_end);
OutputIterator reverse_copy([ep], bi_begin, bi_end, result);
```

Arguments

- An optional std::execution execution policy, ep (default: std::execution ::seq)
- A pair of BidirectionalIterators, bi_begin and bi_end, representing the target sequence
- An OutputIterator, result, representing the destination sequence (if copying)

Complexity

Linear The algorithm invokes swap exactly distance(bi_begin, bi_end)/2 times.

Additional Requirements

- The elements of the target sequence must be swappable.
- If copying, elements of the target sequence must by copyable, and the target and destination ranges cannot overlap.

Example

```
#include <algorithm>

TEST_CASE("reverse") {
```

```
  string stinky = "diaper"; ❶
  reverse(stinky.begin(), stinky.end()); ❷
  REQUIRE(stinky == "repaid"); ❸
}
```

You first construct a string containing the word diaper ❶. Next, you invoke reverse with this string as the target sequence ❷. The result is the word repaid ❸.

sample

The sample algorithm generates random, stable subsequences.

The algorithm samples min(pop_end - pop_begin, n) elements from the population sequence. Somewhat unintuitively, the sample will be sorted if and only if ipt_begin is a forward iterator. It returns the resulting destination sequence's end.

```
OutputIterator sample([ep], ipt_begin, ipt_end, result, n, urb_generator);
```

Arguments

- An optional std::execution execution policy, ep (default: std::execution ::seq)
- A pair of InputIterator objects, ipt_begin and ipt_end, representing the population sequence (the sequence to sample from)
- A OutputIterator, result, representing the destination sequence
- A Distance n representing the number of elements to sample
- A UniformRandomBitGenerator urb_generator, such as the Mersenne Twister std::mt19937_64 introduced in Chapter 12

Complexity

Linear The algorithm's complexity scales with distance(ipt_begin, ipt_end).

Example

```
#include <algorithm>
#include <map>
#include <string>
#include <iostream>
#include <iomanip>
#include <random>

using namespace std;

const string population = "ABCD"; ❶
const size_t n_samples{ 1'000'000 }; ❷
mt19937_64 urbg; ❸

void sample_length(size_t n) { ❹
  cout << "-- Length " << n << " --\n";
```

```
  map<string, size_t> counts; ❺
  for (size_t i{}; i < n_samples; i++) {
    string result;
    sample(population.begin(), population.end(),
           back_inserter(counts), n, urbg); ❻
    counts[result]++;
  }
  for (const auto[sample, n] : counts) { ❼
    const auto percentage = 100 * n / static_cast<double>(n_samples);
    cout << percentage << " '" << sample << "'\n"; ❽
  }
}

int main() {
  cout << fixed << setprecision(1); ❾
  sample_length(0); ❿
  sample_length(1);
  sample_length(2);
  sample_length(3);
  sample_length(4);
}
```

```
-- Length 0 --
100.0 ''
-- Length 1 --
25.1 'A'
25.0 'B'
25.0 'C'
24.9 'D'
-- Length 2 --
16.7 'AB'
16.7 'AC'
16.6 'AD'
16.6 'BC'
16.7 'BD'
16.7 'CD'
-- Length 3 --
25.0 'ABC'
25.0 'ABD'
25.0 'ACD'
25.0 'BCD'
-- Length 4 --
100.0 'ABCD'
```

You first construct a `const string` called `population` containing the letters `ABCD` ❶. You also initialize a `const size_t` called `n_samples` equal to a million ❷ and a Mersenne Twister called `urbg` ❸. All of these objects have static storage duration.

In addition, you initialize the function `sample_length`, which takes a single `size_t` argument called `n` ❹. Within the function, you construct a `map` of `string` to `size_t` objects ❺ that will count the frequency of each `sample` invocation. Within a `for` loop, you invoke `sample` with `population` as the population sequence, a back_inserter to a result string as the destination sequence, n as the sample length, and urbg as the random bit generator ❻.

After a million iterations, you iterate over each element of counts ❼ and print the probability distribution of each sample for the given length n ❽.

Within main, you configure floating-point formatting with fixed and setprecision ❾. Finally, you invoke sample_length with each value from 0 to 4 inclusive ❿.

Because string provides random access iterators, sample provides *stable* (sorted) samples.

WARNING *Notice that the output doesn't contain any unsorted samples like* DC *or* CAB*. This sorting behavior isn't necessarily obvious from the algorithm's name, so be careful!*

shuffle

The shuffle algorithm generates random permutations.

The algorithm randomizes the target sequence such that each possible permutation of those elements has equal probability of appearance.

```
void shuffle(rnd_begin, rnd_end, urb_generator);
```

Arguments

- A pair of RandomAccessIterators, rnd_begin and rnd_end, representing the target sequence
- A UniformRandomBitGenerator urb_generator, such as the Mersenne Twister std::mt19937_64 introduced in Chapter 12

Complexity

Linear The algorithm swaps exactly distance(rnd_begin, rnd_end) - 1 times.

Additional Requirements

The elements of the target sequence must be swappable.

Example

```
#include <algorithm>
#include <map>
#include <string>
#include <iostream>
#include <random>
#include <iomanip>

using namespace std;

int main() {
  const string population = "ABCD"; ❶
  const size_t n_samples{ 1'000'000 }; ❷
  mt19937_64 urbg; ❸
```

```
  map<string, size_t> samples; ❹
  cout << fixed << setprecision(1); ❺
  for (size_t i{}; i < n_samples; i++) {
    string result{ population }; ❻
    shuffle(result.begin(), result.end(), urbg); ❼
    samples[result]++; ❽
  }
  for (const auto[sample, n] : samples) { ❾
    const auto percentage = 100 * n / static_cast<double>(n_samples);
    cout << percentage << " '" << sample << "'\n"; ❿
  }
}
```

```
4.2 'ABCD'
4.2 'ABDC'
4.1 'ACBD'
4.2 'ACDB'
4.2 'ADBC'
4.2 'ADCB'
4.2 'BACD'
4.2 'BADC'
4.1 'BCAD'
4.2 'BCDA'
4.1 'BDAC'
4.2 'BDCA'
4.2 'CABD'
4.2 'CADB'
4.1 'CBAD'
4.1 'CBDA'
4.2 'CDAB'
4.1 'CDBA'
4.2 'DABC'
4.2 'DACB'
4.2 'DBAC'
4.1 'DBCA'
4.2 'DCAB'
4.2 'DCBA'
```

You first construct a `const string` called `population` containing the letters `ABCD` ❶. You also initialize a `const size_t` called `n_samples` equal to a million ❷, a Mersenne Twister called `urbg` ❸, and a `map` of `string` to `size_t` objects ❹ that will count the frequencies of each `shuffle` sample. In addition, you configure floating-point formatting with `fixed` and `setprecision` ❺.

Within a `for` loop, you copy `population` into a new string called `sample` because `shuffle` modifies the target sequence ❻. You then invoke `shuffle` with `result` as the target sequence and `urbg` as the random bit generator ❼, and you record the result within `samples` ❽.

Finally, you iterate over each element in `samples` ❾ and print the probability distribution of each sample ❿.

Notice that, unlike with `sample`, `shuffle` always produces an *unordered* distribution of elements.

Sorting and Related Operations

A *sorting operation* is an algorithm that reorders a sequence in some desired way.

Each sorting algorithm has two versions: one that takes a function object called a *comparison operator* and one that uses `operator<`. A comparison operator is a function object that is invokable with two objects to compare. It returns `true` if the first argument is *less than* the second argument; otherwise, it returns `false`. The sort interpretation of `x < y` is that `x` is sorted before `y`. All the algorithms explained in this section are in the `<algorithm>` header.

NOTE *Notice that `operator<` is a valid comparison operator.*

Comparison operators must be transitive. This means that for any elements `a`, `b`, and `c` the comparison operator `comp` must preserve the following relationship: if `comp(a, b)` and `comp(b, c)`, then `comp(a, c)`. This should make sense: if `a` is ordered before `b` and `b` is ordered before `c`, then `a` must be ordered before `c`.

sort

The `sort` algorithm sorts a sequence (unstably).

NOTE *A stable sort retains the relative, pre-sort ordering of equal elements, whereas an unstable sort might reorder them.*

The algorithm sorts the target sequence in place.

```
void sort([ep], rnd_begin, rnd_end, [comp]);
```

Arguments

- An optional `std::execution` execution policy, `ep` (default: `std::execution::seq`)
- A pair of `RandomAccessIterator`s, `rnd_begin` and `rnd_end`, representing the target sequence
- An optional comparison operator, `comp`

Complexity

Quasilinear O(N log N) where N = `distance(rnd_begin, rnd_end)`

Additional Requirements

The elements of the target sequence must be swappable, move constructible, and move assignable.

Example

```
#include <algorithm>

TEST_CASE("sort") {
  string goat_grass{ "spoilage" }; ❶
  sort(goat_grass.begin(), goat_grass.end()); ❷
  REQUIRE(goat_grass == "aegilops"); ❸
}
```

You first construct a string containing the word spoilage ❶. Next, you invoke sort with this string as the target sequence ❷. The result is that goat_grass now contains the word aegilops (a genus of invasive weeds) ❸.

stable_sort

The stable_sort algorithm sorts a sequence stably.

The algorithm sorts the target sequence in place. Equal elements retain their original ordering.

```
void stable_sort([ep], rnd_begin, rnd_end, [comp]);
```

Arguments

- An optional std::execution execution policy, ep (default: std::execution ::seq)
- A pair of RandomAccessIterators, rnd_begin and rnd_end, representing the target sequence
- An optional comparison operator, comp

Complexity

Polylog-linear $O(N \log^2 N)$ where N = distance(rnd_begin, rnd_end). If additional memory is available, complexity reduces to quasilinear.

Additional Requirements

The elements of the target sequence must be swappable, move constructible, and move assignable.

Example

```
#include <algorithm>

enum class CharCategory { ❶
  Ascender,
  Normal,
  Descender
};

CharCategory categorize(char x) { ❷
  switch (x) {
```

```
    case 'g':
    case 'j':
    case 'p':
    case 'q':
    case 'y':
      return CharCategory::Descender;
    case 'b':
    case 'd':
    case 'f':
    case 'h':
    case 'k':
    case 'l':
    case 't':
      return CharCategory::Ascender;
  }
  return CharCategory::Normal;
}

bool ascension_compare(char x, char y) { ❸
  return categorize(x) < categorize(y);
}

TEST_CASE("stable_sort") {
  string word{ "outgrin" }; ❹
  stable_sort(word.begin(), word.end(), ascension_compare); ❺
  REQUIRE(word == "touring"); ❻
}
```

This example sorts a string using the *ascenders* and *descenders*. In typography, an ascender is a letter with a portion that extends above what is known as the mean line of a font. A descender is a letter with a portion that extends below what is known as the baseline. Letters commonly typed with descenders are *g*, *j*, *p*, *q*, and *y*. Letters commonly typed with ascenders are *b*, *d*, *f*, *h*, *k*, *l*, and *t*. This example seeks a `stable_sort` so that all letters with ascenders appear before all other letters and letters with descenders appear after all other letters. Letters with neither an ascender nor a descender lie in the middle. As a `stable_sort`, the relative ordering of letters with common ascender/descender categorization must not change.

You first define an `enum class` called `CharCategory` that takes on three possible values: `Ascender`, `Normal`, or `Descender` ❶. Next, you define a function that categorizes a given char into a `CharCategory` ❷. (Recall from "Switch Statements" on page 50 that labels "fall through" if you don't include a `break`.) You also define an `ascension_compare` function that converts two given `char` objects into `CharCategory` objects and compares them with `operator<` ❸. Because `enum class` objects convert implicitly to `int` objects and because you define `CharCategory` with its values in the intended order, this will sort letters with ascenders ahead of normal letters ahead of letters with descenders.

Within the test case, you initialize a `string` containing the word `outgrin` ❹. Next, you invoke `stable_sort` with this `string` as the target sequence and `ascension_compare` as the comparison operator ❺. The result is that `word` now contains touring ❻. Notice that t, the only ascender, appears before all the normal characters (which are in the same order as in outgrin), which appear before g, the only descender.

partial_sort

The partial_sort algorithm sorts a sequence into two groups.

If modifying, the algorithm sorts the first (rnd_middle - rnd_first) elements in the target sequence so all elements in rnd_begin to rnd_middle are less than the rest of the elements. If copying, the algorithm places the first min(distance(ipt_begin, ipt_end), distance(rnd_begin, rnd_end)) sorted elements into the destination sequence, and it returns an iterator pointing to the end of the destination sequence.

Basically, a partial sort allows you to find the first few elements of a sorted sequence without having to sort the entire sequence. For example, if you had the sequence D C B A, you could partial sort the first two elements and obtain the result A B D C. The first two elements are the same as if you'd sorted the entire sequence, but the remaining elements aren't.

```
void partial_sort([ep], rnd_begin, rnd_middle, rnd_end, [comp]);
RandomAccessIterator partial_sort_copy([ep], ipt_begin, ipt_end,
                                       rnd_begin, rnd_end, [comp]);
```

Arguments

- An optional std::execution execution policy, ep (default: std::execution ::seq)
- If modifying, a trio of RandomAccessIterators, rnd_begin, rnd_middle, and rnd_end, representing the target sequence
- If copying, a pair ipt_begin and ipt_end representing the target sequence and a pair rnd_begin and rnd_end representing the destination sequence
- An optional comparison operator, comp

Complexity

Quasilinear O(N log N) where N = distance(rnd_begin, rnd_end) * log(distance(rnd_begin, rnd_middle) or distance(rnd_begin, rnd_end) * log(min(distance(rnd_begin, rnd_end), distance(ipt_begin, ipt_end)) for the copy variant

Additional Requirements

The elements of the target sequence must be swappable, move constructible, and move assignable.

Examples

```
#include <algorithm>

bool ascension_compare(char x, char y) {
--snip--
```

```
}

TEST_CASE("partial_sort") {
  string word1{ "nectarous" }; ❶
  partial_sort(word1.begin(), word1.begin() + 4, word1.end()); ❷
  REQUIRE(word1 == "acentrous"); ❸

  string word2{ "pretanning" }; ❹
  partial_sort(word2.begin(), word2.begin() + 3, ❺
               word2.end(), ascension_compare);
  REQUIRE(word2 == "trepanning"); ❻
}
```

You first initialize a string containing the word nectarous ❶. Next, you invoke partial_sort with this string as the target sequence and the fifth letter (a) as the second argument to partial_sort ❷. The result is that the sequence now contains the word acentrous ❸. Notice that the first four letters of acentrous are sorted and that they're less than the remaining characters in the sequence.

In the second example, you initialize a string containing the word pretanning ❹, which you use as the target sequence for partial_sort ❺. In this example, you specify the fourth character (t) as the second argument to partial_sort, and you use the ascension_compare function from the stable_sort example as the comparison operator. The result is that the sequence now contains the word trepanning ❻. Notice that the first three letters are sorted according to ascension_compare and none of the remaining characters in the second argument to partial_sort to z is less than the first three characters.

NOTE *Technically, the* REQUIRE *statements in the preceding example might fail on some standard library implementations. Because* std::partial_sort *isn't guaranteed to be stable, results may vary.*

is_sorted

The is_sorted algorithm determines whether a sequence is sorted.

The algorithm returns true if the target sequence is sorted according to operator< or comp, if given. The is_sorted_until algorithm returns an iterator pointing to the first unsorted element or rnd_end if the target sequence is sorted.

```
bool is_sorted([ep], rnd_begin, rnd_end, [comp]);
ForwardIterator is_sorted_until([ep], rnd_begin, rnd_end, [comp]);
```

Arguments

- An optional std::execution execution policy, ep (default: std::execution ::seq)
- A pair of RandomAccessIterators, rnd_begin and rnd_end, representing the target sequence
- An optional comparison operator, comp

Complexity

Linear The algorithm compares distance(rnd_begin, rnd_end) times.

Examples

```
#include <algorithm>

bool ascension_compare(char x, char y) {
--snip--
}

TEST_CASE("is_sorted") {
  string word1{ "billowy" }; ❶
  REQUIRE(is_sorted(word1.begin(), word1.end())); ❷

  string word2{ "floppy" }; ❸
  REQUIRE(word2.end() == is_sorted_until(word2.begin(), ❹
                                         word2.end(), ascension_compare));
}
```

You first construct a string containing the word billowy ❶. Next, you invoke is_sort with this string as the target sequence, which returns true ❷.

In the second example, you construct a string containing the word floppy ❸. You then invoke is_sorted_until with this string as the target sequence, which returns rnd_end because the sequence is sorted ❹.

nth_element

The nth_element algorithm places a particular element in a sequence into its correct sorted position.

This partial sorting algorithm modifies the target sequence in the following way: the element in the position pointed to by rnd_nth is in that position as if the whole range were sorted. All elements from rnd_begin to rnd_nth-1 will be less than rnd_nth. If rnd_nth == rnd_end, the function performs no operation.

```
bool nth_element([ep], rnd_begin, rnd_nth, rnd_end, [comp]);
```

Arguments

- An optional std::execution execution policy, ep (default: std::execution ::seq)
- A trio of RandomAccessIterators, rnd_begin, rnd_nth, and rnd_end, representing the target sequence
- An optional comparison operator, comp

Complexity

Linear The algorithm compares distance(rnd_begin, rnd_end) times.

Additional Requirements

The elements of the target sequence must be swappable, move constructible, and move assignable.

Example

```
#include <algorithm>

TEST_CASE("nth_element") {
  vector<int> numbers{ 1, 9, 2, 8, 3, 7, 4, 6, 5 }; ❶
  nth_element(numbers.begin(), numbers.begin() + 5, numbers.end()); ❷
  auto less_than_6th_elem = [&elem=numbers[5]](int x) { ❸
    return x < elem;
  };
  REQUIRE(all_of(numbers.begin(), numbers.begin() + 5, less_than_6th_elem)); ❹
  REQUIRE(numbers[5] == 6 ); ❺
}
```

You first construct a vector of int objects containing the number sequence 1 to 10 inclusive ❶. Next, you invoke nth_element with this vector as the target sequence ❷. You then initialize a lambda named less_than_6th_elem, which compares an int with the sixth element of numbers with operator< ❸. This allows you to check that all elements before the sixth element are less than the sixth element ❹. The sixth element is 6 ❺.

Binary Search

Binary search algorithms assume that a target sequence is already sorted. These algorithms have desirable complexity characteristics compared with generic search over an unspecified sequence. Each algorithm explained in this section is in the <algorithm> header.

lower_bound

The lower_bound algorithm finds a partition in a sorted sequence.

The algorithm returns an iterator corresponding to the element result, which partitions the sequence so the elements before result are less than value, whereas result and all elements after it aren't less than value.

```
ForwardIterator lower_bound(fwd_begin, fwd_end, value, [comp]);
```

Arguments

- A pair of ForwardIterators, fwd_begin and fwd_end, representing the target sequence
- A value to partition the target sequence with
- An optional comparison operator, comp

Complexity

Logarithmic If you provide a random iterator, `O(log N)` where `N = distance (fwd_begin, fwd_end)`; otherwise, `O(N)`

Additional Requirements

The target sequence must be sorted according to `operator<` or `comp` if provided.

Example

```
#include <algorithm>

TEST_CASE("lower_bound") {
  vector<int> numbers{ 2, 4, 5, 6, 6, 9 }; ❶
  const auto result = lower_bound(numbers.begin(), numbers.end(), 5); ❷
  REQUIRE(result == numbers.begin() + 2); ❸
}
```

You first construct a `vector` of `int` objects ❶. Next, you invoke `lower_bound` with this `vector` as the target sequence and a `value` of `5` ❷. The result is the third element, `5` ❸. The elements `2` and `4` are less than `5`, whereas the elements `5`, `6`, `6`, and `9` are not.

upper_bound

The `upper_bound` algorithm finds a partition in a sorted sequence.

The algorithm returns an iterator corresponding to the element `result`, which is the first element in the target sequence greater than `value`.

```
ForwardIterator upper_bound(fwd_begin, fwd_end, value, [comp]);
```

Arguments

- A pair of `ForwardIterator`s, `fwd_begin` and `fwd_end`, representing the target sequence
- A `value` to partition the target sequence with
- An optional comparison operator, `comp`

Complexity

Logarithmic If you provide a random iterator, `O(log N)` where `N = distance (fwd_begin, fwd_end)`; otherwise, `O(N)`

Additional Requirements

The target sequence must be sorted according to `operator<` or `comp` if provided.

Example

```
#include <algorithm>

TEST_CASE("upper_bound") {
```

```
  vector<int> numbers{ 2, 4, 5, 6, 6, 9 }; ❶
  const auto result = upper_bound(numbers.begin(), numbers.end(), 5); ❷
  REQUIRE(result == numbers.begin() + 3); ❸
}
```

You first construct a vector of int objects ❶. Next, you invoke upper_bound with this vector as the target sequence and a value of 5 ❷. The result is the fourth element, 6, which is the first element in the target sequence greater than value ❸.

equal_range

The equal_range algorithm finds a range of certain elements in a sorted sequence.

The algorithm returns a std::pair of iterators corresponding to the half-open range equal to value.

```
ForwardIteratorPair equal_range(fwd_begin, fwd_end, value, [comp]);
```

Arguments

- A pair of ForwardIterators, fwd_begin and fwd_end, representing the target sequence
- A value to seek
- An optional comparison operator, comp

Complexity

Logarithmic If you provide a random iterator, O(log N) where N = distance (fwd_begin, fwd_end); otherwise, O(N)

Additional Requirements

The target sequence must be sorted according to operator< or comp if provided.

Example

```
#include <algorithm>

TEST_CASE("equal_range") {
  vector<int> numbers{ 2, 4, 5, 6, 6, 9 }; ❶
  const auto[rbeg, rend] = equal_range(numbers.begin(), numbers.end(), 6); ❷
  REQUIRE(rbeg == numbers.begin() + 3); ❸
  REQUIRE(rend == numbers.begin() + 5); ❹
}
```

You first construct a vector of int objects ❶. Next, you invoke equal_range with this vector as the target sequence and a value of 6 ❷. The result is an iterator pair representing the matching range. The begin iterator points to the fourth element ❸, and the second iterator points to the sixth element ❹.

binary_search

The binary_search algorithm finds a particular element in a sorted sequence.

The algorithm returns true if the range contains value. Specifically, it returns true if the target sequence contains an element x such that neither x < value nor value < x. If comp is provided, it returns true if the target sequence contains an element x such that neither comp(x, value) nor comp(value, x).

```
bool binary_search(fwd_begin, fwd_end, value, [comp]);
```

Arguments

- A pair of ForwardIterators, fwd_begin and fwd_end, representing the target sequence
- A value to seek
- An optional comparison operator, comp

Complexity

Logarithmic If you provide a random iterator, O(log N) where N = distance (fwd_begin, fwd_end); otherwise, O(N)

Additional Requirements

The target sequence must be sorted according to operator< or comp if provided.

Example

```
#include <algorithm>

TEST_CASE("binary_search") {
  vector<int> numbers{ 2, 4, 5, 6, 6, 9 }; ❶
  REQUIRE(binary_search(numbers.begin(), numbers.end(), 6)); ❷
  REQUIRE_FALSE(binary_search(numbers.begin(), numbers.end(), 7)); ❸
}
```

You first construct a vector of int objects ❶. Next, you invoke binary_search with this vector as the target sequence and a value of 6. Because the sequence contains 6, binary_search returns true ❷. When you invoke binary_search with 7, it returns false because the target sequence doesn't contain 7 ❸.

Partitioning Algorithms

A *partitioned sequence* contains two contiguous, distinct groups of elements. These groups don't mix, and the first element of the second distinct group is called the *partition point*. The stdlib contains algorithms to partition sequences, determine whether a sequence is partitioned, and find partition points. Each algorithm explained in this section is in the <algorithm> header.

is_partitioned

The is_partitioned algorithm determines whether a sequence is partitioned.

NOTE *A sequence is partitioned if all elements with some attribute appear before the elements that don't.*

The algorithm returns true if every element in the target sequence for which pred evaluates to true appears before the other elements.

```
bool is_partitioned([ep], ipt_begin, ipt_end, pred);
```

Arguments

- An optional std::execution execution policy, ep (default: std::execution ::seq)
- A pair of InputIterator objects, ipt_begin and ipt_end, representing the target sequence
- A predicate, pred, that determines group membership

Complexity

Linear At most distance(ipt_begin, ipt_end) evaluations of pred

Examples

```
#include <algorithm>

TEST_CASE("is_partitioned") {
  auto is_odd = [](auto x) { return x % 2 == 1; }; ❶

  vector<int> numbers1{ 9, 5, 9, 6, 4, 2 }; ❷
  REQUIRE(is_partitioned(numbers1.begin(), numbers1.end(), is_odd)); ❸

  vector<int> numbers2{ 9, 4, 9, 6, 4, 2 }; ❹
  REQUIRE_FALSE(is_partitioned(numbers2.begin(), numbers2.end(), is_odd)); ❺
}
```

You first construct a lambda called is_odd, which returns true if the given number is odd ❶. Next, you construct a vector of int objects ❷ and invoke is_partitioned with this vector as the target sequence and is_odd as the predicate. Because the sequence contains all its odd numbers placed before its even numbers, is_partitioned returns true ❸.

You then construct another vector of int objects ❹ and again invoke is_partitioned with this vector as the target sequence and is_odd as the predicate. Because the sequence doesn't contain all its odd numbers placed before its even numbers (4 is even and before the second 9), is_partitioned returns false ❺.

partition

The partition algorithm partitions a sequence.

The algorithm mutates the target sequence so it's partitioned according to pred. It returns the partition point. The elements' original ordering isn't necessarily preserved.

```
ForwardIterator partition([ep], fwd_begin, fwd_end, pred);
```

Arguments

- An optional std::execution execution policy, ep (default: std::execution ::seq)
- A pair of ForwardIterators, fwd_begin and fwd_end, representing the target sequence
- A predicate, pred, that determines group membership

Complexity

Linear At most distance(fwd_begin, fwd_end) evaluations of pred

Additional Requirements

The target sequence's elements must be swappable.

Example

```
#include <algorithm>

TEST_CASE("partition") {
  auto is_odd = [](auto x) { return x % 2 == 1; }; ❶
  vector<int> numbers{ 1, 2, 3, 4, 5 }; ❷
  const auto partition_point = partition(numbers.begin(),
                                         numbers.end(), is_odd); ❸
  REQUIRE(is_partitioned(numbers.begin(), numbers.end(), is_odd)); ❹
  REQUIRE(partition_point == numbers.begin() + 3); ❺
}
```

You first construct a lambda called is_odd, which returns true if the given number is odd ❶. Next, you construct a vector of int objects ❷ and invoke partition with this vector as the target sequence and is_odd as the predicate. You assign the resulting partition point into partition_point ❸.

When you invoke is_partitioned on the target sequence with is_odd as the predicate, it returns true ❹. Per the specification of the algorithm, *you cannot rely on the ordering within the groups*, but the partition_point will always be the fourth element, because the target sequence contains three odd numbers ❺.

partition_copy

The partition_copy algorithm partitions a sequence.

The algorithm partitions the target sequence by evaluating pred on each element. All true elements copy into opt_true, and all false elements copy into opt_false.

```
ForwardIteratorPair partition_copy([ep], ipt_begin, ipt_end,
                                    opt_true, opt_false, pred);
```

Arguments

- An optional std::execution execution policy, ep (default: std::execution ::seq)
- A pair of InputIterator objects, ipt_begin and ipt_end, representing the target sequence
- An OutputIterator, opt_true, to receive copies of true elements
- An OutputIterator, opt_false, to receive copies of false elements
- A predicate, pred, that determines group membership

Complexity

Linear Exactly distance(ipt_begin, ipt_end) evaluations of pred

Additional Requirements

- The target sequence's elements must be copy assignable.
- The input and output ranges must not overlap.

Example

```
#include <algorithm>

TEST_CASE("partition_copy") {
  auto is_odd = [](auto x) { return x % 2 == 1; }; ❶
  vector<int> numbers{ 1, 2, 3, 4, 5 }, odds, evens; ❷
  partition_copy(numbers.begin(), numbers.end(),
                 back_inserter(odds), back_inserter(evens), is_odd); ❸
  REQUIRE(all_of(odds.begin(), odds.end(), is_odd)); ❹
  REQUIRE(none_of(evens.begin(), evens.end(), is_odd)); ❺
}
```

You first construct a lambda called is_odd, which returns true if the given number is odd ❶. Next, you construct a vector of int objects containing the numbers from 1 to 5 and two empty vector objects called odds and evens ❷. Next, you invoke partition_copy with numbers as the target sequence, a back _inserter to odds as the output for true elements, a back_inserter to evens as the output for false elements, and is_odd as the predicate ❸. The result is that all of the elements in odds are odd ❹ and none of the elements in evens are odd ❺.

stable_partition

The stable_partition algorithm partitions a sequence stably.

A stable partition might take more computation than an unstable partition, so the user is given the choice.

The algorithm mutates the target sequence so it's partitioned according to pred. It returns the partition point. The elements' original ordering is preserved.

```
BidirectionalIterator partition([ep], bid_begin, bid_end, pred);
```

Arguments

- An optional std::execution execution policy, ep (default: std::execution ::seq)
- A pair of BidirectionalIterators, bid_begin and bid_end, representing the target sequence
- A predicate, pred, that determines group membership

Complexity

Quasilinear O(N log N) swaps where N = distance(bid_begin, bid_end), or O(N) swaps if sufficient memory is available.

Additional Requirements

The target sequence's elements must be swappable, move constructible, and move assignable.

Example

```
#include <algorithm>

TEST_CASE("stable_partition") {
  auto is_odd = [](auto x) { return x % 2 == 1; }; ❶
  vector<int> numbers{ 1, 2, 3, 4, 5 }; ❷
  stable_partition(numbers.begin(), numbers.end(), is_odd); ❸
  REQUIRE(numbers == vector<int>{ 1, 3, 5, 2, 4 }); ❹
}
```

You first construct a lambda called is_odd, which returns true if the given number is odd ❶. Next, you construct a vector of int objects ❷ and invoke stable_partition with this vector as the target sequence and is_odd as the predicate ❸. The result is that the vector contains the elements 1, 3, 5, 2, 4 because this is the only way to partition these numbers while preserving their original within-group order ❹.

Merging Algorithms

Merging algorithms merge two sorted target sequences such that the resulting sequence contains copies of both target sequences and is also sorted. Each algorithm explained in this section is in the `<algorithm>` header.

merge

The `merge` algorithm merges two sorted sequences.

The algorithm copies both target sequences into the destination sequence. The destination sequence is sorted according to `operator<` or `comp` if provided.

```
OutputIterator merge([ep], ipt_begin1, ipt_end1,
                     ipt_begin2, ipt_end2, opt_result, [comp]);
```

Arguments

- An optional `std::execution` execution policy, `ep` (default: `std::execution ::seq`)
- Two pairs of `InputIterators`, `ipt_begin` and `ipt_end`, representing the target sequences
- An `OutputIterator`, `opt_result`, representing the destination sequence
- A predicate, `pred`, that determines group membership

Complexity

Linear At most `N-1` comparisons where `N = distance(ipt_begin1, ipt_end1) + distance(ipt_begin2, ipt_end2)`

Additional Requirements

The target sequences must be sorted according to `operator<` or `comp` if provided.

Example

```
#include <algorithm>

TEST_CASE("merge") {
  vector<int> numbers1{ 1, 4, 5 }, numbers2{ 2, 3, 3, 6 }, result; ❶
  merge(numbers1.begin(), numbers1.end(),
        numbers2.begin(), numbers2.end(),
        back_inserter(result)); ❷
  REQUIRE(result == vector<int>{ 1, 2, 3, 3, 4, 5, 6 }); ❸
}
```

You construct three `vector` objects: two containing sorted `int` objects and another that is empty ❶. Next, you merge the non-empty `vector` and use the empty vector as the destination sequence via a back_inserter ❷. The result contains copies of all the elements from the original sequences, and it too is sorted ❸.

Extreme-Value Algorithms

Several algorithms, called *extreme-value algorithms*, determine minimum and maximum elements or place limits on the minimum or maximum value of an element. Each algorithm explained in this section is in the <algorithm> header.

min and max

The min or max algorithm determines a sequence's extrema.

The algorithms use operator< or comp and return the minimum (min) or maximum (max) object. The minmax algorithm returns both as a std::pair with first as the minimum and second as the maximum.

```
T min(obj1, obj2, [comp]);
T min(init_list, [comp]);
T max(obj1, obj2, [comp]);
T max(init_list, [comp]);
Pair minmax(obj1, obj2, [comp]);
Pair minmax(init_list, [comp]);
```

Arguments

- Two objects, obj1 and obj2, or
- An initializer list, init_list, representing the objects to compare
- An optional comparison function, comp

Complexity

Constant or Linear For the overloads taking obj1 and obj2, exactly one comparison. For the initializer list, at most N-1 comparisons where N is the length of the initializer list. In the case of minmax, given an initializer list, this grows to 3/2 N.

Additional Requirements

The elements must be copy constructible and comparable using the given comparison.

Examples

```
#include <algorithm>

TEST_CASE("max and min") {
  using namespace std::literals;
```

```
  auto length_compare = [](const auto& x1, const auto& x2) { ❶
    return x1.length() < x2.length();
  };

  REQUIRE(min("undiscriminativeness"s, "vermin"s,
              length_compare) == "vermin"); ❷

  REQUIRE(max("maxim"s, "ultramaximal"s,
              length_compare) == "ultramaximal"); ❸

  const auto result = minmax("minimaxes"s, "maximin"s, length_compare); ❹
  REQUIRE(result.first == "maximin"); ❺
  REQUIRE(result.second == "minimaxes"); ❻
}
```

You first initialize a lambda called `length_compare`, which uses `operator<` to compare the lengths of two inputs ❶. Next, you use `min` to determine whether *undiscriminativeness* or *vermin* has lesser length ❷, and you use `max` to determine whether *maxim* or *ultramaximal* has greater length ❸. Finally, you use `minmax` to determine which of *minimaxes* and *maximin* has minimum and maximum length ❹. The result is a pair ❺❻.

min_element and max_element

The `min_element` or `max_element` algorithm determines a sequence's extrema.

The algorithms use `operator<` or `comp` and return an iterator pointing to the minimum (`min_element`) or maximum (`max_element`) object. The `minimax_element` algorithm returns both as a `std::pair` with `first` as the minimum and `second` as the maximum.

```
ForwardIterator min_element([ep], fwd_begin, fwd_end, [comp]);
ForwardIterator max_element([ep], fwd_begin, fwd_end, [comp]);
Pair minmax_element([ep], fwd_begin, fwd_end, [comp]);
```

Arguments

- An optional `std::execution` execution policy, `ep` (default: `std::execution::seq`)
- A pair of `ForwardIterators`, `fwd_begin` and `fwd_end`, representing the target sequence
- An optional comparison function, `comp`

Complexity

Linear For `max` and `min`, at most `N-1` comparisons where `N=distance(fwd_begin, fwd_end)`; for `minmax`, `3/2 N`

Additional Requirements

The elements must be comparable using the given operation.

Examples

```
#include <algorithm>

TEST_CASE("min and max element") {
  auto length_compare = [](const auto& x1, const auto& x2) { ❶
    return x1.length() < x2.length();
  };

  vector<string> words{ "civic", "deed", "kayak",  "malayalam" }; ❷

  REQUIRE(*min_element(words.begin(), words.end(),
                       length_compare) == "deed"); ❸
  REQUIRE(*max_element(words.begin(), words.end(),
                       length_compare) == "malayalam"); ❹

  const auto result = minmax_element(words.begin(), words.end(),
                                     length_compare); ❺
  REQUIRE(*result.first == "deed"); ❻
  REQUIRE(*result.second == "malayalam"); ❼
}
```

You first initialize a lambda called `length_compare`, which uses `operator<` to compare the lengths of two inputs ❶. Next, you initialize a `vector` of `string` objects called `words` containing four words ❷. You use `min_element` to determine the smallest of these words by passing it as the target sequence and `length_compare` as the comparison function (`deed`) ❸, and you use `max_element` to determine the largest (`malayalam`) ❹. Finally, you use `minmax_element`, which returns both as a `std::pair` ❺. The `first` element refers to the shortest `word` ❻, and `second` refers to the longest ❼.

clamp

The `clamp` algorithm bounds a value.

The algorithm uses `operator<` or `comp` to determine whether `obj` is inside the bounds from `low` to `high`. If it is, the algorithm simply returns `obj`; otherwise, if `obj` is less than `low`, it returns `low`. If `obj` is greater than `high`, it returns `high`.

```
T& clamp(obj, low, high, [comp]);
```

Arguments

- An object, `obj`
- A `low` and `high` object
- An optional comparison function, `comp`

Complexity

Constant At most two comparisons

Additional Requirements

The objects must be comparable using the given operation.

Examples

```
#include <algorithm>

TEST_CASE("clamp") {
  REQUIRE(clamp(9000, 0, 100) == 100); ❶
  REQUIRE(clamp(-123, 0, 100) == 0); ❷
  REQUIRE(clamp(3.14, 0., 100.) == Approx(3.14)); ❸
}
```

In the first example, you clamp `9000` to the interval from 0 to 100 inclusive. Because 9,000 > 100, the result is `100` ❶. In the second example, you clamp `-123` to the same interval. Because −123 < 0, the result is `0` ❷. Finally, you clamp `3.14` and because it's within the interval, the result is `3.14` ❸.

Numeric Operations

The `<numeric>` header was discussed in Chapter 12 when you learned about its mathematical types and functions. It also provides algorithms well suited to numeric operations. This section introduces many of them. Each algorithm explained in this section is in the `<numeric>` header.

Useful Operators

Some stdlib numeric operations permit you to pass an operator to customize behavior. For convenience, the `<functional>` header provides the following class templates that expose various binary arithmetic operations through `operator(T x, T y)`:

- `plus<T>` implements addition `x + y`.
- `minus<T>` implements subtraction `x - y`.
- `multiplies<T>` implements multiplication `x * y`.
- `divides<T>` implements division `x / y`.
- `modulus<T>` implements addition `x % y`.

For example, you could add two numbers using the `plus` template, like this:

```
#include <functional>

TEST_CASE("plus") {
  plus<short> adder; ❶
  REQUIRE(3 == adder(1, 2)); ❷
  REQUIRE(3 == plus<short>{}(1,2)); ❸
}
```

You first instantiate a plus called adder ❶, and then you invoke it with the values 1 and 2, which yields 3 ❷. You can also skip the variable entirely and simply use a newly constructed plus directly to achieve the same result ❸.

NOTE *You generally wouldn't use these operator types unless you were using generic code that required them.*

iota

The iota algorithm fills a sequence with incremental values.

The algorithm assigns incremental values beginning with start to the target sequence.

```
void iota(fwd_begin, fwd_end, start);
```

Arguments

- A pair of iterators, fwd_begin and fwd_end, representing the target sequence
- A start value

Complexity

Linear N increments and assignments, where N=distance(fwd_begin, fwd_end)

Additional Requirements

The objects must be assignable to start.

Example

```
#include <numeric>
#include <array>

TEST_CASE("iota") {
  array<int, 3> easy_as; ❶
  iota(easy_as.begin(), easy_as.end(), 1); ❷
  REQUIRE(easy_as == array<int, 3>{ 1, 2, 3 }); ❸
}
```

You first initialize an array of int objects with length 3 ❶. Next, you invoke iota with the array as the target sequence and 1 as the start value ❷. The result is that array contains the elements 1, 2, and 3 ❸.

accumulate

The accumulate algorithm folds a sequence (in order).

NOTE *Folding a sequence means to apply a particular operation over the elements of a sequence while passing the cumulative result along to the next operation.*

The algorithm applies op to start and the target sequence's first element. It takes the result and the target sequence's next element and again applies op, proceeding in this fashion until it visits each element in the target sequence. Loosely, this algorithm adds the target sequence elements and the start value, and it returns the result.

```
T accumulate(ipt_begin, ipt_end, start, [op]);
```

Arguments

- A pair of iterators, ipt_begin and ipt_end, representing the target sequence
- A start value
- An optional binary operator, op, that defaults to plus

Complexity

Linear N applications of op, where N=distance(ipt_begin, ipt_end)

Additional Requirements

The target sequence's elements must be copyable.

Examples

```
#include <numeric>

TEST_CASE("accumulate") {
  vector<int> nums{ 1, 2, 3 }; ❶
  const auto result1 = accumulate(nums.begin(), nums.end(), -1); ❷
  REQUIRE(result1 == 5); ❸

  const auto result2 = accumulate(nums.begin(), nums.end(),
                                  2, multiplies<>()); ❹
  REQUIRE(result2 == 12); ❺
}
```

You first initialize a vector of int objects with length 3 ❶. Next, you invoke accumulate with the vector as the target sequence and -1 as the start value ❷. The result is $-1 + 1 + 2 + 3 = 5$ ❸.

In the second example, you use the same target sequence but a start value of 2 and the multiplies operator instead ❹. The result is $2 * 1 * 2 * 3 = 12$ ❺.

reduce

The reduce algorithm folds a sequence (not necessarily in order).

The algorithm is identical to accumulate except it accepts an optional execution and doesn't guarantee the order of operator applications.

```
T reduce([ep], ipt_begin, ipt_end, start, [op]);
```

Arguments

- An optional std::execution execution policy, ep (default: std::execution ::seq)
- A pair of iterators, ipt_begin and ipt_end, representing the target sequence
- A start value
- An optional binary operator, op, that defaults to plus

Complexity

Linear N applications of op, where N=distance(ipt_begin, ipt_end)

Additional Requirements

- Elements must be movable if you omit ep.
- Elements must copyable if you provide ep.

Examples

```
#include <numeric>

TEST_CASE("reduce") {
  vector<int> nums{ 1, 2, 3 }; ❶
  const auto result1 = reduce(nums.begin(), nums.end(), -1); ❷
  REQUIRE(result1 == 5); ❸

  const auto result2 = reduce(nums.begin(), nums.end(),
                              2, multiplies<>()); ❹
  REQUIRE(result2 == 12); ❺
}
```

You first initialize a vector of int objects with length 3 ❶. Next, you invoke reduce with the vector as the target sequence and -1 as the start value ❷. The result is –1 + 1 + 2 + 3 = 5 ❸.

In the second example, you use the same target sequence but a start value of 2 and the multiplies operator instead ❹. The result is 2 * 1 * 2 * 3 = 12 ❺.

inner_product

The inner_product algorithm computes the inner product of two sequences.

NOTE *An inner product (or dot product) is a scalar value associated with a pair of sequences.*

The algorithm applies op2 to each pair of corresponding elements in the target sequence and sums them together with start using op1.

```
T inner_product([ep], ipt_begin1, ipt_end1, ipt_begin2, start, [op1], [op2]);
```

Arguments

- A pair of iterators, ipt_begin1 and ipt_end1, representing target sequence 1
- An iterator, ipt_begin2, representing target sequence 2
- A start value
- Two optional binary operators, op1 and op2, that default to plus and multiply

Complexity

Linear N applications of op1 and op2, where N=distance(ipt_begin1, ipt_end1)

Additional Requirements

Elements must be copyable.

Example

```
#include <numeric>

TEST_CASE("inner_product") {
  vector<int> nums1{ 1, 2, 3, 4, 5 }; ❶
  vector<int> nums2{ 1, 0,-1, 0, 1 }; ❷
  const auto result = inner_product(nums1.begin(), nums1.end(),
                                    nums2.begin(), 10); ❸
  REQUIRE(result == 13); ❹
}
```

You first initialize two vectors of int objects ❶❷. Next, you invoke inner_product with the two vector objects as the target sequences and 10 as the start value ❸. The result is 10 + 1 * 1 + 2 * 0 + 3 * 1 + 4 * 0 + 4 * 1 = 13 ❹.

adjacent_difference

The adjacent_difference algorithm generates adjacent differences.

NOTE *An adjacent difference is the result of applying some operation to each pair of neighboring elements.*

The algorithm sets the first element of the destination sequence equal to the first element of the target sequence. For each subsequent element, it applies op to the prior element and the current element and writes the return value into result. The algorithm returns the end of the destination sequence.

```
OutputIterator adjacent_difference([ep], ipt_begin, ipt_end, result, [op]);
```

Arguments

- A pair of iterators, ipt_begin and ipt_end, representing target sequence
- An iterator, result, representing the destination sequence
- An optional binary operator, op, that defaults to minus

Complexity

Linear N-1 applications of op, where N=distance(ipt_begin, ipt_end)

Additional Requirements

- Elements must be movable if you omit ep.
- Elements must copyable if you provide ep.

Example

```
#include <numeric>

TEST_CASE("adjacent_difference") {
  vector<int> fib{ 1, 1, 2, 3, 5, 8 }, fib_diff; ❶
  adjacent_difference(fib.begin(), fib.end(), back_inserter(fib_diff)); ❷
  REQUIRE(fib_diff == vector<int>{ 1, 0, 1, 1, 2, 3 }); ❸
}
```

You first two initialize a vector of int objects, one containing the first six numbers of the Fibonacci sequence and another that is empty ❶. Next, you invoke adjacent_difference with the two vector objects as the target sequences ❷. The result is as expected: the first element equals the first element of the Fibonacci sequence, and the following elements are the adjacent differences (1 – 1 = 0), (2 – 1 = 1), (3 – 2 = 1), (5 – 3 = 2), (8 – 5 = 3) ❸.

partial_sum

The partial_sum algorithm generates partial sums.

The algorithm sets an accumulator equal to the first element of the target sequence. For each subsequent element of the target sequence, the algorithm adds that element to the accumulator and then writes the accumulator into the destination sequence. The algorithm returns the end of the destination sequence.

```
OutputIterator partial_sum(ipt_begin, ipt_end, result, [op]);
```

Arguments

- A pair of iterators, ipt_begin and ipt_end, representing the target sequence
- An iterator, result, representing the destination sequence
- An optional binary operator, op, that defaults to plus

Complexity

Linear `N-1` applications of `op`, where `N=distance(ipt_begin, ipt_end)`

Example

```
#include <numeric>

TEST_CASE("partial_sum") {
  vector<int> num{ 1, 2, 3, 4 }, result; ❶
  partial_sum(num.begin(), num.end(), back_inserter(result)); ❷
  REQUIRE(result == vector<int>{ 1, 3, 6, 10 }); ❸
}
```

You first initialize two `vector` of `int` objects, one called `num` containing the first four counting and an empty one called `result` ❶. Next, you invoke `partial_sum` with `num` as the target sequence and `result` as the destination ❷. The first element equals the first element of the target sequence, and the following elements are the partial sums (1 + 2 = 3), (3 + 3 = 6), (6 + 4 = 10) ❸.

Other Algorithms

To keep a long chapter from getting much longer, many algorithms are omitted. This section provides a survey of them.

(Max) Heap Operations

A range of length N is a max heap if for all $0 < i < N$, the $\frac{i-1}{2}$-th element (rounded down) doesn't compare less than the i-th element. These structures have strong performance properties in situations where maximum element lookup and insertions must be fast.

The `<algorithm>` header contains functions that are useful for handling such ranges, such as those in Table 18-1. See [alg.heap.operations] for details.

Table 18-1: Heap-Related Algorithms in the `<algorithm>` Header

Algorithm	Description
`is_heap`	Checks whether a range is a max heap
`is_heap_until`	Finds the largest subrange that is a max heap
`make_heap`	Creates a max heap
`push_heap`	Adds an element
`pop_heap`	Removes the largest element
`sort_heap`	Transforms a max heap into a sorted range

Set Operations on Sorted Ranges

The `<algorithm>` header contains functions that perform set operations on sorted ranges, such as those in Table 18-2. See [alg.set.operations] for details.

Table 18-2: Set-Related Algorithms in the <algorithm> Header

Algorithm	Description
includes	Returns true if one range is a subset of another range
set_difference	Computes the difference between two sets
set_intersection	Computes the intersection of two sets
set_symmetric_difference	Computes the symmetric difference between two sets
set_union	Computes the union of two sets

Other Numeric Algorithms

The <numeric> header contains several more functions in addition to those introduced in the "Numeric Operations" section. Table 18-3 lists them. See [numeric.ops] for details.

Table 18-3: Additional Numerical Algorithms in the <numeric> Header

Algorithm	Description
exclusive_scan	Like partial_sum but excludes the i-th element from the i-th sum
inclusive_scan	Like partial_sum but executes out of order and requires an associative operation
transform_reduce	Applies a function object; then reduces out of order
transform_exclusive_scan	Applies a function object; then calculates an exclusive scan
transform_inclusive_scan	Applies a function object; then calculates an inclusive scan

Memory Operations

The <memory> header contains a number of low-level functions for handling uninitialized memory. Table 18-4 lists them. See [memory.syn] for details.

Table 18-4: Operations for Uninitialized Memory in the <memory> Header

Algorithm	Description
uninitialized_copy uninitialized_copy_n uninitialized_fill uninitialized_fill_n	Copy objects into uninitialized memory
uninitialized_move uninitialized_move_n	Move objects into uninitialized memory
uninitialized_default_construct uninitialized_default_construct_n uninitialized_value_construct uninitialized_value_construct_n	Construct objects in uninitialized memory
destroy_at destroy destroy_n	Destroy objects

Boost Algorithm

Boost Algorithm is a large algorithm library that overlaps partially with the standard library. For space reasons, Table 18-5 lists only a quick reference to those algorithms not already contained in the standard library. Refer to the Boost Algorithm documentation for further information.

Table 18-5: Additional Algorithms Available in Boost Algorithm

Algorithm	Description
boyer_moore boyer_moore_horspool knuth_morris_pratt	Fast algorithms for searching sequences of values
hex unhex	Writes/reads hexadecimal characters
gather	Takes a sequence and moves elements satisfying a predicate into a given position
find_not	Finds the first element in a sequence not equal to a value
find_backward	Like find but works backward
is_partitioned_until	Returns the end iterator for the largest partitioned subsequence that begins with the target sequence's first element
apply_permutation apply_reverse_permutation	Takes an item sequence and an order sequence and reshuffles the item sequence according to the order sequence
is_palindrome	Returns true if a sequence is a palindrome

A NOTE ON RANGES

Chapter 8 introduced range expressions as part of the range-based for loop. Recall from this discussion that a range is a concept that exposes begin and end methods that return iterators. Because you can place requirements on iterators to support certain operations, you can place transitive requirements on ranges so they provide certain iterators. Each algorithm has certain operational requirements, and these are reflected in the sorts of iterators they require. Because you can encapsulate an algorithm's input sequence requirements in terms of ranges, you must understand the various range types to understand each algorithm's constraints.

(continued)

Like concepts, ranges are not yet formally part of C++. Although you'll still get tremendous benefit from understanding the relationship among ranges, iterators, and algorithms, there are two drawbacks. First, algorithms still require iterators as input arguments, so even if a range is at hand, you'll need to extract iterators manually (for example, with `begin` and `end`). Second, as with other function templates, you'll sometimes get spectacularly poor error messages when you violate an algorithm's operational requirements.

Work is underway to introduce ranges into the language formally. In fact, concepts and ranges will likely enter the C++ Standard simultaneously because they dovetail so nicely.

If you want to experiment with one possible implementation of ranges, refer to Boost Range.

FURTHER READING

- *ISO International Standard ISO/IEC (2017) — Programming Language C++* (International Organization for Standardization; Geneva, Switzerland; *https://isocpp.org/std/the-standard/*)
- *The C++ Standard Library: A Tutorial and Reference*, 2nd Edition, by Nicolai Josuttis (Addison-Wesley Professional, 2012)
- "Algorithmic Complexity" by Victor Adamchik (*https://www.cs.cmu.edu/~adamchik/15-121/lectures/Algorithmic%20Complexity/complexity.html*)
- *The Boost C++ Libraries*, 2nd Edition, by Boris Schäling (XML Press, 2014)

19

CONCURRENCY AND PARALLELISM

The Senior Watchdog had her own watchwords:
"Show me a completely smooth operation and I'll show you
someone who's covering mistakes. Real boats rock."
—Frank Herbert, Chapterhouse: Dune

In programming, *concurrency* means two or more tasks running in a given time period. *Parallelism* means two or more tasks running at the same instant. Often, these terms are used interchangeably without negative consequence, because they're so closely related. This chapter introduces the very basics of both concepts. Because concurrent and parallel programming are huge and complicated topics, thorough treatment requires an entire book. You'll find such books in the "Further Reading" section at the end of this chapter.

In this chapter, you'll learn about concurrent and parallel programming with futures. Next, you'll learn how to share data safely with mutexes, condition variables, and atomics. Then the chapter illustrates how execution policies help to speed up your code but also contain hidden dangers.

Concurrent Programming

Concurrent programs have multiple *threads of execution* (or simply *threads*), which are sequences of instructions. In most runtime environments, the operating system acts as a scheduler to determine when a thread executes its next instruction. Each process can have one or more threads, which typically share resources, such as memory, with each other. Because the scheduler determines when threads execute, the programmer can't generally rely on their ordering. In exchange, programs can execute multiple tasks in the same time period (or at the same time), which often results in serious speedups. To observe any speedup from the serial to the concurrent version, your system will need concurrent hardware, for example, a multicore processor.

This section begins with asynchronous tasks, a high-level method for making your programs concurrent. Next, you'll learn some basic methods for coordinating between these tasks when they're handling shared mutable state. Then you'll survey some low-level facilities available to you in the stdlib for unique situations in which the higher-level tools don't have the performance characteristics you require.

Asynchronous Tasks

One way to introduce concurrency into your program is by creating *asynchronous tasks*. An asynchronous task doesn't immediately need a result. To launch an asynchronous task, you use the `std::async` function template in the `<future>` header.

async

When you invoke `std::async`, the first argument is the launch policy `std::launch`, which takes one of two values: `std::launch::async` or `std::launch::deferred`. If you pass `launch::async`, the runtime creates a new thread to launch your task. If you pass `deferred`, the runtime waits until you need the task's result before executing (a pattern sometimes called *lazy evaluation*). This first argument is optional and defaults to `async|deferred`, meaning it's up to the implementation which strategy to employ. The second argument to `std::async` is a function object representing the task you want to execute. There are no restrictions on the number or type of arguments the function object accepts, and it might return any type. The `std::async` function is a variadic template with a function parameter pack. Any additional arguments you pass beyond the function object will be used to invoke the function object when the asynchronous task launches. Also, `std::async` returns an object called a `std::future`.

The following simplified async declaration helps to summarize:

```
std::future<FuncReturnType> std::async([policy], func, Args&&... args);
```

Now that you know how to invoke async, let's look at how to interact with its return value.

Back to the future

A future is a class template that holds the value of an asynchronous task. It has a single template parameter that corresponds with the type of the asynchronous task's return value. For example, if you pass a function object that returns a string, async will return a future<string>. Given a future, you can interact with an asynchronous task in three ways.

First, you can query the future about its validity using the valid method. A valid future has a shared state associated with it. Asynchronous tasks have a shared state so they can communicate the results. Any future returned by async will be valid until you retrieve the asynchronous task's return value, at which point the shared state's lifetime ends, as Listing 19-1 illustrates.

```
#include <future>
#include <string>

using namespace std;

TEST_CASE("async returns valid future") {
  using namespace literals::string_literals;
  auto the_future = async([] { return "female"s; }); ❶
  REQUIRE(the_future.valid()); ❷
}
```

Listing 19-1: The async function returns a valid future.

You launch an asynchronous task that simply returns a string ❶. Because async always returns a valid future, valid returns true ❷.

If you default construct a future, it's not associated with a shared state, so valid will return false, as Listing 19-2 illustrates.

```
TEST_CASE("future invalid by default") {
  future<bool> default_future; ❶
  REQUIRE_FALSE(default_future.valid()); ❷
}
```

Listing 19-2: A default constructed future is invalid.

You default construct a future ❶, and valid returns false ❷.

Second, you can obtain the value from a valid future with its get method. If the asynchronous task hasn't yet completed, the call to get will block the currently executed thread until the result is available. Listing 19-3 illustrates how to employ get to obtain return values.

```
TEST_CASE("async returns the return value of the function object") {
  using namespace literals::string_literals;
  auto the_future = async([] { return "female"s; }); ❶
  REQUIRE(the_future.get() == "female"); ❷
}
```

Listing 19-3: The async function returns a valid future.

You use async to launch an asynchronous task ❶ and then invoke the get method on the resulting future. As expected, the result is the return value of the function object you passed into async ❷.

If an asynchronous task throws an exception, the future will collect that exception and throw it when you invoke get, as Listing 19-4 illustrates.

```
TEST_CASE("get may throw ") {
  auto ghostrider = async(
                      [] { throw runtime_error{ "The pattern is full." }; }); ❶
  REQUIRE_THROWS_AS(ghostrider.get(), runtime_error); ❷
}
```

Listing 19-4: The get method will throw the exception thrown by an asynchronous task.

You pass a lambda to async that throws a runtime_error ❶. When you invoke get, it throws the exception ❷.

Third, you can check whether an asynchronous task has completed using either std::wait_for or std::wait_until. Which you choose depends on the sort of chrono object you want to pass. If you have a duration object, you'll use wait_for. If you have a time_point object, you'll use wait_until. Both return a std::future_status, which takes one of three values:

- future_status::deferred signals that the asynchronous task will be evaluated lazily, so the task will execute once you call get.
- future_status::ready indicates that the task has completed and the result is ready.
- future_status::timeout indicates that the task isn't ready.

If the task completes before the specified waiting period, async will return early.

Listing 19-5 illustrates how to use wait_for to check an asynchronous task's status.

```
TEST_CASE("wait_for indicates whether a task is ready") {
  using namespace literals::chrono_literals;
  auto sleepy = async(launch::async, [] { this_thread::sleep_for(100ms); }); ❶
  const auto not_ready_yet = sleepy.wait_for(25ms); ❷
  REQUIRE(not_ready_yet == future_status::timeout); ❸
  const auto totally_ready = sleepy.wait_for(100ms); ❹
  REQUIRE(totally_ready == future_status::ready); ❺
}
```

Listing 19-5: Checking an asynchronous task's status using wait_for

You first launch an asynchronous task with async, which simply waits for up to 100 milliseconds before returning ❶. Next, you call wait_for with 25 milliseconds ❷. Because the task is still sleeping (25 < 100), wait_for returns future_status::timeout ❸. You call wait_for again and wait for up to another 100 milliseconds ❹. Because the second wait_for will finish after the async task finishes, the final wait_for will return a future_status::ready ❺.

NOTE *Technically, the assertions in Listing 19-5 aren't guaranteed to pass. "Waiting" on page 389 introduced* `this_thread::sleep_for`*, which isn't exact. The operating environment is responsible for scheduling threads, and it might schedule the sleeping thread later than the specified duration.*

An Example with Asynchronous Tasks

Listing 19-6 contains the `factorize` function, which finds all of an integer's factors.

NOTE *The factorization algorithm in Listing 19-6 is woefully inefficient but is good enough for this example. For efficient integer factorization algorithms, refer to Dixon's algorithm, the continued fraction factorization algorithm, or the quadratic sieve.*

```
#include <set>

template <typename T>
std::set<T> factorize(T x) {
  std::set<T> result{ 1 }; ❶
  for(T candidate{ 2 }; candidate <= x; candidate++) { ❷
    if (x % candidate == 0) { ❸
      result.insert(candidate); ❹
      x /= candidate; ❺
      candidate = 1; ❻
    }
  }
  return result;
}
```

Listing 19-6: A very simple integer factorization algorithm

The algorithm accepts a single argument `x` and begins by initializing a set containing 1 ❶. Next, it iterates from 2 to `x` ❷, checking whether modulo division with the `candidate` results in 0 ❸. If it does, `candidate` is a factor, and you add it to the factor set ❹. You divide `x` by the factor you just discovered ❺ and then restart your search by resetting the `candidate` to 1 ❻.

Because integer factorization is a hard problem (and because Listing 19-6 is so inefficient), calls to `factorize` can take a long time relative to most of the functions you've encountered so far in the book. This makes it a prime candidate for asynchronous tasking. The `factor_task` function in Listing 19-7 uses the trusty `Stopwatch` from Listing 12-25 in Chapter 12 to wrap `factorize` and returns a nicely formatted message.

```
#include <set>
#include <chrono>
#include <sstream>
#include <string>

using namespace std;

struct Stopwatch {
```

```
--snip--
};

template <typename T>
set<T> factorize(T x) {
--snip--
}

string factor_task(unsigned long x) { ❶
  chrono::nanoseconds elapsed_ns;
  set<unsigned long long> factors;
  {
    Stopwatch stopwatch{ elapsed_ns }; ❷
    factors = factorize(x); ❸
  }
  const auto elapsed_ms =
             chrono::duration_cast<chrono::milliseconds>(elapsed_ns).count(); ❹
  stringstream ss;
  ss << elapsed_ms << " ms: Factoring " << x << " ( "; ❺
  for(auto factor : factors) ss << factor << " "; ❻
  ss << ")\n";
  return ss.str(); ❼
}
```

Listing 19-7: A `factor_task` function that wraps a call to `factorize` and returns a nicely formatted message

Like `factorize`, `factor_task` accepts a single argument `x` to factorize ❶. (For simplicity, `factor_task` takes an `unsigned long` rather than a templated argument). Next, you initialize a `Stopwatch` within a nested scope ❷ and then invoke `factorize` with `x` ❸. The result is that `elapsed_ns` contains the number of nanoseconds elapsed while `factorize` executed, and `factors` contains all the factors of `x`.

Next, you construct a nicely formatted string by first converting `elapsed_ns` to a count in milliseconds ❹. You write this information into a `stringstream` object called `ss` ❺ followed by the factors of `x` ❻. Then you return the resulting string ❼.

Listing 19-8 employs `factor_task` to factor six different numbers and record the total elapsed program time.

```
#include <set>
#include <array>
#include <vector>
#include <iostream>
#include <limits>
#include <chrono>
#include <sstream>
#include <string>

using namespace std;

struct Stopwatch {
--snip--
```

```
};

template <typename T>
set<T> factorize(T x) {
--snip--
}

string factor_task(unsigned long long x) {
--snip--
}

array<unsigned long long, 6> numbers{ ❶
        9'699'690,
        179'426'549,
        1'000'000'007,
        4'294'967'291,
        4'294'967'296,
        1'307'674'368'000
};

int main() {
  chrono::nanoseconds elapsed_ns;
  {
    Stopwatch stopwatch{ elapsed_ns }; ❷
    for(auto number : numbers) ❸
      cout << factor_task(number); ❹
  }
  const auto elapsed_ms =
           chrono::duration_cast<chrono::milliseconds>(elapsed_ns).count(); ❺
  cout << elapsed_ms << "ms: total program time\n"; ❻
}
--------------------------------------------------------------------------
0 ms: Factoring 9699690 ( 1 2 3 5 7 11 13 17 19 )
1274 ms: Factoring 179426549 ( 1 179426549 )
6804 ms: Factoring 1000000007 ( 1 1000000007 )
29035 ms: Factoring 4294967291 ( 1 4294967291 )
0 ms: Factoring 4294967296 ( 1 2 )
0 ms: Factoring 1307674368000 ( 1 2 3 5 7 11 13 )
37115ms: total program time
```

Listing 19-8: A program using factor_task to factorize six different numbers

You construct an array containing six numbers of varied size and primality ❶. Next, you initialize a Stopwatch ❷, iterate over each element in numbers ❸, and invoke factor_task with them ❹. You then determine the program's runtime in milliseconds ❺ and print it ❻.

The output shows that some numbers, such as 9,699,690, 4,294,967,296, and 1,307,674,368,000, factor almost immediately because they contain small factors. However, the prime numbers take quite a while. Note that because the program is single threaded, the runtime for the entire program roughly equals the sum of the times taken to factorize each number.

What if you treat each factor_task as an asynchronous task? Listing 19-9 illustrates how to do this with async.

```
#include <set>
#include <vector>
#include <array>
#include <iostream>
#include <limits>
#include <chrono>
#include <future>
#include <sstream>
#include <string>

using namespace std;

struct Stopwatch {
--snip--
};

template <typename T>
set<T> factorize(T x) {
--snip--
}

string factor_task(unsigned long long x) {
--snip--
}

array<unsigned long long, 6> numbers{
--snip--
};

int main() {
  chrono::nanoseconds elapsed_ns;
  {
    Stopwatch stopwatch{ elapsed_ns }; ❶
    vector<future<string>> factor_tasks; ❷
    for(auto number : numbers) ❸
      factor_tasks.emplace_back(async(launch::async, factor_task, number)); ❹
    for(auto& task : factor_tasks) ❺
      cout << task.get(); ❻
  }
  const auto elapsed_ms =
             chrono::duration_cast<chrono::milliseconds>(elapsed_ns).count(); ❼
  cout << elapsed_ms << " ms: total program time\n"; ❽
}
```

```
0 ms: Factoring 9699690 ( 1 2 3 5 7 11 13 17 19 )
1252 ms: Factoring 179426549 ( 1 179426549 )
6816 ms: Factoring 1000000007 ( 1 1000000007 )
28988 ms: Factoring 4294967291 ( 1 4294967291 )
0 ms: Factoring 4294967296 ( 1 2 )
0 ms: Factoring 1307674368000 ( 1 2 3 5 7 11 13 )
28989 ms: total program time
```

Listing 19-9: A program using factor_task to factorize six different numbers asynchronously

As in Listing 19-8, you initialize a `Stopwatch` to keep track of how long the program executes ❶. Next, you initialize a `vector` called `factor_tasks` that contains objects of type `future<string>` ❷. You iterate over `numbers` ❸, invoking `async` with the `launch::async` strategy, specifying `factor_task` as the function object, and passing a `number` as the task's argument. You invoke `emplace_back` on each resulting `future` into `factor_tasks` ❹. Now that `async` has launched each task, you iterate over each element of `factor_tasks` ❺, invoke `get` on each `task`, and write it to `cout` ❻. Once you've received values from all the futures, you determine the number of milliseconds it took to run all tasks ❼ and write it to `cout` ❽.

Thanks to concurrency, the total program time of Listing 19-9 roughly equals the maximum task execution time (28,988 ms) rather than the sum of task execution times, as in Listing 19-8 (37,115 ms).

NOTE *The times in Listing 19-8 and Listing 19-9 will vary from run to run.*

Sharing and Coordinating

Concurrent programming with asynchronous tasks is simple as long as the tasks don't require synchronization and don't involve sharing mutable data. For example, consider a simple situation in which two threads access the same integer. One thread will increment the integer while the other decrements it. To modify a variable, each thread must read the variable's current value, perform an addition or subtraction operation, and then write the variable to memory. Without synchronization, the two threads will perform these operations in an undefined, interleaved order. Such situations are sometimes called *race conditions* because the result depends on which thread executes first. Listing 19-10 illustrates just how disastrous this situation is.

```
#include <future>
#include <iostream>

using namespace std;

void goat_rodeo() {
  const size_t iterations{ 1'000'000 };
  int tin_cans_available{}; ❶
  auto eat_cans = async(launch::async, [&] { ❷
    for(size_t i{}; i<iterations; i++)
      tin_cans_available--; ❸
  });
  auto deposit_cans = async(launch::async, [&] { ❹
    for(size_t i{}; i<iterations; i++)
      tin_cans_available++; ❺
  });
  eat_cans.get(); ❻
  deposit_cans.get(); ❼
  cout << "Tin cans: " << tin_cans_available << "\n"; ❽
}
```

```
int main() {
  goat_rodeo();
  goat_rodeo();
  goat_rodeo();
}
--------------------------------------------------------------------------
Tin cans: -609780
Tin cans: 185380
Tin cans: 993137
```

Listing 19-10: An illustration of how disastrous unsynchronized, mutable, shared data access can be

NOTE *You'll get different results on each run of the program in Listing 19-10 because the program has undefined behavior.*

Listing 19-10 involves defining a function called `goat_rodeo`, which involves a catastrophic race condition, and a `main` that invokes `goat_rodeo` three times. Within `goat_rodeo`, you initialize the shared data `tin_cans_available` ❶. Next, you launch an asynchronous task called `eat_cans` ❷ in which a trip of goats decrements the shared variable `tin_cans_available` one million times ❸. Next, you launch another asynchronous task called `deposit_cans` ❹ in which you increment `tin_cans_available` ❺. After launching the two tasks, you wait for them to complete by calling get (the order doesn't matter) ❻❼. Once the tasks complete, you print the `tin_cans_available` variable ❽.

Intuitively, you might expect `tin_cans_available` to equal zero after each task completes. After all, no matter how you order increments and decrements, if you perform them in equal number, they'll cancel. You invoke `goat_rodeo` three times, and each invocation produces a wildly different result.

Table 19-1 illustrates one of the many ways the unsynchronized access in Listing 19-10 goes awry.

Table 19-1: One Possible Schedule for `eat_cans` and `deposit_cans`

eat_cans	deposit_cans	cans_available
Read `cans_available` (0)		0
	Read `cans_available` (0) ❶	0
Compute `cans_available+1` (1)		0
	Compute `cans_available-1` (-1) ❸	0
Write `cans_available+1` (1) ❷		1
	Write `cans_available-1` (-1) ❹	-1

Table 19-1 shows how interleaving reads and writes invites disaster. In this particular incarnation, the read by `deposit_cans` ❶ precedes the write from `eat_cans` ❷, so `deposit_cans` computes a stale result ❸. If this weren't bad enough, it clobbers the write from `eat_cans` when it writes ❹.

The fundamental problem with this data race is *unsynchronized access to mutable shared data*. You might wonder why `cans_available` doesn't update immediately whenever a thread computes `cans_available+1` or `cans_available-1`. The answer lies in the fact that each of the rows in Table 19-1 represents a moment in time when some instruction completes execution, and the instructions for adding, subtracting, reading, and writing memory are all separate. Because the `cans_available` variable is shared and both threads write to it without synchronizing their actions, the instructions get interleaved in an undefined way at runtime (with catastrophic results). In the following subsections, you'll learn three tools for dealing with such situations: mutexes, condition variables, and atomics.

Mutexes

A *mutual exclusion algorithm* (*mutex*) is a mechanism for preventing multiple threads from accessing resources simultaneously. Mutexes are *synchronization primitives* that support two operations: lock and unlock. When a thread needs to access shared data, it locks the mutex. This operation can block depending on the nature of the mutex and whether another thread has the lock. When a thread no longer needs access, it unlocks the mutex.

The `<mutex>` header exposes several mutex options:

- `std::mutex` provides basic mutual exclusion.
- `std::timed_mutex` provides mutual exclusion with a timeout.
- `std::recursive_mutex` provides mutual exclusion that allows recursive locking by the same thread.
- `std::recursive_timed_mutex` provides mutual exclusion that allows recursive locking by the same thread and a timeout.

The `<shared_mutex>` header provides two additional options:

- `std::shared_mutex` provides shared mutual exclusion facility, which means that several threads can own the mutex at once. This option is typically used in scenarios when multiple readers can access shared data but a writer needs exclusive access.
- `std::shared_timed_mutex` provides shared mutual exclusion facility and implements locking with a timeout.

NOTE *For simplicity, this chapter only covers* `mutex`*. See [thread.mutex] for more information about the other options.*

The `mutex` class defines only a single, default constructor. When you want to obtain mutual exclusion, you call one of two methods on a `mutex` object: `lock` or `try_lock`. If you call `lock`, which accepts no arguments and returns `void`, the calling thread blocks until the `mutex` becomes available. If you call `try_lock`, which accepts no arguments and returns a `bool`, it returns immediately. If the `try_lock` successfully obtained mutual exclusion, it returns `true` and the calling thread now owns the lock. If `try_lock` was unsuccessful, it returns `false` and the calling thread doesn't own the lock. To release a mutual exclusion lock, you simply call the method `unlock`, which accepts no arguments and returns `void`.

Listing 19-11 shows a lock-based way to solve the race condition in Listing 19-10.

```
#include <future>
#include <iostream>
#include <mutex>

using namespace std;

void goat_rodeo() {
  const size_t iterations{ 1'000'000 };
  int tin_cans_available{};
  mutex tin_can_mutex; ❶
  auto eat_cans = async(launch::async, [&] {
    for(size_t i{}; i<iterations; i++) {
      tin_can_mutex.lock(); ❷
      tin_cans_available--;
      tin_can_mutex.unlock(); ❸
    }
  });
  auto deposit_cans = async(launch::async, [&] {
    for(size_t i{}; i<iterations; i++) {
      tin_can_mutex.lock(); ❹
      tin_cans_available++;
      tin_can_mutex.unlock(); ❺
    }
  });
  eat_cans.get();
  deposit_cans.get();
  cout << "Tin cans: " << tin_cans_available << "\n";
}

int main() {
  goat_rodeo(); ❻
  goat_rodeo(); ❼
  goat_rodeo(); ❽
}
--------------------------------------------------------------------------
Tin cans: 0 ❻
Tin cans: 0 ❼
Tin cans: 0 ❽
```

Listing 19-11: Using a `mutex` to resolve the race condition in Listing 19-10

You add a `mutex` into `goat_rodeo` ❶ called `tin_can_mutex`, which provides mutual exclusion on the `tin_cans_available`. Inside each asynchronous task, a thread acquires a lock ❷❹ before modifying `tin_cans_available`. Once the thread is done modifying, it unlocks ❸❺. Notice that the resulting number of available tin cans at the end of each run is zero ❻❼❽, reflecting that you've fixed your race condition.

MUTEX IMPLEMENTATIONS

In practice, mutexes are implemented in a number of ways. Perhaps the simplest mutex is a *spin lock* in which a thread will execute a loop until the lock is released. This kind of lock usually minimizes the amount of time between a lock getting released by one thread and acquired by another. But it's computationally expensive because a CPU is spending all of its time checking for lock availability when some other thread could be doing productive work. Typically, mutexes require atomic instructions, such as `compare-and-swap`, `fetch-and-add`, or `test-and-set`, so they can check for and acquire a lock in one operation.

Modern operating systems, like Windows, offer more efficient alternatives to spin locks. For example, mutexes based on *asynchronous procedure calls* allow threads to wait on a mutex and go into a *wait state*. Once the mutex becomes available, the operating system awakens the waiting thread and hands off ownership of the mutex. This allows other threads to do productive work on a CPU that would otherwise be occupied in a spin lock.

In general, you won't need to worry about the details of how mutexes are implemented by your operating system unless they become a bottleneck in your program.

If you're thinking that handling `mutex` locking is a perfect job for an RAII object, you're right. Suppose you forgot to invoke `unlock` on a mutex, say because it threw an exception. When the next thread comes along and attempts to acquire the mutex with `lock`, your program will come to a screeching halt. For this reason, the stdlib provides RAII classes for handling mutexes in the `<mutex>` header. There you'll find several class templates, all of which accept mutexes as constructor parameters and a template parameter corresponding to the class of the mutexes:

- `std::lock_guard` is a non-copyable, non-moveable RAII wrapper that accepts a mutex object in its constructor, where it calls `lock`. It then calls `unlock` in the destructor.
- `std::scoped_lock` is a deadlock avoiding RAII wrapper for multiple mutexes.
- `std::unique_lock` implements a movable mutex ownership wrapper.
- `std::shared_lock` implements a movable shared mutex ownership wrapper.

For brevity, this section focuses on `lock_guard`. Listing 19-12 shows how to refactor Listing 19-11 to use `lock_guard` instead of manual `mutex` manipulation.

```
#include <future>
#include <iostream>
#include <mutex>

using namespace std;
```

```
void goat_rodeo() {
  const size_t iterations{ 1'000'000 };
  int tin_cans_available{};
  mutex tin_can_mutex;
  auto eat_cans = async(launch::async, [&] {
    for(size_t i{}; i<iterations; i++) {
      lock_guard<mutex> guard{ tin_can_mutex }; ❶
      tin_cans_available--;
    }
  });
  auto deposit_cans = async(launch::async, [&] {
    for(size_t i{}; i<iterations; i++) {
      lock_guard<mutex> guard{ tin_can_mutex }; ❷
      tin_cans_available++;
    }
  });
  eat_cans.get();
  deposit_cans.get();
  cout << "Tin cans: " << tin_cans_available << "\n";
}

int main() {
  goat_rodeo();
  goat_rodeo();
  goat_rodeo();
}
--------------------------------------------------------------------------
Tin cans: 0
Tin cans: 0
Tin cans: 0
```

Listing 19-12: Refactoring Listing 19-11 to use `lock_guard`

Rather than using `lock` and `unlock` to manage mutual exclusion, you construct a `lock_guard` at the beginning of each scope where you need synchronization ❶❷. Because your mutual exclusion mechanism is a `mutex`, you specify it as your `lock_guard` template parameter. Listing 19-11 and Listing 19-12 have equivalent runtime behavior, including how long it takes the programs to execute. RAII objects don't involve any additional runtime costs over programming releases and acquisitions by hand.

Unfortunately, mutual exclusion locks involve runtime costs. You might also have noticed that executing Listings 19-11 and 19-12 took substantially longer than executing Listing 19-10. The reason is that acquiring and releasing locks is a relatively expensive operation. In Listings 19-11 and 19-12, the `tin_can_mutex` gets acquired and then released two million times. Relative to incrementing or decrementing an integer, acquiring or releasing a lock takes substantially more time, so using a mutex to synchronize the asynchronous tasks is suboptimal. In certain situations, you can take a potentially more efficient approach by using atomics.

NOTE *For more information about asynchronous tasks and futures, refer to [futures.async].*

Atomics

The word *atomic* comes from the Greek *átomos*, meaning "indivisible." An operation is atomic if it occurs in an indivisible unit. Another thread cannot observe the operation halfway through. When you introduced locks into Listing 19-10 to produce Listing 19-11, you made the increment and decrement operations atomic because the asynchronous tasks could no longer interleave read and write operations on `tin_cans_available`. As you experienced running this lock-based solution, this approach is very slow because acquiring locks is expensive.

Another approach is to use the `std::atomic` class template in the `<atomic>` header, which provides primitives often used in *lock-free concurrent programming*. Lock-free concurrent programming solves data race issues without involving locks. On many modern architectures, CPUs support atomic instructions. Using atomics, you might be able to avoid locks by leaning on atomic hardware instructions.

This chapter doesn't discuss `std::atomic` or how to devise your own lock-free solutions in detail, because it's incredibly difficult to do correctly and is best left to experts. However, in simple situations, such as in Listing 19-10, you can employ a `std::atomic` to make sure that the increment or decrement operations cannot be divided. This neatly solves your data race problem.

The `std::atomic` template offers specializations for all fundamental types, as shown in Table 19-2.

Table 19-2: `std::atomic` Template Specializations for the Fundamental Types

Template specialization	Alias
`std::atomic<bool>`	`std::atomic_bool`
`std::atomic<char>`	`std::atomic_char`
`std::atomic<unsigned char>`	`std::atomic_uchar`
`std::atomic<short>`	`std::atomic_short`
`std::atomic<unsigned short>`	`std::atomic_ushort`
`std::atomic<int>`	`std::atomic_int`
`std::atomic<unsigned int>`	`std::atomic_uint`
`std::atomic<long>`	`std::atomic_long`
`std::atomic<unsigned long>`	`std::atomic_ulong`
`std::atomic<long long>`	`std::atomic_llong`
`std::atomic<unsigned long long>`	`std::atomic_ullong`
`std::atomic<char16_t>`	`std::atomic_char16_t`
`std::atomic<char32_t>`	`std::atomic_char32_t`
`std::atomic<wchar_t>`	`std::atomic_wchar_t`

Table 19-3 lists some of the supported operations for `std::atomic`. The `std::atomic` template has no copy constructor.

Table 19-3: Supported Operations for `std::atomic`

Operation	Description
`a{}` `a{ 123 }`	Default constructor. Initializes value to 123.
`a.is_lock_free()`	Returns true if **a** is lock-free. (Depends on the CPU.)
`a.store(123)`	Stores the value 123 into **a**.
`a.load()` `a()`	Returns the stored value.
`a.exchange(123)`	Replaces the current value with 123 and returns the old value. This is a "read-modify-write" operation.
`a.compare_exchange_weak(10, 20)` `a.compare_exchange_strong(10, 20)`	If the current value is 10, replaces with 20. Returns `true` if the value was replaced. See [atomic] for details on weak versus strong.

NOTE *Specializations for the types in* `<cstdint>` *are also available. See [atomics.syn] for details.*

For the numeric types, the specializations offer additional operations, as listed in Table 19-4.

Table 19-4: Supported Operations for Numeric Specializations of a `std::atomic` **a**

Operation	Description
`a.fetch_add(123)` `a+=123`	Replaces the current value with the result of adding the argument to the current value. Returns the value before modification. This is a "read-modify-write" operation.
`a.fetch_sub(123)` `a-=123`	Replaces the current value with the result of subtracting the argument from the current value. Returns the value before modification. This is a "read-modify-write" operation.
`a.fetch_and(123)` `a&=123`	Replaces the current value with the result of bitwise ANDing the argument with the current value. Returns the value before modification. This is a "read-modify-write" operation.
`a.fetch_or(123)` `a|=123`	Replaces the current value with the result of bitwise ORing the argument with the current value. Returns the value before modification. This is a "read-modify-write" operation.
`a.fetch_xor(123)` `a^=123`	Replaces the current value with the result of bitwise XORing the argument with the current value. Returns the value before modification. This is a "read-modify-write" operation.
`a++` `a--`	Increments or decrements **a**.

Because Listing 19-12 is a prime candidate for a lock-free solution, you can replace the type of `tin_cans_available` with `atomic_int` and remove the `mutex`. This prevents race conditions like the one illustrated in Table 19-1. Listing 19-13 implements this refactor.

```
#include <future>
#include <iostream>
#include <atomic>

using namespace std;

void goat_rodeo() {
  const size_t iterations{ 1'000'000 };
  atomic_int❶ tin_cans_available{};
  auto eat_cans = async(launch::async, [&] {
    for(size_t i{}; i<iterations; i++)
      tin_cans_available--; ❷
  });
  auto deposit_cans = async(launch::async, [&] {
    for(size_t i{}; i<iterations; i++)
      tin_cans_available++; ❸
  });
  eat_cans.get();
  deposit_cans.get();
  cout << "Tin cans: " << tin_cans_available << "\n";
}

int main() {
  goat_rodeo();
  goat_rodeo();
  goat_rodeo();
}
--------------------------------------------------------------------------
Tin cans: 0
Tin cans: 0
Tin cans: 0
```

Listing 19-13: Resolving the race condition using `atomic_int` rather than `mutex`

You replace `int` with `atomic_int` ❶ and remove the `mutex`. Because the decrement ❷ and increment ❸ operators are atomic, the race condition remains solved.

NOTE *For more information about atomics, refer to [atomics].*

You also probably noticed a considerable performance boost from Listing 19-12 to 19-13. In general, using atomic operations will be much faster than acquiring a mutex.

WARNING *Unless you have a very simple concurrent access problem, such as the one in this section, you really shouldn't try to implement lock-free solutions on your own. Refer to the Boost Lockfree library for high-quality, thoroughly tested lock-free containers. As always, you must decide whether a lock-based or lock-free implementation is optimal.*

Condition Variables

A *condition variable* is a synchronization primitive that blocks one or more threads until notified. Another thread can notify the condition variable. After notification, the condition variable can unblock one or more threads so they can make progress. A very popular condition variable pattern involves a thread performing the following actions:

1. Acquire some mutex shared with awaiting threads.
2. Modify the shared state.
3. Notify the condition variable.
4. Release the mutex.

Any threads waiting on the condition variable then perform the following actions:

1. Acquire the mutex.
2. Wait on the condition variable (this releases the mutex).
3. When another thread notifies the condition variable, this thread wakes up and can perform some work (this reacquires the mutex automatically).
4. Release the mutex.

Due to complications arising from the complexity of modern operating systems, sometimes threads can wake up spuriously. Therefore, it's important to verify that a condition variable was in fact signaled once a waiting thread awakens.

The stdlib provides `std::condition_variable` in the `<condition_variable>` header, which supports several operations, including those in Table 19-5. The `condition_variable` supports only default construction, and the copy constructor is deleted.

Table 19-5: Supported Operations of a `std::condition_variable` **`cv`**

Operation	Description
`cv.notify_one()`	If any threads are waiting on **cv**, this operation notifies one of them.
`cv.notify_all()`	If any threads are waiting on **cv**, this operation notifies all of them.
`cv.wait(lock, [pred])`	Given a **lock** on the mutex owned by the notifier, returns when awakened. If supplied, **pred** determines whether the notification is spurious (returns `false`) or real (returns `true`).
`cv.wait_for(lock, [durn], [pred])`	Same as **cv**`.wait` except `wait_for` only waits for **durn**. If timeout occurs and no **pred** is supplied, returns `std::cv_status::timeout`; otherwise, returns `std::cv_status::no_timeout`.
`cv.wait_until(lock, [time], [pred])`	Same as `wait_for` except uses a `std::chrono::time_point` instead of a `std::chrono::duration`.

For example, you can refactor Listing 19-12 so the *deposit cans* task completes before the *eat cans* task using a condition variable, as Listing 19-14 illustrates.

```
#include <future>
#include <iostream>
#include <mutex>
#include <condition_variable>

using namespace std;

void goat_rodeo() {
  mutex m; ❶
  condition_variable cv; ❷
  const size_t iterations{ 1'000'000 };
  int tin_cans_available{};

  auto eat_cans = async(launch::async, [&] {
    unique_lock<mutex> lock{ m }; ❸
    cv.wait(lock, [&] { return tin_cans_available == 1'000'000; }); ❹
    for(size_t i{}; i<iterations; i++)
      tin_cans_available--;
  });

  auto deposit_cans = async(launch::async, [&] {
    scoped_lock<mutex> lock{ m }; ❺
    for(size_t i{}; i<iterations; i++)
      tin_cans_available++;
    cv.notify_all(); ❻
  });
  eat_cans.get();
  deposit_cans.get();
  cout << "Tin cans: " << tin_cans_available << "\n";
}

int main() {
  goat_rodeo();
  goat_rodeo();
  goat_rodeo();
}
---------------------------------------------------------------------------
Tin cans: 0
Tin cans: 0
Tin cans: 0
```

Listing 19-14: Using condition variables to ensure all cans are deposited before they're eaten

You declare a `mutex` ❶ and a `condition_variable` ❷ that you'll use to coordinate the asynchronous tasks. Within the *eat cans* task, you acquire a `unique_lock` to the `mutex`, which you pass into `wait` along with a predicate that returns `true` if there are cans available ❸. This method will release the mutex and then block until two conditions are met: the `condition_variable` awakens this thread and one million tin cans are available ❹ (recall that you must check that all the cans are available because of spurious wakeups).

Within the *deposit cans* task, you acquire a lock on the `mutex` ❺, deposit the cans, and then notify all threads blocked on the `condition_variable` ❻.

Note that, unlike with all the previous approaches, it's impossible for `tin_cans_available` to be negative because the ordering of deposit cans and eat cans is guaranteed.

NOTE *For more information about condition variables, refer to [thread.condition].*

Low-Level Concurrency Facilities

The stdlib's `<thread>` library contains low-level facilities for concurrent programming. The `std::thread` class, for example, models an operating system thread. However, it's best not to use `thread` directly and instead design concurrency into your programs with higher-level abstractions, like tasks. Should you require low-level thread access, [thread] offers more information.

But the `<thread>` library does include several useful functions for manipulating the current thread:

- The `std::this_thread::yield` function accepts no arguments and returns `void`. The exact behavior of `yield` depends on the environment, but in general it provides a hint that the operating system should give other threads a chance to run. This is useful when, for example, there's high lock contention over a particular resource and you want to help all threads get a chance at access.
- The `std::this_thread::get_id` function accepts no arguments and returns an object of type `std::thread::id`, which is a lightweight thread that supports comparison operators and `operator<<`. Typically, it's used as a key in associative containers.
- The `std::this_thread::sleep_for` function accepts a `std::chrono::duration` argument, blocks execution on the current thread until at least the specified duration passes, and returns `void`.
- The `std::this_thread::sleep_until` accepts a `std::chrono::time_point` and returns void. It is entirely analogous to `sleep_for` except it blocks the thread until at least the specified `time_point`.

When you need these functions, they're indispensable. Otherwise, you really shouldn't need to interact with the `<thread>` header.

Parallel Algorithms

Chapter 18 introduced the stdlib's algorithms, many of which take an optional first argument called its execution policy encoded by a `std::execution` value. In supported environments, there are three possible values: `seq`, `par`, and `par_unseq`. The latter two options indicate that you want to execute the algorithm in parallel.

An Example: Parallel sort

Listing 19-15 illustrates how changing a single argument from seq to par can have a massive impact on a program's runtime by sorting a billion numbers both ways.

```
#include <algorithm>
#include <vector>
#include <numeric>
#include <random>
#include <chrono>
#include <iostream>
#include <execution>

using namespace std;

// From Listing 12-25:
struct Stopwatch {
--snip--
};

vector<long> make_random_vector() { ❶
  vector<long> numbers(1'000'000'000);
  iota(numbers.begin(), numbers.end(), 0);
  mt19937_64 urng{ 121216 };
  shuffle(numbers.begin(), numbers.end(), urng);
  return numbers;
}

int main() {
  cout << "Constructing random vectors...";
  auto numbers_a = make_random_vector(); ❷
  auto numbers_b{ numbers_a }; ❸
  chrono::nanoseconds time_to_sort;
  cout << " " << numbers_a.size() << " elements.\n";
  cout << "Sorting with execution::seq...";
  {
    Stopwatch stopwatch{ time_to_sort };
    sort(execution::seq, numbers_a.begin(), numbers_a.end()); ❹
  }
  cout << " took " << time_to_sort.count() / 1.0E9 << " sec.\n";

  cout << "Sorting with execution::par...";
  {
    Stopwatch stopwatch{ time_to_sort };
    sort(execution::par, numbers_b.begin(), numbers_b.end()); ❺
  }
  cout << " took " << time_to_sort.count() / 1.0E9 << " sec.\n";
}
```

```
Constructing random vectors... 1000000000 elements.
Sorting with execution::seq... took 150.489 sec.
Sorting with execution::par... took 17.7305 sec.
```

Listing 19-15: Sorting a billion numbers using `std::sort` with `std::execution::seq` versus `std::execution::par`. (Results are from a Windows 10 x64 machine with two Intel Xeon E5-2620 v3 processors.)

The `make_random_vector` function ❶ produces a `vector` containing a billion unique numbers. You build two copies, `numbers_a` ❷ and `numbers_b` ❸. You sort each `vector` separately. In the first case, you sort with a sequential execution policy ❹, and `Stopwatch` indicates that the operation took about two and a half minutes (about 150 seconds). In the second case, you sort with a parallel execution policy ❺. In contrast, `Stopwatch` indicates that the operation took about 18 seconds. The sequential execution took roughly 8.5 times as long.

Parallel Algorithms Are Not Magic

Unfortunately, parallel algorithms aren't magic. Although they work brilliantly in simple situations, such as with `sort` in Listing 19-15, you must be careful when using them. Any time an algorithm produces side effects beyond the target sequence, you have to think hard about race conditions. A red flag is any algorithm that passes a function object to the algorithm. If the function object has mutable state, the executing threads will have shared access and you might have a race condition. For example, consider the parallel `transform` invocation in Listing 19-16.

```
#include <algorithm>
#include <vector>
#include <iostream>
#include <numeric>
#include <execution>

int main() {
  std::vector<long> numbers{ 1'000'000 }, squares{ 1'000'000 }; ❶
  std::iota(numbers.begin(), numbers.end(), 0); ❷
  size_t n_transformed{}; ❸
  std::transform(std::execution::par, numbers.begin(), numbers.end(), ❹
                 squares.begin(), [&n_transformed] (const auto x) {
                  ++n_transformed; ❺
                  return x * x; ❻
                });
  std::cout << "n_transformed: " << n_transformed << std::endl; ❼
}
```

```
n_transformed: 187215 ❼
```

Listing 19-16: A program containing a race condition due to non-atomic access to `n_transformed`

You begin by initializing two `vector` objects, `numbers` and `squares`, which contain a million elements ❶. Next, you fill one of them with numbers using `iota` ❷ and initialize the variable `n_transformed` to `0` ❸. You then invoke `transform` with a parallel execution policy, `numbers` as your target sequence, `squares` as your result sequence, and a simple lambda ❹. The lambda increments `n_transformed` ❺ and returns the square of the argument `x` ❻. Because multiple threads execute this lambda, access to `n_transformed` must be synchronized ❼.

The previous section introduced two ways to solve this problem, locks and atomics. In this scenario, it's probably best to just use a `std::atomic_size_t` as a drop-in replacement for `size_t`.

Summary

This chapter surveyed concurrency and parallelism at a very high level. In addition, you learned how to launch asynchronous tasks, which allow you to easily introduce multithreaded programming concepts into your code. Although introducing parallel and concurrent concepts into your programs can provide a significant performance boost, you must carefully avoid introducing race conditions that invite undefined behavior. You also learned several mechanisms for synchronizing access to mutable shared state: mutexes, condition variables, and atomics.

EXERCISES

19-1. Write your own spin lock-based mutex called `SpinLock`. Expose a `lock`, a `try_lock`, and an `unlock` method. Your class should delete the copy constructor. Try using a std::lock_guard<SpinLock> with an instance of your class.

19-2. Read about the infamous double-checked locking pattern (DCLP) and why you shouldn't use it. (See the article by Scott Meyers and Andrei Alexandrescu mentioned in the following "Further Reading" section.) Then read about the appropriate way to ensure that a callable gets invoked exactly once using `std::call_once` in [thread.once.callonce].

19-3. Create a thread-safe queue class. This class must expose an interface like `std::queue` (see [queue.defn]). Use a `std::queue` internally to store elements. Use a `std::mutex` to synchronize access to this internal `std::queue`.

19-4. Add a `wait_and_pop` method and a `std::condition_variable` member to your thread-safe queue. When a user invokes `wait_and_pop` and the queue contains an element, it should pop the element off the queue and return it. If the queue is empty, the thread should block until an element becomes available and then proceed to pop an element.

19-5. (Optional) Read the Boost Coroutine2 documentation, especially the "Overview," "Introduction," and "Motivation" sections.

FURTHER READING

- "C++ and The Perils of Double-Checked Locking: Part I" by Scott Meyers and Andrei Alexandrescu (*http://www.drdobbs.com/cpp/c-and-the-perils-of-double-checked-locki/184405726/*)
- *ISO International Standard ISO/IEC (2017) — Programming Language C++* (International Organization for Standardization; Geneva, Switzerland; *https://isocpp.org/std/the-standard/*)
- *C++ Concurrency in Action*, 2nd Edition, by Anthony Williams (Manning, 2018)
- "Effective Concurrency: Know When to Use an Active Object Instead of a Mutex" by Herb Sutter (*https://herbsutter.com/2010/09/24/effective-concurrency-know-when-to-use-an-active-object-instead-of-a-mutex/*)
- *Effective Modern C++: 42 Specific Ways to Improve Your Use of C++ 11 and C++ 14* by Scott Meyers (O'Reilly Media, 2014)
- "A Survey of Modern Integer Factorization Algorithms" by Peter L. Montgomery. *CWI Quarterly* 7.4 (1994): 337–365.

20

NETWORK PROGRAMMING WITH BOOST ASIO

Anyone who has lost track of time when using a computer knows the propensity to dream, the urge to make dreams come true, and the tendency to miss lunch.
—Tim Berners-Lee

Boost Asio is a library for low-level I/O programming. In this chapter, you'll learn about Boost Asio's basic networking facilities, which enable programs to interact easily and efficiently with network resources. Unfortunately, the stdlib doesn't contain a network-programming library as of C++17. For this reason, Boost Asio plays a central role in many C++ programs with a networking component.

Although Boost Asio is the primary choice for C++ developers who want to incorporate cross-platform, high-performance I/O into their programs, it's a notoriously complicated library. This complication combined with an unfamiliarity with low-level network programming might be too overwhelming for newcomers. If you find this chapter obtuse or if you don't need information on network programming, you can skip this chapter.

NOTE *Boost Asio also contains facilities for I/O with serial ports, streams, and some operating system–specific objects. In fact, the name is derived from the phrase "asynchronous I/O." See the Boost Asio documentation for more information.*

The Boost Asio Programming Model

In the Boost programming model, an *I/O context object* abstracts the operating system interfaces that handle asynchronous data processing. This object is a registry for *I/O objects*, which initiate asynchronous operations. Each object knows its corresponding service, and the context object mediates the connection.

NOTE *All Boost Asio classes appear in the* `<boost/asio.hpp>` *convenience header.*

Boost Asio defines a single service object, `boost::asio::io_context`. Its constructor takes an optional integer argument called the *concurrency hint*, which is the number of threads the `io_context` should allow to run concurrently. For example, on an eight-core machine, you might construct an `io_context` as follows:

```
boost::asio::io_context io_context{ 8 };
```

You'll pass the same `io_context` object into the constructors of your I/O objects. Once you've set up all your I/O objects, you'll call the `run` method on the `io_context`, which will block until all pending I/O operations complete.

One of the simplest I/O objects is the `boost::asio::steady_timer`, which you can use to schedule tasks. Its constructor accepts an `io_context` object and an optional `std::chrono::time_point` or `std::chrono_duration`. For example, the following constructs a `steady_timer` that expires in three seconds:

```
boost::asio::steady_timer timer{
  io_context, std::chrono::steady_clock::now() + std::chrono::seconds{ 3 }
};
```

You can wait on the timer with a blocking or a non-blocking call. To block the current thread, you use the timer's `wait` method. The result is essentially similar to using `std::this_thread::sleep_for`, which you learned about in "Chrono" on page 387. To wait asynchronously, you use the timer's `async_wait` method. This accepts a function object referred to as a *callback*. The operating system will invoke the function object once it's time for the thread to wake up. Due to complications arising from modern operating systems, this might or might not be due to the timer's expiring.

Once a timer expires, you can create another timer if you want to perform an additional wait. If you wait on an expired timer, it will return immediately. This is probably not what you intend to do, so make sure you wait only on unexpired timers.

To check whether the timer has expired, the function object must accept a `boost::system::error_code`. The `error_code` class is a simple class that represents operating system–specific errors. It converts implicitly to `bool` (`true` if it represents an error condition; `false` otherwise). If the callback's `error_code` evaluates to `false`, the timer expired.

Once you enqueue an asynchronous operation using `async_wait`, you'll call the `run` method on your `io_context` object because this method blocks until all asynchronous operations are complete.

Listing 20-1 illustrates how to construct and use timers for blocking and non-blocking waits.

```
#include <iostream>
#include <boost/asio.hpp>
#include <chrono>

boost::asio::steady_timer make_timer(boost::asio::io_context& io_context) { ❶
  return boost::asio::steady_timer{
          io_context,
          std::chrono::steady_clock::now() + std::chrono::seconds{ 3 }
  };
}

int main() {
  boost::asio::io_context io_context; ❷

  auto timer1 = make_timer(io_context); ❸
  std::cout << "entering steady_timer::wait\n";
  timer1.wait(); ❹
  std::cout << "exited steady_timer::wait\n";

  auto timer2 = make_timer(io_context); ❺
  std::cout << "entering steady_timer::async_wait\n";
  timer2.async_wait([] (const boost::system::error_code& error) { ❻
    if (!error) std::cout << "<<callback function>>\n";
  });
  std::cout << "exited steady_timer::async_wait\n";
  std::cout << "entering io_context::run\n";
  io_context.run(); ❼
  std::cout << "exited io_context::run\n";
}
```

```
entering steady_timer::wait
exited steady_timer::wait
entering steady_timer::async_wait
exited steady_timer::async_wait
entering io_context::run
<<callback function>>
exited io_context::run
```

Listing 20-1: A program using `boost::asio::steady_timer` for synchronous and asynchronous waiting

You define the `make_timer` function for building a `steady_timer` that expires in three seconds ❶. Within `main`, you initialize your program's `io_context` ❷ and construct your first timer from `make_timer` ❸. When you call `wait` on this timer ❹, the thread blocks for three seconds before proceeding. Next, you construct another timer with `make_timer` ❺, and then you invoke `async_wait` with a lambda that prints `<<callback_function>>` when the timer expires ❻. Finally, you invoke `run` on your `io_context` to begin processing operations ❼.

Network Programming with Asio

Boost Asio contains facilities for performing network-based I/O over several important network protocols. Now that you know the basic usage of `io_context` and how to enqueue asynchronous I/O operations, you can explore how to perform more involved kinds of I/O. In this section, you'll extend what you learned about waiting for timers and employ Boost Asio's network I/O facilities. By the end of this chapter, you'll know how to build programs that communicate over a network.

The Internet Protocol Suite

The Internet Protocol (IP) is the primary protocol for ferrying data across networks. Each participant in an IP network is called a *host*, and each host gets an IP address to identify it. IP addresses come in two versions: IPv4 and IPv6. An IPv4 address is 32 bits, and an IPv6 address is 128 bits.

The Internet Control Message Protocol (ICMP) is used by network devices to send information that supports operation of an IP network. The ping and traceroute programs use ICMP messages to query a network. Typically, end user applications don't need to interface with ICMP directly.

To send data across an IP network, you typically use either the Transmission Control Protocol (TCP) or User Datagram Protocol (UDP). In general, you use TCP when you need to be sure that data arrives at its destination, and you use UDP when you need to be sure that data transits quickly. TCP is a connection-oriented protocol where receivers acknowledge that they've received messages intended for them. UDP is a simple, connectionless protocol that has no built-in reliability.

NOTE *You might be wondering what* connection *means in the TCP/UDP context or thinking that a "connectionless" protocol seems absurd. Here a connection means establishing a channel between two participants in a network that guarantees delivery and order of messages. Those participants perform a handshake to establish a connection, and they have a mechanism for informing each other that they want to close the connection. In a connectionless protocol, a participant sends a packet to another participant without establishing a channel first.*

With TCP and UDP, network devices connect to each other using *ports*. A port is an integer ranging from 0 to 65,535 (2 bytes) that specifies a particular service running on a given network device. This way, a single device can run multiple services and each can be addressed separately. When one device, called a *client*, initiates communication with another device, called a *server*, the client specifies which port it wants to connect to. When you pair a device's IP address with a port number, the result is called a *socket*.

For example, a device with IP address 10.10.10.100 could serve a web page by binding a web server application to port 80. This creates a server socket at 10.10.10.100:80. Next, a device with IP address 10.10.10.200 launches a web browser, which opens a "random high port," such as 55123. This creates a client socket at 10.10.10.200:55123. The client then connects to the server by creating a TCP connection between the client socket and the server socket. Many other processes could be running on either or both devices with many other network connections simultaneously.

The Internet Assigned Numbers Authority (IANA) maintains a list of assigned numbers to standardize the ports that certain kinds of services use (the list is available at *https://www.iana.org/*). Table 20-1 provides a few commonly used protocols on this list.

Table 20-1: Well-Known Protocols Assigned by IANA

Port	TCP	UDP	Keyword	Description
7	✓	✓	echo	Echo Protocol
13	✓	✓	daytime	Daytime Protocol
21	✓		ftp	File Transfer Protocol
22	✓		ssh	Secure Shell Protocol
23	✓		telnet	Telnet Protocol
25	✓		smtp	Simple Mail Transfer Protocol
53	✓	✓	domain	Domain Name System
80	✓		http	Hypertext Transfer Protocol
110	✓		pop3	Post Office Protocol
123		✓	ntp	Network Time Protocol
143	✓		imap	Internet Message Access Protocol
179	✓		bgp	Border Gateway Protocol
194	✓		irc	Internet Relay Chat
443	✓		https	Hypertext Transfer Protocol (Secure)

Boost Asio supports network I/O over ICMP, TCP, and UDP. For brevity, this chapter only discusses TCP because the Asio classes involved in all three protocols are so similar.

NOTE *If you're unfamiliar with network protocols,* The TCP/IP Guide *by Charles M. Kozierok is a definitive reference.*

Hostname Resolution

When a client wants to connect to a server, it needs the server's IP address. In some scenarios, the client might already have this information. In others, the client might have only a service name. The process of converting a service name to an IP address is called *hostname resolution.* Boost Asio contains the boost::asio::ip::tcp::resolver class to perform hostname resolution. To construct a resolver, you pass an io_context instance as the only constructor parameter, as in the following:

```
boost::asio::ip::tcp::resolver my_resolver{ my_io_context };
```

To perform hostname resolution, you use the resolve method, which accepts at least two string_view arguments: the hostname and the service. You can provide either a keyword or a port number for service (refer to Table 20-1 for some example keywords). The resolve method returns a range of boost::asio::ip::tcp::resolver::basic_resolver_entry objects, which expose several useful methods:

- endpoint gets the IP address and port.
- host_name gets the hostname.
- service_name gets the name of the service associated with this port.

If the resolution fails, resolve throws a boost::system::system_error. Alternatively, you can pass a boost::system::error_code reference, which receives the error in lieu of throwing an exception. For example, Listing 20-2 determines the IP address and port for the No Starch Press web server using Boost Asio.

```
#include <iostream>
#include <boost/asio.hpp>

int main() {
  boost::asio::io_context io_context; ❶
  boost::asio::ip::tcp::resolver resolver{ io_context }; ❷
  boost::system::error_code ec;
  for(auto&& result : resolver.resolve("www.nostarch.com", "http", ec)) { ❸
    std::cout << result.service_name() << " " ❹
              << result.host_name() << " " ❺
              << result.endpoint() ❻
              << std::endl;
  }
  if(ec) std::cout << "Error code: " << ec << std::endl; ❼
}
```

```
http www.nostarch.com 104.20.209.3:80
http www.nostarch.com 104.20.208.3:80
```

Listing 20-2: Blocking hostname resolution with Boost Asio

NOTE *Your results might vary depending on where the No Starch Press web servers reside in IP space.*

You initialize an io_context ❶ and a boost::asio::ip::tcp::resolver ❷. Within a range-based for loop, you iterate over each result ❸ and extract the service_name ❹, the host_name ❺, and the endpoint ❻. If resolve encounters an error, you print it to stdout ❼.

You can perform asynchronous hostname resolution using the async_resolve method. As with resolve, you pass a hostname and a service as the first two arguments. Additionally, you provide a callback function object that accepts two arguments: a system_error_code and a range of basic_resolver_entry objects. Listing 20-3 illustrates how to refactor Listing 20-2 to use asynchronous hostname resolution instead.

```
#include <iostream>
#include <boost/asio.hpp>

int main() {
  boost::asio::io_context io_context;
  boost::asio::ip::tcp::resolver resolver{ io_context };
  resolver.async_resolve("www.nostarch.com", "http", ❶
    [](boost::system::error_code ec, const auto& results) { ❷
      if (ec) { ❸
        std::cerr << "Error:" << ec << std::endl;
        return; ❹
      }
      for (auto&& result : results) { ❺
        std::cout << result.service_name() << " "
                  << result.host_name() << " "
                  << result.endpoint() << " "
                  << std::endl; ❻
      }
    }
  );
  io_context.run(); ❼
}
```

```
http www.nostarch.com 104.20.209.3:80
http www.nostarch.com 104.20.208.3:80
```

Listing 20-3: Refactoring Listing 20-2 to use async_resolve

The setup is identical to Listing 20-2 until you invoke async_resolve on your resolver ❶. You pass the same hostname and service as before, but you add a callback argument that accepts the obligatory parameters ❷. Within the body of the callback lambda, you check for an error condition ❸. If one exists, you print a friendly error message and return ❹. In the error-free case, you iterate over the results as before ❺, printing the service_name, host_name, and endpoint ❻. As with the timer, you need to invoke run on the io_context to give the asynchronous operations the opportunity to complete ❼.

Connecting

Once you've obtained a range of endpoints either through hostname resolution or through constructing one on your own, you're ready to make a connection.

First, you'll need a boost::asio::ip::tcp::socket, a class that abstracts the underlying operating system's socket and presents it for use in Asio. The socket takes an io_context as an argument.

Second, you'll need to make a call to the boost::asio::connect function, which accepts a socket representing the endpoint you want to connect with as its first argument and an endpoint range as its second argument. You can provide an error_code reference as an optional third argument; otherwise, connect will throw a system_error exception if an error occurs. If successful, connect returns a single endpoint, the endpoint in the input range to which it successfully connected. After this point, the socket object represents a real socket in your system's environment.

Listing 20-4 illustrates how to connect to No Starch Press's web server.

```
#include <iostream>
#include <boost/asio.hpp>

int main() {
  boost::asio::io_context io_context;
  boost::asio::ip::tcp::resolver resolver{ io_context }; ❶
  boost::asio::ip::tcp::socket socket{ io_context }; ❷
  try  {
    auto endpoints = resolver.resolve("www.nostarch.com", "http"); ❸
    const auto connected_endpoint = boost::asio::connect(socket, endpoints); ❹
    std::cout << connected_endpoint; ❺
  } catch(boost::system::system_error& se) {
    std::cerr << "Error: " << se.what() << std::endl; ❻
  }
}
--------------------------------------------------------------------------------
104.20.209.3:80 ❺
```

Listing 20-4: Connecting to the No Starch web server

You construct a resolver ❶ as in Listing 20-3. In addition, you initialize a socket with the same io_context ❷. Next, you invoke the resolve method to obtain every endpoint associated with *www.nostarch.com* at port 80 ❸. Recall that each endpoint is an IP address and a port corresponding to the host you resolved. In this case, resolve used the domain name system to determine that *www.nostarch.com* at port 80 resides at the IP address 104.20.209.3. You then invoke connect using your socket and endpoints ❹, which returns the endpoint to which connect successfully connected ❺. In the event of an error, resolve or connect would throw an exception, which you would catch and print to stderr ❻.

You can also connect asynchronously with boost::asio::async_connect, which accepts the same two arguments as connect: a socket and an endpoint range. The third argument is a function object acting as the callback, which must accept an error_code as its first argument and an endpoint as its second argument. Listing 20-5 illustrates how to connect asynchronously.

```
#include <iostream>
#include <boost/asio.hpp>

int main() {
  boost::asio::io_context io_context;
```

```
  boost::asio::ip::tcp::resolver resolver{ io_context };
  boost::asio::ip::tcp::socket socket{ io_context };
  boost::asio::async_connect(socket, ❶
    resolver.resolve("www.nostarch.com", "http"), ❷
    [] (boost::system::error_code ec, const auto& endpoint){ ❸
      std::cout << endpoint; ❹
  });
  io_context.run(); ❺
}
```

```
104.20.209.3:80 ❹
```

Listing 20-5: Connecting to the No Starch web server asynchronously

The setup is exactly as in Listing 20-4 except you replace `connect` with `async_connect` and pass the same first ❶ and second ❷ arguments. The third argument is your callback function object ❸ inside of which you print the endpoint to stdout ❹. As with all asynchronous Asio programs, you make a call to `run` on your `io_context` ❺.

Buffers

Boost Asio provides several buffer classes. A *buffer* (or *data buffer*) is memory that stores transient data. The Boost Asio buffer classes form the interface for all I/O operations. Before you can do anything with the network connections you make, you'll need an interface for reading and writing data. For this, you'll need just three buffer types:

- `boost::asio::const_buffer` holds a buffer that cannot be modified once you've constructed it.
- `boost::asio::mutable_buffer` holds a buffer that can be modified after construction.
- `boost::asio::streambuf` holds an automatically resizable buffer based on `std::streambuf`.

All three buffer classes provide two important methods for accessing their underlying data: `data` and `size`.

The `mutable_buffer` and `const_buffer` classes' `data` methods return a pointer to the first element in the underlying data sequence, and their `size` methods return the number of elements in that sequence. The elements are contiguous. Both buffers provide default constructors, which initialize an empty buffer, as Listing 20-6 illustrates.

```
#include <boost/asio.hpp>

TEST_CASE("const_buffer default constructor") {
  boost::asio::const_buffer cb; ❶
  REQUIRE(cb.size() == 0); ❷
}

TEST_CASE("mutable_buffer default constructor") {
```

```
  boost::asio::mutable_buffer mb; ❸
  REQUIRE(mb.size() == 0); ❹
}
```

Listing 20-6: Default constructing `const_buffer` *and* `mutable_buffer` *yields empty buffers.*

Using the default constructors ❶❸, you build empty buffers that have zero `size` ❷❹.

Both `mutable_buffer` and `const_buffer` provide constructors that accept a `void*` and a `size_t` corresponding to the data you want to wrap. Note that these constructors don't take ownership of the pointed-to memory, so *you must ensure that the storage duration of that memory is at least as long as the lifetime of the buffer you're constructing.* This is a design decision that gives you, as the Boost Asio user, maximum flexibility. Unfortunately, it also leads to potentially nasty errors. Failure to properly manage the lifetimes of buffers and the objects they point to will result in undefined behavior.

Listing 20-7 illustrates how to construct buffers using the pointer-based constructor.

```
#include <boost/asio.hpp>
#include <string>

TEST_CASE("const_buffer constructor") {
  boost::asio::const_buffer cb{ "Blessed are the cheesemakers.", 7 }; ❶

  REQUIRE(cb.size() == 7); ❷
  REQUIRE(*static_cast<const char*>(cb.data()) == 'B'); ❸
}

TEST_CASE("mutable_buffer constructor") {
  std::string proposition{ "Charity for an ex-leper?" };
  boost::asio::mutable_buffer mb{ proposition.data(), proposition.size() }; ❹

  REQUIRE(mb.data() == proposition.data()); ❺
  REQUIRE(mb.size() == proposition.size()); ❻
}
```

Listing 20-7: Constructing a `const_buffer` *and a* `mutable_buffer` *using the pointer-based constructor*

In the first test, you construct a `const_buffer` using a C-style string and a fixed length of `7` ❶. This fixed length is smaller than the length of the string literal `Blessed are the cheesemakers.`, so this buffer refers to `Blessed` rather than the entire string. This illustrates that you can select a subset of an array (just as with `std::string_view`, which you learned about in "String View" on page 500). The resulting buffer has size `7` ❷, and if you cast the pointer from `data` to a `const char*`, you'll see that it points to the character `B` from your C-style string ❸.

In the second test, you construct a `mutable_buffer` using a `string` by invoking its `data` and `size` members within the buffer's constructor ❹. The resulting buffer's data ❺ and size ❻ methods return identical data to your original string.

The boost::asio::streambuf class accepts two optional constructor arguments: a size_t maximum size and an allocator. By default, the maximum size is std::numeric_limits<std::size_t> and the allocator is similar to the default allocator for stdlib containers. The streambuf input sequence's initial size is always zero, which Listing 20-8 illustrates.

```
#include <boost/asio.hpp>

TEST_CASE("streambuf constructor") {
  boost::asio::streambuf sb; ❶
  REQUIRE(sb.size() == 0); ❷
}
```

Listing 20-8: Default constructing a streambuf

You default construct a streambuf ❶, and when you invoke its size method, it returns 0 ❷.

You can pass a pointer to a streambuf into a std::istream or std::ostream constructor. Recall from "Stream Classes" on page 524 that these are specializations of basic_istream and basic_ostream that expose stream operations to an underlying sync or source. Listing 20-9 illustrates how to write into and subsequently read from a streambuf using these classes.

```
TEST_CASE("streambuf input/output") {
  boost::asio::streambuf sb; ❶
  std::ostream os{ &sb }; ❷
  os << "Welease Wodger!"; ❸

  std::istream is{ &sb }; ❹
  std::string command; ❺
  is >> command; ❻

  REQUIRE(command == "Welease"); ❼
}
```

Listing 20-9: Writing to and reading from a streambuf

You again construct an empty streambuf ❶, and you pass its address into the constructor of an ostream ❷. You then write the string Welease Wodger! into the ostream, which in turn writes the string into the underlying streambuf ❸.

Next, you create an istream again using the address of the streambuf ❹. You then create a string ❺ and write the istream into the string ❻. Recall from "Special Formatting for Fundamental Types" on page 529 that this operation will skip any leading whitespace and then read the following string until the next whitespace. This yields the first word of the string, Welease ❼.

Boost Asio also offers the convenience function template `boost::asio::buffer`, which accepts a `std::array` or `std::vector` of POD elements or a `std::string`. For example, you can create the `std::string` backed `mutable_buffer` in Listing 20-7 using the following construction instead:

```
std::string proposition{ "Charity for an ex-leper?" };
auto mb = boost::asio::buffer(proposition);
```

The `buffer` template is specialized so if you provide a `const` argument, it will return a `const_buffer` instead. In other words, to make a `const_buffer` out of `proposition`, simply make it `const`:

```
const std::string proposition{ "Charity for an ex-leper?" };
auto cb = boost::asio::buffer(proposition);
```

You've now created a `const_buffer cb`.

Additionally, you can create a dynamic buffer, which is a dynamically resizable buffer backed by a `std::string` or a `std::vector`. You can create one by using the `boost::asio::dynamic_buffer` function template, which accepts either a `string` or a `vector` and returns a `boost::asio::dynamic_string_buffer` or `boost::asio::dynamic_vector_buffer` as appropriate. For example, you can make a dynamic buffer using the following construction:

```
std::string proposition{ "Charity for an ex-leper?" };
auto db = boost::asio::dynamic_buffer(proposition);
```

Although a dynamic buffer is dynamically resizable, recall that the `vector` and `string` classes use an allocator and that allocation can be a relatively slow operation. So, if you know how much data you'll write into a buffer, you might have better performance using a non-dynamic buffer. As always, measuring and experimenting will help you decide which approach to take.

Reading and Writing Data with Buffers

With your new knowledge of how to store and retrieve data using buffers, you can learn how to pull data off a socket. You can read data from active `socket` objects into buffer objects using built-in Boost Asio functions. For blocking reads, Boost Asio offers three functions:

- `boost::asio::read` attempts to read a fixed-size data chunk.
- `boost::asio::read_at` attempts to read a fixed-size data chunk beginning at an offset.
- `boost::asio::read_until` attempts to read until a delimiter, regular expression, or arbitrary predicate matches.

All three methods take a socket as their first argument and a buffer object as their second argument. The remaining arguments are optional and depend on which function you're using:

- A *completion condition* is a function object that accepts an error_code and a size_t argument. The error_code will be set if the Asio function encountered an error, and the size_t argument corresponds with the number of bytes transferred so far. The function object returns a size_t corresponding to the number of bytes remaining to be transferred, and it returns 0 if the operation is complete.
- A *match condition* is a function object that accepts a range specified by a begin and end iterator. It must return a std::pair, where the first element is an iterator indicating the starting point for the next attempt at matching and the second element is a bool representing whether the range contains a match.
- boost::system::error_code reference, which the function will set if it encounters an error condition.

Table 20-2 lists many of the ways you can invoke one of the read functions.

Table 20-2: Arguments for read, read_at, and read_until

Invocation	Description
read(**s**, **b**, [**cmp**], [**ec**])	Reads a certain amount of data from socket **s** into a mutable buffer **b** according to completion condition **cmp**. Sets the error_code **ec** if an error condition is encountered; otherwise, throws a system_error.
read_at(**s**, **off**, **b**, [**cmp**], [**ec**])	Reads a certain amount of data starting from socket **s**, starting from size_t offset **off**, into a mutable buffer **b** according to completion condition **cmp**. Sets the error_code **ec** if an error condition is encountered; otherwise, throws a system_error.
read_until(**s**, **b**, **x**, [**ec**])	Reads data from socket **s** into a mutable buffer **b** until it meets a condition represented by **x**, which can be one of the following: a char, a string_view, a boost::regex, or a match condition. Sets the error_code **ec** if an error condition is encountered; otherwise, throws a system_error.

You can also write data to an active socket object from a buffer. For blocking writes, Boost Asio offers two functions:

- boost::asio::write attempts to write a fixed-size data chunk.
- boost::asio::write_at attempts to write a fixed-size data chunk beginning at an offset.

Table 20-3 shows how to invoke these two methods. Their arguments are analogous to those for the reading methods.

Table 20-3: Arguments for `write` and `write_at`

Invocation	Description
`write(s, b, [cmp], [ec])`	Writes a certain amount of data into socket **s** from a const buffer **b** according to completion condition **cmp**. Sets the `error_code` **ec** if an error condition is encountered; otherwise, throws a `system_error`.
`write_at(s, off, b, [cmp], [ec])`	Writes a certain amount of data from const buffer **b**, starting from `size_t` offset **off**, into socket **s** according to completion condition **cmp**. Sets the `error_code` **ec** if an error condition is encountered; otherwise, throws a `system_error`.

NOTE *There are* many *permutations for invoking the read and write functions. Be sure to read the documentation carefully when you incorporate Boost Asio into your code.*

The Hypertext Transfer Protocol (HTTP)

HTTP is the 30-year-old protocol undergirding the web. Although it's a very complicated protocol to use to introduce networking, its ubiquity makes it one of the most relevant choices. In the next section, you'll use Boost Asio to make very simple HTTP requests. It's not strictly necessary that you have a solid foundation in HTTP, so you can skip this section on first reading. However, the information here adds some color to the examples in the next section and provides references for further study.

HTTP sessions have two parties: a client and a server. An HTTP client sends a plaintext request over TCP containing one or more lines separated by a carriage return and a line feed (a "CR-LF newline").

The first line is the request line, which contains three tokens: an HTTP method, a uniform resource locator (URL), and the HTTP version of the request. For example, if a client wants a file called *index.htm*, the status line might be *GET /index.htm HTTP/1.1*.

Directly following the request line are one or more *headers*, which define the parameters of an HTTP transaction. Each header contains a key and a value. The key must be composed of alphanumeric characters and dashes. A colon plus a space delimits the key from the value. A CR-LF newline terminates the header. The following headers are especially common in requests:

- `Host` specifies the domain of the service requested. Optionally, you can include a port. For example, `Host: www.google.com` specifies *www.google.com* as the host for the requested service.
- `Accept` specifies the acceptable media types in MIME format for the response. For example, `Accept: text/plain` specifies that the requester can process plaintext.

- `Accept-Language` specifies the acceptable human languages for the response. For example, `Accept-Language: en-US` specifies that the requester can process American English.
- `Accept-Encoding` specifies the acceptable encodings for the response. For example, `Accept-Encoding: identity` specifies that the requester can process contents without any encoding.
- `Connection` specifies control options for the current connection. For example, `Connection: close` specifies that the connection will be closed after completion of the response.

You terminate the headers with an additional CR-LF newline. For certain kinds of HTTP requests, you'll also include a body following the headers. If you do, you'll also include `Content-Length` and `Content-Type` headers. The `Content-Length` value specifies the length of the request body in bytes, and the `Content-Type` value specifies the MIME format of the body.

An HTTP response's first line is the *status line*, which includes the HTTP version of the response, a status code, and a reason message. For example, the status line `HTTP/1.1 200 OK` indicates a successful ("OK") request. Status codes are always three digits. The leading digit indicates the status group of the code:

1 (Informational)** The request was received.

2 (Successful)** The request was received and accepted.

3 (Redirection)** Further action is required.

4 (Client Error)** The request was bad.

5 (Server Error)** The request seems okay, but the server encountered an internal error.

After the status line, the response contains any number of headers in the same format as the response. Many of the same request headers are also common response headers. For example, if the HTTP response contains a body, the response headers will include `Content-Length` and `Content-Type`.

If you need to program HTTP applications, you should absolutely refer to the Boost Beast library, which provides high-performance, low-level HTTP and WebSockets facilities. It's built atop Asio and works seamlessly with it.

NOTE *For an excellent treatment of HTTP and its tenant security issues, refer to* The Tangled Web: A Guide to Securing Modern Web Applications *by Michal Zalewski. For all the gory details, refer to the Internet Engineering Task Force's RFCs 7230, 7231, 7232, 7233, 7234, and 7235.*

Implementing a Simple Boost Asio HTTP Client

In this section, you'll implement a (very) simple HTTP client. You'll build an HTTP request, resolve an endpoint, connect to a web server, write the request, and read the response. Listing 20-10 illustrates one possible implementation.

```
#include <boost/asio.hpp>
#include <iostream>
#include <istream>
#include <ostream>
#include <string>

std::string request(std::string host, boost::asio::io_context& io_context) { ❶
  std::stringstream request_stream;
  request_stream << "GET / HTTP/1.1\r\n"
                    "Host: " << host << "\r\n"
                    "Accept: text/html\r\n"
                    "Accept-Language: en-us\r\n"
                    "Accept-Encoding: identity\r\n"
                    "Connection: close\r\n\r\n";
  const auto request = request_stream.str(); ❷
  boost::asio::ip::tcp::resolver resolver{ io_context };
  const auto endpoints = resolver.resolve(host, "http"); ❸
  boost::asio::ip::tcp::socket socket{ io_context };
  const auto connected_endpoint = boost::asio::connect(socket, endpoints); ❹
  boost::asio::write(socket, boost::asio::buffer(request)); ❺
  std::string response;
  boost::system::error_code ec;
  boost::asio::read(socket, boost::asio::dynamic_buffer(response), ec); ❻
  if (ec && ec.value() != 2) throw boost::system::system_error{ ec }; ❼
  return response;
}

int main() {
  boost::asio::io_context io_context;
  try  {
    const auto response = request("www.arcyber.army.mil", io_context); ❽
    std::cout << response << "\n"; ❾
  } catch(boost::system::system_error& se) {
    std::cerr << "Error: " << se.what() << std::endl;
  }
}
--------------------------------------------------------------------------
HTTP/1.1 200 OK
Pragma: no-cache
Content-Type: text/html; charset=utf-8
X-UA-Compatible: IE=edge
pw_value: 3ce3af822980b849665e8c5400e1b45b
Access-Control-Allow-Origin: *
X-Powered-By:
Server:
X-ASPNET-VERSION:
X-FRAME-OPTIONS: SAMEORIGIN
Content-Length: 76199
Cache-Control: private, no-cache
Expires: Mon, 22 Oct 2018 14:21:09 GMT
Date: Mon, 22 Oct 2018 14:21:09 GMT
Connection: close
```

```
<!DOCTYPE html>
<html  lang="en-US">
<head id="Head">
--snip--
</body>
</html>
```

Listing 20-10: Completing a simple request to the United States Army Cyber Command web server

You first define a request function, which accepts a host and an io_context and returns an HTTP response ❶. First, you use a std::stringstream to build a std::string containing an HTTP request ❷. Next, you resolve the host using a boost::asio::ip::tcp::resolver ❸ and connect a boost::asio::ip::tcp::socket to the resulting endpoint range ❹. (This matches the approach in Listing 20-4.)

Then you write your HTTP request to the server you've connected to. You use boost::asio::write, passing in your connected socket and your request. Because write accepts Asio buffers, you use boost::asio::buffer to create a mutable_buffer from your request (which is a std::string) ❺.

Next, you read the HTTP response from the server. Because you don't know the length of the response in advance, you create a std::string called response to receive the response. Eventually, you'll use this to back a dynamic buffer. For simplicity, the HTTP request contains a Connection: close header that causes the server to terminate the connection immediately after it sends its response. This will result in Asio returning an "end of file" error code (value 2). Because you expect this behavior, you declare a boost::system::error_code to receive this error.

Next, you invoke boost::asio::read with the connected socket, a dynamic buffer that will receive the response, and the error_condition ❻. You use boost::asio_dynamic_buffer to construct your dynamic buffer from response. Immediately after read returns, you check for an error_condition other than end of file (which you throw) ❼. Otherwise, you return the response.

Within main, you invoke your request function with the www.arcyber.army.mil host and an io_context object ❽. Finally, you print the response to stdout ❾.

Asynchronous Reading and Writing

You can also read and write asynchronously with Boost Asio. The corresponding asynchronous functions are analogous to their blocking corollaries. For asynchronous reads, Boost Asio offers three functions:

- boost::asio::async_read attempts to read a fixed-size data chunk.
- boost::asio::async_read_at attempts to read a fixed-size data chunk beginning at an offset.
- boost::asio::async_read_until attempts to read until a delimiter, regular expression, or arbitrary predicate matches.

Boost Asio also offers two asynchronous write functions:

- `boost::asio::async_write` attempts to write a fixed-size data chunk.
- `boost::asio::async_write_at` attempts to write a fixed-size data chunk beginning at an offset.

All five of these asynchronous functions accept the same arguments as their blocking counterparts, except their final argument is always a callback function object that accepts two arguments: a `boost::system::error_code` indicating whether the function met an error and a `size_t` indicating the number of bytes it transferred. For the asynchronous `write` functions, you need to determine whether Asio wrote the entire payload. Because these calls are asynchronous, your thread doesn't block while it's waiting for I/O to complete. Instead, the operating system calls your thread back whenever a portion of your I/O request completes.

Because the callback's second argument is a `size_t` corresponding to the number of transferred bytes, you can do the arithmetic to figure out whether you have anything left to write. If there is, you must invoke another asynchronous write function by passing the remaining data.

Listing 20-11 contains an asynchronous version of the simple web client in Listing 20-10. Note that using the asynchronous functions is a bit more complicated. But there's a pattern with callbacks and handlers that's consistent across the request's lifetime.

```
#include <boost/asio.hpp>
#include <iostream>
#include <string>
#include <sstream>

using ResolveResult = boost::asio::ip::tcp::resolver::results_type;
using Endpoint = boost::asio::ip::tcp::endpoint;

struct Request {
  explicit Request(boost::asio::io_context& io_context, std::string host)
      : resolver{ io_context },
        socket{ io_context },
        host{ std::move(host) } { ❶
    std::stringstream request_stream;
    request_stream << "GET / HTTP/1.1\r\n"
                      "Host: " << this->host << "\r\n"
                      "Accept: text/plain\r\n"
                      "Accept-Language: en-us\r\n"
                      "Accept-Encoding: identity\r\n"
                      "Connection: close\r\n"
                      "User-Agent: C++ Crash Course Client\r\n\r\n";
    request = request_stream.str(); ❷
    resolver.async_resolve(this->host, "http",
       [this] (boost::system::error_code ec, const ResolveResult& results) {
         resolution_handler(ec, results); ❸
       });
  }
```

```
  void resolution_handler(boost::system::error_code ec,
                          const ResolveResult& results) {
    if (ec) { ❹
      std::cerr << "Error resolving " << host << ": " << ec << std::endl;
      return;
    }
    boost::asio::async_connect(socket, results,
            [this] (boost::system::error_code ec, const Endpoint& endpoint){
              connection_handler(ec, endpoint); ❺
            });
  }

  void connection_handler(boost::system::error_code ec,
                          const Endpoint& endpoint) { ❻
    if (ec) {
      std::cerr << "Error connecting to " << host << ": "
                << ec.message() << std::endl;
      return;
    }
    boost::asio::async_write(socket, boost::asio::buffer(request),
            [this] (boost::system::error_code ec, size_t transferred){
              write_handler(ec, transferred);
            });
  }

  void write_handler(boost::system::error_code ec, size_t transferred) { ❼
    if (ec) {
      std::cerr << "Error writing to " << host << ": " << ec.message()
                << std::endl;
    } else if (request.size() != transferred) {
      request.erase(0, transferred);
      boost::asio::async_write(socket, boost::asio::buffer(request),
                               [this] (boost::system::error_code ec,
                                       size_t transferred){
                                 write_handler(ec, transferred);
                               });
    } else {
      boost::asio::async_read(socket, boost::asio::dynamic_buffer(response),
                              [this] (boost::system::error_code ec,
                                      size_t transferred){
                                read_handler(ec, transferred);
                              });
    }
  }

  void read_handler(boost::system::error_code ec, size_t transferred) { ❽
    if (ec && ec.value() != 2)
      std::cerr << "Error reading from " << host << ": "
                << ec.message() << std::endl;
  }

  const std::string& get_response() const noexcept {
    return response;
  }
private:
```

```
  boost::asio::ip::tcp::resolver resolver;
  boost::asio::ip::tcp::socket socket;
  std::string request, response;
  const std::string host;
};

int main() {
  boost::asio::io_context io_context;
  Request request{ io_context, "www.arcyber.army.mil" }; ❾
  io_context.run(); ❿
  std::cout << request.get_response();
}
--------------------------------------------------------------------------
HTTP/1.1 200 OK
Pragma: no-cache
Content-Type: text/html; charset=utf-8
X-UA-Compatible: IE=edge
pw_value: 3ce3af822980b849665e8c5400e1b45b
Access-Control-Allow-Origin: *
X-Powered-By:
Server:
X-ASPNET-VERSION:
X-FRAME-OPTIONS: SAMEORIGIN
Content-Length: 76199
Cache-Control: private, no-cache
Expires: Mon, 22 Oct 2018 14:21:09 GMT
Date: Mon, 22 Oct 2018 14:21:09 GMT
Connection: close

<!DOCTYPE html>
<html  lang="en-US">
<head id="Head">
--snip--
</body>
</html>
```

Listing 20-11: An asynchronous refactor of Listing 20-9

You first declare a `Request` class that will handle a web request. It has a single constructor that takes an `io_context` and a `string` containing the host you want to connect with ❶. Just as in Listing 20-9, you create an HTTP GET request using a `std::stringstream` and save the resulting `string` into the `request` field ❷. Next, you use `async_resolve` to request the endpoints corresponding to the requested `host`. Within the callback, you invoke the `resolution_handler` method on the current `Request` ❸.

The `resolution_handler` receives the callback from `async_resolve`. It first checks for an error condition, printing to stderr and returning if it finds one ❹. If `async_resolve` didn't pass an error, `resolution_handler` invokes `async_connect` using the endpoints contained in its `results` variable. It also passes the `socket` field of the current `Request`, which will store the connection that `async_connect` is about to create. Finally, it passes a connection callback as the third parameter. Within the callback, you invoke the `connection_handler` method of the current request ❺.

The connection_handler ❻ follows a similar pattern to the resolution_handler method. It checks for an error condition, and if one exists, it prints to stderr and returns; otherwise, it proceeds to process the request by invoking async_write, which takes three parameters: the active socket, a mutable buffer-wrapping request, and a callback function. The callback function, in turn, invokes the write_handler method on the current request.

Are you seeing a pattern here in these handler functions? The write_handler ❼ checks for an error and proceeds to determine whether the entire request has been sent. If it hasn't, you still need to write some of the request, so you adjust the request accordingly and invoke async_write again. If async_write has written the entire request into socket, it's time to read the response. For this, you invoke async_read using your socket, a dynamic buffer wrapping the response field, and a callback function that invokes the read_handler method on the current request.

The read_handler ❽ first checks for an error. Because your request used the Connection: close header, you expect an end-of-file error (value 2) as in Listing 20-10 and so ignore it. If it encounters a different kind of error, you print it to stderr and return. Your request is complete at this point. (Phew.)

Within main, you declare your io_context and initialize a Request to *www.arcyber.army.mil* ❾. Because you're using asynchronous functions, you invoke the run method on io_context ❿. After io_context returns, you know that no asynchronous operations are pending, so you print the contents of the response on your Request object to stdout.

Serving

Building a server atop Boost Asio is essentially similar to building a client. To accept TCP connections, you use the boost::asio::ip::tcp::acceptor class, which takes a boost::asio::io_context object as its only constructor argument.

To accept a TCP connection using a blocking approach, you use the acceptor object's accept method, which takes a boost::asio::ip::tcp::socket reference, which will hold the client's socket, and an optional boost::error_code reference, which will hold any error conditions that arise. If you don't provide a boost::error_code and an error arises, accept will throw a boost::system_error instead. Once accept returns without error, you can use the socket you passed in to read and write with the same read and write methods you used with the client in the previous sections.

For example, Listing 20-12 illustrates how to build an echo server that receives a message and sends it back uppercased to the client.

```
#include <iostream>
#include <string>
#include <boost/asio.hpp>
#include <boost/algorithm/string/case_conv.hpp>

using namespace boost::asio;

void handle(ip::tcp::socket& socket) { ❶
  boost::system::error_code ec;
  std::string message;
```

```
  do {
    boost::asio::read_until(socket, dynamic_buffer(message), "\n"); ❷
    boost::algorithm::to_upper(message); ❸
    boost::asio::write(socket, buffer(message), ec); ❹
    if (message == "\n") return; ❺
    message.clear();
  } while(!ec); ❻
}

int main()  {
  try {
    io_context io_context;
    ip::tcp::acceptor acceptor{ io_context,
                              ip::tcp::endpoint(ip::tcp::v4(), 1895) }; ❼
    while (true) {
      ip::tcp::socket socket{ io_context };
      acceptor.accept(socket); ❽
      handle(socket); ❾
    }
  } catch (std::exception& e) {
    std::cerr << e.what() << std::endl;
  }
}
```

Listing 20-12: An uppercasing echo server

You declare the `handle` function that accepts a `socket` reference corresponding to a client and handles messages from it ❶. Within a `do-while` loop, you read a line of text from the client into a `string` called `message` ❷, you convert it to uppercase using the `to_upper` function illustrated in Listing 15-31 ❸, and write it back to the client ❹. If the client sent a blank line, you exit from `handle` ❺; otherwise, you clear the contents of the message and loop if no error condition occurred ❻.

Within `main`, you initialize an `io_context` and an `acceptor` so that the program binds to the `localhost:1895` socket ❼. Within an infinite loop, you create a `socket` and call `accept` on the `acceptor` ❽. As long as this doesn't throw an exception, the `socket` will represent a new client, and you can pass this `socket` to `handle` to service the request ❾.

NOTE *In Listing 20-12, the choice was to listen on port 1895. This choice is technically immaterial, as long as no other program running on your computer is currently using that port. However, there are guidelines about how to decide which port your program will listen on. IANA maintains a list of registered ports at* https://www.iana.org/assignments/service-names-port-numbers/service-names-port-numbers.txt *that you might want to avoid. Additionally, modern operating systems typically require that a program have elevated privileges to bind to a port with a value of 1023 or below, a* system port. *The ports 1024 to 49151 don't typically require elevated privileges and are called* user ports. *The ports 49152 to 65535 are the* dynamic/private ports, *which are generally safe to use because they won't be registered with IANA.*

To interact with the server in Listing 20-12, you can use *GNU Netcat*, a network utility that allows you to create inbound and outbound TCP and UDP connections and then read and write data. If you're using a Unix-like system, you probably have it installed. If you don't, see *https://nmap.org/ncat/*. Listing 20-13 shows a sample session that connects to the uppercasing echo server.

```
$ ncat localhost 1895 ❶
The 300 ❷
THE 300
This is Blasphemy! ❷
THIS IS BLASPHEMY!
This is madness! ❷
THIS IS MADNESS!
Madness...? ❷
MADNESS...?
This is Sparta! ❷
THIS IS SPARTA!
❸
Ncat: Broken pipe. ❹
```

Listing 20-13: Interacting with the uppercasing echo server using Netcat

Netcat (`ncat`) takes two arguments: a host and a port ❶. Once you've invoked the program, each line you enter results in an uppercased result from the server. When you type text into stdin, Netcat sends it to the server ❷, which responds in uppercase. Once you send it an empty line ❸, the server terminates the socket and you get a `Broken pipe` ❹.

To accept connections using an asynchronous approach, you use the `async_accept` method on the `acceptor`, which takes a single argument: a callback object that accepts an `error_code` and a `socket`. If an error occurs, the `error_code` contains an error condition; otherwise, the `socket` represents the successfully connected client. From there, you can use the socket in the same way you did in the blocking approach.

A common pattern for asynchronous, connection-oriented servers is to use the `std::enable_shared_from_this` template discussed in "Advanced Patterns" on page 362. The idea is to create a shared pointer to a session object for each connection. When you register callbacks for reading and writing within the session object, you capture a shared pointer "from `this`" within the callback object so that while I/O is pending, the session stays alive. Once no I/O is pending, the session object dies along with all the shared pointers. Listing 20-14 illustrates how to reimplement the uppercasing echo server using asynchronous I/O.

```
#include <iostream>
#include <string>
#include <boost/asio.hpp>
#include <boost/algorithm/string/case_conv.hpp>
#include <memory>
```

```
using namespace boost::asio;

struct Session : std::enable_shared_from_this<Session> {
  explicit Session(ip::tcp::socket socket) : socket{ std::move(socket) } { } ❶
  void read() {
    async_read_until(socket, dynamic_buffer(message), '\n', ❷
            [self=shared_from_this()] (boost::system::error_code ec,
                                       std::size_t length) {
              if (ec || self->message == "\n") return; ❸
              boost::algorithm::to_upper(self->message);
              self->write();
            });
  }
  void write() {
    async_write(socket, buffer(message), ❹
                [self=shared_from_this()] (boost::system::error_code ec,
                                           std::size_t length) {
                  if (ec) return; ❺
                  self->message.clear();
                  self->read();
                });
  }
private:
  ip::tcp::socket socket;
  std::string message;
};

void serve(ip::tcp::acceptor& acceptor) {
  acceptor.async_accept([&acceptor](boost::system::error_code ec, ❻
                                    ip::tcp::socket socket) {
    serve(acceptor); ❼
    if (ec) return;
    auto session = std::make_shared<Session>(std::move(socket)); ❽
    session->read();
  });
}

int main()  {
  try {
    io_context io_context;
    ip::tcp::acceptor acceptor{ io_context,
                                ip::tcp::endpoint(ip::tcp::v4(), 1895) };
    serve(acceptor);
    io_context.run(); ❾
  } catch (std::exception& e) {
    std::cerr << e.what() << std::endl;
  }
}
```

Listing 20-14: An asynchronous version of Listing 20-12

You first define a `Session` class to manage connections. Within the constructor, you take ownership of the `socket` corresponding to the connecting client and store it as a member ❶.

Next, you declare a read method that invokes async_read_until on the socket so it reads into a dynamic_buffer wrapping the message member string up to the next newline character \n ❷. The callback object captures this as a shared_ptr using the shared_from_this method. When invoked, the function checks for either an error condition or an empty line, in which case it returns ❸. Otherwise, the callback converts message to uppercase and invokes the write method.

The write method follows a similar pattern as the read method. It invokes async_read, passing the socket, the message (now uppercase), and a callback function ❹. Within the callback function, you check for an error condition and return immediately if one exists ❺. Otherwise, you know that Asio successfully sent your uppercased message to the client, so you invoke clear on it to prepare for the next message from the client. Then you invoke the read method, which starts the process over.

Next, you define a serve function that accepts an acceptor object. Within the function, you invoke async_accept on the acceptor object and pass a callback function to handle connections ❻. The callback function first invokes serve again using the acceptor so your program can handle new connections immediately ❼. This is the secret sauce that makes the asynchronous handling so powerful on the server side: you can handle many connections at once because the running thread doesn't need to service one client before handling another. Next, you check for an error condition and exit if one exists; otherwise, you create a shared_ptr owning a new Session object ❽. This Session object will own the socket that the acceptor just set up for you. You invoke the read method on the new Session object, which creates a second reference within the shared_ptr thanks to the shared_from_this capture. Now you're all set! Once the read and write cycle ends due to an empty line from the client or some error condition, the shared_ptr reference will go to zero and the Session object will destruct.

Finally, within main you construct an io_context and an acceptor as in Listing 20-12. You then pass the acceptor to your serve function to begin the service loop and invoke run on the io_context to start servicing asynchronous operations ❾.

Multithreading Boost Asio

To make your Boost Asio program multithreaded, you can simply spawn tasks that invoke run on your io_context object. Of course, this doesn't make your program safe, and all the admonitions in "Sharing and Coordinating" on page 647 are in full effect. Listing 20-15 illustrates how to multithread your server from Listing 20-14.

```
#include <iostream>
#include <string>
#include <boost/asio.hpp>
#include <boost/algorithm/string/case_conv.hpp>
#include <memory>
#include <future>
```

```
struct Session : std::enable_shared_from_this<Session> {
--snip--
};

void serve(ip::tcp::acceptor& acceptor) {
--snip--
}

int main() {
  const int n_threads{ 4 };
  boost::asio::io_context io_context{ n_threads };
  ip::tcp::acceptor acceptor{ io_context,
                              ip::tcp::endpoint(ip::tcp::v4(), 1895) }; ❶
  serve(acceptor); ❷

  std::vector<std::future<void>> futures;
  std::generate_n(std::back_inserter(futures), n_threads, ❸
                  [&io_context] {
                    return std::async(std::launch::async,
                                      [&io_context] { io_context.run(); }); ❹
                  });

  for(auto& future : futures) { ❺
    try {
      future.get(); ❻
    } catch (const std::exception& e) {
      std::cerr << e.what() << std::endl;
    }
  }
}
```

Listing 20-15: Multithreading your asynchronous echo server

Your `Session` and `serve` definitions are identical. Within `main`, you declare `n_threads` constant representing the number of threads you'll use to serve, an `io_context`, and an `acceptor` with parameters identical to those in Listing 12-12 ❶. Next, you invoke `serve` to begin the `async_accept` loop ❷.

More or less, `main` is almost identical to Listing 12-12. The difference is that you'll dedicate multiple threads to running the `io_context` rather than just one. First, you initialize a `vector` to store each `future` corresponding to the tasks you'll launch. Second, you use a similar approach with `std::generate_n` to create tasks ❸. As the generative function object, you pass a lambda that invokes `std::async` ❹. Within the `std::async` call, you pass the execution policy `std::launch::async` and a function object that invokes `run` on your `io_context`.

Boost Asio is off to the races now that you've assigned some tasks to running your `io_context`. You'll want to wait for all asynchronous operations to complete, so you call `get` on each `future` you stored in `futures` ❺. Once this loop completes, each `Request` has finished and you're ready to print a summary of the resulting responses ❻.

Sometimes it makes sense to create additional threads and assign them to processing I/O. Often, one thread will suffice. You must measure whether the optimization (and attendant difficulties arising from concurrent code) are worth it.

Summary

This chapter covered Boost Asio, a library for low-level I/O programming. You learned the basics of queuing asynchronous tasks and providing a thread pool in Asio, as well as how to interact with its basic networking facilities. You built several programs, including a simple HTTP client using synchronous and asynchronous approaches and an echo server.

EXERCISES

20-1. Use the Boost Asio documentation to investigate the UDP class analogs to the TCP classes you've learned about in this chapter. Rewrite the uppercasing echo server in Listing 20-14 as a UDP service.

20-2. Use the Boost Asio documentation to investigate the ICMP classes. Write a program that pings all hosts on a given subnetwork to perform network analysis. Investigate *Nmap*, a network-mapping program available for free at *https://nmap.org/*.

20-3. Investigate the Boost Beast documentation. Rewrite Listings 20-10 and 20-11 using Beast.

20-4. Use Boost Beast to write an HTTP server that serves files from a directory. For help, refer to the Boost Beast example projects available in the documentation.

FURTHER READING

- *The TCP/IP Guide* by Charles M. Kozierok (No Starch Press, 2005)
- *Tangled Web: A Guide to Securing Modern Web Applications* by Michal Zalewski (No Starch Press, 2012)
- *The Boost C++ Libraries*, 2nd Edition, by Boris Schäling (XML Press, 2014)
- *Boost.Asio C++ Network Programming*, 2nd Edition, by Wisnu Anggoro and John Torjo (Packt, 2015)

21

WRITING APPLICATIONS

For a bunch of hairless apes, we've actually managed to invent some pretty incredible things.
—*Ernest Cline,* Ready Player One

This chapter contains a potpourri of important topics that will add to your practical understanding of C++ by teaching you the basics of building real-world applications. It begins with a discussion of program support built into C++ that allows you to interact with the application life cycle. Next, you'll learn about Boost ProgramOptions, an excellent library for developing console applications. It contains facilities to accept input from users without your having to reinvent the wheel. Additionally, you'll learn some special topics about the preprocessor and compiler that you'll likely come across when building an application whose source exceeds a single file.

Program Support

Sometimes your programs need to interact with your operating environment's application life cycle. This section covers three major categories of such interactions:

- Handling program termination and cleanup
- Communicating with the environment
- Managing operating system signals

To help illustrate the various facilities in this section, you'll use Listing 21-1 as a framework. It uses a spruced up analog to the `Tracer` class from Listing 4-5 in Chapter 4 to help track which objects get cleaned up in various program termination scenarios.

```
#include <iostream>
#include <string>

struct Tracer { ❶
  Tracer(std::string name_in)
    : name{ std::move(name_in) } {
    std::cout << name << " constructed.\n";
  }
  ~Tracer() {
    std::cout << name << " destructed.\n";
  }
private:
  const std::string name;
};

Tracer static_tracer{ "static Tracer" }; ❷

void run() { ❸
  std::cout << "Entering run()\n";
  // ...
  std::cout << "Exiting run()\n";
}

int main() {
  std::cout << "Entering main()\n"; ❹
  Tracer local_tracer{ "local Tracer" }; ❺
  thread_local Tracer thread_local_tracer{ "thread_local Tracer" }; ❻
  const auto* dynamic_tracer = new Tracer{ "dynamic Tracer" }; ❼
  run(); ❽
  delete dynamic_tracer; ❾
  std::cout << "Exiting main()\n"; ❿
}
```

```
static Tracer constructed. ❷
Entering main() ❹
local Tracer constructed. ❺
thread_local Tracer constructed. ❻
dynamic Tracer constructed. ❼
```

```
Entering run() ❽
Exiting run() ❽
dynamic Tracer destructed. ❾
Exiting main() ❿
local Tracer destructed. ❺
thread_local Tracer destructed. ❻
static Tracer destructed. ❷
```

Listing 21-1: A framework for investigating program termination and cleanup facilities

First, you declare a `Tracer` class that accepts an arbitrary `std::string` tag and reports to stdout when the `Tracer` object is constructed and destructed ❶. Next, you declare a `Tracer` with static storage duration ❷. The `run` function reports when the program has entered and exited it ❸. In the middle is a single comment that you'll replace with other code in the sections that follow. Within `main`, you make an announcement ❹; initialize `Tracer` objects with local ❺, thread-local ❻, and dynamic ❼ storage duration; and invoke `run` ❽. Then you delete the dynamic Tracer object ❾ and announce that you're about to return from `main` ❿.

WARNING *If any of the Listing 21-1 output is surprising, please review "An Object's Storage Duration" on page 89 before proceeding!*

Handling Program Termination and Cleanup

The `<cstdlib>` header contains several functions for managing program termination and resource cleanup. There are two broad categories of program termination functions:

- Those that cause program termination
- Those that register a callback when termination is about to happen

Termination Callback with std::atexit

To register a function to be called when normal program termination occurs, you use the `std::atexit` function. You can register multiple functions, and they'll be called in reverse order from their registration. The callback functions take no arguments and return `void`. If `std::atexit` registers a function successfully, it will return a non-zero value; otherwise, it returns zero.

Listing 21-2 illustrates that you can register an `atexit` callback and it will be called at the expected moment.

```
#include <cstdlib>
#include <iostream>
#include <string>

struct Tracer {
--snip--
};

Tracer static_tracer{ "static Tracer" };
```

```
void run() {
  std::cout << "Registering a callback\n"; ❶
  std::atexit([] { std::cout << "***std::atexit callback executing***\n"; }); ❷
  std::cout << "Callback registered\n"; ❸
}

int main() {
--snip--
}
```

```
static Tracer constructed.
Entering main()
local Tracer constructed.
thread_local Tracer constructed.
dynamic Tracer constructed.
Registering a callback
Callback registered ❸
dynamic Tracer destructed.
Exiting main()
local Tracer destructed.
thread_local Tracer destructed.
***std::atexit callback executing*** ❷
static Tracer destructed.
```

Listing 21-2: Registering an atexit callback

Within `run`, you announce that you're about to register a callback ❶, you do it ❷, and then you announce that you're about to return from `run` ❸. In the output, you can plainly see that the callback occurs after you've returned from `main` and all the non-static objects have destructed.

There are two important admonitions when programming a callback function:

- You must not throw an uncaught exception from the callback function. Doing so will cause `std::terminate` to get invoked.
- You need to be very careful interacting with non-static objects in your program. The `atexit` callback functions execute after `main` returns, so all local, thread local, and dynamic objects will be destroyed at that point unless you take special care to keep them alive.

NOTE *You can register at least 32 functions with `std::atexit`, although the exact limit is implementation defined.*

Exiting with std::exit

Throughout the book, you've been terminating programs by returning from `main`. In some circumstances, such as in multithreaded programs, you might want to exit the program gracefully in some other way, although you should avoid introducing the associated complications. You can use the std::exit function, which accepts a single int corresponding to the program's exit code. It will perform the following cleanup steps:

1. Thread-local objects associated with the current thread and static objects get destroyed. Any atexit callback functions get called.
2. All of stdin, stdout, and stderr get flushed.
3. Any temporary files get removed.
4. The program reports the given status code to the operating environment, which resumes control.

Listing 21-3 illustrates the behavior of std::exit by registering an atexit callback and invoking exit from within run.

```
#include <cstdlib>
#include <iostream>
#include <string>

struct Tracer {
--snip--
};

Tracer static_tracer{ "static Tracer" };

void run() {
  std::cout << "Registering a callback\n"; ❶
  std::atexit([] { std::cout << "***std::atexit callback executing***\n"; }); ❷
  std::cout << "Callback registered\n"; ❸
  std::exit(0); ❹
}

int main() {
--snip--
}
```

```
static Tracer constructed.
Entering main()
local Tracer constructed.
thread_local Tracer constructed.
dynamic Tracer constructed.
Registering a callback ❶
Callback registered ❸
thread_local Tracer destructed.
***std::atexit callback executing*** ❹
static Tracer destructed.
```

Listing 21-3: Invoking std::exit

Within run, you announce that you're registering a callback ❶, you register one with atexit ❷, you announce that you've completed registering ❸, and you invoke exit with argument zero ❹. Compare the program output from Listing 21-3 to the output from Listing 21-2. Notice that the following lines don't appear:

```
dynamic Tracer destructed.
Exiting main()
local Tracer destructed.
```

According to the rules for std::exit, local variables on the call stack don't get cleaned up. And of course, because the program never returns to main from run, delete never gets called. Ouch.

This example highlights an important consideration: you shouldn't use std::exit to handle normal program execution. It's mentioned here for completeness, because you might see it in earlier C++ code.

NOTE *The <cstdlib> header also includes a* std::quick_exit*, which invokes callbacks that you register with* std::at_quick_exit*, which has a similar interface to* std::atexit*. The main difference is that* at_quick_exit *callbacks won't execute unless you explicitly invoke* quick_exit*, whereas* atexit *callbacks will always execute when the program is about to exit.*

std::abort

To end a program, you also have a nuclear option by using std::abort. This function accepts a single integer-valued status code and immediately returns it to the operating environment. No object destructors get called and no std::atexit callbacks get invoked. Listing 21-4 illustrates how to use std::abort.

```
#include <cstdlib>
#include <iostream>
#include <string>

struct Tracer {
--snip--
};

Tracer static_tracer{ "static Tracer" };

void run() {
  std::cout << "Registering a callback\n"; ❶
  std::atexit([] { std::cout << "***std::atexit callback executing***\n"; }); ❷
  std::cout << "Callback registered\n"; ❸
  std::abort(); ❹
}

int main() {
  --snip--
}
```

```
static Tracer constructed.
Entering main()
local Tracer constructed.
```

```
thread_local Tracer constructed.
dynamic Tracer constructed.
Registering a callback
Callback registered
```

Listing 21-4: Calling `std::abort`

Within `run`, you again announce that you're registering a callback ❶, you register one with `atexit` ❷, and you announce that you've completed registering ❸. This time, you invoke `abort` instead ❹. Notice that no output prints after you announce that you've completed callback registration ❶. The program doesn't clean up any objects, and your `atexit` callback doesn't get called.

As you might imagine, there aren't too many canonical uses for `std::abort`. The main one you're likely to encounter is the default behavior of `std::terminate`, which gets called when two exceptions are in flight at once.

Communicating with the Environment

Sometimes, you might want to spawn another process. For example, Google's Chrome Browser launches many processes to service a single browser session. This builds in some security and robustness by piggybacking the operating system's process model. Web apps and plug-ins, for example, run in separate processes, so if they crash, the entire browser doesn't crash. Also, by running the browser's rendering engine in a separate process, any security vulnerabilities become more difficult to exploit because Google locks down that process's permissions in what is known as a sandboxed environment.

std::system

You can launch a separate process with the `std::system` function in the `<cstdlib>` header, which accepts a C-style string corresponding to the command you want to execute and returns an `int` corresponding to the return code from the command. The actual behavior depends on the operating environment. For example, the function will call *cmd.exe* on a Windows machine and */bin/sh* on a Linux machine. This function blocks while the command is still executing.

Listing 21-5 illustrates how to use `std::system` to ping a remote host. (You'll need to update the contents of `command` to a relevant command for your operating system if you're not using a Unix-like operating system.)

```
#include <cstdlib>
#include <iostream>
#include <string>

int main() {
  std::string command{ "ping -c 4 google.com" }; ❶
  const auto result = std::system(command.c_str()); ❷
  std::cout << "The command \'" << command
            << "\' returned " << result << "\n";
}
```

```
--------------------------------------------------------------------------------
PING google.com (172.217.15.78): 56 data bytes
64 bytes from 172.217.15.78: icmp_seq=0 ttl=56 time=4.447 ms
64 bytes from 172.217.15.78: icmp_seq=1 ttl=56 time=12.162 ms
64 bytes from 172.217.15.78: icmp_seq=2 ttl=56 time=8.376 ms
64 bytes from 172.217.15.78: icmp_seq=3 ttl=56 time=10.813 ms

--- google.com ping statistics ---
4 packets transmitted, 4 packets received, 0.0% packet loss
round-trip min/avg/max/stddev = 4.447/8.950/12.162/2.932 ms
The command 'ping -c 4 google.com' returned 0 ❸
```

Listing 21-5: Using `std::system` *to invoke the* `ping` *utility (Output is from macOS Mojave version 10.14.)*

First, you initialize a `string` called `command` containing `ping -c 4 google .com` ❶. You then invoke `std::system` by passing the contents of `command` ❷. This causes the operating system to invoke the `ping` command with the argument `-c 4`, which specifies four pings, and the address `google.com`. Then you print a status message reporting the return value from `std::system` ❸.

std::getenv

Operating environments usually have *environment variables,* which users and developers can set to help programs find important information that the programs need to run. The `<cstdlib>` header contains the `std::getenv` function, which accepts a C-style string corresponding to the name of the environment variable you want to look up, and it returns a C-style string with the contents of the corresponding variable. If no such variable is found, the function returns `nullptr` instead.

Listing 21-6 illustrates how to use `std::getenv` to obtain the *path variable,* which contains a list of directories containing important executable files.

```
#include <cstdlib>
#include <iostream>
#include <string>

int main() {
  std::string variable_name{ "PATH" }; ❶
  std::string result{ std::getenv(variable_name.c_str()) }; ❷
  std::cout << "The variable " << variable_name
            << " equals " << result << "\n"; ❸
}
--------------------------------------------------------------------------------
The variable PATH equals /usr/local/bin:/usr/bin:/bin:/usr/sbin:/sbin
```

Listing 21-6: Using `std::getenv` *to retrieve the path variable (Output is from macOS Mojave version 10.14.)*

First, you initialize a `string` called `variable_name` containing `PATH` ❶. Next, you store the result of invoking `std::getenv` with `PATH` into a string called `result` ❷. Then you print the results to stdout ❸.

Managing Operating System Signals

Operating system signals are asynchronous notifications sent to processes that notify the program that an event occurred. The `<csignal>` header contains six macro constants that represent different signals from the operating system to the program (these signals are operating system agnostic):

- `SIGTERM` represents a termination request.
- `SIGSEGV` represents invalid memory access.
- `SIGINT` represents an external interrupt, such as a keyboard interrupt.
- `SIGILL` represents an invalid program image.
- `SIGABRT` represents an abnormal termination condition, such as `std::abort`.
- `SIGFPE` represents a floating-point error, such as division by zero.

To register a handler for one of these signals, you use the `std::signal` function in the `<csignal>` header. It accepts a single `int` value corresponding to one of the listed signal macros as its first argument. Its second argument is a function pointer (not a function object!) to a function that accepts an `int` corresponding to the signal macro and returning `void`. This function must have C linkage (although most implementations also permit C++ linkage). You'll learn about C linkage later in the chapter. For now, simply prepend `extern "C"` to your function definition. Notice that, due to the asynchronous nature of the interrupts, any accesses to a global, mutable state must be synchronized.

Listing 21-7 contains a program that waits for a keyboard interrupt.

```
#include <csignal>
#include <iostream>
#include <chrono>
#include <thread>
#include <atomic>

std::atomic_bool interrupted{}; ❶

extern "C" void handler(int signal) {
  std::cout << "Handler invoked with signal " << signal << ".\n"; ❷
  interrupted = true; ❸
}

int main() {
  using namespace std::chrono_literals;
  std::signal(SIGINT, handler); ❹
  while(!interrupted) { ❺
    std::cout << "Waiting..." << std::endl; ❻
    std::this_thread::sleep_for(1s);
  }
  std::cout << "Interrupted!\n"; ❼
}
-----------------------------------------------------------------------
Waiting...
Waiting...
```

```
Waiting...
Handler invoked with signal 2.
Interrupted! ❼
```

Listing 21-7: Registering for keyboard interrupts with `std::signal`

You first declare an `atomic_bool` called `interrupted` that stores whether the program has received a keyboard interrupt ❶ (it has static storage duration because you cannot use function objects with `std::signal` and therefore must use a non-member function to handle the callback). Next, you declare a callback handler that accepts an `int` called `signal`, prints its value to stdout ❷, and sets `interrupted` to true ❸.

Within `main`, you set the signal handler for the `SIGINT` interrupt code to `handler` ❹. Within a loop, you wait for the program to get interrupted ❺ by printing a message ❻ and sleeping for a second ❼. Once the program has been interrupted, you print a message and return from `main` ❼.

NOTE *Typically, you can cause a keyboard interrupt on modern operating systems by pressing* CTRL-C.

Boost ProgramOptions

Most console applications accept command line parameters. As you learned in "The Three `main` Overloads" on page 272, you can define `main` to accept the parameters `argc` and `argv`, which the operating environment will populate with the number of arguments and argument contents, respectively. You can always parse these manually and modify your program's behavior accordingly, but there's a better way: the Boost ProgramOptions library is an essential ingredient for writing console applications.

NOTE *All the Boost ProgramOptions classes presented in this section are available in the* `<boost/program_options.hpp>` *header.*

You might be tempted to write your own argument-parsing code, but ProgramOptions is a smarter choice for four reasons:

1. **It's far more convenient.** Once you learn the succinct, declarative syntax of ProgramOptions, you can easily describe fairly complicated console interfaces in a few lines of code.
2. **It handles errors effortlessly.** When the user misuses your program, ProgramOptions tells the user how they misused the program without any additional effort on your part.
3. **It automatically generates a help prompt.** Based on your declarative markup, ProgramOptions creates nicely formatted, easy to employ documentation on your behalf.
4. **It grows beyond the command line.** If you want to draw configuration from config files or environment variables, it's easy to transition from command line arguments.

ProgramOptions comprises three parts:

1. **The options description** allows you to specify the allowed options.
2. **The parsers component** extracts option names and values from the command line, config files, and environment variables.
3. **The storage component** provides you with the interface to access typed options.

In the subsections that follow, you'll learn about each of these parts.

The Options Description

Three main classes comprise the options description component:

- `boost::program_options::option_description` describes a single option.
- `boost::program_options::value_semantic` knows the desired type of a single option.
- `boost::program_options::options_description` is a container for multiple objects of type `option_description`.

You construct an `options_description` to, unsurprisingly, specify a description for the program's options. Optionally, you can include a single string argument in the constructor that describes your program. This will print in the description if you include it, but it will have no functional impact. Next, you use its `add_options` method, which returns a special kind of object of type `boost::program_options::options_description_easy_init`. This class has a special `operator()` that accepts at least two arguments.

The first argument is the name of the option you want to add. ProgramOptions is very smart, so you can provide a long name and a short name separated by a comma. For example, if you had an option called `threads`, ProgramOptions would bind the parameter `--threads` from the command line to this option. If instead you named the option `threads,t`, ProgramOptions would bind either `--threads` or `-t` to your option.

The second argument is the description of the option. You can employ a `value_semantic`, a C-style string description, or both. Because `options_description_easy_init` returns a reference to itself from `operator()`, you can chain these calls together to form a succinct representation of your program's options. Typically, you don't create `value_semantic` objects directly. Instead, you use the convenience template function `boost::program_options::value` to generate them. It accepts a single template parameter corresponding to the desired type of the option. The resulting pointer points to an object that has code to parse text input (from the command line, for example) into the desired type. To specify an option of `int` type, for example, you would invoke `value<int>()`.

The resulting pointed-to object will have several methods that allow you to specify additional information about the option. For example, you can employ the `default_value` method to set the option's default value. To specify that an option of int type should default to 42, you would use the following construction:

```
value<int>()->default_value(42)
```

Another common pattern is an option that can take multiple tokens. Such options are allowed to have spaces between elements, and they'll be parsed into a single string. To allow this, simply use the multitoken method. For example, to specify that an option can take multiple std::string values, you would use the following construction:

```
value<std::string>()->multitoken()
```

If instead you want to allow multiple instances of the same option, you can specify a std::vector as a value, like this:

```
value<std::vector<std::string>>()
```

If you have a Boolean option, you'll use the convenience function boost::program_options::bool_switch, which accepts a pointer to a bool. If a user includes the corresponding option, the function will set the pointed-to bool to true. For example, the following construction will set a bool called flag to true if the corresponding option is included:

```
bool_switch(&flag)
```

The options_description class supports operator<<, so you can create a nicely formatted help dialog without any additional effort. Listing 21-8 illustrates how to use ProgramOptions to create a program_options object for a sample program called *mgrep*.

```
#include <boost/program_options.hpp>
#include <iostream>
#include <string>

int main(int argc, char** argv) {
  using namespace boost::program_options;
  bool is_recursive{}, is_help{};

  options_description description{ "mgrep [options] pattern path1 path2 ..."
}; ❶
  description.add_options()
          ("help,h", bool_switch(&is_help), "display a help dialog") ❷
          ("threads,t", value<int>()->default_value(4),
                      "number of threads to use") ❸
          ("recursive,r", bool_switch(&is_recursive),
                       "search subdirectories recursively") ❹
          ("pattern", value<std::string>(), "pattern to search for") ❺
          ("paths", value<std::vector<std::string>>(), "path to search"); ❻
  std::cout << description; ❼
}
```

```
mgrep [options] pattern path1 path2 ...:
  -h [ --help ]              display a help dialog
  -t [ --threads ] arg (=4)  number of threads to use
  -r [ --recursive ]         search subdirectories recursively
  --pattern arg              pattern to search for
  --path arg                 path to search
```

Listing 21-8: Using Boost ProgramOptions to generate a nicely formatted help dialog

First, you initialize an `options_description` object using a custom usage string ❶. Next, you invoke `add_options` and begin adding options: a Boolean flag indicating whether to display a help dialog ❷, an `int` indicating how many threads to use ❸, another Boolean flag indicating whether to search subdirectories in a `recursive` manner ❹, a `std::string` indicating which `pattern` to search for within files ❺, and a list of `std::string` values corresponding to the `paths` to search ❻. You then write the `description` to stdout ❼.

Suppose that your yet to be implemented mgrep program will always require a `pattern` and a `paths` argument. You could convert these into *positional arguments,* which as their name implies will assign arguments based on their position. To do this, you employ the `boost::program_options::positional_options_description` class, which doesn't take any constructor arguments. You use the `add` method, which takes two arguments: a C-style string corresponding to the option you want to convert to positional and an `int` corresponding to the number of arguments you want to bind to it. You can invoke `add` multiple times to add multiple positional arguments. But the order matters. Positional arguments will bind from left to right, so your first `add` invocation applies to the left positional arguments. For the last positional option, you can use the number `-1` to tell ProgramOptions to bind all remaining elements to the corresponding option.

Listing 21-9 provides a snippet that you could append into `main` in Listing 21-7 to add the positional arguments.

```
positional_options_description positional; ❶
positional.add("pattern", 1); ❷
positional.add("path", -1); ❸
```

Listing 21-9: Adding positional arguments to Listing 21-8

You initialize a `positional_options_description` without any constructor arguments ❶. Next, you invoke `add` and pass the arguments `pattern` and `1`, which will bind the first positional option to the *pattern* option ❷. You invoke `add` again, this time passing the arguments `path` and `-1` ❸, which will bind the remaining positional options to the *path* option.

Parsing Options

Now that you've declared how your program accepts options, you can parse user input. It's possible to take configuration from environment variables, configuration files, and the command line. For brevity, this section only discusses the last.

NOTE *For information on how to obtain configuration from environment variables and configuration files, refer to the Boost ProgramOptions documentation, especially the tutorial.*

To parse command line input, you use the `boost::program_options::command_line_parser` class, which accepts two constructor parameters arguments: an `int` corresponding to *argc*, the number of arguments on the command line, and a `char**` corresponding to *argv*, the value (or content) of the arguments on the command line. This class offers several important methods that you'll use to declare how the parser should interpret user input.

First, you'll invoke its `options` method, which takes a single argument corresponding to your `options_description`. Next, you'll use the positional method, which takes a single argument corresponding to your `positional_options_description`. Finally, you'll invoke `run` without any arguments. This causes the parser to parse the command line input and return a `parsed_options` object.

Listing 21-10 provides a snippet that you could append into `main` after Listing 21-8 to incorporate a `command_line_parser`.

```
command_line_parser parser{ argc, argv }; ❶
parser.options(description); ❷
parser.positional(positional); ❸
auto parsed_result = parser.run(); ❹
```

Listing 21-10: Adding the `command_line_parser` to Listing 21-8

You initialize a `command_line_parser` called `parser` by passing in the arguments from `main` ❶. Next, you pass the `options_description` object to the `options` method ❷ and the `positional_options_description` to the `positional` method ❸. Then you invoke the `run` method to produce your `parsed_options` object ❹.

WARNING *If the user passes input that doesn't parse, for example, because they provide an option that isn't part of your description, the parser will throw an exception that inherits from `std::exception`.*

Storing and Accessing Options

You store program options into a `boost::program_options::variables_map` class, which takes no arguments in its constructor. To place your parsed options into a `variables_map`, you use the `boost::program_options::store` method, which takes a `parsed_options` object as its first argument and a `variables_map` object as its second argument. Then you call the `boost::program_options::notify` method, which takes a single `variables_map` argument. At this point, your `variables_map` contains all the options your user has specified.

Listing 21-11 provides a snippet that you could append into `main` after Listing 21-10 to parse results into a `variables_map`.

```
variables_map vm; ❶
store(parsed_result, vm); ❷
notify(vm); ❸
```

Listing 21-11: Storing results into a `variables_map`

You first declare a `variables_map` ❶. Next, you pass your `parsed_result` from Listing 21-10 and your newly declared `variables_map` to `store` ❷. Then you call `notify` on your `variables_map` ❸.

The `variables_map` class is an associative container that is essentially similar to a `std::map<std::string, boost::any>`. To extract an element, you use `operator[]` by passing the option name as the key. The result is a `boost::any`, so you'll need to convert it to the correct type using its as method. (You learned about `boost::any` in "any" on page 378.) It's crucial to check for any options that might be empty by using the `empty` method. If you fail to do so and you cast the `any` anyway, you'll get a runtime error.

Listing 21-12 provides a snippet that you could append into `main` after Listing 21-10 to parse results into a `variables_map`.

```
if (is_help) std::cout << "Is help.\n"; ❶
if (is_recursive) std::cout << "Is recursive.\n"; ❷
std::cout << "Threads: " << vm["threads"].as<int>() << "\n"; ❸
if (!vm["pattern"].empty()) { ❹
  std::cout << "Pattern: " << vm["pattern"].as<std::string>() << "\n"; ❺
} else {
  std::cout << "Empty pattern.\n";
}
if (!vm["path"].empty()) { ❻
  std::cout << "Paths:\n";
  for(const auto& path : vm["path"].as<std::vector<std::string>>()) ❼
    std::cout << "\t" << path << "\n";
} else {
  std::cout << "Empty path.\n";
}
```

Listing 21-12: Retrieving values from a `variables_map`

Because you use the `bool_switch` value for the `help` and `recursive` options, you simply use those Boolean values directly to determine whether the user has requested either ❶❷. Because `threads` has a default value, you don't need to make sure that it's empty, so you can extract its value using `as<int>` directly ❸. For those options without defaults, such as `pattern`, you first check for `empty` ❹. If those options aren't empty, you can extract their values using `as<std::string>` ❺. You do the same for `path` ❻, which allows you extract the user-provided collection with `as<std::vector<std::string>>` ❼.

Putting It All Together

Now you have all the requisite knowledge to assemble a ProgramOptions-based application. Listing 21-13 illustrates one way to stitch the previous listings together.

```
#include <boost/program_options.hpp>
#include <iostream>
#include <string>

int main(int argc, char** argv) {
  using namespace boost::program_options;
  bool is_recursive{}, is_help{};

  options_description description{ "mgrep [options] pattern path1 path2 ..." };
  description.add_options()
          ("help,h", bool_switch(&is_help), "display a help dialog")
          ("threads,t", value<int>()->default_value(4),
                        "number of threads to use")
          ("recursive,r", bool_switch(&is_recursive),
                         "search subdirectories recursively")
          ("pattern", value<std::string>(), "pattern to search for")
          ("path", value<std::vector<std::string>>(), "path to search");

  positional_options_description positional;
  positional.add("pattern", 1);
  positional.add("path", -1);

  command_line_parser parser{ argc, argv };
  parser.options(description);
  parser.positional(positional);

  variables_map vm;
  try {
    auto parsed_result = parser.run(); ❶
    store(parsed_result, vm);
    notify(vm);
  } catch (const std::exception& e) {
    std::cerr << e.what() << "\n";
    return -1;
  }

  if (is_help) { ❷
    std::cout << description;
    return 0;
  }
  if (vm["pattern"].empty()) { ❸
    std::cerr << "You must provide a pattern.\n";
    return -1;
  }
  if (vm["path"].empty()) { ❹
    std::cerr << "You must provide at least one path.\n";
    return -1;
  }
  const auto threads = vm["threads"].as<int>();
  const auto& pattern = vm["pattern"].as<std::string>();
  const auto& paths = vm["path"].as<std::vector<std::string>>();
```

```
    // Continue program here ... ❺
    std::cout << "Ok." << std::endl;
}
```

Listing 21-13: A complete command line parameter-parsing application using the previous listings

The first departure from the previous listings is that you wrap the call to run on your parser using a try-catch block to mitigate erroneous input provided by the user ❶. If they do provide erroneous input, you simply catch the exception, print the error to stderr, and return.

Once you declare your program options and store them, as in Listings 21-8 to 21-12, you first check whether the user has requested a help prompt ❷. If so, you simply print the usage and exit, because there's no need to perform any further checking. Next, you perform some error checking to make sure the user has provided a pattern ❸ and at least one path ❹. If not, you print an error along with the program's correct usage and exit; otherwise, you can continue writing your program ❺.

Listing 21-14 shows various outputs from your program, which is compiled into the binary mgrep.

```
$ ./mgrep ❶
You must provide a pattern.
$ ./mgrep needle ❷
You must provide at least one path.
$ ./mgrep --supercharge needle haystack1.txt haystack2.txt ❸
unrecognised option '--supercharge'
$ ./mgrep --help ❹
mgrep [options] pattern path1 path2 ...:
  -h [ --help ]             display a help dialog
  -t [ --threads ] arg (=4) number of threads to use
  -r [ --recursive ]        search subdirectories recursively
  --pattern arg             pattern to search for
  --path arg                path to search
$ ./mgrep needle haystack1.txt haystack2.txt haystack3.txt ❺
Ok.
$ ./mgrep --recursive needle haystack1.txt ❻
Ok.
$ ./mgrep -rt 10 needle haystack1.txt haystack2.txt ❼
Ok.
```

Listing 21-14: Various invocations and outputs from the program in Listing 21-13

The first three invocations return errors for different reasons: you haven't provided a pattern ❶, you haven't provided a path ❷, or you provided an unrecognized option ❸.

In the next invocation, you get the friendly help dialog because you provided the `--help` option ❹. The final three invocations parse correctly because all contain a pattern and at least one path. The first contains no options ❺, the second uses the longhand option syntax ❻, and the third uses the shorthand option syntax ❼.

Special Topics in Compilation

This section explains several important preprocessor features that will help you understand the double-inclusion problem, which is described in the following subsection, and how to solve it. You'll learn about different options for optimizing your code by using compiler flags. Additionally, you'll learn how to allow your linker to interoperate with C using a special language keyword.

Revisiting the Preprocessor

The preprocessor is a program that applies simple transformations to source code before compilation. You give instructions to the preprocessor using preprocessor directives. All preprocessor directives begin with a hash mark (`#`). Recall from "The Compiler Tool Chain," on page 5 that `#include` is a preprocessor directive that tells the preprocessor to copy and paste the contents of the corresponding header directly into the source code.

The preprocessor also supports other directives. The most common is the *macro*, which is a fragment of code that's been given a name. Whenever you use that name within C++ code, the preprocessor replaces that name with the contents of the macro.

The two different kinds of macros are object-like and function-like. You declare an object-like macro using the following syntax:

```
#define <NAME> <CODE>
```

where *NAME* is the name of the macro and *CODE* is the code to replace that name. For example, Listing 21-15 illustrates how to define a string literal to a macro.

```
#include <cstdio>
#define MESSAGE "LOL" ❶

int main(){
  printf(MESSAGE); ❷
}
--------------------------------------------------------------------------
LOL
```

Listing 21-15: A C++ program with an object-like macro

You define the macro `MESSAGE` to correspond with the code `"LOL"` ❶. Next, you use the `MESSAGE` macro as the format string to `printf` ❷. After the preprocessor has completed work on Listing 21-15, it appears as Listing 21-16 to the compiler.

```
#include <cstdio>

int main(){
  printf("LOL");
}
```

Listing 21-16: The result of preprocessing Listing 21-15

The preprocessor is nothing more than a copy-and-paste tool here. The macro disappears, and you're left with a simple program that prints `LOL` to the console.

NOTE *If you want to inspect the work that the preprocessor does, compilers usually have a flag that will limit compilation to just the preprocessing step. This will cause the compiler to emit the preprocessed source file corresponding to each translation unit. On GCC, Clang, and MSVC, for example, you can use the* `-E` *flag.*

A function-like macro is just like an object-like macro except it can take a list of parameters after its identifier:

```
#define <NAME>(<PARAMETERS>) <CODE>
```

You can use these *PARAMETERS* within the *CODE*, allowing the user to customize the macro's behavior. Listing 21-17 contains the function-like macro `SAY_LOL_WITH`.

```
#include <cstdio>
#define SAY_LOL_WITH(fn) fn("LOL") ❶

int main() {
  SAY_LOL_WITH(printf); ❷
}
```

Listing 21-17: A C++ program with a function-like macro

The `SAY_LOL_WITH` macro accepts a single parameter named `fn` ❶. The preprocessor pastes the macro into the expression `fn("LOL")`. When it evaluates `SAY_LOL_WITH`, the preprocessor pastes `printf` into the expression ❷, yielding a translation unit just like Listing 21-16.

Conditional Compilation

The preprocessor also offers *conditional compilation*, a facility that provides basic `if-else` logic. Several flavors of conditional compilation are available, but the one you're likely to encounter is illustrated in Listing 21-18.

```
#ifndef MY_MACRO ❶
// Segment 1 ❷
#else
// Segment 2 ❸
#endif
```

Listing 21-18: A C++ program with a conditional compilation

If `MY_MACRO` isn't defined at the point where the preprocessor evaluates `#ifndef` ❶, Listing 21-18 reduces to the code represented by `// Segment 1` ❷. If `MY_MACRO` is `#define`d, Listing 21-18 evaluates to the code represented by `// Segment 2` ❸. The `#else` is optional.

Double Inclusion

Aside from using #include, you should use the preprocessor as little as possible. The preprocessor is extremely primitive and will cause difficult-to-debug errors if you lean on it too heavily. This is evident with #include, which is a simple copy-and-paste command.

Because you can define a symbol only once (a rule appropriately called the *one-definition rule*), you must ensure that your headers don't attempt to redefine symbols. The easiest way to make this mistake is by including the same header twice, which is called the *double-inclusion problem.*

The usual way to avoid the double-inclusion problem is to use conditional compilation to make an *include guard.* The include guard detects whether a header has been included before. If it has, it uses conditional compilation to empty the header. Listing 21-19 illustrates how to put include guards around a header.

```
// step_function.h
#ifndef STEP_FUNCTION_H ❶
int step_function(int x);
#define STEP_FUNCTION_H ❷
#endif
```

Listing 21-19: A step_function.h updated with include guards

The first time that the preprocessor includes step_function.h in a source file, the macro STEP_FUNCTION_H won't be defined, so #ifndef ❶ yields the code up to #endif. Within this code, you #define the STEP_FUNCTION_H macro ❷. This ensures that if the preprocessor includes step_function.h again, #ifndef STEP_FUNCTION_H will evaluate to false and no code will get generated.

Include guards are so ubiquitous that most modern tool chains support the #pragma once special syntax. If one of the supporting preprocessors sees this line, it will behave as if the header has include guards. This eliminates quite a bit of ceremony. Using this construct, you could refactor Listing 21-19 into Listing 21-20.

```
#pragma once ❶
int step_function(int x);
```

Listing 21-20: A step_function.h updated with #pragma once

All you've done here is start the header with #pragma once ❶, which is the preferred method. As a general rule, start every header with #pragma once.

Compiler Optimization

Modern compilers can perform sophisticated transformations on code to increase runtime performance and reduce binary size. These transformations are called *optimizations,* and they entail some cost to programmers. Optimization necessarily increases compilation time. Additionally, optimized code is often harder to debug than non-optimized code, because the optimizer usually eliminates and reorders instructions. In short, you usually want to turn off optimizations while you're programming, but turn them on during testing and in production. Accordingly, compilers typically provide several optimization options. Table 21-1 describes one such example—the optimization options available in GCC 8.3, although these flags are fairly ubiquitous across the major compilers.

Table 21-1: GCC 8.3 Optimization Options

Flag	Description
`-O0 (default)`	Reduces compilation time by turning off optimizations. Yields a good debugging experience but suboptimal runtime performance.
`-O` or `-O1`	Performs the majority of available optimizations, but omits those that can take a lot of (compile) time.
`-O2`	Performs all optimizations at `-O1`, plus nearly all optimizations that don't substantially increase binary size. Compilation might take much longer than with `-O1`.
`-O3`	Performs all optimizations at `-O2`, plus many optimizations that can substantially increase binary size. Again, this increases compilation time over `-O1` and `-O2`.
`-Os`	Optimizes similarly to `-O2` but with a priority for decreasing binary size. You can think of this (loosely) as a foil to `-O3`, which is willing to increase binary size in exchange for performance. Any `-O2` optimizations that don't increase binary size are performed.
`-Ofast`	Enables all `-O3` optimizations, plus some dangerous optimizations that might violate standards compliance. Caveat emptor.
`-Og`	Enables optimizations that don't degrade the debugging experience. Provides a good balance of reasonable optimizations, fast compilation, and ease of debugging.

As a general rule, use `-O2` for your production binary unless you have a good reason to change it. For debugging, use `-Og`.

Linking with C

You can allow C code to incorporate functions and variables from your programs using *language linkage*. Language linkage instructs the compiler to generate symbols with a specific format friendly to another target language. For example, to allow a C program to use your functions, you simply add the `extern "C"` language linkage to your code.

Consider the `sum.h` header in Listing 21-21, which generates a C-compatible symbol for `sum`.

```
// sum.h
#pragma once
extern "C" int sum(const int* x, int len);
```

Listing 21-21: A header that makes the `sum` function available to C linkers

Now the compiler will generate objects that the C linker can use. To use this function within C code, you simply declare the sum function per usual:

```
int sum(const int* x, size_t len);
```

Then instruct your C linker to include the C++ object file.

NOTE *According to the C++ Standard,* pragma *is a method to provide additional information to the compiler beyond what is embedded in the source code. This information is implementation defined, so the compiler isn't required to use the information specified by the pragma in any way.* Pragma *is the Greek root for "a fact."*

You can also interoperate the opposite way: use C compiler output within your C++ programs by giving the linker the C compiler-generated object file.

Suppose a C compiler generated a function equivalent to sum. You could compile using the sum.h header, and the linker would have no problem consuming the object file, thanks to language linkage.

If you have many externed functions, you can use braces {}, as Listing 21-22 illustrates.

```
// sum.h
#pragma once

extern "C" {
  int sum_int(const int* x, int len);
  double sum_double(const double* x, int len);
--snip--
}
```

Listing 21-22: A refactoring of Listing 21-21 containing multiple functions with the extern modifier.

The sum_int and sum_double functions will have C language linkage.

NOTE *You can also interoperate between C++ and Python with Boost Python. See the Boost documentation for details.*

Summary

In this chapter, you first learned about program support features that allow you to interact with the application life cycle. Next, you explored Boost ProgramOptions, which allows you to accept input from users easily using a declarative syntax. Then you examined some selected topics in compilation that will be helpful as you expand your C++ application development horizons.

EXERCISES

21-1. Add graceful keyboard interrupt handling to the asynchronous uppercasing echo server in Listing 20-12. Add a kill switch with static storage duration that the session objects and acceptors check before queueing more asynchronous I/O.

21-2. Add program options to the asynchronous HTTP client in Listing 20-10. It should accept options for the host (like *www.nostarch.com*) and one or more resources (like */index.htm*). It should create a separate request for each resource.

21-3. Add another option to your program in exercise 21-2 that accepts a directory where you'll write all the HTTP responses. Derive a filename from each host/resource combination.

21-4. Implement the mgrep program. It should incorporate many of the libraries you've learned about in Part II. Investigate the Boyer-Moore search algorithm in Boost Algorithm (in the `<boost/algorithm/searching/boyer_moore.hpp>` header). Use `std::async` to launch tasks and determine a way to coordinate work between them.

FURTHER READING

- *The Boost C++ Libraries*, 2nd Edition, by Boris Schäling (XML Press, 2014)
- *API Design for C++* by Martin Reddy (Morgan Kaufmann, 2011)

INDEX

Symbols and Numbers

A

C

D

E

F

G

H

I

J

K

P

Q

R

S

T

U

V

W

X

Y

Z

RESOURCES

Visit *https://nostarch.com/cppcrashcourse/* for updates, errata, and more information.

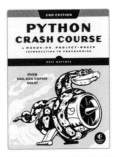